New Ideas in Optimization

ADVANCED TOPICS IN COMPUTER SCIENCE SERIES

Series Editor

Professor V.J. RAYWARD SMITH

School of Information Systems
University of East Anglia
Norwich, UK

This series of texts is aimed at postgraduates and advanced undergraduate students of computer science in colleges and universities. The titles are also invaluable reading for researchers

New Ideas in Optimization

David Corne,

Department of Computer Science, University of Reading

Marco Dorigo,

IRIDIA, Université Libre de Bruxelles

Fred Glover,

MediaOne Chaired Professor, University of Colorado

(Editors)

THE McGRAW-HILL COMPANIES

London · Burr Ridge IL · New York · St Louis · San Francisco · Auckland
Bogotá · Caracas · Lisbon · Madrid · Mexico · Milan
Montreal · New Delhi · Panama · Paris · San Juan · São Paulo
Singapore · Sydney · Tokyo · Toronto

Published by

McGraw-Hill Publishing Company

SHOPPENHANGERS ROAD, MAIDENHEAD, BERKSHIRE, SL6 2QL, ENGLAND

Telephone +44 (0) 1628 502500

Fax: +44 (0) 1628 770224 Web site: http://www.mcgraw-hill.co.uk

---

British Library Cataloguing in Publication Data

A catalogue record for this book is available from the British Library

ISBN 007 709506 5

Library of Congress Cataloguing-in-Publication Data

The LOC data for this book has been applied for and may be obtained from the Library of Congress, Washington, D.C.

Further information on this and other McGraw-Hill titles is to be found at http://www.mcgraw-hill.co.uk

Book's Website address: http://www.mcgraw-hill.co.uk/corne/

Publishing Director: Alfred Waller

Publisher: David Hatter

Typeset by: David Corne

Produced by: Steven Gardiner Ltd

Cover by: Hybert Design

Printed in Great Britain at the University Press, Cambridge

To Stephen Philip Corne and Stephen Philip Corne.

(DC)

To my parents Serena and Roberto.

(MD)

To Diane and Lauren.

(FG)

Contributors

Giovanni Agazzi, *Istituto Dalle Molle di Studi sull'Intelligenza Artificiale (IDSIA), Lugano Switzerland,* agazzi@idsia.ch

Bahram Alidaee, *MIS/POM Area, School of Business Administration, The University of Mississippi, USA,* alidaee@olemiss.edu

Mohammad M. Amini, *Decision Sciences, Fogelman College of Business & Economics, The University of Memphis, Memphis, Tennessee, USA,* mamini@cc.memphis.edu

Regina Berretta, *Instituto de Ciências Matemáticas e de Computação, Universidade de São Paulo, São Carlos, São Paulo, Brazil,* regina@icmsc.sc.usp.br

Vicente Campos, *Departament d'Estadística i Investigació Operativa, Universitat de València, València, Spain,* Vicente.Campos@uv.es

Ken Chisholm, *Department of Computer Studies, Napier University, Edinburgh, Scotland,* ken@dcs.napier.ac.uk

Pablo E. Coll, *Departamento de Computación, Facultad de Ciencias Exactas y Naturales, Universidad Nacional de Buenos Aires, Buenos Aires, Argentina,* pecoll@dc.uba.ar

David Corne, *School of Computer Science, Cybernetics, and Electronic Engineering, University of Reading, England,* D.W.Corne@reading.ac.uk

Gianni Di Caro, *Institut de Recherches Interdisciplinaires et de Développements en Intelligence Artificielle (IRIDIA), Université Libre de Bruxelles, Brussels, Belgium,* gdicaro@iridia.ulb.ac.be

Dipankar Dasgupta, *The Institute for Intelligent Systems, Department of Mathematical Sciences, University of Memphis, Memphis, Tennessee, USA,* dasgupta@msci.memphis.edu

Marco Dorigo, *Institut de Recherches Interdisciplinaires et de Développements en Intelligence Artificielle (IRIDIA), Université Libre de Bruxelles, Brussels, Belgium,* mdorigo@ulb.ac.be

Guillermo A. Durán, *Departamento de Computación, Facultad de Ciencias Exactas y Naturales, Universidad Nacional de Buenos Aires, Buenos Aires, Argentina,* willy@dc.uba.ar

Russ Eberhart, *Purdue School of Engineering and Technology, Indianapolis, Indiana, USA,* eberhart@engr.iupui.edu

Gusz Eiben, *Department of Mathematics and Computer Science, Leiden University, Leiden, The Netherlands,* gusz@cs.leidenuniv.nl

Bernd Freisleben, *Department of Electrical Engineering and Computer Science, University of Siegen, Siegen, Germany,* freisleb@informatik.uni-siegen.de

Luca Maria Gambardella, *Istituto Dalle Molle di Studi sull'Intelligenza Artificiale (IDSIA), Lugano, Switzerland,* luca@idsia.ch

Fred Glover, *MediaOne Chaired Professor, University of Colorado, Colorado, USA,* Fred.Glover@colorado.edu

Prabhat Hajela, *Department of Mechanical Engineering, Aeronautical Engineering, and Mechanics, Rensselaer Polytechnic Institute, Troy, NY, USA,* hajela@rpi.edu

Emma Hart, *Department of Artificial Intelligence, University of Edinburgh, Edinburgh Scotland,* emmah@dai.ed.ac.uk

Jano van Hemert, *Department of Mathematics and Computer Science, Leiden University, Leiden, The Netherlands,* jvhemert@cs.leidenuniv.nl

Diana Holstein, *Facultad de Ciencias Exactas, Universidad Nacional de La Plata, La Plata, Buenos Aires, Argentina,* dholst@ada.info.unlp.ar

James Kennedy, *Bureau of Labor Statistics, Washington, USA,* Kennedy_Jim@bls.gov

Gary A. Kochenberger, *College of Business, University of Colorado, Denver, Colorado, USA,* gkochenberger@castle.cudenver.edu

Manuel Laguna, *Graduate School of Business and Administration, University of Colorado, Boulder, Colorado, USA,* Manuel.Laguna@colorado.edu

Gary B. Lamont, *Department of Electrical and Computer Engineering, Air Force Institute of Technology, Wright-Patterson Air Force Base, Ohio, USA,* lamont@afit.af.mil

Jouni Lampinen, *Department of Information Technology and Production Economics, Faculty of Accounting and Industrial Management, University of Vaasa, Vaasa, Finland,* Jouni.Lampinen@uwasa.fi

Robert Marmelstein, *Department of Electrical and Computer Engineering, Air Force Institute of Technology, Wright-Patterson Air Force Base, Ohio, USA,* marmels@afit.af.mil

Rafael Martí, *Departament d'Estadística i Investigació Operativa, Universitat de València, València, Spain,* Rafael.Marti@uv.es

Peter Merz, *Department of Electrical Engineering and Computer Science, University of Siegen, Siegen, Germany,* pmerz@informatik.uni-siegen.de

René Michel, *Institute for Applied Computer Science and Formal Description Methods (AIFB), University of Karlsruhe (TH), Karlsruhe, Germany,* rmi@aifb.uni-karlsruhe.de

Martin Middendorf, *Institute for Applied Computer Science and Formal Description Methods (AIFB), University of Karlsruhe (TH), Karlsruhe, Germany,* mmi@aifb.uni-karlsruhe.de

Pablo Moscato, *Faculdade de Engenharia Elétrica e de Computação, Departamento de Engenharia de Sistemas, Universidade Estadual de Campinas, Campinas, Brazil,* moscato@densis.fee.unicamp.br

Jan Paredis, *MATRIKS, Universiteit Maastricht, Maastricht, The Netherlands,* jan@riks.nl

Riccardo Poli, *School of Computer Science, University of Birmingham, Birmingham, England,* R.Poli@cs.bham.ac.uk

Kenneth V. Price, *Owl Circle, Vacaville, California, USA,* kvprice@pacbell.net

Colin R. Reeves, *School of Mathematical and Information Sciences, Coventry University, Coventry, England,* C.Reeves@coventry.ac.uk

Rainer Storn, *International Computer Science Institute, Berkeley, California, USA,* storn@icsi.berkeley.edu

Robert G. Reynolds, *Department of Computer Science, Wayne State University, Detroit, Michigan, USA,* reynolds@wsu.edu

Peter Ross, *Department of Artificial Intelligence, University of Edinburgh, Edinburgh, Scotland,* peter@dai.ed.ac.uk

Rafal Salustowicz, *Istituto Dalle Molle di Studi sull'Intelligenza Artificiale (IDSIA), Lugano, Switzerland,* rafal@idsia.ch

Jürgen Schmidhuber, *Istituto Dalle Molle di Studi sull'Intelligenza Artificiale (IDSIA), Lugano, Switzerland,* juergen@idsia.ch

Thomas Stützle, *FG Intellektik, FB Informatik, Technische Universität Darmstadt, Darmstadt, Germany,* tom@intellektik.informatik.tu-darmstadt.de

Éric Taillard, *Istituto Dalle Molle di Studi sull'Intelligenza Artificiale (IDSIA), Lugano Switzerland,* eric@idsia.ch

David A. Van Veldhuizen, *Department of Electrical and Computer Engineering, Air Force Institute of Technology, Wright-Patterson Air Force Base, Ohio, USA,* dvanveld@afit.af.mil

Takeshi Yamada, *NTT Communication Science Laboratories, Kyoto, Japan,* yamada@cslab.kecl.ntt.co.jp

Jun Sun Yoo, *Department of Mechanical Engineering, Aeronautical Engineering, and Mechanics, Rensselaer Polytechnic Institute, Troy, NY, USA,* yooj3@rpi.edu

Ivan Zelinka, *Faculty of Technology, Brno University of Technology, Zlin, Moravia, Czech Republic,* Zelinka@zlin.vutbr.cz

Contents

Acknowledgements

Many people have helped in the process of producing this book, either indirectly through their patience and support, directly via their professional or academic involvement, or both. On the professional side, we want to thank David Hatter, Caroline Howell, and Sarah Cassie at McGraw-Hill, as well as Steve Gardiner at SG Publishing Services for his excellent preef-rooding. On the academic side, we are grateful of course to all of our contributors and co-ordinating editors. In addition to them, Peter Angeline and David Fogel were both helpful in providing ideas for contributions. Also, DC would like to thank Edmund Burke for his forebearance as regards other projects while this book was being finalised, and Chris Hines (who would like to remain anonymous) for technical 'support'.

As regards limitless patience and personal support, DC thanks his parents, Bessie and Mervyn Corne, his wife Anna, and especially his son Stephen. MD thanks all the IRIDIA people and acknowledges support from the Belgian FNRS, of which he is a research associate. FG thanks his wife Diane and daughter Lauren, whose tolerance for the improbable and convoluted schedules of the male member of their household fortunately exceeds all good sense.

Preface

At the time of writing, there are several well-established optimization techniques that are generally useful (that is, they can be easily tailored) for addressing almost any kind of optimization problem, no matter how multi-constrained or complex. These techniques include, for example, evolutionary algorithms, simulated annealing, and tabu search. By 'well-established', we mean that these methods are generally well-known. For example, there are several books in print concerning these techniques, they are widely used in industry and science and they are becoming widely taught at advanced undergraduate and graduate level. This does *not* mean, however, that these techniques are well-understood. Computer scientists and researchers in Artificial Intelligence and related areas are ever more actively investigating these techniques, looking into such questions as to how they can best be tailored to address particular kinds of problems, whether their convergence behaviour or dynamics can be predicted, how they perform in comparison with one-another, and whether we will ever be able to say, *a priori*, which method will be the best basic approach to a given type of optimization problem.

In pursuit of the research efforts hinted at above, researchers in these techniques have in recent years developed a host of new ideas for novel and inspired optimization techniques. This book is about some of the more successful of these new techniques. Almost every one of the techniques described in this book has been found to outperform well-established methods on a particular problem or range of problems. The idea for this book grew mainly from the latter observation. In particular, when this is combined with the fact that several of these new ideas have an inherently interesting and inspiring origin, the need and demand for this book seemed compelling. Hence the present volume, which: (a) introduces a range of new and 'proven' ideas (ant colony optimization, differential evolution immune system methods, memetic algorithms, scatter search) in one coherent text; and (b) also introduces a range of less mature but clearly highly promising new ideas (co-evolutionary constraint satisfaction, cultural algorithms, particle swarm methods, stepwise adaptive weight algorithms, parallel distributed genetic programming, probabilistic incremental program evolution), again, in one coherent text.

Producing this book has been an enjoyable and stimulating activity. We hope that our readers will share that experience!

DC, MD, FG May 1999

Chapter One

Introduction

David Corne, Marco Dorigo, and Fred Glover

1.1 OPTIMIZATION

Optimization is a key topic in computer science, artificial intelligence, operational research, and related fields. Outside these scientific communities the meaning of 'optimization' is rather imprecise: it simply means "doing better". In the context of this book, however, optimization is the process of trying to find the best possible solution to an *optimization problem* within (usually) a given time limit. In turn, an optimization problem is simply a problem for which there are different possible solutions, and there is some clear notion of solution quality. That is, an optimization problem exists when different candidate solutions can be meaningfully compared and contrasted.

Industry and science are rich in such problems. For example, there are many possible ways to design a telecommunications network: which is the most reliable? There are countless ways to organize a factory production schedule: which gives the best throughput? There are a great variety of ways in which a given protein molecule might be structured in three-dimensional space: which has the minimal potential energy? Some such questions are very simple to address. The answer may be easy to find because there are very few possible candidate solutions anyway, and we can simply assess each of them in turn. Or, there may be too many candidates for an exhaustive search, but a fundamental understanding of the problem will either yield the best solution directly, or a quick way to find it.

However, very many optimization problems are fundamentally *hard*. This is the most typical scenario when it comes to realistic and relevant problems in industry or science. The intuitive idea of *hard* corresponds to some quite precise ideas in computer science. Essentially, a 'hard' problem is one for which we cannot *guarantee* to find the best solution in an acceptable amount of time (see Harel [1987] for a readable and thorough introduction to this topic). In practice, however, the quest to solve hard problems is not quite so hopeless as this definition suggests. This is due to the use of *approximate methods*. An approximate method is an algorithm which we use to try to find solutions to (usually) hard optimization problems, and which runs quickly, but which gives no guarantee that the solution it will find is the best possible. Good approximate methods, especially when tailored and customized to work with a particular optimization problem, may often find an optimal (best) solution very quickly.

One very common and practical example of an optimization problem is the school timetabling problem. In general, the problem of generating a school class timetable which satisfies a collection of given constraints (essentially: pupils or teachers should not be in two places at once, rooms should not be double-booked or over-filled, and only certain timeslots should be used for classes) is fundamentally hard. In more formal terms, we say that it is *NP*-hard; this is the set of all problems which, loosely speaking, cannot be guaranteed to be solved in reasonable time by any known method. However, some (but by no means all) of the real-world examples of this problem turn out to be fairly easy to solve in practice. This may be because there happen to be enough rooms of adequate capacity, or few enough classes, or few enough connections between classes (a connection between classes is a constraint which bars them from being scheduled at the same time), or some combination of these. In such cases, approximate methods might tend to find acceptable or even optimal solutions quickly every time (that is, each time it is used at this school before a teaching semester starts). However, as resources and funding become more strained in many educational environments, instances of the school timetabling problem are getting more difficult. In such cases it remains true that approximate methods are still the best way to address them, but we are increasingly challenged towards designing ever more effective such methods. In general, for hard school timetabling and similar problems, we can rarely be confident that the results we achieve are truly optimal – there may well be a better possible solution which makes more efficient use of the available resources. However, progress in optimization – that is, the design of new and better ideas in optimization – will gradually increase our success at such problems.

Another common example is the well-known travelling salesman problem (Lawler et al [1985]). This is the problem of finding the shortest route which visits each of a given collection of points precisely once, returning eventually to the starting point. When the practical instance is actually the problem of a real salesman who needs to plan a day's visits to a small number of nearby locations, the problem might occasionally be simple to solve. This could be because there are so few cities that an exhaustive search can find the best solution in reasonable time. Or, it may be that powerful approximate methods developed especially for this problem, such as the Lin-Kernighan heuristic (Lin & Kernighan [1973]), and particularly Johnson's Iterated Lin-Kernighan method (Johnson [1990]), will often find a good solution quickly. However, there are many settings in which travelling salesman problems occur which are very difficult to solve to optimality. An example is VLSI chip fabrication; here, thousands of holes need to be drilled at certain positions on a silicon chip, and we need to minimize the time it will take to drill them all. Well-developed approximate methods for the problem, such as the two just mentioned, will typically work quite well on such problems, but the failure to guarantee optimal solutions is now a reality; there remains much room for improvement, both in the speed at which solutions are obtained, and in terms of solution quality. In fact, a number of the chapters in this book concern the use of new ideas in optimisation to address the TSP, and thus represent its continuing use as a proving ground for advances in optimization.

Since most real world optimization problems seem to be both fundamentally hard (in the sense of being NP-hard) and also practically hard (in the sense that practical instances of the problem do not happen to be easily solved anyway), research into good approximate methods remains valuable, and continues worldwide. Any new development in optimization which leads to better results on a particular problem, or to new approximate methods which may be applied to a wide range of problems, is of considerable value to science and industry. It may lead to such things as substantial financial savings for corporations, significantly more effective healthcare, or appreciably cheaper and more reliable communications. This collection of ongoing motivations has, over the years, led to a fairly steady stream of ideas for approximate algorithms to solve hard optimization problems. In particular, some of the new ideas over the past decade or so have given improved approaches to many well-known hard optimization problems. We briefly discuss optimization methods, and 'old' and 'new' ideas, in the remainder of this introductory chapter; the succeeding chapters are then devoted to a series of the more recent and pioneering ideas in this field, in most cases presenting results on hard optimization problems which improve significantly over those obtained with more well-established methods. In other cases, the emphasis is on novelty and promise, and ideas which will support established optimization methods or enable new kinds of problem to be tackled.

1.2 STOCHASTIC ITERATIVE METHODS

Optimization methods are the tools used by researchers or practitioners whose task it is to solve an optimization problem. There are a handful of key *types* of optimization method, ranging from specific (designed for and applicable only to a very particular and small class of problems) to general (applicable to almost any optimization problem). What we concentrate on in this book are *stochastic iterative search* methods. These are very much at the 'general' end of the spectrum. These methods usually take on the very general shape of the algorithm in Figure 1.1 (A partial exception occurs for the Scatter Search and Path Relinking approaches of Part Five, which de-emphasize randomization and alternatively incorporate adaptive memory strategies).

---

1. **Begin**: Generate and evaluate an initial collection of candidate solutions S.

2. **Operate**: Produce and evaluate a collection of new candidate solutions S' by making randomized changes to (or 'operating' on) selected members of S.

3. **Renew**: Replace some of the members of S with some of the members of S', and then (unless some termination criterion has been reached) return to 2.

Fig. 1.1: Generalized stochastic iterative search.

These methods tend to be favoured for three main reasons. First, they tend to be rather simple to implement; only a handful of lines of pseudocode, if not actual code, are needed to describe the essential elements of most such methods; Price, for example (in chapter six) emphasizes the compactness of his Differential Evolution algorithm, which is quite surprising when set against its superiority over far more sophisticated methods on at least some problems. Second, they are very general; there is no *a priori* requirement on the kinds of optimization problem which can be addressed. For example, it need not be a differentiable function of real valued parameters, and it need not be expressible in any particular constraint language. Third, they have proved very successful in finding good, fast solutions to hard optimization problems in a great variety of academic, practical, and scientific applications. This success has two aspects. First, when taken 'off the shelf' (if appropriately packaged) a good stochastic iterative search based optimization method can be applied to almost any optimization problem with little or no more effort than is involved in the (obviously necessary) task of writing code which evaluates a candidate solution to that problem. Also, they are successful in the obvious sense that, with such fairly minimal development and implementation, results are often impressive. Second, these techniques provide frameworks which can be easily and richly tailored with specialized heuristics to exploit knowledge about the problem at hand.

Stochastic iterative search methods are all based on the key idea of *generate and test*. Somehow, a candidate solution to the problem at hand is generated. It is then tested for quality. If it is found to be not good enough, then we repeat the process, each time generating a different candidate solution to test. The most obvious version of an iterative generate and test strategy is *random search*. At each iteration, we simply come up with a brand new random solution. However, an enormous variety of optimization methods have been explored which basically follow the generate and test theme, but use more interesting and fruitful ways to guide the generation of new candidate solutions. In these methods, the key is to somehow use information from previously visited solutions to guide the generation of new candidates. Since (in a typical realistic problem) the number of potential candidate solutions is very massively larger than the number we can hope to generate and test in reasonable time, the candidate solution generator component of an optimization method is critical to success.

To design an optimization method is therefore to design a way of dealing with the following question: how can we use information gleaned from previously seen candidate solutions to guide the generation of new ones? In random search, we do not use information from previous solutions at all; performance of random search is consequently very poor. But in current, well-established optimization methods, three proven successful ideas in response to this question are mainly used. These are:

- Idea 1: New candidate solutions are slight variations of previously generated candidates.

- Idea 2: New candidate solutions are generated by recombining aspects of two or more existing candidates.

- Idea 3: The 'parents' from which new candidates are produced (in Ideas 1 or 2) are selected from previously generated candidates via a stochastic and competitive strategy which favours better-performing candidates.

The 'slight variations' mentioned in Idea 1 are achieved by so-called *neighbourhood* or *mutation* operators, also called *move* operators. For example, suppose we are trying to solve a timetabling problem and we encode a solution as a string of numbers such that the *j*th number represents the timeslot given to event *j*. We can simply use a mutation operator which changes a randomly chosen number in the list to a new, randomly chosen value. The 'mutant' timetable is thus a slight variation on its 'parent' timetable. If, instead, we are addressing an instance of the travelling salesman problem, then we would typically encode a candidate solution as a permutation of the cities (or points) to be visited. Our neighbourhood operator in this case might simply be to swap the positions of a randomly chosen pair of cities.

Operators which produce new candidates from two or more existing ones are called *crossover*, *recombination*, or *merge* operators. Some examples of this operation perform straightforward 'cut and splice' operations. Other examples involve more sophisticated strategies, in which, perhaps, two or more parent candidates are the inputs to a self-contained algorithmic search process which outputs one or more new 'child' candidates. Parts Two, Four and Five of this book, respectively on Differential Evolution, Memetic Algorithms, and Scatter Search and Path Relinking, focus in different ways on new ideas for this recombination process.

Finally, a randomized but competetive strategy is used to decide who will be a parent. The strategy is usually that the fitter a candidate is, the more likely it is to be selected to be a parent, and thus be the (at least partial) basis of a new candidate solution.

Well-established optimization methods such as Simulated Annealing (Aarts & Korst [1989]), Tabu Search (Glover [1989, 1990]), Genetic Algorithms (Holland [1975], Goldberg [1989]), and so on, all use at least one of these key ideas. They also involve a great variety of subsidiary features for controlling the course of the search, and adapting the behaviour of the method as the search proceeds. An excellent introduction to a broad collection of these techniques is Reeves [1995]. Next, we briefly recap the main details of these established methods before briefly introducing some of the new ideas which are our main focus.

1.3 ESTABLISHED IDEAS IN OPTIMIZATION

The existing, successful methods in stochastic iterative optimization fall into two broad classes: local search, and population-based search. In local search, a special 'current' solution is maintained, and its neighbours (new candidates only slightly different from it) are explored to find better quality solutions. Occasionally, one of these neighbours becomes the new current solution, and then *its* neighbours are explored, and so forth. The simplest example of a local search method is called hillclimbing (sometimes called random mutation hillclimbing, or stochastic hillclimbing, and so on). Figure 1.2 illustrates it.

---

1. **Begin**: Generate and evaluate an initial 'current' solution s.

2. **Operate**: Change s, producing s', and evaluate s'.

3. **Renew**: If s' is better than s, then overwrite s with s'.

4. **Iterate**: Unless a termination criterion is met, return to 2.

Fig. 1.2: The simple Hillclimbing algorithm.

Hillclimbing essentially iterates Idea 1 by continually producing new candidate solutions which are slight variations of the current solution. It also encapsulates a simple but effective variation on Idea 3: the solution which forms the basis for generating new candidates is always the best solution found so far (actually, a solution whose fitness is the best found so far). More sophisticated local search methods, in different ways, improve on hillclimbing by being more careful, or more clever, in the way that new candidates are generated. In simulated annealing, for example, the difference is basically in step 3: sometimes, we will accept s' as the new current solution, even if it is worse then s. Without this facility, hillclimbing is prone to getting stuck at local peaks – solutions whose neighbours are all worse than the current solution – or plateaux – areas of the solution space where there is considerable scope for movement between solutions of equal goodness, but where very few or none of these solutions has a fitter neighbour. With this facility, simulated annealing – and other local search methods – can sometimes (but certainly not always) avoid such difficulties.

In population-based search, the notion of a single current solution is replaced by the maintenance of a population (a collection) of (usually) different current solutions. New solutions are generated by first selecting members of this population to be 'parents', and then making changes to these parents to produce children. In population-based search, Idea 2 comes into play. Since there is now a collection of current solutions, rather than just one, we can exploit this fact by using two or more from this collection at once as the basis for generating new candidates. Also, the introduction of a population brings with it further opportunities and issues. For example, Idea 3 is now open to more interesting realizations in which we use some strategy or other to *select* which solutions will be parents. Also, when one or more new candidate solutions have been produced, we need a strategy for maintaining the population. That is, assuming that we wish to maintain the population at a constant size (which is almost always the case), some of the population must be discarded in order to make way for some or all of the new candidates produced via mutation or recombination operations. Notice, in particular, that a selection strategy combined with a population maintenance strategy adds up to an overall strategy for implementing a variation on Idea 3. Whereas the selection strategy encompasses the details of how to choose candidates from the population itself, the population maintenance strategy affects what is present in the population, and what therefore is selectable.

There are almost as many population-based optimization algorithms and variants as there are ways to handle the above issues. The key characteristic of population-based algorithms, commonly known as evolutionary algorithms, are the sheer variety of ways which have been used to implement Ideas 1, 2 and 3. A plethora of questions surround these issues which the scientific community is barely beginning to address. For example, is it best to use local search or population based search for a given problem? What kind of selection strategy will work best in general? Can we predict how long a population-based method will take to find the best solution given the population size? If anything, the results of continuing and growing investigation into such questions reveals that it is probably rather naive to expect definitive answers. Instead, we tend to see a considerable degree of problem-dependence; that is, the method which works best on a particular optimization problem may well *not* work best on another, even closely-related problem. One consequence of this general observation which is of particular interest to us here is that it justifies, indeed encourages, the search for new methods. And, indeed, such new methods have emerged often in recent years as researchers worldwide have investigated the many questions surrounding local and population based search.

1.4 NEW IDEAS IN OPTIMIZATION

Continued investigation into local search and population based optimization techniques, and a consequent growing regard for their ability to address realistic problems well, has inspired much investigation of new and novel optimization methods. Often we can express these as different or novel ways of implementing Ideas 1, 2 and 3 of section 1.2, but in other cases this would be quite difficult or inappropriate.

For example, Dorigo (see Part One) has drawn inspiration from the workings of natural ant colonies to derive an optimization method based on ant colony behaviour. This has lately been shown to be remarkably successful on some problems, and there is now a thriving international research community worldwide further investigating the technique. Essentially, the method works by equating the notion of a candidate solution with the route taken by an ant between two (possibly the same) places. Ants leave a trail as they travel, and routes which correspond to good solutions will leave a stronger trail than routes which lead to poor solutions. The trail strength affects the routes taken by future ants. We could view this as a very novel way to implement a combination of Ideas 1, 2 and 3. Essentially, previously generated solutions (routes taken by past ants) affect (via trail strengths) the solutions generated by future ants. However, it makes more sense to view it for what it is – a new and novel idea for optimization inspired by a process which occurs in nature.

Part Two concerns an algorithm called Differential Evolution, developed by Price (see chapter six). Differential Evolution can be easily viewed as a new way to implement Idea 2; that is, it is a novel and highly successful method for recombination of two or more parent solutions. Rather than children combining parts of their parents, in Differential Evolution a child is a linear combination of itself and its parents in which the *difference* between its parents plays a key role. As such, Differential Evolution is necessarily restricted to optimization problems in which solutions are represented by real numbers (or perhaps integers); however, the power of even quite simple Differential Evolution algorithms to solve complex real-world problems provides great compensation for this restriction.

In Part Three, we look at methods based on the workings of the biological immune system. Introduced by Dasgupta (chapter ten), Part Three reveals how the very complex and successful workings of biological immune systems can inspire new ideas in optimization and related fields. This type of method is less clearly seen as an optimization method *per se*, but the chapters in Part Three reveal how immune systems based notions can provide highly effective support to optimization techniques, leading to improved optimization algorithms.

Part Four, introduced by Moscato (chapter fourteen), concerns Memetic Algorithms. This represents one of the more successful emerging ideas in the ongoing research effort to understand population based and local search algorithms. The idea itself is simply to *hybridize* the two types of method, and Memetic Algorithms represent a particular way of achieving the hybridization, and one which has chalked up a considerable number of successes in recent years.

Part Five, introduced by Glover (chapter nineteen), is about Scatter Search, and extensions within that idea named Path Relinking. Scatter Search places a particular focus on Idea 2 – that is, the use of previously generated candidate solutions in the generation of new ones, and, like Differential Evolution, emphasizes the production of new solutions by a linear combination of the 'reference' solutions, although guided instead by combining intensification and diversification themes, and introducing strategies for rounding integer variables. Path relinking introduces considerably more sophistication into how new solutions are generated. Essentially, the idea here is that good material for new candidate solutions can be found by exploring the paths in solution space which link together known good solutions. Both Scatter Search and Path Relinking also exploit adaptive memory strategies.

Finally, in Part Six, we look at a collection of other new methods. Loosely speaking, each of the ideas described in Part Six is in some way 'newer' than those in previous parts; and so, rather than devote a whole Part of this book to each of them, they are collected together as a chapter each in the final Part. In each case, the idea has already led to very promising results in one or more application areas. In chapter twenty-three, Paredis uses an established approach in evolutionary computation – that of coevolution – in a promising and novel way, for addressing constraint satisfaction problems. In chapter twenty-four, Reynolds introduces his novel idea of 'Cultural Algorithms', which employs a model of cultural change within an optimization algorithm, thus providing an additional means to direct and guide the generation of new candidate solutions. Chapter twenty-six, by Eiben and van Hemert, details a simple but extremely effective new algorithm for constrained problems whose focus is on adaptation of the fitness function as the algorithm runs. This simple algorithm has led to some very successful results in graph colouring, one of the classic operations research problems, as well as others. In chapter twenty-seven, Poli introduces his Parallel Distributed Genetic Programming method. This is a technique for evolving parallel, distributed programs to perform particular tasks, which has been shown to compare very favourably with 'canonical' Genetic Programming (Koza 1992]) – the reference 'established method' in this context – on a particular range of benchmark problems. Finally, similar comments can be made about the topic of chapter twenty-eight, in which Salustowicz and Schmidhuber describe their Probabilistic Incremental Program Evolution method. This extends various ideas in evolutionary computation to automatically evolve programs to perform certain tasks, in a way quite different from the way this is done in standard Genetic Programming, and with very promising results so far.

1.5 CONCLUDING REMARKS

There are many more new ideas we could have included in the succeeding chapters. Our selection of what to incorporate in this book is based partly on successful results so far, and partly on what we perceive as the 'generality' of the idea. Several more new ideas and methods fit these criteria quite well. An example along the lines of local search is Guided Local Search (Voudouris & Tsang [1995]), and an example along the lines of population-based search is Population Based Incremental Learning (Baluja & Caruna [1995]). These two particular cases happen to be mentioned in the book – chapter fifteen incorporates Guided Local Search within a Memetic Algorithm approach to the travelling salesman problem, and chapter twenty-eight discusses Population Based Incremental Learning as one of the key inspirations for Probabilistic Incremental Program Evolution. However, several other such developments are inevitably left out of the book; one such, for example, is Variable Neighbourhood Search (Hansen & Mladenovic [1998]), which has proved successful in a number of applications recently.

What is left out is a result of constraints of time and space, but what remains within these pages is, we hope, a collection of some of the more novel and inspired new methods in optimization. We have assembled this material with two purposes in mind: first, to provide in one volume a survey of recent successful ideas in stochastic iterative optimization which can support undergraduate teaching (and beyond) of relevant courses; second, to provide intellectual stimulation and a practical resource for the very many researchers and practitioners in optimization who wish to learn about and experiment with these latest ideas in the field.

Part One
Ant Colony Optimization

Co-ordinating Editor:

Marco Dorigo

Contributors:

Giovanni Agazzi

Gianni Di Caro

Marco Dorigo

Luca Maria Gambardella

René Michel

Martin Middendorf

Thomas Stützle

Éric Taillard

Chapter Two

The Ant Colony Optimization Meta-Heuristic

Marco Dorigo and Gianni Di Caro

2.1 INTRODUCTION

Ant algorithms are multi-agent systems in which the behaviour of each single agent, called *artificial ant* or *ant* for short in the following, is inspired by the behaviour of real ants. Ant algorithms are one of the most successful examples of swarm intelligent systems (Bonabeau et al [1999]), and have been applied to many types of problems, ranging from the classical travelling salesman problem, to routing in telecommunications networks. In this section we will focus on the *ant colony optimization (ACO) meta-heuristic* which defines a particular class of ant algorithms, called in the following *ACO algorithms*.

ACO algorithms have been inspired by the following experience run by Goss et al [1989] using a colony of real ants. A laboratory colony of Argentine ants (*Iridomyrmex humilis*) is given access to a food source in an arena linked to the colony's nest by a bridge with two branches of different length (see Figure 2.1). Branches are arranged in such a way that ants going in either direction (from the nest to the food source or vice versa) must choose between one branch or the other. The experimental observation is that, after a transitory phase which can last a few minutes, most of the ants use the shortest branch. It is also observed that the colony's probability of selecting the shortest branch increases with the difference in length between the two branches. The emergence of this shortest path selection behaviour can be explained in terms of *autocatalysis* (i.e. *positive feedback*) and *differential path length*, and it is made possible by an indirect form of communication, known as stigmergy (Grassé [1959]), mediated by local modifications of the environment.

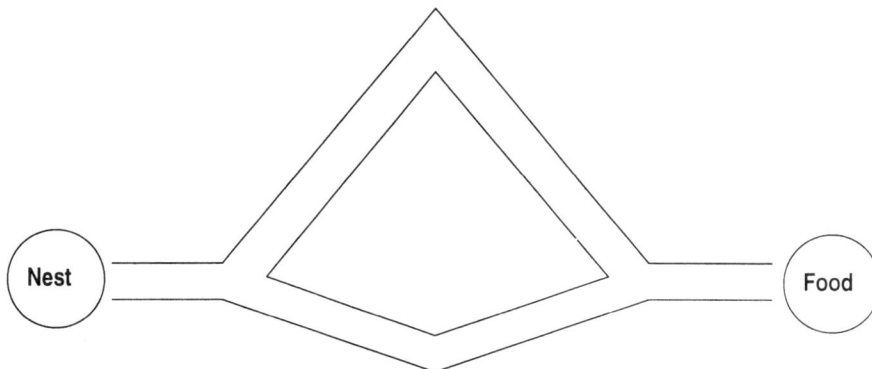

Fig. 2.1: Experimental apparatus for the bridge experiment. Branches have different length. Ants move from the nest to the food source and back.

In fact, Argentine ants, while going from the nest to the food source and vice versa, deposit a chemical substance, called *pheromone*, on the ground. When they arrive at a decision point, such as the intersection between the shorter branch and the longer branch, they make a probabilistic choice which is biased by the amount of pheromone they smell on the two branches. This behaviour has an autocatalytic effect because the very fact of choosing a path will increase the probability that it will be chosen again by future ants. At the beginning of the experiment there is no pheromone on the two branches and therefore ants going from the nest to the food source will choose any one of the two branches with equal probability. Due to differential branch length, the ants choosing the shortest branch will be the first ones to reach the food source. When these ants, in their path back to the nest, reach the decision point, they will see some pheromone trail on the shorter path (this is the trail they released during their forward journey) and will therefore choose the shorter path with higher probability than the longer one. New pheromone will then be released on the chosen path, making it even more attractive for the subsequent ants. While the process iterates, pheromone on the shorter path is deposited at a higher rate than on the longer one. Therefore, the shorter path is more and more frequently selected by ants until, eventually, all ants end up using this path.

In the rest of this chapter we will illustrate how these simple ideas can be engineered and put to work so that a colony of artificial ants can find good solutions to difficult optimization problems. Subsequent chapters in Part One then go into further detail on the application of these ideas to particular problems.

2.2 THE SIMPLE ANT COLONY OPTIMIZATION ALGORITHM

In this section a very simple ant-based algorithm is presented to illustrate the basic behaviour of the ACO meta-heuristic and to put in evidence its basic components. The main task of each artificial ant, similarly to their natural counterparts, is to find a shortest path between a pair of nodes on a graph on which the problem representation is suitably mapped.

Let $G=(N,A)$ be a connected graph with $n=|N|$ nodes. The simple ant colony optimization (S-ACO) algorithm can be used to find a solution to the shortest path problem defined on the graph G, where a solution is a path on the graph connecting a source node f to a destination node d, and the path length is given by the number of hops in the path (see Figure 2.2 for an illustration of this).

Associated with each arc (i, j) of the graph is a variable τ_{ij} called the *artificial pheromone trail*. In the following we will just use the phrase 'pheromone trail' as shorthand for this, or sometimes just 'pheromone'. Pheromone trails are read and written by ants. The amount (intensity) of pheromone trail is proportional to the utility, as estimated by the ants, of using that arc to build good solutions.

Each ant applies a step-by-step constructive decision policy to build solutions to the problem. At each node local information, maintained on the node itself and/or on its outgoing arcs, is used in a stochastic way to decide the next node to move to. The decision rule of an ant k located in node i uses the pheromone trails τ_{ij} to compute the probability with which it should choose node $j \in \mathcal{N}_i$ as the next node to move to (at the beginning of the search process, a small amount of pheromone τ_{ij} is assigned to all the arcs) where $\mathcal{N}_i$ is the set of one-step neighbours of node i:

$$p_{ij}^k = \begin{cases} \dfrac{\tau_{ij}}{\displaystyle\sum_{j \in \mathcal{N}_i} \tau_{ij}} & \text{if } j \in \mathcal{N}_i \\[2ex] 0 & \text{if } j \notin \mathcal{N}_i \end{cases} \qquad (2.1)$$

While building a solution ants deposit pheromone information on the arcs they use. In S-ACO ants deposit a constant amount $\Delta\tau$ of pheromone. Consider an ant that at time t moves from node i to node j. It will change the pheromone value τ_{ij} as follows:

$$\tau_{ij}(t) \leftarrow \tau_{ij}(t) + \Delta\tau \qquad (2.2)$$

By this rule, which simulates real ants' pheromone depositing on arc (i, j), an ant using the arc connecting node i to node j increases the probability that ants will use the same arc in the future. As in the case of real ants, autocatalysis and differential path length are at work to favour the emergence of short paths.

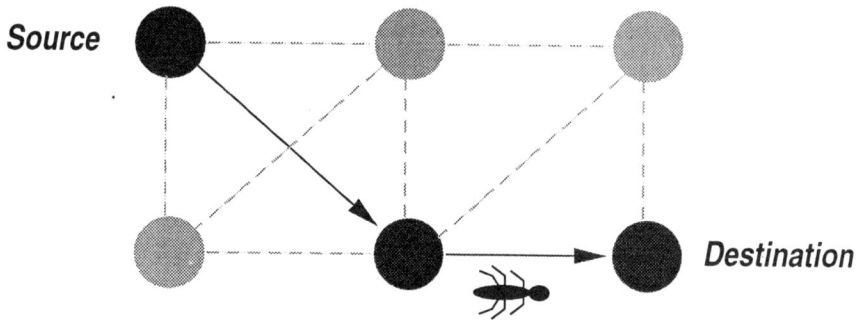

Fig. 2.2: Ants build solutions, that is paths, from a source to a destination node. The ants choosing the solid line path will arrive sooner to the destination and will therefore be the first to bias search of ants moving back to the source node.

To avoid a quick convergence of all the ants towards a sub-optimal path, an exploration mechanism is added: similar to real pheromone trails, artificial pheromone trails 'evaporate'. In this way pheromone intensity decreases automatically, favouring the exploration of different arcs during the whole search process. The evaporation is carried out in a simple way, decreasing pheromone trails exponentially, $\tau \leftarrow (1-\rho)\tau$, $\rho \in (0,1]$, at each iteration of the algorithm. Preliminary experiments run with S-ACO using a simple graph modelling the experimental apparatus of Figure 2.1 have shown that the algorithm effectively finds the shortest path between the simulated nest and food sources. Experiments have also shown that if we increase the complexity of the searched graph, for example by connecting the nest to the food source by means of more than two possible paths, the behaviour of the algorithm tends to become less stable and the value given to parameters becomes critical.

S-ACO must therefore be taken for what it is: a didactic example that, because of its simplicity, has a number of limitations. The algorithms defined in the remainder of this chapter, and those described and employed in chapters three, four and five, all share the basic properties of S-ACO, but are enriched with extra capabilities which help to overcome S-ACO limitations. For example, we can make the amount of pheromone deposited by ants proportional to the quality of the solution built or being generated by the ant so that pheromone information becomes more useful in directing the ants' search. Also, because in many problems some form of heuristic information is available at the nodes, it would be desirable to have ants able to use it.

Another important point is that it would be desirable to enlarge the class of problems that can be attacked by ACO algorithms. S-ACO can be applied only to shortest path problems without additional constraints: If we want to use it to find, for example, a shortest Hamiltonian path on a graph, that is, a path which visits all the nodes once and only once, we need to give our ants at least some limited form of memory.

In the following section we will introduce the ACO meta-heuristic, which builds on the S-ACO model enriching artificial ants with a number of capacities that do not find their counterpart in real ants, but that allow to overcome the above-listed limitations of the simple model.

2.3 THE ACO META-HEURISTIC

ACO algorithms (that is, instances of the ACO meta-heuristic introduced later in this section) can be applied to discrete optimization problems that can be characterized as follows:

- A finite set of N_C *components* $C = \{c_1, c_2, ..., c_{N_C}\}$ is given.

- A finite set L of possible *connections/transitions* among the elements of C is defined over a subset $\tilde{C}$ of the Cartesian product $C \times C$, where:
$$L = \{l_{c_i c_j} \mid (c_i, c_j) \in \tilde{C}\}, \; |L| \leq N_C^2$$

- For each $l_{c_i c_j} \in L$ a *connection cost* function $J_{c_i c_j} \equiv J(l_{c_i c_j}, t)$, possibly parametrized by some time measure t, can be defined.

- A finite set of *constraints* $\Omega \equiv \Omega(C, L, t)$ is assigned over the elements of sets C and L.

- The *states* of the problem are defined in terms of sequences $s = \langle c_i, c_j, ..., c_k \rangle$ over the elements of C (or, equivalently, of L). If S is the set of all possible sequences, the set $\tilde{S}$ of all the (sub)sequences that are feasible with respect to the constraints $\Omega(C, L, t)$, is a subset of S. The elements in $\tilde{S}$ define the problem's *feasible states*. The length of a sequence s, that is, the number of components in the sequence, is expressed by $|s|$.

- A *neighbourhood structure* is defined as follows: state s_2 is said to be a neighbour of s_1 if (i) both s_1 and s_2 are in S, (ii) state s_2 can be reached from s_1 in one logical step, that is, if c_i is the last component in the sequence determining state s_1 there must exist $c_2 \in C$ where $l_{c_1 c_2} \in L$ and $s_2 \equiv \langle s_1, c_2 \rangle$.

- A *solution* ψ is an element of $\tilde{S}$ satisfying all the problem's requirements. A solution is said to be *multi-dimensional* if it is defined in terms of multiple distinct sequences over the elements of C.

- A *cost* $J_\psi(L,t)$ is associated with each solution ψ. $J_\psi(L,t)$ is a function of all the costs $J_{c_i c_j}$ of all the connections belonging to the solution.

Consider the graph $G=(C, L)$ associated with a given discrete optimization problem instance as above defined. The solutions to the optimization problem can be expressed in terms of feasible paths on the graph G. ACO algorithms can be used to find minimum cost paths (sequences) feasible with respect to the constraints Ω. For example, in the travelling salesman problem defined in section 2.4.1, C is the set of cities, L is the set of arcs connecting cities, and a solution ψ is an Hamiltonian circuit.

In ACO algorithms a population (colony) of agents (or ants) collectively solve the optimization problem under consideration by using the above graph representation. Information collected by the ants during the search process is encoded *in pheromone trails* τ_{ij} associated with connections l_{ij} (note that here, and in the following, we simplify notation by setting $l_{c_i c_j} = l_{ij}$). Pheromone trails encode a long-term memory about the whole ant search process. Depending on the problem representation chosen, pheromone trails can be associated to all problem's arcs, or only to some of them. Arcs can also have an associated *heuristic value* η_{ij} representing a priori information about the problem instance definition or run-time information provided by a source different from the ants.

The following is a list of some important general characteristics which pertain to the ant colony as a whole:

- Although each ant is complex enough to find a (probably poor) solution to the problem under consideration, good quality solutions can only emerge as the result of the collective interaction among the ants.

- Each ant makes use only of private information and of information local to the node it is visiting. (Note that in the following, the terms node and component, as well as arc and connection/transition, will be used interchangeably).

- Ants communicate with other ants only in an indirect. way, mediated by the information they read/write in the variables storing pheromone trail values.

- Ants are not adaptive themselves. On the contrary, they adaptively modify the way the problem is represented and perceived by other ants.

The following is a list of properties and characteristics which pertain to individual ants of the colony:

- An ant searches for minimum cost feasible solutions $\hat{J}_\psi = \min_\psi J_\psi(L,t)$.

- An ant k has a memory $\mathcal{M}^k$ that it can use to store information on the path it followed so far. Memory can be used (i) to build feasible solutions, (ii) to evaluate the solution found, and (iii) to retrace the path backward.

- An ant k in state $s_r = \langle s_{r-1}, i \rangle$ can move to any node j in its *feasible neighbourhood* $\mathcal{N}_i^k$. The feasible neighbourhood of a node i is defined as follows:

$$\mathcal{N}_i^k = \{ j \mid (j \in \mathcal{N}_i) \wedge (\langle s_r, j \rangle \in \tilde{S}) \} .$$

- An ant k can be assigned a *start state* s_s^k and one or more *termination conditions* e^k. Usually, the start state is expressed as a unit length sequence, that is, a single component.

- Ants start from the start state and move to feasible neighbour states, building the solution in an incremental way. The construction procedure terminates when, for at least one ant k, at least one of the termination conditions e^k is satisfied.

- An ant k located on node i can move to a node j chosen in $\mathcal{N}_i^k$. The move is selected applying a probabilistic decision rule.

- An ant's probabilistic decision rule is a function of (i) the values stored in a node local data structure $\mathcal{A}_i = [a_{ij}]$, called the *ant-routing table*, obtained by a functional composition of nodes locally available pheromone trails and heuristic values, (ii) the ant's private memory storing its past history, and (iii) the problem constraints.

- When moving from node i to neighbour node j the ant can update the pheromone trail τ_{ij} on the arc (i, j). This is called *online step-by-step pheromone update*.

- Once it has built a solution, the ant can retrace the same path backward and update the pheromone trails on the traversed arcs. This is called *online delayed pheromone update*.

- Once it has built a solution, and, if the case, after it has retraced the path back to the source node, the ant dies, freeing all the allocated resources.

In informal terms, the behaviour of ants during the operation of an ACO algorithm can be summarized as follows. A colony of ants concurrently and asynchronously move through adjacent states of the problem by moving through neighbour nodes of G, as shown in the S-ACO algorithm. The ants move by applying a stochastic local decision policy that makes use of the information contained in the ant-routing tables local to the nodes. By moving, ants incrementally build solutions to the optimization problem being addressed. Once an ant has built a solution, or while the solution is being built, the ant evaluates the (partial) solution and deposits information about its goodness on the pheromone trails of the connections it has used. This pheromone trail information will direct the search process of the future ants.

Besides the activity of the ants themselves, an ACO algorithm includes two more procedures: *pheromone trail evaporation* and *daemon actions* (the daemon actions component is optional). Pheromone evaporation is the process by means of which the pheromone trail intensity on the connections automatically decreases over time. From a practical point of view, pheromone evaporation is needed to avoid a too rapid convergence of the algorithm towards a sub-optimal region. It implements a useful form of *forgetting*, favouring the exploration of new areas of the search space. Daemon actions can be used to implement centralized actions which cannot be performed by single ants. Examples of daemon actions are the activation of a local optimization procedure, or the collection of global information that can be used to decide whether it is useful or not to deposit additional pheromone to bias the search process from a non-local perspective. As a practical example, the daemon can observe the path found by each ant in the colony and choose to deposit extra pheromone on the arcs used by the ant that made the shortest path. Pheromone updates performed in this or similar ways by the daemon are called *offline pheromone updates*.

In Figure 2.3 the ACO meta-heuristic behaviour is described in pseudo-code. The main procedure of the ACO meta-heuristic manages, via the *schedule_activities* construct, the scheduling of the three above discussed components of an ACO algorithm: (i) ants' generation and activity, (ii) pheromone evaporation, and (iii) daemon actions. It is important to note that the *schedule_activities* construct does not specify how these three activities are scheduled and synchronized and, in particular, whether they should be executed in a completely parallel and independent way, or if some kind of synchronization among them is necessary. This leaves the designer the freedom to specify the way these three procedures should interact.

Although ACO algorithms are suitable to find minimum cost (shortest) paths on a graph in general, it is important to note that they are an interesting approach only for those particular shortest path problems for which more classical algorithms like dynamic programming or label correcting methods (Bertsekas [1995]) cannot be efficiently applied. This is the case in many examples of such problems. The following is a list of some particular cases of interest:

- *NP*-hard problems, for which the dimension of the full state-space graph is exponential in the dimension of the problem representation. In this case, ants make use of the much smaller graph G, built from the problem's components, and use their memory to generate feasible solutions which in most ACO implementations are then taken to a local optimum by a problem specific local optimizer.

- Those shortest path problems in which the properties of the problem's graph representation change over time concurrently with the optimization process, that has to adapt to the problem's dynamics. In this case, the problem's graph can even be physically available (like in networks problems), but its properties, like the value of connection costs $J_{c_i c_j}(t)$, can change over time. In this case we conjecture that the use of ACO algorithms becomes more and more appropriate as the variation rate of costs $J_{c_i c_j}(t)$ increases and/or the knowledge about the variation process diminishes.

- Those problems in which the computational architecture is spatially distributed, as in the case of parallel and/or network processing. In cases like these, ACO algorithms can be particularly effective. This is due to their intrinsically distributed and multi-agent nature, which presents a close and exploitable match with these types of architectures.

```
1        procedure ACO_meta-heuristic()
2            while (termination_criterion_not_satisfied)
3                schedule_activities
4                    ants_generation_and_activity();
5                    pheromone_evaporation();
6                    daemon_actions();                      { optional }
7                end schedule_activities
8            end while
9        end procedure


1        procedure ants_generation_and_activity();
2            while available_resources()
3                schedule_the_creation_of_a_new_ant();
4                new_active_ant();
5            end while
6        end procedure


1        procedure new_active_ant()                        { ant lifecycle}
2            initialize_ant();
3            M = update_ant_memory();
4            while (current_state ≠ target_state)
5                A = read_local_ant-routing_table();
6                P = compute_transition_probabilities(A,M,Ω);
7                next_state = apply_ant_decision_policy(P, Ω);
8                move_to_next_state(next_state);
                 if (online_step-by-step_pheromone_update)
9                    deposit_pheromone_on_the_visited_arc();
10                   update_ant_routing_table();
                 end if
11               M = update_internal_state();
12           end while
                 if (online_delayed_pheromone_update)
13               foreach visited_arc ∈ ψ do
14                   deposit_pheromone_on_the_visited_arc();
15                   update_ant_routing_table();
16               end foreach
                 end if
17           die();
18       end procedure
```

Fig. 2.3: The ACO meta-heuristic in pseudo-code, with comments in braces. The procedure daemon_actions() at line 6 of the ACO_meta_heuristic() is optional and refers to centralized actions executed by a daemon possessing global knowledge. In new_active_ant(), target_state (line 4) refers to a complete solution built by the ant. The step-by-step and delayed pheromone updating procedures at lines 9–10 and 14–15 are often mutually exclusive. When both are absent the pheromone is deposited by the daemon.

In the following section we will consider the application of the ACO-meta-heuristic to two paradigmatic problems belonging to the above defined classes of problems: the travelling salesman problem (TSP) and the adaptive routing in communications networks. TSP is the prototypical representative of *NP*-hard combinatorial optimization problems (Garey & Johnson [1979]) where the problem instance is statically assigned and the information is globally available. On the contrary, in the problem of adaptive routing in communications networks an exogenous process (the incoming data traffic) makes the problem instance change over the time, and temporal constraints impose to solve the problem in a distributed way.

Chapters three, four, and five of this book illustrate further applications of the ACO meta-heuristic to *NP*-hard combinatorial optimization problems, while further and more detailed examples of applications to adaptive routing can be found in Di Caro & Dorigo [1998], Di Caro & Dorigo [1998a], Schoonderwoerd et al [1996], and Van der Put [1998].

2.4 ACO FOR THE TRAVELLING SALESMAN PROBLEM

2.4.1 The Travelling Salesman Problem

The travelling salesman problem plays an important role in ant colony optimization because it was the first problem to be attacked by these methods (see Dorigo [1992], Dorigo et al [1991], and Dorigo et al [1996]). The TSP was chosen for many reasons: (i) it is a problem to which the ant colony metaphor is easily adapted, (ii) it is one of the most studied *NP*-hard problems in combinatorial optimization (Lawler et al [1985], Reinelt [1994]), and (iii) it is very easily explained, so that the algorithm behaviour is not obscured by too many technicalities.

The travelling salesman problem, using the terminology introduced in the previous section, can be defined as follows. Let C be a set of components, representing cities, L be a set of connections fully connecting the elements in C, and let $J_{c_i c_j}$ be the cost (length) of the connection between c_i and c_j, that is, the distance between cities i and j. The TSP is the problem of finding a minimal length Hamiltonian circuit on the graph $G=(C,L)$. An Hamiltonian circuit of graph G is a closed tour ψ visiting once and only once all the N_C nodes of G. Its length is given by the sum of the lengths $J_{c_i c_j}$ of all the arcs of which it is composed. Distances need not be symmetric (in an asymmetric TSP $J_{c_j c_i}$ can be different from $J_{c_i c_j}$), and the graph need not be fully connected: if it is not, the missing arcs can be added giving them a very high length.

In the following we will present Ant System, a paradigmatic example of how ACO algorithms can be applied to the TSP. Extensions of Ant System can be found in Bullnheimer et al [1997], Dorigo & Gambardella [1997] and Stützle & Hoos [1997].

2.4.2 Ant System for the TSP

Ant System (AS), which was the first ACO algorithm (Dorigo [1992], Dorigo et al [1991]), was designed as a set of three ant algorithms differing in the way the pheromone trail was updated by ants. Their names were: *ant-density*, *ant-quantity*, and *ant-cycle*. A number of ant algorithms, including the ACO meta-heuristic, have later been inspired by ant-cycle, the best-performing of the three (hereafter, as it has been done in most published papers, we identify Ant System with ant-cycle). Many of these implementations have found interesting and successful applications (see section 2.8, or Dorigo et al [1998] for a more detailed overview).

In Figure 2.4, the new_active_ant() procedure used by the AS algorithm is shown. This can be informally described as follows.

1	**procedure** new_active_ant(ant_identifier)
2	k = ant_identifier ; i = get_start_city() ; $s^k = i$;
3	$\mathcal{M}^k = i$;
4	**while** ($\mid s^k \mid \neq N_C$)
5	**foreach** $j \in \mathcal{N}_i^k$ **do** $read(a_{ij})$ **end foreach**
6	**foreach** $j \in \mathcal{N}_i^k$ **do** $\mid\mathcal{P}\mid_{ij} = p_{ij} = \dfrac{a_{ij}}{\sum_{l \in \mathcal{N}_i^k} a_{il}}$ **end foreach**
7	next_node = apply_probabilistic_rule($\mathcal{P}$, $\mathcal{N}_i^k$);
8	i = next_node ; $s^k = \langle s^k, i \rangle$
9	-
10	-
11	add_i_to_ant_memory($\mathcal{M}^k$)
12	**end while**
13	**foreach** $l_{ij} \in \psi^k$ **do**
14	$\tau_{ij} \leftarrow \tau_{ij} + 1/J_\psi^k$
15	$a_{ij} \leftarrow \dfrac{[\tau_{ij}]^\alpha [\eta_{ij}]^\beta}{\sum_{l \in \mathcal{N}_i^k} [\tau_{il}]^\alpha [\eta_{il}]^\beta}$
16	**end foreach**
17	free_all_allocated_resources();
18	**end procedure**

Fig. 2.4: Pseudo-code of Ant System's new_active_ant() procedure. Line numbers are put in one-to-one correspondence with those of the ACO meta-heuristic pseudo-code of Figure 2.3. Instruction at lines 9 and 10 are empty because no online step-by-step pheromone update is performed. Pheromone evaporation is performed between lines 14 and 15 by the pheromone_evaporation() procedure of Figure 2.3, which is activated by an appropriate synchronization mechanism (not shown in the pseudo-code).

A number $m \leq N_C$ of ants are positioned in parallel on m cities. The ants' start state, that is, the start city, can be chosen randomly, and the memory $\mathcal{M}^k$ of each ant k is initialized by adding the current start city to the set of already visited cities (initially empty). Ants then enter a cycle (Figure 2.4, lines 4 → 12) which lasts N_C iterations, that is, until each ant has completed a tour.

During each step an ant located on node i considers the feasible neighbourhood, reads the entries a_{ij} of the ant-routing table $\mathcal{A}_i$ of node i (Figure 2.4, line 5), computes the transition probabilities (line 6), and then applies its decision rule to choose the city to move to (line 7), moves to the new city (line 8), and updates its memory (line 11).

Once ants have completed a tour (which happens synchronously, given that during each iteration of the while loop each ant adds a new city to the tour under construction), they use their memory to evaluate the built solution and to retrace the same tour backward and increase the intensity of the pheromone trails τ_{ij} of visited connections l_{ij} (lines 13 → 16). This has the effect of making the visited connections become more desirable for future ants. Then the ants die, freeing all the allocated resources. In AS all the ants deposit pheromone and no problem-specific daemon actions are performed. The triggering of pheromone evaporation happens after all ants have completed their tours. Of course, it would be easy to add a local optimization daemon action, like a 3-opt procedure (Lin [1965]); this has been done in most of the ACO algorithms for TSP that have developed after AS (see for example Dorigo & Gambardella [1997], Stützle & Hoos [1999]).

The amount of pheromone trail $\tau_{ij}(t)$ maintained on connection l_{ij} is intended to represent the learned desirability of choosing city j when in city i (which also corresponds to the desirability that the arc l_{ij} belong to the tour built by an ant). The pheromone trail information is changed during problem solution to reflect the experience acquired by ants during problem solving. Ants deposit an amount of pheromone proportional to the quality of the solutions ψ they produced: the shorter the tour generated by an ant, the greater the amount of pheromone it deposits on the arcs which it used to generate the tour. This choice helps to direct search towards good solutions. Note that, as for most of the ACO implementations, there is no per-connection credit assignment: all the connections belonging to a solution receive the same amount of pheromone depending on the quality of the solution the connection is part of.

The memory (or internal state) $\mathcal{M}^k$ of each ant contains the already visited cities and is called a *tabu list*. The term tabu list is used here to indicate a simple memory that contains the set of already visited cities, and has no relation with tabu search (Glover [1989, 1990]). The memory $\mathcal{M}^k$ is used to define, for each ant k, the set of cities that an ant located on city i still has to visit. By exploiting $\mathcal{M}^k$ an ant k can build feasible solutions, that is, it can avoid visiting a city twice. Also, memory allows the ant to compute the length of the tour generated and to cover the same path backward to deposit pheromone on the visited arcs.

The ant-routing table $\mathcal{A}_i = [a_{ij}]$ of node i, where $\mathcal{N}_i$ is the set of all the neighbour nodes of node i, is obtained by the following functional composition of pheromone trails $\tau_{ij}(t)$ and local heuristic values η_{ij}. Note that the heuristic values used are $\eta_{ij} = 1/d_{ij}$, where d_{ij} is the distance between cities i and j. In other words, the shorter the distance between two cities i and j, the higher the heuristic value η_{ij}.

$$a_{ij} = \frac{[\tau_{ij}(t)]^\alpha [\eta_{ij}]^\beta}{\sum_{l \in \mathcal{N}_i}[\tau_{il}(t)]^\alpha [\eta_{il}]^\beta} \quad \forall j \in \mathcal{N}_i \tag{2.3}$$

where α and β are two parameters that control the relative weight of pheromone trail and heuristic value.

The probability $p_{ij}^k(t)$ with which at the t-th algorithm iteration an ant k located in city i chooses the city $j \in \mathcal{N}_i^k$ to move to is given by the following probabilistic decision rule:

$$p_{ij}^k(t) = \frac{a_{ij}(t)}{\displaystyle\sum_{l \in \mathcal{N}_i^k} a_{il}(t)} \tag{2.4}$$

where $\mathcal{N}_i^k \subseteq \mathcal{N}_i$ is the feasible neighbourhood of node i for ant k (that is, the set of cities ant k has not yet visited) as defined by using the ant private memory $\mathcal{M}^k$ and the problem constraints.

The role of the parameters α and β is the following. If $\alpha=0$, the closest cities are more likely to be selected: this corresponds to a classical stochastic greedy algorithm (with multiple starting points since ants are initially randomly distributed on the nodes). If on the contrary $\beta=0$, only pheromone amplification is at work: this method will lead to the rapid emergence of a *stagnation*, that is, a situation in which all ants make the same tour which, in general, is strongly sub-optimal (Dorigo et al [1996]). An appropriate trade-off has to be set between heuristic value and trail intensity.

After all ants have completed their tour, each ant k deposits a quantity of pheromone $\Delta\tau^k(t) = 1/J_\psi^k(t)$ on each connection l_{ij} that it has used, where $J_\psi^k(t)$ is the length of tour $\psi^k(t)$ done by ant k at iteration t:

$$\tau_{ij}(t) \leftarrow \tau_{ij}(t) + \Delta\tau^k(t), \quad \forall l_{ij} \in \psi^k(t), \ k = 1,...,m \tag{2.5}$$

where m is the number of ants at each iteration (maintained constant) and the total number of ants is set to $m = N_C$. Note that these parameters settings, as well as those for α, β and ρ, set respectively to 1, 5 and 0.5, were experimentally found to be good in Dorigo [1992]. This way of setting the value $\Delta\tau^k(t)$ makes it a function of the ant's performance: the shorter the tour done, the greater the amount of pheromone deposited.

After pheromone updating has been performed by the ants, pheromone evaporation is triggered by applying the following rule to all the arcs l_{ij} of the graph G:

$$\tau_{ij}(t) \leftarrow (1 - \rho)\tau_{ij}(t) \tag{2.6}$$

where $\rho \in (0,1]$ is the pheromone trail decay coefficient (the initial amount of pheromone $\tau_{ij}(0)$ is set to a small positive constant value τ_0 on all arcs).

Note that in the original ant system (Dorigo [1992], Dorigo et al [1991]) pheromone evaporation was performed before pheromone updating. The algorithm presented here and the original one are exactly the same if the values $\Delta\tau^k(t)$ used in Equation 2.5 are set to $\Delta\tau^k(t) = 1/((1 - \rho)J_\psi^k(t))$.

2.5 ACO FOR ROUTING IN COMMUNICATIONS NETWORKS

2.5.1 The Routing Problem

The generic routing problem in communications networks can be informally stated as the problem of building and using *routing tables* to direct data traffic so that some measure of network performance is maximized. The choice of a measure of network performance is a function of the type of network and of the provided services. For example, in a packet-switching network performance can be measured by throughput (amount of correctly delivered bits per time unit), and by the distribution of data packet delays.

We can use the terminology introduced in section 2.3 to give a formal definition of the routing problem. Let the sets C and L correspond respectively to the sets of processing nodes and communication links of the real network. Let $G=(C,L)$ be a directed graph, where each node in the set C represents a network node with processing/queuing and forwarding capabilities, and each oriented arc in L is a directional transmission system (link). Each link has associated a cost measure defined by its physical properties and crossing traffic flow. Network applications generate data flows from source to destination nodes. For each node in the network, the local routing component uses the local routing table to choose the best outgoing link to direct incoming data towards their destination nodes. The routing table $\mathcal{R}_i = [r_{ijd}]$ of a generic node i where $\mathcal{N}_i$ is the set of neighbours of i, says to data packets entering node i and directed towards destination node d which should be the next node j in the neighbourhood of i to move to. Routing tables are bi-dimensional because the choice of the neighbour node to which a data packet entering a generic node i should be forwarded is a function of the packet destination node d. Ant-routing tables possess the same bi-dimensional structure: pheromone trails associated to each connection are vectors of $N_C - 1$ values. In fact, ant-routing tables, in all the ACO implementations for routing, are used to build the routing tables by means of implementation-dependent transformations. These vectorial pheromone trails are the natural extension of the scalar trails used for the TSP.

Other important differences with the TSP implementation arise from the different nature of the two problems: (i) each ant is assigned a defined pair (f, d) of start and destination nodes and, discovering a path between f and d, the ant builds only a part of the whole problem solution, defined in terms of paths between all the pairs (i, j) in the network, (ii) the costs associated with the connections are not statically assigned: they depend on the connection's physical properties and on the traffic crossing the connection, that interacts recursively with the routing decisions.

In the following subsection we present S-AntNet, a simplified version of the AntNet algorithm. A detailed description of AntNet can be found in Di Caro & Dorigo [1998], while a more performing extension of it is described in Di Caro & Dorigo [1998a].

2.5.2 S-AntNet

In S-AntNet, each ant searches for a minimum cost path between a pair of nodes of the network. Ants are launched from each network node towards destination nodes randomly selected to match the traffic patterns. Each ant has a source node f and a destination node d, and moves from f to d hopping from one node to the next till node d is reached. When ant k is in node i it chooses the next node j to move to according to a probabilistic decision rule which is a function of the ant's memory and of the local ant-routing table.

Pheromone trails are still connected to arcs, but are memorized in variables associated to arc-destination pairs. That is, each directed arc (i,j) has $N_C - 1$ trail values $\tau_{ijd} \in [0,1]$ associated, one for each possible destination node d an ant located in node i can have (therefore, in general, $\tau_{ijd} \neq \tau_{jid}$). Each arc has also associated an heuristic value $\eta_{ij} \in [0,1]$ independent of the final destination. The heuristic values are set to the following values:

$$\eta_{ij} = 1 - \frac{q_{ij}}{\sum_{l \in \mathcal{N}_i} q_{il}} \tag{2.7}$$

where q_{ij} is the length (in bits waiting to be sent) of the queue of the link connecting node i with its neighbour j.

```
1       procedure new_active_ant(ant_identifier)
2           k = ant_identifier ; i = get_start_node() ; t = get_end_node(); sᵏ = i ;
3           Mᵏ = i;
4           while (i ≠ d)
5               foreach j ∈ Nᵢᵏ do read( aᵢⱼd )  end foreach
```

$$6 \qquad \textbf{foreach } j \in \mathcal{N}_i^k \textbf{ do } |\mathcal{P}|_{ijd} = p_{ijd} = \frac{a_{ijd}}{\sum_{l \in \mathcal{N}_i^k} a_{ild}} \quad \textbf{end foreach}$$

```
7               next_node = apply_probabilistic_rule(P, Nᵢᵏ );
8               i = next_node ; sᵏ = ⟨sᵏ,i⟩
9               -
10              -
11              add_i_to_ant_memory(Mᵏ);
12          end while
13          foreach lᵢⱼ ∈ ψᵏ do
14              τᵢⱼd ← τᵢⱼd + Δτᵏ ;
```

$$15 \qquad a_{ijd} \leftarrow \frac{w\,\tau_{ijd} + (1-w)\eta_{ij}}{w + (1-w)(|\mathcal{N}_i^k|-1)} ;$$

```
16          end foreach
17          free_all_allocated_resources();
18      end procedure
```

Fig. 2.5: Pseudo-code of S-AntNet's new_active_ant() procedure. Line numbers correspond with those of the ACO meta-heuristic pseudo-code of Figure 2.3. Instructions at lines 9 and 10 are empty since no online step-by-step pheromone update is performed. Update of pheromone trails and ant-routing tables is done by the ant during its backward path toward the origin node (lines 13 → 16). Pheromone evaporation is performed between lines 14 and 15 by the pheromone_evaporation() procedure of Figure 2.3, which is activated by an appropriate synchronization mechanism (not shown in the pseudo-code).

In S-AntNet, as well as in most other implementations of ACO algorithms for routing problems, the daemon component (line 6 of the ACO meta-heuristic of Figure 2.3) is not present.

The local ant-routing table $\mathcal{A}_i$ is obtained by a functional composition of the local pheromone trails τ_{ijd} and heuristic values η_{ij}. While building the path to the destination, ants move using the same link queues as data. In this way ants experience the same delays as data packets and the time T_{fd} elapsed while moving from the source node f to the destination node d can be used as a measure of the path quality. The overall 'goodness' of a path can be evaluated by an heuristic function of the trip time T_{fd} and of a local adaptive statistical model maintained in each node. In fact, paths need to be evaluated relative to the network status because a trip time T judged of low quality under low congestion conditions could be an excellent one under high traffic load. Once the generic ant k has completed a path, it deposits on the visited nodes an amount of pheromone $\Delta\tau^k(t)$ proportional to the goodness of the path it built. To this purpose, after reaching its destination node, the ant moves back to its source nodes along the same path but backward and using high priority queues, to allow a fast propagation of the collected information.

During this backward path from d to f the ant k increases the pheromone trail value $\tau_{ijd}(t)$ of each connection l_{ij} previously used while it was moving from f to d. The pheromone trail intensity is increased by applying the following rule:

$$\tau_{ijd}(t) \leftarrow \tau_{ijd}(t) + \Delta\tau^k(t) \tag{2.8}$$

The reason the ant updates the pheromone trails during its backward trip is that, before it can compute the amount of pheromone $\Delta\tau^k(t)$ to deposit on the visited arcs it needs to complete a path from source to destination to evaluate it.

After the pheromone trail on the visited arc has been updated, the pheromone value of all the outgoing connections of the same node i, relative to the destination d, evaporates (note that in this case the decay factor is chosen so that it operates a normalization of the pheromone values which continue therefore to be usable as probabilities):

$$\tau_{ijd}(t) \leftarrow \frac{\tau_{ijd}(t)}{(1 + \Delta\tau^k(t))}, \quad \forall j \in \mathcal{N}_i \tag{2.9}$$

where $\mathcal{N}_i$ is the set of neighbours of node i.

As we said, S-AntNet's ant-routing table $\mathcal{A}_i = [a_{ijd}(t)]$ of node i is obtained, as usual, by the composition of the pheromone trail values with the local heuristic values. This is done as follows:

$$a_{ijd}(t) = \frac{w\tau_{ijd}(t) + (1-w)\eta_{ij}}{w + (1-w)/(|\mathcal{N}_i|-1)} \tag{2.10}$$

where $j \in \mathcal{N}_i$, d is the destination node, $w \in [0,1]$ is a weighting factor and the denominator is a normalization term.

The ants' decision rule is then defined as follows. Let ant k be located on node i and be directed towards node d. If there is at least one city in the ant's current location neighbourhood that ant k has not visited yet, then the ant chooses the next node $j \in \mathcal{N}_i$ with the following probability (however note that, in S-AntNet, differently from what happens in Ant System, the neighbourhood and the feasible neighbourhood are the same; that is, $\mathcal{N}_i^k \equiv \mathcal{N}_i$):

$$p_{ijd}^k(t) = \begin{cases} a_{ijd}(t) & \text{if } j \notin \mathcal{M}^k \\ 0 & \text{if } j \in \mathcal{M}^k \end{cases} \tag{2.11}$$

otherwise, a city $j \in \mathcal{N}_i$ is chosen with uniform probability: $p_{ijd}^k(t) = 1/|\mathcal{N}_i|$.

In other words, ants try to avoid cycles (Equation 2.11) but, in the case all the nodes in i's neighbourhood have already been visited by the ant, the ant has no choice and it has to re-visit a node, generating in this way a cycle. In this case the generated cycle is deleted from the ant memory, and so the ant forgets completely about it. Considering the stochasticity of the decision rule and the evolution in the traffic conditions, it is very unlikely that the ant repeats the same cycle over and over again.

2.6 PARALLEL IMPLEMENTATIONS

The population-oriented nature of ACO algorithms makes them particularly suitable to parallel implementation. In particular, it is at least in principle possible to exploit three different types of parallelism: (i) parallelism at the level of ants, (ii) parallelism at the level of data, and (iii) functional parallelism. Parallelism at the level of ants, which is probably the most obvious way of parallelizing an ACO algorithm, consists in considering a number $\mathcal{NC}$ of colonies, $\mathcal{NC} > 1$, each applied to the same problem instance. Colonies can be allowed or not to exchange information on the search process. Parallelism at the level of data consists in splitting the considered problem in a number of subproblems in the data domain, each one solved by a colony of ants. Last, functional parallelism could be easily obtained in an ACO algorithm by letting the procedures ants_generations_and_activity(), pheromone_evaporation(), and daemon_actions() (lines 4–6 of the ACO_meta-heuristic() procedure of Figure 2.3) perform their activities concurrently, maybe exchanging synchronization signals. Obviously, functional parallelism can be combined with the other two types of parallelism. Currently, all the parallel implementations of ACO algorithms use ant level parallelism. These implementations are briefly reviewed in the following.

- The first parallel versions of an ACO algorithm was Bolondi and Bondanza's implementation of AS for the TSP on the Connection Machine CM-2 (Hillis [1982]). The approach taken was that of attributing a single processing unit to each ant (Bolondi & Bondanza [1993]). Unfortunately, experimental results showed that communication overhead can be a major problem with this approach on fine grained parallel machines, since ants spend most of their time communicating to other ants the modifications they did to pheromone trails. As a result, the algorithm's performance was not impressive and scaled up very badly when increasing the problem dimensions.

- Better results were obtained on a coarse grained parallel network of 16 transputers (Bolondi & Bondanza [1993], Dorigo [1993]). In this implementation, Bolondi and Bondanza divided the colony into $\mathcal{NC}$ subcolonies, where $\mathcal{NC}$ was set to be the same as the number of available processors. Each subcolony acted as a complete colony and implemented therefore a standard AS algorithm. Once each subcolony completed an iteration of the algorithm, a hierarchical broadcast communication process collected the information about the tours of all the ants in all the subcolonies and then broadcast this information to all the $\mathcal{NC}$ processors. In this way, a concurrent update of the pheromone trails was performed. The speed-up obtained with this approach was nearly linear with the number of processors and this behaviour was shown to be rather stable for increasing problem dimensions.

- More recently, Bullnheimer et al [1997a] proposed two coarse grained parallel versions of AS called Synchronous Parallel Implementation (SPI) and Partially Asynchronous Parallel Implementation (PAPI). SPI is basically the same as the one implemented on transputers by Bolondi and Bondanza, while in PAPI pheromone information is exchanged among subcolonies every fixed number of iterations done by each subcolony. The two algorithms have been evaluated by simulation. The findings show that PAPI performs better than SPI, where performance was measured by running time and speedup. This is probably due to

PAPI's reduced communication caused by the less frequent exchange of pheromone trail information among subcolonies. More experiments are needed to compare the quality of results produced by the SPI and the PAPI implementations.

- An interesting aspect of any ant level parallel implementation is the type of pheromone trail information that should be exchanged between the $\mathcal{NC}$ subcolonies and how this information should be used to update the subcolony's trail information. Krüger et al [1998] considered: (i) the exchange of the global best solution: every subcolony uses the global best solution to choose where to add pheromone trail; (ii) the exchange of the local best solutions: every subcolony receives the local best solution from all other subcolonies and uses it to update pheromone trails; and (iii) the exchange of the total trail information: every colony computes the average over the trail information of all colonies. That is, every colony r ($1 \leq r \leq \mathcal{NC}$) sends τ^r to the other colonies and afterwards computes (where $\tau^r = [\tau_{ij}^r]$ is the trail information of subcolony r):

$$\tau_{ij}^r = \sum_{h=1}^{\mathcal{NC}} \tau_{ij}^h, \ 1 \leq i, j \leq n$$

Preliminary results indicate that methods (i) and (ii) are faster and give better solutions than method (iii).

- The execution of parallel independent runs is the easiest way to obtain a parallel algorithm and, obviously, it is a reasonable approach when the underlying algorithm is randomized. Stützle [1998] presents computational results for the execution of parallel independent runs on up to ten processors of his $\mathcal{MMAS}$ algorithm (Stützle & Hoos [1997], Stützle & Hoos [1997a]). His results show that the performance of $\mathcal{MMAS}$ improves with the number of processors.

2.7 ANTS, PHEROMONES, AND SOLUTIONS EVALUATION

In this section we discuss some of the most characteristic aspects of ACO algorithms. In particular, we focus on the way solutions generated by ants are evaluated, the way these evaluations are used to direct, via pheromone trail laying, ants' search, and on the importance of using a colony of ants.

Implicit and explicit solution evaluation

In ACO algorithms solutions generated by ants provide feedback to direct the search of future ants entering the system. This is done by two mechanisms. The first one, which is common to all ACO algorithms, consists of an *explicit* solution evaluation. In this case some measure of the quality of the solution generated is used to decide how much pheromone should be deposited by ants. The second one is a kind of *implicit* solution evaluation. In this case, ants exploit the differential path length (DPL) effect of real ants foraging behaviour. That is, the fact that if an ant chooses a shorter path then it is the first to deposit pheromone and to bias the search of forthcoming ants.

It turns out that in geographically distributed problems, like network problems, implicit solution evaluation based on the DPL effect can play an important role. In fact, as it was shown, for example, in Di Caro & Dorigo [1997, 1998], where explicit solution evaluation was switched off by setting the amount of pheromone deposited by ants to a constant value independent of the cost of the path built by the ant, it is possible to find good solutions to network problems just exploiting the DPL effect. Quite obviously, it has also been shown that coupling explicit and implicit solution evaluation (by making the amount of pheromone deposited proportional to the cost of the solution generated) improves performance.

The fact that the DPL effect can be exploited only in geographically distributed network problems is due to efficiency reasons. In fact, the distributed nature of nodes in routing problems allows the exploitation of the DPL effect in a very natural way, without incurring in any additional computational costs. This is due both to the decentralized nature of the system and to the inherently asynchronous nature of the dynamics of a real communications network.

On the contrary, this is not the case in those combinatorial optimization problems in which the most natural way to implement ACO algorithms is by using a colony of synchronized ants. That is, ants that synchronously add elements to the solution they are building. Of course, it would in principle be possible to have asynchronous ants, in the sense explained above, also in combinatorial optimization problems. The difficulty with this is the computational inefficiencies introduced by the computational overhead necessary to have independent, asynchronous ants. These inefficiencies can outweigh the gains which arise due to the exploitation of the DPL effect (this was, for example, the case of the asynchronous implementation of an ACO algorithm for the TSP reported in Cottarelli & Gobbi [1997]).

Explicit solution evaluation and pheromone laying

As we said before, after an ant has built a solution the cost of the built solution is used to compute the amount of pheromone the ant should deposit on the visited edges. In Ant System, for example, each ant deposits an amount of pheromone inversely proportional to the cost of the solution it generated. Obviously, this is only one of the possible choices and many implementations of ACO algorithms for the TSP or other combinatorial optimization problems exist that use different functional forms of the solution cost to decide how much pheromone the ants, or the daemon, should deposit. A problem which arises in routing problems, and in general in any problem where the characteristics of the problem change in unpredictable ways during problem solution, is that there is no simple way to evaluate a solution and therefore to decide how much pheromone ants should deposit. A way out to this problem, which is used by AntNet (Di Caro & Dorigo [1997], Di Caro & Dorigo [1998]), is to use ants to learn online a model of the network status that can be used to evaluate how good the solutions found by ants are.

Number of ants

The exact number of ants to be used is a parameter that must usually be set experimentally. Fortunately, ACO algorithms seem rather robust to the number of ants used. We will therefore limit our discussion to the following question: Why use a colony of ants (that is,

$m > 1$) rather than one single ant? In fact, although a single ant is capable of generating a solution, efficiency considerations suggest that the use of a colony can be a desirable choice. This is particularly true for geographically distributed problems, since the differential length effect exploited by ants in the solution of such problems can only arise with a colony of ants. It is also interesting to note that in routing problems ants solve $\hat{N} < N_C^2$ shortest path problems, and a colony should be used for each of these problems.

On the other hand, in the case of combinatorial optimization problems in which ants move synchronously, the use of m ants that build θ solutions each (that is, the ACO algorithm is run for θ iterations) could be equivalent, at least in principle, to the use of one ant that generates $m\theta$ solutions. Nevertheless, empirical evidence suggests that the performance of the algorithm is at its optimal level when the number m of ants is set to a value $M > 1$, where M is, in general, dependent on the class of problems to which the algorithm is applied.

2.8 OTHER ACO META-HEURISTIC APPLICATIONS

There are now available numerous successful implementations of the ACO meta-heuristic (Figure 2.3) applied to a number of different combinatorial optimization problems. These are listed in Table 2.1, ordered by application problem and chronologically. The most studied problems have been the travelling salesman, the quadratic assignment (QAP) and routing in telecommunication networks. For all of these problems, ACO algorithms are competitive with the best available heuristic approaches. In particular:

- For the particularly important class of quadratic assignment problems which model real world problems, ACO algorithms are currently one of the most performing heuristics available. Chapter three presents an overview of the available ACO algorithms for the QAP.

- Results obtained by the application of ACO algorithms to the TSP are very encouraging (see Stützle & Dorigo [1999] for an overview of applications of ACO algorithms to the TSP): they are often better than those obtained using other general-purpose heuristics like evolutionary computation or simulated annealing. Also, when adding to ACO algorithms rather unsophisticated local search procedures based on 3-opt (Lin [1965]) the quality of the results obtained (Dorigo & Gambardella [1997], Stützle [1998a]) is close to that obtainable by much more sophisticated methods. More research will be necessary to assess whether ACO algorithms can reach the performance of state-of-the-art algorithms like Iterated Lin-Kernighan (see Johnson & McGeoch [1997]).

- An ACO algorithm called AntNet (Di Caro & Dorigo [1998, 1998a]) outperformed a number of state-of-the-art routing algorithms for packet-switching networks on a set of benchmark problems.

Table 2.1: List of current applications of ACO algorithms. Classified by application and chronologically ordered.

Problem	Year	Main References	Algorithm Name(s)
Travelling salesman	1991	Dorigo [1992], Dorigo et al [1991, 1996]	AS
	1995	Gambardella & Dorigo [1995]	Ant-Q
	1997	Dorigo & Gambardella [1997, 1997a]	ACS, ACS-3-Opt
	1997	Stützle & Hoos [1997, 1997a]	$\mathcal{MMAS}$
	1997	Bullnheimer et al [1997a]	Asrank
Quadratic assignment	1994	Maniezzo et al [1994]	AS-QAP
	1997	Gambardella et al [1997]	HAS-QAP[a]
	1998	Maniezzo [1998]	ANTS-QAP
	1998	Taillard [1998]	FANT
	1999	Stützle & Hoos [1999], Stützle & Dorigo [chapter three, this volume]	$\mathcal{MMAS}$-QAP
	1999	Maniezzo & Colorni [1999]	AS-QAP[b]
Vehicle routing	1996	Bullnheimer & Strauss [1996], Bullnheimer et al [1997b, 1998]	AS-VRP
	1999	Gambardella et al [chapter five, this volume]	MACS-VRPTW
Connection-oriented network routing	1996	Schoonderwoerd et al [1996, 1997]	ABC
	1998	White et al [1998]	ASGA
	1998	Di Caro & Dorigo [1998b]	AntNet-FS
	1998	Bonabeau et al [1998]	ABC-smart ants
Connection-less network routing	1997	Di Caro & Dorigo [1997, 1998, 1998a]	AntNet, AntNet-FA
	1997	Subramanian et al [1997]	Regular ants
	1998	Heusse et al [1998]	CAF
	1998	Van der Put [1998], Van der Put & Rothkrantz [1999]	ABC-backward
Sequential ordering	1997	Gambardella & Dorigo [1997]	HAS-SOP
Graph colouring	1997	Costa & Hertz [1997]	ANTCOL
Shortest common supersequence	1998	Michel & Middendorf [1998]	AS-SCS
	1999	Michel & Middendorf [chapter four, this volume]	AS-SCS-L
Frequency assignment	1998	Maniezzo& Carbonaro [1998]	ANTS-FAP
Generalized assignment	1998	Ramalhinho Lourenço & Serra [1998]	MMAS-GAP
Multiple knapsack	1999	Leguizamón & Michalewicz [1999]	AS-MKP
Optical networks	1999	Navarro Varela & Sinclair [1999]	ACO-VWP
Single machine total tardiness	1999	Bauer et al [1999]	ACS-SMTTP

[a] HAS-QAP is an ant algorithm which does not follow all the aspects of the ACO metaheuristic.
[b] This is a variant of the original AS-QAP.

Very interesting results have been obtained also for:

- The sequential ordering problem (finding the shortest Hamiltonian path on a graph which satisfies a set of precedence constraints on the order in which nodes are visited). When applied to this problem HAS-SOP, an ACO algorithm coupled to a local search routine, has been found to improve upon many of the best known results on a wide set of benchmark problems (Gambardella & Dorigo [1997]).
- The shortest common supersequence problem and the vehicle routing problem. These two problems, as well as the ACO algorithms proposed for their solution, are the subject of chapters four and five.

Finally, ACO algorithms have also been applied to the graph colouring problem, for which reasonably good, although not state-of-the-art results were obtained.

2.9 A SHORT OVERVIEW OF THE REMAINDER OF PART ONE

Part One includes three further chapters dedicated to applications of ACO algorithms to some important and difficult combinatorial optimization problems. Although these are introduced and discussed in detail in the forthcoming chapters, it is interesting here to show how they can be cast in the ACO meta-heuristic framework.

2.9.1 The Quadratic Assignment Problem

The quadratic assignment problem can be stated as follows. Consider a set of n activities that have to be assigned to n locations. A matrix $\mathcal{D} = [d_{ij}]$ gives distances between locations, where d_{ij} is the distance between location i and location j, and a matrix $\mathcal{F} = [f_{hk}]$ characterizes flows among activities (transfers of data, material, humans, etc.), where f_{hk} is the flow between activity h and activity k. An assignment is a permutation π of $\{1,...,n\}$, where $\pi(i)$ is the activity that is assigned to location i. The problem is to find a permutation $\tau*$ which minimizes the sum of the products of the flows among activities by the distances between their locations. Note that the TSP can be seen as a particular case of the QAP: the items are the integers between 1 and n, while the locations are the cities to be visited. The problem is then to assign a different number to each city in such a way that the tour visiting the cities ordered according to their assigned number has minimal length.

In chapter three, the QAP is represented as follows. The set C of components comprises activities and locations. Transitions are from activities to locations and vice versa. Typically, an ant first chooses an activity, then a location to which to assign the activity, then another activity, and so forth, until all activities have been assigned. Activities and locations are chosen from the feasible neighbourhood, that is, from activities (locations) not yet assigned. Typically, in AS-QAP and $\mathcal{MMAS}$-QAP for example, pheromone trails are associated with transitions from activities to locations (that is, to the choice of the location to which to assign an activity), but not with transitions from locations to activities (which are chosen by some probabilistic or heuristic rule that is not a function of pheromone trails). Obviously, nothing prevents us from defining an ACO algorithm in which transitions from locations to activities are also a function of pheromone trails.

2.9.2 The Shortest Common Supersequence Problem

Given a set L of strings over an alphabet Σ, the shortest common supersequence problem consists in finding a string of minimal length that is a supersequence of each string in L. A string B is a supersequence of a string A if B can be obtained from A by inserting in A zero or more characters. Consider for example the set $L = \{bbbaaa, bbaaab, cbaab, cbaaa\}$. The string *cbbbaaab* is a shortest supersequence. Ants build solutions by repeatedly removing symbols from the front of the strings in L and appending them to the supersequence under construction. In practice, each ant maintains a vector of pointers to the front of the strings (where the front of a string is the first character in the string not yet removed) and moves in the space of the feasible vectors. Here the representation used by the ACO algorithm is the following. The components are the vectors of pointers, the transitions are implicitly defined by the rules which govern the way characters can be removed from the string fronts, and the constraints are implicitly defined by the ordering of the characters in the strings.

2.9.3 The Vehicle Routing Problem

Vehicle routing problems (VRPs) are a class of problems in which a set of vehicles has to serve a set of customers minimizing a cost function and subject to a number of constraints. The characteristics of the vehicles and of the constraints determine the particular type of VRP. The VRP considered in chapter five is called vehicle routing problem with time windows (VRPTW): Let $G = (N, A)$ be a complete directed graph, where $N = \{n_0,...,n_n\}$ is the set of nodes, and $A = (i, j) : i \neq j$ is the set of arcs. Node n_0 represents a depot, while the other nodes represent customers' locations. A weight $t_{ij} \geq 0$, representing the travel time from node n_i to node n_j, is associated with each arc (i, j). A demand $q_i \geq 0$ $(q_0 = 0)$ and a service window $[b_i, e_i]$, with $e_i \geq b_i \geq 0$, are associated with each customer n_i. The objective is to find minimum cost vehicle routes such that (i) every customer is visited exactly once by exactly one vehicle, (ii) every customer is visited during its time window, (iii) for every vehicle the total demand does not exceed the vehicle capacity Q, and (iv) every vehicle starts and ends its tour in the depot. The particular VRPTW considered in chapter five uses a hierarchical cost function: the first goal is to minimize the number of vehicles used, while the second goal is to minimize the total travel times. A solution with a lower number of vehicles is always preferred to a solution with a higher number of tours even if the travel time is higher. It is easy to see that VRPs and TSPs are closely related: a VRP consists of the solution of many TSPs with common start and end city (that is, the depot). As in the TSP, ants build their solutions by sequentially visiting all the cities: the problem's components are the cities, while the transitions can be associated to the arcs. The feasible neighbourhood is given by the set of unvisited cities and pheromone trails are associated to arcs.

Acknowledgements

We are grateful to Thomas Stützle for critical reading of a draft version of this article. Marco Dorigo acknowledges support from the Belgian FNRS, of which he is a Research Associate. This work was supported by a Marie Curie Fellowship awarded to Gianni Di Caro (CEC-TMR Contract N. ERBFMBICT 961153).

Chapter Three

ACO Algorithms for the Quadratic Assignment Problem

Thomas Stützle and Marco Dorigo

3.1 INTRODUCTION

The quadratic assignment problem (QAP) is an important problem in theory and practice. Many practical problems like backboard wiring (Steinberg [1961]), campus and hospital layout (Dickey & Hopkins [1972], Elshafei [1977]), typewriter keyboard design (Burkard & Offermann [1977]), scheduling (Geoffrion & Graves [1976]) and many others can be formulated as QAPs. The QAP can best be described as the problem of assigning a set of facilities to a set of locations with given distances between the locations and given flows between the facilities. The goal then is to place the facilities on locations in such a way that the sum of the product between flows and distances is minimal.

More formally, given n facilities and n locations, two $n \times n$ matrices $A = [a_{ij}]$ and $B = [b_{rs}]$, in which a_{ij} is the distance between locations i and j, and b_{rs} is the flow between facilities r and s, the QAP can be stated as follows:

$$\min_{\psi \in S(n)} \sum_{i=1}^{n} \sum_{j=1}^{n} b_{ij} a_{\psi_i \psi_j} \tag{3.1}$$

In Equation 3.1, $S(n)$ is the set of all permutations (corresponding to the assignments) of the set of integers $\{1, \ldots, n\}$, and ψ_i gives the location of facility i in the current solution $\psi \in S(n)$. Here $b_{ij} a_{\psi_i \psi_j}$ describes the cost contribution of simultaneously assigning facility i to location ψ_i and facility j to location ψ_j. In the following we denote with J_ψ the objective function value of permutation ψ.

The term *quadratic* stems from the formulation of the QAP as an integer optimization problem with a quadratic objective function. Let x_{ij} be a binary-valued variable which takes value 1 if facility i is assigned to location j and 0 otherwise. Then the problem can be formulated as follows:

$$\min \sum_{i=1}^{n} \sum_{j=1}^{n} \sum_{l=1}^{n} \sum_{k=1}^{n} a_{ij} b_{kl} x_{ik} x_{jl} \tag{3.2}$$

subject to the constraints $\sum_{i=1}^{n} x_{ij} = 1$, $\sum_{j=1}^{n} x_{ij} = 1$, and $x \in \{0,1\}$.

The QAP is an *NP*-hard optimization problem (Sahni & Gonzalez [1976]); even finding a solution within a factor of $1+\varepsilon$ of the optimal one remains *NP*-hard. It is considered as one of the hardest optimization problems as general instances of size $n \geq 20$ cannot be solved to optimality. Therefore, to practically solve the QAP one has to apply heuristic algorithms which find very high quality solutions in relatively short computation time. Several such heuristic algorithms have been proposed which include algorithms like Simulated Annealing (Burkard & Rendl [1984], Connolly [1990]), Tabu Search (Battiti & Tecchiolli [1994], Skorin-Kapov [1990], Taillard [1991]), Genetic Algorithms (Fleurent & Ferland [1994], Merz & Freisleben [1997], Tate & Smith [1995]), Evolution Strategies (Nissen [1994]), GRASP (Li et al [1994]), Ant Algorithms (Gambardella et al [1999], Maniezzo [1998], Maniezzo & Colorni [1999], Maniezzo et al [1994], Stützle [1997], Stützle & Hoos [1999]), and Scatter Search (Cung et al [1997]).

In particular, for structured, real-life instances, Ant Colony Optimization (ACO) algorithms are currently one of the best performing algorithms. Since the first application of Ant System to the QAP (Maniezzo et al [1994]), several improved applications have been proposed. These include direct improvements over this first application (Maniezzo & Colorni [1999]), the application of improved ACO algorithms (Maniezzo [1998], Stützle [1997], Stützle & Hoos [1999], Taillard & Gambardella [1997]), and an ant based algorithm (Gambardella et al [1999]), called HAS-QAP. Except for HAS-QAP, the Ant System application to the QAP and all the proposed improvements on it fit into the framework of the ACO meta-heuristic (see chapter two for a detailed outline of the ACO meta-heuristic). HAS-QAP has the particularity of using pheromone trail information to *modify* complete solutions instead of constructing new solutions from scratch.

In this chapter we give an overview of the existing applications of the ACO meta-heuristic to the QAP and present computational results which confirm that ACO algorithms are among the best performing algorithms for this problem. The chapter is structured as follows. We first outline how the ACO meta-heuristic can be applied to solve QAPs. Then we present the implementations of the ant algorithms for the QAP and discuss the common features of these approaches and their differences. To exemplify the computational results obtained with ACO algorithms, we compare the performance of $\mathcal{MMAS}$, one of the improved ACO algorithms, to that obtained using HAS-QAP and other algorithms proposed for the QAP.

3.2 APPLYING THE ACO META-HEURISTIC TO THE QAP

To apply the ACO meta-heuristic to a problem, it is convenient to represent the problem by a graph $G=(C, L)$, where C are the components and L is the set of connections (see chapter two). To represent the QAP as such a graph, the set of components C is given by the facilities and locations part of the problem description, and the set of connections L may fully connect the components. The construction of an assignment of facilities to locations can then – in the most general case – be interpreted as an ant's walk, guided by pheromone trail information (associated with the transitions) and possibly by locally available heuristic information. The ant's walk additionally has to obey certain constraints to ensure that a feasible solution is generated. In the case of the QAP, such a feasible solution assigns every facility to exactly one location and every location is assigned exactly one facility. Hence, a feasible solution ψ to the QAP consists of n couplings (i, j) of facilities and locations.

For the practical application of the ACO meta-heuristic to the QAP it is convenient to use a fixed assignment direction, for example, to assign facilities to locations (or locations to facilities). Then, facilities are assigned by the ants in some order, which we refer to as the *assignment order*, to locations. An ant iteratively applies the following two steps until it has constructed a complete solution. In a first step the ant chooses a facility which should be assigned next. In a second step the chosen facility is assigned to some location. Pheromone trails and heuristic information may be associated with both steps. With respect to the first step, the pheromone trails and heuristic information may be used to learn an appropriate assignment order (obviously, the assignment order may influence the performance of the algorithm). Concerning the second step, the pheromone trail τ_{ij} and the heuristic information η_{ij} associated with the couplings between facility i and location j determines the desirability of putting facility i on location j. After all ants have generated a feasible solution and possibly improved it by applying a local search, ants are allowed to deposit pheromone, taking into consideration the quality of the solutions.

3.3 AVAILABLE ACO ALGORITHMS FOR THE QAP

Since the first application of Ant System (Dorigo et al [1991], Dorigo [1992], Dorigo et al [1996]), and the seminal work on ACO applied to the QAP (Maniezzo et al [1994]), several improved ACO applications to this problem have been proposed by various authors. Despite the differences among these algorithms, they share at least two important common aspects.

One aspect concerns solution construction. All the proposed ant algorithms for the QAP associate pheromone trails τ_{ij} only to couplings of the form $\psi_i = j$, hence, τ_{ij} can be interpreted as the desirability of assigning facility i to location j. Concerning the assignment order, all the proposed algorithms assume that it is either fixed throughout the run of the algorithm (possibly chosen according to some heuristic information, as in Maniezzo et al [1994], Maniezzo & Colorni [1999], and Maniezzo [1998]) or it is chosen randomly according to a uniform distribution (Stützle [1997], Stützle & Hoos [1999], Taillard & Gambardella [1997]).

The second aspect is that all the proposed algorithms improve the ants' solutions using a local search algorithm (see section 3.4 for details on the local search algorithms applied). Hence, these algorithms are hybrid algorithms combining solution construction by (artificial) ants with local search algorithms. Such a combination may be very interesting. Constructive algorithms often result in a poor solution quality compared to local search algorithms. On the other side, it has been noted that repeating local searches from randomly generated initial solutions results for most problems in a considerable gap to the optimal solution (Johnson & McGeoch [1997]). Yet, past experience has shown that the combination of a probabilistic, adaptive construction heuristic with local search may yield significantly improved solutions (Boese et al [1994], Dorigo & Gambardella [1997], Stützle & Hoos [1999]). ACO algorithms are such adaptive construction heuristics, in the sense that a colony of ants modifies the solution representation assigning higher pheromone trail strength to connections (here, corresponding to couplings of facilities to locations), which are contained in better solutions. During the solution construction ants preferably select couplings which have a high pheromone strength and by combining such couplings they generate promising starting solutions for the local search algorithm. An additional advantage of using ant algorithms is that, by generating good initial solutions, the subsequent local search needs far fewer iterations to reach a local optimum. Thus, for a given time limit many more local searches can be run than by starting from randomly generated solutions.

Additionally, all ACO algorithms applied to the QAP apply the procedures of the ACO meta-heuristic in a specific order (see Figure 2.3 in chapter two). They first construct solutions, then improve the generated solutions by a local search algorithm, and finally update the pheromone trails. In fact, most of the best performing ACO algorithms for *NP*-hard combinatorial optimization problems follow this specific scheme and apply local search, which is an optional feature of the ACO meta-heuristic, to improve solutions (Dorigo & Gambardella [1997], Gambardella & Dorigo [1997], Stützle & Hoos [1999], Stützle [1998a]). An exception are the current applications to network routing and the application to the shortest common supersequence problem, presented in chapter four of this book.

In the following we present the available ant algorithms for the QAP in more detail. We first discuss those which are in fact instantiations of the ACO meta-heuristic defined in chapter two and then outline concisely the HAS-QAP algorithm, which does not use solution construction. The details of the local search algorithms applied by each of the approaches are given in section 3.4.

3.3.1 Ant System for the QAP

Ant System (AS) is the first ACO algorithm which has been applied to the QAP (see chapter two for an outline of its application to the travelling salesman problem); we refer to it in the following as AS-QAP (Maniezzo et al [1994], Dorigo et al [1996]). In AS-QAP the assignment order is determined by a pre-ordering of the facilities, as explained below. Then, at each step a facility i is assigned probabilistically to some location j preferring locations with a high pheromone trail τ_{ij} and promising heuristic information η_{ij}.

Heuristic information

The heuristic information on the potential goodness of an assignment is determined in AS-QAP as follows. Two vectors d and f are calculated in which the ith components represent respectively the sum of the distances from location i to all other locations and the sum of the flows from facility i to all other facilities. The lower d_i, the distance potential of location i, the more central the location, the higher f_i, the flow potential of facility i, the more important is the facility. Next a coupling matrix $\mathbf{E} = f \cdot d^T$ is calculated, whose elements are $e_{ij} = f_i \cdot d_j$. Then, the heuristic desirability of assigning facility i to location j is given by $\eta_{ij} = 1 / e_{ij}$. The motivation for using this type of heuristic information is that, intuitively, good solutions will place facilities with high flow potential on locations with low distance potential.

Solution construction

A solution is constructed as follows. In AS-QAP facilities are sorted in non increasing order of the flow potentials. At each construction step an ant k assigns the next still unassigned facility i to a free location j with a probability given by:

$$p_{ij}^k(t) = \frac{[\tau_{ij}(t)]^\alpha [\eta_{ij}]^\beta}{\sum_{l \in \mathcal{N}_i^k} [\tau_{il}(t)]^\alpha [\eta_{il}]^\beta}, \quad \text{if } j \in \mathcal{N}_i^k \tag{3.3}$$

where $\tau_{ij}(t)$ is the pheromone trail at iteration t, α and β are parameters which determine the relative influence of the pheromone strength and the heuristic information, and $\mathcal{N}_i^k$ is the feasible neighbourhood of node i, that is, only those locations that are still free (note that these probabilities sum to 1 over the feasible neignbourhood). The single steps are repeated until a complete assignment is constructed.

Pheromone update

The pheromone trail update applied to all couplings is done according to the following equation:

$$\tau_{ij}(t+1) = \rho \cdot \tau_{ij}(t) + \sum_{k=1}^{m} \Delta \tau_{ij}^k \tag{3.4}$$

where ρ, with $0 \leq \rho < 1$, is the persistence of the pheromone trail, so that $(1-\rho)$ represents the evaporation. The parameter ρ is used to avoid unlimited accumulation of the pheromone trails and allows the algorithm to forget previously done bad choices. $\Delta \tau_{ij}^k$ is the amount of pheromone ant k puts on the coupling (i, j); it is given by:

$$\Delta \tau_{ij}^k = \begin{cases} Q / J_\psi^k & \text{if facility } i \text{ is assigned to location } j \text{ in the solution of ant } k \\ 0 & \text{otherwise} \end{cases} \tag{3.5}$$

where ψ^k is the kth ant solution, J_ψ^k its objective function value, and Q is the amount of pheromone deposited by an ant.

A first improvement of AS-QAP is presented in Maniezzo & Colorni [1999] and we refer to it as AS2-QAP. AS2-QAP differs mainly in the way the heuristic information is calculated and in the different way of calculating the probability of assigning facilities to locations. Yet, since a further improvement over AS2-QAP, called ANTS-QAP and presented in the next section, performs generally better, we do not present the details of AS2-QAP. For the sake of completeness, we will indicate the common features between AS2-QAP and the algorithm presented in the next section.

3.3.2 The ANTS algorithm applied to the QAP

In Maniezzo [1998] a substantially improved ACO algorithm called ANTS is introduced, presenting its application to the QAP. In the following we refer to this algorithm as ANTS-QAP. According to Maniezzo [1998] the term ANTS derives from the fact that the proposed algorithm can be interpreted as an **A**pproximate **N**ondeterministic **T**ree **S**earch since it shares several elements with an approximated Branch & Bound procedure. In fact, in Maniezzo [1998] the ANTS algorithm is extended to an exact algorithm; we refer the interested reader to the original reference for details. In the following we only present the heuristic algorithm.

The ANTS framework introduces several modifications with respect to AS. The most significant modification is the use of lower bounds on the solution cost of the completion of a partial solution to compute dynamically changing heuristic values η_{ij}. Further modifications are the use of a different action choice rule and a modified trail update rule.

Use of lower bounds

In ANTS-QAP lower bounds on the completion cost of a partial solution are used to give heuristic information on the attractiveness of adding a specific coupling (i, j). This is achieved by tentatively adding the coupling to the current partial solution and by estimating the cost of a complete solution containing that coupling by means of a lower bound. This estimate is then used to influence the probabilistic decisions taken by the ant during the solution construction: the lower the estimate the more attractive is the addition of a specific coupling. Using lower bounds for the heuristic information presents several advantages like the elimination of possible moves if the cost estimation is larger than the so far best found solution. Yet, the lower bound is calculated at each construction step of an ant and, hence, the lower bounds should be efficiently computable.

In ANTS-QAP the Gilmore–Lawler lower bound (GLB, see Gilmore [1962], Lawler [1963]) is computed at the start of the algorithm. Along with the lower bound computation one gets the values of the dual variables corresponding to the constraints when formulating the QAP as an integer programming problem (see Equation 3.2). A disadvantage of the GLB is the relatively high computational complexity, which is of $\mathcal{O}(n^3)$. To decrease the computational effort associated with the lower bound computations, in ANTS-QAP a weaker lower bound than GLB is proposed, called LBD. This lower bound has the advantage of having a computational complexity of $\mathcal{O}(n)$. For details on the lower bound computation we refer to Maniezzo [1998]. In AS2-QAP lower bounds are used in the same way as in ANTS, but in AS2-QAP the GLB is used in each construction step. The computational results presented in Maniezzo [1998] show that using this weaker lower bound is sufficient to guide the ants' solution construction.

Solution construction

In ANTS-QAP a pre-ordering of the locations is given by the values of the dual variables which are obtained when computing the GLB for an instance. Given a location j, ant k decides to assign facility i to this location with the probability given by Equation 3.6. Note that the same action choice rule is also used in AS2-QAP.

$$p_{ij}^k(t) = \frac{\alpha \cdot \tau_{ij}(t) + (1-\alpha) \cdot \eta_{ij}}{\sum_{l \in \mathcal{N}_j^k} \alpha \cdot \tau_{lj}(t) + (1-\alpha) \cdot \eta_{lj}}, \quad \text{if } i \in \mathcal{N}_j^k \tag{3.6}$$

An advantage of Equation 3.6 is that, compared to Equation 3.3, one parameter is eliminated. Additionally, simpler operations which are faster to compute, like multiplications instead of exponentiations, are applied. Here, $\mathcal{N}_j^k$ is the feasible neighbourhood, and, again, the probabilities sum to 1 over the feasible neighbourhood (defined by the facilities which are not yet assigned to any location). Also note that in this formulation the pre-ordering is done on locations instead of facilities. Obviously, it is also possible to use a pre-ordering of the facilities like in AS-QAP.

Pheromone update

The pheromone update in ANTS-QAP does not use pheromone evaporation, that is, we have $\tau_{ij}(t+1) = \tau_{ij}(t) + \sum_{k=1}^{m} \Delta\tau_{ij}^{k}$, where:

$$\Delta\tau_{ij}^{k} = \begin{cases} \tau_0 \cdot (1 - \dfrac{J_{\psi}^{k} - LB}{J_{avg} - LB}) & \text{if facility } i \text{ is given location } j \text{ in ant } k\text{'s solution} \\ 0 & \text{otherwise} \end{cases} \qquad (3.7)$$

J_{avg} is the moving average of the last l solutions provided by the ants and LB is the value of the GLB which is calculated at the start of the algorithm. If an ant's solution is worse than the current moving average, the pheromone trail strength of the couplings constructed by the ants is decreased; if the ant's solution is better, the pheromone trail strength is increased. The additional effect of using Equation 3.7 is a dynamic scaling of the objective function differences which may be advantageous if in later stages of the search the absolute difference between the ant's solution qualities become smaller.

3.3.3 $\mathcal{MMAS}$ for the QAP

$\mathcal{MMAS}$ is an improvement over AS, first proposed applying it to the TSP (Stützle & Hoos [1997], Stützle & Hoos [1997a]) and subsequently to the QAP; referred to in the following as $\mathcal{MMAS}$-QAP. The modifications introduced by $\mathcal{MMAS}$ with respect to AS are the following. First, to exploit the best solutions found in an iteration or during the run of the algorithm, after each iteration only one ant is allowed to add pheromone. This ant may be the *iteration-best* or the *global-best* ant. Second, to avoid search stagnation (that is, the situation where all the ants follow the same path – Dorigo et al [1996]), the allowed range of the pheromone trail strengths is limited to the interval $[\tau_{min}, \tau_{max}]$, that is, $\forall \tau_{ij} \; \tau_{min} \leq \tau_{ij} \leq \tau_{max}$. Lastly, the pheromone trails are initialized to the upper trail limit, which causes a higher exploration at the start of the algorithm (Stützle [1998a]).

Construction of solutions

In $\mathcal{MMAS}$-QAP, at each construction step, ant k first randomly chooses a facility i among those not yet assigned, and then places it on a free location j with a probability given by:

$$p_{ij}^{k}(t) = \frac{\tau_{ij}(t)}{\sum_{l \in \mathcal{N}_i^{k}} \tau_{il}(t)}, \text{ if } j \in \mathcal{N}_i^{k} \qquad (3.8)$$

It is noteworthy that $\mathcal{MMAS}$ does not make use of any heuristic information. As shown in the $\mathcal{MMAS}$ application to the TSP (Stützle & Hoos [1999]), the heuristic information is not necessary to achieve high quality solutions when solutions are improved by local search. Not using heuristic information additionally eliminates one parameter and, thus, reduces the effort for parameter tuning. (Note that in an early application of $\mathcal{MMAS}$ to the QAP the pseudo-random proportional action choice rule (Dorigo & Gambardella [1997]) was used for the solution construction. This rule makes with probability q the best possible choice according to the search experience. That is, facility i is put on a location j, for which τ_{ij} is maximal. With probability $1-q$ the location is chosen according to Equation 3.8. For the experimental results presented in section 3.5 we do not use the pseudo-random-proportional action choice rule, that is, we simply set $q = 0$).

Update of pheromone trails

After all ants have constructed a solution, the pheromone trails are updated according to:

$$\tau_{ij}(t+1) = \rho \cdot \tau_{ij}(t) + \Delta \tau_{ij}^{best} \qquad (3.9)$$

where:

$$\Delta \tau_{ij}^{best} = \begin{cases} 1/J_{\psi}^{best} & \text{if facility } i \text{ has location } j \text{ in solution } \psi^{best} \\ 0 & \text{otherwise} \end{cases} \qquad (3.10)$$

where J_{ψ}^{best} is the objective function value of ψ^{best}. ψ^{best} may be either the *iteration-best* solution ψ^{ib}, or the best solution found during the run of the algorithm, the *global-best* solution ψ^{gb}. Hence, if in the best solutions facilities are often put on specific locations, these couplings will have a high amount of pheromone. A judicious choice in the use of either ψ^{ib} or ψ^{gb} for the pheromone trail update may help to improve the algorithm's performance. In general, best results are obtained if the frequency of choosing ψ^{gb} increases during the run of the algorithm (Stützle [1998a]). Additionally one has to ensure that the pheromone trail strength respects the limits. If after the pheromone update we have $\tau_{ij} > \tau_{max}$, we set $\tau_{ij} = \tau_{max}$; analogously, if $\tau_{ij} < \tau_{min}$ we set $\tau_{ij} = \tau_{min}$.

Additional diversification features

For the $\mathcal{MMAS}$ application to the QAP an additional technique to increase the diversification of the search is used. In particular, if the search progress is only very small, the pheromone trails are reinitialized to τ_{max}.

3.3.4 FANT

In Taillard & Gambardella [1997], another ACO algorithm is proposed for the QAP, which is called Fast Ant System (FANT). In FANT solutions are constructed in the same way as in $\mathcal{MMAS}$-QAP using the action choice rule given in Equation 3.8, that is, also no heuristic information is used. FANT differs from the other approaches presented so far in two main aspects, the number of ants used and the management of pheromone trails.

Number of ants

FANT makes use of only one ant, that is, no population is used. The use of a single ant allows the algorithm to find good solutions fast (also due to the choice of the local search algorithm – see section 3.4). Yet, using only one ant appears to be rather a specific parameter setting than an important novelty of the algorithm.

Pheromone update

Like ANTS-QAP, FANT does not use pheromone trail evaporation. Initially, all pheromone trails are set to one and after each iteration pheromone is added as follows:

$$\tau_{ij}(t+1) = \tau_{ij}(t) + r \cdot \Delta\tau_{ij} + r* \cdot \Delta\tau_{ij}^{gb} \tag{3.11}$$

where $\Delta\tau_{ij} = 1$ for every coupling (i, j) which is part of the solution generated in the current iteration, $\Delta\tau_{ij}^{gb} = 1$ for every coupling of the global-best solution ψ^{gb}, and r and $r*$ are two parameters. The value of r may be modified during the algorithm's run (initially it is set to one), while the value of $r*$ is kept fixed. The two parameters determine the relative reinforcement provided by the current solution and by the global-best one. In two occasions the pheromone trails are updated in a different way from the above described rule. (i) If the global best solution has been improved, parameter r is set to one and the pheromone trails are erased and all set to one (intensification of the search around the global best solution). (ii) If the ant constructs a solution which is the same as ψ^{gb}, r is increased by one and again all pheromone trails are erased and set to r (diversification of the search by decreasing the relative weight of ψ^{gb}).

3.3.5 HAS-QAP

HAS-QAP (Gambardella et al [1999]), although inspired by previous work on ant algorithms, differs rather strongly from the previously presented ACO algorithms. In fact, it is not really an instance of the ACO meta-heuristic. The major difference is that pheromone trails are not used to construct new solutions from scratch but to modify the current solutions.

Solution modification

In HAS-QAP each ant represents a complete solution and pheromone trails are used to direct the modification of the ants' current solutions. Modification consists in repeating R of the following swaps of facilities. First, a facility i is randomly chosen. Then, a second facility $j \neq i$ is chosen and their locations ψ_i and ψ_j are exchanged. The second facility j is chosen as follows. With probability $1-q$, where q is a parameter, it is chosen to maximize $\tau_{j\psi_i^k} + \tau_{i\psi_j^k}$ (exploitation); with probability q the second index j is chosen with probability:

$$p_{ij}^k(t) = \frac{\tau_{i\psi_j^k}(t) + \tau_{j\psi_i^k}(t)}{\sum_{l \neq i}(\tau_{i\psi_l^k}(t) + \tau_{l\psi_i^k}(t))} \tag{3.12}$$

After a solution has been modified, local search is applied to the so generated solution. In this sense, HAS-QAP is similar in spirit to iterated local search algorithms (Martin et al [1991], Stützle [1998a]) in which a local search algorithm is repeatedly applied from mutations of the current solution. In HAS-QAP additional features of search intensification and diversification are added, but we refer to Gambardella et al [1999] for a detailed description of the techniques used.

Pheromone update

In HAS-QAP only the global-best solution is allowed to add pheromone. The pheromone update follows Equation 3.9, where:

$$\Delta\tau_{ij}^{best}(t) = \begin{cases} Q / J_{\psi}^{gb} & \text{if facility } i \text{ has location } j \text{ in solution } \psi^{gb} \\ 0 & \text{otherwise} \end{cases} \tag{3.13}$$

where Q is a parameter which determines the amount of pheromone added by the global best solution.

3.3.6 Synopsis

As indicated at the beginning of this section, the proposed ant algorithms for the QAP have some common features like the use of local search to improve solutions and that pheromone trails are only associated to couplings of facilities and locations. Yet, they also differ in certain aspects of how the ideas of the ACO meta-heuristic are put to work. In Table 3.1 we summarize some of the general differences concerning the presence of heuristic information, the use of a population, whether pheromone evaporation is used (by using evaporation we refer to lowering the pheromone trail strength after each algorithm iteration by a constant factor; if an algorithm does not use pheromone evaporation, it typically uses other additional techniques like reinitialization of pheromones or similar to avoid stagnation of the search), or whether solutions are constructed from scratch. Apart from these differences, the presented algorithms also differ in several specific details like discussed before. We note in addition that current experience suggests that to obtain very good performance, heuristic information is not absolutely necessary if solutions are improved by local search (Stützle & Hoos [1999], Stützle [1998a]).

Table 3.1: Summary of the characteristics discussed in this section. √ means that the feature is used or present and ¬ means that it is not used.

Feature	AS-QAP	ANTS-QAP	$\mathcal{MMAS}$-QAP	FANT-QAP	HAS-QAP
Heuristic	√	√	¬	¬	¬
Population	√	√	√	¬	√
Evaporation	√	¬	√	¬	√
Solution construction	√	√	√	√	¬

3.4 LOCAL SEARCH FOR THE QAP

Local search starts from some initial assignment and repeatedly tries to improve the current assignment by local changes. If in the neighbourhood of the current assignment a better one ψ' is found, it replaces the current assignment and the local search is continued from ψ'.

In the QAP case, the neighbourhood of a permutation ψ is typically defined by the set of permutations which can be obtained by exchanging two of the facilities. The objective function difference $\Delta(\psi,r,s)$ obtained by exchanging two facilities ψ_s and ψ_r can be computed in $\mathcal{O}(n)$ time, using Equation 3.14 (Taillard [1995]):

$$\Delta(\psi,r,s) = b_{rr} \cdot (a_{\psi_s\psi_s} - a_{\psi_r\psi_r}) + b_{rs} \cdot (a_{\psi_s\psi_r} - a_{\psi_r\psi_s}) +$$
$$b_{sr} \cdot (a_{\psi_r\psi_s} - a_{\psi_s\psi_r}) + b_{ss} \cdot (a_{\psi_r\psi_r} - a_{\psi_s\psi_s}) +$$
$$\sum_{k=1,k \neq r,s}^{n} (b_{kr} \cdot (a_{\psi_k\psi_s} - a_{\psi_k\psi_r}) + b_{ks} \cdot (a_{\psi_k\psi_r} - a_{\psi_k\psi_s}) + \tag{3.14}$$
$$b_{rk} \cdot (a_{\psi_s\psi_k} - a_{\psi_r\psi_k}) + b_{sk} \cdot (a_{\psi_r\psi_k} - a_{\psi_s\psi_k}))$$

Notice that if both matrices A and B are symmetric with a null diagonal, the formula can be simplified using the facts that $a_{rs} = a_{sr}$ and that $b_{\psi_r\psi_s} = b_{\psi_s\psi_r}$. The effect of a particular swap can be evaluated faster using information from preceding iterations. Let ψ' be the solution which is obtained by exchanging facilities r and s in solution ψ, then for swapping facilities u and v, with $(\{u,v\}\cap\{r,s\}=\varnothing)$, the move can be evaluated in constant time (Taillard [1995]):

$$\Delta(\psi',u,v) = \Delta(\psi,r,s)$$
$$+ (b_{ru} - b_{rv} + b_{sv} - b_{su}) \cdot (a_{\psi_s\psi_u} - a_{\psi_s\psi_v} + a_{\psi_r\psi_v} - a_{\psi_r\psi_u}) \tag{3.15}$$
$$+ (b_{ur} - b_{vr} + b_{vs} - b_{us}) \cdot (a_{\psi_u\psi_s} - a_{\psi_v\psi_s} + a_{\psi_v\psi_r} - a_{\psi_u\psi_r})$$

The simplest local search algorithm based on the above described neighbourhood is iterative improvement, in the following referred to as 2-opt. Iterative improvement can be implemented using a *first-improvement* or a *best-improvement* pivoting rule. While in the first case an improving move is immediately performed, in the second case the whole neighbourhood is examined and a move which gives the best improvement is chosen. Best-improvement 2-opt for the QAP benefits from the fact that the effect of exchanging two facilities can be calculated fast using the information of previous iterations (see Equation 3.15); the first iteration is of complexity $\mathcal{O}(n^3)$, while the subsequent iterations can be done in $\mathcal{O}(n^2)$. With first-improvement 2-opt usually more moves have to be performed to reach a local minimum and every complete neighbourhood scan is of complexity $\mathcal{O}(n^3)$. Yet, first improvement algorithms can be executed faster if only a limited number of iterations are performed or additional techniques like *don't look bits* (Bentley [1992]) are applied. Additionally, by examining the neighbourhood in random order, different local optima may be obtained also when starting from the same initial solution.

A disadvantage of iterative improvement algorithms is that they stop at the first local minimum encountered. This disadvantage may be avoided by using *short* runs of tabu search (TS) (Taillard [1991], Battiti & Tecchiolli [1994]) or simulated annealing (SA) (Burkard & Rendl [1984], Connolly [1990]), which allow the local search to leave local minima (the reason such runs must be short is clear, since in a hybrid ACO algorithm the local search algorithm will be applied several times). Generally, TS or SA will return solutions of better quality than a single application of 2-opt, yet at the cost of longer computation times. Hence, for a given amount of computing time one faces the following tradeoff: Is it worthwhile to apply fewer times a local search algorithm which, on average, returns better quality solutions or one better applies more often a weaker local search algorithm? The latter may be advantageous to faster identify regions of the search space with high quality solutions. Additionally, 2-opt benefits from the good solutions generated by ACO algorithms in later stages of the search and only few improvement steps are necessary to reach a local minimum.

The ant algorithms presented here use the following local search algorithms. In AS-QAP, best-improvement 2-opt and short runs of SA have been applied, while in AS2-QAP and ANTS-QAP only best-improvement 2-opt is applied. The computational results presented with AS-QAP in Maniezzo et al [1994] suggested that better performance can be obtained by using SA. In $\mathcal{MMAS}$-QAP, short runs of the robust tabu search (Ro-TS) (Taillard [1991]) and best-improvement 2-opt are applied. HAS-QAP and FANT both make use of a truncated version of first-improvement 2-opt. In particular, at most two complete scans of the neighbourhood are done. Hence, although the local search does not necessarily return a locally optimal solution, it is guaranteed to be fast. The experimental results presented in the following section for $\mathcal{MMAS}$-QAP will show that the appropriate choice of the local search algorithm depends strongly on the QAP instance type.

3.5 EXPERIMENTAL RESULTS

In this section we report on the experimental results obtained with $\mathcal{MMAS}$ on some QAP instances from QAPLIB (http://fmatbhp1.tu-graz.ac.at/~karisch/qaplib) and compare them with robust tabu search (Ro-TS) (Taillard [1991]), a genetic hybrid algorithm (GH) proposed in Fleurent & Ferland [1994], and HAS-QAP (Gambardella et al [1999]). In Taillard [1995] it was argued that the type of problem instance has a strong influence on the performance of the different algorithms proposed for solving the QAP. We first introduce the most important aspects of the different problem types following the description in Taillard [1995]. We show that the instance type has a strong influence on which local search algorithm should be used in $\mathcal{MMAS}$-QAP. In particular we use $\mathcal{MMAS}$-QAP either with 2-opt (referred to as $\mathcal{MMAS}$-QAP$_{2\text{-opt}}$) or with short robust tabu search runs of length $4n$, where n is the problem dimension (referred to as $\mathcal{MMAS}$-QAP$_{TS}$). Then, we present the computational results and compare them to the above mentioned algorithms.

3.5.1 Parameter Settings

Suitable parameter settings for $\mathcal{MMAS}$-QAP were determined in some preliminary experiments. We use $m = 5$ ants (all ants apply local search to the solution they generate) and $\rho = 0.8$. The low number of ants is motivated by the fact that local search for larger QAP instances is computationally rather demanding, but a reasonable number of iterations should be performed to learn the pheromone trails. The most important aspect concerning possible values of the trail strength is that they have to be in a reasonable interval around the expected amount of pheromone deposited by the trail update. Hence, an interval of allowed values is determined to reflect this intuition. We set:

$$\tau_{\max} = \frac{1}{1-\rho} \cdot \frac{1}{J_\psi^{gb}}$$

where J_ψ^{gb} is the objective function value of the global best solution (this setting corresponds to the maximum possible trail level for longer runs). The lower trail limit is set at $\tau_{\min} = \tau_{\max} / 2n$.

When 2-opt is applied, we use a specific schedule to alternate the pheromone trail update between ψ^{gb} and ψ^{ib} (see also section 3.3.3). Let u^{gb} indicate that every u^{gb} iterations ψ^{gb} is used to add pheromone. Then we set u^{gb} to 3 in the 11 first iterations, to 2 up to iteration 25, and from then on we set it to 1. By shifting the emphasis from the iteration best to the global best solution for trail update, we are shifting from a stronger exploration of the search space to an exploitation of the best solution found so far. After a reinitialization of the pheromone trails, we again apply the given schedule from the start. When applying tabu search, preliminary experiments suggested that updating pheromone trails using ψ^{gb} in every second iteration gives reasonably good results.

3.5.2 Types of QAP Instances

According to Taillard [1995], the benchmark instances of the QAP available in QAPLIB can be classified into the following four classes (see also Table 3.2):

   (i) *Unstructured, randomly generated*: Instances with the distance and flow matrix entries generated randomly according to a uniform distribution (among those are instances taixxa used in section 3.5.4). These are among the hardest to solve exactly. Nevertheless, most iterative search methods find solutions which lie within 1-2% of the best known solutions relatively quickly (Taillard [1995]).

   (ii) *Unstructured, with grid-distances*: Instances whose distance matrix is defined as Manhattan distance between grid points on an $n_1 \times n_2$ grid and with random flows.

   (iii) *Real-life instances*: 'Real-life' instances from practical applications of the QAP. Among those are the instances of Steinberg [1961] (instances ste36x), instances of a layout problem for a hospital (Krarup & Pruzan [1978], instances kra30x), instances corresponding to the layout of typewriter keyboards (Burkard & Offermann [1977], instances bur26x), and a new type of instance proposed in Taillard [1995]. The real-life instances have in common that the flow matrices have (in contrast to the previously mentioned randomly generated instances) many zero entries and the remaining entries are clearly not uniformly distributed.

   (iv) *Real-life like instances*: Because the real-life instances in QAPLIB are mainly of rather small size, a type of randomly generated problems has been proposed in Taillard [1995] (instances taixxb). These instances are generated in such a way that the matrix entries resemble the distribution found in real-life problems.

In order to differentiate among the classes of QAP instances the flow dominance *fd* may be used. It is defined as the coefficient of variation of the flow matrix entries multiplied by 100. That is: $fd(B) = 100\,\sigma / \mu$, where:

$$\mu = \frac{1}{n^2} \cdot \sum_{i=1}^{n} \sum_{j=1}^{n} b_{ij} \quad \text{and} \quad \sigma = \sqrt{\frac{1}{n^2 - 1} \cdot \sum_{i=1}^{n} \sum_{j=1}^{n} (b_{ij} - \mu)^2}$$

Table 3.2: Dominance values for some QAPLIB instances used in the experiments. Dominance values are given for the first A and the second B matrix ($dd(A)$ and $fd(B)$ respectively) as in QAPLIB. Instances are ordered according to the four classes described.

Instance	dd(A)	fd(B)	Instance	dd(A)	fd(B)
Unstructured, randomly generated (i)			**Real-life instances (iii)**		
Tai40a	63.10	60.23	bur26a	15.09	274.95
Tai50a	60.75	62.24	kra30a	49.22	149.98
Tai60a	61.41	60.86	kra30b	49.99	149.98
Tai80a	59.22	60.38	ste36a	55.65	400.30
Unstructured, grid instances (ii)			ste36b	100.79	400.30
Nug30	52.75	112.48	**Real-life like instances (iv)**		
Sko56	51.46	110.53	tai40b	66.75	317.22
Sko64	51.18	108.38	tai50b	73.44	313.91
Sko72	51.14	107.13	tai60b	76.83	317.82
Sko81	50.93	106.61	tai80b	64.05	323.17

In case few facilities comprise a large part of the overall flow, this is indicated by a high flow dominance. Randomly generated problems according to a uniform distribution have a rather low flow dominance, whereas real-life problems, in general, have a rather high flow dominance. Analogously to the flow dominance also a *distance dominance* (dd) can be defined. In Table 3.2 we give dominance values for both matrices of some instances of each type. Obviously, real-life instances and the randomly generated real-life like instances have considerably higher dominance values for at least one of the matrices.

3.5.3 Which Local Search?

ACO algorithms for the QAP are hybrid algorithms which combine two components: solution construction by artificial ants and local search algorithms. Here we focus on the influence of the local search algorithm on the final performance and show that no single best choice for the local search algorithm exists. In particular, the type of the QAP instance has a strong influence on which local search algorithm should be applied. We exemplify this aspect in the case of applying $\mathcal{MMAS}$ to the QAP. In Figure 3.1 we present the average solution quality as a function of computation time, averaged over 10 independent runs, of $\mathcal{MMAS}$-QAP $_{2\text{-opt}}$ and $\mathcal{MMAS}$-QAP $_{TS}$. Additionally we present results for a multiple descent approach (MD) that restarts the local search from randomly generated initial solutions. The average solution quality is measured on instance tai50a (class (i) as defined above) and on instance tai50b (class (iv) as defined above). The two instances show largely different flow dominance values (see Table 3.2).

Two important observations can be made from the experimental results. First, it seems that $\mathcal{MMAS}$ is able to guide the local search towards better solutions since the results with $\mathcal{MMAS}$ are better than those of the multiple descent approach using the same local search technique. Second, the local search algorithm which should be used by $\mathcal{MMAS}$–QAP strongly depends on the instance type. For instance, for tai50a tabu search gives significantly better solution quality than 2-opt. On the contrary, for instance tai50b

$\mathcal{MMAS}$-QAP$_{\text{2-opt}}$ outperforms $\mathcal{MMAS}$-QAP$_{\text{TS}}$. In case of the structured instance tai50b it pays off to use more often a rather simple local search procedure to identify the preferred locations of the facilities instead of the more computation intensive tabu search procedure that yields slightly better local optima. The computational results of the next section confirm this observation.

3.5.4 Computational Results

We now present our computational results for the application of $\mathcal{MMAS}$-QAP to a wide range of QAP instances taken from QAPLIB. We only used instances with $n \geq 20$, since smaller instances are easily solved. When using tabu search for the local search component we allow a total of 250 applications of tabu search. For $\mathcal{MMAS}$-QAP$_{\text{2-opt}}$ we stop the algorithm either after a maximum number of 1000 local search applications or after the same computation time as needed by $\mathcal{MMAS}$-QAP$_{\text{TS}}$.

We compare $\mathcal{MMAS}$-QAP to the robust tabu search algorithm (Ro-TS), to a genetic hybrid method (GH) which uses short tabu search runs, and to HAS-QAP. In Taillard [1995] it was shown that GH performed best for structured instances of class (iii) and (iv), whereas tabu search algorithms like Ro-TS performed best on the unstructured instances (classes (i) and (ii)). Ro-TS is allowed $1000 \cdot n$ iterations, resulting in similar run-times to $\mathcal{MMAS}$-QAP$_{\text{TS}}$. In GH, 250 short robust tabu search runs of the same length as in $\mathcal{MMAS}$-QAP$_{\text{TS}}$ are applied. Hence, the computation times are comparable. HAS-QAP is allowed 1000 applications of the truncated first-improvement local search technique. Since in Gambardella et al [1999] it is noted that computation times for HAS-QAP are similar to those of GH, the HAS-QAP results are also roughly comparable as regards computation times with those of $\mathcal{MMAS}$. In fact, experience suggests that HAS-QAP takes roughly 75% of the time used by $\mathcal{MMAS}$. The results reported for HAS-QAP and GH are taken directly from Gambardella et al [1999].

The computational results presented in Table 3.3 are for instances of type (i) and (ii), and in Table 3.4 for those of type (iii) and (iv). The average solution quality is reported, measured as the percentage deviation from the best known solution and obtained in 10 runs of the algorithms; best results are indicated in bold. In general, which method performs best depends strongly on the instance type. For the instances of type (i) and (ii) the hybrids using short tabu search runs and Ro-TS show the best performance (note that, in Taillard [1995], variants of strict tabu search have been shown to perform best on instances of type (i)). $\mathcal{MMAS}$-QAP$_{\text{2-opt}}$ and HAS-QAP perform significantly worse than Ro-TS, GH, and $\mathcal{MMAS}$-QAP$_{\text{TS}}$ on these instances.

On the real-life (like) instances, the performance characteristics of the algorithms are very different. Here, $\mathcal{MMAS}$-QAP$_{\text{2-opt}}$ and HAS-QAP show much improved performance and, in fact, $\mathcal{MMAS}$-QAP$_{\text{2-opt}}$ is the best algorithm for instances taixxb and bur26x. For example, for all instances bur26x the best known solution value is found in every run. $\mathcal{MMAS}$-QAP$_{\text{2-opt}}$ finds these best known solutions (which are conjectured to be optimal) on average in 3.8 seconds on a SUN UltraSparc I processor (167Mhz). Neither $\mathcal{MMAS}$-QAP$_{\text{TS}}$ nor Ro-TS could find the best known solutions in all runs. In Ro-TS, for example, the best solutions of each run were only found on average after 18.5 seconds. For instances taixxb the Ro-TS performs, except for the smallest instances, significantly worse than the $\mathcal{MMAS}$ hybrids or HAS-QAP. Only on the kra30x and ste36a instances can Ro-TS catch up with the other algorithms.

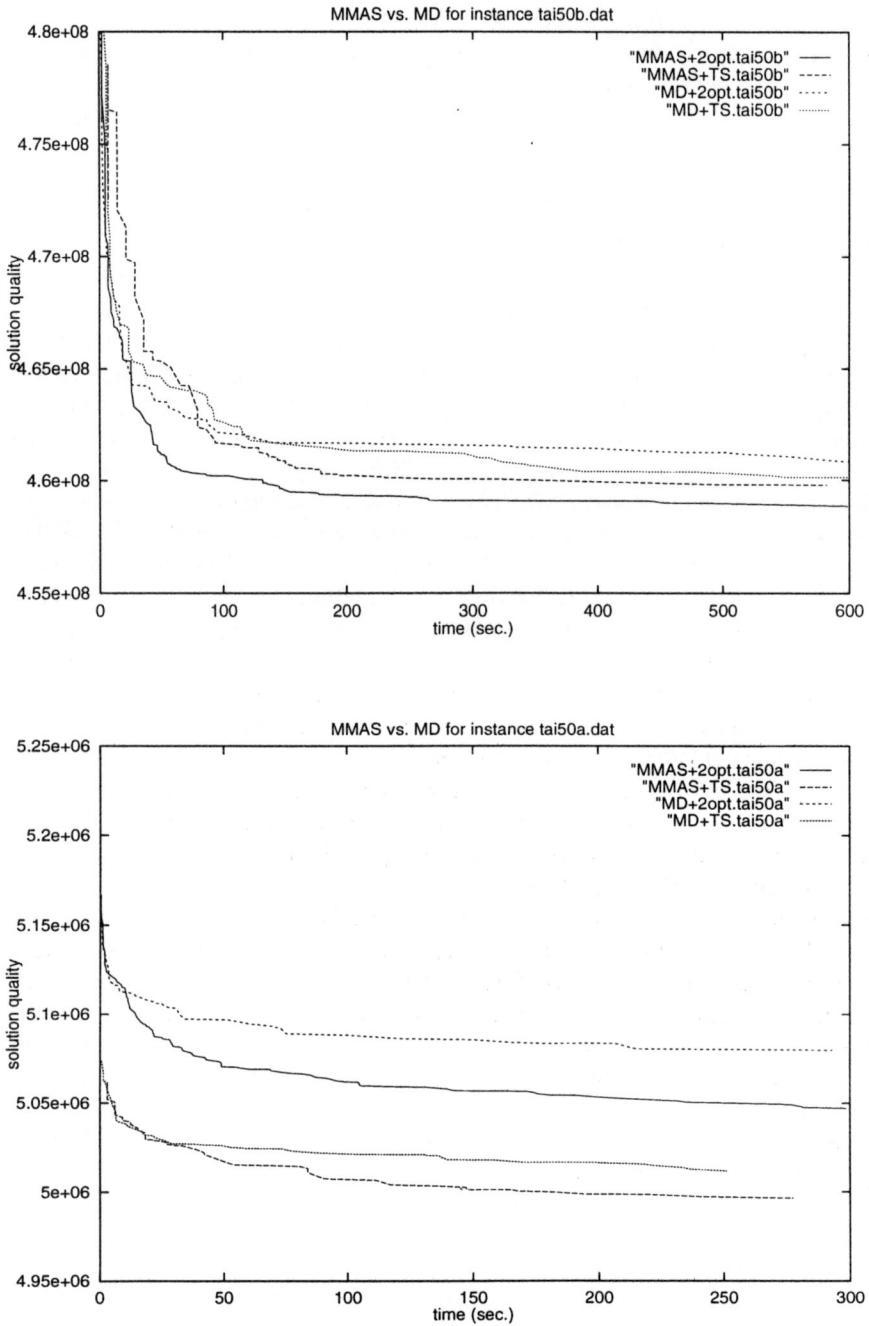

Fig. 3.1: Average solution quality development on tai50a (above) and tai50b (below) for $\mathcal{MMAS}$-QAP$_{\text{2-opt}}$, $\mathcal{MMAS}$-QAP$_{\text{TS}}$, multiple descent with 2-opt (MD$_{\text{2-opt}}$), and multiple descent with short tabu searches (MD$_{\text{TS}}$). Best results are in bold. See text for more details.

Table 3.3: Experimental results for heuristic algorithms on unstructured QAP instances (classes (i) and (ii)). We give the average excess from the best known solutions over 10 independent runs of the algorithms. Best results are in bold. See text for details.

Instance	Ro-TS	GH	HAS-QAP	$\mathcal{MMAS}$-QAP$_{TS}$	$\mathcal{MMAS}$-QAP$_{2\text{-opt}}$
Random problems with uniformly distributed matrix entries					
tai20a	**0.108**	0.268	0.675	0.191	0.428
tai25a	**0.274**	0.629	1.189	0.488	1.751
tai30a	0.426	0.439	1.311	**0.359**	1.286
tai35a	**0.589**	0.698	1.762	0.773	1.586
tai40a	0.990	**0.884**	1.989	0.933	1.131
tai50a	1.125	**1.049**	2.800	1.236	1.900
tai60a	1.203	**1.159**	3.070	1.372	2.484
tai80a	0.900	**0.796**	2.689	1.134	2.103
random flows on grids					
nug30	0.013	**0.007**	0.098	0.026	0.042
sko42	0.025	**0.003**	0.076	0.015	0.104
sko49	0.076	**0.040**	0.141	0.067	0.150
sko56	0.088	**0.060**	0.101	0.068	0.118
sko64	0.071	0.092	0.129	**0.042**	0.171
sko72	0.146	0.143	0.277	**0.109**	0.243
sko81	0.136	0.136	0.144	**0.071**	0.223
sko90	**0.128**	0.196	0.231	0.192	0.288

Interestingly, using a simple local search procedure is sufficient to yield very high quality solutions on the structured instances. Hence, for these instances it seems to be better to apply more often a local search procedure in order to identify promising regions of the search space. In fact, the ACO algorithms are able to exploit the structure of the real life (like) QAP instances and are able to guide the local search towards high quality solutions. Once such a promising region is identified it is rather easy to find very high quality solutions. Notice that, for the instances taixxb with $n \leq 60$ in almost every run the best-known solutions - conjectured to be optimal - are found. Since $\mathcal{MMAS}$-QAP$_{TS}$ and GH show similar performance characteristics, our results also suggest that replacing the tabu search runs used in GH with a 2-opt local search should allow the genetic algorithm to find better quality solutions in the same computation time. In fact, this has been done in Taillard & Gambardella [1997] and their computational results confirm our conjecture.

One might conjecture that flow (distance) dominance could help to identify which algorithm should be used on a particular instance. When both flow and distance dominance are low, the best choice appears to be using algorithms like $\mathcal{MMAS}$-QAP$_{TS}$, GH, or Ro-TS, while for high flow and/or distance dominance, the best would be to apply a hybrid algorithm with a fast local search. Although such a simple rule would work reasonably well, exceptions occur. For example, although instance ste36a has the highest flow dominance among the real-life instances, $\mathcal{MMAS}$-QAP$_{TS}$ and even Ro-TS give slightly better average performance than $\mathcal{MMAS}$-QAP$_{2\text{-opt}}$.

Table 3.4: Experimental results for heuristic algorithms on structured QAP instances (classes (iii) and (iv)). We give the average excess from the best known solutions over 10 independent runs of the algorithms. n.a. indicates that an algorithm has not been applied to a specific instance. Best results are in bold. See text for details.

Instance	Ro-TS	GH	HAS-QAP	$\mathcal{MMAS}$-QAP$_{TS}$	$\mathcal{MMAS}$-QAP$_{2\text{-opt}}$
		real-life instances			
bur26a-h	0.002	0.043	**0.0**	0.006	**0.0**
kra30a	0.268	**0.134**	0.630	**0.134**	0.314
kra30b	**0.023**	0.054	0.071	**0.023**	0.049
ste36a	0.155	n.a.	n.a.	**0.036**	0.181
ste36b	0.081	n.a.	n.a.	**0.0**	**0.0**
		randomly generated real-life like instances			
tai20b	**0.0**	**0.0**	0.091	**0.0**	**0.0**
tai25b	**0.0**	**0.0**	**0.0**	**0.0**	**0.0**
tai30b	0.107	0.0003	**0.0**	**0.0**	**0.0**
tai35b	0.064	0.107	0.026	0.051	**0.0**
tai40b	0.531	0.211	**0.0**	0.402	**0.0**
tai50b	0.342	0.214	0.192	0.172	**0.002**
tai60b	0.417	0.291	0.048	**0.005**	**0.005**
tai80b	1.031	0.829	0.667	0.591	**0.096**

It should be mentioned here that also in the applications of AS-QAP, AS2-QAP, and ANTS-QAP very good performance compared to other algorithms is obtained, with the ANTS-QAP approach performing best. For example, in Maniezzo [1998] the performance of ANTS-QAP has been compared to robust tabu search and GRASP (Li et al [1994]): The computational results show that ANTS-QAP was the best on all the instances tested. Note however that the results presented in Maniezzo [1998] are not directly comparable to the ones presented here due to the different experimental setup.

In summary, the results show that algorithms based on the ACO meta-heuristic are currently among the best available algorithms for real-life, structured QAP instances.

Acknowledgements

This work was supported by a Marie Curie Fellowship awarded to Thomas Stützle (CEC-TMR Contract No. ERB4001GT973400). Marco Dorigo acknowledges support from the Belgian FNRS, of which he is a Research Associate.

Chapter Four

An ACO Algorithm for the Shortest Common Supersequence Problem

René Michel and Martin Middendorf

4.1 INTRODUCTION

In this chapter we describe how to apply the ACO meta-heuristic to a well-known string problem, namely the Shortest Common Supersequence (SCS) problem.

The algorithmic solution of string problems is an important and intensively investigated area of computer science. One reason for this is that many objects or processes in nature can be described in an abstract way by a string of characters. An important example is the genetic information of living creatures which is stored basically in large DNA molecules. These molecules are long sequences formed by four different elements called nucleotides. Hence DNA molecules can be viewed as a string over a four-symbol alphabet. Another example comes from mechanical engineering. In this context a product is represented by the series of operations applied to it during the construction process.

An important string problem in these areas is to find for a given set of strings a string that can serve as a good representative for the set. 'Good' means here that every string in the set can be obtained from the representative by doing only deletions of characters. In this case the string found is called a *supersequence* of the given set of strings.

Example 4.1: Consider a set of DNA strings from different species. A question concerning the evolution of these species is what can be said about the DNA string of an (unknown) common ancestor. If we assume for simplicity that the only mutations which have occurred during the evolutionary process that created these species were deletions of nucleotides from the ancestor's DNA, then the ancestor's DNA string must be a supersequence of the given DNA strings. Since mutations are rare events, it is reasonable to assume that the ancestor DNA is a short(est) supersequence.

Example 4.2: Consider a set of workpieces $\{S_1, S_2, S_3\}$ one wants to produce. Each workpiece is characterised by the sequence of operations necessary to produce it: $S_1 = bcbacb$, $S_2 = caac$, $S_3 = bbacac$. The problem is to construct a conveyer belt on which the three workpieces can be produced. Assume this conveyer belt consists of a sequence of three types of machines. Each machine can perform one operation on an arriving workpiece or can let the workpiece pass unchanged. The operations that a machine performs are determined by its type – either a or b or c. Our problem is now to find a feasible sequence of machines for the conveyer belt. Clearly, such a sequence is feasible if and only if it is a supersequence. See Figure 4.1 for a possible solution and how the strings S_1, S_2 and S_3 can be embedded into it. For economical reasons one is usually interested in finding a shortest supersequence. For our example it can be shown that the sequence *bcbacacb* with only eight machines is a shortest one.

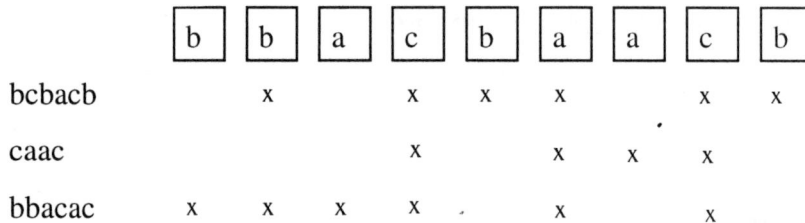

	b	b	a	c	b	a	a	c	b
bcbacb		x		x	x	x		x	x
caac				x		x	x	x	
bbacac	x	x	x	x		x		x	

Fig. 4.1: A conveyer belt for the products of Example 4.2.

Informally, the *Shortest Common Supersequence* (SCS) problem can be stated as follows. Given a set L of strings over an alphabet Σ, find a shortest string that is a supersequence of L.

The SCS problem is a computationally hard problem. It is known to be NP-hard and remains NP-hard under severe restrictions to the problem instances. For example, when every string has length two (Timkovsky [1990]) or when the size of the alphabet is two (Räihä & Ukkonen [1981]) and every given string is of the simple form $0^p 10^q 10^r$ for integers p, q, r (Middendorf [1994]). The SCS problem is even difficult to approximate in the following sense: For every $\varepsilon > 0$, it is not possible to find a polynomial time algorithm which computes a supersequence that is at most $1 + \varepsilon$ times longer than the optimal one (if $P \neq NP$). This holds even if the alphabet size is two (Bonnizoni et al [1994]).

Optimal algorithms based on dynamic programming or branch and bound exist for the SCS problem (see Fraser [1995]). However, the dynamic programming algorithms are successful only for a very small number of strings, because otherwise their space requirement is too large. Branch-and-Bound algorithms need too much time to be practical, except for strings over very small alphabets.

Two kinds of 'classical' heuristics have been proposed for the SCS problem. The first class of heuristics repeatedly removes a pair of strings from L, computes a shortest supersequence of this pair (e.g. by dynamic programming), and puts the obtained supersequence into the set L. This process is repeated until L contains only one string. The heuristics in this class differ in their strategies for selecting the pairs of strings and work well for problem instances with a small number of strings.

The second class of heuristics, which are more interesting for the work presented in this chapter, build a supersequence starting from the empty string as follows. When a new symbol – say a – is appended to the supersequence, the heuristic looks at the first character of every string in L (that is, the *front*) and removes every a from the front of the strings in L. This process is repeated until all strings are exhausted. Heuristics of this kind differ in the criteria used to decide which symbol is appended next to the superserquence. The Majority Merge heuristic always chooses the most frequent symbol from the front (Foulser et al [1992]). A variant of Majority Merge called L-Majority Merge weighs each character of a string in L with the length of the suffix starting with that character (i.e., the length of the remaining string beginning with the character itself). Then it computes for each symbol the sum of the weights of all its occurrences in the front and selects the symbol with the largest sum (Branke et al [1998]). The idea is that it is more urgent to remove characters from the long strings than from the short strings.

A genetic algorithm (called GA-SCS) for the SCS problem has been developed by Branke et al [1998]. GA-SCS is based on the L-Majority Merge heuristic. The general idea was to use a heuristic for SCS that is influenced by many parameters and then optimize the parameter values by the genetic algorithm. To make L-Majority Merge parameter dependent, a parameter is assigned to every character of each string in the given instance of the SCS problem. The used variant of L-Majority Merge always chooses a symbol to append for which the sum of the products of the parameter value with the weight of every occurrence in the front is maximal. The task of the genetic algorithm was then to find a good parameter setting.

4.2 THE AS-SCS ALGORITHM

ACO algorithms, described at length in chapter two, solve optimization problems heuristically by a colony of cooperating artificial ants that search for good solutions. Ants cooperate indirectly by dynamically changing the representation of the problem instance in such a way that the following ants are guided towards good solutions.

A standard approach for the design of ACO algorithms is to find a suitable graph representation of the problem to be solved. Usually, a path in the graph corresponds to the outcome of a sequence of decisions that are made by an ant when constructing a solution. In this case, a direct correspondence between a path in the graph and a solution of the problem can be established. Ants that found a solution deposit some amount of artificial pheromone along the edges of the path in the graph that corresponds to the solution – the amount of pheromone depends on the solution quality. Each decision made by an ant depends on two factors: (i) the amount of pheromone that was placed on the edges of the graph that correspond to the possible outcomes of the decision and (ii) the quality of the possible outcomes measured by a heuristic. This approach was used in the first ACO algorithm called Ant System (AS) (Dorigo [1992], Dorigo et al [1991]) to solve the travelling salesman problem and later in several other ant algorithms for permutation problems that were inspired by Ant System (e.g. for the quadratic assignment problem, see chapter three) and machine scheduling problems such as the flow shop problem (Stützle [1998b]) and the job shop problem (Dorigo et al [1996]).

AS-SCS, the ACO algorithm described in the following, works directly on the problem instance L. In AS-SCS the ants are guided by a Majority Merge type heuristic. To explain the approach let us consider for simplicity the functioning of an ant that does not use any trail information to search for a supersequence. This ant applies a probabilistic version of the Majority Merge heuristic to find a supersequence and a corresponding embedding of the strings from L into it. Every decision of the ant depends exactly on the symbols occurring in the actual front. The next symbol to append to the supersequence is chosen randomly such that the probability for a symbol to be chosen equals the proportion of its occurrences in the characters of the front. If the ant chooses a as the next symbol to append to the supersequence then each occurrence of a in the front has in a sense 'supported' this decision. Then all 'a's are removed from the front. When the whole supersequence is constructed every character of a string in L is embedded into exactly one character of the supersequence. That means it has supported successfully exactly one decision of the ant. Consequently, during the trail update phase of AS-SCS – which is done offline by the daemon (see ACO metaheuristic, chapter two, Figure 2.3) – some amount of pheromone is placed onto every character of each string in L. A certain amount of pheromone is provided for each character s of the supersequence. This amount of pheromone is then distributed equally among all characters of the strings in L which caused s to be appended. Thus each decision of the ant to append a character to the supersequence influences the update of several pheromone values during the pheromone trail update phase. In a figurative sense this means that the ants in AS-SCS produce pheromone trails consisting of a varying number of lanes. Characters that are embedded early into the supersequence (that is, they supported successfully an early decision) receive more pheromone than characters which are embedded later into the supersequence. This is because following ants will then prefer symbols to append next to the supersequence for which the corresponding characters in the front have been embedded early by other ants. Therefore, the amount of pheromone provided for a character of the supersequence depends on the characters position – the nearer it lies to the beginning of the supersequence the more pheromone is provided. The rest of this section describes this in more detail.

We need some notation for a detailed description of AS-SCS. Let $L = \{S_1, ..., S_n\}$ be the set of n input strings over an alphabet Σ. The character at position j of string i is denoted by s_{ij} and τ_{ij} is the amount of pheromone placed on s_{ij}. During initialisation τ_{ij} is set to 1. Let m ants be searching the solution space. Every ant $k \in \{1, ..., m\}$ uses a state vector $\bar{v}^k = \{v_1^k, v_2^k, ..., v_n^k\}$ to keep track of the progress of the computation of its supersequence S^k. The state vector $\bar{v}^k$ points to characters in the front of the strings (see Example 4.3).

Example 4.3: In a 2-string problem a vector (3,5) would describe a state where the 2 leading characters of string S_1 and the 4 leading characters of string S_2 are already embedded in S^k, whereas the third character of string S_1 and the fifth character of string S_2 are still waiting for a suitable extension of S^k before they can be embedded.

At the beginning of each iteration all elements of state vector $\bar{v}^k$ are set to 1. The computation of a supersequence S^k is completed when $\bar{v}^k = \bar{v}_{fin}$, where $\bar{v}_{fin}$ is the set $\{|S_1|+1, |S_2|+1, ..., |S_n|+1\}$ and $|S_i|$ is the length of string S_i for i from 1 to n. The candidate-set:

$$C^k = \{a \in \Sigma \mid \exists i : a = s_{iv_i^k}\}$$

denotes the set of symbols occurring in the actual front of the strings and therefore are possible candidates to be appended to S^k next. For every symbol $a \in C^k$ the sum of the amount of pheromone placed on its occurrences in the front is denoted by $\tau^k(a)$:

$$\tau^k(a) \leftarrow \sum_{i \in \mathcal{I}^k : s_{iv_i^k} = a} \tau_{iv_i^k} \qquad (4.1)$$

where $\mathcal{I}^k$ denotes the set of indices for which $v_i^k < |S_i|+1$ holds.

In the following we describe one iteration of the algorithm from the point of view of some arbitrary ant k. Initially, the state vector $\bar{v}^k$ is $(1, 1, ..., 1)$, S^k is the empty string, and C^k contains exactly the symbols occurring at the beginning of the input strings. As long as the state vector $\bar{v}^k$ is different from $\bar{v}_{fin}$ the following three steps are repeated:

1. Ant k chooses a symbol $a \in C^k$ according to the Pseudo-Random-Proportional Action Choice Rule with threshold q_0 (see Dorigo & Gambardella [1997]): if the value of a random variable q that is uniformly distributed over $[0,1]$ is equal or less than q_0, $0 < q_0 < 1$, the ant chooses the symbol $a \in C^k$ with maximum value $[\tau^k(a)]^\alpha$; otherwise, the symbol a is chosen according to the following probability distribution:

$$p(a, \vec{v}^k) \leftarrow \frac{[\tau^k(a)]^\alpha}{\sum\limits_{a' \in C^k} [\tau^k(a')]^\alpha} \tag{4.2}$$

where α is a parameter which controls the variance of the distribution.

2. The symbol a is appended to the supersequence:

$$\mathcal{S}^k \leftarrow \mathcal{S}^k a \tag{4.3}$$

3. The new state vector $\vec{v}^k$ is calculated. Let $\mathcal{M}^k(|\mathcal{S}^k|)$ be the set of characters $s_{iv_i^k}$ in the front which are equal to the symbol a, that is, the symbol that equals the $|\mathcal{S}^k|$th character in $\mathcal{S}^k$. For each i from 1 to n set:

$$v_i^k \leftarrow \begin{cases} v_i^k + 1 & \text{if } s_{iv_i^k} \in \mathcal{M}^k(|\mathcal{S}^k|) \\ v_i^k & \text{otherwise} \end{cases} \tag{4.4}$$

Then, once each ant has generated a valid supersequence $\mathcal{S}^k$ of the given input strings, the values $\Delta\tau_{ij}^k$ for each ant's contribution to the update of the pheromone trails are computed:

1. The total amount of pheromone ant k places on the trail is:

$$\Theta^k \leftarrow f(rank(k)) \cdot \frac{1}{|\mathcal{S}^k|} \tag{4.5}$$

where $1/|\mathcal{S}^k|$ measures the quality of the found supersequence and $f(rank(k))$ is a factor that depends on the rank of the supersequence found by ant k – ranking is done with respect to the lengths of the supersequences found by all ants.

2. The contribution of ant k to the update of the trail is computed as follows. Note, that every character of a string in L is contained in exactly one set $\mathcal{M}^k(l), l \in [1:|\mathcal{S}^k|]$. As argued above, the total amount of pheromone added for the characters in a set $\mathcal{M}^k(l)$ depends on l – the smaller l is, the more pheromone is added. This is because the smaller l is the earlier the characters in $\mathcal{M}^k(l)$ have been embedded in the supersequence and a high pheromone value gives a character a better chance to be chosen early by following ants. To every character in a set $\mathcal{M}^k(l)$ the same amount of pheromone is added. Formally, for all $l \in \{1,2,...,|\mathcal{S}^k|\}$ and each character $s_{ij} \in \mathcal{M}^k(l)$:

$$\Delta\tau_{ij}^k \leftarrow \frac{\Theta^k}{|\mathcal{M}^k(l)|} \cdot 2 \cdot \frac{|\mathcal{S}^k| - l + 1}{|\mathcal{S}^k|^2 + |\mathcal{S}^k|} \tag{4.6}$$

In Step 2, note that, since:

$$\sum_{l=1}^{|S^k|}(|S^k|-l+1) = \frac{|S^k|^2+|S^k|}{2}$$

it is easy to verify that the total amount of pheromone placed by ant k is indeed Θ^k.

At the end of the iteration, when all ants have performed the steps described above, the overall amount of new trail is calculated as follows:

$$\Delta\tau_{ij} \leftarrow \sum_{k=1}^{m}\Delta\tau_{ij}^k \tag{4.7}$$

The update of the trail values τ_{ij} is done according to the following formula:

$$\tau_{ij} \leftarrow (1-\rho)\cdot\tau_{ij}+\chi\cdot\Delta\tau_{ij} \tag{4.8}$$

where χ is a parameter which allows to scale the amount of pheromone put onto the trail and $\rho \in (0,1]$ is a value which determines the *evaporation* rate of the trail information.

4.3 VARIATIONS AND EXTENSIONS

Some variations and extensions of AS-SCS are described in this section.

4.3.1 Weighting Pheromone Values

Instead of the Majority Merge heuristic it is also possible to use other heuristics of the same type to guide the ants on their way to good solutions. This requires only to change Equation 4.1 accordingly. For example, to weight the pheromone values according to the L-Majority Merge heuristic, Equation 4.1 is changed to:

$$\tau^k(a) \leftarrow \sum_{i\in\mathcal{I}^k:s_{iv_i^k}=a}\tau_{iv_i^k}(|S_i|-v_i^k+1) \tag{4.9}$$

4.3.2 A Lookahead Function as Heuristic

To direct the decisions of the ants ACO algorithms often use – in addition to the pheromone values – heuristic values. In AS-SCS the heuristic values are computed by means of a *lookahead function* which takes into account the influence of the choice of the next symbol to be appended to the supersequence on the quality of the states reachable during the following iteration. Therefore, when deciding whether or not to append some symbol a an ant does not only calculate the probability according to the corresponding pheromone value but also makes one step lookahead by evaluating in some way the state that would result from this decision. Here it computes the maximum amount of pheromone placed on the occurrences of a symbol in the new front:

$$\eta(\vec{v}^k, a) \leftarrow \max_{a' \in \vec{C}^k} \vec{\tau}^k(a') \qquad (4.10)$$

where $\vec{C}^k$ and $\vec{\tau}^k$ denote respectively the candidate-set and the amount of pheromone in the new state that is obtained from vector $\vec{v}^k$ if symbol a is chosen.

To make use of this heuristic value η the calculation of the transition probabilities is changed accordingly. Equation 4.2 is changed to (parameter β controls the influence of η):

$$p(a, \vec{v}^k) \leftarrow \frac{[\tau^k(a)]^\alpha \cdot [\eta(\vec{v}, a)]^\beta}{\sum_{a' \in C^k} ([\tau^k(a')]^\alpha \cdot [\eta(\vec{v}, a')]^\beta)} \qquad (4.11)$$

Instead of using one step lookahead to compute η as described above it is also possible to use a deeper lookahead.

4.3.3 Island Model

For the ant algorithm described here an *island model* approach is used. The island model is a concept that is often used for genetic algorithms. The idea is to have several colonies of ants working on the same problem instance independently most of the time. This means every colony lays its own pheromone trail which is not accessible to ants of other colonies. After a certain number of iterations some exchange of best solutions between the colonies is done. If a colony receives a solution that is better than the best solution found so far by the colony, the received solution becomes the new best found solution. It influences the colony because during the trail update phase some new pheromone is always put on the trail that corresponds to the best found solution. This can be viewed as an elitist strategy where an 'elitist' ant is added to the colony that always 'finds' the best found solution. In AS-SCS every colony receives the overall best solution found so far.

Two different types of colonies are used: 'forward colonies' and 'backward colonies'. The difference is that the backward colonies work not on the set L but on the reverse instance which contains the reverse of every string from L. Clearly, when a forward colony and a backward colony exchange a solution it has to be reversed.

4.4 RESULTS

In this section we report on the results of several tests run with AS-SCS. The tests compare the performance of AS-SCS with the performance of L-Majority Merge and the genetic algorithm GA-SCS. As test instances we used (i) sets of random strings of equal and different lengths where each character was chosen uniformly from Σ, (ii) a set of similar strings, and (iii) two special instances. Sets of random strings are instances which exhibit neither a special relation between the strings nor special internal structures in the strings which could influence the algorithms behaviour in some very specific way. Similar strings are important for applications, for example, when comparing DNA strings of closely related species or when producing several variants of the same product. The special sets of strings were created such that the heuristic L-Majority Merge performs bad on it. Also the optimum solution is known for them. In particular, the following test instances were used:

- Random strings (equal or different length).
    - T-R1: 16 random strings of length 160, alphabet size 16.
    - T-R2: 4 random strings of length 80 and 4 of length 40, alphabet size 16.

- Similar Strings.
    - T-S: 16 random strings of length 80 obtained as randomly chosen substrings of one random string of length 100, alphabet size 16.

- Special cases.
    - T-W1: 9 strings a^{40}, 4 strings $b^{13}a^{27}$, 2 strings $b^{26}a^{14}$, 1 string $b^{39}a$.
    - T-W2: 8 strings $a^{20}b^{20}$, 8 strings $b^{20}c^{20}$.

The test runs were done with AS-SCS using the L-Majority Merge heuristic. The following parameter values have been used (if not stated otherwise): $\alpha = \beta = 9$, $\rho = 0.5$, $\chi = 1000$, and $q_0 = 0.9$. Every iteration was done with 4 colonies (2 backward and 2 forward colonies) of 16 ants each. The following f values which control the influence of an ant on the trail update were used: $f(1)=f(2)=4$, $f(3)=f(4)=3$, $f(5)=f(6)=2$, $f(7)=f(8)=1$, and $f(9)= \ldots = f(16)=0$. Note that the rank of an ant is computed with respect to the other ants in its colony. Hence in every iteration the eight best ants in each colony put new pheromone on the trail. In addition, we used one elitist ant in each colony which puts new pheromone on the trail of the best solution found so far. For the elitist ant $f(0)=5$ was used. Every 8th iteration the global best solution that has been obtained is sent to all colonies. All reported results are averaged over 25 runs (5 runs of AS-SCS on each of 5 different problem instances; the same 5 problem instances were used for comparing the different algorithms) with 150 iterations each. In the following AS-SCS (AS-SCS-L, AS-SCS-L2) denotes the ant algorithm without lookahead (with lookahead of depth 1, with lookahead of depth 2 respectively). Similarly, LM (LM-L, LM L2) denotes the L-Majority Merge heuristic without lookahead (with lookahead of depth 1 and 2 respectively).

A comparison of the performance of AS-SCS with the L-Majority Merge heuristic and the genetic algorithm GA-SCS on random and similar strings can be found in Table 4.1. The table shows that AS-SCS is slightly better on T-R1 than GA-SCS and that both algorithms perform similar on T-R2 and T-S. But it should be noted that AS-SCS is much faster than GA-SCS (AS-SCS used less than a minute on a Pentium-II 300MHz processor compared to a few hours for GA-SCS on a 486-50 processor). Also AS-SCS and GA-SCS are better than LM. The superiority of AS-SCS over LM is small on random strings of equal length (4.53%) and medium on the random strings of different length (11.99%). In general, on random strings L-Majority Merge is a good heuristic because it makes locally optimal decisions. This strategy cannot be too bad because basically the remaining strings are again random. On similar strings the improvement over LM is quite large (38.34%) and AS-SCS often found a supersequence of length 100 which is supposed to be optimal.

The additional lookahead function improved the results of AS SCS and LM on the random strings significantly (the relative improvement over LM grows from 4.53% (11.99%) for AS-SCS to 20.04% (19.10%) for AS-SCS-L2 on T-R1 (T-R2). Clearly the additional lookahead takes time (on a Pentium-II 300 MHz Processor AS-SCS needs less than one minute, AS-SCS-L about 20 minutes, and AS-SCS-L2 about 2 hours for T-R1). But on T-R1 the ant algorithm AS-SCS-L2 is better, even after only one iteration, than AS-SCS after 150 iterations.

When available computation time limited it might be better to use the L-Majority Merge heuristic with deep lookahead than to use the ant algorithm with small or no lookahead. This is indeed true for random strings (compare Table 4.1 with the results from Table 4.2). The reason is that L-Majority Merge fits very well for random strings as was explained above. But the situation is different for similar strings where L-Majority Merge with deep lookahead is worse than the ant algorithm without lookahead (see Tables 4.1 and 4.2).

The performance of AS-SCS, LM, and GA-SCS on the special instances is shown in Table 4.3. The optimal strings are $a^{40}b^{39}$ for T-W1 and $a^{20}b^{20}c^{20}$ for T-W2. For both instances the optimal string cannot be found by LM. But AS-SCS, as well as GA-SCS, were able to find the optimal supersequence.

Table 4.1: Results on random and similar strings. We report the length of the best solution and the relative improvement over LM. Averages over 25 runs (5 runs on each of 5 problem instances). AS-SCS, AS-SCS-L, and AS-SCS-L2 stopped after 150 iterations, while GA-SCS stopped when all individuals have the same fitness.

$|\Sigma|$	LM	LM-L	LM-L2	GA-SCS	AS-SCS	AS-SCS-L	SC-SCS-L2
T-R1	985.2	907.8	872.8	965.5	940.6	875.0	787.8
	0%	7.86%	11.41%	2.0%	4.53%	11.19%	20.04%
T-R2	296.8	274.8	260.8	260.2	261.2	245.8	240.1
	0%	7.41%	12.13%	12.33%	11.99%	17.18%	19.10%
T-S	166.4	152.0	129.8	100.0	102.6	102.7	100.5
	0%	8.65%	22.0%	39.9%	38.34%	38.28%	39.60%

Table 4.2: Heuristic LM with different depth of lookahead. We report the length of the solution and the relative improvement over LM without lookahead.

Problem	0	1	2	3	4	5	6
T-R1	985.2	907.8	872.8	849.0	840.4	829.0	816.8
	0%	7.86%	11.41%	13.82%	14.7%	15.85%	17.09%
T-S	166.4	152.0	129.8	117.4	128.2	118.0	118.8
	0%	8.65%	22.0%	29.45%	22.96%	29.09%	28.61%

Table 4.3: Results on the special instances. We report the length of the best solution. Averages over 25 runs (5 runs on each of 5 problem instances). AS-SCS stopped after 150 iterations, while GA-SCS stopped when all individuals have the same fitness.

Problem	Optimum	LM	GA-SCS	AS-SCS
T-W1	79	91	79	79
T-W2	60	79	60	60

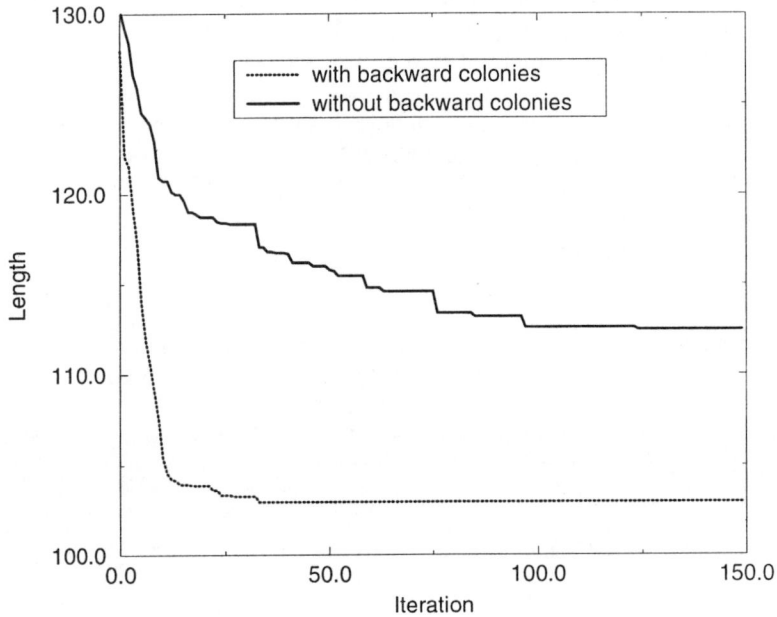

Fig. 4.1: Results of AS-SCS-L with/without 'backward colonies' on T-S.

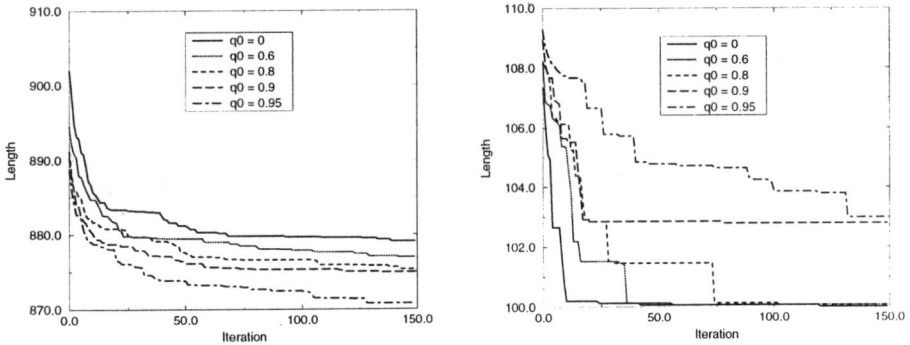

Fig. 4.2: Results of AS-SCS-L on T-R1 (left) and T-S (right) for different values of q_0.

It should be noted that the performance of AS-SCS when doing no pheromone update (that is, when the pheromone trail strength τ_{ij} is always 1 for every $i \in [1:n]$, $j \in [1:|S_i|]$) is worse than its performance when doing it. The difference is larger on similar strings than on random strings because the random strings are in a way good for 'random' ants without trail information.

To use a combination of forward and backward colonies is of no benefit on random strings over using only forward colonies. But on similar strings the combination of forward and backward colonies becomes clearly an advantage (see Figure 4.1).

Another difference between the behaviour of AS-SCS on random strings and similar strings concerns the influence of the threshold parameter of the Pseudo-Random-Proportional Action Choice Rule on the solution quality. While on random strings the quality improves with a growing threshold value (that is, for increasing value of q_0, see left part of Figure 4.2) the opposite holds for the case of similar strings (see right part of Figure 4.2). This indicates that it is advantageous to stay quite close to the greedy solution when searching for good solutions for random strings, in contrast to the case for similar strings.

In conclusion, as shown by the results reported here, it appears that AS-SCS is a promising alternative to classical heuristics and genetic algorithms for the shortest common supersequence problem. This is particularly true for strings that are not purely random strings, suggesting additional benefits of using AS-SCS style methods for realistic applications of this type.

Chapter Five

MACS-VRPTW: A Multiple Ant Colony System for Vehicle Routing Problems with Time Windows

Luca Maria Gambardella, Éric Taillard and Giovanni Agazzi

5.1 INTRODUCTION

This chapter presents MACS-VRPTW, a Multiple Ant Colony System for Vehicle Routing Problems with Time Windows. MACS-VRPTW is based on Ant Colony System (ACS – Gambardella & Dorigo [1996], Dorigo & Gambardella [1997,1997a]) and, more generally, on Ant Colony Optimization (ACO), a new metaheuristic approach inspired by the foraging behaviour of real colonies of ants.

The basic ACO idea (see chapter two and Dorigo et al [1998] for a detailed description of the ACO metaheuristic) is that a large number of simple artificial agents are able to build good solutions to hard combinatorial optimization problems via low-level based communications. Real ants cooperate in their search for food by depositing chemical traces (pheromones) on the floor. An artificial ant colony simulates this behaviour (Dorigo et al [1991, 1996]). Artificial ants cooperate by using a common memory that corresponds to the pheromone deposited by real ants. This artificial pheromone is one of the most important components of ant colony optimization and is used for constructing new solutions.

In the ACO metaheuristic, artificial pheromone is accumulated at run-time during the computation. Artificial ants are implemented as parallel processes whose role is to build problem solutions using a constructive procedure driven by a combination of artificial pheromone, problem data and a heuristic function used to evaluate successive constructive steps.

Recently, many ACO algorithms have been proposed to solve different types of combinatorial optimization problems. In particular, ACO algorithms have been shown to be very efficient when combined with specialized local search procedures to solve the symmetric and asymmetric travelling salesman problems (TSP/ATSP, Dorigo & Gambardella [1997, 1997a], Stützle [1998a], Stützle & Dorigo [1999]), the sequential ordering problem (SOP, Gambardella & Dorigo [1997]), the quadratic assignment problem (QAP, Gambardella et al [1999], Taillard & Gambardella [1997]), the bi-quadratic assignment problem and the p-median problem (Taillard [1998]).

One of the most efficient ACO based implementations has been Ant Colony System (ACS – Gambardella & Dorigo [1996], Dorigo & Gambardella [1997, 1997a]) that introduced a particular pheromone trail updating procedure useful to intensify the search in the neighbourhood of the best computed solution. This chapter presents an ACS extension able to solve the vehicle routing problem with time windows (VRPTW).

The VRPTW is defined as the problem of minimizing time and costs in case a fleet of vehicles has to distribute goods from a depot to a set of customers. The VRPTW considered in this chapter minimizes a multiple, hierarchical objective function: the first objective is to minimize the number of tours (or vehicles) and the second is to minimize the total travel time. A solution with a lower number of tours is always preferred to a solution with a higher number of tours even if the travel time for the low number of tours solution is higher. This hierarchical objective view of the VRPTW is very common in the literature, and in cases where problem constraints are very tight (for example when the total capacity of the minimum number of vehicles is very close to the total volume to deliver or when customers' time windows are narrow), both objectives can be antagonistic. For example, the minimum travel time solution can include a number of vehicles which is greater than that of the solution with minimum number of vehicles (see e.g. Kohl et al [1997]).

In order to adapt the ACS for these multiple objectives the idea is to define two ACS colonies, each dedicated to the optimization of a different objective function. In MACS-VRPTW the colonies cooperate by exchanging information through pheromone updating. MACS-VRPTW is shown to be competitive with the best existing methods both in terms of solution quality and computation time. Moreover, MACS-VRPTW improves the best solutions known for some problem instances of the literature.

The remainder of this chapter is organized as follows: First, vehicle routing problems are introduced by presenting a formal definition of the capacitated vehicle routing problem (CVRP), and then providing a definition for the vehicle routing problem with time windows (VRPTW). Second, ACS main characteristics are analyzed by explaining how ACS has been applied to the travelling salesman problem (TSP). Then, we explain how the ACS is extended to deal with the VRPTW, and the resulting MACS-VRPTW system is investigated by presenting its main components. Last, numerical results are reported and some conclusions are drawn.

5.2 VEHICLE ROUTING PROBLEMS

The most elementary version of the vehicle routing problem is the capacitated vehicle routing problem (CVRP). The CVRP is described as follows: n customers must be served from a unique depot. Each customer asks for a quantity q_i of goods ($i = 1,..., n$) and a vehicle of capacity Q is available to deliver goods. Since the vehicle capacity is limited, the vehicle has to periodically return to the depot for reloading. In the CVRP, it is not possible to split customer delivery. Therefore, a CVRP solution is a collection of tours where each customer is visited only once and the total tour demand is at most Q. From a graph theoretical point of view the CVRP may be stated as follows: Let $G = (C, L)$ be a complete graph with node set $C = \{c_0, c_1, c_2, ..., c_n\}$ and arc set $L = \{(c_i, c_j) : c_i, c_j \in C, i \neq j\}$. In this graph model, c_0 is the depot and the other nodes are the customers to be served. Each node is associated with a fixed quantity q_i of goods to be delivered (a quantity $q_0 = 0$ is associated with depot c_0). To each arc (c_i, c_j) is associated a value t_{ij} representing the travel time between c_i and c_j. The goal is to find a set of tours of minimum total travel time. Each tour starts from and terminates at the depot c_0, each node c_i ($i = 1,..., n$) must be visited exactly once, and the quantity of goods to be delivered on a route should never exceed the vehicle capacity Q.

One of the most successful exact approaches for the CVRP is the *k-tree* method of Fisher [1994] that succeeded in solving a problem with 71 customers. However, there are smaller instances that have not been exactly solved yet. To treat larger instances, or to compute solutions faster, heuristic methods must be used. Among the best heuristic methods are tabu searches (Taillard [1993], Rochat & Taillard [1995], Rego & Roucairol [1996], Xu & Kelly [1996], Toth & Vigo [1998]) and large neighbourhood search (Shaw [1998]).

The CVRP can be extended in many ways. For example a service time s_i for each customer (with $s_0 = 0$) and a time limit over the duration of each tour can be considered. An important extension of the CVRP that is the subject of this chapter is the vehicle routing problem with time windows (VRPTW). In addition to the mentioned CVRP features, this problem includes, for the depot and for each customer c_i $(i = 0,...,n)$ a time window $[b_i, e_i]$ during which the customer has to be served (with b_0 the earliest start time and e_0 the latest return time of each vehicle to the depot). The tours are performed by a fleet of v identical vehicles. The additional constraints are that the service beginning time at each node c_i $(i = 1,...,n)$ must be greater than or equal to b_i, the beginning of the time window, and the arrival time at each node c_i must be lower than or equal to e_i, the end of the time window. In case the arrival time is less than b_i, the vehicle has to wait till the beginning of the time window before starting servicing the customer.

In the literature the fleet size v is often a variable and a very common objective is to minimize v. This objective is related to the real situation in which driver salaries are variable costs for the company or when the company has to rent vehicles to perform deliveries.

Usually, two different solutions with the same number of vehicles are ranked by alternative objectives such as the total travelling time or total delivery time (including waiting and service times). These objectives are also used for companies owning a fixed fleet of vehicles.

A number of exact and heuristic methods exist for the VRPTW. Among exact methods, that of Kohl et al [1997] is one of the most efficient and succeeded in solving a number of 100 customers instances. Note that exact methods are more efficient in case the solution space is restricted by narrow time windows since less combinations of customers are possible to define feasible tours. The most successful heuristic methods for the VRPTW are Adaptive Memory Programs (see Taillard et al [1998] for an introduction to Adaptive Memory Programming), Embedding Tabu Searches (Rochat & Taillard [1995], Taillard et al [1997], Badeau et al [1997]), Guided Local Search (Kilby et al [1999]) and Large Neighbourhood Search (Shaw [1998]); note that the method of Taillard et al [1997] can also be viewed as a kind of Large Neighbourhood Search.

5.3 ANT COLONY SYSTEM

This section introduces and presents the original Ant Colony System (ACS) (Gambardella & Dorigo [1996], Dorigo & Gambardella [1997, 1997a]) applied to the travelling salesman problem (TSP). Indeed, MACS-VRPTW has been proposed to solve a VRPTW where both the number of vehicles and the travel time have to be minimized. This multiple objective minimization is achieved by using two artificial ant colonies based on ACS.

The TSP is the problem of finding a shortest closed tour which visits all the cities in a given set. ACS is applied to the TSP by associating two measures to each arc of the TSP graph: the closeness η_{ij} and the pheromone trail η_{ij}. Closeness, defined as the inverse of the arc length, is a static heuristic value, that never changes for a given problem instance, while the pheromone trail is dynamically changed by ants at runtime. Therefore, the most important component of ACS is the management of pheromone trails. These pheromone trails are used, in conjunction with the objective function, for constructing new solutions. Informally, the levels of pheromon on the trails give a measure of how desirable it is to insert a given arc in a solution. Pheromone trails are used for both exploration and exploitation. Exploration concerns the probabilistic choice of the components used to construct a solution: a higher probability is given to elements with a strong pheromone trail. Exploitation chooses the component that maximizes a blend of pheromone trail values and heuristic evaluations.

The ACS goal is to find a shortest tour. In ACS, m ants build tours in parallel, where m is a parameter of the method. Each ant is randomly assigned to a starting node and has to build a solution, that is, a complete tour. A tour is built node by node: each ant iteratively adds new nodes until all nodes have been visited. When ant k is located in node i, it chooses the next node j probabilistically from the set of feasible nodes $\mathcal{N}_i^k$ (that is, in this case, the set of nodes that still have to be visited). The probabilistic rule used to construct a tour is the following. With a probability q_0 the next node will be chosen via exploitation, while with a probability $(1 - q_0)$ the next node will be chosen via exploration. In the case of exploitation, a node with the highest value of $\tau_{ij} \cdot [\eta_{ij}]^\beta$ is chosen, where j is a feasible node. In the case of exploration, a node j is chosen with a probability p_{ij} proportional to $\tau_{ij} \cdot [\eta_{ij}]^\beta$. This probability p_{ij} is given in Equation 5.1.

$$
p_{ij} = \begin{cases} \dfrac{\tau_{ij} \cdot [\eta_{ij}]^\beta}{\sum_{l \in \mathcal{N}_i^k} \tau_{il} \cdot [\eta_{il}]^\beta} & \text{if } j \in \mathcal{N}_i^k \\ \\ 0 & \text{otherwise} \end{cases}
\tag{5.1}
$$

where β and q_0 are parameters: β weighs the relative importance of the heuristic value, while q_0 ($0 \leq q_0 \leq 1$) determines the relative importance of exploitation versus exploration: the smaller q_0 the higher the probability to use the rule described with Equation 5.1.

Once each ant has built a complete solution, this solution is tentatively improved upon by using a local search procedure. Next, the best solution found from the beginning of the trial is used to update the pheromone trails. Then, the process is iterated by starting again m ants until a termination condition is satisfied. ACS terminates when at least one of the following conditions becomes true: a fixed, pre-determined maximum number of solutions has been generated, a fixed amount of CPU time has elapsed, or no improvement has been achieved during a given number of iterations.

In ACS, the pheromone trail is updated both locally and globally. Local updating is performed during the construction of solutions, while global updating is performed at the completion of the constructive phase. In brief, the overall effect of local updating is to dynamically change the desirability of edges for future ants: every time an ant uses an edge the quantity of pheromone associated with this edge is decreased and the edge therefore becomes less attractive. On the other hand, global updating is used to intensify the search in the neighbourhood of the best solution computed.

In ACS, only the best solution found so far is used to influence global modifications of the pheromone trail. This updating strategy (Gambardella & Dorigo [1995, 1996], Dorigo

& Gambardella [1997, 1997a]) has been proved to be more efficient than the updating strategy used in the early Ant System (AS) (Dorigo et al [1991, 1996]). In this early method, all of the constructed solutions were used to update the pheromone trails. The rationale for only using the best-so-far solution for global updating is that in this way a 'preferred route' is memorized in the pheromone trail matrix, and future ants will use this information to generate new solutions in a neighbourhood of this preferred route. The phermone trail values τ_{ij} are therefore updated in the way indicated below in Equation 5.2.

$$\tau_{ij} = (1 - \rho) \cdot \tau_{ij} + \rho / J_{\psi}^{gb} \qquad \forall (i, j) \in \psi^{gb} \qquad (5.2)$$

where ρ $(0 \le \rho \le 1)$ is a parameter of the method and J_{ψ}^{gb} is the length of ψ^{gb}, the shortest path generated since the start of the computation. This global updating procedure is applied at the end of each cycle, that is, each time the constructive phase has been completed.

Local updating is performed as follows. When an ant moves from node i to node j, the amount of pheromone trail currently on arc (i, j) is decreased according to the rule:

$$\tau_{ij} = (1 - \rho) \cdot \tau_{ij} + \rho \cdot \tau_0 \qquad (5.3)$$

where τ_0 is the initial value of trails. It was found that $\tau_0 = 1/(n \cdot J_{\psi}^{h})$ is a good value for this parameter where J_{ψ}^{h} is the length of the initial solution produced by the nearest neighbour heuristic (Flood [1956]) and n is the number of nodes.

An interesting aspect of the local updating method is that, while edges are visited by ants, Equation 5.3 makes their trail diminish, making them gradually less and less attractive, and therefore preferring the exploration of not yet visited edges, consequently enhancing diversity in solution generation.

5.4 MACS-VRPTW FOR VEHICLE ROUTING PROBLEMS WITH TIME WINDOWS

Although VRPs can be seen as relatively direct extensions of the travelling salesman problem, the first ant system for vehicle routing problems has been designed only very recently; this was done by Bullnheimer et al [1997b, 1999]. They considered the most elementary version of the problem, called the capacitated vehicle routing problem (CVRP). In this chapter we consider a more elaborate type of vehicle routing problem which involves two objective functions: (i) the minimization of the number of tours (or vehicles), and (ii) the minimization of the total travel time. Minimization of the number of tours or vehicles always takes precedence over minimization of the total travel time, as was explained earlier in section 5.2.

This hierarchical objectives VRPTW is very common in the literature but sometimes it is mixed up with other VRPTW variants that consider only one objective (for example, Kohl et al [1997] consider instances built on the same data set as hierarchical objectives VRPTW instances, but with travel time as unique objective).

In the MACS-VRPTW algorithm (Figures 5.1 and 5.2) both objectives are optimized simultaneously by coordinating the activities of two ACS based colonies. The goal of the first colony, ACS-VEI, is to try to diminish the number of vehicles used, while the second colony, ACS-TIME, optimizes the feasible solutions found by ACS-VEI. Both colonies use independent pheromone trails but collaborate by sharing the variable ψ^{gb} managed by MACS-VRPTW. Initially, ψ^{gb} is a feasible VRPTW solution found with a nearest neighbour heuristic. Then, ψ^{gb} is improved by the two colonies. When ACS-VEI is activated, it tries to find a feasible solution with one vehicle less than the number of vehicles used in ψ^{gb}. The goal of ACS-TIME is to optimize the total travel time of solutions that use as many vehicles as vehicles used in ψ^{gb}. ψ^{gb} is updated each time one of the colonies computes an improved feasible solution. In case the improved solution contains fewer vehicles than the vehicles used in ψ^{gb}, MACS-VRPTW kills ACS-TIME and ACS-VEI. Then, the process is iterated and two new colonies are activated, working with the new, reduced number of vehicles.

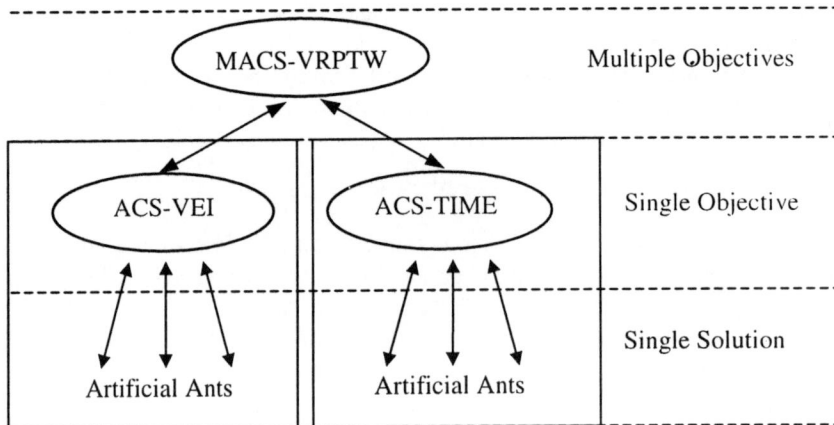

Fig. 5.1: Architecture of MACS-VRPTW.

```
procedure MACS-VRPTW()
                                                              {Initialize}
    ψ^gb ← feasible initial solution with unlimited number of vehicles
            produced  with a nearest neighbour heuristic
    repeat                                                   { Main Loop }
        v   ←  #active_vehicles ( ψ^gb )
        activate  ACS-VEI(v – 1)
        activate  ACS-TIME(v)
        while ACS-VEI and ACS-TIME are active
            wait for improved solution ψ from ACS-VEI or ACS-TIME
            ψ^gb ← ψ
            if #active_vehicles( ψ^gb ) < v then
                    kill  ACS-TIME  and  ACS-VEI
        end while
    until a stopping criterion is met
```

Fig. 5.2: Pseudo-code of MACS-VRPTW(): Multiple Ant Colony System for Vehicle Routing Problems with Time Windows. ψ^{gb} is the best feasible solution, with lowest number of vehicles and shortest travel time. The procedure #active_vehicles (ψ) computes the number of active vehicles in the feasible solution ψ.

5.4.1 ACS-TIME and ACS-VEI colonies

The working principles of ACS-VEI and ACS-TIME colonies are described in Figure 5.3 and Figure 5.4.

```
procedure ACS-TIME(v)
                                                          {Initialize }
    initialize pheromone and data structures using v
      repeat                                              { Cycle }
        for each ant k
                                          { construct a solution ψk }
            new_active_ant(k, local_search=TRUE, 0)
        end for each
                            { Update the best solution if it is improved }
        if ∃k : ψk is feasible and Jψk < Jψgb then
            send ψk to MACS-VRPTW()
                        {perform global updating according to Equation 5.2}
        τij = (1 − ρ)·τij + ρ/Jψgb          ∀(i, j) ∈ ψgb
    until a stopping criterion is met
```

Fig. 5.3: Pseudo-code of ACS-TIME: Travel time minimization Parameter v is the smallest number of vehicles for which a feasible solution has been computed.

ACS-TIME colony (Figure 5.3) is a traditional ACS based colony whose goal is to compute a tour as short as possible. In ACS-TIME m artificial ants are activated to construct problem solutions $\psi^1,...,\psi^m$. Each solution is built by calling the new_active_ant procedure, a constructive procedure explained in detail in section 5.4.3 that is similar to the ACS constructive procedure designed for the TSP. When $\psi^1,...,\psi^m$ have been computed, they are compared to ψ^{gb} and, in case one solution is better, it is sent to MACS-VRPTW. MACS-VRPTW uses this solution to update ψ^{gb}. After solutions generation, the global updates are performed using Equation 5.2 and ψ^{gb}.

ACS-VEI colony (Figure 5.4) searches for a feasible solution by maximizing the number of visited customers. ACS-VEI starts its computation using $v-1$ vehicles, that is, one vehicle fewer than the smallest number of vehicles for which a feasible solution has been computed (that is, the number of vehicles in ψ^{gb}). During this search the colony produces unfeasible solutions in which some customers are not visited. In ACS-VEI, the solution computed since the beginning of the trial with the highest number of visited customers is stored in the variable $\psi^{ACS-VEI}$. A solution is better than $\psi^{ACS-VEI}$ only when the number of visited customers is increased. Therefore ACS-VEI is different from the traditional ACS applied to the TSP. In ACS-VEI the current best solution $\psi^{ACS-VEI}$ is the solution (usually unfeasible) with the highest number of visited customers, while in ACS applied to TSP the current best solution is the shortest one.

In order to maximize the number of customers serviced, ACS-VEI manages a vector IN of integers. The entry IN_j stores the number of time customer j has not been inserted in a solution. IN is used by the constructive procedure new_active_ant for favouring the customers that are less frequently included in the solutions. In ACS-VEI, at the end of each cycle, pheromone trails are globally updated with two different solutions: $\psi^{\text{ACS-VEI}}$, the unfeasible solution with the highest number of visited customers and ψ^{gb}, the feasible solution with the lowest number of vehicles and the shortest travel time. Experiments have shown that a double update greatly improves performance. Indeed, the updates with $\psi^{\text{ACS-VEI}}$ are not increasing the trails toward the customers that are not included in the solution. Since ψ^{gb} is feasible, the updates with ψ^{gb} are increasing trails toward all customers.

---

procedure ACS-VEI(s)

                    { Initialize }

initialize pheromone and data structures using s

  $\psi^{\text{ACS-VEI}} \leftarrow$ initial solution with s vehicles produced with a nearest neighbour heuristic.   { $\psi^{\text{ACS-VEI}}$ is not necessary feasible }

  repeat   { Cycle }

    for each ant k

                 { construct a solution ψ^k }

      new_active_ant(k, local_search=FALSE, IN)

      $\forall$ customer $j \notin \psi^k$: $IN_j \leftarrow IN_j + 1$

    end for each

           { update the best solution if it is improved }

    if $\exists k$: #visited_customers(ψ^k) > #visited_customers($\psi^{\text{ACS-VEI}}$) **then**

      $\psi^{\text{ACS-VEI}} \leftarrow \psi^k$

      $\forall j$: $IN_j \leftarrow 0$ { reset IN }

      if $\psi^{\text{ACS-VEI}}$ is feasible **then**

        send $\psi^{\text{ACS-VEI}}$ to MACS-VRPTW()

          { perform global updating according to

            Equation 5.2 using both $\psi^{\text{ACS-VEI}}$ and ψ^{gb} }

    $\tau_{ij} = (1 - \rho) \cdot \tau_{ij} + \rho / J_\psi^{\text{ACS-VEI}}$ $\forall (i, j) \in \psi^{\text{ACS-VEI}}$

    $\tau_{ij} = (1 - \rho) \cdot \tau_{ij} + \rho / J_\psi^{\text{gb}}$ $\forall (i, j) \in \psi^{\text{gb}}$

  until a stopping criterion is met

Fig. 5.4: Procedure ACS-VEI: Number of vehicles minimization. Parameter s is set to $v-1$, that is, one vehicle less than the smallest number of vehicles for which a feasible solution has been computed. #visited_customers (ψ) computes the number of customers that have been visited in solution ψ.

5.4.2 Solution Model

MACS-VRPTW uses a solution model in which each ant builds a single tour (Figure 5.5). A solution is represented as follows: First, the depot with all its connections to/from the customers is duplicated a number of times equal to the number of available vehicles. Distances between copies of the depot are set to zero. This approach makes the vehicle routing problem closer to the traditional travelling salesman problem.

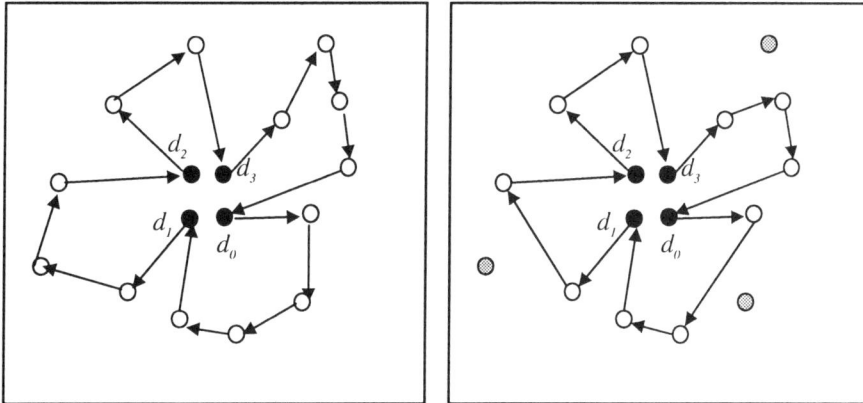

Fig. 5.5: Feasible (left) and unfeasible (right) solutions for a vehicle routing problem with four duplicated depots and four active vehicles.

So, in both the TSP and this model, a feasible solution is a path that visits all nodes exactly once. Figure 5.5 shows a solution represented as a single tour. Duplicated depots $(d_0,...,d_3)$ are black points while clients are white points. All duplicated depots have the same coordinates but they have been split to clarify the picture. An advantage of such a solution representation is that the trails in direction of the duplicated depots are less attractive than in the case of a single depot (due to the pheromone update rules). This positively affects the quality of solutions produced by the constructive procedure.

5.4.3 Solution Constructive Procedure

ACS-VEI and ACS-TIME both use the new_active_ant constructive procedure shown in Figure 5.6, which is similar to the ACS constructive procedure designed for the TSP. Each ant starts from a randomly chosen copy of the depot and, at each step, moves to a not yet visited node that does not violate time window or vehicle capacity constraints. The set of available nodes, in case the ant is not located in a duplicated depot, also includes not yet visited duplicated depots. An ant at node i chooses probabilistically the next node j by using exploration and exploitation mechanisms. The attractiveness η_{ij} is computed by taking into account the travelling time t_{ij} between nodes i and j, the time window $[b_i, e_i]$ associated with node j and the number of times IN_j node j has not been inserted in a solution. When new_active_ant is called by ACS-TIME, the variables IN are not used and the corresponding parameter is set to zero.

Each time an ant moves from one node to another, a local update of the pheromone trail is executed according to Equation 5.3. Last, at the end of the constructive phase, if the solution is incomplete (some customers may be omitted) it is tentatively completed by performing further insertions. The insertion is executed by considering all the non visited customers sorted by decreasing delivery quantities. For each customer the the best feasible insertion (shortest travel time) is sought, until no further feasible insertion is possible. Also, ACS-TIME uses a local search procedure to improve the feasible solutions. The local search uses moves similar to CROSS (Taillard et al [1997]), and is based on the exchange of two sub-chains of customers, one of which may eventually be empty.

---

procedure new_active_ant(k, local_search, IN)

{Initialize}

put ant k in a randomly selected duplicated depot i.

$\psi k \leftarrow \langle i \rangle$

$current\_time_k \leftarrow 0,\ load_k \leftarrow 0$

loop   {ant k builds a tour and stores it in ψk }

{ Starting from node i compute the set $\mathcal{N}_i^k$ of feasible nodes (all nodes j still to be visited and such that $current\_time_k$ and $load_k$ are compatible with time windows $[b_i, e_i]$ and delivery quantity q_i of customer j), then $\forall j \in \mathcal{N}_i^k$ compute the attractiveness η_{ij} as follows: }

$$delivery\_time_j \leftarrow \max\{current\_time_k + t_{ij}, b_j\}$$
$$delta\_time_{ij} \leftarrow delivery\_time_j - current\_time_k$$
$$distance_{ij} \leftarrow delta\_time_{ij} \cdot (e_j - current\_time_k)$$
$$distance_{ij} \leftarrow \max\{1.0, (distance_{ij} - IN_j)$$
$$\eta_{ij} \leftarrow 1.0 / distance_{ij}\ \eta_{ij}$$

{ Choose probabilistically the next node j using η_{ij} in exploitation and exploration (Equation 5.1) mechanisms: }

$\psi k \leftarrow \psi k + \langle j \rangle$

$current\_time_k \leftarrow delivery\_time_j$

$load_k \leftarrow load_k + q_j$

if j is a depot **then** $current\_time_k \leftarrow 0$ and $load_k \leftarrow 0$

$\tau_{ij} \leftarrow (1 - \rho)\tau_{ij} + \rho\tau_0$ { Local pheromone updating (Equation 5.3) }

$i \leftarrow j$ { New node for ant k }

until $\mathcal{N}_i^k = \{\}$ { End the loop when no more feasible nodes are available}

{ In this step path ψk is extended by tentatively inserting non visited customers }

$\psi k \leftarrow$ insertion_procedure(ψk)

{ In this step feasible paths are optimized by a local search procedure. The parameter local_search is TRUE in ACS-TIME and it is FALSE in ACS-VEI }

if $local\_search$ = TRUE **and** ψk is feasible **then**

$\psi k \leftarrow$ local_search_procedure(ψk)

Fig. 5.6: The procedure new_active_ant; this is the procedure by which ant k constructs a solution, used by ACS-VEI and ACS-TIME.

5.5 NUMERICAL RESULTS

This section reports on computational results showing the efficiency of MACS-VRPTW. MACS-VRPTW has been tested on a classical set of 56 benchmark problems (Solomon [1987]) composed of six different problem types (C1,C2,R1,R2,RC1,RC2). Each data set contains between eight to twelve 100-node problems. The names of the six problem types have the following meaning. Problem sets C have clustered customers whose time windows were generated based on a known solution. Problem sets R have customers location generated uniformly randomly over a square. Problem sets RC have a combination of randomly placed and clustered customers. Problem sets of type 1 have narrow time windows and small vehicle capacity. Problem sets of type 2 have large time windows and large vehicle capacity. Therefore, the solutions of type 2 problems have very few routes and significantly more customers per route.

Experiments are made by executing, for each problem data, 3 runs that are stopped after a fixed computation time. Solutions are then averaged for each problem type and the result is reported in the tables. Experiments have been done with the following parameter settings: $m = 10$ ants, $q_0 = 0.9$, $\beta = 1$ and $\rho = 0.1$. The code was written in C++.

Tables 5.1 and 5.2 compare MACS-VRPTW with a number of the best methods available for the VRPTW. The methods considered are: the Adaptive Memory Programming of Rochat & Taillard [1995] (RT), the Large Neighbourhood Search of Shaw [1998] (SW), the Guided Local Search of Kilby et al [1999] (KPS), the Alternate K-exchange reduction of Cordone & Wolfler-Calvo [1997] (CW) and the Adaptive Memory Programming of Taillard et al [1997] (TB). Tables 5.1 and 5.2 provide 3 columns for each data set: the average number of vehicles (which is main goal), the average tour length, and the computation time (in seconds). The computational times cannot be directly compared for different reasons. First, the authors have used different computers; second, some methods (RT and TB) were designed to solve harder problems than the VRPTW and implementations specifically designed for the VRPTW might be faster.

Table 5.1: Performance comparison among the best VRPTW algorithms for different computational time (in seconds) on problem sets R1, C1 and RC1. RT = Rochat & Taillard [1995], SW = Shaw [1998], KPS = Kilby et al [1999], CW = Cordone & Wolfler-Calvo [1997], TB = Taillard et al [1997].

	R1			C1			RC1		
	Veh	Dist	Time	Veh	Dist	Time	Veh	Dist	Time
	12.55	1214.80	100	10	828.40	100	12.46	1395.47	100
MACS-	12.45	1212.95	300	10	828.38	300	12.13	1389.15	300
VRPTW	12.38	1213.35	600	10	828.38	600	12.08	1380.38	600
	12.38	1211.64	1200	10	828.38	1200	11.96	1385.65	1200
	12.38	1210.83	1800	10	828.38	1800	11.92	1388.13	1800
	12.83	1208.43	450	10	832.59	540	12.75	1381.33	430
RT	12.58	1202.00	1300	10	829.01	1600	12.50	1368.03	1300
	12.58	1197.42	2700	10	828.45	3200	12.33	1269.48	2600
	12.45	1198.37	900	–	–	–	12.05	1363.67	900
SW	12.35	1201.47	1800	–	–	–	12.00	1363.68	1800
	12.33	1201.79	3600	–	–	–	11.95	1364.17	3600
KPS	12.67	1200.33	2900	10	830.75	2900	12.12	1388.15	2900
CW	12.50	1241.89	1382	10	834.05	649	12.38	1408.87	723
	12.64	1233.88	2296	10	830.41	2926	12.08	1404.59	1877
TB	12.39	1230.48	6887	10	828.59	7315	12.00	1387.01	5632
	12.33	1220.35	13774	10	828.45	14630	11.90	1381.31	11264

Table 5.2: Performance comparison among the best VRPTW algorithms for different computational time (in seconds) on problem sets R2, C2, and RC2. Refer to the heading of Table 5.1 for the meaning of abbreviations used.

		R2			C2			RC2	
	Veh	Dist	Time	Veh	Dist	Time	Veh	Dist	Time
	3.05	971.97	100	3	593.19	100	3.38	1191.87	100
MACS-	3.00	969.09	300	3	592.97	300	3.33	1168.34	300
VRPTW	3.00	965.37	600	3	592.89	600	3.33	1163.08	600
	3.00	962.07	1200	3	592.04	1200	3.33	1153.63	1200
	3.00	960.31	1800	3	591.85	1800	3.33	1149.28	1800
	3.18	999.63	1600	3	595.38	1200	3.62	1207.37	1300
RT	3.09	969.29	4900	3	590.32	3600	3.62	1155.47	3900
	3.09	954.36	9800	3	590.32	7200	3.62	1139.79	7800
KPS	3.00	966.56	2900	3	592.29	2900	3.38	1133.42	2900
CW	2.91	995.39	1332	3	591.78	292	3.38	1139.70	946
	3.00	1046.56	3372	3	592.75	3275	3.38	1248.34	1933
TB	3.00	1029.65	10116	3	591.14	8187	3.38	1220.28	5798
	3.00	1013.35	20232	3	590.91	16375	3.38	1198.63	11596

Table 5.3: Average of the best solutions computed by different VRPTW algorithms. Best results are in bold. RT= Rochat & Taillard [1995]), TB= Taillard et al [1997]), CR=Chiang and Russel (1993), PB=Potvin and Bengio (1996), TH= Thangiah et al. (1994).

	R1		C1		RC1		R2		C2		RC2	
	VEI	DIST	VEI	DIST	VEI	DIST	VEI	DIST	VEI	DIST	VEI	DIST
MACS-VRPTW	**12.00**	1217.73	**10.00**	**828.38**	11.63	1382.42	**2.73**	967.75	3.00	**589.86**	3.25	1129.19
RT	12.25	1208.50	**10.00**	**828.38**	11.88	1377.39	2.91	961.72	3.00	**589.86**	3.38	1119.59
TB	12.17	1209.35	**10.00**	**828.38**	**11.50**	1389.22	2.82	980.27	3.00	**589.86**	3.38	1117.44
CR	12.42	1289.95	10.00	885.86	12.38	1455.82	2.91	1135.14	3.00	658.88	3.38	1361.14
PB	12.58	1296.80	10.00	838.01	12.13	1446.20	3.00	1117.70	3.00	589.93	3.38	1360.57
TH	12.33	1238.00	10.00	832.00	12.00	1284.00	3.00	1005.00	3.00	650.00	3.38	1229.00

MACS-VRPTW was executed on a Sun UltraSparc 1 167MHz, 70 Mflop/s (Dongarra, 1997), RT used a 15 Mflop/s Silicon Graphics computer, SW used a 63 Mflop/s Sun UltraSparc, KPS used a 25Mflops/s DEC Alpha, CW used a 18 Mflop/s Pentium and TB used a 10 Mflop/s Sun Sparc 10. Table 5.1 provides computational results for MACS-VRPTW when stopped after 100, 300, 600, 1200 and 1800 seconds. The RT, SW and TB iterative methods were also stopped after different computation times while KPS and CW provide results for a unique computation time.

In Tables 5.1 and 5.2 it is shown that MACS-VRPTW is very competitive: for C1 and RC2 types it is clearly the best method and it is always among the best methods for the other problem sets. A characteristic of MACS-VRPTW is that it is able to produce relatively good solutions in a short amount of time.

Table 5.3 reports the average of the best solutions obtained in all our experiments. Similar results were also provided by other authors. In addition to the methods of Rochat & Taillard [1995] (RT) and Taillard et al [1997] (TB) already compared in Tables 5.1 and 5.2, Table 5.2 includes the results of the hybrid method of Chiang & Russel [1993] (CR), the genetic algorithm of Potvin & Bengio [1996] (PB), and the hybrid method of Thangiah et al [1994] (TH). With the exception of RC1 type problem, MACS-VRPTW has been able to produce the best results for all other problem types.

During this experimental campaign, the best solution known of a number of problem instances have been improved. The value of these new best solutions are reported in Table 5.4. In addition to the VRPTW instances the ACS-TIME colony has been tested on CVRP instances. In Table 5.4 are also reported new best solution value for CVRP problem instances tai*nnn* used in Rochat & Taillard [1995], where *nnn* stands for the number of customers.

Table 5.4: New best solution values computed by MACS-VRPTW. *RT*= Rochat & Taillard [1995], *S* = Shaw [1998], *TB*= Taillard et al [1997]

Problem	source	Old Best		New Best	
		vehicles	length	vehicles	length
r112.dat	RT	10	953.63	**9**	982.140
r201.dat	S	4	1254.09	4	**1253.234**
r202.dat	TB	3	1214.28	3	**1202.529**
r204.dat	S	2	867.33	2	**856.364**
r207.dat	RT	3	814.78	**2**	894.889
r208.dat	RT	2	738.6	2	**726.823**
r209.dat	S	3	923.96	3	**921.659**
r210.dat	S	3	963.37	3	**958.241**
rc202.dat	S	4	1162.8	**3**	1377.089
rc203.dat	S	3	1068.07	3	**1062.301**
rc204.dat	S	3	803.9	3	**798.464**
rc207.dat	S	3	1075.25	3	**1068.855**
rc208.dat	RT	3	833.97	3	**833.401**
tai100a.dat	RT	11	2047.90	11	**2041.336**
tai100c.dat	RT	11	1406.86	11	**1406.202**
tai100d.dat	RT	11	1581.25	11	**1581.244**
tai150b.dat	RT	14	2727.77	14	**2656.474**

5.6 CONCLUSIONS

This chapter introduced MACS-VRPTW, a new Ant Colony Optimization based approach to solve vehicle routing problems with time windows. In particular, MACS-VRPTW has been designed to solve vehicle routing problems with two objective functions: (i) the minimization of the number of tours (or vehicles) and (ii) the minimization of the total travel time, where number of tours minimization takes precedence over travel time minimization. MACS-VRPTW introduces a new methodology for optimizing multiple objective functions. The basic idea is to coordinate the activity of different ant colonies, each of them optimizing a different objective. These colonies work by using independent pheromone trails but they collaborate by exchanging information. This is the first time a multi-objective function minimization problem is solved with a multiple ant colony optimization algorithm.

MACS-VRPTW is shown to be competitive with the best existing methods both in terms of solution quality and computation time and has been able to improve the best solutions known for a number of problem instances of the literature.

Acknowledgements

This research has been partially supported by the Swiss National Science Foundation project 21–52557.97 'Adaptive Memory Programming for Dynamic Optimization Problems'.

Part Two

Differential Evolution

Co-ordinating Editor:

Kenneth Price

Contributors:

Ken Chisholm

Jouni Lampinen

Kenneth Price

Rainer Storn

Ivan Zelinka

Chapter Six:

An Introduction to Differential Evolution

Kenneth V. Price

6.1 EVOLUTIONARY ALGORITHMS FOR NUMERICAL OPTIMIZATION

Differential Evolution (DE) is a simple yet powerful population-based, direct-search algorithm for globally optimizing functions defined on totally ordered spaces, including especially functions with real-valued parameters. Real parameter optimization comprises a large and important class of practical problems in science, engineering and business. Finding answers to questions like, 'Which parameter values most closely model the observed data?', 'Which recipe optimizes the yield of a chemical process?' and 'Which portfolio maximizes return on investment?' can improve product reliability, enhance process efficiency and save money. More generally, given an *objective function* $f(\vec{x})$, defined on a space of D real-valued *object variables* $[x_j]^T = \vec{x} \in \mathrm{R}^D$, $j = 1,2,...,D$, at what location $\vec{x}^*$ does $f(\vec{x})$ reach an extreme value? Without loss of generality, it is sufficient to consider only those cases in which the extreme is a minimum, since any maximization task can be inverted into a minimization problem simply by multiplying $f(\vec{x})$ by -1.

Object variables are system parameters that represent the degrees of freedom over which a designer has control. Similarly, the objective function (sometimes called a 'cost', or 'fitness' function) evaluates how well a given vector of object variables satisfies design objectives. For example, the object variables of an optical system would include the curvature and position of each lens surface in the design. The corresponding objective function would measure the residual aberrations that any given configuration of lenses generates. The goal, in this case, would be to find a set of lens curvatures and separations that minimizes image defects.

When confronted with a difficult optimization task, the method of first choice will usually be a problem-specific heuristic. By incorporating expert knowledge into their design, such techniques invariably achieve superior performance when compared to general methods like Evolutionary Algorithms (EAs). For example, if the objective function is a linear polynomial, then efficient methods exist, like the simplex method and Karmakar's algorithm, which can provide globally optimal solutions for problems containing hundreds, even thousands, of variables. If the objective function is not a linear polynomial and if problem-specific methods are not available, then an appeal is usually made to the Levenberg-Marquardt algorithm, branch-and-bound methods, or to real-valued, simplex derivatives like that of Nelder and Mead. Unfortunately, functional pathologies like non-linearity, noise, high dimensionality, *multi-modality* (multiple local optima), *epistasis* (parameter interaction), constraints, flatness and non-differentiability, either alone or in combination, can easily render these deterministic methods impotent. As stochastic algorithms, EAs have the potential to overcome many of these limitations, but if they do not incorporate problem-specific knowledge into their design, their performance will likely be sub-par. Fortunately, knowledge that the optimization process will be restricted to the domain of totally ordered spaces and in particular to the space of continuous variation, is itself problem-specific information that can be used to enhance an EA's performance without jeopardizing its status as a general-purpose numerical optimizer.

$$G = 0$$

$$initialize\ P_G := \{\vec{x}_{1,G}, \vec{x}_{2,G}, ..., \vec{x}_{NP,G}\}$$

$$evaluate\ P_G : \{f(\vec{x}_{1,G}), f(\vec{x}_{2,G}), ..., f(\vec{x}_{NP,G})\}$$

do (until termination criteria are met or $G=G_{max}$)

{

$$P_G' = mutate(P_G)P_G$$

$$P_G'' = recombine(P_G')$$

$$evaluate\ P_G'' = \{f(\vec{x}_{1,G}''), f(\vec{x}_{2,G}''), ..., f(\vec{x}_{NP,G}'')\}$$

$$select\ P_{G+1}\ from\ P_G''\ and\ P_G$$

$$G = G + 1$$

}

Fig. 6.1: Outline for a typical Evolutionary Algorithm (EA)

While the value of evolutionary algorithms as general-purpose numerical optimizers has often been questioned (Hart & Belew [1991], Salomon [1997], De Jong [1993]), much of this criticism has (justifiably) been based on results obtained with combinatorial algorithms that were not originally designed for the task. Like a chain, a successful numerical optimization algorithm will only be as effective as its weakest link, and within the context of real parameter global optimization, integer encoding, non-isomorphic search strategies, non-scaling mutation operators and susceptibility to coordinate rotation are all 'weak links' that can significantly degrade performance. Even once these design challenges have been adequately addressed, an effective global optimizer must still find a way to accommodate the peculiarities posed by each objective function without becoming victimized by them. To this end, DE introduces a novel, self-referential mutation scheme that is not only elegantly simple, but also remarkably effective.

Unlike EAs that rely on the output of a predefined probability distribution function, DE drives mutation with the differences of randomly sampled pairs of object vectors: $\vec{x}_{r1} - \vec{x}_{r2}$. Obviously, the distribution of these object vector differences is determined by the distribution of the object vectors themselves. Moreover, the way in which object vectors are distributed depends primarily on their response to the objective function's topography. Consequently, the biases in the way DE tries to improve object vectors match those implicit in the function it is optimizing. Instead of falling easy prey to the generic pathologies listed above, DE's simple mutation scheme has proven itself to be remarkably resistant to them. In addition to being robust, DE is also:

- fast, simple, easy to use ('tune') and modify;
- effective, with superior global optimization ability;
- inherently parallel;

- precision limited only by floating point format;
- efficient, using only $\mathcal{O}(n)$ processes; no sorting or matrix multiplication;
- uses self-referential mutations, no predefined probability distribution to specify;
- effective on, and very easily adapted for integer, discrete and mixed parameter optimization;
- does not require that the objective function be differentiable;
- operates on flat surfaces;
- works with noisy, epistatic and time-dependent objective functions;
- can provide multiple solutions in a single run;
- can provide co-evolutionary solutions for games and simulations;
- effective in nonlinear constraint optimization in conjunction with penalty functions.

Assuming for the moment that DE actually works, the question will immediately arise as to why such a simple method should work at all. After a brief, first glimpse of DE, an attempt is made to answer this question with an in-depth look at the rationale behind DE's critical design choices. Not every design decision is completely determined by rational principles, however, so several versions of DE are presented that are primarily distinguished by the crossover schemes they use. Next, the dynamics of DE are explored in a set of simple experiments which are designed to provide some insight into how the factors controlling DE are related and how they affect performance. Based on these observations, some guidelines for choosing DE's control parameters are then provided. The extension of DE to include integer, discrete and mixed optimization problems is briefly discussed, along with a few comments regarding DE and constrained optimization. After a challenge to theorists, the prospects for the future development of DE are considered.

6.2 DE: AN OVERVIEW

In many ways, DE is a typical EA, like that of Figure 6.1. DE generates a randomly distributed initial population $P_{G=0}$ of NP D-dimensional object variable vectors $x_{j,i,G}$:

$$P_G = \left\{ \vec{x}_{1,G}, \vec{x}_{2,G}, ..., \vec{x}_{i,G}, ..., \vec{x}_{NP,G} \right\}, \quad \vec{x}_{i,G} = x_{j,i,G}$$

$$x_{j,i,G=0} = x_j^{(lo)} + rand_j[0,1] \cdot \left(x_j^{(hi)} - x_j^{(lo)} \right) \tag{6.1}$$

$$i = 1,2,...NP, \quad NP \geq 4, \quad j = 1,2,...,D$$

The term $rand_j[0,1]$ represents a uniformly distributed random variable that ranges from zero to one. The subscript j indicates that a new random value is generated for each value of j; that is, for each object variable. If the subscript is i, then the random value is generated just once for each vector (for example, line 2, Equation 6.2). The superscripts hi and lo denote upper and lower initial parameter bounds, respectively.

After initialization, the population is subjected to repeated generations, $G = 1,2,...,G_{max}$ of mutation, recombination and selection. DE employs both mutation and recombination to create one 'child', or trial vector $u_{j,i,G+1}$, for each 'parent' vector $x_{j,i,G}$, as Equation 6.2 shows:

$$r_1, r_2, r_3 \in \{1,2,...,NP\},$$

(randomly selected, except : $r_1 \neq r_2 \neq r_3 \neq i$)

$$j_{rand} = \text{int}(rand_i[0,1) \cdot D) + 1$$

for $(j = 1; j \leq D; j = j+1)$

{

    if $(rand_j[0,1) < CR \vee j = j_{rand})$

        $u_{j,i,G+1} = v_{j,i,G+1} = x_{j,r3,G} + F \cdot (x_{j,r1,G} - x_{j,r2,G})$

    else

        $u_{j,i,G+1} = x_{j,i,G}$

}   (6.2)

The indices r_1, r_2 and r_3 are randomly chosen population indices that are mutually different and also different from i, which indexes the current (parent) object vector. Consequently, the population size, NP, must be greater than 3. Both CR and F are user-specified control variables. Because it represents a probability, CR ranges from 0 to 1. F, however, is a scaling factor that typically belongs to the interval: $(0,1+)$. Observe that when $rand_j[0,1]$ is less than CR or if $j = j_{rand}$, the child parameter is a linear combination of three randomly chosen vectors; otherwise, the child parameter is inherited directly from its parent. The condition that '$\vee j = j_{rand}$' is included in order to ensure that the child vectors will differ from their parents by at least one parameter (for example, in the case that we have $CR = 0$).

After each child vector is evaluated by the objective function, its cost is compared to the cost of its parent. If the child vector has an equal or lower cost to the parent vector, it replaces its parent vector in the population; otherwise, if the child's cost is greater than the cost of its parent, then the parent vector is retained. Equation 6.3 illustrates this simple decision process:

$$\vec{x}_{i,G+1} = \begin{cases} \vec{u}_{i,G+1} & \text{if} \quad f(\vec{u}_{i,G+1}) \leq f(\vec{x}_{i,G}) \\ \vec{x}_{i,G} & \text{otherwise} \end{cases} \tag{6.3}$$

With the membership of the next generation thus selected, the evolutionary cycle in DE repeats until either the task is solved, all vectors converge to a point, or no improvement is seen after many generations.

Figure 6.2 puts Equations 6.1–6.3 into context and illustrates that DE's most compact representation is as a vector formula. In fact, the number of characters in Figure 6.2 is not much greater than what is required for the generalized EA outlined in Figure 6.1. Unlike the outline in Figure 6.1, however, the prescription in Figure 6.2 is fully functional. Even the C-language implementation of this algorithm that appears in Appendix 6.A is not much more elaborate and requires fewer than 30 lines of code. Note that in the C-language, indices begin with 0, whereas the vector formulation (Equations 6.1, 6.2, and 6.3, and Figures 6.1 and 6.2) indexes the first element with 1. The schematic diagram in Figure 6.3 provides an alternative way to visualize DE in which the flow of control details are emphasized. Figure 6.4 illustrates the same procedure (*DE/rand/1/bin*) graphically in terms of a vector diagram.

Input : $D, G_{max}, NP \geq 4, F \in (0,1+), CR \in [0,1]$, and initial bounds : $\vec{x}^{(lo)}, \vec{x}^{(hi)}$.

Initialize : $\begin{cases} \forall i \leq NP \wedge \forall j \leq D : x_{j,i,G=0} = x_j^{(lo)} + rand_j[0,1] \cdot \left(x_j^{(hi)} - x_j^{(lo)}\right) \\ i = \{1,2,...,NP\}, \quad j = \{1,2,...,D\}, \quad G=0, \quad rand_j[0,1] \in [0,1] \end{cases}$

$\begin{cases} \text{While } G < G_{max} \\ \quad \forall i \leq NP \begin{cases} \text{Mutate and recombine :} \\ \quad r_1, r_2, r_3 \in \{1,2,...,NP\}, \text{randomly selected, except :} r_1 \neq r_2 \neq r_3 \neq i \\ \quad j_{rand} \in \{1,2,...,D\}, \text{randomly selected once each } i \\ \quad \forall j \leq D, u_{j,i,G+1} = \begin{cases} x_{j,r_3,G} + F \cdot \left(x_{j,r_1,G} - x_{j,r_2,G}\right) \\ \qquad \text{if } \left(rand_j[0,1) < CR \vee j = j_{rand}\right) \\ x_{j,i,G} \text{ otherwise} \end{cases} \\ \text{Select :} \\ \quad \vec{x}_{i,G+1} = \begin{cases} \vec{u}_{i,G+1} & \text{if } f\left(\vec{u}_{i,G+1}\right) \leq f\left(\vec{x}_{i,G}\right) \\ \vec{x}_{i,G} & \text{otherwise} \end{cases} \end{cases} \\ G = G+1 \end{cases}$

Fig. 6.2: Equations 6.1—6.3 in context: *DE/rand/1/bin*

6.3 ENCODING AND OPERATORS: DYNAMIC RANGE AND ADJACENCY

Many EAs attempting numerical optimization have chosen to encode continuous parameters as binary integers. The integer format, however, is unable to efficiently represent the wide dynamic range of parameter values so often encountered in numerical optimization tasks. If a computation is expected to cover a dynamic range that extends over many orders of magnitude, then very large integers will be needed to represent the full spectrum of values, yet most bits will not be significant in the final result. This waste of resources can be avoided by encoding object vectors as floating-point numbers.

More problematic than the limited dynamic range of binary integers is their failure, in conjunction with logical operators, to preserve the order of the continuum's topology. Very often, EAs that encode parameters as binary integers modify them with logical operators, like the exclusive OR, which inverts, or 'flips' bits. This encoding/operator combination, however, does not map consecutive integers to adjacent points in the space of object variables. Because the space of R^n is also *totally (linearly) ordered*, any two elements, *a* and *b*, can be arranged so that either $a \geq b$ or $b \geq a$. Resorting to a binary integer representation and logical operators discards this useful information, effectively transforming a problem with order into a harder combinatorial one.

Consider, for example, the consecutive integers: 15, 16 and 17, with binary representations: 01111, 10000 and 10001, respectively. Even though 16 is adjacent to both 15 and 17, 5 bits must be inverted to move between 16 and 15, while only 1 bit must be flipped to move between 16 and 17. This disparity between the natural order of the object vector space and its implementation makes an incremental search using logical operators difficult, since any number of bits may have to be flipped to move between adjacent points in parameter space. *Gray codes* circumvent this problem by mapping the integers to an alternative binary representation that allows adjacent integers to be transformed into one another by a single bit-flip. Gray-coded integers, however, still lack the ability to handle a wide dynamic range.

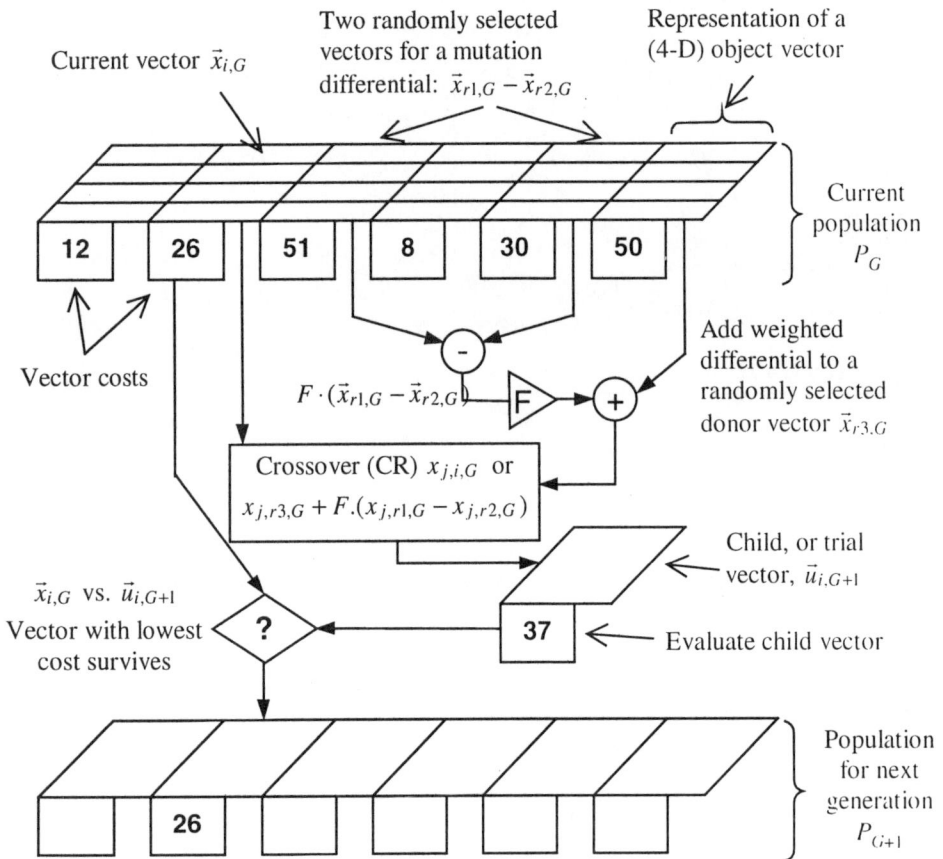

Fig. 6.3: Schematic representation of the algorithm: *DE/rand/1/bin.*

Instead of modifying the binary encoding scheme to accommodate logical operators, a simpler solution to this 'adjacency' problem is to retain traditional binary encoding and replace logical operators with arithmetic ones. By using addition, 16 can be transformed into 17 by adding 1, or into 15 by adding −1. Integers can remain encoded in their traditional format because addition, with its cascading bits, ensures that small differences between object vectors map to small (arithmetic) differences between their encoded counterparts. Since they are just scaled, binary-coded integers, the same adjacency-preserving benefits of arithmetic operators also accrue to floating-point formatted numbers. For these reasons, DE encodes real parameter data as ordinary floating-point numbers and manipulates them with standard floating-point arithmetic routines.

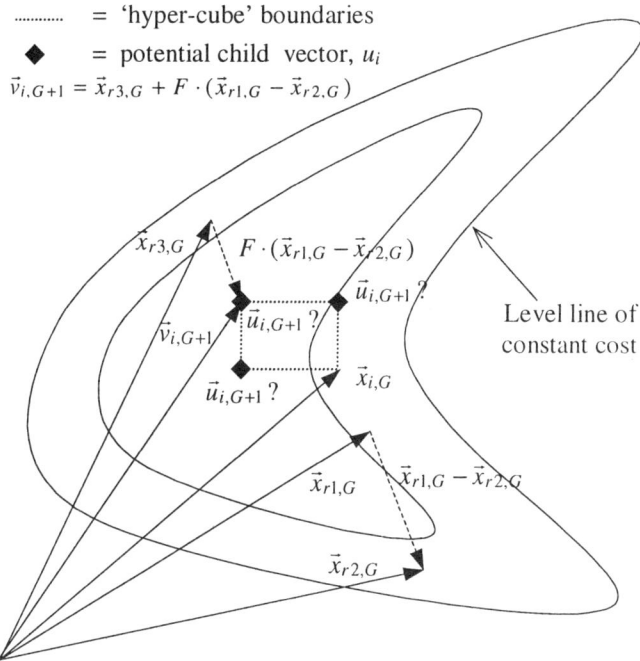

Fig. 6.4: A graphical view of *DE/rand/1/bin*.

6.4 POPULATION STRUCTURE AND PARAMETER BOUNDS

DE uses a population of fixed size primarily as a matter of convenience and there is no *a priori* reason for this choice. The population is implemented as an *NP*-by-*D* floating-point array, where *NP* is the number of object vectors in the population and *D* is the number parameters in an object vector. To implement DE in parallel, two arrays of object vectors are maintained. One array is for the current parent population and the other is for constructing the next generation of contending child vectors. Isolating the current and competing generations eliminates memory conflicts when executing DE in parallel. If execution is sequential, a single array can be used, with successful child vectors (constructed in a temporary vector) immediately replacing their parents. No dramatic difference in performance between the one- and two-array methods has been observed. Population members can also be updated asynchronously (e.g., randomly) if the sequential model is used.

As Equation 6.1 suggests, object vectors should be initialized by randomly selecting their parameters with a uniform distribution from a search space with well-defined limits. In practice, initial parameter bounds are often determined by physical constraints. If not, then initial upper and lower parameter bounds should be large enough to encompass the locations of suspected global optima. Once they have been used for initializing parameters, bounds may, in many cases, be ignored to allow DE to expand its search beyond the initially prescribed limits if the population is drawn there by the dynamics of the objective function. Limits, however, may occasionally be necessary to avoid the flight to infinity, especially if flat, or nearly flat 'surfaces' are involved. If a good solution is already in hand, DE can be initialized with object vectors that are normally distributed around the nominal solution, although it is difficult to recommend this practice, since it may overly localize the search. The important point to remember is that initial parameter values should be randomly distributed in some way, since it is the differences between object variables that drive DE. If an infeasible object vector is generated during the initialization process, it can be rejected and reinitialized, or it can be accepted into the population if it is assigned a penalty that is higher than the highest objective function value among initial, feasible object vectors.

If a new parameter value is proposed which exceeds a strict boundary limit, then several options exist for resetting the parameter to an allowed value. The simplest method is to set the parameter equal to the limit it exceeded. Even though this method has worked well in practice, it should probably be avoided, since it has the potential to decrease the diversity of the population. Alternatively, an out-of-bounds parameter can be reset by reinitializing it. While this certainly keeps the parameters diverse, it is, perhaps, an extreme solution for maintaining diversity. A good compromise is to reset the offending parameter to a point midway between its pre-mutation/crossover value and the bound that it violated. Equation 6.4 shows how to use this method to reset the jth parameter of the ith child vector, $u_{j,i,G+1}$:

$$u_{j,i,G+1} = \begin{cases} \left(x_{j,i,G} + x_j^{(lo)}\right)\big/2 & \text{if } u_{j,i,G+1} < x_j^{(lo)} \\ \left(x_{j,i,G} + x_j^{(hi)}\right)\big/2 & \text{if } u_{j,i,G+1} > x_j^{(hi)} \\ u_{j,i,G+1} & \text{otherwise} \end{cases} \tag{6.4}$$

This technique allows bounds to be approached asymptotically while minimizing the amount of disruption that results from resetting out-of-bounds values.

6.5 MUTATION

Before detailing DE's approach to mutation, it will first be helpful to understand some of the special demands that real parameter optimization places on a mutation algorithm. These demands can be formalized as a set of design principles to which all viable EA optimizers should adhere. A brief examination of how one alternative EA optimizer realizes these principles helps to establish a frame of reference for understanding DE. Because it is so simple, *using* DE requires neither a knowledge of the design principles upon which it is based, nor another EA for comparison, but knowing what makes real parameter global optimization challenging and seeing how complex existing methods have become in order to meet those challenges, makes the effectiveness of DE's simple mutation scheme all the more intriguing.

In the context of real parameter optimization, mutation refers to the process of adding a randomly generated increment to one or more parameters of an existing object vector. The goal of an efficient mutation scheme is to generate increments, or steps, that move existing object vectors in the right direction by the right amount at the right time. Achieving this goal depends critically on the characteristics of the distribution that generates the steps. The problem is, however, that no single generating distribution can exhibit the versatility required to efficiently exploit the contours of every objective function landscape. Despite this uncertainty, there is one characteristic that every viable generating function will display: a zero mean. Generating mutation steps with an unbiased distribution eliminates the possibility that object vectors will acquire a drift that is an artifact of the step-generating process.

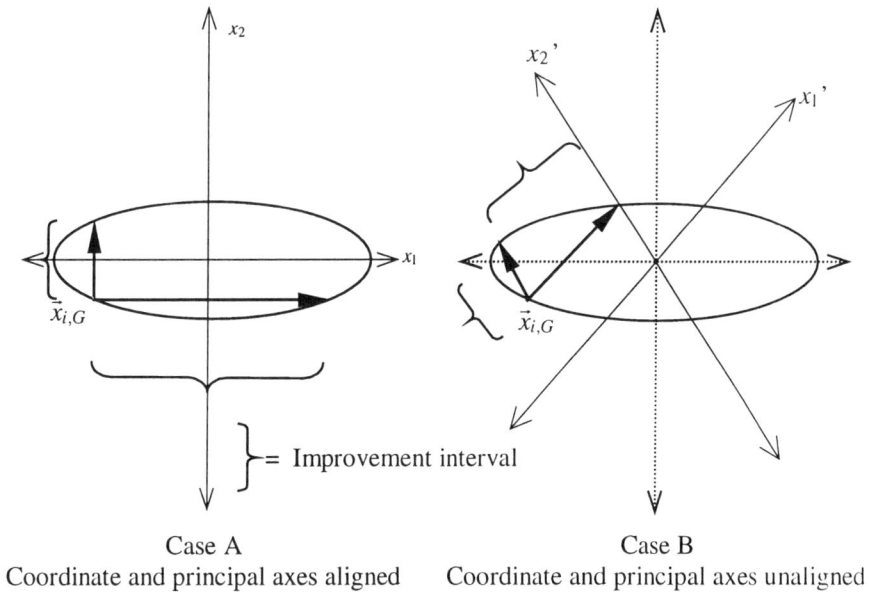

Case A
Coordinate and principal axes aligned

Case B
Coordinate and principal axes unaligned

Fig. 6.5: Rotating coordinate axes away from the principal axes of the ellipse results in smaller intervals of improvement.

Assuming that a compromise (typically, Gaussian) zero-mean generating distribution is deemed acceptable, a method must still be devised for tailoring mutation step sizes to suit each object vector parameter. Suppose, for example, that the objective function is the ellipsoid of Equation 6.5

$$f(\vec{x}) = x_1^2 + a_0 x_2^2 \tag{6.5}$$

Figure 6.5 plots a contour of this function as an elliptical, 'level line' of constant cost. For the vector at $\bar{x}_{i,G}$, there is a well-defined range of mutation step sizes that will result in improvement. In particular, any move from $\bar{x}_{i,G}$ to a point interior to the level line upon which $\bar{x}_{i,G}$ is situated will yield an object vector of lower cost. As Case A in Figure 6.5 shows, this 'improvement interval' for $\bar{x}_{i,G}$ is different in each coordinate direction and depends on the eccentricity of the ellipse. Although large steps are suitable for searching the long axis of the ellipse, when applied along the direction of the short axis they cause child vectors to overshoot the region of acceptability. To compensate, the step size can be reduced, but then performance will suffer because the smaller steps will no longer be able to exploit the maximum rate of improvement along the long axis. It is clear that in the case of the ellipsoid, no single step size can efficiently search all dimensions. Consequently, any mutation scheme that hopes to efficiently search distorted spaces like the ellipsoid must do so by scaling a distribution of mutation step sizes to the appropriate magnitude for each parameter of the objective function.

It is not just the scale of mutation steps that needs to be tuned, but also their orientations. Consider what happens when the coordinate axes are rotated away from the principal axes of the ellipse. As Case B in Figure 6.5 shows, rotation significantly decreases the interval of improvement along the long axis and marginally decreases it along the short axis. Thus, rotation slows the optimization process because the steps most likely to result in improvement are typically smaller than when the principal axes of the ellipse and the coordinate axes are aligned.

Rotation not only slows progress by decreasing the available interval of improvement along coordinate axes, it also eliminates the possibility of using low mutation rates to quickly optimize *separable* functions. If it is separable, a D-dimensional function can be decomposed into D one-dimensional tasks whose solutions can be discovered independently. These partial solutions can then be conjoined to locate the solution to the function's D-dimensional version. For example, the ellipse in Case A of Figure 6.5, (Equation 6.5) is separable. The special alignment that exists between its principal axes and the coordinate axes allows the 2D ellipsoid to be decomposed into two, one-dimensional functions:

$$f_1(x_1) = x_1^2 \tag{6.6}$$

$$f_2(x_2) = a_0 x_2^2 \tag{6.7}$$

whose minima are easily found to be:

$$f_1(x_1^*) = 0, \ x_1^* = 0 \tag{6.8}$$

$$f_2(x_2^*) = 0, \ x_2^* = 0 \tag{6.9}$$

Furthermore, the conjunction of these two solutions locates the minimum of the two-dimensional ellipsoid:

$$f(\vec{x}^*) = f(x_1^*, x_2^*) = (0,0) \tag{6.10}$$

For an EA, generating trial vectors that differ from existing vectors by a single parameter value is the stochastic equivalent of solving the D, one-dimensional problems as arbitrarily scheduled tasks. Using this optimal, 'one-parameter-at-a-time' strategy, EAs can solve separable problems in $\mathcal{O}(D \ln D)$ time (Salomon [1996]).

If, however, the principal axes of a separable function are arbitrarily rotated away from coincidence with coordinate axes, parameters become dependent and the function is no longer (in general) decomposable. In the case of the ellipse, rotation transforms Equation 6.5 into Equation 6.11, corresponding to Case B of Figure 6.5:

$$f(\vec{x}) = x_1^2 + a_1 x_1 x_2 + a_0 x_2^2 \tag{6.11}$$

The cross term $a_1 x_1 x_2$ expresses the parameter dependence known as *epistasis*. Although the one-parameter-at-a-time strategy is optimal on separable functions, when applied to epistatic functions, it is even less efficient than a random search (Salomon [1996]). Thus, rotation not only decreases search efficiency by decreasing intervals of improvement, it also eliminates the possibility that low mutation rates can be used to discover a solution quickly. Since most real-world functions of interest are more likely to be epistatic than separable, viable EAs must be capable of perturbing *all* parameters with correlated mutations.

In summary, an efficient mutation scheme for real parameter optimization should:

- Use a zero-mean distribution for generating mutation vectors
- Dynamically scale the distribution to suit each parameter
- Correlate mutations to ensure rotational invariance

Given all these demands and the indescribable variety of objective function landscapes, how can a mutation scheme be devised that will satisfy these criteria? For over 30 years, the answer provided by *Evolution Strategies* has been: 'self-adaptation'.

6.5.1 The Evolution Strategy

The Evolution Strategy (ES) was originally developed by Rechenberg and Schwefel at the Technical University of Berlin beginning in 1964 (Rechenberg [1973], Schwefel [1981]). Early applications included real parameter shape optimization problems (Klockgether & Schwefel [1977]). ES takes a self-adaptive approach to the problem of scaling and orienting mutation vectors. Imagine that each object vector, $\bar{x}_{i,G}$, is paired with a strategy vector, $\vec{\sigma}_{i,G}$, whose components are used to scale the output of a pre-defined, multivariate probability distribution. In the ES, strategy variables co-evolve along side their corresponding object vectors and are themselves subject to mutation, recombination and selection. Typically, strategy vectors are changed according to the rule given in Equation 6.12, whereas object vectors are mutated are according to Equation 6.13:

$$\sigma_{j,i,G+1} = \sigma_{j,i,G} \cdot \exp\left(\tau' \cdot N_i(0,1) + \tau \cdot N_j(0,1)\right)$$

$$\tau = \left(\sqrt{2\sqrt{D}}\right)^{-1} \quad \tau' = \left(\sqrt{2D}\right)^{-1}$$

(6.12)

$$u_{j,i,G+1} = x_{j,i,G} + \sigma_{j,i,G+1} \cdot N_j(0,1)$$

(6.13)

The term, $N(0,1)$ stands for a normally (Gaussian) distributed variable with a zero mean and a standard deviation of 1. $N_j(0,1)$ indicates that a new random value is generated for each parameter while $N_i(0,1)$ refers to a random value that is generated just once for each vector. Unlike the Gaussian distribution that drives the evolution of the object vectors, strategy vectors are usually perturbed by log-normal noise. The constants τ' and τ sometimes have to be adjusted away from their nominal values. Scaling the multivariate distribution with the strategy vector transforms the surface of constant probability for placing an offspring from a sphere to an ellipsoid that is aligned with the coordinate axes (Figure 6.6). By using a zero-mean distribution and by providing a means for dynamically adapting step sizes to each parameter, ES clearly satisfies the first two of the three demands listed above. Correlating mutations, however, calls for a more extensive strategy.

The ES correlates mutations by extending the self-adaptive approach to include covariance terms (Schwefel [1981]). The simple vector of strategy variables is now replaced by a full *D-by-D strategy matrix* that adds $D(D-1)/2$ rotation angles to the D, scale factors from the strategy vector. These angles are initially random, but as they evolve, they orient the mutation ellipsoid in the direction that is most likely to produce an acceptable object vector (Figure 6.6). While strategy *vectors* require only as much memory as do the object variables themselves, strategy *matrices* require D times as much memory. In addition, a full vector-matrix multiplication must be performed for each newly-proposed object vector. For large values of D, this can strain computational resources, since the routine involves an $\mathcal{O}(D^2)$ process. While ES's adaptive approach works well for relatively small problems, its limits are quickly discovered once larger and more demanding (e.g., multi-modal epistatic) functions are encountered.

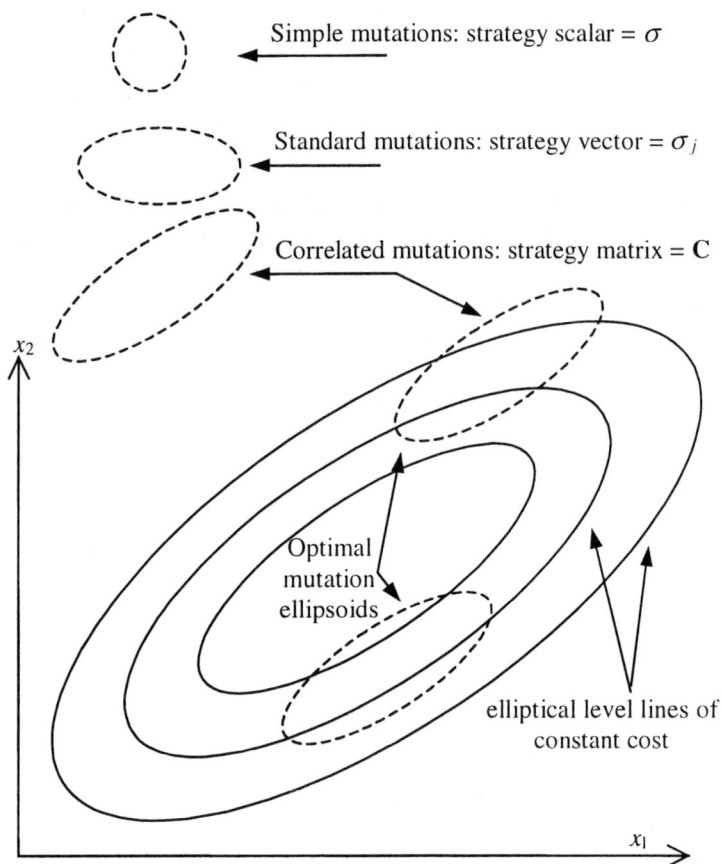

Fig. 6.6: Optimal mutation ellipsoids of equal probability for placing an offspring occur when they are similar to, and aligned with, the (elliptical) function's level lines.

6.5.2 Differential Mutation

Whereas an ES generates mutation vectors by adaptively scaling and correlating the output of pre-defined, multivariate probability distribution, DE just randomly samples the object vector population for them. As Equation 6.14 shows, DE mutates an object vector by **adding the weighted difference of a randomly chosen pair of object vectors to it:**

$$r_1, r_2 \in \{1, 2, ..., NP\}, \text{randomly selected, except} : r_1 \neq r_2 \neq i$$

$$\vec{u}_{i,G+1} = \vec{x}_{i,G} + k_\mu \cdot (\vec{x}_{r1,G} - \vec{x}_{r2,G})$$

(6.14)

The possibility: $r_1 = r_2$ can safely be eliminated, since no mutation even occurs with this combination of indices. Also, the cases: $r_1 = i$ and $r_2 = i$ are excluded because they effectively transform Equation 6.14 into a crossover procedure. In fact, DE's simple mutation scheme is often mistaken for *arithmetic crossover* and a comparison of Equations 6.14 and 6.15 shows why:

$$r_3 \in \{1, 2, ..., NP\}, \text{randomly selected, except} : r_3 \neq i$$

$$\vec{u}_{i,G+1} = \vec{x}_{i,G} + k_\chi \cdot (\vec{x}_{r3,G} - \vec{x}_{i,G})$$

(6.15)

Equation 6.14 is the DE mutation operation, whereas Equation 6.15 is the formula for arithmetic crossover. The difference, of course, is that Equation 6.15 is a general linear combination of two vectors, whereas Equation 6.14 is a special case of a linear combination of three vectors. Actually, this case of mistaken identity nicely illustrates the fact that DE takes the same approach to mutation as some EAs take to recombination. In both cases, new vectors are generated that are linear combinations of existing object vectors. Thus, DE is a consistent evolutionary approach to real parameter optimization in which both mutation and recombination are simple operations that randomly sample linear combinations of object vectors.

Despite their similarity, the processes defined by Equations 6.14 and 6.15 search the space of object vectors in very different ways. For example, the arithmetic crossover of Equation 6.15 provides a way for $\vec{x}_{i,G}$ to become more like another vector in the population. In particular, the special case $k_\chi = 1$ effectively transforms Equation 6.15 into a *replacement operation* that attempts the wholesale substitution of $\vec{x}_{r3,G}$ for $\vec{x}_{i,G}$. For other values of k_χ, Equation 6.15 limits the search for a new $\vec{x}_{i,G}$ to points along one of the $NP-1$ axes that join $\vec{x}_{i,G}$ with every other vector in the population (Figure 6.7). The randomly chosen index $r3$ determines which axis will be searched, while k_χ determines which point on the chosen axis is actually tested. Furthermore, when added to $\vec{x}_{i,G}$, the increment: $k_\chi \cdot (\vec{x}_{r3,G} - \vec{x}_{i,G})$ moves $\vec{u}_{i,G}$ either toward, or away from $\vec{x}_{r3,G}$. As such, any constant value of k_χ other than zero introduces a bias into the search by consistently moving each vector either closer to $(0 < k_\chi \leq 1)$, or further away from $(k_\chi < 0, k_\chi > 1)$, other object vectors in the population.

Unlike the steps generated by Equation 6.15, the mutation vectors produced by Equation 6.14 do not contain any reference to $\vec{x}_{i,G}$. In its place is a second, randomly chosen object vector, the inclusion of which expands the number of search axes to: $(NP-1)(NP-2)/2$ (Figure 6.7). Furthermore, since random sampling assures that each differential, $\vec{x}_{r1,G} - \vec{x}_{r2,G}$, occurs as often as does its opposite, $\vec{x}_{r2,G} - \vec{x}_{r1,G}$, the distribution that Equation 6.14 generates is guaranteed to exhibit a zero mean. Consequently, a constant value of k_μ scales the magnitude of the step sizes but does not bias the search like k_χ does in Equation 6.15. Additionally, there is no value of k_μ for which Equation 6.14 becomes a replacement operation, so the population's diversity cannot be threatened in this way.

In DE, the scaling factor k_μ in Equation 6.14 is held constant during optimization and has traditionally been referred to as 'F' to distinguish it as one of DE's control variables. In all optimizations to date, effective values for F have come from the range: $F \in (0,1]$ but, of course, larger values can be used should they be needed. A comparison of Equations 6.13 and 6.14 shows that $F \cdot (\vec{x}_{r1,G} - \vec{x}_{r2,G})$ plays the same role in DE as $\vec{\sigma}_{i,G+1} \cdot N_j(0,1)$ does in

ES. Unlike the pre-defined probability distribution used by ES, however, DE's distribution of vector differentials is automatically *self-scaling*. Therefore, while $\bar{\sigma}_{i,G+1}$ must adapt to the *absolute* scale of mutations, F only needs to modify their *relative* magnitude.

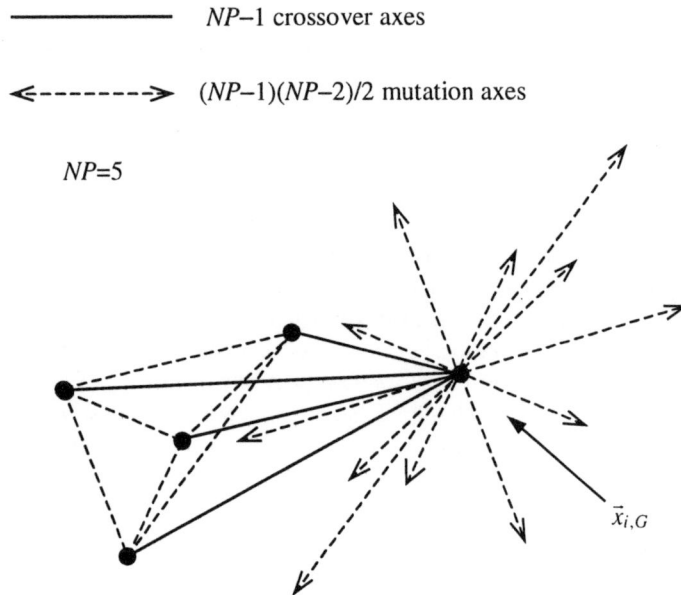

Fig. 6.7: Crossover and mutation vectors for $\bar{x}_{i,G}$ defined by a 5-member population.

To understand how DE scales mutation step sizes to suit each parameter, reconsider the case of the ellipsoidal objective function. Figure 6.8 shows the population of object vectors as a distribution of points encompassing the ellipse. In practice, all object vectors do not fall on the same level line, but will instead be distributed about a level line that represents their average cost. This, at least, is the distribution that is expected for system that is not too far from equilibrium. The sheaf of vectors under the ellipse in Figure 6.8 is the actual set of difference vectors that the pictured distribution of object vectors generates. It is immediately apparent that the distribution of object vector differences is itself elliptical and models the ideal mutation distribution as well as the population sample models the ellipse. In each dimension, mutations of various sizes exist, but in each case they exhibit a scale that is comparable to each parameter's interval of improvement. By inspection, it is also clear that the scaling constant F is typically less than unity, since mutations are perhaps twice as large as what is optimal (for this somewhat generic, unimodal function *only*).

Not only is the DE mutation scheme capable of dynamically scaling individual step sizes, it is also impervious to the effects of coordinate system rotation. Although rotation transforms the coordinates of object vectors, it does not change their locations relative to one another or with respect to the contours of the cost function. Consequently, object vectors will still be found clustered about a level line even after rotation. As a result, the mutation distribution generated by object vector pairs will always have the same orientation as the level lines, and this is a necessary condition for optimal mutation (Figure 6.6)

(Rudolph [1992]). It is also clear why F is the same multiplier for all parameters, since changing the scale factor for each parameter would arbitrarily rotate the difference vector and destroy the correlation imparted to it by the fitness landscape. The insensitivity of DE to the effects of coordinate rotation can be seen in Figure 6.9, which shows the average number of function evaluations needed to resolve the minimum of a very eccentric, 10-dimensional ellipsoid (Equation 6.16) to an error of $\varepsilon = 1.0e-6$, over a range or rotation angles.

$$f_{ellip.}(\vec{x}) = \sum_{j=1}^{D=10} 10^{j-1} \cdot x_j^2, \quad \varepsilon = 1.0e-6, \quad \vec{x}^{(lo)} = -10, \quad \vec{x}^{(hi)} = 10 \qquad (6.16)$$

The data for Figure 6.9 are 20-trial averages generated using mutation but no recombination. P_m is the probability that a parameter will be mutated. Only when all parameters are mutated ($P_m = 1$) is the time required to resolve the optimum invariant with respect to coordinate rotation.

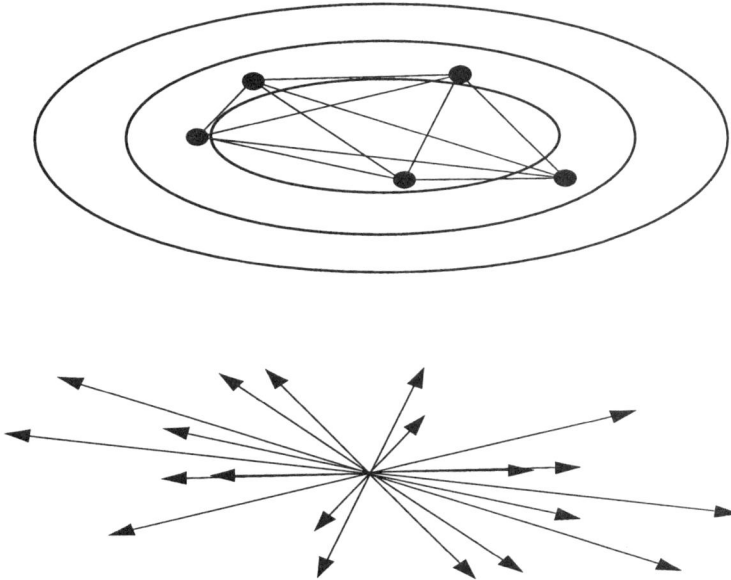

Fig. 6.8: The DE mutation distribution generated by points scattered about a level line

6.5.3 Universal Global Mutations

In an ES, each object vector uses its own strategy matrix to scale and correlate the output of a multivariate distribution. As such, each correlation matrix tends to reflect only local information about the neighbourhood of the object vector to which it is assigned. By contrast, DE mutates all object vectors with same universal distribution. Because of the ellipsoid's symmetry, there is little difference between ES's optimal mutation ellipsoids and DE's universal distribution as a comparison of Figures 6.6 and 6.8 shows. In this special case, all strategy matrices should be the same for all points on the same level line and generate identical ellipsoids of equal probability for placing an offspring that all share the same orientation as the principal axes of the ellipse (Rudolph [1992]).

The difference between the two approaches becomes more clear once a second ellipse (with a different orientation and eccentricity) is added to the fitness landscape (see Figure 6.10). The existence of one ellipse does not (substantially) alter the correlation matrices for object vectors adapting to the other ellipse, and *vice versa*. In each basin of attraction, the ES strategy will continue to provide each object vector with locally optimal mutations that are self-adapted to each object vector's local environment. However, while local self-adaptation ensures rapid local improvement, it does not correlate global information.

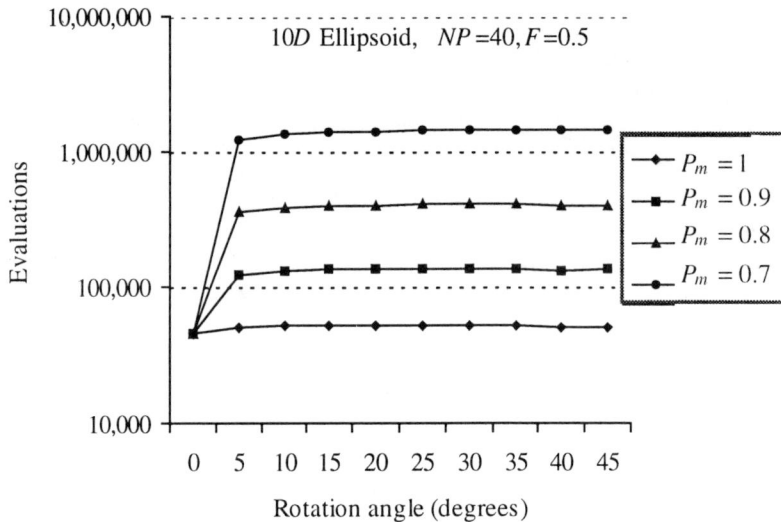

Fig. 6.9: Function evaluations to reach 1.0e-6 as a function of the coordinate rotation angle. Here, *Pm* stands for the probability that a parameter is mutated.

The situation is quite different in DE, since all of the object vectors are mutated by the same distribution. If object vectors occupy both ellipsoids, then DE's universal distribution will contain a mixture of mutation vectors (see Figure 6.10). Mutations which are generated by a pair of vectors belonging to one ellipse will not necessarily be effective when added to an object vector in the other ellipse, and *vice versa*. The frequency with which such inappropriate vector pairs are chosen for a differential depends on the shape of the ellipses, and it also depends on how the population is proportioned between them. A natural weighting exists, with the relevant mutation pairs being chosen most often for object vectors in the most populated ellipse. No claim is made here that this universal distribution, or the weightings it generates, is optimal; it is noted here, however, that this distribution has worked very well in practice.

In addition to the two, superimposed sets of locally correlated mutation vectors, DE's universal distribution also includes differentials whose contributing object vectors are taken from different ellipses. The inclusion of these large-scale mutations provides DE with what can be considered to be *globally correlated* mutations (see Figure 6.10). Unlike the simple ellipsoids of equal probability for placing an offspring generated by the ES strategy, the sheaf of mutation vectors that DE generates, although relatively sparse, is capable of a far greater complexity than the symmetry of a simple mutation ellipsoid can express. The addition of these large-scale, inter-basin mutations is apparently what gives DE its exceptional performance as a global optimizer.

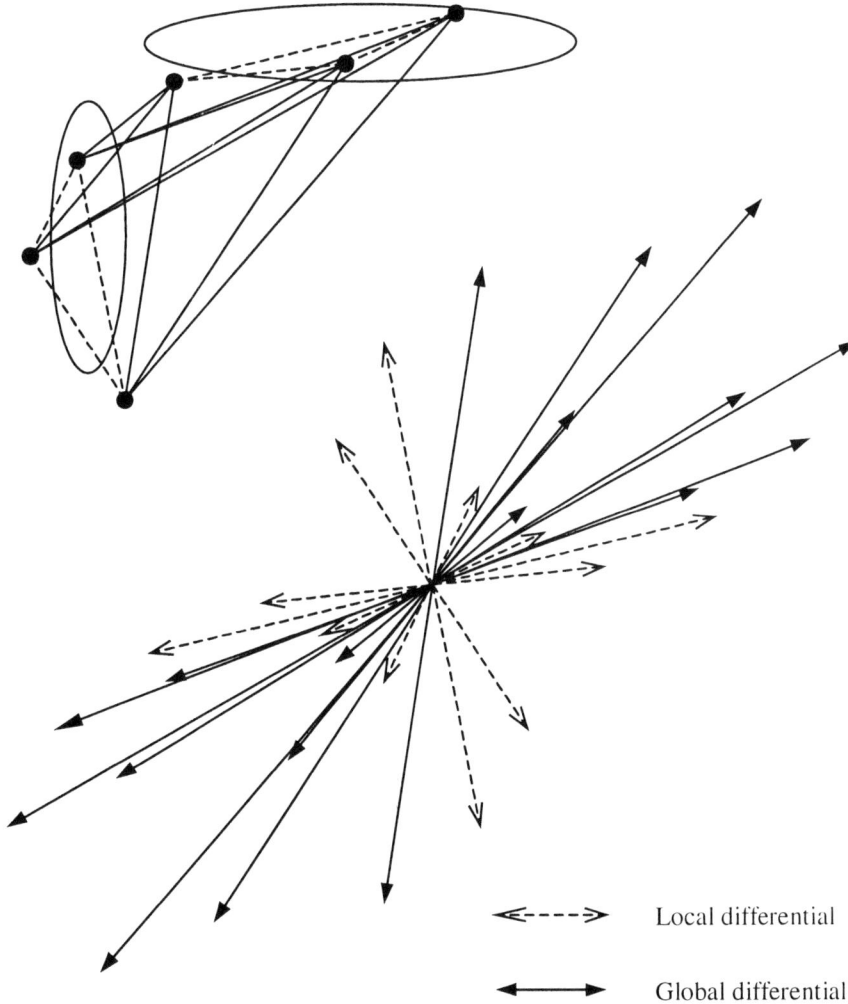

Fig. 6.10: DE's universal distribution superimposes locally and globally correlated mutations

Table 6.1 compares the effectiveness of DE's mutation scheme directly to the method of correlated self-adaptive mutations using some very simple test functions. The results in the first column are for Meta-Evolutionary Programming (Saravanan & Fogel [1996]), which for these experiments used the same method of correlated mutations as does an ES

(Schwefel [1981]).   To ensure a fair comparison, only the MEP's mutation scheme (Equations 6.12, 6.13) was replaced by the DE mutation formula (Equation   6.14). Otherwise, the two EAs are identical, using tournament selection and no recombination operators. Implementation details of the MEP algorithm and function definitions can be found in Saravanan & Fogel [1996]. The results clearly show that for these simple test functions, DE's sampled mutations were significantly more effective in every case than the method of adaptive strategies.

Table 6.1: Performance of an MEP with self-adaptive correlated mutations *vs.* one using DE's self-referential mutations.

Function	Dim.	MEP: LN-EP(2.5)		MEP: $0.5 \cdot (x_{i,r1,G} - x_{i,r2,G})$	
		Mean Best	Std. Dev.	Mean Best	Std. Dev.
Sphere	3	1.995e-10	1.417e-09	1.605e-16	2.225e-16
Rosenbrock	2	3.824e-15	8.999e-14	5.612e-46	5.883e-45
Bohachevsky	2	6.862e-16	3.045e-15	6.147e-20	2.289e-19
Sphere	20	4.646e-05	4.315e-04	1.998e-07	1.084e-07
Shifted Sphere	20	5.556e-05	5.741e-04	1.971e-07	1.067e-07
Ackley	20	9.295e-01	9.179e-01	1.381e-04	3.700e-05

6.6 SELECTION

A selection scheme is a criterion that specifies under what conditions newly proposed vectors can enter the population. For example, *tournament* selection determines the membership of the next generation by holding a series of competitions between randomly chosen pairs of vectors. Typically, competing vectors are selected from the combined parent-offspring population and those vectors that score the most wins are allowed to advance. This particular mechanism was used to obtain the results of Table 6.1 and is favoured by advocates of MEP. Alternatively, ES uses a *deterministic* selection scheme in which only the best-performing members of the combined parent-offspring populations advance. It should be noted that there are several variations to both of these methods and numerous other selection schemes have been proposed as well. One disadvantage shared by both tournament selection and the deterministic ES scheme is the computational expense of sorting the population at the end of each generation.

By contrast, DE's selection criterion could not be simpler (Equation 6.3). If the child vector $\vec{u}_{i,G+1}$ does not equal or improve on its parent $\vec{x}_{i,G}$ then $\vec{x}_{i,G}$ remains in the population for at least one more generation and will not be displaced by any other vector. Allowing $\vec{u}_{i,G+1}$ to replace $\vec{x}_{i,G}$ when both have the same cost enables object vectors to move along level lines. One consequence of adopting Equation 6.3 as an acceptance criterion is that neither the cost of individual population members, nor the total cost of the population ever increases. More importantly though, DE's scheme spares the selection process the additional chore of globally reallocating the population's resources.

In most EAs, the effects of selection and recombination are subtly intertwined because both processes contribute to the global transport of information and resources. For example, both MEP's tournament selection and ES's deterministic scheme will replace a poorly performing object vector with a superior one irrespective of the dominant vector's origin. This activity produces a high degree of selective pressure that can quickly move vectors to promising locales from anywhere in the search space. By contrast, global transport of a vector in DE occurs only as a result of mutation or recombination because a parent vector can only be replaced by the child it spawns and not by just any other better performing member. Consequently, DE's selection scheme simply demands that each individual vector get better, leaving the main task of globally reallocating resources to recombination.

6.7 RECOMBINATION

Mutation is primarily responsible for keeping a population robust and for searching new territory. Recombination, or crossover, is a complementary process that reinforces prior successes by building child vectors out of existing object vector parameters. There is considerable debate over the power of recombination, but evidence exists that uniform recombination cannot reduce the $\mathcal{O}(D \ln D)$ computational complexity that genetic algorithms exhibit when applied to separable functions (Mühlenbein & Schlierkamp-Voosen [1993]). Nevertheless, recombination can provide a significant speed-up, so as a practical matter, it is usually worth the effort.

Early versions of DE, such as the scheme elaborated in Equation 6.2, use a special, non-uniform, discrete recombination procedure in which parameters for $\bar{x}_{i,G}$'s potential replacement $\bar{u}_{i,G+1}$ are taken either from $\bar{x}_{i,G}$ itself or from a mutated 'donor' vector, $\bar{v}_{i,G+1}$. Both exponential and binomial processes have been invoked to control the frequency with which $\bar{v}_{i,G+1}$ is chosen over $\bar{x}_{i,G}$ as a source of parameters for the child vector $\bar{u}_{i,G+1}$. Both processes are mediated by a user-defined crossover constant CR which, like NP and F, is held constant throughout the optimization process. The binomial scheme used in Equation 6.2 takes parameters from $\bar{v}_{i,G+1}$ *every time* that $rand_j[0,1) < CR$; otherwise, the parameter comes from $\bar{x}_{i,G}$. By contrast, the exponential scheme takes child vector parameters from $\bar{x}_{i,G}$ until the *first time* that $rand_j[0,1) < CR$, at which point the remaining parameters are taken from $\bar{v}_{i,G+1}$. To ensure that parent and child vectors differ by at least one parameter, both the binomial and exponential schemes always take one parameter from $\bar{v}_{i,G+1}$, even when $CR = 0$. The two decision procedures are also the same when $CR = 1$, since both will use: $\bar{u}_{i,G+1} = \bar{v}_{i,G+1}$. Code for both of these processes appears in Appendix 6.A. Since both processes have proven effective, it is difficult to recommend one over the other based on experience, but the ability of the binomial process to search all corners of the hyper-cube defined by $\bar{x}_{i,G}$ and $\bar{v}_{i,G+1}$ suggests that it should be the method of first choice.

For intermediate values of CR, the binomial method introduces many more donor parameters into the child vector than does an exponential distribution operating with the same value of CR. Consequently, it is important when reporting results to specify not only CR, but also the process to which it refers. To facilitate this reporting, a simple nomenclature scheme was developed that provides a shorthand for referencing a variety of DE models. For example, *DE/rand/1/bin* (Figures 6.2, 6.3, 6.4 and Appendix 6.A) is shorthand for a *D*ifferential *E*volution algorithm in which *rand*omly chosen donor vectors are mutated and then discretely recombined with parameters from $\bar{x}_{i,G}$ using a *binomial* distribution. The '*1*' in *DE/rand/1/bin* stands for the number of vector pairs that contribute to the mutation vector.

Early experiments with filter designs and chemical process control suggested that 4-vector, 2-differential mutation in conjunction with $F = 0.5$ was an especially robust combination (Price [1996], Wang [1997]). In particular, the model: *DE/best/2/exp*, which uses an *exp*onential process, proved very effective, probably because of the increased speed of convergence that comes from constantly using the *best* performing population member as the donor. Subsequent investigations, however, suggest that both the use of a 2-differential mutation vector and the constant use of the best-so-far vector as a donor are, perhaps, ill-advised in the general case. Adding vector differentials appears to destroy their correlation which in turn can degrade performance while the bias introduced by a heavy dependence on the best-so-far vector often leads to premature convergence unless prohibitively large populations are used.

The discrete recombination scheme used in these early versions of DE simply copies child parameters directly from their donors. For child parameters to be general linear combinations of other object vector parameters requires an operation like arithmetic crossover (Equation 6.15). Enlarging the scope of crossover to include arithmetic crossover endows recombination with the ability to explore the space between and beyond the corners of the hyper-cube to which a search driven by discrete recombination is restricted. Arithmetic crossover also permits DE to search along axes defined by those pairs of object vectors that were explicitly excluded by Equation 6.14. More importantly, though, arithmetic crossover is a rotationally invariant search procedure, whereas discrete recombination is not.

Discretely recombining the parameters of two vectors generates potential child vectors that lie on the corners of a *D*-dimensional hyper-cube. Figure 6.11, Case A illustrates a two-dimensional example in which the hyper-cube is a rectangle defined by the vectors: $\bar{x}_{i,G}$ and $\bar{x}_{r3,G}$. The remaining two corners of the rectangle are potential child vectors, each of which inherits one coordinate from each of the defining vectors. Rotation, however, transforms the coordinates of both vectors and thus changes the projected shape of the hyper-cube, as Figure 6.11, Case B illustrates. The only two corners of the hyper-cube that remain unchanged by rotation are the ones occupied by the vectors that define the hyper-cube. The location of all other corners depends on the orientation of the coordinate system. In the case of the ellipse in Figure 6.11, it can be seen that when compared to the child vectors in Case A, the options generated in Case B are not as well-placed.

Discrete recombination is not a rotationally invariant process because different parameters can be inherited from different vectors. For a child vector's prescription to be rotationally invariant, *all* of its parameters must be taken from the same point in the space of object vectors. In *DE/rand/1/bin*, this can only be done when $CR = 1$. This limitation can be overcome by replacing the discrete recombination formula prescribed in Equation 6.2 (*DE/rand/1/bin*) with the arithmetic crossover scheme defined by Equation 6.15. The resulting algorithm, *DE/current-to-rand/1*, generates vectors that are rotationally invariant, linear combinations of the *current* vector $x_{j,i,G}$, and a *rand*omly chosen donor $x_{j,r3,G}$. The final DE version descriptor indicating either *exp* or *bin* is not necessary since CR is implicitly equal to 1 and not used. The exquisitely simple prescription given in Equation 6.17 below combines Equations 6.14 and 6.15 and is illustrated graphically in Figure 6.12.

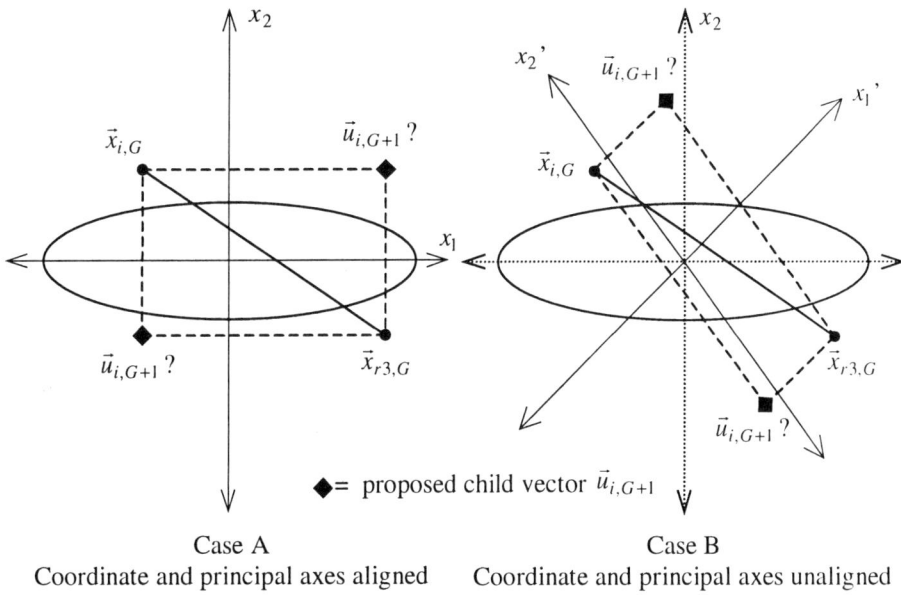

Case A
Coordinate and principal axes aligned

Case B
Coordinate and principal axes unaligned

Fig. 6.11: Coordinate rotation shifts the location of potential child vectors generated by discrete recombination. Linear combinations of $\vec{x}_{i,G}$ and $\vec{x}_{r3,G}$ remain unaltered.

$$\vec{u}_{i,G+1} = \vec{x}_{i,G} + K \cdot (\vec{x}_{r3,G} - \vec{x}_{i,G}) + F \cdot (\vec{x}_{r1,G} - \vec{x}_{r2,G})$$

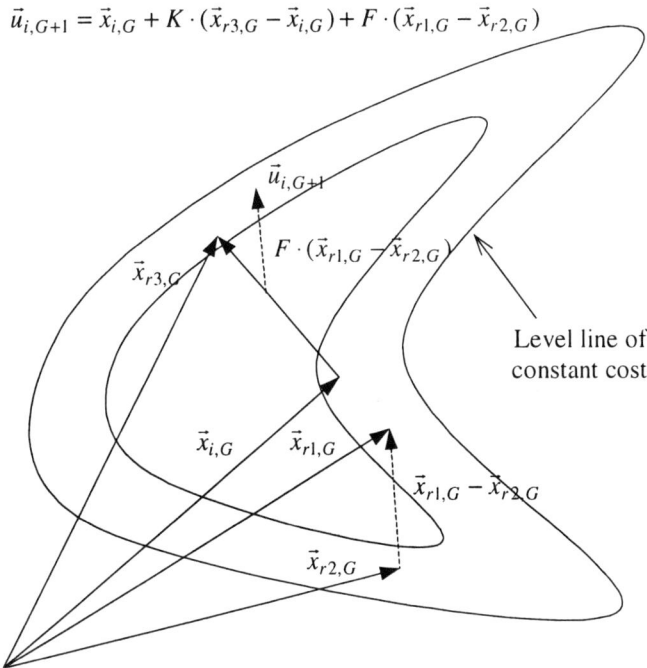

Fig. 6.12: DE/current-to-rand/1.

$$r_1, r_2, r_3 \in \{1,2,..., NP\}, \text{randomly selected, except} : r_1 \neq r_2 \neq r_3 \neq i$$
$$\vec{u}_{i,G+1} = \vec{x}_{i,G} + K \cdot (\vec{x}_{r3,G} - \vec{x}_{i,G}) + F \cdot (\vec{x}_{r1,G} - \vec{x}_{r2,G}) \qquad (6.17)$$

Like its mutation counterpart F, the coefficient of combination K has proven to be an effective control variable when it is held to a user-specified constant throughout the optimization process. Traditionally, $K \in [-0.5,1.5]$, but experiments with DE have not demonstrated any benefit to using values outside the more restricted range: $[0,1]$. In fact, it is *almost* always sufficient for K to be chosen with a uniform random distribution from the interval: $[0,1]$. When $K = 1$, the formulation in Equation 6.17 reduces to the model: *DE/rand/1/bin* with $CR = 1$. When $K = 0$, the algorithm in Equation 6.17 reduces to a mutation-only model. Code for this and several other versions of DE (e.g., *DE/current-to-rand/1/bin*) can be found in Appendix 6.A.

6.8 DE DYNAMICS

Understanding the dynamic interplay between NP, K and F, can help simplify the selection of effective control variable combinations for *DE/current-to-rand/1* (Equation 6.17). To provide some insight into DE's dynamics, the results of two simple experiments are presented. The first experiment uses the two-array, mutation-only version ($K = 0$) to locate the minimum of a 10-dimensional, spherical objective function:

$$f(\vec{x}) = \sum_{j=1}^{D=10} x_j^2, \quad \varepsilon = 1.0\text{e-}6, \quad \vec{x}^{(lo)} = -1000, \quad \vec{x}^{(hi)} \doteq 1000 \qquad (6.18)$$

Figure 6.13 plots the population size, NP, *versus* the average number of function evaluations that DE needed to resolve the minimum of the sphere to within 1.0e−6. Results, obtained for several values of F, show two simple trends. The most obvious is that for constant F, the number of function evaluations required to resolve the sphere to the specified error ε is proportional to NP, that is:

$$Evals_\varepsilon \propto NP \ln NP \qquad (6.19)$$

Notice, however, that in the case of the sphere, deviations from this relationship appear for small values of F ($F \leq .2$) in conjunction with small populations. The second trend suggested by the data in Figure 6.13 is that the rate of convergence slows dramatically as F increases.

To explore the effect that F has on the time it takes to resolve the sphere's minimum, a second experiment was conducted using a logarithmic scale to plot the number of objective function evaluations as a function of F. Results for two different settings of K are plotted in Figure 6.14, but in each case, $NP = 40$. The results for the mutation-only model ($K = 0$) most clearly illustrate that when F is large, the time to reach the specified error grows exponentially with F:

$$Evals_\varepsilon \propto NP \cdot e^F NP \ln NP, \quad F \gg 1 \qquad (6.20)$$

Figure 6.14 also shows that this relationship remains valid even when crossover is used ($K = 1$). Curiously, convergence was not regular for $F = 1$, $K = 1$, so no point was plotted. In every other case, all 100 trials located the minimum with the specified degree of error.

Even though the spherical test function on which Equation 6.20 is based is not representative of the highly-constrained, multi-modal functions that confound engineers and scientists, the relationship it expresses appears to be universal within the context of DE. This is not a proven fact, but merely an empirical observation.

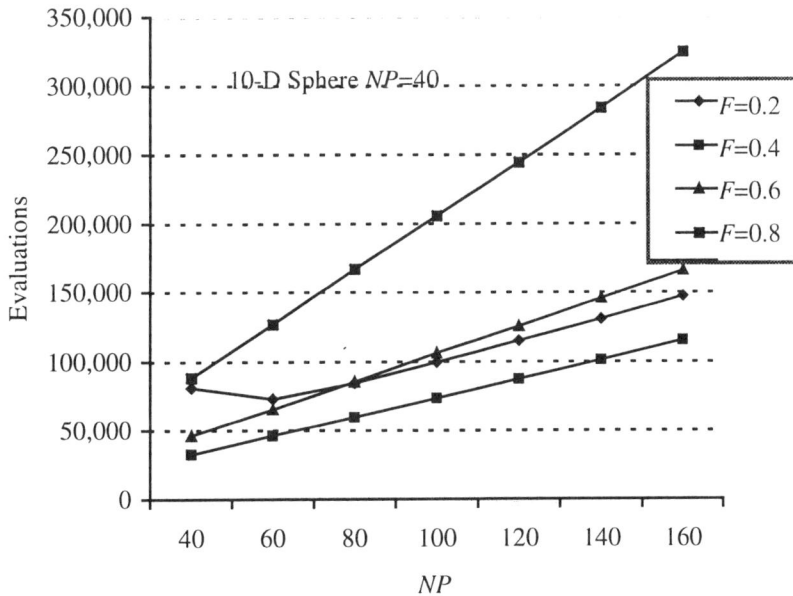

Fig. 6.13: Solution time *versus* population size for various values of *F*.

6.9 USER GUIDELINES

Because DE is comparatively robust, selecting a set of control variables that will solve an arbitrary problem has seldom proven difficult. Not only can a single setting solve a range of problems, a single problem can usually be solved with a broad range of settings. The best approach is to run a few trials with different standard settings and use the feedback that these trials provide to refine the selection of control variables. Of course, if function evaluation times are very long, it will be important to minimize the amount of experimentation required to find effective control variables. To this end, the following guidelines are proposed.

CR: Discrete crossover probability- version selection

If the objective function is known to be separable, then $CR = 0$ in conjunction with *DE/rand/1/bin* will undoubtedly be very effective. Indeed, almost any value of *CR* should work on separable functions. In reality, there are degrees of epistasis, so intermediate values of *CR* may also prove useful. Odds are, though, that if an appeal is being made to an evolutionary optimizer, then the problem at hand is probably not separable. As with the real-world design problems featured in the following chapters on DE, values of *CR* close to, or equal to 1 appear to be the rule. Consequently, *DE/current-to-rand/1* is recommended as the method of first choice and *CR*, which is implicitly equal to 1, does not need not be specified. The proven ability of *DE/rand/1/bin* and of the more complex *DE/current-to-rand/1/bin*, however, suggests that they should not be excluded from consideration if *DE/current-to-rand/1* should fail to perform adequately.

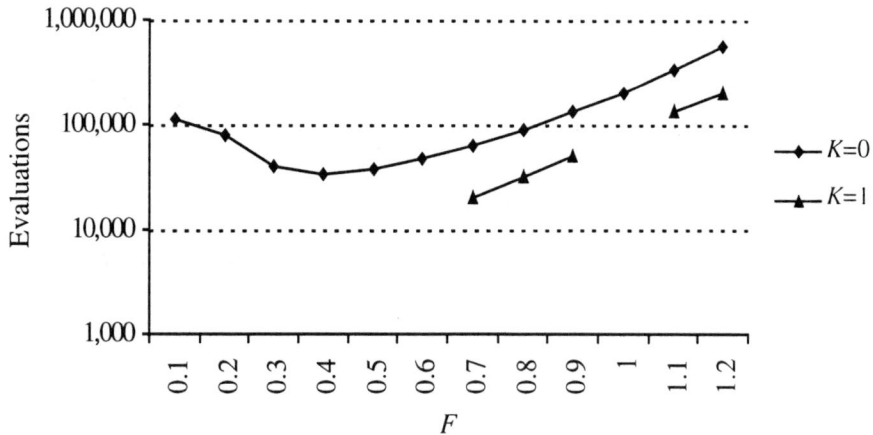

Fig. 6.14: Solution time *versus F* for fixed *NP*=40.

NP: Population size

Based on Equation 6.19, it is obvious that in order to achieve the highest possible speed of convergence, the population size *NP* should be as small as possible. If, however, *NP* becomes too small, then the probability of either *premature convergence* or *stagnation* can become significant. Stagnation refers to a condition in which the population stops evolving while still distributed across the fitness landscape. Premature convergence, a very common problem in both local search and population-based algorithms refers to the condition in which all vectors coalesce towards a single, non-optimal point. Both of these conditions can usually be overcome by increasing the value of *NP*. In real-world engineering problems, a population size of *NP* = 20*D* will probably be more than adequate. Indeed, populations as small as 5*D* are often possible, although optimal solutions using *NP* < 2*D* should not be expected.

Some tasks, such as determining the weights in a neural network, involve hundreds or thousands of variables. For such problems, very good results are still possible even though memory resources will probably limit population sizes to far less than 20*D*. In addition, functions with very many (thousands/millions) of local minima appear to require populations on the order of up to 100*D*. Indeed, the optimal population size for a given problem is probably not even a linear function of dimension. Even so, for the problems with 30 dimensions or less upon which these recommendations are based, *NP* = 20*D* has proven to be a reliable starting point.

K and F: Coefficient of combination (k_χ) and mutation scale factor (k_μ)

These two control variables appear to be quite closely related. In fact, experience shows that it is often possible to successfully optimize a function using the same value for each. The range over which *K=F* is effective may be quite narrow, however, so it is often simpler to set them independently. Even though *K* is continuous, it usually suffices to set it to one of three discrete values: 0, 0.5, or 1. Only rarely will *K* need to be more carefully chosen. Frequently, choosing *K* randomly from the range: [0,1] once per vector (*not* once per parameter) is very effective, but more control than this technique provides will probably be necessary for hard problems.

K=0 corresponds to a mutation-only DE. The lack of crossover-induced selective pressure when *K* = 0 means that both *F* and *NP* can be relatively small without putting the population's diversity at risk. Even though the mutation-only model uses smaller populations and scale factors than do crossover models, convergence for the mutation-only model is typically slower than when $K \geq 0.5$ or 1. Furthermore, if either *NP* or *F* becomes too small, the population can stagnate. Although it is relatively slow, the mutation-only DE model converges to reliably good solutions in the majority of test functions to which it has been applied.

When *K* = 0.5 or 1.0, *F* will typically have to be 0.5 or greater to oppose the inward pressure that sampling only the space between object vectors generates. Indeed, in several cases, the combination: *K* = 0.5, *F* = 0.5 appears to exploit a kind of dynamic balance between the contraction caused by *K* = 0.5 and the outward, diffusive pressure exerted when *F* = 0.5. More commonly, though, when $K \geq 0.5$, *F* will be in the range 0.6–0.8. Smaller values of *F* tend to cause premature convergence unless very large populations are employed.

For a general recommendation, start with: *DE/current-to-rand/1*, *NP* = 20*D*, *K* = 0.5, *F* = 0.8. If convergence seems premature, then increase *NP* and/or *F*, and/or *decrease K*. If the population stagnates, then increase *NP* and/or *F*, and/or choose *K* randomly from the interval: [0,1]. If none of these alternatives works, try *DE/rand/1/bin* in conjunction with a small value of *CR*. Table 6.2 is a summary of the recommended values for each of DE's control parameters. Recommendations are based on limited experimental evidence, so experimentation is *strongly* encouraged.

Table 6.2: Guide for choosing DE's initial control variable settings.

Control Variable	Lo	Hi	Best?	Comments
NP: Population size	2*D*	100*D*?	20*D*	100*D* if highly multi-modal
F: Scaling factor	0.0	1.0+	0.3–0.9	$F \geq 0.5$ if $K \geq 0.5$ (?)
CR: Crossover probability	0.0	1.0	0.8–1.0	*CR*=0 separable, *CR*=1 epistatic
K: Coefficient of combination	−0.5	1.5	0, 0.5, 1.0	Try a random *K* in [0,1]

6.10 MIXED VARIABLE OPTIMIZATION

In addition to being an effective global optimizer for functions with continuous variables (Storn & Price [1997]), DE has also demonstrated an equal ability to optimize problems with integer, discrete and even mixed variables. Such problems are particularly common in engineering where otherwise continuous design variables are limited to a discrete set of commercially available values. Optical design, for example, involves all three types of variables. The number of lens surfaces is a positive integer variable, but both the curvature and the position of a lens are continuous variables. Furthermore, optical glass is commercially available only in a limited number of compositions, so the index of refraction of each lens is effectively a discrete variable with irregularly spaced values.

The most common approach to optimizing mixed-variable objective functions is to treat all variables as continuous. Once the continuous problem has been optimized, real values that correspond to discrete and integer variables can be rounded-off to the nearest available value. In practice, this method often gives less than optimal results because no attempt is made during optimization to evaluate only realizable systems. When generating child vectors, DE also treats all object vector parameters as real variables, but continuous values corresponding to integer and discrete variables are rounded-off to the nearest available value before each child vector is evaluated. This way, only realizable systems provide feedback to the optimization process. It is important to round-off only in the context of evaluating a child vector. To keep the population robust, successful child vectors must enter the population with all of the precision with which they were generated.

Despite the simplicity of this approach to mixed variable optimization, DE consistently outperforms competing methods, as Lampinen and Zelinka demonstrate in their chapter on DE and mechanical engineering design optimization. Their chapter also includes an alternative strategy for handling discrete variables. Since Lampinen and Zelinka extensively discuss how to modify DE for mixed variable optimization, this topic will not be explored further in this Introduction.

6.11 CONSTRAINTS

Sometimes, finding an objective function's global minimum is not enough. It may be, for example, that the 'optimal' object vector violates one or more constraints that must be satisfied. Safety codes, mechanical interference and size limitations are common ways in which 'hard' constraints enter into optimization problems. Probably the simplest example of a hard constraint is the bound-constraint. In an optical system, for example, no lens can have an index of refraction less than 1, or a thickness less than or equal to zero. Consequently, both the thickness of a lens and its index of refraction have strict lower bounds that are physically constrained to realizable values. When a parameter is strictly bound-constrained, then DE should not be allowed to search beyond that bound. Any child parameter generated out of bounds should be reset by one of the methods described in section 6.4, Equation 6.4.

Even if an object vector satisfies all constraints, the possibility often exists that it cannot be evaluated. For example, a ray of light being traced through a proposed optical system might be refracted to an angle that causes it to miss the next lens surface and exit the system prematurely. Consequently, such a ray provides no information about the optical system at all and the evaluation routine will typically result in an exception. To handle such exceptions, DE should be instructed to reject these *indeterminate* child vectors as would be the case if their cost were prohibitively high.

Unlike the rejection of indeterminate vectors or the enforcement of strict boundary constraints, not all constraints are 'hard'. In many cases, constraint violations will be inevitable, so the emphasis then shifts to minimizing the extent to which these violations must be tolerated. One way to implement these 'soft' constraints is with *penalty functions*. Penalty functions are modifications to the objective function that cause an object vector's cost to increase with both the magnitude and number of its constraint violations. Even though constraints complicate the process of formulating a cost function, they are often necessary, since without them, some problems will be insurmountable. As R. Storn points out in his chapter on DE for digital filter design, the inclusion of problem-specific knowledge into the design of the objective function can be crucial to success. Since both R. Storn and Lampinen and Zelinka elaborate soft constraint-handling methods, a further discussion of this topic is deferred to them.

6.12 FINAL THOUGHTS

DE appears to be one of the first evolutionary algorithm to do 'useful work', i.e., work that in the past could only be accomplished by a human expert with specialized software. For example, armed only with DE and a ray tracing program, it is possible to design complex optical systems with only the most rudimentary knowledge of optical design. In one experiment, the author designed a Maksutov-Schmidt telescope with a two-element, air-spaced field flattener on a PC in a single afternoon. This particular optical design problem involved 14 variables, boundary constraints, indeterminate object vectors and, like most optical designs, was multimodal and highly epistatic. The same scenario has been repeated in the field of digital filter design, as R. Storn demonstrates in chapter seven. Filters that would otherwise require specialized methods to design can routinely be configured using DE and well-designed penalty functions.

It is not just the power of DE as a global optimizer that gives it such promise as a design tool, but also its versatility. DE is very easily extended to mixed variable optimization and to problems involving multiple, non-linear constraints. Unlike many global optimizers, the objective function does not have to be continuous, nor is gradient information required for DE to work. Indeed, the objective function itself can be specified in a relative way, as K. Chisholm has done in order to apply DE to the problem of co-evolving strategies for playing checkers ('draughts'). Since the objective function for this problem is the number of wins in round-robin play, and since many games are drawn (tied), the objective function is very noisy. Despite this, DE is still able to evolve improved strategies. The same can be expected in other applications in which the objective function is only reliable on average. Furthermore, DE is inherently parallel. Consequently, solutions to design problems involving computationally expensive objective functions can be accelerated by distributing the computational load across a network of processors.

The convergence of power and versatility in an algorithm as trivially simple as DE ought to make any student of the theory of computation curious. To date, no convergence proof exists for DE. Although its self-referential nature makes DE easy to understand, the same lack of absolutes complicates the analysis of DE's dynamics, since each function exhibits its own unique behaviour. Even if theoretical results are slow in materializing, extensive experimentation ought to reveal the extent of the relationship between NP, K and F, if any. Indeed, holding these control variables constant during optimization is almost certainly not an optimal strategy, so a more effective algorithm may be possible if these quantities can be adaptively tuned, or if rules can be developed to facilitate the selection of effective combinations.

The ability of functions to resolve their own optima is indeed a mysterious process. Fortunately, understanding this process is not a prerequisite for exploiting its power. With just a few lines of code, DE enables non-specialists to discover effective solutions to nearly intractable problems without appealing to expert knowledge or specialized design algorithms. For most engineers and scientists with real-world problems to solve, this will enough. Others, however, will wonder why.

Acknowledgements

The author would like to thank David W. Corne at the University of Reading, U.K., for his interest in DE and especially for the invitation to include Differential Evolution in this book. Gratitude is also extended to Dr. R. Storn for his helpful comments regarding the draft for this Introduction. Additional thanks go out to J. Lampinen, I. Zelinka and K. Chisholm not only for their work on this chapter, but also for their friendship and continued interest in DE.

APPENDIX 6.A: A C-STYLE PROGRAM FOR THE ALGORITHM: *DE/RAND/1/BIN* IMPLEMENTED WITH A SINGLE ARRAY

Input: D = number of parameters
            NP = population size
            F = scale factor, $F \in (0,1+)$
            K = coefficient of combination, $K \in [0,1]$, e.g., K = 0, .5, or 1.
            CR = crossover control constant, $CR \in [0,1]$
            Gmax = maximum number of generations
            hi[ ], lo[ ] = upper and lower initial parameter bounds, respectively
            rand(0,1) returns a uniformly distributed random number from the range: [0,1).

```
  generation = 0;
  for ( i = 0;  i < NP;  i++ )
  {   for ( j = 0;  j < D;  j++ )  x[i][j] = lo[j] + rand(0,1) * ( hi[j] - lo[j] );
      cost[i] = your_function( &x[i][0]  );
  }
  do
  { for ( i = 0;  i < NP;  i ++ )     /*  Population index, i, begins with 0  */
      {
            do r1 = ( int )( rand(0,1 ) * NP ); while (r1 == i );
            do r2 = ( int )( rand(0,1 ) * NP ); while (r2 == i || r2 == r1 );
            do r3 = ( int )( rand(0,1 ) * NP ); while (r3 == i || r3 == r1 || r3 == r2 );

/*  Begin version: DE/rand/1/bin  */

            j=( int )( rand(0,1) * D );
            for ( k = 1;  k <= D;  k++ )
            {   if ( rand(0,1) < CR || k == D) temp[j] = x[r3][j] + F * ( x[r1][j] - x[r2][j] );
                else temp[j] = x[i][j];

            /*   check bounds ?   */
                j = ( j+1 ) % D;  /*   % = modulo; index j runs from 0 to D-1   */
            }
/*  End version: DE/rand/1/bin  */

            score = your_function( &temp[0]  );
            if ( score <= cost[i] )
            {   for ( j = 0; j < D;  j++ )  x[i][j] = temp[j];
                cost[i] = score;
            }
      }
      generation += 1;
  } while ( generation  < Gmax );
  /* End code */
```

```
/*  Alternative Versions  */

/*  Begin version: DE/current-to-rand/1  */

        for ( j = 0; j < D; j ++ )
        {     temp[j] = x[i][j] + K * ( x[r3][j] - x[i][j] ) + F * ( x[r1][j] - x[r2][j] );

            /*  check bounds ?  */
        }

/*  End version: DE/current-to-rand/1  */


/*  Begin version: DE/rand/1/exp  */

        j=( int )( rand(0,1) * D );
        flag = 0;
        for ( k = 1;  k <= D;  k++ )
          {
            if ( rand(0,1) < CR || k== D) flag=1;
            if (flag == 1) temp[j] = x[r3][j] + F * ( x[r1][j] - x[r2][j] );
              else temp[j] = x[i][j];

            /*  check bounds ?  */

            j = ( j+1 )%D; /*  % = modulo; index j runs from 0 to D-1   */
          }
/*  End version: DE/rand/1/exp  */

/*  Begin version: DE/current-to-rand/1/bin  */

        j=( int )( rand(0,1) * D );
          for ( k = 1;  k <= D;  k++ )
          {
            if ( rand(0,1) < CR || k == D)
            {
                temp[j] = x[i][j] + K * ( x[r3][j] - x[i][j] ) + F * ( x[r1][j] - x[r2][j] );
            }
            else temp[j] = x[i][j];

            /*  check bounds ?  */

            j = ( j+1 ) % D; /*  % = modulo; index j runs from 0 to D-1   */
          }

/*  End version: DE/current-to-rand/1/bin  */
```

Chapter Seven

Designing Digital Filters with Differential Evolution

Rainer Storn

7.1 AN INTRODUCTION TO LINEAR DIGITAL FILTERS

As its name implies, a filter is a device that filters out unwanted signals in order to retrieve information. A well-known example from nature is the human ability to understand the spoken words of a person at a cocktail party, even though dozens of other people are also talking. Other, more technical examples of filtering are: the recovery of deep-space signals which are buried in thermal noise, the filtering of images to facilitate edge detection, the division of frequency bands to allow more than one radio station to transmit information, the adjustment of treble and bass in high-fidelity amplifiers, and so on. In the early days of the electronics industry, filters were mainly built from analog components like inductors, capacitors and resistors. With the invention of the transistor and the integrated circuit, 'active' filters became feasible which in turn led to a reduction in both filter size and cost for many applications. Unfortunately, the main disadvantages of analog components remained. Tight manufacturing tolerances, temperature drift and changing properties during a filter's life cycle still made it expensive to build high-precision devices. With the advent of digital technology, this scenario underwent a significant transformation and long-term, stable filters with exactly predictable properties became economically feasible. Today, the linear versions of digital filters are the most important representatives of this exciting technology.

We now provide a very brief introduction to the theory of linear digital filters so that the reader can understand the design choices to be made. A more complete description of and introduction to the topic of digital filters can be found in a number of textbooks, including Mitra & Kaiser [1993] and Rabiner & Gold [1975].

The most common linear digital filters transform a real-valued input sequence: $x_n = \{x_0, x_1, x_2,...\}$ into a real-valued output sequence: $y_n = \{y_0, y_1, y_2,...\}$. Only the three basic building blocks shown in Figure 7.1 are needed to construct any linear digital filter. The building blocks are the *unit delay*, the *multiplier* and the *adder/subtracter*. The unit delay, symbolized by z^{-1}, has a deep mathematical meaning that will be briefly mentioned later. The unit delay can also be thought of as a one-element queue that stores an incoming numerical value at the current time instant and then passes it on at the following time instant. Concerning the multiplier, we will confine our discussion to real-valued coefficients a_i only.

Unit Delay $x_n \longrightarrow \boxed{z^{-1}} \longrightarrow x_{n-1}$

Multiplier $x_n \longrightarrow \triangleright^{a_i} \longrightarrow a_i x_n$

Adder/Subtracter $\begin{array}{c} x_n \searrow^{+} \\ \quad \bigcirc \longrightarrow x_n \pm z_n \\ z_n \nearrow_{\pm} \end{array}$

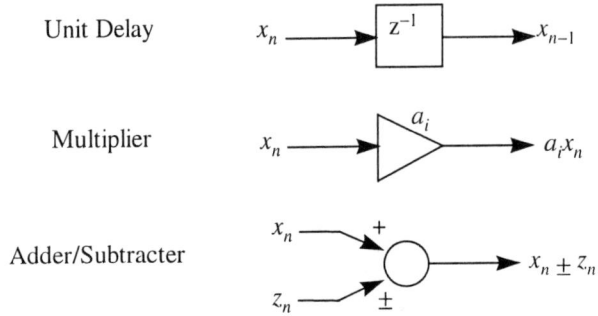

Fig. 7.1: The basic elements of linear digital filters.

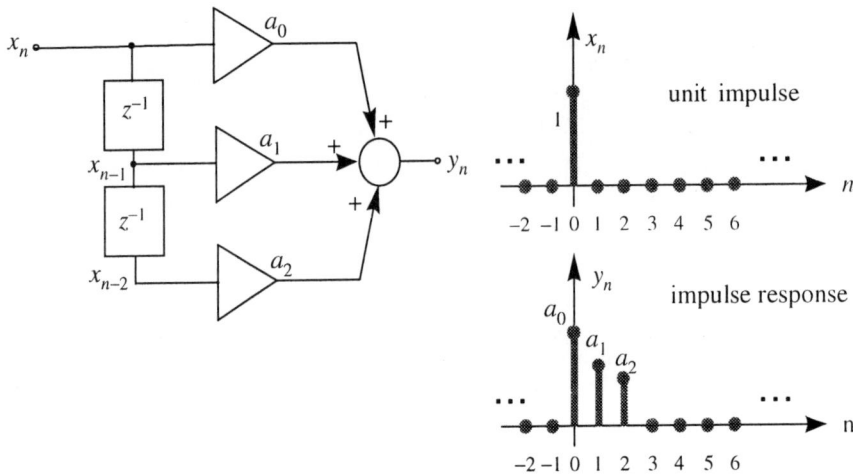

Fig. 7.2: Example for a finite impulse response (FIR) filter.

Linear digital filters which have a single input and a single output come in two flavours: finite impulse response (FIR) filters and infinite impulse response (IIR) filters. Of these two types of filter, FIR-filters are simpler to analyze and understand. Figure 7.2 illustrates a simple example of an FIR-filter that has two delay elements, one adder and three multipliers: a_0, a_1, a_2. The arrangement of the basic elements of a filter as shown in Figure 7.2 is called a flowgraph. If we count time with the index, n, and if we denote the input signal at the nth instant as x_n, we can derive from Figure 7.1 and Figure 7.2 that the output signal, y_n, is:

$$y_n = x_n \cdot a_0 + x_{n-1} \cdot a_1 + x_{n-2} \cdot a_2 \tag{7.1}$$

When the input signal x_n is the unit impulse (Figure 7.2), the output signal y_n consists of only three, non-zero samples and the response to the input signal falls to zero in a finite time. This behaviour gives this structure its name: *finite impulse response* filter. We can also analyze the above structure in terms of the Z-transform, which can be written as:

$$X(z) = Z\{x_n\} \tag{7.2}$$

An important theorem of the Z-transform is:

$$z^{-k} \cdot X(z) = Z\{x_{n-k}\} \tag{7.3}$$

which we can use together with the flowgraph of Figure 7.2 to derive the equation:

$$Y(z) = X(z) \cdot a_0 + X(z) \cdot z^{-1} \cdot a_1 + X(z) \cdot z^{-2} \cdot a_2 \tag{7.4}$$

We can now define the *transfer function H(z)* as:

$$H(z) = \frac{Y(z)}{X(z)} = a_0 + z^{-1} \cdot a_1 + z^{-2} \cdot a_2 \tag{7.5}$$

Because the highest power of z^{-1} in Equation 7.5 is 2, we say that the *degree* of the FIR-filter is 2. In the general case of an FIR-filter, we get:

$$H(z) = \sum_{i=0}^{N-1} a_i \cdot z^{-i} \tag{7.6}$$

which has a degree of $N-1$.

Now that we have a picture of what an FIR-filter is, we can more easily understand the IIR-filter. A simple example of an IIR-filter is shown in Figure 7.3. If we again apply a unit impulse to the digital filter, we see that the first output sample y_0 is just the un-delayed unit impulse and that this value is also stored in the delay element. At the next time instant, $n=1$, the input signal x_n is zero and only the value 1 from the delay element, weighted by the coefficient b, contributes to the adder; hence, the next output sample is b. This value is again stored in the unit delay, and so on. We can easily verify that the unit impulse response is infinite as a result of the recursive structure of the filter. Omitting the time domain equation, we inspect the Z-transform of the output signal $Y(z)$ to get:

$$Y(z) = X(z) + Y(z) \cdot z^{-1} \cdot b \tag{7.7}$$

or:

$$H(z) = \frac{Y(z)}{X(z)} = \frac{z}{z-b} \tag{7.8}$$

The general form $H(z)$ of an IIR-filter is:

$$H(z) = \frac{\displaystyle\sum_{n=0}^{N} a_n \cdot z^{-n}}{1 + \displaystyle\sum_{m=1}^{M} b_m \cdot z^{-m}} = a_0 \cdot \frac{\displaystyle\prod_{n=1}^{N} (z - z_{0_n})}{\displaystyle\prod_{m=1}^{M} (z - z_{p_m})} \cdot z^{M-N} \tag{7.9}$$

and the degree is defined as max(N,M).

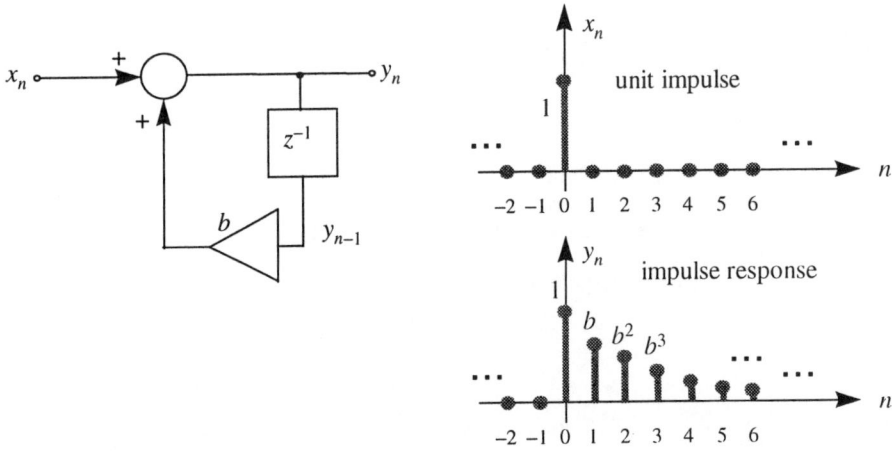

Fig. 7.3: Example of an infinite impuse response (IIR) filter.

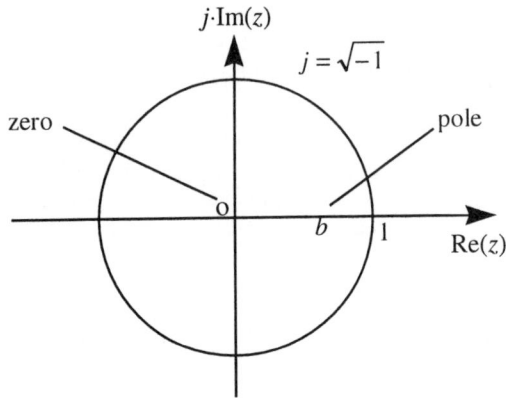

Fig. 7.4: Pole-Zero diagram for the IIR-filter of Figure 7.3.

Since z is generally a complex number, we can draw the Pole-Zero diagram of Equation 7.8 in the complex z-plane (Figure 7.4). We see that $H(z)$ has a singularity (or pole) at $z=b$. Without proof, we state that all poles of an IIR-filter must be inside the unit circle of the complex z-plane in order for the filter to be stable.

Since z is complex, we can rewrite Equation 7.8 as:

$$H(z) = \frac{z}{z-b} = \frac{\text{Re}(z) + j \cdot \text{Im}(z)}{\text{Re}(z) - b + j \cdot \text{Im}(z)} \qquad (7.10)$$

where j is the square root of -1. From Equation 7.10, we can compute the magnitude of the transfer function as:

$$|H(z)|= \frac{\sqrt{\mathrm{Re}(z)^2 + \mathrm{Im}(z)^2}}{\sqrt{(\mathrm{Re}(z)-b)^2 + \mathrm{Im}(z)^2}} \tag{7.11}$$

A graphical representation of Equation 7.11 with $b=0.8$ is shown in Figure 7.5.

Without proof, we now state the relationship between Fourier- and Z-Transforms:

$$z = e^{j2\pi\Omega} = \cos(2\pi \cdot \Omega) + j \cdot \sin(2\pi \cdot \Omega) \tag{7.12}$$

where:

$$\Omega = \frac{f}{f_s} \tag{7.13}$$

The variable f denotes the *natural frequency*, while f_s is called the *sampling frequency*. The sampling frequency determines the time interval $T_s = 1/f_s$, which elapses between two successive signal samples x_{n-1} and x_n. We are now interested in the *frequency response* $H(e^{j2\pi\Omega})$, which for the IIR-filter of Equation 7.10 and Figure 7.3 is:

$$H(e^{j2\pi\Omega}) = \frac{e^{j2\pi\cdot\Omega}}{e^{j2\pi\cdot\Omega}-b} \tag{7.14}$$

Hence, we get Equation 7.15 below, which is represented graphically in Figure 7.6.

$$\left|H(e^{j2\pi\Omega})\right| = A(\Omega) = \frac{1}{\sqrt{(\cos(2\pi\Omega)-b)^2 + \sin^2(2\pi\Omega)}} \tag{7.15}$$

A comparison of Figures 7.5 and 7.6 reveals that the curve in Figure 7.6 matches the one that $|H(z)|$ in Equation 7.11 leaves on the cylinder: $\mathrm{Re}^2(z)+\mathrm{Im}^2(z)=1$.

Two other important quantities in filter design are the *phase angle* (Equation 7.16) and *group delay* (Equation 7.17).

$$\varphi(\Omega)= arc\left(H\left(e^{j2\pi\cdot\Omega}\right)\right) \tag{7.16}$$

$$G(\Omega)= -\frac{d\varphi(\Omega)}{d\Omega} \tag{7.17}$$

In filter design problems, some or all of the quantities, $A(\Omega)$, $\varphi(\Omega)$ and $G(\Omega)$ are subject to constraints.

7.2 FILTER DESIGN WITH DIFFERENTIAL EVOLUTION

A wide variety of specialized and efficient methods for designing digital filters have been developed over the past decades (Mitra & Kaiser [1993], Rabiner & Gold [1975], Rorabaugh [1993]) so it is justified to ask why these devices should be designed at all with a general-purpose optimizer like DE. There are several good reasons why this might be advantageous:

1. The filter design problem at hand might be so unusual that no specialized design procedure exists.

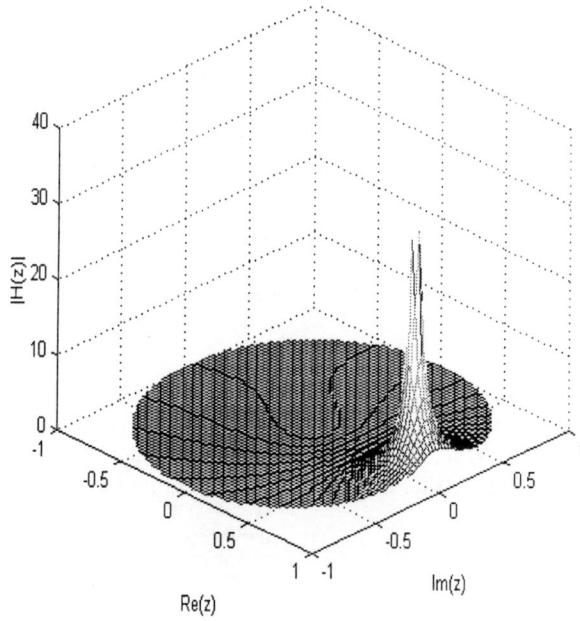

Fig. 7.5: Graphical representation of Equation 7.11 with b=0.8.

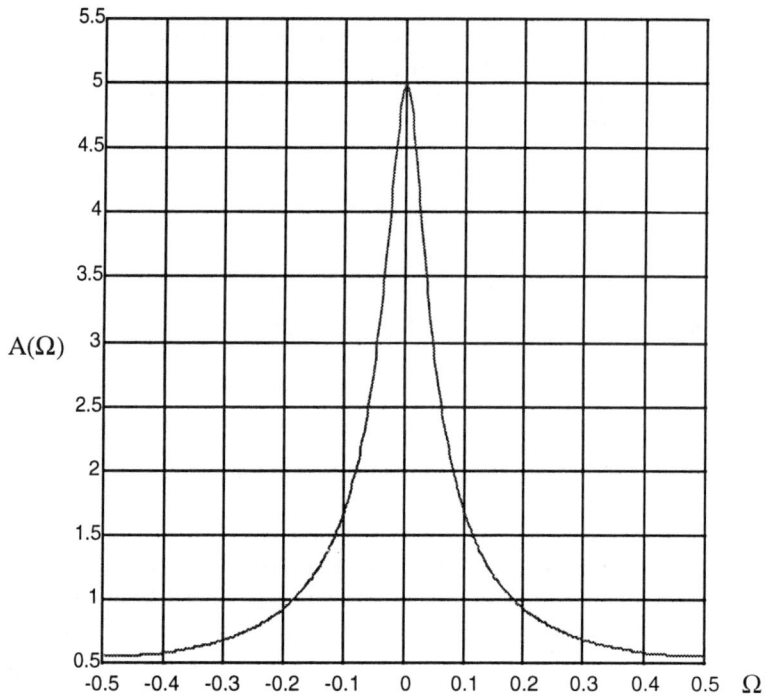

Fig 7.6: $A(\Omega)$ from Equation 7.15 for $\Omega \in [-0.5, 0.5]$.

2. Although there might be a specialized design procedure, it may not be easily accessible. The reason for this could be that although a journal paper is available, the source code is not. Even if the code is available, a high price tag could render it uneconomical.

3. The designer simply doesn't know whether or not a specialized design procedure exists. Designing the filter with DE might actually take less time than would be needed to conduct a search for a problem-specific design method.

4. The designer is not an expert at the task and has only a basic knowledge of digital filter design.

In the following sections, we present two examples in which Differential Evolution is applied to the problem of digital filter design. The first example is the design of an IIR-filter with unusual constraints for which specialized design methods exist. The design software, however, is not generally available, so this example is representative of case 2 above. The second example is also a representative of case 2 and involves designing a pair of filters.

7.3. EXAMPLE 7.1: DESIGNING AN IIR-FILTER WITH CONSTRAINTS IN BOTH MAGNITUDE AND GROUP DELAY

IIR-filters are generally chosen in cases where tight requirements for the magnitude response are imposed, but where neither the phase angle nor the group delay plays a major role. In cases where linear, or approximately linear phase is required, one usually resorts to FIR-filters because they can provide piece-wise exactly linear phase, i.e., piece-wise constant group delay. On some occasions, however, FIR-filters will incur an unnecessarily high realization expense. Consider, for example, the graphics codec for sample rate reduction (ITU-CCIR [1985]), whose magnitude and group delay specifications are depicted in Figure 7.7.

The specifications of Figure 7.7 can be fulfilled by a linear phase FIR-filter of degree 61 (Haase [1989]). Since the tight passband specifications for the magnitude can be fulfilled with an IIR-filter of relatively low degree, it seems worthwhile to try and meet the specifications of Figure 7.7 with an IIR approach, even though the group delay specifications will enforce a filter degree which is higher than what is needed for fulfilling the magnitude requirements alone. The goal is to achieve an overall reduced realization expense and a lower overall filter delay. It has been shown in Keinath [1992] that the IIR-filter degree can be reduced to 10 with specialized design methods that simultaneously consider magnitude and phase requirements. Specialized methods for IIR-filter design in the complex domain, however, are seldom readily available and they have the additional disadvantage of being difficult to implement. Hence, this design problem is an attractive candidate for solution by DE.

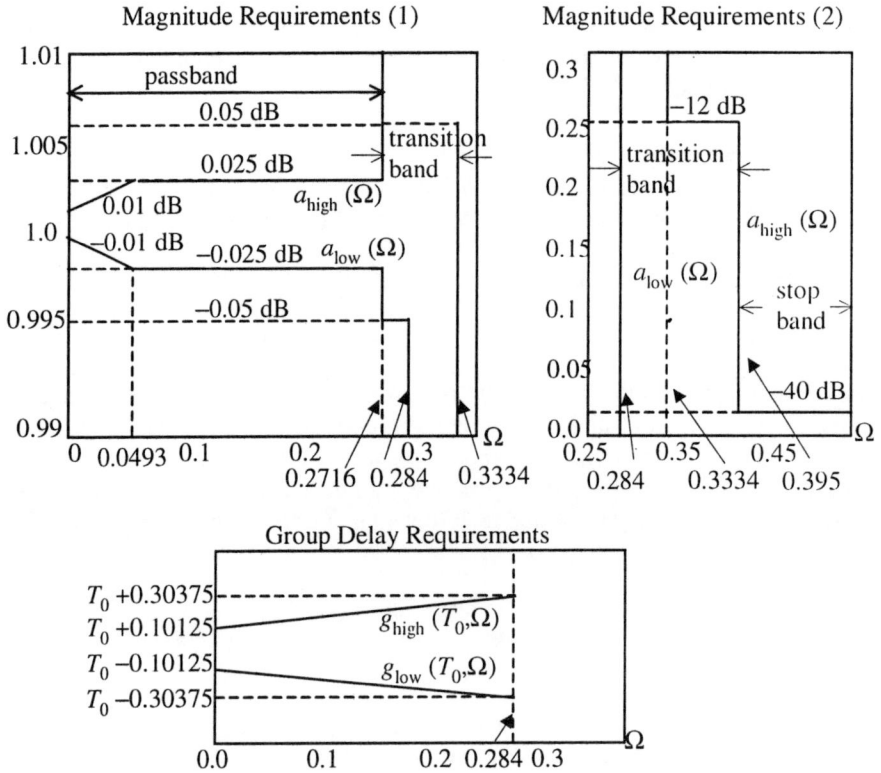

Fig. 7.7: Tolerance schemes for the magnitude and group delay of a graphics codec (ITU-CCIR [1985]). The qualifier 'dB' indicates a logarithmic value according to $20 \cdot \log_{10}(...)$. 'T' denotes the time normalized by T_s.

7.4 DESIGNING THE COST FUNCTION

The general transfer function for IIR-filters of Equation 7.9 exhibits the zeroes:

$$z_{0_n} = r_{0_n} \cdot e^{j2\pi\Phi_{o_n}}, \quad n = 1,2,...,N \tag{7.18}$$

as well as the poles:

$$z_{p_m} = r_{p_m} \cdot e^{j2\pi\Phi_{p_m}}, \quad m = 1,2,...,M \tag{7.19}$$

with:

$$r_{0_n}, r_{p_m}, \Phi_{0_n}, \Phi_{p_m} \in [0,1] \tag{7.20}$$

For the case in which Equation (7.9) exhibits only real filter coefficients a_n and b_m, the zeroes and poles of $H(z)$ are either real, or appear in complex conjugate pairs.

As was done in Keinath [1992], the graphics codec specifications from Figure 7.7 will be met by cascading a seventh-order linear phase FIR-pre-filter and an IIR-filter of order 10 with an overall magnitude response:

$$A_{GC}(\Omega) = \sum_{v=0}^{3} f_v \cdot 2\cos(\pi\Omega(v-3.5)) \cdot$$

$$\cdot \frac{\prod_{i=1}^{5}\sqrt{1-2r_{0_i} \cdot \cos(2\pi(\Omega-\Phi_{0_i}))+r_{0_i}^2}}{\prod_{j=1}^{4}\sqrt{1-2r_{p_j} \cdot \cos(2\pi(\Omega-\Phi_{p_j}))+r_{p_j}^2}} \cdot$$

$$\cdot \frac{\prod_{i=1}^{5}\sqrt{1-2r_{0_i} \cdot \cos(2\pi(\Omega+\Phi_{0_i}))+r_{0_i}^2}}{\prod_{j=1}^{4}\sqrt{1-2r_{p_j} \cdot \cos(2\pi(\Omega+\Phi_{p_j}))+r_{p_j}^2}} \cdot a_0$$

(7.21)

and a group delay of:

$$G_{GC}(\Omega) = 1.75 - \sum_{i=1}^{5}\frac{1-r_{0_i} \cdot \cos(2\pi(\Omega-\Phi_{0_i}))}{1-2r_{0_i} \cdot \cos(2\pi(\Omega-\Phi_{0_i}))+r_{0_i}^2}$$

$$- \sum_{i=1}^{5}\frac{1-r_{0_i} \cdot \cos(2\pi(\Omega+\Phi_{0_i}))}{1-2r_{0_i} \cdot \cos(2\pi(\Omega+\Phi_{0_i}))+r_{0_i}^2}$$

$$+ \sum_{j=1}^{4}\frac{1-r_{p_j} \cdot \cos(2\pi(\Omega-\Phi_{p_j}))}{1-2r_{p_j} \cdot \cos(2\pi(\Omega-\Phi_{p_j}))+r_{p_j}^2}$$

$$+ \sum_{j=1}^{4}\frac{1-r_{p_j} \cdot \cos(2\pi(\Omega+\Phi_{p_j}))}{1-2r_{p_j} \cdot \cos(2\pi(\Omega+\Phi_{p_j}))+r_{p_j}^2}$$

(7.22)

Figure 7.8 shows the flowgraph of just the IIR-filter.

As in Keinath [1992], the FIR-filter coefficients remain fixed, set to the values:

$$f_v = \{-0.033271, -0.019816, 0.169865, 0.415454\}$$

(7.23)

leaving only the radii and angles of poles and zeroes of the IIR part, as well as the constant a_0 as free parameters. The value a_0 in Equation 7.21, however, is a redundant parameter and should be held constant during the optimization process. Otherwise, the optimization procedure has infinitely many global optima from which to choose. Hence, the only parameters that are varied in the cost function are the radii, the angles of zeroes and the poles of the IIR-filter. Note that since the time constant T_0 in Figure 7.7 is not constrained, it will be a result of the design process.

Since this IIR-filter will be fashioned by a general-purpose function minimizer, the design objective must be restated as a cost function, which when minimized, yields the desired solution. The main part of the cost function is simply the value of the maximum absolute deviation of either the magnitude response: Equation 7.21, or the group delay: Equation 7.22, whichever deviation is greater. In addition, several penalties are included in the cost function which reflect special knowledge about the filter design problem. These penalties realize the following constraints:

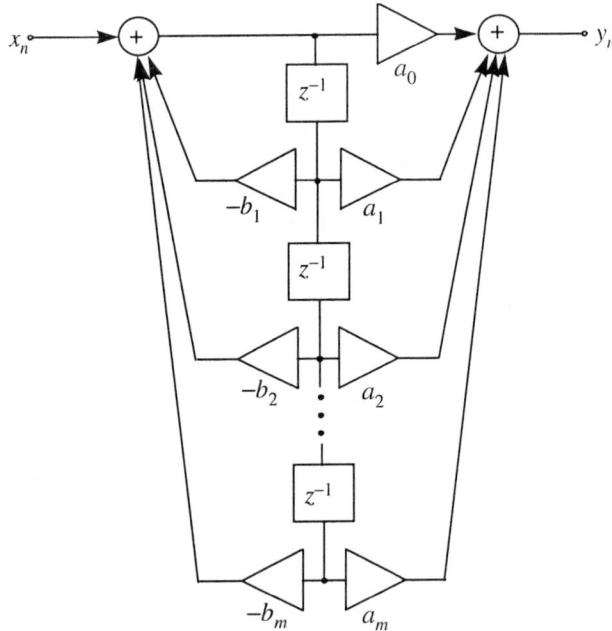

Fig. 7.8: Flowgraph of the IIR-filter which must be designed for $M=10$.

(1) All parameters must be positive. Although this restriction is not necessary for the angles Φ_{0_i}, Φ_{p_j}, it avoids redundant angle values.
(2) The radii r_{p_j} of the poles must be < 1 to ensure the stability of the IIR-filter.
(3) The angles Φ_{p_j} of the poles must be ≤ 0.284 because it doesn't make sense to locate poles in either the transition or stop bands of a filter.
(4) The radii r_{0_i} of the zeroes must be ≥ 1 to allow for phase compensation in the passband.
(5) The angles Φ_{0_i} of the zeroes must be ≤ 0.5 to avoid redundant angle values.

Violations are penalized by adding a positive value to the cost function. The magnitude of the penalty depends on the extent of the corresponding violation. The greater the violation is, the larger the penalty value will be. We now can build the cost function, $f(\underline{x})$, where $\underline{x}$ is the parameter vector:

$$\underline{x} = (x_1, x_2, ..., x_{18})^{\mathrm{T}} \tag{7.24}$$

with the mapping:

$$x_i = r_{0_i}, \quad i = 1,2,3,4,5 \tag{7.25}$$

$$x_{i+5} = \Phi_{0_i}, \quad i = 1,2,3,4,5 \tag{7.26}$$

$$x_{i+10} = r_{p_i}, \quad i = 1,2,3,4 \tag{7.27}$$

$$x_{i+14} = \Phi_{p_i}, \quad i = 1,2,3,4 \tag{7.28}$$

The mathematical formulation of the cost function $f(\underline{x})$ is:

$$f(\underline{x}) = \max\big(dev(A_{GC}(\Omega)), dev(G_{GC}(\Omega))\big) + \sum_{\mu=1}^{5} P_{\mu} \tag{7.29}$$

where:

$$dev(A_{GC}(\Omega)) = \max \begin{cases} A_{GC}(\Omega) - a_{high}(\Omega) & \text{if} \quad A_{GC}(\Omega) > a_{high}(\Omega) \\ a_{low}(\Omega) - A_{GC}(\Omega) & \text{if} \quad A_{GC}(\Omega) < a_{low}(\Omega) \\ 0 & \text{otherwise} \end{cases} \tag{7.30}$$

and

$$dev(G_{GC}(\Omega)) = \max \begin{cases} G_{GC}(\Omega) - g_{high}(T_0,\Omega) & \text{if} \quad G_{GC}(\Omega) > g_{high}(T_0,\Omega) \\ g_{low}(T_0,\Omega) - G_{GC}(\Omega) & \text{if} \quad G_{GC}(\Omega) < g_{low}(T_0,\Omega) \\ 0 & \text{otherwise} \end{cases} \tag{7.31}$$

In Equation 7.31, T_0 is always adjusted so that the maximum deviation from the requirements in Figure 7.7 is minimal. To realize the constraints listed above, the penalty terms P_{μ} in Equation 7.29 are computed as:

$$P_1 = \sum_{i=1}^{18} \begin{cases} 20000 - 100 \cdot x_i & \text{if} \quad x_i < 0 \\ 0 & \text{otherwise} \end{cases} \qquad \text{(all parameters} > 0) \tag{7.32}$$

$$P_2 = \sum_{i=1}^{5} \begin{cases} 2 + \dfrac{100}{x_i + 10^{-10}} & \text{if} \quad x_i < 1 \\ 0 & \text{otherwise} \end{cases} \qquad \text{(radii of zeroes} \geq 1) \tag{7.33}$$

$$P_3 = \sum_{i=6}^{10} \begin{cases} 2 + 100 \cdot x_i & \text{if} \quad x_i > 0.5 \\ 0 & \text{otherwise} \end{cases} \qquad \text{(angles of zeroes} \leq 0.5) \tag{7.34}$$

$$P_4 = \sum_{i=11}^{14} \begin{cases} 2 + 100 \cdot x_i & \text{if} \quad x_i \geq 1 \\ 0 & \text{otherwise} \end{cases} \qquad \text{(radii poles} < 1) \tag{7.35}$$

$$P_5 = \sum_{i=15}^{18} \begin{cases} 2 + 100 \cdot x_i & \text{if} \quad x_i > 0.284 \\ 0 & \text{otherwise} \end{cases} \qquad \text{(angles of poles} \leq 0.284) \tag{7.36}$$

A parameter vector $\underline{x}$ for which the cost function $f(\underline{x})$ is zero solves the filter design problem. The above example illustrates an important finding which has been experienced in all DE filter designs so far: the proper choice of the cost function is crucial; that is, a lot of knowledge about digital filters must be included into the design of the cost function to get a satisfactory result. The incorporation of knowledge into filter design means that the search space of the cost function is narrowed to those regions where it makes sense to perform a search. If this is not done, DE has enormous difficulties in finding a design solution.

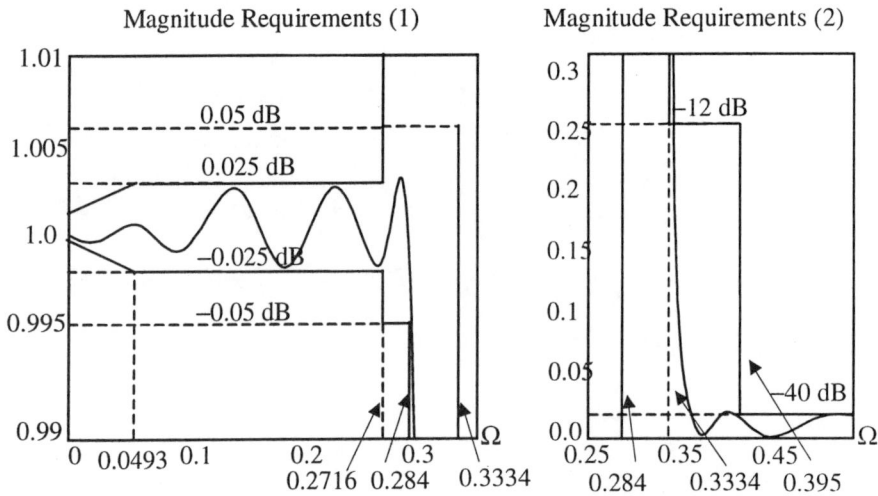

Fig. 7.9: Magnitude response of the filter design solution for $a_0 = 0.00390625$.

7.5. RESULTS FOR DESIGN EXAMPLE 7.1

The optimization task stated above was undertaken using the DE strategy: DE/current-to-best/1/exp in which the ith trial vector for generation G+1, $\vec{v}_{i,G+1}$, is created according to:

$$\vec{v}_{i,G+1} = \vec{x}_{i,G} + K \cdot (\vec{x}_{best,G} - \vec{x}_{i,G}) + F \cdot (\vec{x}_{r1,G} - \vec{x}_{r2,G}) \qquad (7.37)$$

The DE settings were: $NP=300$, $K=F=0.85$, $CR=1.0$ with $a_0 = 2^{-8} = 0.00390625$.

All parameters were initialized with uniformly distributed, randomly chosen, real values between 0 and 1. In order to properly detect the maximum of Equations 7.22 and 7.23, all functions were sampled at 100 equi-distant points in the pass band: $\Omega \in [0, 0.2716]$. To increase computational speed, only 20 sample points were used in the transition bands and stop band: $\Omega \in [0.395, 0.5]$. No particular effort was made to achieve the fastest possible convergence. With the above settings, the filter was designed after 1146 generations, corresponding to a total of 344,100 cost function evaluations. Overall computing time was several hours on a 486DX computer with 50MHz clock frequency. The resulting magnitude and group delay responses are depicted in Figures 7.9 and 7.10.

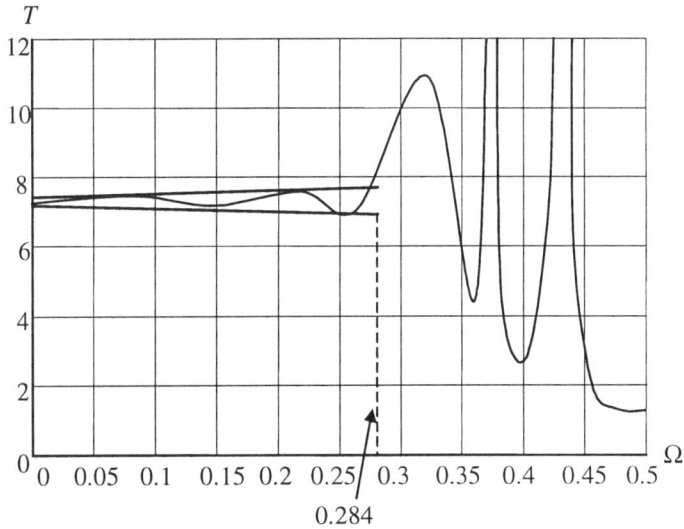

Fig. 7.10: Group delay response of the filter design solution for $a_0 = 0.00390625$.

The corresponding values produced for each parameter in this case are as follows:

$x_1 = 1.620493889$ $x_2 = 1.006124616$ $x_3 = 1.016987443$

$x_4 = 2.498671532$ $x_5 = 1.919012547$ $x_6 = 0.2243566662$

$x_7 = 0.3745155931$ $x_8 = 0.4304945767$ $x_9 = 0.02474720217$

$x_{10} = 0.1109348238$ $x_{11} = 0.636967894$ $x_{12} = 0.4702593982$

$x_{13} = 0.408888042$ $x_{14} = 0.8722907901$ $x_{15} = 0.2370584458$

$x_{16} = 0.125761658$ $x_{17} = 0.05192748457$ $x_{18} = 0.3109594584$

The design can be recomputed for many different values of the parameter a_0. An additional example is provided below, using the same DE strategy, with parameter setttings $NP=300$, $F=K=0.85$, $CR=1.0$, and $a_0 = 0.01$. In this case, DE needed 930 generations, or 279,300 function evaluations. The corresponding parameter values resulting from the optimization are:

$x_1 = 1.70534277$ $x_2 = 1.019881606$ $x_3 = 1.558364391$

$x_4 = 1.001873851$ $x_5 = 1.829733968$ $x_6 = 0.1320674717$

$x_7 = 0.3776784241$ $x_8 = 0.2309984416$ $x_9 = 0.4321155548$

$x_{10} = 0.04620760679$ $x_{11} = 0.636967894$ $x_{12} = 0.3932341039$

$x_{13} = 0.6438843012$ $x_{14} = 0.8722907901$ $x_{15} = 0.3089904487$

$x_{16} = 0.1219726913$ $x_{17} = 0.05192748457$ $x_{18} = 0.124328509$

The magnitude and group delay responses are shown in Figures 7.11 and 7.12.

Magnitude Requirements (1)   Magnitude Requirements (2)

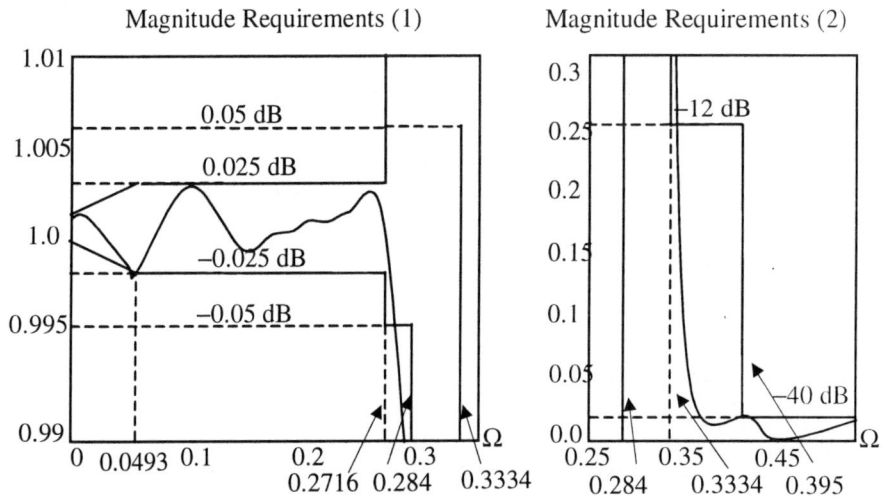

Fig. 7.11: Magnitude response of the filter design solution for $a_0 = 0.01$.

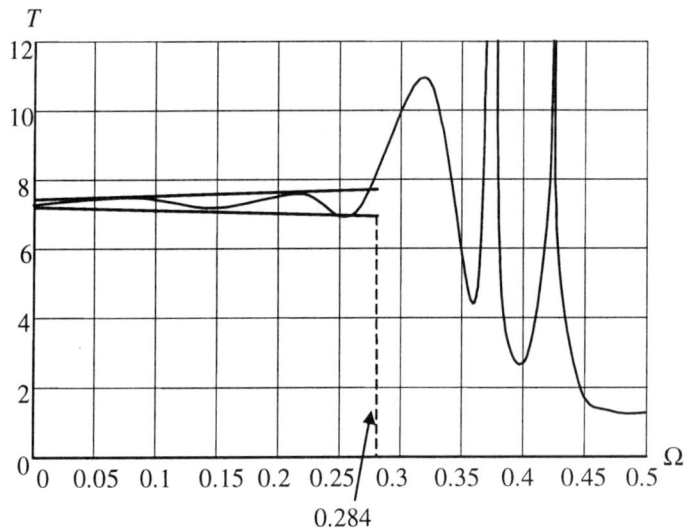

Fig. 7.12: Group delay response of the filter design solution for $a_0 = 0.01$.

It should be noted that the design of this filter is an extremely difficult task. An entire PhD dissertation has been devoted to the problem of designing IIR-filters with constraints in magnitude and group delay (Keinath [1992]). This makes it even more interesting that the above design problem could be solved with a general-purpose optimizer like DE.

7.6 EXAMPLE 7.2: DESIGNING FILTERS FOR A HOWLING REMOVAL UNIT

In order to demonstrate its applicability to real-world problems, DE has been used to design a howling removal unit (Storn [1996]). Two filters, a bandpass filter (Figure 7.13) and a lowpass filter (Figure 7.14) are needed for the unit.

Low computational complexity is one of the most important requirements for filters in this application, since the unit must operate in a real-time environment with limited resources. Therefore, it was crucial to design both the bandpass and lowpass filters with a minimum degree. To this end, the bandpass design was chosen to be a recursive digital filter (IIR-filter), whose transfer function had to meet specific magnitude constraints defined by a tolerance scheme. The lowpass filter was designed as a transversal filter (FIR-filter) without the usual linear phase requirement. The lowpass filter also had to meet magnitude specifications defined by a tolerance scheme. DE was chosen for both problems because, like case 2) in the list of motivations, specialized design software was unavailable.

The cost function for both the bandpass and the lowpass filters was defined to be:

$$f(\underline{x}) = \max\left(dev(A(\Omega)), \sum_{\mu=1}^{5} P_{\mu} \right) \tag{7.38}$$

with the following definition of the penalties P_{μ} :

a) For all parameters $par[i]$:

$$P_1 = 20{,}000 + par[i] * 100 \quad \text{if} \quad par[i] < 0$$

b) For all $par[i]$ denoting the radius of a zero of the transfer function:

$$P_2 = 2 + \frac{100}{|par[i] + 1.e - 7|} \quad \text{if} \quad par[i] < 1$$

c) For all $par[i]$ denoting a zero angle:

$$P_3 = 2 + par[i] * 100 \quad \text{if} \quad par[i] < 0.5$$

d) For all $par[i]$ denoting a pole radius:

$$P_4 = 2 + par[i] * 100 \quad \text{if} \quad par[i] >= 1$$

e) For all $par[i]$ denoting a pole angle:

$$P_5 = 2 + par[i] * 100 \quad \text{if} \quad par[i] \in \text{stopband of filter}$$

This cost function is similiar in structure to the one in the previous example. The sole difference is that in this example, only the largest penalty term contributes to the cost function, whereas in the previous example, all penalty terms contributed. This difference, however, is not really crucial to the design of any of these filters.

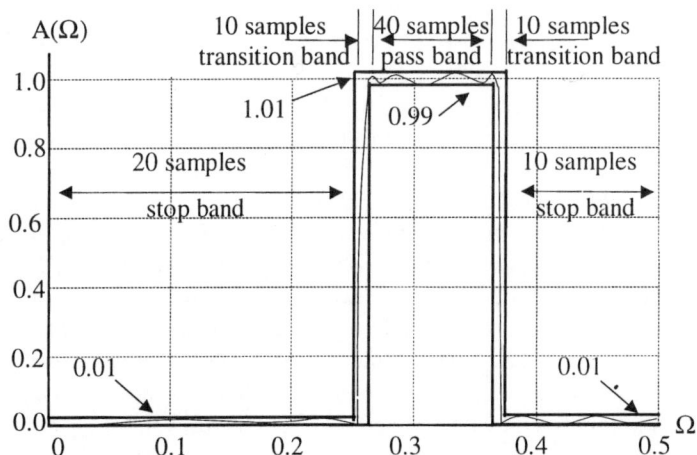

Fig. 7.13: Magnitude response of the bandpass filter after the design process.

To determine the deviation from the tolerance scheme, the magnitude response of each filter was sampled in the frequency domain. The number of samples that were used is indicated in Figures 7.13 and 7.14 which also show the final results of the design. The bandpass filter of Figure 7.14 was obtained using DE/best/exp/2, with $NP=300$, $F=0.5$ and $CR=1.0$. All parameters were initialized uniformly at random from the interval $[-2, +2]$. The entire design took 2,210,400 evaluations of the bandpass transfer function. A total of 24 parameters were used, including 6 zero radii, 6 zero angles, 6 pole radii and 6 pole angles in the complex z-plane (Rorabaugh [1993]). The overall gain constant a_0 was set to 0.005. The magnitude response still violates some parts of the tolerance scheme slightly, but the design was satisfactory for the howling remover. It should be noted that this filter with a degree of 6, achieved using DE, compares very favourably to designs obtained with traditional methods (in this case, the method of Yule Walker equations which needed a filter degree of 8). The coefficients according to Equation 7.9) of the bandpass filter are:

$a_0 = 0.005$ $a_1 = 0.006996762473$ $a_2 = -0.003461699001$

$a_3 = -0.02366392873$ $a_4 = -0.03755615279$ $a_5 = -0.03418922052$

$a_6 = 0.000384441606$ $a_7 = 0.05557145923$ $a_8 = 0.09735714644$

$a_9 = 0.1028533131$ $a_{10} = 0.0807185173$ $a_{11} = 0.04386262968$

$a_{12} = 0.01305463538$

$b_0 = 1.0$ $b_1 = 4.279090405$ $b_2 = 12.04419518$

$b_3 = 23.46417618$ $b_4 = 36.34767914$ $b_5 = 44.66229248$

$b_6 = 45.55633163$ $b_7 = 37.81253433$ $b_8 = 26.03436661$

$b_9 = 14.18435287$ $b_{10} = 6.132423401$ $b_{11} = 1.824242473$

$b_{12} = 0.3591913283$

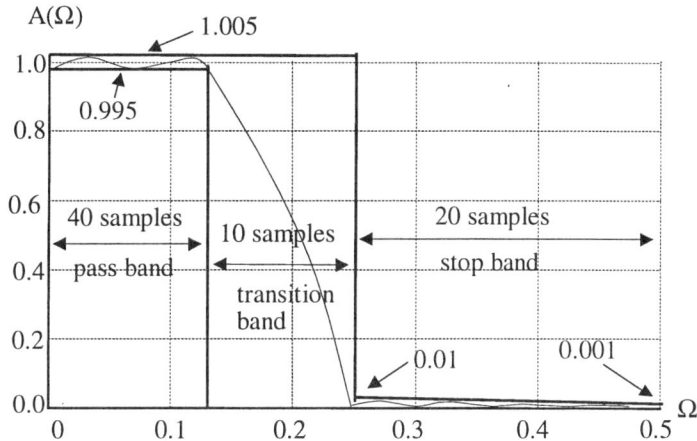

Fig. 7.14: Magnitude response of the lowpass filter after the design process.

The lowpass filter result of Figure 7.14 was obtained using DE/best/exp/2, with $NP=200$, $F=0.5$ and $CR=1.0$. Again, all parameters were initialized uniformly at random from the interval [-2, +2]. The design took 83,800 evaluations of the lowpass transfer function. A total of 16 parameters were used, including 8 zero radii and 8 zero angles in the complex z-plane. The overall gain constant a_0 was set to 0.005. DE accomplished the design with a filter of degree of 16, whereas the traditional least squares design needed a degree of 19. The coefficients according to Equation 7.6 are as follows:

$$a_0 = 0.005 \qquad a_1 = 0.01574276 \qquad a_2 = 0.005165873$$
$$a_3 = -0.05204853 \qquad a_4 = -0.1178162 \qquad a_5 = -0.1039745$$
$$a_6 = 0.03941562 \qquad a_7 = 0.2424996 \qquad a_8 = 0.3597494$$
$$a_9 = 0.3087258 \qquad a_{10} = 0.1521918 \qquad a_{11} = 0.0273716$$
$$a_{12} = -0.0009015155 \qquad a_{13} = 0.02845241 \qquad a_{14} = 0.04708275$$
$$a_{15} = 0.03073536 \qquad a_{16} = 0.007710777$$

7.7 FINAL THOUGHTS

It has been shown that DE can be used to design linear digital filters which, in general, is a very difficult task for a general-purpose optimizer. The key to success in this domain has been a properly designed cost function that includes the maximum deviation from the specifications as well as penalty terms to narrow the search and ensure filter stability. It was also beneficial to increase the penalty value as constraint violations increased. All optimizations were supported by continuous graphical monitoring of the parameter values as well as the corresponding transfer function of the lowest-cost vector. It was observed that DE control variable settings that produced rapid progress initially usually ended up causing the population to stagnate. The best indication of a successful optimization was a moderate improvement rate with the parameter values of the current best vector changing often and to a significant extent, especially at the beginning of the optimization.

Chapter Eight

Mechanical Engineering Design Optimization by Differential Evolution

Jouni Lampinen and Ivan Zelinka

8.1 INTRODUCTION

Most non-linear optimization methods assume that objective function variables are continuous. In practical engineering design work, however, problems are common in which some, or all, of the design parameters are discrete or integer variables. Discrete variables often occur because a design element is only available in a limited set of standard sizes. For example, the thickness of steel plate, the diameter of copper pipe, the size of a screw, the pitch of a gear tooth, the size of a roller bearing, etc. are often limited to a set of commercially available standard sizes. Integer variables occur in problems with identical design elements. Examples of integer variables include the number of: teeth on a gear, bolts or rivets needed to fix a structure, heat exchanger tubes, cooling fins on a heat sink, parallel V-belts in a transmission, coils of a spring, etc.

It is clear that a large fraction of engineering design optimization problems fall into the category of *mixed integer-discrete-continuous, non-linear programming* problems. Even so, the most frequently discussed methods in the literature are for solving continuous problems. Generally, continuous problems are considered to be easier to solve than discrete ones, suggesting that the presence of any non-continuous variables considerably increases the difficulty of finding a solution. In practice, problems containing integer or discrete variables are usually solved as though they were continuous with the nearest available discrete values then being chosen. In most such cases, this technique produces a result that is often quite far from optimal. The reason for using this approach is based on an appreciation of commonly used current methods. It is still commonly believed that there are no efficient, effective, robust, and easy-to-use non-linear programming methods currently available that are capable of handling mixed variables.

Another source of difficulty encountered in practical engineering design optimizations involves constraint handling. Real-world limitations frequently impose multiple, non-linear and non-trivial constraints on a design. Constraints can limit the feasible solutions to only a small subset of the design space.

In response to these demands, a novel approach for solving mixed integer-discrete-continuous, non-linear engineering design optimization problems has been developed based on the recently introduced Differential Evolution (DE) algorithm (see chapter six). This investigation describes the techniques needed to handle boundary constraints as well as those needed to simultaneously deal with several non-linear and non-trivial constraint functions. After introducing these techniques, three illustrative and practical numerical examples are presented. The first example designs a gear train with a specified gear ratio, the second problem minimizes the manufacturing cost of a pressure vessel, and the third example uses DE to design a coil spring with a minimum amount of steel. The mixed-variable methods used to solve these problems are discussed in detail and compared with published results obtained with other optimization methods for the same problems. Even though this investigation only focuses on engineering design applications, we note that DE can be applied, in principle at least, to solve any mixed integer-discrete-continuous optimization task.

8.2 MIXED INTEGER DISCRETE-CONTINUOUS NLP

A mixed integer-discrete-continuous, non-linear programming problem can be expressed as follows:

Find

$$X = \{x_1, x_2, x_3, ..., x_D\} = [X^{(i)}, X^{(d)}, X^{(c)}]^T$$

to minimize

$$f(X)$$

subject to constraints

$$g_j(X) \le 0, \quad j = 1, ..., m$$

and subject to boundary constraints

$$x_i^{(L)} \le x_i \le x_i^{(U)}, \quad i = 1, ..., D$$

where

$$X^{(i)} \in R^i, \ X^{(d)} \in R^d, \ X^{(c)} \in R^c$$

(8.1)

In Equation 8.1, $X^{(i)}$, $X^{(d)}$ and $X^{(c)}$ denote feasible subsets of integer, discrete and continuous variables, respectively. The above formulation is general and basically the same for all types of variables and only the structure of the design domain distinguishes one problem from another. While both integer and discrete variables have a discrete nature, only discrete variables can assume floating-point values. In practice, it is not uncommon for the discrete values of a feasible set to be unevenly spaced. This is the main reason why integer and discrete variables often handled differently.

Some researchers also define a further, fourth class of variables, so-called 'zero-one' (binary) variables. These variables can only assume the integer values, 0 or 1. This class of variables is important for many applications because it is capable of expressing many practically relevant machine states, such as a switch that can be either on or off, or a valve that can be either open or closed, or a device that is either connected or not, a clutch that is open or closed, and so forth. For this investigation, the class of binary-integer variables is treated as a special case of integer variables.

8.3 DIFFERENTIAL EVOLUTION

Price and Storn first introduced the Differential Evolution (DE) algorithm a few years ago. chapter six of this book provides a comprehensive and modern introduction to the method.

DE can be classified as an *evolutionary optimization algorithm*. At present, the best known representatives of this class are *genetic algorithms* (Goldberg [1989]) and *evolution strategies* (Schwefel [1995]). Currently, there are several variants of DE. The particular version used throughout this investigation is the *DE/rand/1/bin* scheme. The extension of DE to mixed-parameter optimization will be described in detail, but this particular scheme will be mentioned only briefly, since more detailed descriptions are provided in chapter six and Storn & Price [1997, 1997a]. Since the DE algorithm was originally designed to operate on continuous variables, the optimization of continuous problems is discussed first, while the manner in which this method has been adapted to handle integer and discrete variables is explained later.

Generally, the function to be optimized, f, is of the form:

$$f(X) : R^D \rightarrow R \qquad (8.2)$$

The optimization goal is to minimize the value of this *objective function f(X)*,

$$\min(f(X)) \qquad (8.3)$$

by optimizing the values of its parameters:

$$X = (x_1,...,x_D), \quad X \in R^D \qquad (8.4)$$

where X denotes a vector composed of D objective function parameters. Usually, the parameters of the objective function are also subject to lower and upper boundary constraints, $x^{(L)}$ and $x^{(U)}$ respectively:

$$x_j^{(L)} \leq x_j \leq x_j^{(U)}, \quad j = 1,...,D \qquad (8.5)$$

As with all evolutionary optimization algorithms, DE operates on a population, P_G, of candidate solutions, not just a single solution. In particular, DE maintains a population of constant size that consists of NP, real-valued vectors, $X_{i,G}$, where i indexes the population and G is the generation to which the population belongs.

$$P_G = X_{i,G}, \quad i = 1,...,NP, \quad G = 1,...,G_{\max} \qquad (8.6)$$

Additionally, each vector contains D real parameters (*chromosomes of individuals*):

$$X_{i,G} = x_{j,i,G}, \quad i = 1,...,NP, \quad j = 1,...,D \qquad (8.7)$$

In order to establish a starting point for optimum seeking, the population must be initialized. Often there is no more knowledge available about the location of a global optimum than the limits of the problem variables. In this case, a natural way to seed the initial population, $P_{G=0}$, is with random values chosen from within the given boundary constraints:

$$P_0 = x_{j,i,0} = rand_j[0,1] \cdot (x_j^{(U)} - x_j^{(L)}) + x_j^{(L)}, \quad i = 1,...,NP, \quad j = 1,...,D \qquad (8.8)$$

where $rand_j[0,1]$ denotes a uniformly distributed random value within range: [0.0,1.0] that is chosen anew for each j.

DE's self-referential population reproduction scheme is different from the population reproduction schemes employed by most other evolutionary algorithms. From the first generation forward, vectors in the current population P_G are randomly sampled and combined to create candidate vectors for the subsequent generation P_{G+1}. The population of candidate vectors, or 'trial' vectors $P'_{G+1} = U_{i,G+1} = u_{j,i,G+1}$ is generated as follows in Equation 8.9. Also see chapter six for further detail.

$$u_{j,i,G+1} = \begin{cases} v_{j,i,G+1} = x_{j,r_3,G} + F \cdot (x_{j,r_1,G} - x_{j,r_2,G}) & \text{if} \quad rand_j[0,1) \le CR \vee j = k \\ x_{j,i,G} & \text{otherwise} \end{cases}$$

where

$$i = 1,...,NP, \quad j = 1,...,D \qquad\qquad (8.9)$$

$k \in \{1,...,D\}$,   random parameter index, chosen for each i

$r_1, r_2, r_3 \in \{1,...,NP\}$,   randomly selected, except : $r_1 \ne r_2 \ne r_3 \ne i$

$CR \in [0,1], \quad F \in (0,1]$

The randomly chosen indexes, r_1, r_2 and r_3 are different from each other and also different from the running index i. New, random, integer values for r_1, r_2 and r_3 are chosen for each value of i, i.e. for each individual. The index k refers to a randomly chosen chromosome which is used to ensure that each individual trial vector $U_{i,G+1}$ differs from its counterpart in the previous generation $X_{i,G}$ by at least one parameter. A new random integer value is assigned to k prior to the construction of each trial vector, i.e. for each value of the index i.

F and CR are DE control parameters. Like NP, both values remain constant during the search process. F is a real-valued factor in range (0.0,1.0+] that scales the differential variations. The upper limit on F has been empirically determined. Values of F greater than unity, while possible, do not appear to be productive. CR is a real-valued crossover factor in range [0.0,1.0] that controls the probability that a trial vector parameter will come from the randomly chosen, mutated vector $v_{j,i,G+1}$ instead of from the current vector $x_{j,i,G}$. Generally, both F and CR affect the convergence velocity and robustness of the search process. Their optimal values are dependent both on objective function characteristics and on the population size, NP. Usually, suitable values for F, CR and NP can be found by trial-and-error after a few tests using different values. Practical advice on how to select control parameters NP, F and CR can be found in chapter six, in Storn [1996], and Storn & Price [1997, 1997a].

DE's selection scheme also differs from other evolutionary algorithms. The population for the next generation P_{G+1} is selected from the current population P_G and the child population, according to the following rule:

$$X_{i,G+1} = \begin{cases} U_{i,G+1} = u_{j,i,G+1} & \text{if} \quad f(U_{i,G+1}) \le f(X_{i,G}) \\ X_{i,G} & \text{otherwise} \end{cases} \qquad (8.10)$$

Thus, each individual of the temporary population is compared with its counterpart in the current population. Assuming that the objective function is to be minimized, the vector with the lower objective function value wins a place in the next generation's population. As a result, all the individuals of the next generation are as good or better than their counterparts in the current generation. The interesting point concerning DE's selection scheme is that a trial vector is only compared to one individual, not to all the individuals in the current population.

8.4 CONSTRAINT HANDLING

8.4.1 Boundary constraints

In boundary constrained problems, it is essential to ensure that parameter values lie inside their allowed ranges after reproduction. A simple way to guarantee this is to replace parameter values that violate boundary constraints with random values generated within the feasible range:

$$u_{j,i,G+1} = \begin{cases} rand_j[0,1] \cdot (x_j^{(U)} - x_j^{(L)}) + x_j^{(L)} & \text{if } u_{j,i,G+1} < x_j^{(L)} \vee u_{j,i,G+1} > x_j^{(U)} \\ u_{j,i,G+1} & \text{otherwise} \end{cases}$$

where

$$i = 1,...,NP, \quad j = 1,...,D$$

(8.11)

This is the method that was used for this work. Another, less efficient method for keeping trial vectors within bounds is to regenerate the offending parameter value according to Equation 8.9 as many times as is necessary to satisfy the boundary constraint. It should also be mentioned that DE's generating scheme can extend its search beyond the space defined by initial parameter limits (Equations 8.8 and 8.9) if allowed to do so. This can be a beneficial property for unconstrained optimization problems because optima that are outside of the initialized range can often be located.

8.4.2 Constraint functions

We use a soft-constraint (penalty) approach to implement the constraint functions. A constraint function introduces a measure that gauges the distance to the feasible region. This approach is not used, however, to reject unfeasible solutions (as it is in the case of hard-constraints). One possible soft-constraint approach involves formulating the objective function as follows:

$$f_{cost}(X) = (f(X) + a) \cdot \prod_{i=1}^{m} c_i^{b_i}$$

where

$$c_i = \begin{cases} 1.0 + s_i \cdot g_i(X) & \text{if } g_i(X) > 0 \\ 1 & \text{otherwise} \end{cases}$$

$$s_i \geq 1, \quad b_i \geq 1, \quad \min(f(X)) + a > 0$$

(8.12)

The constant a ensures that only non-negative values will be assigned to $f(X)$. When the value of a is set high enough, it does not otherwise affect the search process. The constant s scales the constraint function $g(X)$ while the exponent b serves to modify the overall shape of the optimization surface. Generally, higher values of the constants s and b are used when the range of the constraint function $g(X)$ is expected to be low. Usually, setting $s=1$ and $b=1$ works satisfactorily. Ordinarily, if one of the constraint functions $g_i(X)$ remains violated after the optimization run, it will be necessary to rerun the process using higher values for s_i and/or b_i.

In many real-world engineering design optimizations, the number of constraint functions is relatively high and the constraints are often non-trivial. It may well be, for example, that feasible solutions comprise only a small subset of the space. Feasible solutions may also divide the search space into isolated 'islands'. Further, the user may easily define totally conflicting constraints so that no feasible solutions exist at all. Even so, if two or more constraints conflict so that no feasible solution exists, DE can find the nearest feasible solution. In the case of non-trivial constraints, the user can often judge which of the constraints are conflicting on the basis of the nearest feasible solution. It is then possible to redesign the objective function in order to address these issues, or reconsider the problem setting itself in order to resolve the conflict.

Another benefit of the soft-constraint based approach is that the search space remains continuous. Multiple hard constraints often split the search space into many separated islands of feasible solutions. This discontinuity introduces stalling points for some genetic searches and also raises the possibity of new, locally optimal areas near the island borders. For these reasons, a soft-constraint approach is considered essential. It should be mentioned here that many traditional optimization methods are only able to handle problems which have only hard-constraints. For evolutionary optimization, the soft-constraint method was found to be a natural approach.

8.5 HANDLING INTEGER AND DISCRETE VARIABLES

In its canonical form, the Differential Evolution algorithm is only capable of handling continuous variables. Extending it to optimize integer variables, however, is very easy and requires only a couple of simple modifications. First, integer values should be used to evaluate the objective function, even though DE itself still works internally with continuous floating-point values. Thus:

$$f(y_i), \quad i = 1, \ldots, D$$

where

$$y_i = \begin{cases} x_i & \text{for continuous variables} \\ INT(x_i) & \text{for integer variables} \end{cases} \qquad (8.13)$$

$$x_i \in X$$

$INT()$ is a function for converting a real value to an integer value by truncation. Truncation is performed here for evaluating trial vectors and for handling boundary constraints. Truncated values are not elsewhere assigned. Thus, DE works with a population of continuous variables regardless of the corresponding object variable type. This is essential for maintaining the diversity of the population and the robustness of the algorithm.

Instead of Equation 8.8, integer variables should be initialized as follows:

$$P_0 = x_{j,i,0} = rand_j[0,1] \cdot (x_j^{(U)} - x_j^{(L)} + 1) + x_j^{(L)}, \quad i = 1, \ldots, NP, \quad j = 1, \ldots, D \qquad (8.14)$$

Additionally, instead of Equation 8.11, boundary constraints for integer variables should be handled according to the prescription provided in Equation 8.15 below:

$$u_{j,i,G+1} = \begin{cases} rand_j[0,1] \cdot (x_j^{(U)} - x_j^{(L)} + 1) + x_j^{(L)} & \text{if} \quad INT(u_{j,i,G+1}) < x_j^{(L)} \\ & \qquad\qquad \vee INT(u_{j,i,G+1}) > x_j^{(U)} \\ u_{j,i,G+1} & \text{otherwise} \end{cases}$$

where $\qquad\qquad\qquad\qquad\qquad\qquad\qquad\qquad\qquad\qquad\qquad\qquad$ (8.15)

$$i = 1,...,NP, \quad j = 1,...,D$$

Discrete values can also be handled in a straightforward manner. Suppose that the subset of discrete variables $X^{(d)}$ contains l elements that can be assigned to variable x:

$$X^{(d)} = x_i^{(d)}, \quad i = 1,...,l$$

where $\qquad\qquad\qquad\qquad\qquad\qquad\qquad\qquad\qquad\qquad\qquad\qquad$ (8.16)

$$x_i^{(d)} < x_{i+1}^{(d)}$$

Instead of the discrete value x_i itself, we may assign its index i to x. Now the discrete variable can be handled as an integer variable that is boundary constrained to range $1,...,l$. To evaluate the objective function, the discrete value x_i is used instead of its index i. In other words, instead of optimizing the value of the discrete variable directly, we optimize the value of its index i. Only during evaluation is the indicated discrete value used. Once the discrete problem has been converted into an integer one, the previously described methods for handling integer variables can be applied (Equations 8.13–8.15).

8.6 NUMERICAL EXAMPLES

To discover the effectiveness of the techniques proposed in sections 8.4 and 8.5, three numerical examples were optimized using DE and the soft-constraint approach (Table 8.1). These non-linear, engineering design optimization problems with discrete, integer and continuous variables were first investigated by Sandgren [1990] and subsequently by many other researchers (Fu et al [1991], Loh & Papalambros [1991, 1991a], Zhang & Wang [1993], Chen & Tsao [1993], Li & Chou [1994], Wu & Chow [1995], Lin et al [1995], Thierauf & Cai [1997], Cao & Wu [1997]) who applied a variety of optimization techniques (Table 8.2). These problems represent optimization situations involving discrete, integer and continuous variables that are similar to those encountered in everyday mechanical engineering design tasks. As the problems are clearly defined and fairly easy to understand, they form a suitable basis for comparing alternative optimization methods.

Table 8.1: Summary of test problems.

			Number of Variables		
Example	Description	Total	Discrete	Integer	Continuous
8.1	Design of a Gear Train	4	0	4	0
8.2	Design of a Pressure Vessel	4	2	0	2
8.3	Design of a Coil Spring	3	1	1	1

Table 8.2: Alternative methods used to solve the test problems.

Solution technique	Reference
Branch & Bound using Sequential Quadratic Programming	Sandgren [1990]
Integer-Discrete-Continuous Non-Linear Programming	Fu et al [1991]
Sequential Linearization Algorithm	Loh & Papalambros [1991, 1991a]
Simulated Annealing	Zhang & Wang [1993]
Genetic Algorithm	Chen & Tsao [1993]
Non-Linear Mixed-Discrete Programming	Li & Chou [1994]
Meta-Genetic Algorithm	Wu & Chow [1995]
Modified Genetic Algorithm	Lin et al [1995]
Two-level Parallel Evolution Strategy	Thierauf & Cai [1997]
Evolutionary Programming	Cao & Wu [1997]
Differential Evolution	this chapter

8.6.1 Example 8.1: Designing a gear train

The first example problem is to optimize the gear ratio for the compound gear train arrangement shown in Figure 8.1. The gear ratio for a reduction gear train is defined as the ratio of the angular velocity of the output shaft to that of the input shaft. In order to produce the desired overall gear ratio, the compound gear train is constructed out of two pairs of gearwheels, d–a and b–f. The overall gear ratio i_{tot} between the input and output shafts can be expressed as:

$$i_{tot} = \frac{\omega_o}{\omega_i} = \frac{z_d z_b}{z_a z_f} \qquad (8.17)$$

where ω_o and ω_i are the angular velocities of the output and input shafts, respectively, and z denotes the number of teeth on each gearwheel.

The optimization problem is to find the number of teeth for gearwheels d, a, b and f in order to produce a gear ratio i_{tot} as close as possible to the target ratio: $i_{trg} = 1/6.931$. For each gear, the minimum number of teeth is 12 and the maximum is 60.

The problem is formulated as follows:

Find
$$X = (x_1, x_2, x_3, x_4) = (z_d, z_b, z_a, z_f), \quad x \in \{12, 13, \ldots, 60\}$$
to minimize
$$f(X) = (i_{trg} - i_{tot})^2 = \left(\frac{1}{6.931} - \frac{x_1 x_2}{x_3 x_4} \right)^2 \qquad (8.18)$$
subject to
$$12 \le x_i \le 60, \quad i = 1,2,3,4.$$

Thus, the goal is to find optimum values for four integer variables that will minimize the squared difference between the desired gear ratio i_{trg} and current gear ratio i_{tot}. For this problem, each variable is subject only to upper and lower boundary constraints.

The gear train problem was solved using the *DE/rand/1/bin* strategy with control settings of: *NP*=100, *F*=0.60 and *CR*=1.00. The integer techniques described in section 8.4.1 were invoked to handle boundary constraints. Because no constraint functions were involved, the objective (cost) function was simply defined to be the squared error, i.e. *f(X)*:

$$f_{cost}(X) = f(X) \tag{8.19}$$

Table 8.3 lists the various gear train solutions and compares DE's result with those reported in Sandgren [1990], Fu et al [1991], Loh & Papalambros [1991a], Zhang & Wang [1993], Lin et al [1995], Wu & Chow [1995], and Cao & Wu [1997]. We can observe from Table 8.3 that the solution found by DE was equally as good as the best solution in the literature. In addition, it should be noted that DE provided different results from run to run with the same objective function value (Table 8.4).

By inspecting Equation 8.18, it is obvious that there are four global optima. Because DE can work with a population of solutions rather than just a single solution, it is capable of finding multiple global optima for this problem. By using a sufficiently large population, it is possible to obtain all four alternative solutions in a single run. Despite that, only one solution was extracted from the population of the last generation because the other three solutions can be found in a trivial way based on one solution and the symmetry of Equation 8.18. In practice, however, there exist optimization tasks with multiple global optima that cannot be detected so simply.

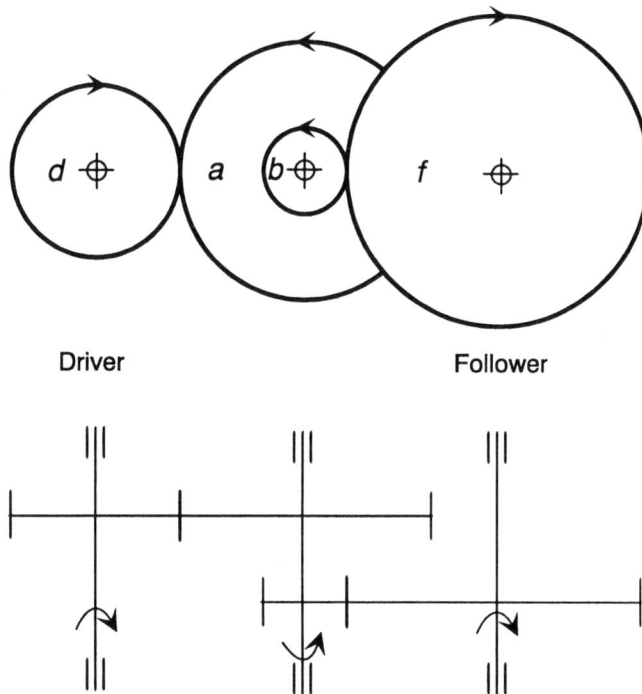

Fig. 8.1: Compound gear train for Example 8.1.

Table 8.3: Best solutions for the gear train problem. S90 = Sandgren [1990], F91 = Fu et al [1991], L91 = Loh & Papalambros [1991a], Z93 = Zhang & Wang [1993], L95 = Lin et al [1995], W95 = Wu & Chow [1995], C97 = Cao & Wu [1997], TC = this chapter.

Item	Optimum Solution								Type of variable
	S90	F91	L91	Z93	L95	W95	C97	TC*	
x_1 (z_d)	18	14	19	30	19	19	30	16	integer
x_2 (z_b)	22	29	16	15	16	16	15	19	integer
x_3 (z_a)	45	47	42	52	49	43	52	43	integer
x_4 (z_f)	60	59	50	60	43	49	60	49	integer
$f(x)$	5.7×10^{-6}	4.5×10^{-6}	0.233×10^{-6}	2.36×10^{-9}	**2.7×10^{-12}**	**2.7×10^{-12}**	2.36×10^{-9}	**2.7×10^{-12}**	
Gear Ratio	0.146666	0.146411	0.144762	0.144231	0.144281	0.144281	0.144231	0.144281	
Error [%]	1.65	1.17	0.334	0.034	0.00114	0.00114	0.034	0.00114	

Table 8.4: Alternative solutions for the gear train problem found by DE.

Solution	z_d	z_b	z_a	z_f
1	19	16	43	49
2	16	19	43	49
3	19	16	49	43
4	16	19	49	43

One may wonder why a single, globally optimal solution is not always sufficient when multiple global optima exist. One reason is that the sensitivity of the objective function to small changes in its variables may be different at the alternative optimal points. In practice, it is often important to select the most robust solution, i.e. that with the least sensitivity to noise. For example, it is possible that the optimized design variables cannot effectively be manufactured. Alternatively, the design parameters may change during the lifetime of the machine due, for example, to normal wear of its components. In cases such as these, robust global optima are to be preferred over optima which display high sensitivity to design implementation errors.

Results for DE were recorded after 300 generations, corresponding to 30,000 evaluations of the objective function. The computation time required was 0.81 seconds using a PC with an AMD K6-233 MHz processor (SPECfp95 rating 5.5 (SPEC [1995])). In order to evaluate the robustness of the DE algorithm, 100 independent trials were performed. All of these runs yielded the reported value of $f(X)$. As mentioned, different solutions were obtained from run to run because of the existence of multiple global optima. These alternative solutions are illustrated in Table 8.4.

8.6.2 Example 8.2: Designing a pressure vessel

The second example is to design a compressed air storage tank with a working pressure of 3,000 psi and a minimum volume of 750 ft^3. As Figure 8.2 shows, the cylindrical pressure vessel is capped at both ends by hemispherical heads. Using rolled steel plate, the shell is to be made in two halves that are joined by two longitudinal welds to form a cylinder. Each head is forged and then welded to the shell.

The objective in this example is to minimize the manufacturing cost of the pressure vessel. The manufacturing cost of the pressure vessel is a combination of material cost, welding cost and forming cost. Refer to Sandgren [1990] for more details on how cost is determined. The design variables which apply in this example are shown in Figure 8.2. Variables L and R are both continuous while T_s and T_h are both discrete. The thickness of the shell, T_s, and the head, T_h, are both required to be set at standard sizes. For this example, steel plate was available in thicknesses which were multiples of 0.0625 inch. The problem can be formulated as follows:

Find
$$X = (x_1, x_2, x_3, x_4) = (T_s, T_h, R, L)$$
to minimize
$$f(X) = 0.6224 x_1 x_3 x_4 + 1.7781 x_2 x_3^2 + 3.1611 x_1^2 x_4 + 19.84 x_1^2 x_3$$
subject to
$$g_1(X) = 0.0193 x_3 - x_1 \leq 0 \tag{8.20}$$
$$g_2(X) = 0.00954 x_3 - x_2 \leq 0$$
$$g_3(X) = 750.0 \times 1728.0 - \pi x_3^2 x_4 - \frac{4}{3} \pi x_3^3 \leq 0$$
$$g_4(X) = x_4 - 240.0 \leq 0$$
$$g_5(X) = 1.1 - x_1 \leq 0$$
$$g_6(X) = 0.6 - x_2 \leq 0$$

The objective function, $f(X)$, represents the total manufacturing cost of the pressure vessel as a function of the design variables. The constraints $g_1, ..., g_6$ quantify the restrictions to which the pressure vessel design must adhere. These limits arise from a variety of sources. For example, the minimal wall thickness of the shell T_s (g_1) and heads T_h (g_2) with respect to the shell radius are limited by the pressure vessel design code. The volume of the vessel must be at least the specified 750 ft^3 (g_3). Available rolling equipment limits the length of the shell, L, to no more than 20 feet (g_4). According to the pressure vessel design code, the thickness of the shell T_s is not to be less than 1.1 inches (g_5) and the thickness of the head T_h is not to be less than 0.6 inches (g_6).

The DE control variables used to solve the pressure vessel design problem were: $NP=20$, $F=0.70$ and $CR=0.90$. The problem statements do not define the boundaries for the design variables, but the constraints g_4, g_5 and g_6 are pure boundary constraints, so they were handled as lower boundary constraints for x_1 and x_2 and as an upper boundary constraint for x_4, respectively. The lower boundaries for x_3 and x_4 can be set to zero, since common sense demands that they must be non-negative values. The upper boundaries for x_1, x_2 and x_3, however, must still be specified in order to define the search space. Consequently, these bounds were arbitrarily set high enough to make it highly probably that the global optimum lies inside of the defined search space. Since the possibility existed that the global optimum was outside of the initially defined search space, these estimated bounds were used only for initializing the population according to Equation 8.11. DE was then allowed to extend the search beyond these boundaries. The possibility of using this kind of 'loose' boundary constraint for variables is one of the advantages of DE. In practical engineering design work, it is not unusual for one or more boundaries to be unknown and the distance to the optimum cannot be reliably estimated. The boundary constraints used for each variable are shown in Table 8.5. The other constraints g_1, g_2 and g_3 were handled as constraint functions.

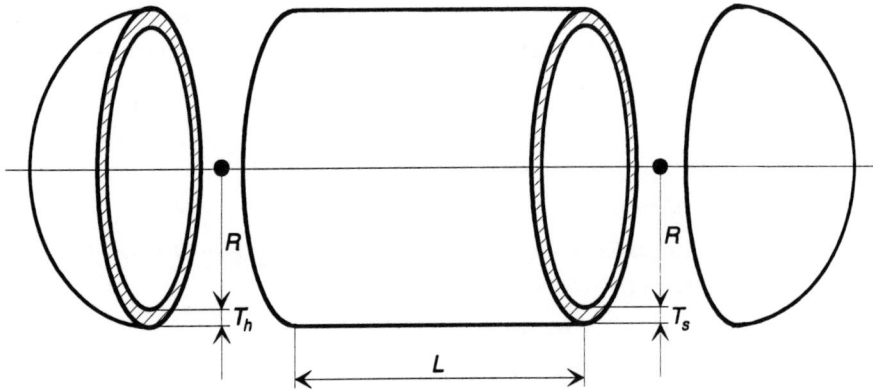

Fig. 8.2: Pressure vessel for Example 8.2.

The cost function for DE was formulated as follows:

$$f_{\text{cost}}(X) = f(X) \cdot \prod_{i=1}^{3} c_i^2$$

where

$$c_i = \begin{cases} 1.0 + s_i \cdot g_i(X) & \text{if} \quad g_i(X) > 0 \\ 1 & \text{otherwise} \end{cases}$$

$$s_1 = 1.0 \cdot 10^{10}, \; s_2 = s_3 = 1.0$$

(8.21)

Notice that it is not necessary to evaluate the constraint functions g_4, g_5 and g_6 because they were handled as boundary constraints and DE was not allowed to generate a candidate vector that violated any of them.

In researching this problem, at least three different formulations were found in the literature. To enable a more comprehensive comparison with the other methods, all three cases were solved using DE. Case A is an exception to the problem statements above, since all of the variables are treated as continuous. In Table 8.6, DE's results for Case A are compared to those reported in Sandgren [1990] and Fu et al [1991]. Case B is formulated according the original problem statements. The results and comparisons of DE with Sandgren [1990], Fu et al [1991], Loh & Papalambros [1991a], and Wu & Chow [1995] are in Table 8.7. Case C, reported in Table 8.8, also differs from the original problem statements. For some unknown reason, Li & Chou [1994], Thierauf & Cai [1997], and Cao & Wu [1997] have used a slightly reformulated constraint-function g_5 as follows:

$$g_5(X) = 1.0 - x_1 \le 0 \qquad\qquad (8.22)$$

Table 8.5: Boundary constraints used for the pressure vessel example.

Lower limitation	Constraint	Upper limitation
Constraint g_5	$1.1 \le x_1 \le 12.5$	Roughly guessed*
Constraint g_6	$0.6 \le x_2 \le 12.5$	Roughly guessed*
Non-negative value of x_3	$0.0 \le x_3 \le 240.0$	Roughly guessed*
Non-negative value of x_4	$0.0 \le x_4 \le 240.0$	Constraint g_4

*The value of this boundary is not given among the problem statements. Thus, the value is estimated roughly and used only for initialization of population. DE was allowed to extend the search beyond this limit.

This modification extends the region of feasible solutions and also makes it possible to obtain a significantly lower objective function value. All of the solutions of Li & Chou [1994], Thierauf & Cai [1997], and Cao & Wu [1997] lie in the extended region of the search space. Because of that, they cannot be fairly compared with the results obtained using Sandgren's original problem statements (Sandgren [1990]). Thus, Cases A, B and C are not comparable because they represent differently formulated problems.

As Tables 8.6–8.8 show, DE found a better solution for each pressure vessel design problem than the best solution found in the literature. Computations were carried out to 500 generations in all three cases, corresponding to 10,000 evaluations of the cost function. Computation took 0.35 seconds on a PC with an AMD K6-233 MHz processor (SPECfp95 rating 5.5 [SPEC95]). One hundred independent runs were performed for each case and all trials yielded the reported value of $f(X)$ or (marginally) better. In addition, all solutions were within the feasible design domain.

Table 8.6: Optimal solutions for the pressure vessel problem. Case A: all variables are treated as continuous. S90 = Sandgren [1990], F91 = Fu et al [1991], TC = this chapter.

Item	Optimum solution, Case A			Type of variable
	S90	F91	TC	
x_1 (T_s) [inch]	1.1	1.100001	1.100000	Continuous
x_2 (T_h) [inch]	0.6	0.600016	0.600000	Continuous
x_3 (R) [inch]	47.7008	48.35145	56.99482	Continuous
x_4 (L) [inch]	117.701	111.9893	51.00125	Continuous
$g_1(X)$	0.179	0.166818	9.0314×10^{-17}	
$g_2(X)$	0.145	0.138743	0.056269	
$g_3(X)$	0.0	18.0	2.1316×10^{-11}	
$g_4(X)$	122.299	128.0107	189.00	
$f(X)$ [$]	**7867.0**	**7790.588**	**7019.031**	
	100.0%	99.0%	89.2%	

Table 8.7: Optimal solutions for the pressure vessel problem. Case B: solved according to the original problem statements (Sandgren [1990]). S90 = Sandgren [1990], F91 – Fu et al [1991], L91 = Loh & Papalambros [1991a], W95 = Wu & Chow [1995], TC = this chapter.

Item	Optimum solution, Case B*					Type of variable
	S90	F91	L91	W95	TC	
x_1 (T_s) [inch]	1.125	1.125	1.125	1.125	1.125	Discrete
x_2 (T_h) [inch]	0.625	0.625	0.625	0.625	0.625	Discrete
x_3 (R) [inch]	48.97	48.38070	58.2901**	58.1978	58.29016	Cont.
x_4 (L) [inch]	106.72	111.7449	43.693	44.2930	43.69266	Cont.
$g_1(X)$	0.179	0.191250	1.068×10^{-6}	0.001782	4.8355×10^{-17}	
$g_2(X)$	0.1578	0.163449	0.068912	0.069793	0.068912	
$g_3(X)$	3.0	75.8750	0.429283	974.5829	1.6087×10^{-11}	
$g_4(X)$	133.284	128.2551	196.3070	195.7070	196.3073	
$f(X)$ [$]	**7982.5**	8048.619	**7197.734****	7207.497	<u>7197.729</u>	
	100.0%	100.8%	90.2%**	90.3%	90.2%	

*In Zhang & Wang [1993] and Lin et al [1995] it is reported that the value of $f(X) = 7197.7$ was reached. Because neither a more accurate result, nor details of the result were provided, they are not included in this comparison.
**No values for constraint functions were reported in Loh & Papalambros [1991a]. Also, the optimum solution was too inaccurately reported to reconstruct the results properly. The reported value $x_3 = 58.290$, causes a violation of constraint g_3. Because of that, 58.2901 was used here for reconstructing the constraint functions and target function values. In Loh & Papalambros [1991a], a value of $f(X) = 7197.7$ was originally reported.

Table 8.8: Optimal solutions for pressure vessel problem, Case C: different constraint-function, g_5, with respect to the original problem statements (Sandgren [1990]). L94 = Li & Chou [1994], C97 = Cao & Wu [1997], T97 = Thierauf & Cai [1997], TC = this chapter.

Item	Optimum solution, Case C				Type of variable
	L94	C97	T97	TC	
x_1 (T_s) [inch]	1.000	1.000	1.000	1.000	Discrete
x_2 (T_h) [inch]	0.625	0.625	0.625	0.625	Discrete
x_3 (R) [inch]	51.250	51.1958	51.812	51.81347	Cont.
x_4 (L) [inch]	90.991	90.7821	84.591	84.57853	Cont.
$g_1(X)$	1.011	0.0119	0.000	8.8688×10^{-17}	
$g_2(X)$	0.136	0.1366	0.131	0.13070	
$g_3(X)$	18759.754	13584.5631	15.000	7.5602×10^{-11}	
$g_4(X)$	149.009	149.2179	155.409	155.422	
$f(X)$ [$]	**7127.3**	7108.6160	7006.9	<u>7006.358</u>	
	100.0%	99.7%	98.3%	98.3%	

8.6.3 Example 8.3: Designing a coil compression spring

The third example involves the design of a coil compression spring. The spring is illustrated in Figure 8.3. The design objectives for this spring are that it is to be a helical compression spring to which a strictly axial and constant load will be applied. The objective is to minimize the volume of spring steel wire needed to manufacture the spring. The design variables are the number of spring coils N, the outside diameter of the spring D, and the spring wire diameter d. This example contains integer, discrete and continuous variables. The number of spring coils N is an integer variable and the outside diameter D is a continuous variable. Additionally, the spring wire diameter d is only available in the standard (discrete) sizes shown in Table 8.9.

Table 8.9: Allowable spring steel wire diameters for the coil spring design problem

0.009	0.0095	0.0104	0.0118	0.0128	0.0132
0.014	0.015	0.0162	0.0173	0.018	0.020
0.023	0.025	0.028	0.032	0.035	0.041
0.047	0.054	0.063	0.072	0.080	0.092
0.105	0.120	0.135	0.148	0.162	0.177
0.192	0.207	0.225	0.244	0.263	0.283
0.307	0.331	0.362	0.394	0.4375	0.500

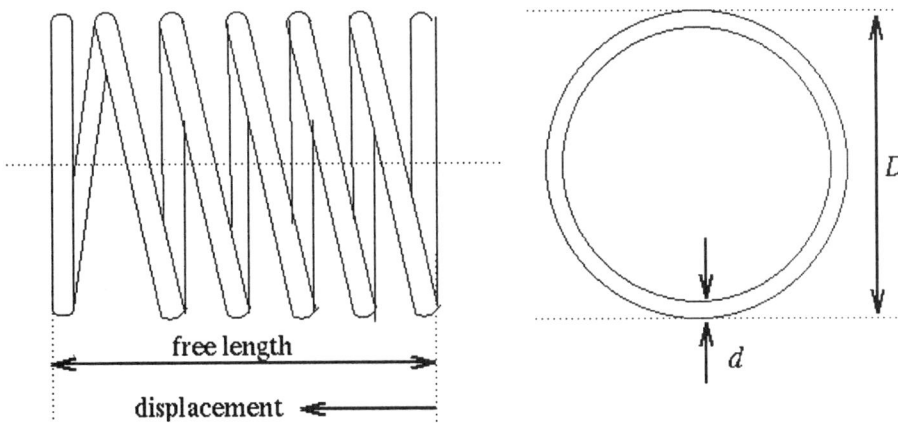

Fig. 8.3: Coil spring for Example 8.3.

The problem is formulated as follows in Equation 8.23:

Find

$$X = (x_1, x_2, x_3) = (N, D, d)$$

to minimize

$$f(X) = \frac{\pi^2 x_2 x_3^2 (x_1 + 2)}{4}$$

subject to

$$g_1(X) = \frac{8 C_f F_{max} x_2}{\pi x_3^3} - S \le 0$$

$$g_2(X) = l_f - l_{max} \le 0$$

$$g_3(X) = d_{min} - x_3 \le 0$$

$$g_4(X) = x_2 - D_{max} \le 0$$

$$g_5(X) = 3.0 - \frac{x_2}{x_3} \le 0$$

$$g_6(X) = \sigma_p - \sigma_{pm} \le 0$$

$$g_7(X) = \sigma_p + \frac{F_{max} - F_p}{K} + 1.05(x_1 + 2)x_3 - l_f \le 0$$

$$g_8(X) = \sigma_w - \frac{F_{max} - F_p}{K} \le 0$$

where

$$C_f = \frac{4(x_2 / x_3) - 1}{4(x_2 / x_3) - 4} + \frac{0.615 x_3}{x_2} \le 0$$

$$K = \frac{G x_3^4}{8 x_1 x_2^3} \qquad\qquad (8.23)$$

$$\sigma_p = \frac{F_p}{K}$$

$$l_f = \frac{F_{max}}{K} + 1.05(x_1 + 2)x_3$$

The objective function $f(X)$ computes the volume of spring steel wire as a function of the design variables. The design constraints are specified as follows (for more detail see Sandgren [1990], Wu & Chow [1995], and Siddall [1982]):

(a) The maximum working load is: $F_{max} = 1000.0$ lb.
(b) The allowable maximum shear stress is: $S = 189000.0$ psi (g_1).
(c) The maximum free length is: $l_{max} = 14.0$ inch (g_2).
(d) The minimum wire diameter is: $d_{min} = 0.2$ inch (g_3).
(e) The maximum outside diameter of the spring is: $D_{max} = 3.0$ inch (g_4).
(f) The pre-load compression force is: $F_p = 300.0$ lb.
(g) The allowable maximum deflection under pre-load is: $\sigma_{pm} = 6.0$ inch (g_6).
(h) The deflection from pre-load to maximum load position is: $\sigma_w = 1.25$ inch (g_8).
(i) Combined deflections must be consistent with length, i.e., the coils should not touch under the load at which the maximum spring deflection occurs (g_7).
(j) The shear modulus of the material is: $G = 11.5 \times 10^6$.

(k) The spring is guided, so the buckling constraint is bypassed.

(l) The outside diameter of the spring D should be at least three times greater than the wire diameter d to avoid lightly wound coils (g_5).

The following DE settings solved the coil spring problem: $NP=40$, $F=0.90$ and $CR=0.90$. Although the problem statements do not define design variable boundaries, the constraints g_3 and g_4 are pure boundary constraints and were treated as a lower boundary constraint for x_3 and as an upper boundary constraint for x_2 respectively. Further, g_5 can also be handled as a boundary constraint. To define the search space, the other boundary constraints were chosen based on the problem statements and the simple geometric limitations elaborated in Table 8.10. The remaining constraints were handled as soft-constraint functions.

Table 8.10: Boundary constraints used for the coil spring example.

Lower limitation	Constraint	Upper limitation
At least one spring coil is required to form a spring.	$1 \leq x_1 \leq \dfrac{l_{max}}{d_{min}}$	Upper and lower surfaces of unloaded spring coils touch each other.
Constraints g_3 and g_5 together	$3d_{min} \leq x_2 \leq D_{max}$	Constraint g_4
Constraint g_3	$d_{min} \leq x_3 \leq \dfrac{D_{max}}{3}$	Constraints g_4 and g_5 together

The cost function for DE was formulated as follows:

$$f_{cost}(X) = f(X) \cdot \prod_{i=1}^{2} c_i^3 \cdot \prod_{i=6}^{8} c_i^3$$

where

$$c_i = \begin{cases} 1.0 + s_i \cdot g_i(X) & \text{if} \quad g_i(X) > 0 \\ 1 & \text{otherwise} \end{cases}$$

$$s_1 = s_2 = s_6 = 1.0, \; s_7 = s_8 = 1.0 \cdot 10^{10}$$

(8.24)

Constraint functions g_3, g_4 and g_5 did not have to be evaluated because they were handled as boundary constraints and DE was not allowed to generate a candidate vector that violated any of them.

Tables 8.11 and 8.12 compare DE's solution with results obtained by other researchers. Two different versions of the coil spring problem were solved. Case A (Table 8.11) reports the solutions generated when all variables are assumed to be continuous. Case B (Table 8.12) reports the mixed-variable solution according to the problem statements above. In both cases, DE obtained a better solution than the best solution found in the literature. In order to demonstrate the robustness of the DE algorithm, 100 independent optimization trials were performed for both Cases A and B. All trials yielded the reported $f(X)$ value or better. All of the solutions were also within the feasible region of the design space. The number of generations was 650 in both cases, corresponding to 26,000 function evaluations. The computation time was 0.94 seconds on a PC with an AMD K6-233 MHz processor with SPECfp95 rating 5.5 (SPEC [1995]).

Table 8.11: Optimal solutions for the coil spring problem. Case A: continuous. S90 = Sandgren [1990], TC = this chapter.

Item	Optimum solution, Case A		Type of variable
	S90	TC	
x_1 (N) [l]	9.1918	7.117621	Continuous
x_2 (D) [inch]	1.2052	1.372407	Continuous
x_3 (d) [inch]	0.2814	0.2909652	Continuous
$g_1(X)$	5.000	3.35959×10^{-10}	
$g_2(X)$	9.065	1.62759	
$g_3(X)$	0.08138	0.090965	
$g_4(X)$	1.7947	1.62759	
$g_5(X)$	1.2833	1.71674	
$g_6(X)$	5.4643	5.46429	
$g_7(X)$	0.0	2.28983×10^{-16}	
$g_8(X)$	0.0	3.96737×10^{-12}	
$f(X)$ [inch^3]	**2.6353**	**2.61388**	
	100.0%	99.2%	

Table 8.12: Optimal solutions for the coil spring problem. Case B: discrete. S90 = Sandgren [1990], C93 = Chen & Tsao [1993], W95 = Wu & Chow [1995], TC = this chapter.

Item	Optimum solution, Case B				Type of variable
	S90	C93	W95	TC	
x_1 (N) [l]	10	9	9	9	Integer
x_2 (D) [inch]	1.180701	1.2287	1.227411	1.2230410	Continuous
x_3 (d) [inch]	0.283	0.283	0.283	0.283	Discrete
$g_1(X)$	54309	415.969	550.993	1008.8114	
$g_2(X)$	8.8187	8.9207	8.9264	8.94564	
$g_3(X)$	0.08298	0.08300	0.08300	0.083000	
$g_4(X)$	1.8193	1.7713	1.7726	1.77696	
$g_5(X)$	1.1723	1.3417	1.3371	1.32170	
$g_6(X)$	5.4643	5.4568	5.4585	5.46429	
$g_7(X)$	0.0	0.0	0.0	2.67581×10^{-16}	
$g_8(X)$	0.0	0.0174	0.0134	5.07515×10^{-16}	
$f(X)$ [inch^3]	**2.7995**	2.6709	2.6681	**2.65856**	
	100.0%	95.4%	95.3%	95.0%	

In general, a robust search and high convergence velocity are conflicting objectives. To illustrate this, an experiment was performed with Case B using alternative values for DE's control parameters that were selected to favor a high convergence velocity rather than a robust search. Using control settings of: $NP=40$, $F=0.70$ and $CR=0.80$, DE found the optimum in 200 generations (8,000 function evaluations). Compared to the original settings of: $NP=40$, $F=0.90$ and $CR=0.90$, the new settings increased convergence velocity by 325%. Only 5 out of 100 independent trials ended up with a result that was worse than that reported in Table 8.12. Thus, a significantly faster convergence in Case B was achieved by sacrificing some robustness.

8.7 CONCLUSIONS

Based on the results of this three-problem test suite, DE appears to be a promisingly efficient, effective and robust optimization algorithm. Additionally, DE is both easy to implement and easy to use. DE was capable of optimizing all integer, discrete and continuous variables, and it was able to handle non-linear objective functions with multiple non-trivial constraints. Furthermore, high quality solutions were obtained in every case. In all test problems, the solution found by DE was better than or equal to the best solution found by any of the competing methods. Although the problems in this test set had generally been considered to be rather difficult, they were not sufficiently difficult to test DE's limits.

To evaluate and demonstrate DE's robustness, 100 independent trials were performed for each case studied. In every instance, all runs yielded the reported $f(X)$ value or better. In addition, all of the solutions were within the feasible region of the design space. Because of that, it can be concluded that DE is a robust design algorithm for mixed parameter global optimization.

DE's ability to solve a problem is not particularly sensitive to the values of its control parameters NP, F and CR. Typically, it is sufficient to choose the values for the control parameters F and CR as multiples of 0.1 and the population size, NP, as a multiple of 10. Similarly, the number of generations to be evaluated was chosen to be a multiple of 50. In the pressure vessel and coil spring design examples, the same control parameters were used for differently formulated versions of the test problems. Notice that exactly the same values of NP, F and CR were effective for solving both the continuous and discrete versions of the problems!

The values of NP, F and CR, however, still affect the convergence velocity and robustness of the algorithm. In this investigation, values were selected to favour robustness rather than convergence velocity. Because computationally inexpensive objective functions were used, the highest possible convergence velocity was not important. Despite this, convergence was still relatively fast in all cases. It is possible, however, to increase the convergence velocity significantly by favouring fast convergence over robustness.

It is sometimes argued that evolutionary optimizers require a large number of objective function evaluations. Before deciding whether or not this is true for DE, some further facts should be considered. Each of the real-world optimization problems discussed here can be solved on an ordinary PC using less than 1 second of computation time. Furthermore, this test problem set contains problems that are too difficult for most existing optimization methods. Unfortunately, insufficient data was available to accurately compare the number of objective function evaluations required by other methods to those required by DE. For some unknown reason, the large majority of the articles to which this investigation refers did not report the number of function evaluations properly. Besides, the number of objective function evaluations would be important only if the competing algorithm is, in fact, capable of finding the optimal solution.

Based on experience, DE seems to be better at locally fine-tuning a solution than traditional binary-encoded genetic algorithms. This property appeared especially when continuous parameters were the subject of optimization. This advantage appears not to decrease the capability of DE for global exploration, as is the case with many other methods. DE also seems capable of producing useful results with much lower population sizes than traditional genetic algorithms require. Despite its small population sizes and greedy selection criterion, DE displayed a relatively low risk of premature convergence. As a result, DE required less than one tenth as many objective function evaluations as did a simple genetic algorithm.

Some optimization methods require a feasible initial solution as a starting point for a search. Preferably, this feasible solution should be rather close to a global optimum to ensure that the algorithm does not converge to a local minimum. If non-trivial constraints are imposed, it may be difficult or impossible to provide a feasible initial solution. The efficiency, effectiveness and robustness of many methods are often highly dependent on the quality of the starting point. The combination of DE with the soft-constraint approach does not require any initial solution, but it can still take advantage of a high quality initial solution if one is available. For example, initializing DE with normally distributed variations of a good solution creates a population that is biased towards the feasible region of the search space.

If there are no feasible solutions in the search space, as is the case for totally conflicting constraints, DE with the soft-constraint approach is still able to find the nearest feasible solution. This is important in practical engineering design work because often many non-trivial constraints are involved.

Because the current test problem set did not uncover any major limitation of the DE algorithm, a larger problem set should be the subject of a future investigation. Since the goal of this article was primarily to introduce and demonstrate this novel approach, the convergence properties of DE were neither studied, nor discussed comprehensively. In order to create a more complete picture of DE's properties, a more difficult set of problems should be the focus of future studies.

Another interesting topic is the fact that DE works with more than just one candidate solution. When multiple global optima exist, as was the case in the gear train example, multiple solutions can be found by performing only a single run of DE. In the case of multi-objective problems, the use of a population enables DE to locate multiple points from a Pareto-front instead of only a single Pareto-optimal solution.

DE was targeted to fill a gap in the field of mixed discrete-integer-continuous optimization where no really satisfactory methods appeared to be available. As this investigation demonstrates, DE has proven to be very effective for this purpose. Despite being in its infancy, DE has great potential to become a widely used, multipurpose optimization tool for solving a broad range of practical engineering design problems.

Chapter Nine

Co-evolving Draughts Strategies with Differential Evolution

Ken Chisholm

9.1 INTRODUCTION

The original work of Samuel [1959] on machine learning with the game of draughts (checkers) is almost 40 years old. It was, however, the more recent work of the *Chinook* (Schaeffer et al [1992]) checkers program team at the University of Alberta in the 1990s that inspired the author to look at the problem of optimising the board-evaluation function using a Genetic Algorithm (GA). The *Chinook* team has now virtually 'solved' the draughts end-game by creating an enormous database of solved boards (Lake et al [1994]). The openings are also relatively well understood, leaving the mid-game as an area where, due to the size of the search space, pure processing power and prodigious storage are not sufficient for an exhaustive search. It was felt, therefore, that this area of game playing was still worth investigating using GAs. The goal was to see if such an approach could improve on, or at least match, Samuel's rather tailored technique of machine learning that helped enable his program to play at county level.

The fundamental problem in what Samuel [1959] called, 'the generalised learning process', is to find an optimal set of board-evaluation coefficients for the game of draughts despite the inherently noisy game-playing environment. Instead of the hill-climbing techniques originally used by Samuel, this investigation attacked the problem with a co-evolutionary computational process. Both a simple GA and the more recent Differential Evolution (DE) algorithm were used to co-evolve board strategies. Results suggest that DE is an effective way to search for optimal strategies despite the presence of noise in the game-playing environment.

9.2 HISTORICAL BACKGROUND: BASIC GAME-PLAYING ALGORITHMS

Most standard game-playing programs for two-person, zero-sum board games such as draughts and chess use a limited, look-ahead tree (Shannon [1950]) with a mini-max search (Levy & Newborn [1991]). Usually, some form of tree pruning, such as alpha-beta cut-off (Knuth & Moore [1975]), is used to reduce the number of moves that must be considered. Figure 9.1 illustrates a sample portion of a mini-max search tree that uses alpha-beta pruning.

The board-evaluation function rates the terminal boards (or leaf nodes) at the horizon of the search tree. Normally, the principle of hot-pursuit (Turing [1953]) is used to locally extend the search-tree to ensure that the boards to which the board-evaluation function is applied are relatively stable and not so badly affected by the horizon effect (Berliner

[1973]). Hot-pursuit essentially causes all pending 'takes' to be completed before a board is evaluated. This is particularly important in draughts, since the rules of the game dictate that so-called, 'take-moves', *must* be carried out if they are available. For more details, see Turing [1953] and Shannon [1950a] which, although they discuss algorithms for playing computer chess, are also applicable to playing draughts.

The static board-evaluation function is essentially a weighted-sum of *feature* scores based on the various properties of the board. The features used to evaluate a terminal board are board properties that have traditionally been considered to be important by human players, such as: number of pieces, mobility count, centre-control, advancement of pieces, etc. (See Samuel's first paper [1959] and Appendix 9.A for a further discussion of these board features.)

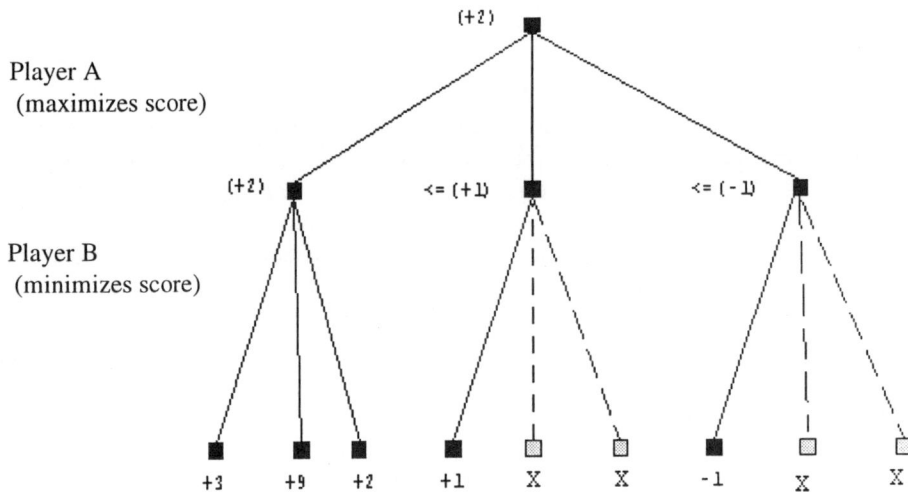

Fig. 9.1: A sample mini-max search tree.

The score for a board is a simple linear polynomial, usually represented as follows:

$$\text{Board score} = (w_1 f_1) + (w_2 f_2) + ... + (w_n f_n)$$

$$\text{Term}_1 \quad \text{Term}_2 \quad \quad \text{Term}_n$$

(9.1)

The features $(f_1,...,f_n)$ used in this board-evaluation function are usually based on human strategic knowledge of the game that has accumulated over decades (or even centuries) of analysis (Belasco[1973], Fortman [1982]). Even so, the relative weights $(w_1,...,w_n)$ assigned to these features can still fruitfully be analysed using optimisation techniques like hill-climbing. In his first paper, Samuel presented a very impressive method for generalised learning based on hill-climbing. This was certainly a considerable *tour-de-force* for its time. Samuel also reported how various board features could be viewed as connected in some way (such as centre control and mobility, for example) and treated as a single feature for the purpose of analysis. For practical reasons, the number of these 'binary-connected' terms that Samuel considered had to be limited and somewhat hard-coded into the program.

In his second paper, Samuel [1967] presented a novel method for extending feature groupings with what he called 'signature tables'. These tables allowed the connectivity between features to include tertiary and even hierarchical groupings. The author believes that the nature of the GA approach to this search space enables the connectivity of the various features to be captured and produced in a fairly direct manner.

9.3 BASIC CO-EVOLUTIONARY LEARNING PROCESS USING A SIMPLE GA

The approach taken here is use a GA to evolve a set of weights for the polynomial in Equation (1). The weights themselves represent the genetic material processed by the GA (Holland [1975], Goldberg [1989]). To assess the quality of candidate solutions, a draughts-playing program, *DRAFT5-UK,* was pressed into service. *DRAFT5-UK* is the descendant of a draughts-playing program that was written by the author almost 25 years ago as an undergraduate AI project (Chisholm [1976]). Originally designed to investigate various methods for achieving better rote-learning techniques, such as partial-board matching during end-games, *DRAFT5-UK* has been extended, tuned, translated and ported many times over the years and is the main engine for the research reported here. *DRAFT5-UK* is written in ANSI C and currently runs on UNIX systems and PCs under MS-DOS. The system has a graphical front-end which incorporates the facility to suggest moves for a human opponent.

As with most draughts and chess programs, *DRAFT5-UK* was written so that it could play against itself by alternately searching and moving for black and then for white. The self-playing ability of *DRAFT5-UK* enables a pool of individuals with different weights to play against each other in a draughts tournament. By maintaining a collection of differing weights in a two-dimensional array, it is possible to simulate a pool of 'players' whose strategies are defined by their board evaluation weights. (See Figure 9.2 for a sample set of individuals and their associated weights).

												Generation 6
Fitness	Piece	King	Mob	KMob	Back	Cent	KCent	Adv1	DBLSq	Near	Exch	MOVE
0	1200	2000	140	140	140	140	140	140	660	5	140	240
23	1081	1917	17	25	22	1	110	85	85	4	128	7
22	416	1564	85	79	131	49	118	65	349	1	104	70
21	896	1564	17	25	74	49	118	138	230	1	104	70
20	734	1068	86	91	74	12	69	65	365	5	136	163
19	786	630	23	137	57	70	35	17	75	1	118	171
18	896	1564	7	91	74	49	118	138	230	1	104	150
18	416	1621	23	91	26	49	47	65	85	1	104	150
18	469	1564	7	79	131	49	118	65	85	1	70	70
17	384	1621	140	19	117	75	89	22	412	4	70	38
17	416	1564	7	25	131	49	118	138	230	1	104	150

Fig. 9.2: A sample pool of board feature weights.

The fitness function (Angeline & Pollack [1993]) used in this GA is simply the number of wins an individual achieves in an all-play-all, round-robin (RR) draughts tournament. When compared to a simple knockout tournament, for example, the RR tournament format provides a more accurate estimate about the playing ability of an individual strategy. Even with this RR tournament format, the evaluation function is somewhat noisy. This, unfortunately, slows down each experiment because many games must be played each generation to obtain accurate strategy evaluations. The RR approach, however, is thought to be absolutely necessary because of the high probability that a draughts game will end in a draw. Drawn games are very common in draughts tournaments, even with human players and particularly with automatic game-playing programs such as *DRAFT5-UK*. For example, in the 42-game Tinsley-*Chinook* match for the World Draughts Championship in 1993 (Schaeffer et al [1993]), there were 33 draws, 6 wins for Dr. Tinsley and 2 wins for *Chinook*, with one game not played at the end of the match. It should, however, be noted that draws are not quite so common in games that involve opponents who are not of this exceptional calibre. The reward of half a point for a drawn game was discounted, as it was felt that this reward would serve to reduce the effectiveness of searching for aggressive end-game strategies.

Initial experiments used a simple rank-based selection scheme and an 'elitist' crossover technique that preserved the best 'player' from each generation. To help maintain diversity, the gene pool was occasionally divided into divisions, with genes being appropriately promoted between divisions at the end of each generation. This had the desirable side effect of ensuring that opponents of an appropriate calibre are used in each match and is somewhat similar to the notion of *hosts* and *parasites* used in the experiments of Rosin & Belew [1995]. Trials with elitism, *competitive fitness sharing* and *Hall of Fame* techniques (Rosin & Belew [1997]) were also used to produce the greatest increase in performance in the fewest number of generations. This version of the *DRAFT5* draughts program became known as *DRAFT5-GA*. The basic GA is outlined in Appendix 9.B.

9.4. RESULTS AND ANALYSIS OF INITIAL GA EXPERIMENTS

Each experiment was carried out 10 times in an attempt to minimise the evaluation noise from *DRAFT5-UK*. For a pool size of 60, a full RR tournament required 3600 games each generation, or 180,000 games for every 50-generation experiment. Each individual game takes about 2 seconds, so each experiment takes approximately 4 days on a 200 MHz Pentium. In order for these experiments to be feasible on a reasonable time scale, the look-ahead search limit for *DRAFT5-UK* was set to two moves plus hot-pursuit. Due to the time-consuming nature of evaluating strategies, a gene pool of more than 60 members was not considered.

A sample, 'top ten', from the final (50th) generation is shown in Figure 9.3. In passing, it can be seen that the board feature weights show signs of convergence. Perhaps the most encouraging result from these initial experiments was the fact that the King Weight was always approximately 1.5 times the (ordinary) Piece Weight. This is the generally accepted ratio given in many draughts books for human players and was, in fact, the ratio used by Samuel in his studies. This ratio means that three (ordinary) pieces will be exchanged for two kings, if by so doing some positional advantage is obtained.

Another positive result is that the values for the lesser weights such as mobility, centre control, cramping and advancement, are also very similar to those determined by years of fine-tuning *DRAFT5-UK* using human opponents. (In retrospect, it is felt that a very slow form of hill-climbing was in effect being performed). Additionally, *DRAFT5-UK* played some games against human opponents using these GA-calculated weights with some considerable success.

Generation: 50

Fitness	Piece	King	Mob	KMob	Back	Cent	KCent	Adv1	DBLSq	Near	Exch	MOVE
0	1200	2000	140	140	140	140	140	140	660	5	140	240
30	989	1590	74	53	65	22	127	83	385	1	79	203
29	904	1590	74	5	65	33	127	137	385	1	79	123
28	904	1590	74	107	65	33	127	92	385	2	79	98
28	904	1590	133	76	65	35	127	83	473	1	79	98
26	904	1692	74	126	73	33	127	137	385	1	79	98
26	927	1692	74	5	65	58	127	137	385	2	79	89
26	933	1590	74	5	65	41	127	83	405	1	128	140
25	933	1590	74	85	65	33	127	137	378	2	79	98
25	904	1692	74	5	4	33	107	92	385	3	53	98
24	927	1692	138	126	19	28	24	83	385	3	79	98

Fig. 9.3: A sample 'top ten' weights from the final (50th) generation pool.

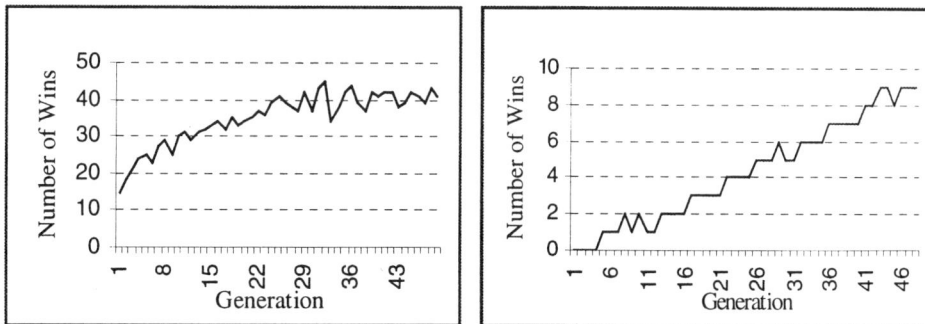

Fig. 9.4: Fitness growth of *DRAFTS-GA* (left) and of *DRAFT5-GA* vs. *DRAFT5-UK* (right).

9.5 MEASURING THE IMPROVEMENT OF *DRAFT5-GA*

In the area of draughts and chess, the skill of a human player (and indeed, a program) is usually determined by competitions against other players (or programs) in tournaments. This and the work of Donnelly et al. with the game of GO (Donnelly et al [1994]), suggested a more absolute method for measuring the improvement of *DRAFT5-GA*. Using the GA described in Appendix 9.B, a set of experiments was conducted in which the tournament winner of each generation was preserved in a finalists pool. At the end of 50 generations, these generation winners competed against each other in a final round-robin tournament to determine whether or not the GA had successfully evolved improved strategies for *DRAFT5-GA*. The graph in Figure 9.4 (left) shows the number of wins by generation winners plotted against generation number.

Figure 9.4 indicates that there is a general trend of slow improvement with a fair degree of local variability superimposed. As with the work of Donnelly et al., it is felt that one of the main factors affecting these results is the difficulty of obtaining perfect fitness information. As we indicated earlier, this is partly a result of the fact that drawn games are very common in draughts.

Another set of experiments was conducted using a slight variation of the performance measure described above. In this set of experiments, the winner of each generation was entered into a 40 game match against the original, hand-tuned *DRAFT5-UK*. The results of this set of experiments were, as Figure 9.4 (right) illustrates, also quite promising. Once again, it can be seen that there is a general trend of improvement with some superimposed local variability. For further details regarding *DRAFT5-GA*, the interested reader is referred to Chisholm & Bradbeer [1997].

9.6 DIFFERENTIAL EVOLUTION: *DRAFT5-DE*

On discovering the work of Storn & Price [1997, 1997a] on Differential Evolution (DE), it was thought that this novel technique would be both appropriate and efficient for optimising the board evaluation coefficients. DE has been demonstrated to be an effective global optimiser by the work of Storn & Price [1996] at the IEEE's First International Competition on Evolutionary Optimisation (ICEO). Although DE placed third behind two deterministic methods of limited applicability, it nevertheless proved to be the fastest evolutionary algorithm among contest entries (Bersini et al [1996]). The author was also encouraged to pursue this evolutionary algorithm because it was reported by Price [1996] that DE was relatively immune to the sort of noisy fitness functions that characterise these co-evolutionary draughts experiments.

To use DE, it was first necessary to change the coefficients of the linear polynomial from the integers used in previous research, to real numbers. This version of *DRAFT5-GA* based on DE came to be known as *DRAFT5-DE*. Figure 9.5 lists some results from the fourth generation of a typical experimental run. Note that 'players' are not ranked in the DE algorithm. Consequently, the individuals in Figure 9.5 are not shown in order of fitness, as was the case with the previous GA experiments. For additional information and a much fuller description of Differential Evolution, the interested reader is directed to chapter six as well as the various other papers on the topic by Price [1994, 1996, 1997] and also Storn & Price [1997].

As with *DRAFT5-GA*, generation winners from *DRAFT5-DE* were pitted against one another in a RR tournament to determine if each generation winner was indeed an improvement over previous champions. The graph in Figure 9.6 (left) plots the number of wins achieved by each generation winner in the play-offs *versus* the generation number. By comparing the fitness growth of *DRAFT5-GA* in Figure 9.4 (left) with that of *DRAFT5-DE* in Figure 9.6 (left), it can be seen that *DRAFT5-DE* produced a higher rate of improvement that exhibited less variability. Differential Evolution achieved both a higher learning rate (particularly during the initial generations) and a better overall fitness after 50 generations than did *DRAFT5-GA*.

										Generation: 4
Fitness	Piece	King	Mob	KMob	Back	Cent	KCent	Adv1	DBLSq	Near
Range: 1200	2000	140	140	140	140	140	140	660	5	
1	65.8	1029.0	58.7	102.9	79.4	73.0	136.8	51.3	8.9	4.2
4	202.6	1347.0	101.9	63.3	84.7	115.2	1.3	4.2	187.1	4.8
3	1061.8	49.0	121.7	23.7	43.4	112.2	9.4	138.1	366.6	3.7
2	314.2	1591.0	66.4	132.0	119.7	57.4	107.4	18.8	425.4	5.7
4	997.0	713.0	5.1	83.6	30.8	74.2	18.1	114.1	262.4	5.0
0	26.2	589.0	133.7	114.7	39.6	45.1	79.0	89.3	315.8	3.5
5	657.2	1177.0	101.2	66.0	61.2	22.0	101.1	126.6	431.3	1.9
2	724.6	321.0	64.7	74.5	92.3	69.2	102.4	116.9	549.5	1.2

Fig. 9.5: Sample of a *DRAFT5-DE* population after 4 generations (features, 'Exch' and 'MOVE' are not shown).

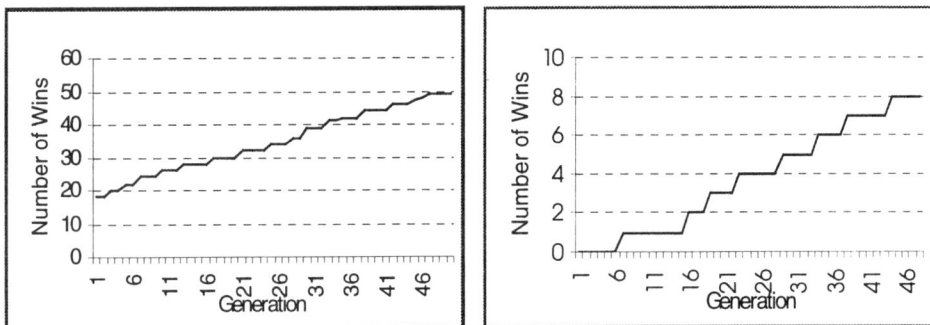

Fig. 9.6: Fitness growth of *DRAFT5-DE* (left) and *DRAFT5-DE* vs. *DRAFTS-UK* (right).

To confirm the increase in the playing ability of *DRAFT5-DE* and to further compare the rate of improvement with a more absolute standard, generation winners were also played against *DRAFT5-UK* in a 40 game match. Figure 9.6 (right) shows the number of wins achieved by each generation winner in these final play-offs. Clearly, the co-evolutionary learning process has still not produced a version of the draughts playing program that is better than *DRAFT5-UK*. This is to be expected, since *DRAFT5-UK*'s hill-climbing model has sometimes used the sophisticated move-by-move correlation methods described by Samuel [1959, 1967]. A move-by-move fitness function is thought to be a fruitful line of research for some further DE experiments. Furthermore, *DRAFT5-DE*'s steady rate of improvement appears unabated after 50 generations, suggesting that longer experiments need to be conducted before a judgement can be made regarding the ultimate playing ability of the strategies evolved by this method.

In game-playing programs like the Checkers World Championship calibre *Chinook* (Schaeffer et al [1992, 1993]), a different set of coefficients for the board evaluation function is employed for each phase of the game. Literature about draughts and chess describes how the opening game, mid-game and end-game phases can be quite different because the importance of certain features changes during play (Fortman [1982], Levy & Newborn [1991]). In fact, *Chinook* (Lake et al [1994]) goes even further and divides the game into four phases of play, each of which uses its own board evaluation function. To reduce computation time, this investigation considered only the three classical phases (the opening, mid-game and end-game). This version of *DRAFT5-DE* with three equal phases of board evaluation is referred to as: *DRAFT5-3P*.

9.7 A MULTIPHASE EVALUATION FUNCTION: *DRAFT5-3P*

The number of phases is a user-defined parameter that can easily be changed. Indeed, evolving the most effective number of phases might itself be the focus of some future GA-based experimentation. Presently, the number of pieces that remain on the board determines the game phase. Although the game has, in this case, been partitioned equally into the three phases, finding an optimal way to partition the game into phases based on the number of remaining pieces is another strategy variable that could conceivably be evolved using a meta-GA.

For this multiphase experiment, each chromosome in the gene pool was expanded to a 2-dimensional array. An entry in a player's 2-D array denotes the value for that board parameter coefficient during the specified phase of the game. Figure 9.7 shows a sample of an initial gene pool from *DRAFT5-3P*. In this case, the gene pool has been inoculated (Surrey & Radcliffe [1996]) with values for the *PIECE* and *KING* coefficients that are recommended in draughts books (Fortman [1982]) and AI literature (Samuel [1959, 1967]). Restricting the search space this way both speeds computation and allows the search to concentrate on the *positional* aspects of the game, a topic that is still a matter of much discussion. Future DE experiments, however, should include both of these coefficients in the evolutionary process, as it is felt that the value of a *PIECE* (and of a *KING*, to a slightly lesser extent) may also change subtly during the course of a game.

DRAFT5-3P's rate of improvement was studied in the same manner as was done for both *DRAFT5-GA* and *DRAFT5-DE*. The rate of improvement of the generation winners after the final RR play-offs appears in Figure 9.8 (left). The results of playing each generation winner against the normal version of *DRAFT5-UK* are presented in Figure 9.8 (right).

It should be noticed that the rate of learning is initially slower initially than it was for *DRAFT5-DE*. This is to be expected, since the number of coefficients to be determined for each player increases from 12 in *DRAFT5-DE* to 30 in *DRAFT5-3P*. Once again, since the learning rate is sustained through the final generation, it seems likely that, given time, still better strategies will evolve. Work is under way to resolve this question.

9.8 CONCLUSIONS AND FUTURE WORK

It has been shown that this co-evolutionary approach to machine learning enables a draughts-playing program to significantly improve its playing ability, in a manner similar to the hill-climbing approach taken by Samuel in his earlier experiments. The first major conclusion that can be drawn from this research is that DE was both effective and efficient in a co-evolutionary, competitive context, both in terms of the overall learning rate and the comparative performance. Furthermore, DE appeared to search the range of the search space in an efficient manner. It is felt that this is mainly due to the form of mutation that is fundamental to DE. This echoes the findings of Price [1997] concerning the considerable speed of execution and overall functionality of DE against the functions of the 2nd ICEO (Bersini et al [1996]). These experiments also appear to confirm the claim of Price [1997] that DE is relatively immune to a somewhat noisy fitness function, which was the certainly the case during these experiments.

Generation: 1										
(Phase)	Piece	King	Mob	KMob	Back	Cent	Kcent	Adv1	DBLSq	Near
'Player' #1	(Fitness = 9)									
P1	1000.0	1500.0	58.7	102.9	79.4	73.0	136.8	51.3	8.9	4.2
P2	1000.0	1500.0	101.9	63.3	84.7	115.2	1.3	4.2	187.1	4.8
P3	1000.0	1500.0	121.7	23.7	43.4	112.2	9.4	138.1	366.6	3.7
'Player' #2	(Fitness = 6)									
P1	1000.0	1500.0	66.4	132.0	119.7	57.4	107.4	18.8	425.4	5.7
P2	1000.0	1500.0	5.1	83.6	30.8	74.2	18.1	114.1	262.4	5.0
P3	1000.0	1500.0	133.7	114.7	39.6	45.1	79.0	89.3	315.8	3.5
'Player' #3	(Fitness = 5)									
P1	1000.0	1500.0	101.2	66.0	61.2	22.0	101.1	126.6	431.3	1.9
P2	1000.0	1500.0	111.2	52.4	67.4	74.4	6.6	40.2	36.0	5.6
P3	1000.0	1500.0	26.1	90.2	115.9	38.1	120.8	41.9	30.0	1.1

Fig. 9.7: A sample gene pool showing chromosomes for a 3-phase evaluation function (not all features are shown).

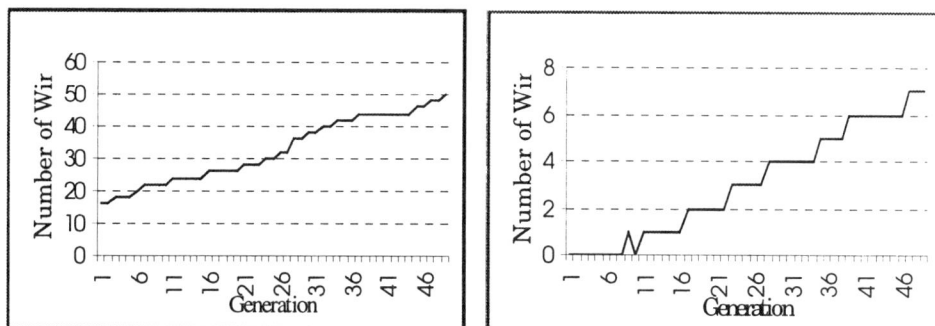

Fig. 9.8: Fitness growth of *DRAFT5-3P* (left) and *DRAFT5-3P* vs. *DRAFT5-UK* (right).

Experiments with *DRAFT5-3P* have naturally lead to the idea of using trees and other non-linear functions to evaluate boards. The use of structures similar to the GA-determined decision trees of Kennedy et al [1997], is also thought to be a fruitful line for future research. This idea resembles the hierarchical *signature tables* described in Samuel's later work [1967], but with the considerable advantage that the tree structures can be evolved almost automatically. This could, at least partially, lead to the semi-automatic generation of new feature parameters for the board evaluation function - the often stated '*Holy Grail*' of machine learning in game-playing programs, ever since the early 1960's (Samuel [1959, 1967], Berliner [1973]).

Further experiments also need to be carried out using DE to evolve an optimal multiphase board evaluation function. Hopefully, future experiments using faster hardware and parallel processing systems will extend the search depth and permit bigger populations to evolve longer. The distributed model of computation suggested by Lake et al [1994] uses a network of workstations and is thought to be a possible solution·to this problem. In the longer term, the goal is to extend this work into several areas of game theoretic research and to apply DE to the practical problems that arise in economics and the stock markets (Gargano et al [1993]).

Acknowledgements

The author would like to acknowledge the many helpful discussions and detailed communications with Kenneth Price and also several members of the GA group at Napier University who made helpful suggestions and comments regarding earlier drafts of this paper.

APPENDIX 9.A: BOARD FEATURE DESCRIPTIONS

PIECE – This parameter is credited with 1 for each (ordinary) piece of the side being considered.

KING – This parameter is credited with 1 for each king of the side being considered.

MOB – This parameter is credited with 1 for each possible move that is available to the (ordinary) pieces of the side being considered.

KMOB – This parameter is credited with 1 for each possible move that is available to the king pieces of the side being considered.

BACK – This parameter is credited with 1 if are no active kings on the board and the two Back Row Bridge squares (1 and 3, or 30 and 32) in the back row are occupied by pieces of the side being considered.

CENT – This parameter is credited with 1 for each of the following squares: 11, 12, 15, 16, 20, 21, 24 and 25) which are occupied by a piece of the side under consideration.

KCENT – This parameter is credited with 1 for each of the following squares: 11, 12, 15, 16, 20, 21, 24 and 25) which are occupied by a king of the side under consideration.

ADV1 – This parameter is credited with 1 for each piece that can move onto the 8th row (to become a king).

DBLSQ – This parameter is credited with 1 if the material credit is less than 9 and a piece is in either of the double corner squares and the side under consideration is behind in material.

NEAR – This parameter is credited with a cramping coefficient (based on the sum of the Manhattan distances from other pieces on the board) if the total material credit is less than 9 and the side under consideration is ahead in material.

EXCH – This parameter is credited with 1 if there are fewer pieces on the board than before the look-ahead was carried out and the side under consideration is ahead in material, with no relative change in strength.

MOVE – This parameter is credited with 1 if pieces are even, with a total piece count (2 for ordinary men and 3 for kings) of less than 24, and if an odd number of pieces are in the move system, defined as those vertical files starting on squares 1, 2, 3 and 4. ('The Move' is a very old property of draughts mentioned in the literature that causes one side or the other to have good 'momentum'.)

APPENDIX 9.B: THE BASIC DRAUGHTS ROUND-ROBIN TOURNAMENT GA

```
/* Basic Draughts tournament GA - version 1 */
Max_Number_Of_Generations = 50
Pool_Size = 30
Mutation_Rate = 10

/* Initialise the pool of weights with random numbers */
for i = 1 to Pool_Size do
  for j = 1 to Chromosome_length do
    Pool[i, j] = random(allowed range)

/* Carry out generations of RR draughts tournaments with GA */
for  g = 1 to Max_Number_of_ Generations do
{   /* Evaluate fitness of Pool of draughts players (using RR matches) */
    for i = 1 to Pool_Size do {
      for j = 1 to Pool_Size do {
        if (i # j) then  {
              Copy Pool[i] weights to 'Player A' evaluation function
              Copy Pool[j] weights to 'Player B' evaluation function
              result = draughts ( Player A  vs. Player B)
              if result = 1 then Pool[i].fitness = Pool[i].fitness + 1
              if result = 2 then Pool[j].fitness = Pool[j].fitness + 1
          }
        }
      }
    }
    Sort Pool of Players based on the Fitness from RR Draughts Tournament
    Elite = Pool[1]                /* Preserve best player          */
    Select ()                      /* Standard proportional selection */
    Crossover (ProbXover=0.8)      /* Single point crossover        */
    for m = 1 to Mutation_Rate do  Mutate_Pool  /* ProbMutate = 0.15  */
    Pool[Pool_Size] = elite        /* Insert elite back in Pool     */
    Display and store result
}
```

Part Three

Immune System
Methods

Co-ordinating Editor:

Dipankar Dasgupta

Contributors:

Dipankar Dasgupta

Prabhat Hajela

Emma Hart

Gary Lamont

Robert Marmelstein

Peter Ross

David Van Veldhuizen

Jun Sun Yoo

Chapter Ten

Information Processing in the Immune System

Dipankar Dasgupta

10.1 INTRODUCTION

The natural immune system is a distributed system with several functional components positioned in strategic locations throughout the body. It deploys a multi-level defence against invaders through non-specific (innate) and specific (acquired) immune mechanisms. The lymphocyte is the main type of immune cell participate in the immune response that posses the attributes of specificity, diversity, memory, and self/non-self recognition. Other cells called phagocytic cells – neutrophils, eosinophils, basophils, monocytes – are accessory immune cells whose primary function is to provide facilities to detect and eliminate antigen.

There are two subclasses of the lymphocyte – T and B, each having its own function. The primary lymphoid organs (bone marrow, thymus) provide sites where lymphocytes mature and become antigenically committed. In particular, T lymphocytes develop in bone marrow and travel to thymus to mature; whereas B lymphocytes develop and mature within the bone marrow. The secondary lymphoid organs (spleen, lymph nodes) function to capture antigen and to provide sites where lymphocytes interact with that antigen to stimulate immune response.

Immune response includes a series of chain reactions similar to the 'domino effect', i.e. antigenic presence (such as viruses, bacteria, extracts or metabolites of infectious agents, or vaccines) trigger the first component, messenger molecules (lymphokine) which in turn activates the next component (B-cells) which in turn activates the next component, and so on., until the reaction is complete. Among the excited components are the B-cells, each of which can recognize one particular antigen. When a B-cell recognizes an antigen in the presence of lymphokine, it undergoes clonal expansion and differentiation; some daughter cells become plasma cells that produce antibodies against the antigen, others become memory cells.

The natural immune system is a great source of inspiration for developing intelligent problem-solving techniques, and there are a few computation models based on immunological principles (Dasgupta & Attoh-Okine [1997]). However, most of these computational models emulated one or the other functional components of the immune system. For example, the immune network based on idiotypic model (Jerne [1973]) primarily considered the mechanisms of B-cells in formulating the hypothesis, whereas the negative selection algorithm (Forrest et al [1994]) assumes T-cell mechanisms as its computation power. In some studies, genetic algorithms have been used to model somatic mutation and gene recombination – the process by which antibodies are evolved to recognize a specific antigen. Other researchers (Segel [1997]) viewed the immune system as an autonomous decentralized system and made some useful comparisons between the immune system and autonomous decentralized systems.

The immune system can also be viewed as a multi-agent system (Dasgupta [1998]) where the functionalities and the capabilities of different types of immune agents (cells and molecules) vary. These agents move and interact freely in the environment with other agents to regulate the immune response. Accordingly, they can mutually recognize each other's activities and can produce specific response to provide maximum protection against foreign antigens.

10.2 CIRCULATORY MECHANISMS

The immune system consists of a variety of specialized cells, enzymes, and other serum proteins which are spread throughout the body. The immune cells, in particular lymphocytes, undergo constant levels of recirculation through the blood, lymph nodes, lymphoid organs (spleen, thymus, bone marrow, glands), and tissue spaces. Studies show that lymphocytes circulates through blood for 2–12 hours before appearing in a particular lymphoid organ (Kuby [1994]). This feature allows a maximum number of antigenically committed lymphocytes to encounter and interact with antigen within a relatively short period of time in order to generate a specific immune response. Different populations of lymphocytes recirculate at primary and secondary lymphoid organs and is carefully controlled to ensure that appropriate populations of B- and T-cells (naive, effector and memory) are recruited into different locations. This differential migration of lymphocyte subpopulations at different locations of the body is called *trafficking* or *homing*. As lymphocytes recirculate, they tend to home to various secondary lymphoid organs. The secondary lymphoid organs trap antigens and present them in pieces on the surface of antigen-presenting cells (APC) to be recognized by the immune cells. These organs provide specialized micro-environment to support clonal expansion and differentiation of antigen-activated lymphocytes into effector and memory cells. Interestingly, memory cells exhibit selective homing to the type of tissue in which they first encountered the antigen. Presumably this ensures that a particular memory cell will return to the location where it is most likely to re-encounter a subsequent antigenic challenge.

Experiments have shown that when a particular antigen is injected, T-cells specific for that antigen disappear from the circulation within 48 hours, suggesting that all the specific T-cells encounter (event driven) the antigen in peripheral lymph organs and cease recirculating within that time period. This process is closely regulated to assure steady-state levels of each different type of immune cells. Accordingly, cell division and differentiation of each cell lineages is balanced through programmed cell death by apoptosis. Such decisions can satisfy the basic needs of increased sophistication without centralized control.

10.3 REGULATORY MECHANISMS

The mechanisms of immune response are complex and self-regulatory. These regulation mechanisms include multiple positive- and negative-feedback loops to modulate the type, magnitude, and duration of the response. The regulation of immune responses (i.e. specific immunity) can broadly be divided into two branches – the humoral immunity which is mediated by B-cells and their products (antibody-mediated), and the cellular immunity mediated by T-cells. Both branches follow similar sequence of steps as defence strategies –

proliferation, activation, induction, differentiation and secretion, attack, suppression, and memory, however, they do in different ways. When an antigen enters the body, self-regulatory mechanisms determine (influenced by prior exposure to antigen) the branch of the immune system to be activated, the intensity of the response, and its duration. Specifically, regulation of both humoral and cellular immunity is conducted by a population of T-cells referred to as either helper or suppressor cells which either augment or suppress immune responses. These T-cells regulate immune responses by release of soluble molecules (mediators), such as lyphokines, cytokines, interleukins in order to activate B-cells and other immune cells. Subsequently, B-cells follow one of two pathways: they either differentiate directly into plasma cells, which are basically antibody-secreting factories, or they give rise to germinal centres, specialized structures within lymphoid organs where they undergo somatic mutation (a process called affinity maturation). The importance of the self-regulatory mechanisms is also evident from clonal expansion (inhumoral immunity) with continued antigen presence and reduction of those specific immune cells after clearance of antigens. Such a control of antibody production is thought of as an idiotypic regulatory network (Jerne [1973]) connected by the complementarity of receptors and epitopes. According to this network theory, as an antibody or receptor is produced in response to an antigen, the variable region of antibodies or receptors can induce the formation of a second set of antibodies or cell receptors with specificity against the first set. The second set of receptors or antibodies are called anti-idiotypes, and they can suppress production of the original set. Subsequent anti-idiotypes can then be formed against the second set and, as the process continues with formation of additional anti-idiotypes, these interactions produce a regulatory network. The idiotype network theory suggests that the immune system represents a complex circuitry of interacting B- and T-cells that functions either to enhance or to suppress immune activation. However, the complexity of the idiotype network has made it difficult to predict whether administration of anti-idiotype antibodies or T-cells bearing anti-idiotype receptors up-regulate or down-regulate immune responsiveness (Kuby [1994]).

Moreover, the clonal expansion and proliferation of B-cells are closely regulated (with a co-stimulation) in order to prevent uncontrolled immune response. This second signal helps to ensure tolerance and judge between dangerous and harmless invaders. So the purpose of this accompanying signal in identifying a non-self is to minimize false alarm and to generate decisive response in case of a real danger.

10.4 MEMORY MECHANISMS

The basis of learning in the immune system is the generation of long-lived memory cells at the end of primary response (first encounter of an antigen). The persistent population of memory cells is the mechanism by which the immune system remembers. These memory cells circulate in the body as relatively quiescent cells for the life of the organism. Memory cells carry on their surface the particular immunoglobulin that will strongly bind to a particular reinvading antigen. Because of these memory cells, responds to subsequent encounters are much faster and effective. Memory cells are differentiable from virgin immune cells (newly generated) by their cell-surface marker (CD44) that they programmed to make (Lodish et al [1997; chapter 27]).

The existence of immunological memory is the basis for vaccination, and the reason why adults are less susceptible to infectious diseases (since they already encountered) than are children. The mechanism(s) by which memory cells persist is not well understood, even by immunologists. One theory is that memory cells live for a long time. Another is that memory cells are restimulated at some low level. A number of mechanisms for restimulation have been proposed. Jerne [1973] proposed the idiotypic network theory in which cells co-stimulate each other in a way that mimics the presence of the antigen. Another theory is that small amounts of the residual antigen are retained in lymph nodes or in follicular dendritic cells. Others suggested that related environmental antigens provide cross-stimulation (see for details Smith et al [1999]).

10.5 ARTIFICIAL IMMUNE SYSTEMS

These immunological mechanisms have inspired the development of several computational models (Dasgupta [1999]). A brief survey of some of these models may be found elsewhere (Dasgupta & Attoh-Okine [1997]). Forrest et al [1994] developed a negative-selection algorithm for change detection based on the principles of self-nonself discrimination. This algorithm works on similar principles, generating detectors randomly, and eliminating the ones that detect self, so that the remaining T-cells can detect any non-self. This self and non-self (computational) algorithm, the representative of a two-component model, appears to be very useful in some applications.

There exist other models which emulate different immunological aspects, for example, Smith et al [1999] argued that immunological memory belongs to the same class of associative memories as Kanerva's sparse distributed memory (SDM). They showed the correspondence between B- and T-cells in the immune system and hard locations in a SDM. In particular, their work demonstrated that B- and T-cells perform a sparse coverage of all possible antigens in the same way that hard locations perform a sparse coverage of all possible addresses in a SDM.

Researchers have also been studied immunogenetic approaches (evolving antibodies using genetic algorithms) for more than a decade (Forrest & Perelson [1991], Hightower et al [1995]). Farmer et al [1986] compared the immune system with learning classifier systems. Bersini & Varela [1991] used the recruitment mechanism of the immune system to accelerate the parallel and local hill climbing. In particular, they developed an IRM (Immune Recruitment Mechanism) and GIRM (Genetic IRM) to recruit a candidate from a certain population in the shape space. There exist other computation models emulating different immunological principles, for example, its ability to detect common patterns in a noisy environment (Forrest et al [1993]), its ability to discover and maintain coverage of diverse pattern classes (Smith et al [1993]), and its ability to learn effectively, even when not all antibodies are expressed and not all antigens are presented. In some studies, genetic algorithms have been used to model somatic mutation – the process by which antibodies are evolved to recognize a specific antigen (Hightower et al [1996]).

Hajela and others (Hajela & Lee [1996], Hajela et al [1997]) recently used a genetic search for immune network design in solving structural optimization problems. Hajela et al's work is also the subject of chapter thirteen. Other researchers investigated artificial immune systems for scheduling (Hart et al [1998]); this work is the also the subject of chapter twelve. Potter & De Jong [1998] reported a method for concept learning in which a coevolutionary genetic algorithm was applied to the construction of an immune system whose antibodies can discriminate between examples and counter-examples of a given concept.

10.6 SUMMARY

This chapter has briefly described various information processing properties of the immune system. The main role of the immune system is to recognize all cells (or molecules) within the body and categorize those cells as self or non-self. The non-self cells are further categorized in order to induce an appropriate type of defensive mechanism.

From an information-processing perspective, the immune system is a highly parallel intelligent system. It uses learning, memory, and associative retrieval to solve recognition and classification tasks. Its learning takes place through recruitment mechanism which is partly an evolutionary process similar to biological evolution. Immune response is self-regulatory, i.e. there is no central organ that controls the functions of the immune system. Immune response can also be either local or systemic, depending on the route and property of the antigenic challenge. All these feature make the system very robust in order to respond to the unexpected and the ability to remember that response.

The mechanism of the immune system has inspired the development of some useful computational models. As the field is growing, researchers applying the models in many areas including computer security, data mining, machine learning, fault detection, etc. Like other biologically motivated systems (such as neural networks, evolutionary algorithms), immunity-based systems have much to offer in real-world problem solving.

In the remaining chapters of Part Three, a number of applications or potential applications of these new ideas are described. First, chapter eleven describes an architecture for a computer virus immune system which intends to play a similar role for computers that our own immune system provides for us. This is perhaps the most immediate, yet quite intriguing and exciting, application of these information processing ideas. Chapters twelve and thirteen then focus on ways of using immune system ideas for more traditional optimization tasks. Chapter twelve describes how immune systems ideas have recently been studied in application to job-shop scheduling problems; the idea here is that an evolutionary computation method can produce an artificial immune system which greatly aids the process of rescheduling when circumstances require it. In chapter thirteen, immune systems ideas are used in enhancing the performance of an evolutionary algorithm for optimizing structures.

Acknowledgements

This work is supported by the faculty research grant (FY'98) of the University of Memphis.

Chapter Eleven

A Distributed Architecture for a Self-Adaptive Computer Virus Immune System

Gary B. Lamont, Robert E. Marmelstein, David A. Van Veldhuizen

11.1 INTRODUCTION

Computer viruses are widely acknowledged as a significant computer threat. It is difficult to quantify this threat, but indications are that it is becoming more and more widespread. Two qualitative trends are recognized and accepted: the 'birth rate' of new viruses is high and increasing, and accelerating computer interconnectivity and interoperability enhances the capabilities of viruses to spread (Kephart et al [1997]). These factors make it increasingly difficult for existing anti-virus products to keep pace with threat proliferation. Observe that the combinatorics associated with the ability to identify, classify and eliminate computer viruses, and repair their damage, is overwhelming. In response to this situation several research efforts are using Biological Immune Systems (BISs) as a model for developing techniques which identify, attack, and eradicate viruses from computer systems. Of particular interest to researchers is the computational emulation of BIS self-adaptation mechanisms to combat previously unseen viruses in unpredictable and unsecured user environments. Other discussions on the association of BIS concepts with computer immune systems are found in Forrest et al [1994], and Kephart et al [1997].

This discussion examines how modelling the human BIS as a hierarchical distributed information processing system can be used to protect against computer viruses (Marmelstein et al [1998]). We begin in section 11.2 by summarizing key facets of the human BIS and associate this model with Computer Virus Immune System (CVIS) requirements and implementation challenges. Contemporary research in this field is examined and evaluated in section 11.3.

This analysis culminates in section 11.4, where we discuss Intelligent Agents (IAs) and their possible employment in the proposed distributed CVIS architecture. Finally, we present our conclusions and future work in section 11.5.

11.2 IMMUNE SYSTEM MODELLING AND REQUIREMENTS

In this section we explore the suitability of the human BIS as a model for an adaptive CVIS. This is accomplished by identifying the principal components of the BIS and using them to define CVIS requirements. The term BIS refers to all processes protecting against foreign pathogens, thus including the innate immune process at birth with continuing antibody adaptation to environmental pathogens including vaccination (*active immune system*). In a *passive immune system*, antibodies are injected directly into the body, an example being mother–child antibody transfers. Note that the BIS is not an absolute system such that it finds all pathogens, but is only partially able to protect the body against *all* pathogens.

11.2.1 BIS Overview

The human BIS is a vast and unique network of molecules and cells. The primary function of the human BIS is to protect the body against foreign microorganisms (or antigens) such as viruses, bacteria, and parasites. The basic but imperfect process via which each BIS accomplishes this task is extensively described (with detailed pedagogical diagrams) by a number of authors including Stryer [1995] and Marrack & Kappler [1993]. Rather than reiterate these detailed discussions of a BIS's multi-layered structure, here we will explain our simplifed BIS model which has two major components: *extracellular* and *intracellular* at our CVIS modeling level.

Extracellular BIS

We treat the extracellular BIS as the following high level set of interacting components (generator/suppresser, detector, classifier, purger, BIS memory, adaptation process). These are each described next, and a consideration of their interactions with each other is illustrated in Figure 11.1.

Generator/Suppresser: The diversity of antibodies evolves from a random generation of B-cell types, self/non-self discrimation, and identification of families of antigens, thus resulting in a robust detection system. The diversity of BIS antigen receptors is accomplished through combining memory genes (stem cells) in a random manner in the bone marrow eventually generating pro-B-cells that are winnowed for self/non-self with support of 'helper' T-cells. Thus, self-identified cells are suppressed. Each antibody producing B-cell can make a specific antibody as determined by its DNA base sequence as reflected in five general classes of antibodies (Stryer [1995]). The distinctive DNA sequence determines the amino acid sequence of its antibody which are replicated on the B-cell's surface.

Detector: General detectors discriminate between entities that are part of the host (self) and those that are foreign (non-self). B-cell detectors use receptors to identify an antigen (foreign pathogen invader) through a molecular bond; such an antigen binding to a antibody on the surface of the B-cell is associated with exceeding an *affinity* threshold for detection. The specific affinity is usually not for the entire antigen, but only for a particular antigen site called the *epitope*.

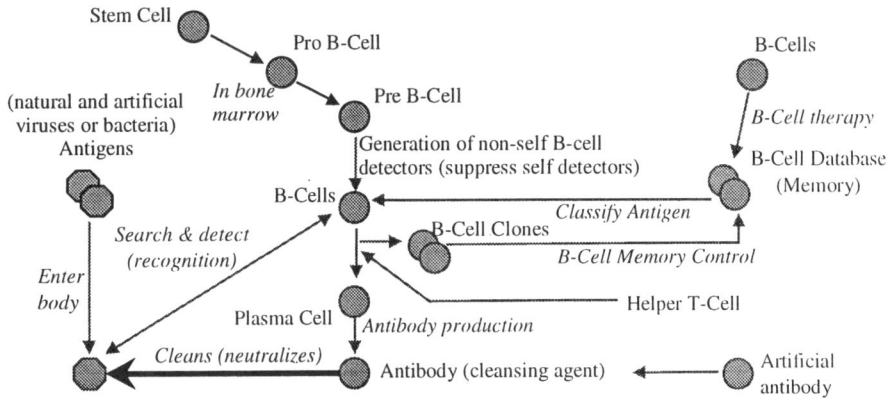

Fig. 11.1: Extracellular BIS (High Level). This is a very simplified model of the extracellular human immune system (BIS) which is a natural distributed and parallel system. The BIS' processes include determining self/non-self; search, detection and classification of antigens; and generating appropriate antibodies used for cleansing, and cloning (dividing) B-cells for memory.

Classifier: Once an antigen is detected, classifiers in the B-cell determine its unique type. Correct classification of the antigen is essential to formulating an effective immune response through release of appropriate antibodies. Once classified, a 'large' number of antibodes are released from the B-cell that successfully identified an antigen. The B-cell then divides into clones that are mutated in a process known as *affinity maturation*.

Purger: B-cells produce specific antibodies that can block (neutralize) antigens by filling their receptors. Since they also can 'mark' an antibody, other cells such as macrophages are constructed that attack or binded with the marked antigen and eliminate it. The particular antigen purging or cleansing process is dependent on B-cell structure and results of detector and classifier actions.

BIS Memory: Distributed memory (e.g. lymphocytes – *lymphocyte* is a general term encompassing both B- and T-cells in the circulating blood supply) stores successful B-cell threat responses (mutated B-cell clones) for future reference. We defined this subprocess as B-cell BIS 'memory control/management'. When faced with another instance of a given antigen, BIS memory is used for detection and classification via antigen receptors to produce the most effective B-cell response. The persistent BIS B-cell memory seems to react using associative memory constructs.

Adaptation Process: The adaptation process modifies BIS components to optimize overall system performance. Each unique BIS is of course imperfect in that every pathogen (antigen) is not uniquely identified. Literature indicates that the BIS contains far fewer genes (about 10^6) than the estimated number of pathogens (10^{16}; Janeway [1997]). Also, finite body resources must be managed in order to adapt to all critical activities. While there is no centralized physical mechanism responsible for this adaptation, its effect on BIS components is observed in a myriad of distributed processes. For example, lymphocytes evolve via reactions to surrounding cells. As depicted in Figure 11.1, pre-B-cells are generated that reflect both self and non-self patterns. Cells detecting self are then suppressed by 'helper' T-cells. This process, known as *negative selection* (Stryer [1995]), eliminates lymphocytes that would attack host cells.

Intracellular BIS

The intracellular BIS system attempts to find antigens existing within living human cells. In order to accomplish this task, the infected cell transports segments or fragments of the antigen to its surface through the action of Major Histocompatibility Complex (MHC) protein molecules. These surface fragments, bonded with the MHC, are identified through receptors on 'Killer' T-cells or CD8 cells which evolve out of the thymus (see Figure 11.2). These Killer T-cells then eliminate the infected cell by physical or chemical action. The intracellular BIS system also generates 'Helper' T-cells or CD4 cells that are an integral element of the self/non-self detector as indicated in the figure. CD4 cells promote inflammation by inducing B-cells to produce antibodies. The generation of T-cell types depends upon the form of MHC (I or II).

Additional BIS Components

Other BIS bacterial infection fighting elements include the *complement system* consisting of over 10 circulating proteins (e.g. inactive and non-functional). By definition, this immunity element is a complement to the antibody approach. It is thought to be an important BIS element in that it generates proteins which indirectly influence extracellular and intracellular processes.

In general, each human BIS is robust in its distributed nature, is able to react to new antigens in a scalable fashion up to a limit of pathogens, and is usually 'fail-safe' (autoimmunity and allergic attacks are exceptions). Because of these characteristics we use the BIS model to develop a hierarchical CVIS design for very complex information processing systems.

11.2.2 Nature of the Computer Threat

Like its biological counterpart, a computer virus can spread from host to host of an information processing system through a variety of methods. With regard to these methods, deterministic viruses can be classified into three major categories: file infectors, boot-sector viruses, and macro viruses. These virus types are usually stealth or semi-stealth in nature. File infectors are normally installed in memory during system initialization or when operating system commands are executed. Once resident they can attach themselves to legitimate programs and files. Boot-sector viruses infect their namesake sector on a given disk. When an infected disk is booted, the virus is loaded into memory and spreads by infecting other disks inserted into the machine. Macro viruses inhabit executable 'macro' files of widely used application programs (such as Microsoft Excel™). Running these infected macros then also executes the virus. Each of these virus types can cause considerable system damage – based upon virus classification.

Software innovations can also undermine computer security. While they make it possible to automate more computer functions, they may also contribute to the spread of viruses while acting on the user's behalf. Thus, an e-mail agent may automatically unleash a virus by opening infected attachments (Etzioni & Weld [1994], Maes [1994]). The Internet, while being a valuable information resource, is simultaneously a possible virus source. Internet browsers make it all too easy to download even infected encrypted files; combining browsers and agents further compounds virus transmission through interconnectivity and interoperability in the present-day computer network domain. Also,underlining protocols and self-encryption code can be contaminated.

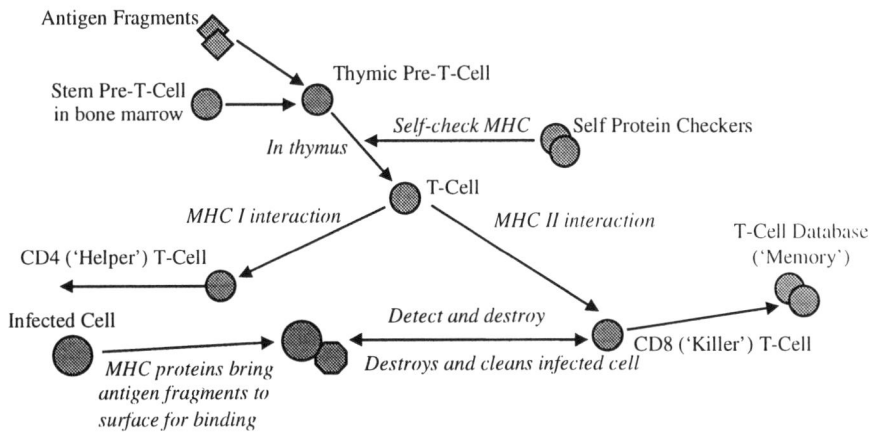

Fig. 11.2: Intracellular BIS (High Level).

11.2.3 CVIS Requirements

Many anti-virus utilities operate by scanning files for bit patterns (called *signatures*) known to belong to a specific virus; these utilities are called signature scanners. In addition, deductive techniques (such as heuristic scanning) use 'rules of thumb' to identify programs exhibiting virus-like behaviour or other anomalies. While reliable, these methods use static knowledge bases that may not describe newer viruses. The result is a continual update cycle required to cope with newer viral threats.

This situation implies a more robust computer security system is needed; we suggest a *silicon*-based immune system automatically and inductively adapting to counter new viral threats. Such a system must possess analogous components to those of its BIS biological counterpart in order to perform necessary functions. These components are described below and are depicted in Figure 11.3 using a data-flow format. Figure 11.4 reflects the CVIS algorithmic view.

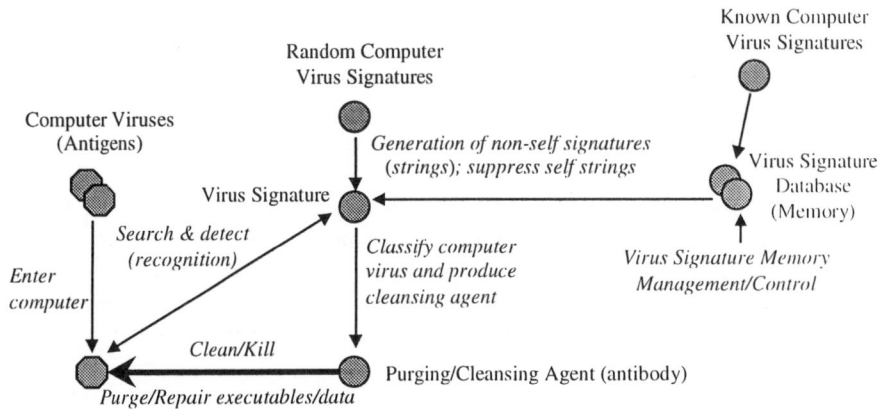

Fig. 11.3: Generic CVIS Data-Flow Diagram. Searching for and detecting computer viruses over all possible computer data settings is highly combinatoric. Also, the choice of deleting or repairing an infected executable or data file depends upon the particular application and computational environment.

Generate/Suppress Virus: Generate a random collection of possible computer virus signatures with possible combination operators to generate new signatures. Compare signatures to a prior determined self strings and remove self signatures as shown in Figure 11.5. Of course, determination of self can be done with an absolute or partial view.

Detect Virus: Detect viral presence (non-self) in the host through string pattern recognition. Detection must occur regardless of whether or not the virus was previously encountered; viruses are identified through a scanning technique (e.g. signature correlation) or a system trace approach. Although a set of detectors could be changing (random mutation) in a random manner in order to react to *all* possible antigens, this is generally impossible because of spatial and temporal constraints. Thus, detectors are generally 'imperfect' so they may detect an extensive variety of possible computer viruses.

Classify Virus: Isolate the computer virus and uniquely identify it based on its characteristics. Use the virus' signature to locate infected host resources (executables, data files, or memory). If the virus cannot initially be accurately classified, extract its signature from an infected entity.

Purge Virus: Purge the virus from all infected resources or remove the resource. Identify damaged system resources (perhaps as part of the purge process) and restore to uninfected state (if possible) or replace from some integrity database.

Augment Virus Database: If the virus was not previously encountered, store all relevant information needed to recognize it in future. Control of the number of virus signatures is accomplished by limiting the number stored in the database.

The adaptation process algorithmic structure for a simple CVIS performing the previous tasks is shown in Figure 11.4. This approach is easily implemented as reflected in many contemporary virus-protection systems. The algorithmic details of the self/non-self process along with virus memory management control are discussed in section 11.4.4.

11.2.4 CVIS Implementation Challenges

Given BIS complexity, significant technical obstacles stand in the way of an equivalent CVIS implementation. Perhaps the most challenging of these is the task of replicating a BIS's inherent parallelism. Consider that in a BIS, lymphocytes are distributed throughout the body's circulatory system. Since each lymphocyte acts as an independent agent the search for antigens (non-self) within the host is highly parallel. In contrast, a number of factors limit the extent to which a search for viruses can be parallelized within most computer architectures. Some of these factors include: number of available system processors, competition between tasks for processor time, and bottlenecks in accessing shared resources (such as disk drives and memory).

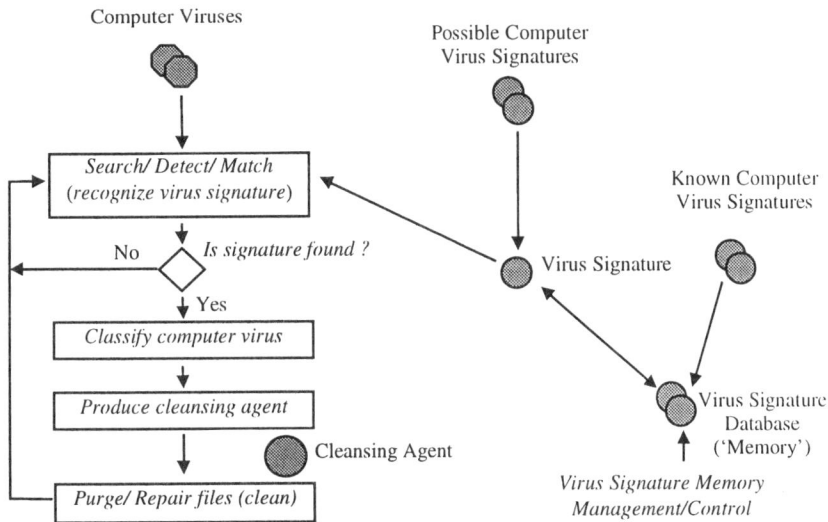

Fig. 11.4: The Generic CVIS Algorithm.

The CVIS should have distributed control, include multi-layer security, minimize autoimmunity (attacking self), limit overreaction (allergy), provide diverse operation implementations, and be self-adaptive in a dynamic software environment. All CVIS activities should be autonomous and disposable due to the dynamic architecture (both software and hardware) of contemporary computer systems.

Implementing an artificial adaptation mechanism is another major challenge in BIS emulation. Because a CVIS is a finite discrete system modelled at a certain level of abstraction, it lacks the evolutionary adaptation mechanism of the multi-layered BIS. Thus, several factors complicate the CVIS adaptation mechanism design. For example, what aspect of the CVIS should evolve? Candidate components include virus detection, virus purge, and damage repair. Whichever is chosen, it is critical to ensure that the cure is not worse than the disease. In addition, the computational overhead of testing candidate solutions for the large number of existing viruses clearly make it impractical to implement a complete CVIS on a single system.

One could also use the intracellular BIS model for virus detection and elimination. Equivalent MHC proteins (string patterns) would probe files and bind with unknown strings. This combined information would then be evaluated by a classifier as to the existence of a virus signature. If identified as a known virus the file would be repaired or destroyed and replaced. If a new virus signature was discovered, an analysis process would attempt to build the complete virus signature from string fragments. This new virus would then be classified and appropriate antibodies generated throughout the CVIS. In this regard, a high level CVIS status evaluation should be available on a continuing basis.

11.3 CURRENT COMPUTER VIRUS IMMUNE SYSTEM RESEARCH

The BIS model has recently generated considerable interest as a source of computer virus fighting techniques. In their survey of artificial immune system research, Dasgupta & Attoh-Okine [1997] cite the CVIS research of Forrest et al [1994,1997] and that of Kephart [1994] and Kephart et al [1997]. Contemporary research of each of these major CVIS researchers can be found at www.cs.unm.edu and www.av.ibm.com respectively. This section evaluates each approach's suitability for specific aspects of our CVIS.

11.3.1 Self/Non-Self Determination

Forrest's work concerns methods for distinguishing legitimate computer resources from those corrupted by a computer virus. This is primarily accomplished via *detectors* monitoring important data. These detectors are randomly generated binary strings of fixed size. Given detector strings are complemented by equally sized segments of protected data; this operation's output determines whether the data has been improperly modified. Thus, detectors act as self/non-self discriminators for protected data. Figure 11.5 indicates the algorithmic flow of this approach and shows the dynamic, continuing evaluation of self/non-self strings.

While elegant in its simplicity, Forrest's algorithm has significant drawbacks. Perhaps most serious is the overhead of generating sufficient detectors to monitor a given data size N_s. Even though a large data set can be monitored using a small number of detectors N_r, only a small percentage of an initial randomly generated detector pool, N_{ro}, proves to be useful. This percentage is determined by the probability P_M that two strings of size l match at r contiguous locations, and the desired reliability P_f of the detector. Thus, given Equation 11.1 with P_M and P_f fixed, N_{ro} must increase exponentially (as a function of N_s) in order to yield N_r valid detectors.

$$N_{ro} = \frac{-\ln P_f}{P_M \times (1 - P_M)^{N_s}} \qquad (11.1)$$

This algorithm's computational overhead further increases if it becomes necessary to protect frequently changing data files. To stay current the system must generate new detectors whenever changes to protected resources occur. It's easily seen that the combinatorics become overwhelming. However, this approach can be made more viable by generating the self/non-self detectors from an infected portion of the file. The resulting detectors are then used to check for the presence of a specific *virus* instead of non-self. Thus, we shift the detectors' purpose from protecting a specific piece of data to virus classification and file integrity inspection. Since a given virus is unlikely to change this variation has much lower overhead than Forrest's method.

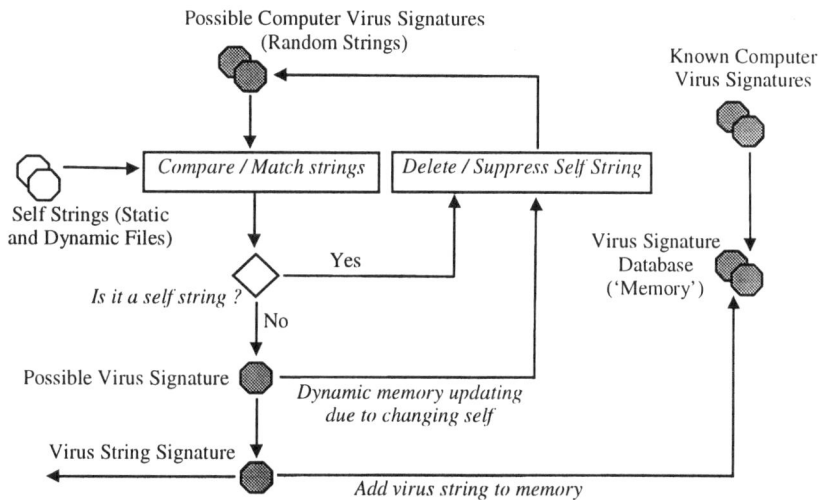

Fig. 11.5: Self/Non-Self Determination Algorithm. This provides the static/dynamic generation/deletion of non-self strings by suppressing self strings (see Forrest et al). We propose the inverse, directly generating non-self strings from infected files.

Constructive induction and machine learning techniques Cardinale & O'Donnell [1999] are other research approaches used to determine self/non-self. For example, constructive induction creates new hypotheses by manipulating current logical rules from a knowledge base, old hypotheses, or other appropriate information; new hypotheses are then evaluated and ordered based upon their ability to achieve the system goal. The initial results of this investigation indicate that constructive induction virus detection provides for distinguishing between changing positive and negative instances of self with the use of byte patterns. In regard to machine learning, logical and spatial operators were able to construct new attributes and thus distinguish between self and non-self with varying degrees of accuracy.

Observe that the constructive induction technique is very similar to a Genetic Programming approach using decision trees for evolving logical computer programs (Koza [1992]). Even with a small, static (architecture and software) contemporary computer system, finding a non-unique program to identify self/non-self has a high complexity measure when considering the required number of system and application software bits. All the approaches are very computationally intensive since computer systems and their resident applications are continuously upgraded.

Another approach employs an expert system using deductive reasoning to determine self/non-self (Dasgupta & Attoh-Okine [1997]). An associated distributed knowledge base is used with logical reasoning to determine the rationale for 'out-of-threshold' activity.

However, a shortfall of all these approaches is that they employ a static pattern matching process, which may be ineffective or even inefficient in dynamic environments.

Also, one can propose alternative algorithms that trade off space and time complexity to generate an ample number of detectors in a given environment. By making these genetic, computational overhead can be reduced at the expense of accuracy (absolute vs partial detection). Whether this genetic approach is feasible depends upon the problem domain and desired performance. With all the approaches, self-anomalies could be incorporated into the virus detector's database too, but knowing that they require an a priori computational cost.

11.3.2 Virus Decoy Programs

The approach of Kephart et al [1997] uses decoys to detect computer viruses via a 'baiting' scheme. Decoys are programs whose sole purpose is to become infected by some virus. This approach uses negative selection as embodied in Forrest's et al approach, but enjoys several advantages over their approach. Since there is no reason for a decoy program to change, the risk of a false positive detection (inherent in Forrest et al.'s algorithm) is practically zero. In addition, because the decoys' file structure is known, virus code can be automatically isolated and its signature extracted. Lastly, the decoy method avoids the overhead of generating new detectors every time protected data changes. The algorithmic essence of this approach is represented in Figure 11.6. It should be noted that the papers of Kephart et al also include system components relating to automatic generation of virus signatures and repair procedures for infected host files. Note that such decoys could be employed as a first step in an adaptive response to a new virus once other mechanisms indicate the existence of a contaminated host file.

Despite its advantages the decoy approach is not without risk. There is no guarantee any virus will attack a decoy in a given time period (if at all). Additionally, the longer it takes a decoy to become infected, the more damage a virus can cause to other system programs. It is then preferable that the decoy possess attributes maximizing its probability of infection. Because these characteristics are virus dependent, decoys must be generic (attracting many viruses) or specialized (for a specific virus). Another drawback is this method's usefulness only for detection and not for classification. As a result, it must be used in conjunction with another method to identify detected viruses.

11.4 TOWARDS AN ADAPTIVE CVIS

As discussed earlier, a CVIS must be adaptive in order to effectively protect against an ever changing virus population. However, as indicated in section 11.2.4, significant technical obstacles stand in the way of achieving such a capability. To overcome these problems we propose a multi-level distributed architecture designed to manage the enormous computational burdens associated with a CVIS implementation, but yet not intrusive or obstructive to the user. This is accomplished primarily through network coordination and communication of autonomous IAs at three levels: local, network, and global in order to provide distributed viral analysis. This section first discusses IAs and presents our proposed architecture, followed by a comprehensive overview of the interlocking hierarchical scheme.

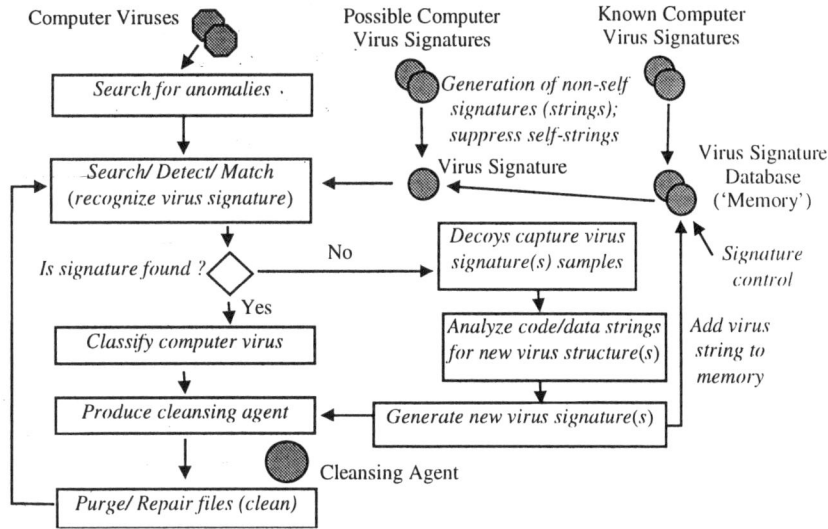

Fig. 11.6: Virus Decoy Algorithm. The decoy system is based upon the BIS' intracellular processes (see Kephart et al [1997]). Cleansing agents (antibodies) may be stored in a database and produced a priori.

11.4.1 Mobile and Distributed Intelligent Agents

The concept of IAs plays an integral role in the architectural design of our hierarchical CVIS. In order to understand this role, the generic structure of an autonomous mobile agent is discussed first with applications to our architecture following.

The concept of an IA evolves from the object-oriented software design process. Agent structures can take on a variety of internal and external characteristics (Karmouch [1998]) reflecting various aspects of human intelligence. In general, an autonomous IA has a number of goals, a scope of competence, and the ability to collaborate and communicate with other agents, objects, and even humans. General agent implementation issues include data/agent transfer mechanisms, naming and addressing, control, communication, security, privacy, coordination, stability, performance, scalability, portability, resource management, authority, and legality (Pham & Karmouch [1998]). In essence, most of these agent characteristics need to be addressed as critical implemented constructs in order to achieve the objectives of our hierarchical CVIS architecture.

Mobile agents must be transportable from one hardware device to another in a specific heterogeneous environment. Such mobility of binary agent images is managed at a meta-level by an appropriate distributed system. This mobile agent system is then a client/server combination which provides for obtaining, executing, and exporting agent images. However, intelligent agents must embody appropriate and complex interfaces in order to transcend the hierarchy within heterogeneous OS environments. For example, such a distributed IA system requires various secure interoperability OS protocols such as those found in Internet communication processing. Implementation consideration and performance evaluation must be given to the underlying communication process (message passing – MPI, PVM or threads – DCOM, COBRA). Although many detailed mobile agent designs have been proposed, here we focus only on their use in a CVIS.

Based upon the generic BIS lymphocytes and the associated CVIS functions presented earlier, the generic autonomous IA types in the proposed system would include: monitoring (detect), action (classify, produce, repair, update), communicator, helper, killer (destroy, purge, clean), and suppressor agents. Such agents would have three general modes of operation (Dasgupta [1998]): sensing, recognition, and response. The design of these agents and their modes of operation would naturally follow an object-oriented standard.

11.4.2 IAs and the CVIS Architecture

In the three-tiered architecure of our hierarchical CVIS (see Figure 11.7), the IAs take on a variety of collaboration/communication tasks. The dynamic client/server role of each element of the proposed CVIS depends upon the particular IA task being executed. The IAs are described using the previous nomenclature, and their major tasks, classified in terms of global level (strategic) or local level (tactical), are shown in Table 11.1.

11.4.3 Local Level

An IA at the local level controls all of the CVIS-related activities for an individual computer system (or node). Because we desire to minimize the CVIS processing overhead on each node, only those functions which are necessary for *tactical* virus protection are performed at this lower level.

Table 11.1: IA Roles in the CVIS.

CVIS Level	Major Tasks
Local Level (tactical)	Self/Non-self Detection: Model user/software activity (e.g., access, execution, and file/disk/memory size patterns)
	Monitor for abnormal activity (e.g., exceeding pattern thresholds)
	Determine causes of threshold violations
	Monitor disk/file/memory changes
	Detect and classify virus signatures
	Eliminate viruses and repair data, files, ...
	Analyze system vulnerability Network Level
	Classify virus signatures (decoys)
	Distribute virus alerts to network computer systems:
	Exchange virus signatures with low-level computers
	Report results of processing detected virus infections
Global Level (strategic)	Generate and adapt virus detectors (e.g., strings, weights): Download virus fighting software resources (e.g., detectors) to network as required
	Download virus information from external sources
	Evaluate and report overall system status

```
┌─────────────────────────────┐
│ Global Level:               │
│   Resource Adaptation       │
│   Detector Generation       │
│   Resource Warehouse        │
└─────────────────────────────┘
```

```
┌─────────────────────────┐        Messages:  ⬆    Messages:
│ Network Level:          │        Resource        Resource Request
│   Virus Classification  │                        Infected Decoy
│   Alert Generation      │                        Metrics        ⬇
│   Metrics Reporting     │
└─────────────────────────┘
```

```
┌─────────────────────────┐        Messages:  ⬆    Messages:
│ Local Level:            │        Resource        Resource Request
│   Vulnerability Analysis│        Virus Alert     Infected File  ⬇
│   Virus Detection       │
│   Virus Elimination     │
│   System Repair         │
└─────────────────────────┘
```

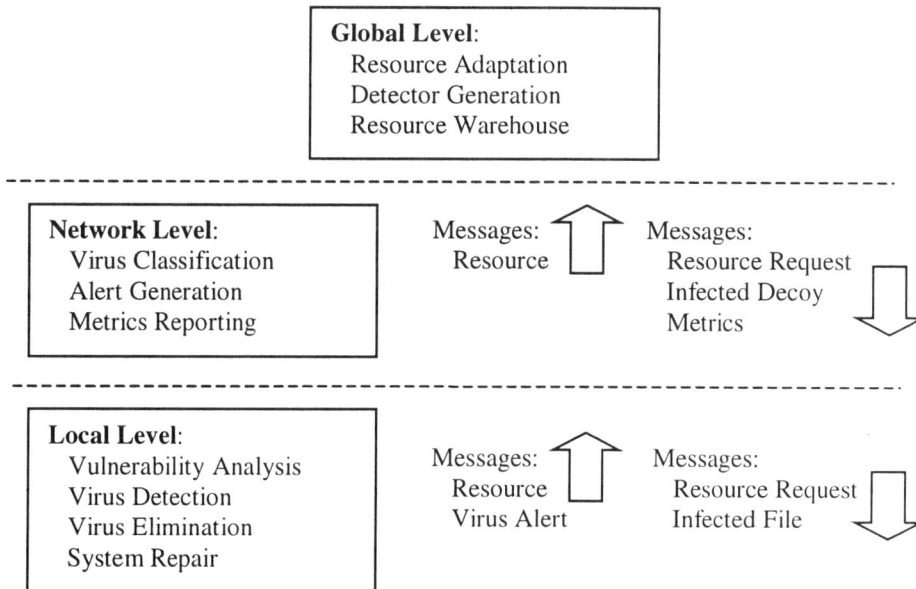

Fig. 11.7: Distributed CVIS Architecture.

Virus Detection and Classification

Virus detection is accomplished in part by using Kephart's decoy approach (section 11.3.2). A local IA manages decoys resident on a given node, in particular determining the number and type of decoys needed for the node's protection. It schedules them for execution, and periodically checks each decoy for infection. If an infected decoy is found the contaminated file is sent to the network level for virus classification. This approach provides multiple and redundant virus capture mechanisms. Also, we suggest that generic and specific virus signature pattern matching techniques be employed to 'quickly' find known and unknown viruses. Thus, the virus classification process for these techniques should be placed at the local level for efficiency. Many CVIS researchers indicate that such a combined approach would also be more effective in an overall CVIS design. Multilevels of detection and classification are proposed with the overall design.

Virus Elimination

After the network IA has classified the virus, it sends the local IA the set of detectors needed to identify the detected virus. As discussed in section 11.3, this enables the remaining files on the system to be tested for infection.

System Repair

If possible, the local IA tries to repair infected files. This process is initiated if a repair routine exists (at the global level) for a given virus. If none is available the file is deleted and replaced with its most recent (uninfected) backup.

Vulnerability Analysis

Scanning the system configuration attempts to uncover deficiencies in the current virus protection level. Since the local IA tracks known network threats it uses the audit's results in requesting resources to improve the node's threat readiness.

The local IA's functionality depends heavily on its interaction with the network and global levels. While the local IA performs functions with relatively low processing overhead (e.g. executing and checking decoys), more complex functions (e.g. virus classification, signature extraction, and decoy evolution) are performed by dedicated platforms at higher CVIS levels. In terms of information exchange, the local IA routes all requests for virus fighting resources (e.g. decoys, detectors, file repair routines) through its associated network IA. The local IA is sent the resources corresponding to its request in turn. Alerts are also received at the local level regarding viruses discovered in the network. These alerts trigger vulnerability audits which are the basis for resource requests. The guiding principle is that the local IA is responsible for maintaining the resource configuration needed to successfully counter viruses on its particular node.

11.4.4 Network Level

Our architecture's network level contains nodes characterized by a high degree of interaction. It is expected that nodes at this level exhibit one or more of the following characteristics: they share a large number of resources, they are connected by a local or wide area network, and they support a common organization. Under these conditions an infection appearing in one node can quickly spread throughout the network. As a result, a key network IA purpose is to insure its local IAs are informed of any virus found in the network. In addition, the network level acts as a conduit for resource transfers between the local and global CVIS levels. The network IA performs several activities.

Virus Classification (Decoys)

When network IAs receive infected decoy files (from their local IAs), they attempt to classify the embedded virus. This is done by checking the infected decoy portion against the library of detectors for each virus on file. If a match is found, the appropriate detector set is sent to the local IAs for virus elimination. Infected files that cannot be identified are forwarded to the global level. In order to provide antibody diversity within memory resources (see Figure 11.8), we use an informative entropy measure ($p \cdot \log p$) associated with each string element (gene) and sum over all genes (Mori et al [1996]). The intent is to maximize entropy while limiting memory requirements using a Genetic Algorithm (see section 11.4.5). This simple Genetic Algorithm (GA) model uses *somatic* (body) recombination and *somatic* mutation operators to provide search diversity. These associated operators employ an *affinity* measure between antigens and antibodies based upon gene connectiveness to determine individual parent selection. In a particular application, the GA convergence rate might be extensive, but the assumed time constraints of most computational environments should permit the CVIS to operate in the background permitting the long-term evolutionary process to be successful.

Threat Alert Distribution

A network IA also distributes alerts about viruses detected in the network. An alert is issued when a local IA detects a virus and the infected file is forwarded to the network IA. If the network IA can classify the virus it sends alert messages and detectors to all local IAs within its span of control.

Metrics Reporting

The network IA reports its success (or lack thereof) in processing detected infections. For example, a decoy successfully attracting a virus is reported to the global CVIS level. These reports are used as metrics (at the global level) gauging the overall fitness of a given resource within the CVIS.

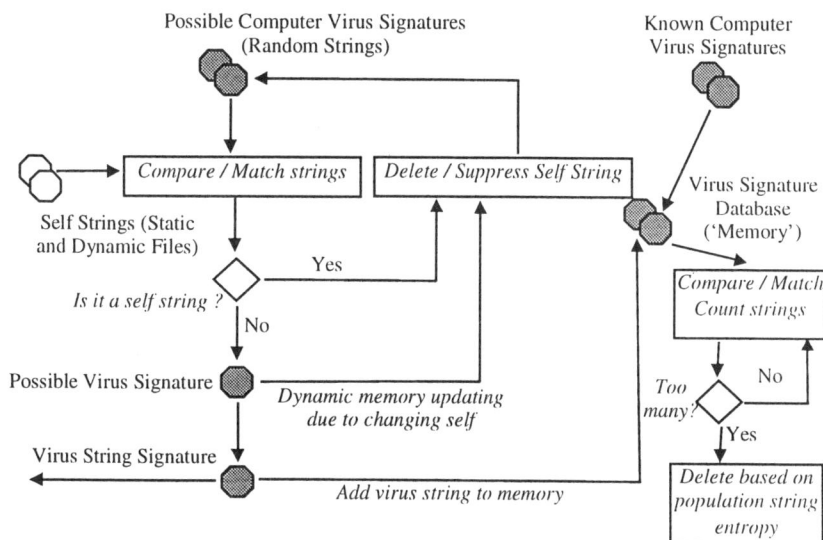

Fig. 11.8: Self/Non-Self determination algorithm with GA component. The GA provides virus signature diversity within a given database. This keeps the database size 'reasonable'.

11.4.5 Global Level

The apex of our architecture hierarchy is the *strategic* global level. Activity at this level is focused on generating and adapting virus-fighting resources and evaluating overall system status. Once developed, the viral immune resources can be distributed and become operational throughout the network via the IAs. In this sense, the global level acts as a warehouse for resources found to be useful at the lower levels of the CVIS architecture and reports on their effectiveness and status.

Application of Evolutionary Algorithms

Evolutionary algorithms (EAs) are used at the global level as a means of resource adaptation. As an example, we explain how decoys are evolved within our architecture. Recall that decoys are used for detecting viruses on a host node. We propose a Genetic Algorithm (GA) to improve the performance of two decoy types: virus specific and generic. This GA is defined using the general model provided by Bäck [1996; page 122] as follows:

$$GA = (I, \Phi, \Omega, \Psi, s, \iota, \mu, \lambda) \tag{11.2}$$

where I corresponds to individuals, Φ the fitness function, Ω the GA probabilistic operators, Ψ the generation transition function, s the selection operator, ι the termination criteria, μ the number of parents, and λ the number of offspring.

Our approach is to use all networks linked to the CVIS as a laboratory for evaluating the decoy population. In our GA instantiation, the chromosome (I) is composed of attributes affecting the decoy's behaviour; these include Processor Duty Cycle (PDC), file size and name, directory location, and priority. Once a population of individuals is generated, they are randomly downloaded to applicable local IAs. At that point we begin to collect statistics on each individual's fitness.

Fitness is computed based on decoy type. In the virus specific case, fitness is dependent upon how quickly the decoy attracts a virus. We define this metric by counting the number of files found to be infected by the virus relative to the PDC amount used by the decoy (Equation 11.3). Thus a decoy containing infection with low PDC maximizes its fitness. For the generic decoy case (Equation 11.4), given N viruses and $M(i)$ nodes infected by the ith virus, we compute fitness by averaging Φ_1 for each node affected. Using this approach we maximize Φ_2 for each decoy based on the number of viruses it detects.

$$\Phi_1 = \frac{1 - PDC}{\text{Number of Infected Files} + 1} \tag{11.3}$$

$$\Phi_2 = \frac{1}{N} \sum_{i=1}^{N} \begin{pmatrix} 0, & \text{if } M(i) = 0 \\ \frac{1}{M(i)} \sum_{j=1}^{M(i)} \Phi_1 & \text{if } M(i) > 0 \end{pmatrix} \tag{11.4}$$

The above process need not be computationally intensive. Consider that weeks (or even months) may elapse before a critical mass of metrics are collected justifying a new generation of decoys. This enables a single, dedicated platform at the global level to manage a large decoy population. Virus priorities determine the proportion of processing resources devoted to the GA (with newer viruses receiving highest priority). Since a virus may never become extinct, the GA's priority can be decreased in proportion to the time the CVIS has been free of viruses. This approach is substituted for a fixed GA termination criteria. Other GA parameters are to be defined upon implementation.

Generation of Virus Detectors

Our CVIS design adapts to new viruses by learning how to classify them through continued learning by example (induction) with the GA meta-level process. Recall that infected files which cannot be classified are sent to the global level. The global IA isolates infected portions of the decoy and attempts to match them to a known virus; if this fails the infection is cataloged as a new virus. Accordingly, using a GA, self/non-self detectors for the new virus are generated. These are then forwarded to the network IAs facilitating classification of future instances of the same virus. Of course, this approach is predicated upon static virus signatures. On the other hand, the GA could classify all known viruses at the global level providing possible better effectiveness.

11.4.6 CVIS Modelling of BIS Morphisms

In section 11.2 we proposed the human BIS as a model for an adaptive CVIS. Our architecture successfully implements key model elements as reflected in the unique BIS/CVIS figures or flow diagrams. At a high level of observation, the BIS has five interacting components: detectors, classifiers, purgers, memory, and an adaptation process which map pedagogically to our explicit CVIS model. Other researchers as referenced have also proposed somewhat similar but abstract relationships.

CVIS detectors are produced by the global IA, and used by network and local IAs. Classification is performed at both the network and global levels. Local system repair emulates cleansing agent actions. Memory is distributed across the CVIS' levels, and finally, our CVIS implementation automatically adapts to new viral threats. The proposed CVIS architecture *in toto* thus executes the key BIS components in a silicon environment.

Specific computational concerns with the proposed hierarchical architecture include the impact of message passing overhead between levels, decoy programs if used as the sole detection mechanism may fail to locate viruses within an appropriate time frame.

11.5 CONCLUSIONS AND FUTURE WORK

We have proposed a distributed CVIS architecture based on its biological counterpart, the BIS (both extracellular and intracellular views). This design makes extensive use of effective and efficient low-level virus fighting approaches developed by others. What distinguishes our work is that we have modified the techniques (specifically addressing virus detection and classification) and augmented them with new technologies (such as EAs and IAs), resulting in a comprehensive autonomous CVIS design capable of adapting to new viral strains. Further, we have illustrated how the distributed nature of our CVIS architecture mitigates the enormous computational burden of this task and provides an effective and efficient computer immunology system.

One should continue analyzing and designing various aspects of the proposed CVIS architecture including parameter optimization and intelligent mobile agent implementations along with consideration of more refined BIS elements. Specific focus would compare mobile agent structure to static agent structure effectiveness and efficiencies, movement of appropriate IA detection, classification and purging operations between levels for real-time applications. Also, the statistical aspects of evolutionary algorithms in general provide tantalizing techniques to obtain adaptive CVIS architectures with improved performance.

Because of the extensive programming aspects of the proposed CVIS, we suggest a comprehensive real-world development based on it be standardized, implemented, and validated by an appropriate agency such as the Air Force Information Warfare Center, the CERT Coordination Center, or the National Computer Security Association.

Chapter Twelve

The Evolution and Analysis of a Potential Antibody Library for Use in Job-Shop Scheduling

Emma Hart and Peter Ross

12.1 INTRODUCTION

The biological immune system defends the body against pathogens and other toxins that may be harmful. Remarkably, despite the fact that the body has fairly limited genetic resources, and there are an almost infinite number of possible pathogens, the immune system is able to react rapidly and efficiently to both those antigens it has previously encountered, as well as entirely new ones.

An analogy can be made to a manufacturing scheduling environment: while a factory is running, many environmental changes occur which will result in any pre-planned schedules having to be altered. The nature of these changes is varied and covers an almost unlimited range of possibilities. Some events occur frequently and are predictable, whilst others are completely unpredictable. For example, certain parts required to complete a job may arrive later than expected, a customer may suddenly demand a job to be completed earlier than planned, or a machine may break down and be unable to be used for some period of time. An efficient scheduling system should be able to react quickly to such changes, and either alter the current schedule or rapidly produce a new schedule to take such changes into account, so that manufacturing continues in an efficient manner.

Although there has been a great deal of previous work in the job-shop scheduling domain, almost all of it has concentrated on producing schedules that are as close to optimal schedules as possible, in the sense that some objective is minimizd. However, such schedules are often extremely fragile, in that a minor change in conditions can render the schedule useless.

Ideally we wish to maintain a scheduling system that not only can produce robust schedules that are resilient to minor changes, but can also produce sets of schedules that together cover all the contingencies that may occur, both foreseeable, and unforeseeable.

12.2 PREVIOUS APPROACH

Previous work described in Hart et al [1998] investigated the potential for the use of an immune-system methodology in the job-shop scheduling domain. Assume there are j jobs; each job is to be processed on some or all of m machines, in some job-specific order. The length of time each job spends on a machine, p_{jm}, is also job-specific. We applied the immune-system analogy in the following manner:

Antigen: let an antigen represent a set of conditions describing a possible scenario in the factory for which a schedule must be produced. That is, the antigen defines the expected arrival time of each job, and the date by which each job must be finished. A set of antigens, called the antigen universe, thus represents possible scenarios/contingencies that can occur, and can cover a wide range of conditions.

Antibody: let an antibody represent a list of instructions for creating a schedule, given the conditions described by an antigen.

Matching: an antigen and antibody are said to 'match' if the schedule produced using the instructions given by the antibody and the information supplied by the antigen results in no job completing after the job due-date defined by the antigen.

Match-Score: this represents the maximum number of time units a job is late in the schedule produced as a result of matching antibody and antigen. A perfect schedule has match-score 0; the higher the match-score, the worse the schedule.

Thus, the aim was to create an immune system that could rapidly and efficiently produce schedules to cope with a particular set of circumstances encountered in the factory at a given time.

12.2.1 Representation of the Immune System

The immune system model used was based on that described by Hightower et al [1995, 1996]. In this model, the genetic material required to produce an antibody molecule is stored in a set of antibody libraries. Each library contains a set of 'components' or fragments of antibody.

An antibody is produced by combining a randomly selected component from each library. Thus, an immune system containing l libraries, each with c components, can produce c^l different antibodies – this is known as the potential antibody repertoire. If the components in each library are genetically dissimilar, then the scope for producing a diverse range of antibodies is increased. A genetic algorithm is used to evolve the components of the immune libraries.

Each component of our scheduling immune system represented a partial list of instructions for creating a small part of a complete schedule. An indirect schedule representation, first described in Fang et al [1993] was chosen to ensure that randomly combining components from the libraries would result in a valid schedule. The representation was as follows:

A complete schedule is represented by jm genes. Alleles have values between 1 and the largest job number j. A string provides instructions for building a legal schedule as follows; a string 'abcd...' is interpreted as 'put the first untackled task of the ath uncompleted job into the earliest place where it will fit in the schedule, then place the first untackled task of the bth uncompleted job into the earliest place it will fit in the developing schedule...'. The task of constructing the actual schedule is handled by a schedule builder which maintains a circular list of uncompleted jobs, and a list of untackled tasks for each job. The notion of ath uncompleted job is taken modulo the length of the circular list, and hence the representation is always valid, regardless of the alleles present in the genotype. This lends itself to straightforward reproductive operators and is particularly suitable for an immune-library representation where random components are combined to produce a complete schedule.

12.2.2 Performance of the Immune System

A variety of experiments, discussed in detail in Hart et al [1998] showed that a GA could be used to successfully evolve a set of immune libraries. The system was evaluated by attempting to induce a 'response' (schedule) from the immune system by presenting it with a set of scheduling conditions (antigen). The response mechanism was straightforward :

Until a satisfactory schedule is found or a maximum of 2000 evaluations reached:

- Randomly select a segment from each library to form an antibody
- Apply a sequence of random mutations to the antibody
- Evaluate the schedule produced by applying the instructions in the antibody to the data in the antigen.

Tests were done first using the original antigens that had been used to evolve the immune-system, and then with several antigen universes which contained previously unencountered antigens. The results were encouraging. Fang's GA tends to need 20×10^3 evaluations to find a satisfactory schedule. Tests using the evolved AISs require at most 2×10^3 evaluations. Figure 12.1 shows the average quality of the best schedule found by Fang's GA at each evaluation (averaged over 10 trials) and compares it to the average quality of the schedules found using an evolved AIS after only 2×10^3 evaluations, for one of the test antigens. Detailed results for 40 different antigens are given in Hart et al [1998].

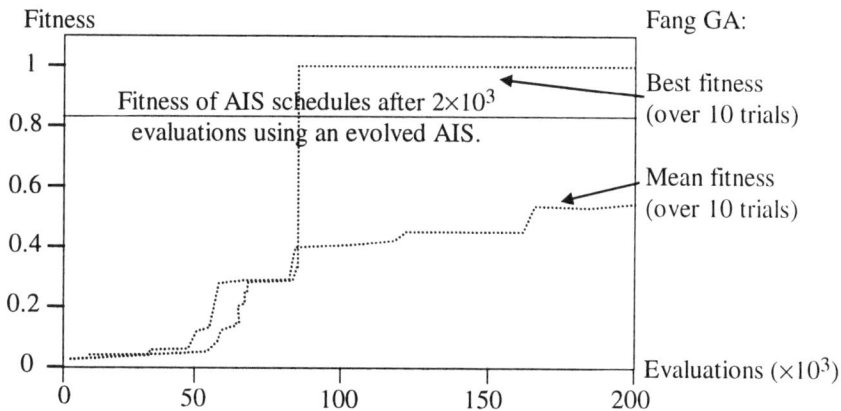

Fig. 12.1: Comparison of AIS schedule quality criteria to the quality of those schedules found by Fang's method (Fang et al [1993]).

12.3 PROBLEMS WITH THE PREVIOUS APPROACH

Although this early work indicated that the approach outlined above had some potential as a method for generating and storing good 'parts' of schedules, there are two obvious flaws. These were concerned with the choice of representation, and with the underlying time complexity of the approach arising from combinatorial explosion:

Representation: the information contained in a single library component changes its meaning according to the components preceding it in an antibody. It would be preferable if a component retained its meaning regardless of the other components it combined with. However, it is difficult to envisage a representation in which this would be true and yet combining random components would still lead to feasible antibodies.

Combinatorics: the major flaw in the approach lies in the method used to retrieve antibodies from the fully evolved immune system. Selecting random components and combining them to produce antibodies results in an antibody search space of size c^l. There could be considerable variation in quality across this space, and yet it could be counterproductive to spend much effort searching it. In the experiments described, the antibody search-space was size 3125 (5^5), which is small compared to the number of schedule evaluations generally required by a GA to solve such a problem, which is often of the order of 20,000 (see Fang et al [1993] and Lin et al [1997]). However, in large problems which require larger immune systems, the combinatorics may become intractable.

Moreover, analysis of data supplied by real companies relating to their scheduling problems, for example Hart et al [1998a] reveals that similar scenarios often crop up over and over again, and as a result there are known methods for dealing with them. An experienced scheduler can quickly piece together new schedules using prior knowledge gained from past experiences. Therefore, the problem is generally not to produce a new schedule starting from scratch, but to select and draw on prior experiences to adapt to the new situation.

12.4 USING HISTORICAL INFORMATION IN THE PRESENT AND FUTURE

Thus, we conjecture that although a variety of conditions may arise that all require a new schedule to be implemented, the conditions are often predictable. Further, although many slight deviations from the norm arise, it is rare to have to radically reschedule. For instance, consider the following situations, typical to a large variety of scheduling problems:

Typical patterns of customer requests can be predicted for different times of the year, remaining reasonably constant from year to year, and hence result in predictable schedules.

Certain machines commonly break down or require maintenance. If the situation is encountered regularly, there are known procedures and schedules for coping with such events. A scheduler gains some intuition regarding sequences of events which tend to produce good schedules when performed in some particular order in many situations.

Jobs arriving from certain other factories or other parts of the same factory tend to arrive early or (more often) late. Again, an experienced scheduler has knowledge of how to deal with these situations.

Thus it appears reasonable that in many real-life situations, not only are there a certain number of predictable scenarios which require rescheduling, but as many of the events are foreseeable and common, there are known procedures from dealing with them. Therefore, a set of historical schedules or partial schedules is made available for use when trying to reschedule.

If we examine the set of practical schedules that are used for the commonly occurring scenarios, then one notices various types of patterns occurring across subsets of the schedules. For instance, simply considering the order in which jobs are processed on machines it becomes obvious that there are particular groups of jobs (of varying size) that tend to occur in close proximity or in some particular order in more than one schedule. For example, common job sequences may be observed, such as 'operation a always occurs directly before operation b', or 'operations a,b,c tend to occur in a group in many schedules, but in different permutations'.

Thus, if a set of common patterns or parts of schedules could be built up using the knowledge encapsulated in past schedules, then these patterns can be used as building blocks when constructing a new schedule. Using good building blocks ought to be an efficient and rapid way of calculating a new schedule, as the scheduling process would take account of useful information learned in the past.

Although the job-sequences on each machine are an obvious candidate for observing patterns, there are other attributes of the system in which patterns may be observed, for example distribution of idle times on machines. In the remainder of this article, we consider only the task of recognizing sequences in job orders on each machine to illustrate the point. Thus, an antigen can be considered to represent the sequence of jobs on a particular machine, given a particular scenario, and an antibody represents a short sequence of jobs that is common to more than one machine.

12.5 IMMUNE SYSTEMS AND PATTERN RECOGNITION

Previous work by Forrest et al [1993], and Smith et al [1993], has shown that an immune system model combined with a genetic algorithm can be used to evolve a set of antibodies that recognize a range of diverse, binary antigen strings. This work showed that an immune system model could both detect common patterns (schemas in the binary case) in a noisy environment and also maintain diversity in that many types of antibody evolved in niches, each niche responsible for recognizing a particular antigen. Moreover, they showed that it was possible to control the evolution of the antibodies to be either specialist (i.e the antibody only recognised a single specific antigen), or generalist (i.e the antibody recognized a wide range of antigens) by varying the parameters of the genetic algorithm. This is precisely the function that needs to be realized by our pattern recognizing antibodies in the scheduling domain, but using non-binary strings.

12.5.1 Emergent Fitness Sharing

Smith and Forrest propose an emergent fitness sharing algorithm to encourage evolution of diverse antibodies. The algorithm is shown below.

1. Choose an antigen at random.

2. Choose a sample of size sigma of the antibody population, at random and without replacement.

3. Each antibody in the sample is matched against the chosen antigen, using a match-function M to compute its match-score.

4. The antibody in the sample with the highest match score has its match score added to its fitness. The fitness of all other antibodies remains unchanged.

5. Repeat from step (1) for typically three times the number of antigens.

The hypothesis proposed by Smith et al [1993] and validated in Forrest et al [1993] is that for small σ, generalist antibodies will evolve that match all antigens (to some degree), and for high σ a number of specialist antibodies will evolve, each of which matches a different antigen.

In the context of scheduling, our proposed sequence-recognizing AIS should produce antibodies that are in some ways a compromise between the generalist and specialist antibodies described earlier. For example, it is unlikely that a common sequence of jobs will be observed in all schedules, and hence the completely generalist antibody is unlikely to exist. However, it seems important to find patterns that are common to as many schedules as possible. At the other extreme, highly specialist antibodies that represent patterns occurring in only one schedule are necessary to deal with the particular conditions represented by the schedule, but are less useful as general building blocks for constructing a schedule given any scenario.

Therefore, the ideal set of building blocks or antibodies will contain several diverse patterns. Some of these patterns occur in only one schedule, and some of them match a subset of the known schedules. These subsets of known schedules may intersect or they may be disjoint. Hence, we are interested in two particular attributes of the antibody population:

Overlap: This is a measure of how many antigens a given antibody matches. This provides some measure of how common the pattern represented by the antibody is in the schedule set.

Redundancy: This is a measure of the number of different antibodies matching an antigen. It is important to look for more that one antibody which matches the same schedule, as a schedule may contain several sequences, each of which is common to different subset of the remaining schedules.

The idea is illustrated in Figure 12.2 which shows a population of antibodies, and their ability to match 4 antigens, labelled A,B,C and D.

Preliminary work by the authors (Hart & Ross [1999]) investigated the amount of overlap and redundancy occurring when a population of 500 binary antibodies was evolved using a genetic algorithm. This involved an antigen universe containing up to nine diverse, binary antigens of length 64, using the method described by Forrest. Figure 12.3 shows the number of antibodies in the final population that matched each individual antigen in the case where there were nine antigens, with the shaded fraction indicating how many of those antibodies were unique. A match is said to occur if at least $m\%$ of the bits in the antigen and antibody match, where m is the match-threshold. The figure shows the results obtained at a low match-threshold of 50%, and at a higher match-threshold of 70%. It is clear from the figure that at high match-thresholds, small niches of antibodies occur, but also that there is a high proportion of diversity within the niche. This is promising for the proposed scheduling system.

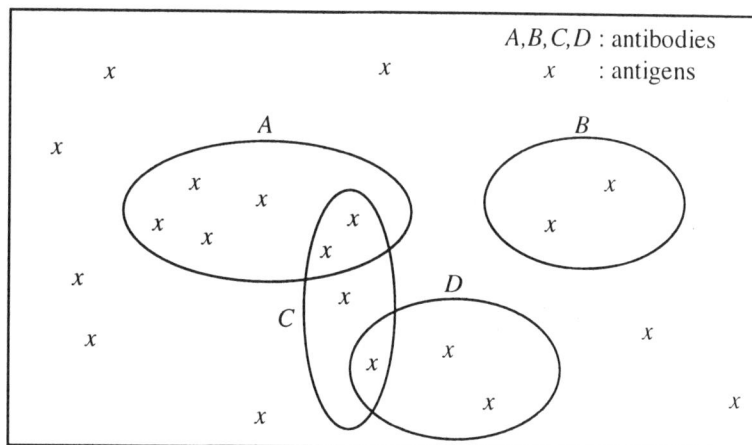

Fig. 12.2: A population of antobodies, showing how they match 4 antigens A, B, C, D.

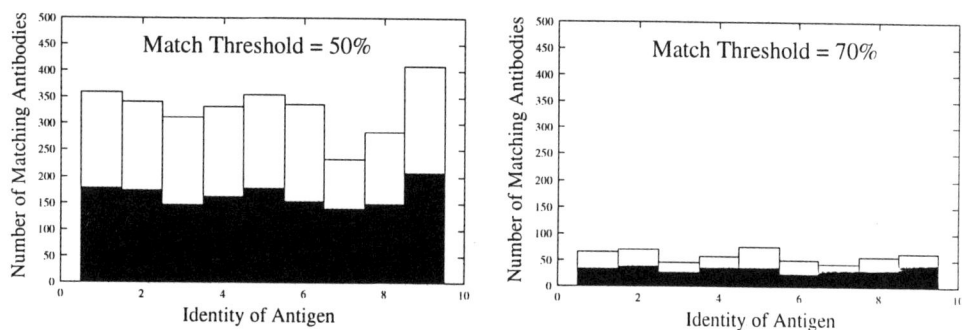

Fig. 12.3: Graphs show the effect of redundancy when using a GA to evolve antibodies matching binary antigens. The shaded portion of the graph represents the fraction of unique antibodies found.

We also examined the amount of overlap in the same populations, by measuring how many of the antibodies in the final population *that match at least one antigen* match more than one antigen. We found that, with a match threshold of 70%, 93% of the antibodies which matched anything matched only one antigen, with the remaining 7% matching two antigens. With the match threshold at 50%, however, the figures are quite different. All antibodies which matched anything matched at least four antigens. To the nearest percentage point, 14% matched only four, 23% matched five, 20% matched six, 39% matched seven, and the remaining 2% matched eight. Clearly, if the match threshold is high, there is very little overlap between antibodies. This is not particularly convenient for our scheduling systems.

The results of these investigations led us to make some modifications to the basic system proposed by Forrest when implementing our scheduling AIS. We modify both the emergent-sharing fitness function and the match-function in order to attempt to encourage more overlap as well as maintaining some level of redundancy and niche formation. The system is now described, with all modifications highlighted.

12.6 AN AIS MODEL FOR PATTERN RECOGNITION IN SCHEDULING

This section describes an implementation of an artificial immune system to recognize patterns in scheduling data. We refer to this system in the remainder of this article as PRAIS – Pattern Recognising Artificial Immune System.

12.6.1 Test Data

Ten test-scenarios were generated from a base problem – jb11 from Morton & Pentico [1993] – extensively used in the GA-scheduling community as a benchmark. jb11 contains 15 jobs to be scheduled on five machines, each job with differing arrival and due-dates.

The test-scenarios were produced by applying a mutation operator with probability 0.2 to each of the arrival dates given in the base problem. The mutation operator randomly changed the arrival date, with the caveat that the new arrival-date was still at least p_t days before the expected due-date, where p_t was the processing time of the job.

Satisfactory schedules were then found for each of the scenarios, using a genetic algorithm described in Fang et al [1993]. From each schedule, we produce five antigens, where each antigen corresponds to the sequence of jobs on one of the machines. An antigen is thus a sequence of integers of length j. This gives us five antigen universes, one for each machine, with each universe containing 10 antigens. Thus, an independent set of antibodies is discovered for each machine.

12.6.2 Antibody Representation

An antibody is represented by a sequence of integers, of length l, where $l < j$. We choose l to be significantly less than j as it is expected that by using a shorter antibody it will be easier to maintain a high degree of match between antibody and antigen. Also, we expect that the common patterns will consist of short sequences of jobs. The method in which such antibodies might be used to construct schedules is described later.

We also add a wild-card allele, '*', to facilitate incomplete matching. A wild-card can match any job. This has the advantage that if many of the common job-sequences are shorter than the chosen antibody length l, a partially matching antibody will have high fitness. Also, it may be possible to observe patterns of the form 'a**b', i.e where the common jobs are not consecutive. The initial antigen population is generated completely at random. An antibody is not allowed to contain duplicate jobs, but may contain multiple copies of the wild-card allele.

12.6.3 The Matching Algorithm

An antibody is matched against an antigen by aligning the two strings. If the antibody is shorter than the antigen, then a match-score is calculated for every possible alignment position. A possible alignment is any alignment in which every gene of the antibody is aligned with every gene of the antigen. This is illustrated in Figure 12.4.

Antigen	1	2	3	4	5	6	7	8	9	Match Score
	3	4	6	7	8					0
		3	4	6	7	8				0
Antibody			3	4	6	7	8			10
				3	4	6	7	8		15
					3	4	6	7	8	0

Fig. 12.4: Possible antibody/antigen alignments, and the resulting match-score.

The match-score is calculated by counting the number of matches between antigen and antibody genes in the alignment. An exact match contributes a score of five, whereas a wild-card match contributes a score of one to prevent the evolution of all wild-card genes.

The reason for allowing multiple binding-sites is that a job-sequence described by the antibody may occur at any position in an antigen. This is also a feature observed in the biological immune system, where both antibody and antigen have multiple binding sites.

12.6.4 Emergent Fitness Sharing Function

As we wish to encourage occurrence of overlapping antibodies in the system, we modify steps (1) and (3) of the function described in section 12.5.1 so that a sample of antigens of size τ is selected without replacement for testing against the antibodies. The match-score of an antibody is summed over each antigen it is tested against, to give its total fitness.

12.6.5 Parameters and Operators

A genetic algorithm based on GENESIS (Grefenstette [1984]) is used to evolve the antibody population. The modified emergent fitness sharing function is used, with a population of size 100. Reproduction of antibodies takes place via one of three crossover operators, depending on the relationship between the two parent antibodies:

Order-Based Crossover (OX): if the parents are permutations of each other, then a well known permutation-based crossover operator, Davis' order-based crossover (OX) is used (Davis [1985]).

2pt-Crossover: if the parents have no genes in common, (excluding wild cards) and the parents differ outside of a randomly chosen cross-segment, use 2pt crossover.

Overlap-Crossover: used if one parent overlaps the other, as shown in Figure 12.5. In this case, align the parents so that the matching regions line up, and then read from the left most position. If only one parent has a gene at a position, use that in the child, if both parents have a gene at the position, select randomly from either parent. Continue reading from left to right until the child is of the required length. In Figure 12.5, matching regions are underlined and shown in bold, and genes which can be chosen from either parent are shown in italics.

In addition, a mutation operator is always applied (that is, with a probability of 1) which has a small possibility of randomly mutating each gene.

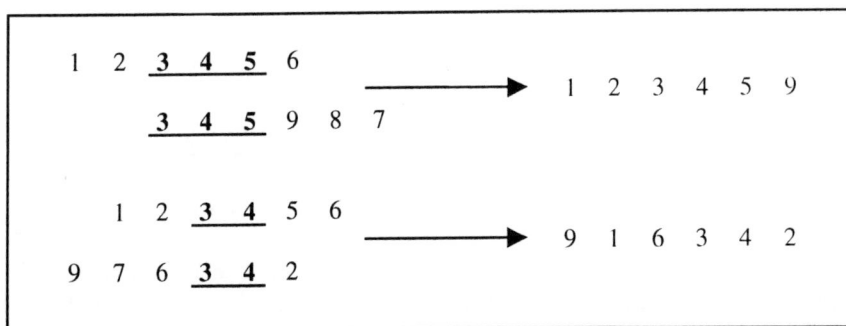

Fig. 12.5: Overlap Crossover: the figure shows examples of two overlapping configurations of parent antibodies and the resulting child antibody in each case.

12.7 EXPERIMENTAL RESULTS

Many experiments were performed to identify good settings for the three main parameters: the antibody sample size σ, the antigen sample size τ, and the length of the antibody l. Here we report results with antibodies of size 5, i.e 1/3 the length of the antigen string. As a separate set of antibodies are evolved for each machine, we illustrate our results here using only one of the machines, machine 1. The set of antigens used is shown in Table 12.1.

12.7.1 Experimental Parameters

All reported experiments were performed using a population of size 100, with the length of each antibody in the population equal to five jobs. Each experiment was run for 250 generations and was repeated ten times. The mutation rate in each case was $1/l = 0.2$. Details of the settings for σ and τ are described in the succeeding sections.

The initial experiments were performed to answer several questions concerning whether the evolved antibodies will be useful pattern recognizers in the context of scheduling.

- How many antigens are matched by at least one antibody?
- How many unique antibodies are found?
- What is the average number of antigens matched by an antibody?
- How many alleles are represented in the set of antibody patterns?

Table 12.1: The antigens representing the job-orders found on machine-1 in 10 different scenarios.

Antigen	Job Order													
a	1	2	7	4	3	9	6	8	14	5	13	12	10	11	15
b	1	3	4	7	6	8	2	5	9	12	10	11	13	14	15
c	1	3	5	4	2	8	9	6	14	7	10	11	12	13	15
d	1	4	14	2	8	6	9	3	7	5	10	12	11	13	15
e	1	4	3	12	7	8	2	6	5	9	10	11	14	15	13
f	1	4	3	7	6	11	2	5	8	9	10	12	13	15	14
g	1	4	6	8	3	2	9	7	5	14	13	10	11	15	12
h	2	8	6	4	7	12	3	9	1	5	10	11	14	15	13
i	3	1	6	2	7	8	9	4	5	11	10	12	13	15	14
j	3	2	7	1	6	9	5	4	15	8	10	11	14	12	15

12.7.2 How many antigens are matched by at least one antibody?

The extent of the match between the evolved antibodies and the antigens in the universe can be measured by calculating the match-score between each antibody and each antigen, and defining a match to have occurred if the match-score is greater than some threshold value m. Table 12.2 shows the average number of antigens (from the universe containing 10 antigens) that were not matched by any antibody, for match-threshold m ranging from 2 to 5. The match-threshold is defined as the number of non wild-card places in which the antigen and antibody match. Experiments are performed over a range of values for σ and τ, the size of the antibody and antigen samples respectively.

Table 12.2: Mean number of antigens (out of a possible 10) not matched by *any* antibody.

Match Threshold	$\tau = 1$ σ			$\tau = 4$ σ			$\tau = 8$ σ		
	5	10	30	5	10	30	5	10	30
2	0.9	0	0.0	2.2	0.9	0.0	3.5	2.5	0.9
3	5.3	2.6	1.6	5.4	3.2	2.0	5.5	4.7	4.1
4	8.7	7.1	5.2	7.8	7.3	6.3	8.6	8.1	8.2
5	9.7	9.5	8.8	9.5	9.5	8.7	9.7	9.6	9.5

For certain combinations of values there are no antibodies that match some of the antigens. This is particularly noticeable as τ increases. With high τ, antibodies that successfully match more than one antigen are rewarded most highly. But, in many antigen-universes, it may be impossible to detect common patterns between certain subsets of antigen, and so the completely generalist antibody may not exist. Examining the antigen universe for machine 1 suggests this is indeed the case – e.g. if subsets of eight antigens are selected, no common pattern may be found. Similarly, low σ also encourage generalist antibodies to evolve, so we may expect poor performance if the value of σ is too low.

12.7.3 Unique Antibodies

The ultimate aim is to acquire a collection of unique antibodies, each of which represents some commonly occurring pattern in the antigen-universe. The more unique patterns we can detect, the more useful the antibodies will be as building blocks for constructing new schedules. Therefore, the final population of antibodies is examined to determine the exact number of unique antibodies that match an antigen with a match-score which is greater or equal to the match-threshold. Table 12.3 shows the results obtained by counting the number of unique antibodies that match in exactly 2,3,4 and 5 places and summing the results. It is clear that number of unique antibodies decreases as τ is increased, and increases as σ increases. This is unsurprising, due to the same arguments outlined in section 12.7.1. Note however that having multiple copies of a matching antibody may ultimately be useful in the response phase when the antibodies are selected for building a schedule – if we consider the number of copies of an antibody in the population as analogous to a concentration, then this concentration can be used as a measure of probability of picking the antibody when trying to reconstruct a schedule. This has strong parallels with the real immune system in which the concentration of an antibody that can bind successfully to an invading pathogen rapidly increases during the secondary response phase (Roitt et al [1998]).

12.7.4 Overlap

We have shown that it is possible to evolve a set of unique antibodies, and also that those antibodies tend to match at least one antigen. Finally, in order to establish the generality of the antibodies in the final population, we record the number of antigens matched by each antibody in the population. As noted previously, the most useful set of antibodies will contain antibodies that have a high degree of *general* characteristics, i.e. each antibody matches more than one antigen. Figure 12.6 shows the number of antibodies that match n antigens, where n takes values between 1 and 10. The diagram contrasts the results obtained for a match-threshold of 2 and using a fixed antibody sample size $\sigma = 30$ for various values of τ. Clearly, more antigens are matched at high values of τ, as expected.

Table 12.3: Number of unique antobodies in final population for match thresholds ≥ 2.

Antibody Sample Size, σ	Antigen Sample Size, τ			
	2	4	6	8
5	23.8	23.7	20.0	17.7
10	38.6	28.0	24.5	20.5
30	58.4	44.4	24.9	39.7

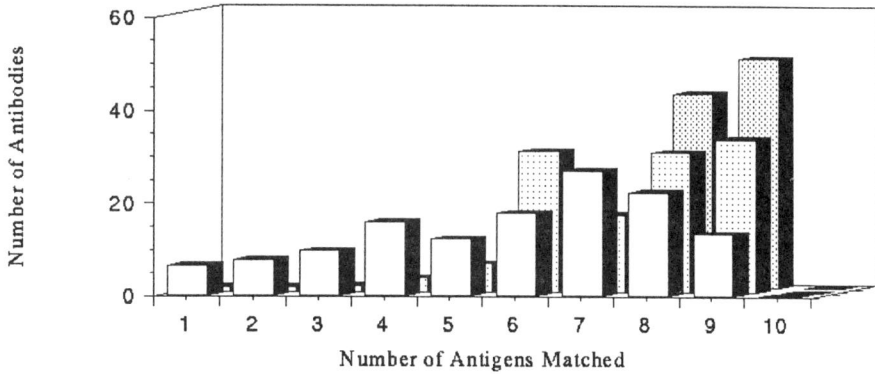

Fig. 12.6: Match threshold 2: antibodies matching more than one antigen for antibody sample size = 30. Antigen sample size is 1 (foireground), 2 (middle), and 4 (background).

It is interesting to observe how the number of antibodies matching more than 1 antigen rises with time. Figure 12.7 summarises experiments where m is varied from 2 to 5, for populations of antibodies in which antibody length is varied from 1 to 5. When the match-threshold is equal to the antibody length, there is rapid increase in the number of matching antibodies in the $m = 2$ case after which the number remains relatively constant. For $m = 3$, the number rises steadily. For values of $m < l$, in each case, there is an immediate increase at the start of each run to a level which is maintained throughout the remainder of the experiment. The initial rise is more pronounced when m is significantly less than l.

12.7.5 Unique Alleles

The greater the number of alleles that are represented by the antibodies, the more useful the patterns will be in constructing new schedules, since these antibody building blocks will cover more parts of the schedule. The exact number of alleles expected to occur in the final antibodies will depend of course on the nature of the antigen-universe; for some universes, there may only be a few alleles which belong to common pattern sequences. Recall that for machine 1, there are 15 possible alleles. Table 12.4 compares the number of unique alleles found in matching antibodies for three different values of σ, given a match-threshold ≥ 2. For small values of σ, very generalist antibodies evolve, representing only a few alleles. However, as σ is increased, the number of alleles represented increases as small clusters of more specialist alleles begin to evolve.

Table 12.4: Mean number of alleles represented in final population for given σ.

	Antibody Sample Size, σ		
	5	10	30
Mean no. of alleles represented	5.6	7.5	9.1

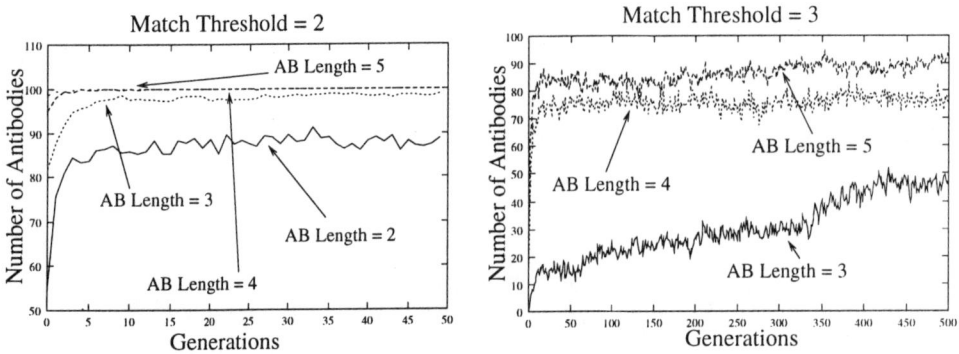

Fig. 12.7: Antibodies matching more than one antigen with $m=2$ (left) and $m=3$ (right).

12.8 THE IMMUNE RESPONSE

We have described how an immune system model combined with a GA using emergent-fitness sharing can be used to evolve a set of antibodies (job-sequences) that match or partially match a set of antigens (schedules). Somehow, we would now like to use these antibodies as building blocks to rapidly construct a schedule in response to changing environmental conditions at the factory. This is analogous to how the real immune system initiates an immune-response in order to counter foreign invaders or pathogens: in an on-going process, the immune system continually manufactures antibodies which circulate through the body, using information encoded in its germline DNA. If an antibody detects an invader, then a response is mounted in which the concentration of the recognising antibody rapidly increases. The next section briefly describes the salient concepts in the natural system and how they are modelled in this case by our scheduling AIS. The reader is referred to Roitt et al [1998] for a detailed description of the natural immune system.

12.8.1 The DNA Germline

The immune system manufactures B-cells which produce antibodies. B-cells are formed by combining light and heavy chains of protein, coded for by the germline DNA of the immune system. Heavy chains are formed by combining three different types of gene from the germline to make a single functional gene unit. The light chain is formed from two variable gene types, plus a constant, non-variable region. The diagram shown in Figure 12.8 is an extremely simplified representation of the process of manufacturing of a heavy chain. Genes from the germline DNA are recombined at random to produce a link which becomes part of the B-cell DNA. This is transcribed and translated via messenger RNA and finally combined with a light chain to form the completed B-Cell which can secrete antibody. The huge diversity of antibodies that are produced is due to this variable recombination of genes to form each chain, and the fact that there are many different light chains and many different heavy chains which can come together in any combination.

Now consider the scheduling AIS. This introduces a rather confusing shift in terminology than that used in sections 12.6 and 12.7 – the *antibodies* produced by the pattern recognition process described in those sections can be considered as *genes* on the germline strands of DNA. Each *gene* represents a sequence of jobs that appears in one or more of the antigens (schedules) in the antigen universe. Combining several of these genes results in this case in a *schedule*, rather than in B-cell DNA.

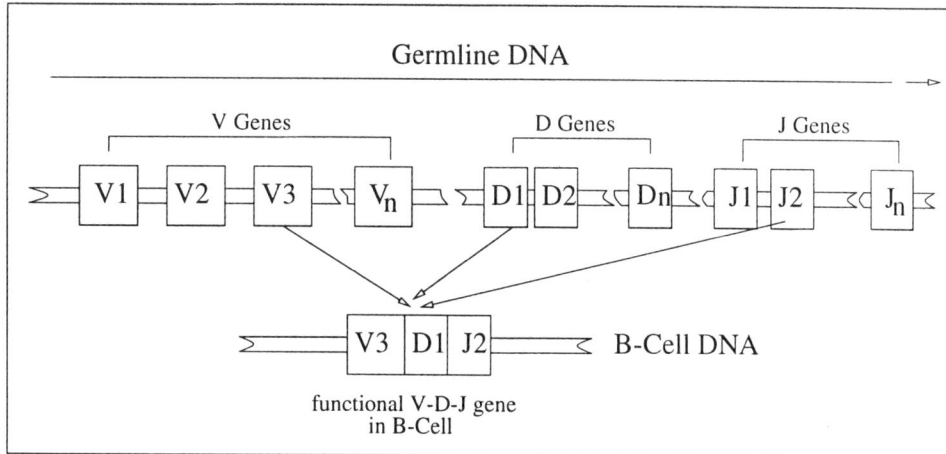

Fig. 12.8: Production of B-Cell DNA from germline DNA.

Thus, we can model the mechanisms used by the real immune system to produce B-Cells to produce schedules. Both systems have a mechanism for continually producing antibodies from a germline. In the real system, those antibodies that recognize pathogens are proliferated. In the scheduling system, antibodies that recognize and react to a specific set of environmental conditions are proliferated. The environmental conditions may simply consist of a set of jobs to be processed, with associated processing-times, arrival-times, and due-dates. In this case, the immune system must produce a complete schedule. On the other hand, the conditions may also define a partially completed schedule, in addition to the information about the jobs. In this case, the immune system must complete the schedule. Therefore, two areas need to be addressed:

1. Using the genes evolved by PRAIS, how can the germline be constructed?
2. How can antibodies be produced from the germline?

The remaining sections describe an immune-system model, CLARISA (CLassification via ARtificial Immune System Analogy), originally implemented by the authors to solve pattern recognition and classification problems, and adapted to solve scheduling problems (Hart et al [1998]). Work is currently in progress to test the efficiency of this system.

12.8.2 Forming the Germline

A simple and very general germline can be formed using all of the output from PRAIS. However, given a specific antigen, it is straightforward to construct an individual germline, especially tailored to produce antibodies that correspond to that antigen only. The process itself is efficient, and results in a more efficient response.

Consider an antigen which consists of a partial sequence of jobs on a machine, plus information regarding the jobs and operations that have yet to be scheduled on that machine. Define the universal set U to be the set of all jobs that are processed on the machine. Define the set A to be the subset of jobs in U that have already been processed. Let S be the set of antibodies output from PRAIS, which are of length l.

1. Select from S all antibodies Ab that consist solely of jobs not yet scheduled. Add this to the germline G.
2. Select from S all antibodies Ab that overlap with A, where an overlap is said to occur if the first n jobs in Ab are equal to the last n jobs in A, where $n \leq l$, and the remaining $(l-n)$ jobs in Ab do not occur in A. Add Ab to the germline G.
3. Add to G any jobs that are not yet included in G, and exist in U.

The germline now contains sufficient information to complete the partial schedule defined by the antigen and can now be used to produce antibodies, i.e schedules in this case. Each *antibody* from S added to G is now referred to as a gene in the germline.

12.8.3   Generating Antibodies from the Germline

The germline may contain c genes. Assume that there are j jobs to be scheduled. Examining all possible combinations of individual jobs would result in $j!$ schedules being evaluated. Although c may be $\geq j$, there are less than $c!$ valid combinations of genes from the germline – as each gene in G contains more than one job, selection of a gene immediately precludes a large number of genes from being selected for inclusion in the same antibody. As well as examining fewer schedules, we are also taking advantage of prior knowledge and past experience when constructing the schedules.

The diversity of antibodies produced by the natural immune system can be attributed to six major recombination mechanisms. The same mechanisms can be employed to produce a diverse range of schedules in the scheduling system. Each method is now discussed briefly, indicating its relationship to the scheduling system.

Multiple genes in the germline: This is the major mechanism for maintaining diversity. As the germline contains multiple genes (thus incorporating some degree of redundancy), many valid combinations of genes can produce feasible schedules.

Somatic Mutation: Somatic mutation occurs as B-cells reproduce to produce clones of themselves. Mutations in some genes result in clones which are slightly different to the parent B-cell. This is easily modelled in a scheduling context – minor mutations can be introduced into completed schedules produced from the germline by use of a swap or shift operator for example.

Somatic Recombination: Mistakes made during gene recombination may result in imperfect recombination, where the final protein contains elements encoded by different gene segments. This is equivalent to genes combining with either some overlap, or with missing genes, resulting in a combination that is shorter than the sum of the combining genes. This is illustrated in Figure 12.9.

Gene Conversion: In the natural immune system, sections of DNA from a number of pseudo-gene regions may be copied into the new gene-link to alter the DNA sequence. This can modelled by considering the single jobs added to the germline in step (3) of the algorithm described in section 12.8.2 to be pseudo-genes, and copying one of these pseudo-genes over a random element of another gene during recombination.

Nucleotide Addition: During the joining of two genes when producing B-cell DNA, extra genes may be inserted between them, coding for additional amino acids. As in the previous paragraph, we can consider the single-job genes added to G as a nucleotides, and insert one of these genes in-between two other genes during recombination.

Joining of Light and Heavy Chains: The discussion so far has concentrated on producing and using a germline for a single machine. Of course, a separate germline for each machine in the problem is required. Each machine can be considered equivalent to a chain in the natural system – whereas the natural system manufactures an antibody by combining heavy and light chains, the scheduling system produces complete schedules by combining the schedules of each machine.

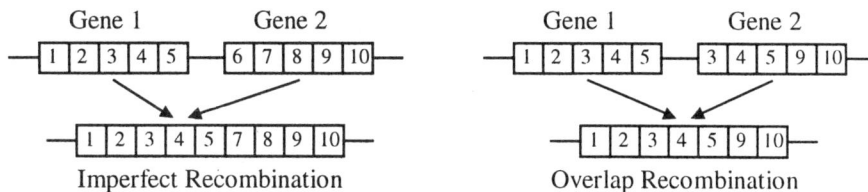

Gene 1   Gene 2   Gene 1   Gene 2

| 1 | 2 | 3 | 4 | 5 | | 6 | 7 | 8 | 9 | 10 | | 1 | 2 | 3 | 4 | 5 | | 3 | 4 | 5 | 9 | 10 |

| 1 | 2 | 3 | 4 | 5 | 7 | 8 | 9 | 10 | | 1 | 2 | 3 | 4 | 5 | 9 | 10 |

Imperfect Recombination   Overlap Recombination

Fig. 12.9: Somatic recombination of genes.

12.8.4 Evaluating Schedules

A range of antibodies (schedules) can be produced from the germline by employing a mixture of the methods described above. In the natural immune system, antibodies are selected according to the extent with which they can bind to invading antigen. In the scheduling system, schedules can be evaluated against some pre-defined objective (such as maximum tardiness, makespan etc.) and the schedule with the best objective chosen as the 'winning' schedule.

12.8.5 Immunological Memory

The natural antibody response consists of two phases. In the primary response, antibodies are produced from the germline – some will bind to the antigen and are cleared from the circulation, others that are not specific to the antigen are naturally catabolized. During the secondary response, which follows soon after, the affinities of the antibodies for the antigen are much higher. The capacity to mount a secondary response is based on immunological memory. The cellular basis of such memory lies in the expansion of populations of antigen-specific cells during the primary response so that there is an increased frequency of highly specific resting B-cells in the blood stream capable of responding to that antigen in the future. These cells can remain in the bloodstream for extremely long periods of time. This memory can be exploited by vaccination, in the artificial as well as the natural model, for example see Smith et al [1997].

Thus, the scheduling AIS can be primed with the schedules that correspond to the antigens that were used in PRAIS to evolve the germline. These ready-made complete schedules can be immediately tested to see if they fit the environmental conditions described by a new antigen. If the new antigen represents a partially completed schedule, then the partial schedule is compared to the completed schedules, and if they are consistent the partial schedule can be immediately completed.

Furthermore, any new schedules generated from the germline that are deemed to successfully match an antigen are also allowed to mature into memory-cells, and added to a memory bank. Thus, the memory of the system gradually increases as the system is used. Just as in the real system, memory cells eventually die off if they are not activated, thus the system is allowed to forget little used schedules.

12.9 CONCLUSIONS

We have described how two different immune system models can be used to address scheduling problems in manufacturing. In the first of these models, called PRAIS, a population of antibodies is evolved that recognizes common patterns of job-sequences in a set of schedules currently used by a factory corresponding to variety of situations. These antibodies are then used as genes in a germline of artificial DNA which is then used to produce schedules to cope with new environmental conditions, using methods analogous to those used by the natural immune system to produces B-Cells from DNA.

We report successful results using PRAIS to recognize patterns. Work is currently in progress to determine how successfully the modified version of CLARISA (a free version of CLARISA is planned for general distribution via the WWW, and will be made available via this book's WWW page) is in producing new schedules for new situations, and the precise function and importance of each of the germline recombination mechanisms described.

The immune system metaphor provides an important new approach to tackling real-world problems. Solutions to such problems often require robust and rapid solutions which are of acceptable quality. These characteristics are commonly not addressed by many current optimization techniques, which concentrate on providing optimal solutions which are often fragile. The natural immune-system contains all of the features necessary to produce solutions containing these characteristics. It is postulated that future work can and will exploit these features in an artificial system.

Chapter Thirteen

Immune Network Modelling in Design Optimization

Prabhat Hajela and Jun Sun Yoo

13.1 INTRODUCTION

Genetic algorithms (GAs), patterned after Darwin's postulate of 'survival of the fittest', have been used as a search strategy in a number of structural optimization problems (Hajela [1990], Le Riche & Haftka [1993], Hajela & Lee [1995], Hartmann & Grill [1996]). The search process is robust and can be used in problems with nonconvex or disjoint design spaces (Lin & Hajela [1993]), and where a mix of discrete, integer, and continuous design variables makes it difficult to generate gradient information required by more traditional optimization methods. While designed primarily for unconstrained search, the method has been extended for use in constrained optimization problems and in problems involving multiple conflicting criteria. The focus has also shifted towards the use of genetic algorithms in large dimensionality design problems, where computational efficiency is a major concern. Intuitively, it stands to reason that any variation of the approach that builds on the exploitative characteristics of the basic GA would have the best chances of success. This chapter describes a GA based modelling of another biological process, the immune system, and of its implementation in problems of design optimization. A principal advantage of the immune system simulation is in its seamless integration into a GA based search for an optimal design.

In biological immune systems, foreign cells and molecules, denoted as antigens, are recognized and eliminated by type-specific antibodies. The task of recognizing antigens is formidable due to the very large number of possible antigens; it is estimated (Smith et al [1993]) that the immune system has been able to recognize at least 10^{16} antigens. This pattern recognition capability is impressive, given that the genome contains about 10^{5} genes, and the immune system must use segments of these to construct antibodies for all possible antigens that are likely to be encountered; in a typical mammal, there are between 10^{7} and 10^{8} different antibodies. In biological systems, this recognition problem translates into a complex geometry matching process. The antibody molecule region contains a specialized portion referred to as the paratope which is used for identifying other molecules. The amino acids from which the paratope is constructed to determine its shape and hence also the shape of the antigen molecules that can attach to the paratope. The antibody, therefore, can have a geometry that is specific to a particular antigen (specialist) or is capable of partial match and capturing of a broader group of antigens (generalist). The antibody molecule is schematically shown in Figure 13.1. The specific region on any molecule to which the paratopes can attach is referred to as the epitope.

The genetic information for an antibody is encoded by separate gene segments, each of which is drawn from a library of gene segments. For this combinatorial mechanism to function effectively, the contents of the libraries must act cooperatively and partition the antigen recognition task evenly among the segments. This cooperative partitioning requires some organization, and an evolutionary approach has been used for this purpose. The approach is similar to that used in GAs; the main difference is in the choice of the fitness function. In immune systems, the fitness of an individual would be determined by its ability to recognize either a specific or a broader group of antigens. The chapter next describes an implementation of immune system modeling in the context of a GA based search. This is followed with specific applications of immune network modeling in design optimization; a single structural optimization problem is selected for each of these implementations.

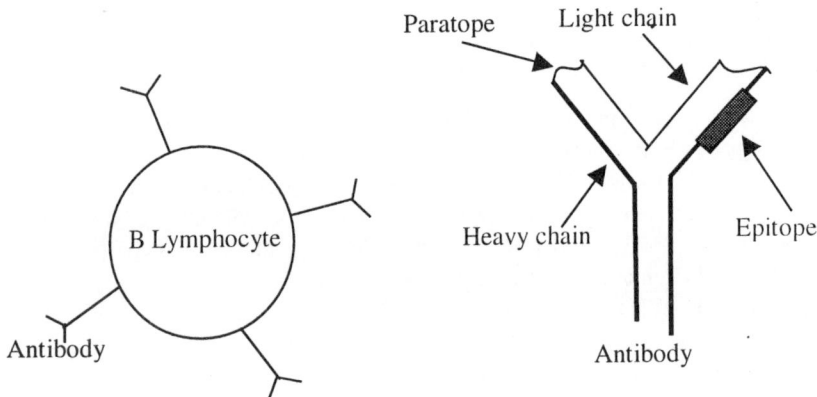

Fig. 13.1: Antibody in biological immune system

13.2 IMMUNE SYSTEM MODELLING

The immune system model described herein is based on the use of binary string structures to represent both the antigen and antibody molecules. While this is a gross simplification of the biological model where genes are specified by a four-letter DNA alphabet, and where antibody-antigen pairings are based on complex matching of three-dimensional shapes, it fits more naturally into a GA based design optimization strategy.

The simulation is initiated by first defining a scalar measure of the degree of match between binary bit string representations of the antibodies and antigens. The match can be measured either in terms of similarity or complementarity in the string structures. Different levels of complexity can be built into the development of such a matching function, including the number of matches on a bit-by-bit basis and/or the length of contiguously matched substrings. If antibodies are to be developed that are a match of the antigens, a simple numerical measure that quantifies similarity for use in immune system modeling is to count the number of matching bits between a pair of strings as:

$$Z = \sum_i t_i$$

where $t_i=1$ if there is a match at the ith location of the two strings, and is 0 otherwise. A larger value of Z indicates a higher degree of match between the two strings. If a randomly distributed population of antibodies is exposed to a specific antigen, maximization of Z using a traditional GA simulation would result in an antibody population that matches the antigen. Reversing the definition of t_i would result in the evolution of an antibody population that is complementary to the antigen.

The more interesting problem is in modelling the dynamics of the immune system when there are multiple antigens for which covering antibodies must be generated. The antibody pool can evolve to produce multiple copies of strings that match each of the present antigens. These antibodies would be termed as specialists, designed specifically for a particular antigen. Alternatively, it is also possible to evolve the antibody population into a generalist, which maximally covers all of the antigens. The manner in which the antigens are selected and exposed to the antibodies has a dominant effect on whether specialist or generalist antibodies are produced (Smith et al [1993]) in the immune system simulation. Both of these antibody types are relevant in the context of design optimization, and the simulation strategies for their generation are summarized here for completeness.

Consider first a scenario in which a number of different antigens exist, and an antibody population must be evolved to provide generalist antibodies that provide maximum coverage of the antigens with the least number of antibodies; in the limit, this would result in a single antibody that maximally covers all of the antigens. A numerical process that would produce the desired effect is initiated by randomly initializing the population of antibodies and by specifying an antigen pool. The following stepwise procedure is adopted.

Step 1: Initialize the fitness of all antibodies to zero.
Step 2: Compute the fitness of the antibody pool based on similarity to the antigens (or based on complementarity); this requires the following specific steps:
    (a) An antigen is selected at random.
    (b) A sample of antibodies of size μ is selected from the antibody pool without replacement.
    (c) The match score of each antibody is computed by comparing against the selected antigen, and the antibody with the highest score has the match score added to its fitness value; the fitness of the other antibodies is unchanged.
    (d) The antibodies are then returned to the antibody population, and the process repeated a number of times (typically two to three times the antibody population size).
Step 3: Based on the fitness computed in Step 2, a GA simulation is conducted with prescribed probabilities of crossover and mutation to evolve the antibody population through one generation of evolution.
Step 4: The process is then repeated from Step 1 till convergence in the antibody population is attained.

It turns out that the ability of the approach to develop either generalists, specialists, or both, is dependent upon the selection of the control parameter μ which denotes the sample size. A large sample size μ will facilitate the exposure of most antibodies to all antigens, particularly if the rate of sampling of the antigens does not contain a bias. In this case, the match scores of prospective antibodies that are specific to the sampled antigens will be higher, and these antibodies would evolve in the immune network simulation. On the other hand, the use of smaller sample size decreases the probability of a prospective antibody from being exposed to the different antigens. In this case, the tendency of the immune network simulation is to develop a generalist antibody, as the match scores of such antibodies will dominate the evolutionary process. In fact, increasing sample size would result in the appearance of a few specialists until ultimately, with a large enough sample size, the specialists would completely dominate the antibody evolution.

13.3 IMPLICATIONS IN GA BASED DESIGN OPTIMIZATION

GA based optimization employs a stochastic sampling strategy to identify design characteristics associated with a high level of fitness, and evolves these features over subsequent generations of simulated evolution into those that maximize design fitness. The approach is initiated by generating a starting population of designs, where each design is represented by a string like structure, much like the chromosome structure in biological organisms. Through stochastic transformation operators of selection, crossover, and mutation, the population of designs is evolved many times (generations) to some optimal state. A commonly used string like representation of designs is to denote each variable of the design as a binary bit string, and to append these individual strings head-to-tail to construct a single string of '0's and '1's that represents the total design.

The approach is ideally well-suited for minimizing or maximizing an unconstrained function, and, in general, its extension to the constrained optimization problem is obtained through the use of the penalty function approach. While easy to implement, the penalty function approach has been shown to be sensitive to the choice of algorithm parameters. This sensitivity typically results in an increased number of function evaluations required for convergence. Alternative methods for handling design constraints in genetic search have been explored in a number of recent studies (Michalewicz & Janikow [1991], Hajela & Yoo [1996]).

When binary bit strings are employed for design representation in GA based search, the number of design alternatives represented by an L-digit string is 2^L, and for the search to be efficient, sufficient sampling of these designs must be done at each stage of the design process. In design problems where each discrete variable can assume a value from a large number of alternatives or where continuous variables must be represented with a high degree of precision, the string lengths become quite long, necessitating large population sizes and the accompanying loss in efficiency.

A multistage search (Lin & Hajela [1993]), wherein the granularity of the genetic algorithm based search is varied through a successive increase in the precision with which a design space is represented, provides one alternative to working with large population sizes. In this approach, a relatively smaller population is first used to identify promising regions of the design space; the design space itself is represented in a coarse granular manner in this early stage. Once the promising regions of the search space are identified, a biased search with higher precision of design space representation is conducted within those regions. Similar strategies in GA search have been described in other work as dynamic parameter encoding (Schraudolph & Belew [1992]). Another approach which assigns significance to the previous generations of evolution in genetic search is referred to as directed crossover (Lin & Hajela [1993]). In theory, if a binary string of length L is used for representing the design, a population size that is in proportion to the string length would have to be selected. If however, only a smaller fraction, $isig*L$ ($0<isig<1$) of the bits in the string were really significant to the search process, the population size could be reduced accordingly. The primary motivation behind the directed crossover strategy, therefore, is to identify significant bit positions and constrain the crossover operation to these bit locations.

Both of these strategies are premised on the assumption that the gross schema-patterns in strings that correspond to near-optimal designs begin to assert themselves relatively early in the GA solutions, and identification of these schemas coupled with an opportunistic use of this information, can assist in speeding up the convergence rate of the GA. The immune network simulation affords another approach that belongs to the category of such schemes.

Subsequent sections of this chapter focus on showing adaptations of the immune network model in the problem of accounting for constraints in GA based search, to enhance the convergence characteristics of the GA, in multicriterion design, and as a coordination strategy in decomposition based design methods where the GA is used as the search engine.

13.4 IMMUNE NETWORKS FOR CONSTRAINT HANDLING IN GA

In the initial stages of a GA search, a typical population contains a mix of both feasible and infeasible designs. In the penalty function approach, the fitness measure of infeasible designs is penalized through the use of a penalty function proportional to the amount of constraint violation. This is both problem dependent and extremely sensitive to user specified parameters; previous studies have shown that choice of parameters can bias the GA search to suboptimal designs. The immune network model can be used for constraint handling by interweaving the immune model simulation in the GA based search. The string like representation of infeasible designs are denoted as the population pool of antibodies which must be evolved to reflect characteristics of the feasible designs (antigens). This simulation co-adapts the infeasible design representations to the structure of feasible designs, and may therefore be considered as a step which reduces constraint violations in the population. Note that in this process, both GA simulations are performed using unconstrained scalar functions to define fitness – the objective function for the optimization problem is used to define the fitness measure in the GA based approach for optimal design, and the Z function (matching function) described earlier used as a fitness measure for the embedded immune system simulation.

For the initial population of designs generated at random, each design is evaluated to compute its objective function value and a cumulative measure of constraint violation as:

$$\sum \{\max(0, g_j(x))\}^2$$

The feasible and infeasible designs are separated and each group ranked in an order which places the best objective function value at the top of the scale. A fraction of the feasible designs are selected and denoted as the antigen population. Using these antigens, the infeasible designs are used as the starting population of antibodies and subjected to an immune system simulation which promotes the production of generalist antibodies. The net output from this simulation is a subpopulation of designs with a reduction in the level of constraint violations. The initially feasible designs are then combined with multiple copies of the best constraint conditioned designs to conduct a traditional GA simulation with the objective function as the only measure of fitness. After a generation of GA evolution, the population is re-evaluated for objective function and constraint values, and the process repeated till convergence. The flow diagram for this process is shown in Figure 13.2.

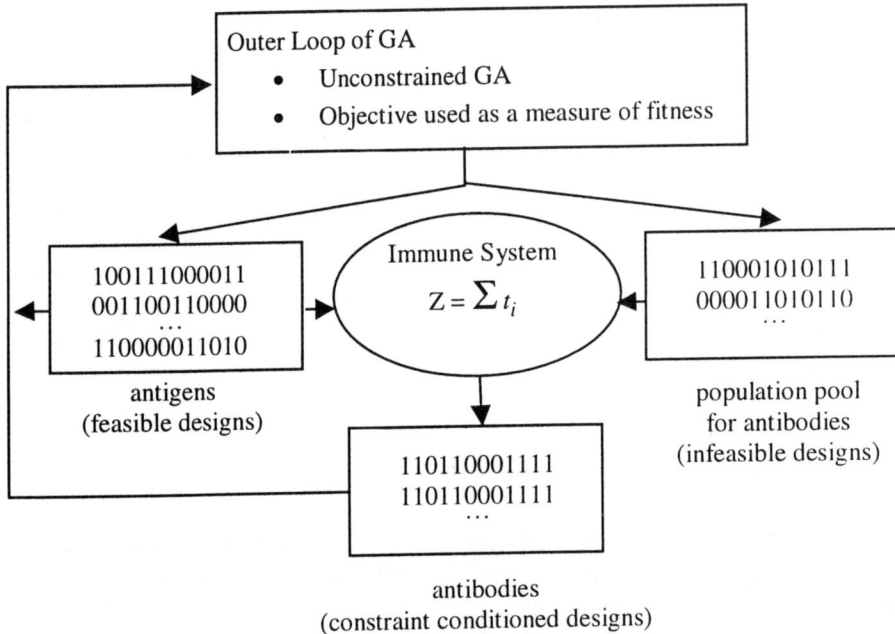

Fig. 13.2: Procedure for constraint handling using immune networks.

In this schema adaptation process, infeasible designs which may have good objective function values are forced to adapt schema that contribute to design feasibility from an antigen population (of feasible designs). The efficiency of the process, therefore, depends upon the selection of infeasible designs that are exposed to the antigens during the immune system simulation. Numerical experimentation supports the use of those infeasible designs for which the objective function value is close to the average objective function value of the antigen pool. In this instance, design features that determine goodness of objective function value would be similar for the antibodies and antigens – the infeasible designs would inherit those features of the antigens (feasible designs) that promote constraint satisfaction. It is important to note that the immune system simulation does not require computation of the objective or constraint functions, and is therefore efficient from a computational standpoint.

13.5 IMMUNE NETWORKS IN GA BASED SEARCH

We next turn our attention to the use of immune network simulation in accelerating the convergence characteristics of the genetic algorithm by biasing the search in those regions which are identified to be promising at the early stages of the search process. A stepwise procedure describing this adaptation is as follows.

Step 1: A population of designs is randomly generated.

Step 2: The fitness function, a composite measure of the objective function and a penalty associated with constraint violation, is obtained for the entire population.

Step 3: Members within the top 3% of the population obtained at the end of Step 2 are designated as the antigens, and the entire population (including the antigens) is defined as the starting population of antibodies.

Step 4: Using an antibody sample size μ smaller than the number of antigens, the degree of match Z is obtained for each member of the population according to the steps described earlier. This promotes the development of generalist antibodies.

Step 5: The match score of each design is used as a fitness measure in a traditional selection or reproduction operation. During this reproduction operation, the size of the population is unchanged.

Step 6: The crossover and mutation operations are performed on the new population of antibodies formed in Step 5.

Step 7: The process is then repeated from Step 2 with an intent of evolving the population to maximize the Z function and cycled to convergence.

It is important to note that this process (shown schematically in Figure 13.3) is somewhat different from the traditional GA implementation. In the latter, the fitness function is the composite measure of objective function value and the design constraints, and this is used in the selection or reproduction stage of the GA evolution. In the present work, this composite measure is only used to identify the antigens to which the population must adapt. The immune network simulation is conducted to determine a measure of schema similarity between all members of the population and the selected antigens, and a GA used to evolve the population with the intent of maximizing this similarity function. It stands to reason that the sample size μ be chosen to be smaller than the number of antigens so the solution obtained at the end of the immune network simulation will be a generalist.

13.6 IMMUNE NETWORKS IN MULTICRITERION DESIGN

A general mathematical statement of the multicriterion design problem is as follows:

$$\min_{X \in \Omega} \overline{f}(X) \tag{13.1}$$

where $\overline{f}(X)$ and Ω denote the objective function and the feasible set, respectively, and:

$$\overline{f}(X) = \{f_1(X), f_2(X), \cdots, f_m(X)\} \tag{13.2}$$

$$\Omega = \{X \in R^n | g(X) \le 0, \quad h(X) = 0\} \tag{13.3}$$

In the above, m is the number of objective criteria that are to be minimized, and n is the number of design variables. The vector functions $g(X)$ and $h(X)$ define the inequality and equality constraints, respectively. An ideal solution for each criterion would be obtained by minimizing each separately, without regard to the others. In general, however, criteria must be traded-off against each other, and this brings one to the subject of constructing a weighted composite objective function as follows.

$$f(X) = w_1 f_1 + w_2 f_2 + \ldots + w_m f_m, \quad \text{with } \sum w_i = 1 \tag{13.4}$$

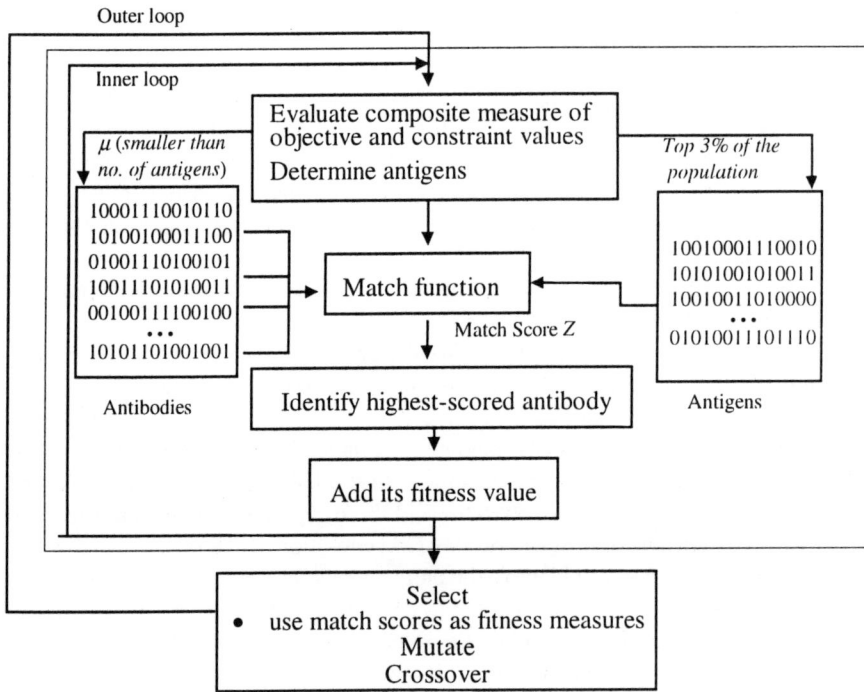

Fig. 13.3: Procedure for improving GA convergence characteristics using immune networks.

Since the weighting schedule is rarely known precisely, it is always advantageous to generate a front of compromise designs, with each point on the front representing a particular weighting choice. One simple approach to generate the front of Pareto optimal solutions to multicriterion optimization problems is to minimize the weighted composite objective function of Equation 13.4 for different sets of weights. Another intuitive approach is to minimize the difference between the individual objective functions and their corresponding ideal solutions. The ideal solution of each objective function can be determined by optimizing each of the objective functions independently. If the ideal solutions are defined as $f_1^*, f_2^*, \ldots f_m^*$, then for an arbitrary design x, the normalized distance of each component of the objective functions from its ideal optimum is given as follows.

$$d_i(x) = \frac{f_i(x) - f_i^*}{f_i^*} \qquad i = 1, \ldots m \qquad (13.5)$$

Now, the problem can be solved by minimizing the composite of all deviations as follows,

$$\text{Minimize} \quad \{ \max_{i=1,\ldots,m} [w_i d_i(x)] \} \qquad (13.6)$$

for multiple sets of weighting coefficients; the optimal solutions obtained in this manner would constitute the front of Pareto optimum solutions. In using the immune network simulation to develop a front of Pareto optimal designs, the basic idea is to treat good designs corresponding to different weighting criteria coefficients as antigens, and to evolve sub-populations of designs that cover each of these antigens. In other words, the feature of immune system simulation that encourages the growth and stabilization of specialist antibodies is required in this problem. A summary of how this is accomplished is as follows.

Step 1: Randomly generate a population of designs.

Step 2: Formulate a number of different weight combinations that can be expected to span the Pareto optimal front.

Step 3: Evaluate each design in the population for its objective values corresponding to each of the chosen weighting combinations.

Step 4: Combine the objective and constraint values to obtain a composite measure of each design, and for each of the weight combinations.

Step 5: For each combination of weights, identify the designs with the best composite measure.

Step 6: Defining the identified designs of Step 5 as antigens and the whole population as a pool for antibodies (including the antigens), implement the immune system simulation as described earlier to generate specialist antibodies.

13.7 IMMUNE NETWORKS IN DECOMPOSITION-BASED DESIGN

An alternative approach to adapting GA search for large scale design problems (long string lengths) is based on partitioning the problem into an appropriate number of subproblems; a reasonable approach for partitioning is one where balanced subsets of design variables are assigned to different subproblems, and where each subproblem would be responsible for meeting the system level design objectives and for satisfying constraints most critically affected by the design variables of that subproblem.

Consider the design problem to be formulated in terms of a design variable vector X. Also, let the design constraints $g_j(X)$ belong to the global constraint set G. The vector X and constraint set G are said to define a system level problem that is formulated as follows:

$$\text{Min or Max} \quad F(X)$$
$$\text{subject to} \quad G \equiv \{g_j(X), \ j = 1,..., NCON\} \leq 0 \tag{13.7}$$

Assume further that the best topology for decomposing the problem domain resulted in three subproblems A, B, and C, and the design variables and constraints for each of these subproblems are denoted by X_A, X_B, X_C, and g_A, g_B, and g_C, respectively. The objective function $F(X)$ for each of the subproblems is the same, and is the system level objective function. The system level problem of Equation 13.7 is now represented by the following three subproblems.

$$\text{Min or Max} \quad F(X)$$
$$\text{subject to} \quad g_i(X_i) \leq 0, \quad X_k = const \tag{13.8}$$
$$i,k = A, B, \text{ or } C \quad i \neq k$$

The GA strategy in each subproblem works with shorter string lengths, and hence smaller population sizes are required in each subproblem. The principal challenge in this approach arises from the fact that the constraint sets identified for a particular subproblem, are not completely independent of the design variables that may have been assigned to another subproblem. This issue of coordinating the solutions among the several subproblems is addressed through the use of the immune network simulation as follows.

After partitioning of the design variable vector for each subsystem has been performed, genetic evolution is carried out in each subsystem in parallel, with the fitness function described in terms of the system level objective function. Only those subsections of the chromosome string which correspond to the design variables for a particular subsystem are subject to change in that subsystem evolution. This process can be carried out in each subsystem (in parallel if hardware permits) for a fixed number of generations. Next, a fraction of most fit strings from each subsystem are introduced as antigens for which a generalist immune system simulation is performed in all other subsystems. This serves as a correction step that introduces compatibility between the different subpopulations. A schematic of the process flow is shown in Figure 13.4. The approach has been used in the multidisciplinary design of rotor blades (Lee & Hajela [1996]), and in a dual structure-control optimization problem (Lee & Hajela [1997]).

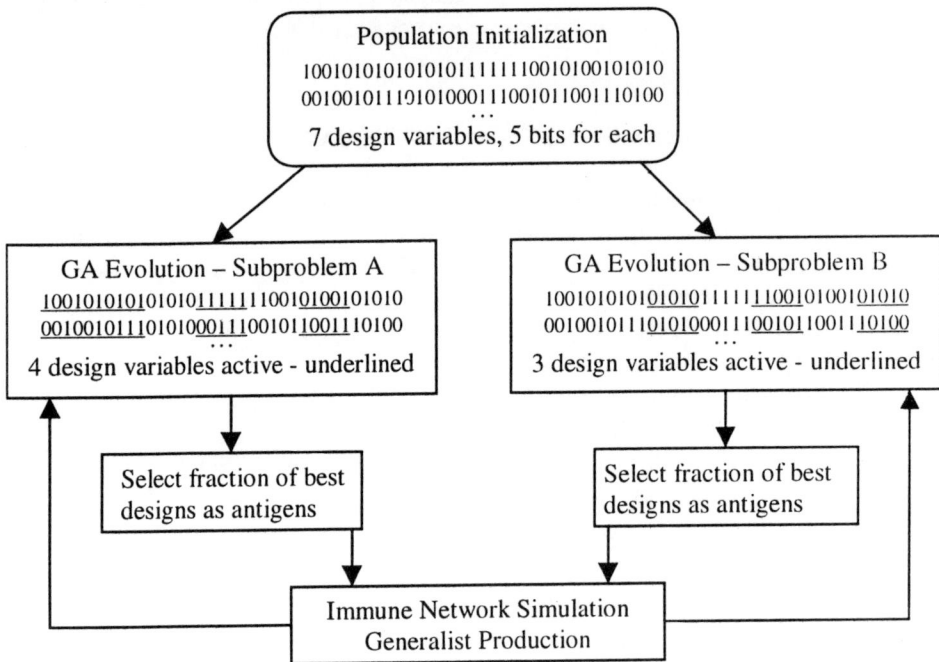

Fig. 13.4: Schematic flow diagram for coordination in decomposition based design using the immune network simulation.

13.7.1 An Illustrative Problem

The optimal sizing of a 10-bar truss, the geometry and applied loads for which are shown in Figure 13.5, will be used to illustrate the use of immune network modeling in some of the applications described in previous sections. Each cross-sectional area of the truss elements was considered as an independent design variable and these were sized to obtain a minimum weight structure. A load $P = 100$ *kips* was applied at nodes 3 and 5 in the directions of displacements d_6 and d_8 and allowable constraints on maximum stresses in the bar elements in both tension and compression of ± 25 *kpsi*, and allowable limits on selected nodal displacements were specified in this design problem. The material was aluminum with a density $\rho = 0.1$ *lb/in³*, Young's modulus of 10×10^6 *lb/in²*, and a length $l = 360$ *in*.

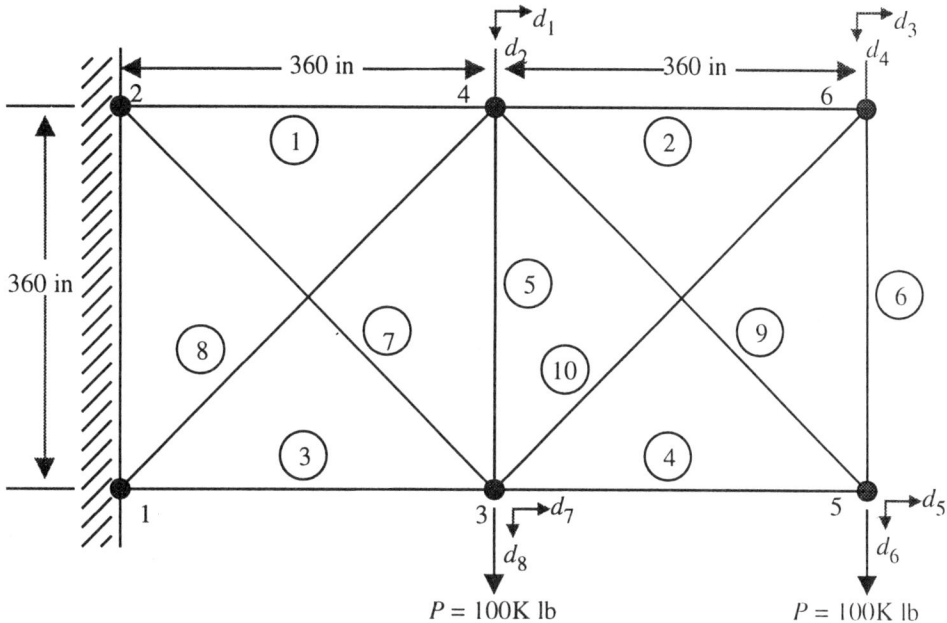

Fig. 13.5: Planar 10-bar truss structure.

Enhanced GA Convergence:

The performance of the immune network based convergence-enhancement strategy was compared with a plain GA implementation and with use of efficiency enhancing strategies such as directed crossover and multistage search. Each cross-sectional area, with a lower and upper bound of 0.01 in² and 12.0 in², respectively, was represented by a 10-bit binary string, with consequent precision of 0.01173 in² for each design variable. A population size of 200 was used in the GA simulation. Probabilities of crossover and mutation of 0.8 and 0.02 were specified for plain GA, directed crossover, and multistage approaches while the immune network simulation approach used 0.8 and 0.005. In the directed crossover strategy, the crossover gain was recorded for the first eight generations iterations and a genetic search with 50% regular crossover and 50% directed crossover was performed. In the multistage search method, four stages of genetic search were implemented using precisions of design variable representation of 1.0, 0.2, 0.05, and 0.01173 in², respectively. Also, the best 25% of the population at the end of each stage was used to seed the population for the next stage. An antibody sample size of 4 and antigen population of 6 were chosen for the immune network simulation which allowed the population to converge to a generalist. A total of 80,000 function evaluations were allowed in each simulation and the results obtained are summarized in Table 13.1 for eight different simulations using different random number seeds. On average, the advanced strategies improve upon the plain GA, even for a relatively small-sized problem. The multistage search produces the best overall objective but also shows the largest variance in the optimized solutions from the mean. The immune network modelling process generated good results consistently. The best overall objective was similar to the one obtained in the multistage search. Both the mean and the deviation of optimal objective values were the lowest for the immune network approach which suggests that it is not only effective in locating the optimal solution but also less dependent on the random number seed. When the immune network approach is implemented in design problems of higher dimensionality, the improvement in the convergence rate is further amplified as the method is designed to identify the gross schema-patterns that correspond to best design strings early in the search process.

Table 13.1: Best objective values for 10-bar truss problem

Trial number	Plain GA	Directed Crossover	Multistage	Immune
	Optimal Objective			
1	1617.6	1620.8	1599.2	1636.8
2	1780.8	1772.8	1608.0	1612.8
3	1704.0	1712.0	1699.2	1660.8
4	1699.2	1700.8	1808.0	1686.4
5	1656.0	1667.2	1704.0	1608.0
6	1670.4	1659.2	1659.2	1664.0
7	1712.0	1672.0	1603.2	1608.0
8	1676.8	1668.8	1643.2	1659.2
Mean	1689.6	1684.2	1665.5	1642.0
Standard deviation	46.7556	45.0681	70.7555	29.9912
Best results	1617.6	1620.8	1599.2	1608.0

Constraint Handling in GA Search

In this study, the problem formulation for the 10 bar truss was modified in that prescribed limits on stresses of $\sigma_{all} = 25$ kpsi were used for each of the bar elements except for element 9, for which allowable stress $\sigma_{all} = 75$ kpsi was adopted. Lower and upper bounds on each variable were set as 0.01 in^2 and 10.0 in^2, respectively. Each variable was represented by a 10-bit binary string, with a consequent precision of 0.01 in^2.

A number of numerical experiments were performed to determine the parameters needed to define the immune system simulation. First, a fraction Φ of feasible designs with best objective function value were drawn from the population, and their average objective function value was computed. A number of feasible designs N_{feas} closest in objective function value were then selected a fraction Γ of these were selected to be antigens.

Experiments were conducted to assess the performance of the constraint handling procedure with different values of Φ and Γ. Values of $\Phi = 0.5$ and $\Gamma = 0.4$-0.6 perform best from a standpoint of consistently converging to a near optimal solution. Lower values of Φ are intuitively expected to perform better as the infeasible designs would adapt features of better feasible designs. For $\Phi = 0.5$ and different values of Γ, the convergence trends for the objective function using the immune system modelling approach were found to be reliably better than when using a standard GA with a penalty function approach. Some oscillatory behaviour exists in the earlier generations of evolution, where some infeasibility is introduced due to the use of the objective function as the sole measure of fitness. However, the optimal objective function values obtained in each of the immune system based simulations were similar and consistently superior to those obtained in the plain GA approach using penalty terms. Further, the convergence history indicates that a near-optimal feasible design was consistently obtained much earlier in the evolution process. Additional details pertaining to these simulations are available in Hajela & Lee [1996].

Multicriterion Design

In this application, the objective to minimize a weighted sum of the structural weight f_1, and the vertical displacement f_2, indicated by degree of freedom d_6 in Figure 13.5. The constraints were maximum allowable deflections $d_{1max} = 3$ *in*, $d_{2max} = 1.5$ *in*, $d_{3max} = 0.8$ *in*, and $d_{4max} = 0.8$ *in*. Experiments were conducted to compare the traditional with the immune network based approach. The mean results from several runs of the new approach were compared with those obtained from the traditional approach, where a separate GA run was required for each different combination of weighting coefficients. In the immune network strategy, the number of antigens representing each weighting combination and the sample size were selected as 11 and 33, respectively. Since the sample size is three times the number of antigens, the antibody population converges to a set of specialists. For the test problem, lower and upper bounds of 0.1 in^2 and 20 in^2 were specified for all cross sectional areas. A total string length of 30 allowed these design variables to be represented by a precision of 2.843 in^2. The population size was 200, the crossover and mutation rates were 0.6 and 0.01 respectively, and the GA was stopped after 40,000 function evaluations. Results were encouraging. The mean error computed over all sets of weighting coefficients and multiple independent trials was around 3%, supporting the effectiveness of the proposed strategy. Fuller details are available in Yoo & Hajela [1999].

13.8 CLOSING REMARKS

This chapter has described an adaptation of an unconstrained genetic search to simulate the mechanics of the biological immune system. The intrinsic strengths of the immune system simulation reside in a schema recognition and adaptation capability, and can be used advantageously in improving the performance of genetic algorithms in design optimization problems. The use of immune system modeling in GA based design optimization is presented in the context of four specific applications - to enhance the convergence characteristics of GAs, in direct handling of design constraints, in multicriterion design problems, and facilitating co-ordination in decomposition based design.

Part Four

Memetic Algorithms

Co-ordinating Editor:

Pablo Moscato

Contributors:

Regina Berretta

Pablo Coll

Guillermo Durán

Bernd Freisleben

Diana Holstein

Peter Merz

Pablo Moscato

Chapter Fourteen

Memetic Algorithms: A Short Introduction

Pablo Moscato

14.1 INTRODUCTION

We use the generic denomination of *Memetic Algorithms* (MAs) to identify a broad class of metaheuristics (i.e. general purpose methods aimed to guide an underlying heuristic) which constitutes one of the most successful approaches for combinatorial optimization; in particular for the approximate solution of NP optimization problems. In the last decade we have seen it evolve from being a competitive technique (compared with other Evolutionary Computation approaches) to be an unrivalled methodology in several problem domains.

A key feature, present in most MAs implementations, is the use of a population-based search which intends to use all available knowledge about the problem. This knowledge is incorporated in the form of heuristics, approximation algorithms, local search techniques, specialized recombination operators, truncated exact methods, and many other ways.

In essence, most MAs can be interpreted as a *cooperative-competitive* strategy of optimizing agents (Norman & Moscato [1989]). Their success can probably be explained as being a direct consequence of the *synergy* of the different search approaches incorporated.

The first MA we implemented with M.G. Norman in 1988 (Norman & Moscato [1989]) can be regarded as a hybrid of traditional Genetic Algorithms (GAs) and Simulated Annealing (SA). Part of the initial motivation was to find a way out of the limitations (which were evident for us at the time) of both techniques on a well-studied combinatorial optimization problem the Min Euclidean Travelling Salesman Problem (MIN ETSP). However, the original inspiration of our first implementation came from computer game tournaments (Hofstadter [1983]) used to study the evolution of cooperation (Axelrod & Hamilton [1981]; see also Nowak & Sigmund [1998] and Nakamaru et al [1998] for more recent developments in this field).

Our approach had several features which anticipated many current algorithms. The competitive phase of the algorithm was based on the new allocation of search points in a configuration phase, a process involving a battle for survival followed by what we called *clonation*, which has a strong similarity with the more recent 'go with the winners' algorithms (Aldous & Vazirani [1994], Peinado & Lengauer [1997]). The optimizing agents were arranged with a topology similar to a two-dimensional lattice.

Due to our computer experiments, we soon acquired an insight on the particular relevance that a *spatial* organization, when coupled with an appropiate set of rules, had for the overall search process. A few months later, we discovered that we shared similar views with other researchers (Mühlenbein [1991], Gorges-Schleuter [1991]), and other authors proposing *island models* for GAs. Spatialization is nowadays recognized as a very important feature, a 'catalyser' responsible for a variety of phenomena (Nakamaru et al [1998, 1998a]). Its study has already led, in some cases, to some proper undecidability results (Grim [1997]).

About a year later, in 1989, we identified several authors who were also pioneering the introduction of heuristics to improve the solutions before recombining them (Mühlenbein et al [1988], Gorges-Schleuter [1989]; also see other references and the discussion in Moscato [1989]). Particularly coming from the GA field, several authors were introducing problem-domain knowledge in a variety of ways. In Moscato [1989] we introduced the denomination of *memetic algorithms* for this type of metaheuristic, and we suggested that *cultural evolution* can be a better working metaphor to escape from the biologically constrained thinking imperant at that time.

The name came after the introduction of the word 'meme' by R. Dawkins in the last chapter of his book 'The Selfish Gene'. In his own words:

> Examples of memes are tunes, ideas, catch-phrases, clothes fashions, ways of making pots or of building arches. Just as genes propagate themselves in the gene pool by leaping from body to body via sperms or eggs, so memes propagate themselves in the meme pool by leaping from brain to brain via a process which, in the broad sense, can be called imitation.

Dawkins [1990]

Today, memetic algorithms, albeit under different names, have a remarkable record of success in a variety of classical NP Optimization problems like: Graph Partitioning (Bui & Moon [1996], Merz & Freisleben [1998]), Max Independent Set (Aggarwal et al [1997], Hifi [1997], Sakamoto et al [1997]) Bin-Packing (Reeves [1996]), Min Graph Colouring (Costa et al [1995], Fleurent & Ferland [1996], Dorne & Hao [1998], Galinier & Hao [1998]), Set Covering (Beasley & Chu [1996]), Parallel Machine Scheduling (Cheng & Gen [1997]), Min Generalised Assignment (Chu & Beasley [1997]), Multidimensional Knapsack (Beasley & Chu [1998]), Nonlinear Integer Programming (Taguchi et al [1998]) Quadratic Assignment (Carrizo et al [1992], Merz & Freisleben [1997]) Set Partitioning (Levine [1996]), and particularly on the Min Travelling Salesman Problem (Gorges-Schleuter [1989, 1991a], Moscato & Norman [1992], Freisleben & Merz [1996, 1996a], Merz & Freisleben [1997a]). The reader familiar with the theory of *NP*-Completeness would recall that most of them are 'classical' as they have already appeared in Karp's notorious 1972 paper on the reducibility of combinatorial problems. In many cases the authors claim that they have developed the best heuristic for the problem at hand. This is a most remarkable fact, since these problems have a long-standing tradition and a wide variety of different algorithmic techniques have been tested on them.

Other applications of Memetic Algorithms include: Partial Shape Matching (Ozcan & Mohan [1998]), The Binary Perceptron Learning Problem (Moscato [1993]), Kauffman *NK* Landscapes (Merz & Freisleben [1998a]), Maintenance Scheduling (Burke & Smith [1997]), Timetabling (Burke et al [1995], Paechter et al [1996]), and Sport Games Scheduling (Costa [1995]). This list is very limited; its only aim is to show the wide applicability of the approach.

14.1.1 Local Search

Since most implementations of MAs currently use local search methods, it should be wise to first briefly define the formal notion of *computational problems* and *local search* techniques for addressing them. We will also formally define what a *local search problem* is. The definitions of local search problems and algorithms are less tight than those used for the definition of the associated complexity classes, and we will try to make them compatible with those from Yannakakis' recent survey on computational complexity of local search (Yannakakis [1997]).

A *computational problem* P has an input domain set I_P of *instances* and for each instance $x \in I_P$ we can establish a set $ans_P(x)$ of corresponding *answers*. This relationship is completely arbitrary, and is the first part of our algorithmic problem solving decisions. However, for obvious reasons, it is wise that we ensure that there exists a subset $sol_P(x) \subseteq ans_P(x)$ which identifies the *feasible* (sometimes called 'acceptable' or 'valid') solutions to problem P.

An algorithm *solves* problem P if on input $x \in I_P$ it outputs any member $y \in sol_P(x)$ (an acceptable solution), or in case $sol_P(x)$ is empty it reports that no such y exists. If every $sol_P(x)$ has zero, one or more elements we have a *search problem*.

A *combinatorial optimization problem* is a special kind of search problem where every instance $x \in I_P$ has a set $sol_P(x)$ of finite cardinality and every solution $y \in sol_P(x)$ has associated an *objective function* $m_P(y, x)$ and a *goal* (which can be either 'Max' or 'Min'). The optimization search problem is to find the feasible solution $y^* \in sol_P(x)$ that minimizes (or maximizes, depending on the associated goal for P) the value of the objective function. Associated with an optimization problem we can derive a *decision* problem. In this case, for every instance the answer is either 'Yes' or 'No'. To formulate the problem, instead of trying to find the best solution of instance x, we ask whether x has a solution having measure at most B (or, 'at least' when the goal is to maximize). This problem is known as the *underlying decision version* or *underlying language*.

For the reader who might not feel familiar with the discussion that will follow, we recommend a fast and appropriate introduction containing necessary definitions for the topic from Bovet & Crescenzi [1994]. We can then define a *decision problem* Π as a triple (I_P, ans_P, π) where I_P is the set of words that encode instances of problem P, ans_P is a function that maps an instance $x \in I_P$ into a finite set $ans_P(x)$ of words that encode possible solutions of x, and π is a *predicate* such that, for any instance x and for any possible solution $y \in ans_P(x)$, $\pi(x, y) = \textbf{true}$ if and only if $y \in sol_P(x)$ (i.e. if y is a feasible solution for instance x of problem P). To solve a decision problem (I_P, ans_P, π) consists in deciding, for a given instance $x \in I_P$, whether the set of solutions y which appear in *both* $ans_P(x)$ and $sol_P(x)$ is not empty.

For the discussion, we might focus on problems in which we seek the y^* that minimizes the objective function over all $y \in sol_P(x)$. Therefore, we view the objective function $m_P(y^*, x)$ as the 'minimum price' or *cost* of solution y^* given instance x for problem P.

As an example, we can consider the Min Graph Colouring problem since it will be the topic of chapter eighteen. It can be stated as follows: given a graph $G = (V, E)$ (the graph G is the particular instance $x \in I_P$), the problem (P) is to find a *valid colouring* of the graph G (a solution $y \in sol_P(x)$) such that it minimizes (the 'goal') the number of colours that are needed (the number of colours is our cost function $m_P(y, x)$). A valid colouring of G is an assignment of one colour to each node such that there is no pair of vertices i and j linked with an edge to which the same colour has been assigned. We remark that $sol_P(x)$ represents valid colourings of G, while $ans_P(x)$ can represent unfeasible colourings. There are infinite numbers of ways of generating $ans_P(x)$ sets. The first one that immediately comes to mind is to allow edges with both end nodes coloured with the same colour. Others might include more than one colour assigned to each node, non-integer colour numbers, etc. There is actually no limit for the $sol_P(x) \subseteq ans_P(x)$ relationship that can be found in implementations which appear in practice.

We now need to define three entities before we can discuss what a local search problem is. They are the search space, the neighbourhood relation, and the guiding function. All of them are related with the chosen representation (we may also say 'mathematical encoding') of the computational problem. We must stress here one important issue: a proper selection of the representation is probably the most decisive step upon which almost all success or failure of the heuristic approach will find its fundamental cause. We will also see that a computational problem upon which we have fixed a mathematical encoding and we have defined these three entities can give rise to a *local search problem*. Note that a single computational problem P, can be the source of different local search problems for different definitions of this triple.

Search Space and valid representations

Given a computational problem P, we associate to each instance of $x \in I_P$ a search space $S_P(x)$, with the following properties.

- Each element $s \in S_P(x)$ represents an answer in $ans_P(x)$.

- For decision problems: at least one element of $sol_P(x)$ that stands for a 'Yes' answer is represented by one element in $S_P(x)$.

- For optimization problems: at least one *optimal* element y^* of $sol_P(x)$ is represented by one element in $S_P(x)$.

Note that the first requirement refers to $ans_P(x)$ and not to $sol_P(x)$. If these requirements have been achieved, we say that we have a *valid representation* or *valid formulation* of the problem. For simplicity, we will just write S to refer to $S_P(x)$ when x and P are clear from the context. Furthermore, we will refer to elements of S as *configurations*.

Neighbourhood Relation

Given a problem P, an instance $x \in I_P$ and a search space S for it, it is possible to assign to each element $s \in S$ a set $\mathcal{N}(s) \subseteq S$ of neighbouring configurations of S. The set $\mathcal{N}(s)$ is called the neighbourhood of S and each member $s' \in \mathcal{N}(s)$ is called a *neighbour* of S. We remark that the neighbourhood depends on the instance, so the notation $\mathcal{N}(s)$ is a simplified form of $\mathcal{N}_P(s,x)$ since it is clear from the context.

The elements of $\mathcal{N}(s)$ need not be listed explicitly. In most of the implementations of local search, they are implicitly defined by referring to a set of possible *moves*, which define transitions between configurations. Moves are usually defined as 'local' modifications of some part of S. This 'locality' is one of the key ingredients of local search, and actually it has also given the name to the whole search paradigm. A good rule of thumb is that successful implementations of local search based heuristics are in general associated with a smooth landscape of the objective function in relation with the chosen neighbourhood. We will just mention this in passing, since these concepts will be the subject of chapter sixteen where they will be covered in depth. Chapter sixteen will discuss formal definitions and will deal with the study of fitness landscapes in MAs and its particular relevance for the search processes.

Note that from the definition above there is no implication that local search is bounded to 'closeness' under some kind of distance relationship between configurations. It is possible to give examples of more complex neighbourhood definitions which can be used as well (a reader familiar with local search techniques for the Travelling Salesman Problem (TSP) might recall the λ-change upon which the Lin-Kernighan algorithm relies).

Another important feature to be considered when selecting moves is their *ergodicity*, that is, the ability, given any $s \in S$ to find a sequence of transitions that can reach all other configurations in S. Sometimes this property is self-evident and its existence, for a given representation, does not need to be explicitly proved. For instance, that is the case if the search space is a set of all permutations of different symbols (as it is generally used for TSP and some scheduling problems) and the moves are the generators of the group of permutations.

Guiding Function

The *guiding function* F_g associates to each configuration $s \in S$ a value $F_g(s)$ that assesses the quality of the solution. If we have a decision problem, the guiding function F_g is generally based on the so-called 'distance to feasibility', which is generally *ad hoc*, 'designed' in such a way as to account for the number of constraints that are violated.

For optimization problems, it is also necessary that the guiding function must be closely related to the objective function of the problem. After all, the objective function of the problem is part of our input data and, as such, it is out of our algorithmic reach. However, in many implementations of MAs for optimization problems a guiding function is defined as a weighted sum of the value of the objective function and the distance to feasibility (which accounts for the constraints). Typically, a higher weight is assigned to the constraints, so as to give preference to feasibility over optimality.

In some optimisation problems, the search space S is defined in such a way that it only encodes feasible solutions. In this case, the guiding function generally coincides with the objective function of the problem. However, there are other alternatives. In chapter fifteen, we will discuss an implementation of an MA based on Guided Local Search, which uses a guiding function based on a penalization scheme which is dynamically updated during the search process.

14.1.2 Local Search Algorithms

A *local search algorithm* starts from a configuration $s_0 \in S$, and iterates using at each step a transition based on the neighbourhood of the current configuration. Popular metaphors abound, the most commonly used is that the process is a 'navigation' in the search space. The initial configuration can be constructed by some other algorithm or generated at random. In most implementations, the selection of the next configuration (among the set of neighbours) is based on the guiding function which accounts for the number of violated constraints, and, for optimization problems, it is also based on the objective function. Due to these characteristics, the approach is metaphorically called 'Hillclimbing'.

The selection of the particular type of moves to use does certainly depend on the specific characteristics of the problem and the representation chosen (see for example chapter seventeen which concerns the number partitioning problem). There is no general advice for this, since it is a matter of the available computer time for the whole process as well as other algorithmic decisions that include ease of coding, etc. In some cases some moves are conspicuous, for example it can be the change of the value of one single variable or the swap of the values of two different variables. Sometimes the 'step' may also be composed of a chain of transitions. For instance, in relation with MAs, Radcliffe and Surry introduced the concept of *Binomial Minimal Mutation*, where the number of mutations to perform is selected according to a certain binomial distribution (Radcliffe & Surry [1994]).

14.1.3 Local Search Problems and *PLS*-Completeness

The increasing relevance that local search has in the approximate solution of many *NP*-hard problems has led to a formal characterisation of computational complexity classes (Johnson et al [1988]). To build such a theory, an indisoluble relationship between a problem P and a local search algorithm on a neighbourhood $\mathcal{N}$ must be established. Then a local search problem can be defined as a five-tuple (I_P, sol_P, m_P, $goal$, $\mathcal{N}_P$), where I_P is the set of instances of problem P, $sol_P(x)$ is the set of feasible solutions of $x \in I_P$, $m_P(y,x)$ is the objective function for $y \in sol_P(x)$ while $goal$ can be either *Max* or *Min*, and $\mathcal{N}_P(y,x)$ is the neighbourhood relationship that associates a set of different feasible solutions with any $y \in sol_P(x)$. In short, we can call it $P/\mathcal{N}$ and an associated complexity class has been established:

Definition 14.1:

A *local search problem* ($P/\mathcal{N}$) is in class *PLS* (for Polynomial Local Search) if there are three polynomial-time algorithms, which we will call *starter*, *evaluator*, and *l-engine* (for 'local engine'), with the following properties:

- Given an input x (formally a string $x \in \{0,1\}^*$), the starter determines whether $x \in I_P$ and in this case produces an acceptable solution $y_0 \in sol_P(x)$.

- Given an instance $x \in I_P$ and an input y, the evaluator determines whether $y \in sol_P(x)$ and in this case computes $m_P(y,x)$.

- Given an instance $x \in I_P$ and an acceptable solution $y \in sol_P(x)$, the l-engine determines whether y is a local optimum, and if it is not it outputs a neighbour $y' \in \mathcal{N}_P(y,x)$ with strictly better value of m_P; that is, $m_P(y',x) < m_P(y,x)$ for a minimization problem, and $m_P(y',x) > m_P(y,x)$ for a maximization problem.

Note that the first thing the algorithms do is to check if they have received a valid input and they also do that in polynomial-time. It is important to remark that the definition above includes the problems of local optimality arising in linear programming, maximum matching, minimum spanning tree, and other problems for which exist polynomial-time algorithms that find the optimal solution. It is obvious that the definition embodies an *iterative improvement* procedure by iterating in the application of the l-engine (the *hill-climbing* procedures).

It is conjectured that the class *PLS* does not contain *NP*-hard problems. It has been proven that if a *PLS* problem is *NP*-hard, then $NP = co\text{-}NP$, a fact which is considered very unlikely (Yannakakis [1997]). The complexity class co-*NP* is the class of decision problems whose complement is in the class *NP*. For instance, the Hamiltonian Cycle is a member of *NP* (see: http://www.densis.fee.unicamp.br/~moscato/Hamilton.html). Its complement would be the decision problem given by the question: 'Is a given graph non-Hamiltonian?', which belongs to co-*NP*.

The introduction of the *PLS*-Complete class has led to many interesting results and many open challenges (Johnson et al [1988], Schäffer & Yannakakis [1991], Yannakakis [1997]). Note also that in the formal definition of the *PLS* class the authors have restricted the discussion to $S \equiv sol_P(x)$ and $F_g(y, x) \equiv m_P(y, x)$.

If *P/N* and *P?N'* are two local search problems, then a *PLS*-reduction from *P/N* to *P?N'* consists of two polynomial-time computable functions t_1 and t_2 such that:

- t_1 maps instances x of *P/N* to instances $t_1(x)$ of *P?N'*;

- let y' be a solution of instance $t_1(x)$, then t_2 maps pairs of the form (y', x) to solutions in $sol_P(x)$;

- for all instances x of P, if y'_{lo} is a local optimum for instance $t_1(x)$ of P', then $t_2(y'_{lo}, x)$ is a local optimum for x.

If the two functions t_1 and t_2 satisfy the conditions above, we say that *P/N PLS-reduces* to *P'/N'*. As a corollary, if there is a polynomial-time algorithm for finding local optima for *P'/N'* and *P/N PLS*-reduces to *P'/N'*, then there is also a polynomial-time algorithm for finding local optima for *P/N*.

Reductions compose and this helps relate the difficulty of one problem to another via a chain of *PLS*-reductions. This leads to the introduction of another complexity class. A problem in *PLS* is called *PLS-complete* if every problem in *PLS* can be *PLS*-reduced to it.

Sophie Fischer studied the computational complexity of several local search problems. She has addressed the following question: 'Given an instance of a local search problem, and a start solution s_0, is there a locally optimal solution s' that can be reached from s_0 within a polynomial number of local search steps?'. The problem is clearly in *NP* and the question, for several problems in *PLS*, was proved *NP*-complete (Fischer [1995]). In a previous paper, Papadimitriou et al [1990] had considered the following (different) problem: 'Given a local search problem and a start solution s_0, how hard is to compute a locally optimal solution s' reachable from s_0?'. They proved that the problem is PSPACE-hard for some problems in *PLS*. We refer the reader to the excellent survey by M. Yannakakis (Yannakakis [1997]) which covers in depth several issues of interest.

14.1.4 Parallel Local Search

A variety of metaheuristics have been proposed to guide a single, local search-based optimizer. They include variants of simulated annealing and basic tabu search (Glover [1994]) techniques as well as the so-called GRASP methods. On the contrary, memetic algorithms, as well as parallel hillclimbing and go-with-the-winners algorithms, can be distinguished by the use of more than one optimizer.

There are many ways by which local search algorithms can be parallelized. The starter, evaluator, and l-engine algorithms might have steps which can be efficiently separated in independent threads, generally due to *domain decomposition* of the instance x. However, we may use many local search processes instead of just one. With reference to agent-driven software engineering, we generally refer to this approach as the use of an interactive population of optimizing agents, instead of a single optimizer. It can be proved that: 'if $prob(M,t)$ is the probability of *not* having found a solution with relative excess ε in t time units with M *independent* walks, and $prob(1,t)= e^{-\lambda t}$ where λ is a positive real number, then $prob(M,t)=prob(1,Mt)$'. Theoretical analysis on these issues can be found in Shonkwiler & van Vleck [1994] and Ferreira & Zerovnik [1993] (see also Verhoeven & Aarts [1995]).

As a result, the so-called *population approaches* (Moscato [1993]) seem natural candidates for concurrent processing and perfectly fit many parallel computer architectures. Since processes can run independently on different processors, there are no critical concerns about the speed of the interconnection network. However, for almost a decade we have been advocating for the use of *interactions* between the processes as a way to improve the performance of the search. This approach has led to our work in memetic algorithms which is the subject of the next section.

14.2 MEMETIC ALGORITHMS

14.2.1 A Bit of History

In 1988, when we started investigating this field, we were first interested in providing some evidence that a set of loosely independent but interactive local search processes could benefit from periodic competitive and cooperative interactions (Norman & Moscato [1989]). Although we were relying on qualitative results using the TSP as a representative test-bed, we soon conjectured (based on our computational experiments) that our approach was improving the results obtained by totally independent processes. In other words, we were obtaining superlinear speed up, which improves over the linear speed-up for totally independent processes promised by the theorem indicated in the previous section.

In our first MA, most of the total time was spent by the local search independent processes running on different processors. Since the time needed to coordinate the interactions was negligible in comparison with the periods of independent local search the algorithm was perfect for MIMD parallel computers (hypercubes, transputer systems, etc.) as well as heterogeneous multicomputers (like networks of workstations). Part of our later work was to try to establish MAs as the most suitable methodology for programming a combinatorial optimization metaheuristic in message-passing parallel systems as opposed to the traditional approach based on domain decomposition.

14.2.2 Formalization

An intuitive notion, useful but not always true, is that of seeing an MA as a GA over the subspace of local optima given by a certain neighbourhood definition $\mathcal{N}$ associated with some local search algorithm. This has led to alternative names for particular MAs like *knowledge-augmented* GAs, *Lamarckian* evolutionary algorithms, *hybrid* GAs, *genetic local search*, etc. However, some examples of MAs can hardly fit this metaphor, a conspicuous case being *scatter search* (see chapter nineteen, and Glover [1995]; we acknowledge that the question of inclusion works two ways. Scatter search originated the ideas of using guided improvement and repair of combined solutions over a decade before the MA taxonomy was introduced. Our inclusion of SS within MAs reflects the goal of embracing, definitionally, a wide range of methods within a common classification).

We think that seeing MAs as a GA restricted to local minima is too narrow a definition. But, it is wise to continue using some of the terminology of GAs whenever applicable. For instance, Radcliffe and Surry, in their representation-independent formalization of local-search-based MAs (Radcliffe & Surry [1994]), start their formalism by making reference to a *representation function* ρ that, given any solution $y \in sol_P(x)$, returns a *chromosome* $\rho(y)$ in the space of *genotypes* $S(\rho)$. They remark that ρ is injective. This means that every y is represented by one unique chromosome $\rho(y)$ but it does not need to be surjective (there might be chromosomes that do not correspond to any $y \in sol_P(x)$). It is clear that the space of genotypes is related to our previous definition of the search space S. The only difference is that in our definition of valid representations we do accept those which can leave out some optimal solutions provided that *at least one* should be present.

We do not intend here to give formal definitions for what a *gene* is in the context of Evolutionary Computation methods. However, it might be relevant to mention that '(graph)-genetic' and '(set)-allelic' representations have been used in many implementations of MAs. Radcliffe [1994] has made an attempt to formalize these notions. We will suppose the reader has some familiarity with GAs and the *genetic representation* (Radcliffe & Surry [1994]) which is the widely used array (ordered pairs) of gene numbers and their corresponding allele values. We can extend their definition by remarking that in the general case there might exist an adjacency relation between genes which can be encoded as a graph. For instance, it is not uncommon to find representations based on cycles or trees and operators acting via operations in those subgraphs. In the (set)-allelic representations (Radcliffe & Surry [1994]), a chromosome is a set of values drawn from some universal set $\mathcal{A}$. It is interesting to remark that in our formal definition for recombination neither a definition of gene nor meme will be required.

14.2.3 Recombination

Regarding the definition of the *PLS* class, we can analogously define another class which we will call *PMA* (for *Polynomial Merger Algorithms*) by reference to three similar algorithms to the ones that define *PLS*. In essence, the class definition particularly depends on an algorithm tentatively called *k-merger*. It receives as input a set S_{par} of $k \geq 2$ acceptable solutions (informally called 'parents') and will create at least one acceptable solution. The creation of this new solution will be a process with many restrictions involving the detection, the preservation or avoidance, and the feasible combination of *features* already present in the parent solutions.

The *k-merger* is said to be *blind* if it does not use any information from the input instance of problem P. We denote as $\mathcal{M}_P(S_{par}, x) \subseteq sol_P(x)$ the set of all possible outputs given by the *k-merger* algorithm if it receives as input the pair (S_{par}, x) for problem P. We will say that a problem $P/\mathcal{M}$ belongs to *PMA* if there exist three polynomial-time algorithms *p*-starter, *p'*-evaluator, and *k-merger* (where p and k are integer numbers such that $p' \geq p \geq k \geq 2$) that satisfy the following properties:

- Given an input x the p-starter determines whether $x \in I_P$ and in this case produces a set of p different acceptable solutions $\{y_1, y_2, ..., y_p\} \subseteq sol_P(x)$.

- Given an instance $x \in I_P$ and an input (formally a string in $\{0, 1\}^*$), the p'-evaluator determines whether this input represents a set of feasible solutions, i.e. $\{y_1, y_2, ..., y_p\} \subset sol_P(x)$, and in that case it computes the value of the objective function associated to each one of them, i.e. $m_P(y_j, x)$ for each j from 1 to p'.

- Given an instance $x \in I_P$ and a set of k acceptable solutions $S_{par} \subseteq sol_P(x)$, the k-merger determines whether S_{par} is a k-merger optimum; if not it does the following:

  - For each $y \in S_{par}$, it solves n_1 polynomial-time decision problems $\{\Pi_1(y), ..., \Pi_{n_1}(y)\}$, yielding a $k \times n_1$ matrix D of Boolean coefficients formed by the output of all these decision problems, i.e. $D_{ij} = \Pi_j(y_i)$.

  - It creates a set of n_2 constraints C which can be partitioned into two subsets, i.e. $C = C_{in} \cup C_{out}$. Each $c \in C$ is represented by a predicate π_c such that its associated decision problem $\Pi_c(y)$ can be solved in polynomial-time for all $y \in sol_P(x)$. Any predicate π_c is a polynomial-time computable function that has as input the Boolean matrix D and the instance x. It is required that at least one predicate π_c^* is to be a non-constant function of at least two different elements of S_{par}.

  - It outputs at least one offspring, i.e. another acceptable solution $y' \in \mathcal{M}_P(S_{par}, x)$ which has a strictly better objective function value (i.e. $m_P(y', x) < \max\{m_P(y_1, x), m_P(y_2, x), ..., m_P(y_k, x)\}$ for a minimization problem, and $m_P(y', x) > \min\{m_P(y_1, x), m_P(y_2, x), ..., m_P(y_k, x)\}$ for a maximization problem) subject to:

$$\max_{y' \in sol_P(x)} [(\sum_{(c \in C_{in}) \wedge \Pi_c(y')} w_c) - (\sum_{(c \in C_{out}) \wedge \Pi_c(y')} w_c)] \qquad (14.1)$$

It is clear from the requirements we have just enunciated that the k-merger algorithm has an analogy with the definition of the l-engine algorithm introduced before. The set $\mathcal{M}_P(S_{par}, x)$ can be also interpreted as a 'neighbourhood', not for a single solution, but for a set of k (at least two) acceptable solutions instead. Not surprisingly, since this set can be viewed as an extension of the concept of neighbourhood, algorithms that only rely in recombination and mutation (like standard GAs) have been considered by some authors as members of the local search family. It is certainly a debatable classification.

In general, we will refer to a k-merger algorithm as a *recombination operator*. Another suitable name for it would have been *k-recomb-engine*. A recombination operator is *blind* if it is a k-merger algorithm and only has as input the set S_{par} and a set of values of the guiding function associated to each element of the set. We will say that the recombination is *myopic* if it does not use all the information of x.

We will say that a 2-merger algorithm is a crossover operator if it is blind, and if its computational complexity is low (that is, at most $\mathcal{O}(|N| \log(|N|))$ where $|N|$ is a measure of the size of the input – recall that a k-merger algorithm has as input the set S_{par} and the instance x). The definition adopted here for 'crossover' is arbitrary, reflecting the general use of the term in the evolutionary computing literature. In search for examples of crossover operators we can mention the well-known one-point-crossover, two-point crossover, or generalized N-point crossover (Radcliffe & Surry [1994]).

Having defined recombination in such a general way, there are several differences with other nature-based approaches. In Radcliffe [1994] a recombination operator was defined as *pure* if given a set of $k \geq 2$ identical solutions it returns the same solution. Note that from the definitions above, in the case of all identical parents, the k-merger algorithm would either declare the set S_{par} to be a k-merger optimum or give a strictly better solution. Note also that we do not restrict recombination to satisfy $S_{par} \subseteq M_P(S_{par}, x)$.

Another difference with biologically-inspired algorithms, is that we do not restrict the recombination operator to be a symmetric function of its arguments. For instance, given two parent solutions $y_1, y_2 \in sol_P(x)$, it is possible that $M_P(y_1, y_2, x) \neq M_P(y_2, y_1, x)$. A k-merger algorithm will be called *parent-symmetric* if the set $\mathcal{M}_P(S_{par}, x)$ is the same for all the $k!$ permutations of the k input parents' names. Note that most implementations of GAs use parent-symmetric recombination.

Our definition conveys another generalization with important consequences for the notorious problem of premature convergence in many GAs. For biologically-inspired methods, in general the offspring of a 2-merger algorithm is more similar to the parents (assuming an appropiate distance measure d) than the two parents are to each other. This can be written as:

$$\max\{d(y_1, y'), d(y_2, y')\} \leq d(y_1, y_2) \quad \forall y' \in \mathcal{M}_P(y_1, y_2, x) \tag{14.2}$$

This is an unnecessary restriction for recombination in MAs and we do not require it. It is valid, however, for the uniform crossover operator when the Hamming distance is used as a metric. Even the weaker restriction, with 'min' instead of 'max' is not required.

It is easy to see that the class *PMA* is not empty. For instance, let the problem P be the task of finding the minimum weight spanning tree of a graph $G(V, E)$. Let $sol_P(G(V, E))$ be the set of all spanning trees of G. There exists an exact neighbourhood (for local search) where two spanning trees are neighbours if one can be obtained from the other by exchanging one edge from another. Relying on this characterization for a neighbourhood relationship $\mathcal{N}$, the problem can be solved by a local search algorithm, and $P/\mathcal{N} \in PLS$. Based on that definition of $\mathcal{N}$ it is easy to create a polynomial-time p-starter and p'-evaluator algorithms. It is easy to see that a k-merger algorithm for this problem can be constructed using Prim's or Kruskal's algorithms running on a graph $G'(V', E')$ where $V' = V$ and E' is the set formed by the union of all edges in the input set S_{par}. This k-merger cannot be blind since the Prim's or Kruskal's algorithms would need knowledge of part of the input instance x (the graph G), since at least it will need the weight of the edges in E'. For the sake of brevity, we leave to the reader the corresponding analysis for linear programming and maximum matching.

14.2.4 Local-Search-based Memetic Algorithms

Sometimes it is easy to come up with many different ways of creating efficient, i.e. polynomial-time, starter, evaluator, l-engine, and k-merger algorithms (or heuristics) for an arbitrary computational problem P. This said, it is possible to define local search-based memetic algorithms (LS-based MAs) by reference to them. In general, LS-based MAs have been applied as a heuristic to approximately solve problems which had been proved to be *NP*-hard. In these cases, any LS-based MA, after fixation of any parameters that it may have, must be considered as a heuristic (an instantation of a general metaheuristic) for the problem of interest.

```
Begin
        InitializePopulation Pop using FirstPop()
        Foreach individual i ∈ Pop do i ← Local-Search-Engine(i)
        Foreach individual i ∈ Pop do i ← Evaluate(i)
        Repeat                              /* Generations Loop */
                parfor j := 1 to #recombinations do
                        selectToMerge a set Spar ⊆ Pop ;
                        offspring ← Recombine(Spar,x) ;
                        offspring ← Local-Search-Engine(offspring) ;
                        Evaluate(offspring) ;
                        addInPopulation individual offspring to Pop ;
                endparfor
                parfor j ←1 to #mutations do
                        selectToMutate an individual i ∈ Pop ;
                        im ← Mutate(i) ;
                        im ← Local-Search-Engine(im) ;
                        Evaluate(im) ;
                        addInPopulation individual im to Pop ;
                endparfor
                Pop ← SelectPop(Pop);
                if Pop has converged then Pop ← RestartPop(Pop);
        until termination-condition = True;
End
```

Fig. 14.1: The Local-Search-Based Memetic Algorithm.

The pseudocode of a LS-based MAs in Figure 14.1 will certainly help to clarify the general structure. It uses some reserved words which can be interpreted as follows. For instance, the **initializePopulation** command can be executed in different ways. Some MAs would use the starter algorithm (or a set of them if more than one is known), or, if possible, it is somehow randomized in order to generate a set of good initial solutions. The function Local-Search-Engine(), receives as input an individual and tries to improve it by iteratively using the l-engine algorithm. At each iteration it returns a better individual until that is no longer possible. Note that there is no need to evaluate the guiding function F_g (using the Evaluate() algorithm) until we got a local optimum.

After the initial population has been created, at least one recombination is done. Some MAs ask all individuals to be involved in recombinations, so #recombinations need not be specified as a parameter. In the pseudocode we have used **parfor** to indicate operations which can be executed in parallel if possible. The **selectToMerge** command is executed by selecting a subset of individuals for input to the k-merger algorithm. Some MAs use a random function, while others use a more complex approach. For instance, there are some authors who also advocated for the benefits of using a structured population for interaction of individuals (Gorges-Schleuter [1989, 1991], Mühlenbein [1991], Moscato [1993]).

A new individual is created by recombining the selected individuals according to the Recombine() function. This can start a variety of procedures, ranging from a single application of any available efficient (i.e. polynomial-time) k-merger algorithm up to more complex recombination operators (which means that they need not be efficient) such as the more systematic searches in $\mathcal{M}$ (Aggarwal et al [1997]). Afterwards, it is optimized and added (or not) to the population according to some criteria.

Analogously, a number of individuals are subjected to some mutations. Sometimes the Mutate() function is implemented as a random process based on the same neighbourhood definition implicit by the l-engine. This is not the general rule and other forms of mutation are possible. Again, the individual is reoptimized at the end of the mutation process and added or not to the population.

The SelectPop() function will act on the population, having the effect of reducing its size. The selection of this subset is not always determined by the objective or the guiding function. It may be biased by other features of the individuals, like the interest of maximizing some measure of diversity of the selected set. Again, this can be implemented in a variety of ways. The convergence of the population is sometimes decided by reference to a 'diversity-crisis', a measure which indicates, below a certain threshold, that the whole population has very similar configurations. When the population has converged, a RestartPop() function is used. In general, the best individual (or 'incumbent solution') is kept, and a new population is created using some randomized method. All individuals in the population are optimized and evaluated afterwards, and the whole process is repeated.

The termination-condition can also be implemented in many ways. It can be a time-expiration or generation-expiration criteria as well as more adaptive procedures, like some dynamic measure of lack of improvement.

14.3 MEMETIC ALGORITHMS IN PRACTICE

14.3.1 Early Approaches

We have mentioned elsewhere that a paper by Kase and Nishiyama (Kase & Nishiyama [1964]) describes work with some resemblance to a population approach for a layout problem (a set of 'players' of a certain 'game') which uses some type of recombination. However, it might be possible to uncover earlier references. For instance, Papadimitriou & Steiglitz [1982, page 484] cite Dunham et al [1961] as 'an early description of local search'. This paper has an intriguing title: 'Design by Natural Selection'. We have not had access to a copy of the article yet to analyse it, but this exemplifies the interest on evolutionary approaches as early as 1961. An excellent source which collects together examples of evolutionary computation ideas in early work is contained in Fogel [1998].

The TSP was the problem that inspired several MAs prior to 1988, possibly due to the fact that the researchers soon recognised the limitations of traditional GAs. Starting with the work by Brady [1985], other authors like Suh & van Gucht [1987], Liepins & Hilliard [1987], and Grefenstette [1987], soon were on the track of incorporating more problem-specific information in their algorithms. A major step forward was made by Mühlenbein et al [1988], Mühlenbein [1989], and Gorges-Schleuter [1989]. Most of these papers have been recently reviewed in Johnson & McGeoch [1997]; other references to early MAs (such as the work of Kauffman & Levin [1987] and other papers on the quadratic assignment problem) can be found in Moscato [1989].

14.3.2 Other MAs

After 1989, several papers on MAs appeared, generally referred as 'non-traditional GAs', or 'hybrid GAs'. Of particular relevance was the work by Eshelman [1991], Eshelman & Schaffer [1991], Braun [1991], and Ulder et al [1991]. A better insight on the dynamics of the MA of Moscato & Norman [1992] was obtained with a visualization tool. The software allowed the user to see the trajectories of individuals in a high-dimensional space by properly projecting them in a two or three-dimensional space (Hofmann [1992]).

It is beyond the scope of this chapter to survey the whole area. An up-to-date bibliography of MAs is maintained at the Memetic Algorithms' Home Page, along with much other information related to MAs. This page is located at the following address: http://www.densis.fee.unicamp.br/~moscato/memetic_home.html. This book's web page also contains links to the Memetic Algorithms' Home Page and additional relevant resources.

14.3.3 Fitness Landscape Analysis

In Moscato [1989] we first discussed the relevance that the hypothesis of correlation of local minima had on the overall success or failure of MAs. This subject was later studied by several researchers (Manderick et al [1991], Mathias & Whitley [1992], Moscato [1993], Dzubera & Whitley [1994], Merz & Freisleben [1998a]). Since its relevance is nowadays being more recognized (Reeves [1998]), we considered it as a very important topic, and chapter sixteen of this book is entirely dedicated to it. We therefore refer the reader to chapter sixteen for discussion of fitness landscape analysis with reference to supporting the design of the various components of a memetic algorithm.

14.4 FUTURE DIRECTIONS

It seems reasonable that one of the most important issues in memetic algorithms is to continue finding new ways to implement *negative knowledge* in them. This may seem paradoxical but it is not. Quoting M. Minsky:

> We tend to think of knowledge in positive terms – and of experts as people who know what to do. But a 'negative' way to seem competent is, simply, never to make mistakes.

Minsky [1994]

In essence, this is what heuristics do best, so certainly there is no paradox here. Ways of adding knowledge to population-based search (Radcliffe [1994], Aggarwal et al [1997], Gen & Cheng [1997], Beasley & Chu [1998], Bui & Moon [1998]) have been an early concern for some authors (Grefenstette [1987], Liepins & Hilliard [1987], Suh & van Gucht [1987], Moscato [1989]).

However, a key issue is related with the representation of the problem. Here is another place where 'negative expertise' would certainly help. Quoting Minsky's paper once again:

In the earliest theories about AI, for example, we emphasized the importance of heuristics for generating efficient search trees. This can be done either by pruning initially larger trees or by suppressing those branches right from the start – that is, by not thinking of them in the first place. When you decide to leave a room, you don't even think of jumping out the window. Thus, a positive system forces us to generate and test, whereas a negative-based system could more efficiently shape the search space from the start. To do this efficiently, we would have to invent ways to compile each new search generator, perhaps on the basis of previously learned negative prototypes.

Minsky [1994]

It may be possible that a future generation of MAs will work in at least two levels and two time scales. In the short-timescale, a set of agents would be searching in the search space associated to the problem while the long-time scale adapts the heuristics associated with the agents. Our work with D. Holstein (chapter fifteen) might be classified as a first step in this promising direction. However, it is reasonable to think that more complex schemes evolving solutions, agents, as well as representations, will soon be implemented.

We can read in a well-known textbook on combinatorial optimization:

> The strategy developed by Lin [1965] for the TSP is to obtain several local optima and then identify edges that are common to all of them. These are then fixed, thus reducing the time to find more local optima.

Papadimitriou & Steiglitz [1982]

It is intriguing that such an strategy, which has been around for more than three decades, is still not accepted by some researchers regardless of all empirical evidence of the benefits of memetic algorithms which exploit, by using recombination, the correlation of local optima (Moscato [1989, 1993], Mühlenbein [1991], Boese [1995]; see also chapter sixteen for extra references). We remark that it is one of the basic mechanisms for recombination of solutions. Memetic algorithms research should be conducted to provide more systematic, and also more efficient, recombination procedures.

Also in Papadimitriou & Steiglitz [1982] we can read:

> As is common with heuristics, one can also argue for exactly the opposite idea. Once such common features are detected, they are *forbidden* rather than fixed. This justification is the following: If we fear that the global optimum is escaping us, this could be because our heuristic is 'fooled' by this tempting features. Forbidding them could finally put us on the right track towards the global optimum. This is called *denial* in Steiglitz & Weiner [1968].

Papadimitriou & Steiglitz [1982]

We note that this strategy also appears in many MA implementations, e.g. in Merz and Freislebens' *Distance Preservation* recombination operator for the TSP. It is also part of the spirit that inspires the *Guided Local Search* MA (see chapter fifteen) as well as the tabu search metaheuristic. Our novel memetic recombination procedures involving 'rebel' and 'obsequent' 'behaviours' also take into account this design strategy. They are introduced in chapter seventeen, which investigates MAs on the number partitioning problem.

At the time of writing this chapter, Applegate, Bixby, Cook, and Chvatal have established a new breakthrough result for the TSP. They have solved to optimality an instance of the TSP of 13,509 cities corresponding to all U.S. cities with populations of more than 500 (see: http://www.crpc.rice.edu/CRPC/newsArchive/tsp.html). The approach, according to Bixby, '...involves ideas from polyhedral combinatorics and combinatorial optimization, integer and linear programming, computer science data structures and algorithms, parallel computing, software engineering, numerical analysis, graph theory, and more'. This is definitely the same philosophy of MAs, that of a synergy of different approaches. However, we wonder if the connection is even stronger. We wonder if the word 'more' does also employ some kind of recombination or other type of evolutionary processes. In Johnson & McGeoch [1997, page 301] it is suggested that part of the approach has an analogy with multi-parent recombination. From the complete graph with all edges, a subgraph is formed with the union of the edges of a selected elite of tours generated with the Iterated Lin-Kernighan algorithm, which is possibly the most powerful single-agent local search heuristic for the TSP. Since the resulting graph is sufficiently sparse and well-structured, an optimal tour in this subgraph can be computed.

For the practitioner, a word of advice is recommended here. Solving TSP problem instance usa13509 demanded three Digital AlphaServer 4100s (with a total of 12 processors) and a cluster of 32 Pentium-II PCs. The complete calculation took about three months of computer time, and involved the joint work of four of the most prominent researchers in the field of combinatorial optimization, putting their skills together for many years. According to the authors the code has certainly more than 1,000 pages and implemented state-of-the-art techniques from a wide variety of scientific fields. If this approach includes some form of recombination, it may possibly be classified as an MA too. In that case, it would probably be the most complex MA ever built. Simpler forms of MAs can certainly be more easily implemented if we require only approximate optimality.

Regarding local search and its variants, Lewis and Papadimitriou affirm:

> Explaining and predicting the impressive empirical success of some of these algorithms is one of the most challenging frontiers of the theory of computation today.

> Lewis & Papadimitriou [1997]

We conclude this introduction to Part Four by expressing our hope that the work in MAs, and in particular their empirical performance, can also motivate researchers to work towards establishing such a predictive theory.

Acknowledgements

I would like to acknowledge N. Krasnogor for several useful comments and remarks made on a draft version of this chapter. Also I benefit from useful discussions with other members of the *MemePool* Project, in particular with R. Berretta, L. Buriol, P.M. França, D. Holstein, A.S. Mendes, M.G. Norman, and A. Schaerf. Many thanks to all the authors who are helping to make the Memetic Algorithms' Home Page a useful resource. Although this chapter is not a survey, I apologize to anyone inadvertently left out. This work is supported by FAPESP, Brazil.

Chapter Fifteen

Memetic Algorithms using Guided Local Search: A Case Study

Diana Holstein and Pablo Moscato

15.1 INTRODUCTION

The Guided Local Search technique introduced by Voudouris & Tsang [1995, 1998] and Voudouris [1997] was designed to be conceptually simple and aimed to be applicable to a wide range of combinatorial optimization problems. We may say that these two aspects, as well as the first computational results using it, were responsible for attracting us to investigate its use in connection within the memetic algorithms (MAs) methodology. Simplicity is a common theme with other metaheuristics, like Simulated Annealing, and basic Tabu Search implementations. However, the simplicity of the mechanisms proposed to control the so-called 'exploration vs. exploitation' or 'diversification vs. intensification' issues (another common theme in metaheuristics) was certainly intriguing. We soon concluded that it was worth the effort of analysing how best to incorporate it into MAs.

Regarding the issue of computational comparison of heuristics, we believe in one saying originally attributed to the late Richard Feynman, the Nobel Prize Laureate in Physics. Allegedly he has said: 'The first principle is that you must not fool yourself, and you are the easiest person to fool'. Although the saying was certainly not directed to the metaheuristic research community at the time (actually it was given at the 1974 Commencement address at Caltech), it has certainly helped us to have it in mind when studying a new methodology. It is an omnipresent warning to avoid our unconscious bias towards proving something, specifically that one method is better than another one. We also support the *good practice* strategy of first experimenting new methodologies on well-known problems, instead of rather obscure problems for which, although they might be of some practical or economical impact, not enough literature is available. For these reasons, we started investigating the Guided-LS-powered MAs using the Travelling Salesman Problem as our test-bed. The selection was also due to our own experience with a variety of metaheuristics developed for this problem.

15.1.1 Guided Local Search

The main objective of this chapter is to illustrate how the Guided Local Search (Guided-LS) technique can be used as a powerful Local-Search-Engine() algorithm for the LS Based Memetic Algorithm proposed in the previous chapter. In this chapter we will make all efforts to continue with the same mathematical notation used in chapter fourteen. This said, we refer to it for the necessary definitions. For instance, when we refer to the Local-Search-

Engine() procedure we are talking about the procedure described in the pseudo-code for *Local-Search-based MAs* which was discussed in section 14.2.4 (Figure 14.1).

Given a search space S and any configuration $s \in S$, the latter has with it some information encoded in its *features*. We can define that a solution (analogously, a configuration) feature of s (analogously, S) is any non-trivial property exhibited by the solution (configuration). A property is non-trivial if it is not exhibited by all candidate solutions (configurations).

The main idea behind Guided-LS is that, given a search space S, we can control the search process by reference to these properties, which are implicit from the features of S. Again, this is a common theme with Tabu Search which aims to control the search by reference to *attributes* of the solutions.

The selection of what can constitute a feature is generally easy since they tend to be quite conspicuous from the problem domain and the representation chosen. For each feature f_k we have an indicator function Ind_k, such that $Ind_k = 1$ if S exhibits feature f_k, and $Ind_k = 0$ otherwise.

Given a problem P with an objective function $m_P(y, x)$ which maps every configuration $y \in sol_P(x)$ to a numerical value, we can construct a guiding function F_g of the form:

$$F_g(s) = m_P(y, x) + \lambda \sum_{k=1}^{M} p_k Ind_k(s) \tag{15.1}$$

where the variable p_k is a *penalty counter* (generally implemented as an integer value) for feature f_k which is proportional to the number of times it was penalized. All p_k are initialized to zero at the start (we have M of them). The value of λ is a parameter which balances the impact of the penalties with respect to the original objective function (the length of the tour). We will explain later how this value is generally set.

For each f_k a cost value ($cost_k$) is assigned which helps to rate its significance relative to other features. The main idea is that when a search is trapped in a local minimum of the Local-Search-Engine() we want to guide, we would systematically *fade out* features which have contributed to the current state through penalizing them. There is a risk here, that of constantly penalizing the most significant features. This is controlled with the introduction of yet another function for each feature ($util_k$) which takes account how many times each present features have been penalized in the past. Those features which maximize $util_k$ are selected to be penalized. We have:

$$util_k(s) = Ind_k(s) \times \frac{cost_k}{1 + p_k} \tag{15.2}$$

where the denominator obviously includes protection in case of a zero penalty count.

15.2 THE GUIDED-LS BASED MEMETIC ALGORITHM

In our description of the algorithm, we will make reference to the Local Search Based Memetic Algorithm pseudo-code of Figure 14.1 in section 14.2.4.

We need to explain the methodology we used for our experiments. Our interest was to see to which extent can we improve a very simple local search heuristic with the application of three different metaheuristics: (a) a memetic algorithm which does not use the ideas of Guided LS, (b) a Guided LS algorithm which uses only one individual (thus not a single recombination of solutions is used in this case), and (c) a Guided-LS based MA which combines features of both.

We were aware of the excellent results of P. Merz and B. Friesleben with their MA for TSP. Their algorithm relies on the Lin-Kernighan local search technique which is a very powerful technique for this problem. Their latest MA is probably one of the best heuristic methods for the TSP (Merz & Freisleben [1997a]). However, if we were using the same local search method we were pretty sure that we would have a problem to test the benefits of the Guided LS. Being the basic memetic algorithm (and the basic l-engine technique) too good (and our available computers too slow at the time of starting this project) we would face a problem to test the benefits of the introduction of the Guided LS. We then decided to have a relatively worse l-engine algorithm and see how it can be improved. We tried to emulate the situation where you have a problem such that it is easy to design some kind of naive local search algorithm of limited power but easy to code. These decisions were taken being severely limited by our practical limitations for the experimentation.

For a better comparison, we have selected all other algorithmic decisions of the MA to be most of the time equal to those used by Merz and Freisleben. That would help us to have their paper as a valid benchmark. However, in our implementation, no effort was taken to optimise the code. The results presented here will have only one purpose in mind, that of being a pedagogical example of how to integrate Guided LS within the MA framework.

In the next subsections we will show how the 'reserved words' from the pseudo-code of the LS-based MA (Figure 14.1) are interpreted in this implementation.

15.2.1 The Initialization Procedures

The **initializePopulation** command creates a set of 20 individuals. There is no population structure. Each individual will have one configuration. Each one of the configurations S represents a feasible solution $y \in sol_P(x)$. The search space S is composed of all the permutations of N_c different symbols (where N_c denotes the number of cities of instance x, each symbol corresponding to one city number). Different configurations may actually represent the same solution in this case.

The FirstPop() procedure creates the first individual (let's say individual $ind=1$) by generating a random permutation of the N_c symbols (this is our *starter* algorithm in this case since any random permutation corresponds to a valid solution). After that, the first individual is used as the input of the l-engine algorithm, which will be explained later in section 15.2.3. Then all other individuals are generated as follows: starting with the second individual ($ind=2$) we create individual ind by first receiving a copy of individual $ind-1$ which we modify with a specific heuristic called *random chain of 2-changes*. As with the first one, we apply the l-engine algorithm to the newly created individual.

The *random chain of 2-changes* modifying heuristic starts by selecting one edge of the tour at random with uniform probability and deleting it. From that edge, it selects and also deletes three other edges such that the four strings containing edges which have not been deleted have approximately the same number of edges. If (c_i, c_{i+1}), (c_j, c_{j+1}), (c_k, c_{k+1}) and (c_m, c_{m+1}) are the deleted edges (found in that order in the original tour) they are replaced with the new edges (c_i, c_j), (c_{i+1}, c_k), (c_{j+1}, c_m) and (c_{k+1}, c_{m+1}).

15.2.2 The Regularization Parameter

For the MA which uses GLS we have associated a regularization parameter λ to each one of the individuals of the population. For the purposes of a fair comparison, and regarding the computational results of Voudouris & Tsang [1995], we have decided to apply the following formula:

$$\lambda = 0.3 \cdot \frac{L(initial\_tour)}{N_c} \qquad (15.3)$$

where $L(initial\_tour)$ is the length of the tour associated to that individual (after the first optimization phase using only the l-engine procedure) and N_c is the number of cities.

15.2.3 The Local-Search-Engine() Procedure

The Local-Search-Engine() uses as basic l-engine a variant of the well-known algorithm which creates 2-opt tours. In our implementation we have made use of several variants of the technique which have been introduced by Bentley [1992] and discussed in depth in Johnson & McGeoch [1997].

The main difference is that since we are using Guided-LS, the l-engine accepts or rejects transitions regarding the guiding function and not the original $m_P(y,x)$, i.e. the tour length. For instance, the new distance matrix combining the penalties can be written as:

$$D_{ij} = d_{ij} + \lambda p_{ij} \qquad (15.4)$$

where p_{ij} is the penalty associated with the edge between cities i and j. Since the l-engine relies on the calculation of the changes of the guiding function, they are calculated with the following formula:

$$\Delta F_g(\Delta s) = \Delta m_P(\Delta y, x) + \lambda \sum_{k}^{M} p_k \Delta Ind_k(\Delta s) \qquad (15.5)$$

15.2.4 The Recombine() Procedure

Selection of parents

The *#recombinations* value is set to 10, and each time the **selectToMerge** command is called, it selects two solutions to be recombined; i.e. we are using a 2-merger algorithm in this case. One of them is always the incumbent solution (the best one so-far found). Since there is no population structure, there is no other constraint for selecting the second parent and all other 19 parents are available. Then it is selected using a random uniform probability among the other 19 solutions.

Recombination

The basic recombination procedure we have used is tentatively called *Multiple Fragment-Nearest Neighbour Repair Edge Recombination*, and it is an example of an efficient 2-

merger algorithm as described in chapter fourteen. It receives two valid solutions (two tours) and creates an offspring tour. Given two parent tours having edge sets A and B respectively, all edges common to both parents (i.e. edges in $A \cap B$) are selected to be part of the offspring. We then list edges in $(A-B) \cup (B-A)$ and list them in increasing order regarding their lengths, arbitrarily breaking ties. Starting with the first one of the list we test if we can add it to the offspring. Each subsequent addition must avoid the generation of an unfeasible tour, so we need to prohibit the creation of a *subtour* (a closed cycle with fewer than the total number of cities) or a *bifurcation* (a city that has three edges incident on it). In those cases, that edge is not added and the procedure continues using the next one in the list. If after completion of this step we still do not have a complete tour (we have a set of disconnected multi-edge strings or isolated cities), we proceed with a *patching* operation. Instead of using the *Karp-patching* mechanism (Moscato & Norman [1992], Moscato [1993]) we resort to the simpler idea of running the nearest-neighbour constructive heuristic on the set of cities which have none or only one edge (the so-called *endpoints* of the set of substrings).

---

procedure (Guided) Local-Search-Engine
begin
    $iter = 0$;
    foreach feature k **do** $p_k \leftarrow 0$;
    repeat

$$F_g(s) = m_P(y,x) + \lambda \sum_k^M p_k Ind_k \; ;$$

$$s_{iter+1} = l - engine(s_{iter}, F_g(s_{iter})) \; ;$$

        foreach feature k **do** $util_k \leftarrow Ind_k \cdot \dfrac{cost_k}{1 + p_k} \; ;$

        foreach feature k which maximizes $util_k$ **do** $p_k = p_k + 1$;
        $iter = iter + 1$;
    until guidedLS-termination-condition = True;
  return the best-so-far found solution regarding $m_p(x, y)$

Fig. 15.1: The (Guided) Local-Search-Engine() Algorithm.

15.2.5 Adding New Individuals to the Population

To preserve the diversity of the population, the **addInPopulation** command checks that there is no other individual with the same offspring value already in *Pop*. If so, the tour to be introduced is altered by randomly performing a chain of 2-changes. This procedure is analogous to the one used to create the initial population by the FirstPop() procedure.

15.2.6 The Mutate() Procedure

The *#mutations* parameter was set to 1. The **selectToMutate** command selects at random one individual from *Pop* and it uses the *double-bridge move* (Johnson & McGeoch [1997]). This removes the four edges (c_i, c_{i+1}), (c_j, c_{j+1}), (c_k, c_{k+1}), and (c_m, c_{m+1}) and inserts four new edges (c_i, c_{k+1}), (c_j, c_{m+1}), (c_k, c_{i+1}), and (c_m, c_{j+1}) to create another valid tour.

15.2.7 The SelectPop() and RestartPop() Procedures

The SelectPop() procedure works by selecting the best 20 individuals (regarding the cost function only). If for three consecutive generations the incumbent solution did not improve, population-converged is set to **True**, and we assumed that the Guided-LS procedure is no longer able to produce better solutions.

We have decided not to implement any RestartPop() procedure to first analyse the performance of the methods without recurring to it. However, we point out one out of many ways in which such a procedure might have been implemented based on running the Recombine() procedure 19 times. In each of the 19 calls, one of the input parent configurations is the 'best' individual and all the other configurations are mutated and recombined with it. The 'best' here is a relative measure, meaning that it is the individual which has improved the most (regarding the objective function) since the last time the RestartPop() procedure was called.

15.3 COMPUTATIONAL RESULTS

15.3.1 TSPLIB Instances

We first tested the behaviour of the three metaheuristics using a set of 23 instances from TSPLIB. We may consider them in the small-medium size range since the number of cities varies between 48 and 783. The optimum solution is known in all cases. We present results of only one run for each instance, so we can only comment on some basic qualitative preliminary results.

For a baseline comparison, we have run 300 times a multi-start version of the basic LS heuristic and the best result is reported. We counted the number of attempted 2-changes and we have run the MA, the GLS and the Guided-LS MA algorithms until we have reached that value. This was the stopping criterion used. The results are given in Table 15.1.

What we first note is that the basic local search was not able to find an optimal solution in any case. When an algorithm has found an optimal solution we print the value of the objective function (the length of the tour) in boldface. In all cases the number between brackets shows the relative percentual gap over the optimum solution. Eye inspection of the table clearly shows that the MA has found only six times the optimum, but that behaviour is not very robust. This is understandable since we have not done much to find a good strategy for the MA without Guided-LS. The Guided-LS did significantly better, finding the optimum 13 times out of 23 runs. However, it is the Guided-LS based MA which seems more robust, finding 17 times the optimum solution. However, the Guided-LS algorithm alone seems to better handle the last five instances in comparison with the Guided-LS MA, with the exception of instance p654.tsp where the gap is higher.

Table 15.1: Computational results using TSPLIB instances.

Instance	Cities	Opt.	LS Heuristic	MA	GLS MA	GLS
att48	48	10628	10638 (0.09)	**10628 (0.0)**	**10628 (0.0)**	**10628 (0.0)**
st70	70	675	687 (1.78)	681 (0.89)	**675 (0.0)**	**675 (0.0)**
eil76	76	538	555 (3.16)	**538 (0.0)**	**538 (0.0)**	539 (0.19)
rd100	100	7910	8131 (2.79)	8045 (1.71)	**7910 (0.0)**	**7910 (0.0)**
kroe100	100	22068	22572 (2.28)	22073 (0.02)	**22068 (0.0)**	**22068 (0.0)**
krod100	100	21294	21923 (2.95)	21536 (1.14)	**21294 (0.0)**	**21294 (0.0)**
kroc100	100	20749	21018 (1.30)	**20749 (0.0)**	**20749 (0.0)**	**20749 (0.0)**
krob100	100	22141	22323 (0.82)	22220 (0.36)	**22141 (0.0)**	**22141 (0.0)**
kroa100	100	21282	21387 (0.49)	**21282 (0.0)**	**21282 (0.0)**	**21282 (0.0)**
eil101	101	629	648 (3.02)	634 (0.79)	**629 (0.0)**	**629 (0.0)**
bier127	127	118282	120434 (1.82)	118361 (0.07)	**118282 (0.0)**	118313 (0.03)
pr136	136	96772	99160 (2.47)	97009 (0.24)	**96772 (0.0)**	96781 (0.01)
pr144	144	58537	59281 (1.27)	**58537 (0.0)**	**58537 (0.0)**	**58537 (0.0)**
kroa150	150	26524	27361 (3.16)	26528 (0.02)	**26524 (0.0)**	**26524 (0.0)**
u159	159	42080	43018 (2.23)	**42080 (0.0)**	**42080 (0.0)**	**42080 (0.0)**
d198	198	15780	16368 (3.73)	15867 (0.5)	15808 (0.18)	15816 (0.23)
krob200	200	29437	30774 (4.54)	29956 (1.76)	**29437 (0.0)**	**29437 (0.0)**
lin318	318	42029	44508 (5.90)	42558 (1.26)	**42029 (0.0)**	42062 (0.08)
pcb442	442	50778	53993 (6.33)	51242 (0.91)	50926 (0.29)	50808 (0.06)
att532	532	27686	29566 (6.79)	28314 (2.27)	27744 (0.21)	27716 (0.11)
u574	574	36905	39691 (7.55)	37112 (0.56)	37153 (0.67)	36978 (0.20)
p654	654	34643	38522 (11.2)	35662 (2.94)	34674 (0.09)	34879 (0.68)
rat783	783	8806	9468 (7.52)	8920 (1.29)	8834 (0.32)	8809 (0.03)
Mean			3.62	0.73	0.08	0.07
Hits opt			–	(6/23)	(17/23)	(13/23)

15.3.2 Fractal Instances

We have also run some experiments on a set of fractal instances of the TSP (Mariano et al [1995], Norman & Moscato [1995], Moscato & Norman [1998]). The situation in this case shows a relatively similar situation although the Guided-LS procedure now seems to be failing more often in finding the optimum solution. The Guided-LS MA found the optimum (or conjectured optimum) 7 times out of 8. The notorious exception is an instance called MNPeano (Moscato & Norman [1998], see Figure 15.2) where Guided-LS has found a solution of cost 460, around 7% above optimality. It is interesting to note the contrast with lin318.tsp and pcb442.tsp (both similarly sized) where the gaps are significantly lower.

Although these issues require further investigation, we conjecture that the high number of edges which have the same length in these instances might conspire against the Guided-LS navigation strategy. We point out that we consider it necessary to use both the TSPLIB instances and *also* use other type of instances (like the fractal ones) for the computational experiments in order to produce more robust metaheuristics (Moscato & Norman [1998]).

Table 15.2: Computational results on Fractal Instances.

Instance	Cities	LS Heuristic	MA	GLS MA	GLS
snowf1-2	294	294	279	**276**	278
flowsnk2	294	258	255	**254**	**254**
fassp1-2	320	**320**	**320**	**320**	**320**
mnpeano3	364	459	**428**	441	460
daveven4	486	474	449	**443**	452
qtour2-3	500	516	501	**500**	503
spnsk5	729	808	**715**	**715**	722
koch1-4	768	939	**715**	**715**	**715**
Hits opt:		–	(4/8)	(7/8)	(3/8)

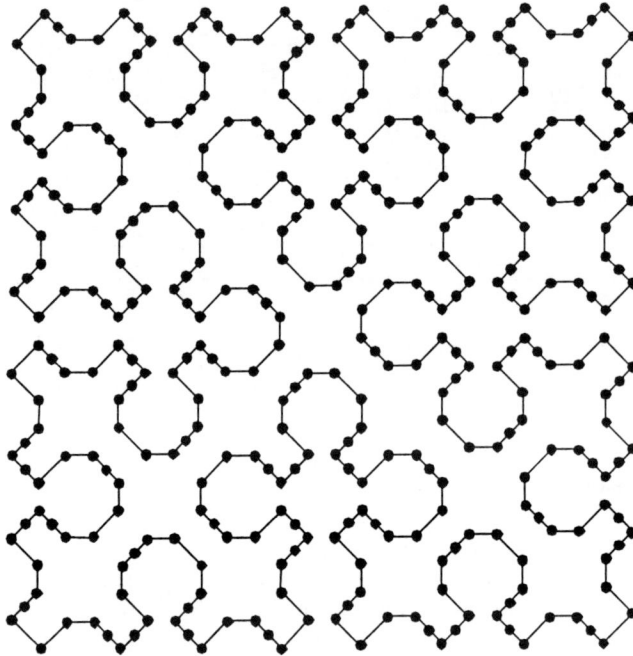

Fig. 15.2: Optimum of mnpeano3 (Norman & Moscato [1995], Moscato & Norman [1998]).

15.4 CONCLUSIONS

When we started this research project in 1996, we were first interested in evaluating the benefits of including Guided-LS in a memetic algorithm. We have found that it is really straightforward to implement and the resulting metaheuristic is very robust. Indeed, we have been caught by surprise with the performance of the combined method. We believe that it is clear that MAs can benefit from the inclusion of more evolved forms of Guided-LS for each individual agent. We also believe that we could benefit from the characteristics of the basic Guided-LS metaheuristic to provide a different search mechanism for the individuals. One way of doing this, for instance, would be by letting each individual work on different features. Another interesting research direction would be to make a co-evolutionary MA, in which we search both for better guiding heuristics and configurations at the same time (though the adaptations would proceed at different time-scales). Better guiding heuristics can be created by adapting the penalizations as well as evolving different features.

We have also tested the behaviour for diferent values of the regularisation parameter λ. We have found that, at least in this case, the performance of the Guided-LS MA was not too sensitive. If this does not generalise to some other problem domain, we remark that it may be also subject to the use of some adaptation scheme during the search. However, we recognized that more tests on the TSP are necessary, principally to make the basic Guided-LS more robust. This should be done using some other types of instances, like the fractal instances proposed here (see our discussion on methodological issues in Moscato & Norman [1998]), but other types of distributions such as those proposed by Bentley should be used.

We also remark here that the Guided-LS MA results presented in this chapter do not outperform the MA implemented by Merz & Freisleben [1997a]. However, we must remark that although we have used a very weak local search heuristic for the TSP (a simplified form of the 2-opt heuristic) we have been able to solve many instances to optimality. The approach used by Merz and Freisleben involved the more powerful Lin-Kernighan heuristic and a specially developed recombination operator which is tailored to preserve diversity. A recent paper reports new improved results with a 'single agent' Guided-LS (Voudouris & Tsang [1998]). There is a good basis to hope that better, more robust and efficient MAs based on these techniques will be developed in the near future. The Travelling Salesman Problem appears to be a good example of a leading case.

Acknowledgements

We want to thank C. Voudouris and E. Tsang for sending us their papers before publication. P.M.'s work is supported by FAPESP, Brazil.

Chapter Sixteen

Fitness Landscapes and Memetic Algorithm Design

Peter Merz and Bernd Freisleben

16.1 INTRODUCTION

The notion of fitness landscapes has been introduced to describe the dynamics of evolutionary adaptation in nature (Wright [1932]) and has become a powerful concept in evolutionary theory. Fitness landscapes are equally well suited to describe the behaviour of heuristic search methods in optimization, since the process of evolution can be thought of as searching a collection of genotypes in order to find the genotype of an organism with highest fitness and thus highest chance of survival.

Thinking of a heuristic search method as a strategy to 'navigate' in the fitness landscape of a given optimization problem may help in predicting the performance of a heuristic search algorithm if the structure of the landscape is known in advance. Furthermore, the analysis of fitness landscapes may help in designing highly effective search algorithms. In the following we show how the analysis of fitness landscapes of combinatorial optimization problems can aid in designing the components of memetic algorithms. However, some of the presented concepts can also be utilized for the development of other search algorithms, including genetic algorithms and neighbourhood search algorithms (e.g. simulated annealing and tabu search).

16.2 FITNESS LANDSCAPES OF COMBINATORIAL PROBLEMS

In combinatorial optimization, the number of (candidate) solutions of a given problem is finite. Due to the fact that the complete enumeration of the search space is in many cases impractical (many combinatorial optimization problems are known to be *NP*-hard (Garey & Johnson [1979]), only a small fraction of all solutions can be evaluated and thus the structure of the problem must be exploited to find optimum or near optimum solutions. To identify the structure of a given problem, the idea of fitness landscape analysis appears to be a promising approach.

16.2.1 Combinatorial Optimization Problems

An example of a combinatorial optimization problem addressed in this chapter is the famous *travelling salesman problem* (TSP) in which a salesman tries to find a shortest closed tour to visit a set of N cities under the condition that each city is visited exactly once

(Lawler et al [1985]). Thus, the TSP consists of finding a permutation π of the set $\{1, 2, 3, \ldots, n\}$ that minimizes the quantity:

$$C(\pi) = \sum_{i=1}^{n-1} d_{\pi(i),\pi(i+1)} + d_{\pi(n),\pi(1)} \qquad (16.1)$$

where d_{ij} denotes the distance between cities i and j.

Another well-known combinatorial optimization problem is the graph bi-partitioning problem (GBP), which can be stated as follows. Given a undirected graph $G=(V,E)$, the GBP is to find a partition of the nodes in two equally sized sets such that the number of edges between nodes in the different sets is minimized. More formally, the problem is to minimize:

$$c(V_1, V_2) = |\, e(V_1, V_2)\,|, \quad \text{with} \quad e(V_1, V_2) = \{(i, j) \in E : i \in V_1 \wedge j \in V_2\} \qquad (16.2)$$

where $c(V_1, V_2)$ is referred to as the cut size of the partition.

In the *quadratic assignment problem* (QAP; see also chapter three), n facilities have to be assigned to n locations at minimum cost. Given a set $\Pi(n)$ of all permutations of $\{1,2,\ldots,n\}$ and two $n\times n$ matrices $A = a_{ij}$ and $B = b_{ij}$, the task is to minimize the quantity:

$$C(\pi) = \sum_{i=1}^{n} \sum_{j=1}^{n} a_{ij} b_{\pi(i)\pi(j)}, \qquad \pi \in \Pi(n) \qquad (16.3)$$

Matrix A can be interpreted as a distance matrix, i.e. a_{ij} denotes the distance between location i and location j, and B is referred to as the flow matrix, i.e. b_{kl} represents the flow of materials from facility k to facility l. The TSP and the GBP are special cases of the QAP.

The *NK*-model of Kauffman & Levin [1987] and Kauffman [1993] defines a family of fitness landscapes which can be tuned by two parameters: N and K. While N determines the dimension of the search space, K specifies the degree of epistatic interactions of the genes constituting a genome. Each point in the fitness landscape is represented by a bit string of length N and can be viewed as a vertex in the N-dimensional hypercube. The fitness f of a point $b = (b_1,\ldots,b_n)$ is defined as follows:

$$f(b) = \frac{1}{N} \sum_{i=1}^{N} f_i(b_i, b_{i1}, \ldots, b_{iK}) \qquad (16.4)$$

where the fitness contribution f_i of gene i depends on its allele b_i and the alleles of K other genes $b_{i1}, b_{i2}, \ldots, b_{iK}$. The function f_i assigns a uniformly distributed random number between 0 and 1 to each of its 2^{K+1} inputs (all possible combinations of values of these $K+1$ binary genes). The values for $i1,\ldots,iK$ are chosen randomly from $\{1, \ldots, N\}$.

16.2.2 Fitness Landscape Definition

To define a fitness landscape for a given problem instance, a real valued fitness has to be assigned to each of the solutions $s \in S$ of the search space. Furthermore, we need to find an arrangement of the solutions or genotypes in the genotypical space to form a landscape. The spatial structure of the landscape can be defined by a metric d, which assigns to each pair of solutions a distance value $d(\cdot, \cdot)$.

More formally, a fitness landscape of a problem instance for a given combinatorial optimization problem is a triple $\mathcal{L}=(S, f, d)$ and consists of a set of points (solutions) S, a fitness function f which assigns a real-valued fitness to each of the points in S and a distance metric d which assigns a real-valued distance value between pairs of points in S, and for which it is required that:

$$d(s,t) \geq 0, \quad d(s,t) = 0 \Leftrightarrow s = t, \quad d(s,t) \leq d(s,u) + d(u,t) \quad \forall s,t,u \in S$$

Furthermore, when s and t are distinct, $d_{min} \leq d(s,t) \leq d_{max}, \forall s,t \in S$. The fitness landscape can be interpreted as a graph $G_{\mathcal{L}} = (V, E)$ with vertex set $V = S$ and edge set $E = \{(s, s') \in S \times S \mid d(s,s') = d_{min}\}$. The diameter of the landscape is the maximum distance between two points in the graph and is denoted $diam\, G_{\mathcal{L}}$, thus $d_{max} = diam\, G_{\mathcal{L}}$. The topology of the graph is, of course, problem dependent. For example, for NK-landscapes the graph is a Hamming graph, for the graph bi-partitioning problem the graph is a Johnson graph, and for the travelling salesman problem the graph is a Cayley graph (see Stadler [1995] for details).

For any instance of a given problem, there are many fitness landscapes, since many metrics can be defined on the set of all solutions to a given problem. The easiest and most straightforward definition of a distance function may be the following. Consider an elementary operator ω that transforms a solution s into a solution s'. The associated distance metric $d_\omega(s,t)$ is defined as the minimum number of applications of ω required to obtain t from s. Usually, the operator modifies a solution only slightly, e.g. by changing a single gene of the genotype. For example, in binary coded problems, such an operator is the bit-flip operator which flips one bit at a time. To obtain one solution from the other, all differing bits have to be flipped, one by one. The number of times the bit-flip operator has to be applied is the number of different bits, and the distance metric induced by the operator is known as the Hamming distance $d_H(x, y) = \Sigma_i (x_i \oplus y_i)$ between bit vectors.

In the TSP, for example, an elementary operator is the edge-exchange operator which exchanges two edges contained in the current solution by two new edges maintaining feasibility. Applied twice, the operator generates a solution that has either zero, three or four edges not contained in the original tour, depending on the choice of the edges in the second application of the operator. If one or two edges are removed that have previously been inserted, the number of different edges is fewer than four. So, instead of counting the number of applications of the edge-exchange operator, the number of different edges between two tours appears to be a better suited distance measure for the TSP.

16.2.3 Properties of Fitness Landscapes

For both performance prediction and memetic algorithm design, it becomes crucial to identify landscape characteristics which influence the effectiveness of heuristic search methods. The following landscape properties are known to have a strong influence:

- the fitness differences between neighbouring points in the landscape (ruggedness),
- the number of local optima (peaks in the landscape),
- the distribution of the local optima in the search space, and
- the topology of the basins of attraction of the local optima.

Several methods have been proposed to 'measure' these properties. Some of them are presented in the following.

Autocorrelation Functions of Fitness Landscapes

The landscape ruggedness is an important property, since a smooth landscape where fitness varies only slightly along a random walk (the random application of an elementary operator) can be easily optimized by heuristic search algorithms. If small moves in a landscape lead to high fitness changes, the landscape is said to be rugged.

To measure the ruggedness of a fitness landscape, several methods have been proposed, for example the correlation functions proposed by Weinberger [1990]. The *autocorrelation function* (Stadler [1992], Weinberger [1990]) is defined as:

$$\zeta(d) = \frac{\langle f(x)f(y)\rangle_{d(x,y)=d} - \langle f\rangle^2}{\langle f^2\rangle - \langle f\rangle^2} \qquad (16.5)$$

where $\langle x\rangle$ denotes the mean of all x_i. It defines the correlation of points at distance d in the search space.

Alternatively, Weinberger suggested using random walks to investigate the correlation structure of a landscape. The *random walk correlation function* (Stadler [1995, 1996], Weinberger [1990]) of a time series $\{f(x, t)\}$ is:

$$r(s) = \frac{\langle f(x_t)\rangle\langle f(x_{t+s})\rangle - \langle f\rangle^2}{\langle f^2\rangle - \langle f\rangle^2} \qquad (16.6)$$

It defines the correlation of two points s steps away along a random walk through the fitness landscape. Based on these definitions, the correlation length ℓ (Stadler [1996]) of the landscape can be defined as:

$$\ell = -\frac{1}{\ln(|r(1)|)} = -\frac{1}{\ln(|\zeta(1)|)} \qquad (16.7)$$

for $r(1), \zeta(1) \neq 0$. If the landscape is *statistically isotropic*, i.e. the time series $\{f(x, t)\}$ forms a stationary random process, then a single random walk is sufficient to obtain $r(s)$. If a time series is *isotropic*, *Gaussian* and *Markovian*, then the corresponding landscape is called an AR(1) landscape, and the random walk correlation function is of the form $r(s) = r(1)^s = e^{-s/\ell}$ with ℓ being the correlation length of the landscape. For example, AR(1) landscapes are found in the *NK*-model and the TSP (Weinberger [1990]). Figure 16.1 shows $r(s)$ for an AR(1) landscape of the instance tai100a of the QAP.

The correlation length is a well suited measure for comparing landscapes for a given problem instance. The higher the correlation length, the smoother the landscape and hence the easier the search for an algorithm based on the underlying neighbourhood of the landscape, since neighbouring points have a higher correlation. Table 16.1 provides an overview of various fitness landscapes and their correlation lengths. These were obtained theoretically and have been confirmed by experiments (Stadler [1995, 1996]).

tai100a

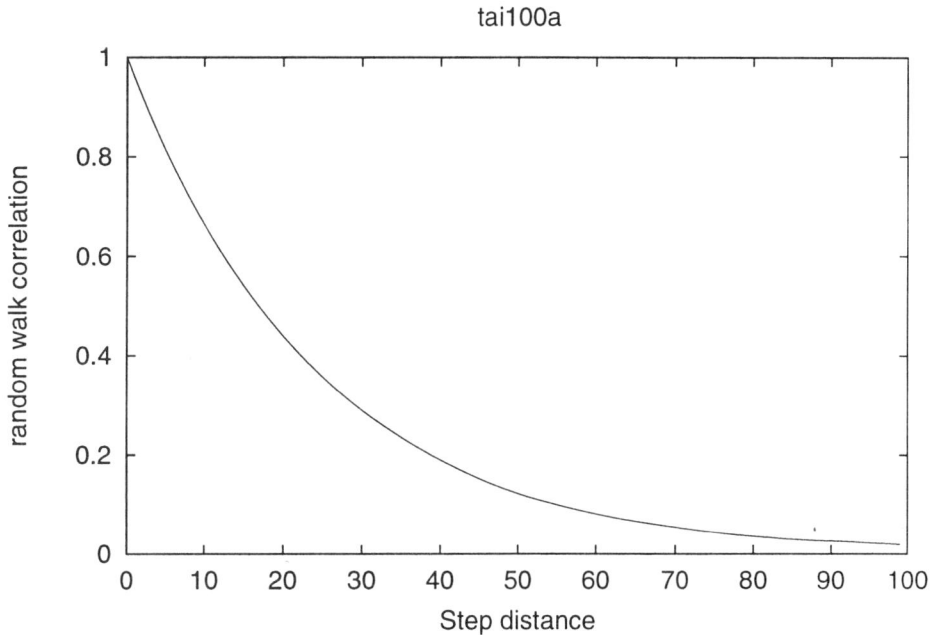

Fig. 16.1: Random walk correlation function for the QAP instance tai100a.

Table 16.1: Correlation measures in fitness landscapes of selected combinatorial optimization problems

Problem	Metric	$diam\ G_{\mathcal{L}}$	$|\mathcal{N}|$	ℓ
TSP	Edge-exchange	$n-1$	$(n-1)n/2$	$n/2$
	Node-exchange	$n-1$	$(n-1)n/2$	$n/4$
NK	Hamming	N	$n-1$	$n/(k+1)$
GBP	Exchanges	$n/2$	$(n-1)n/2$	$\sim n/8$
	α-Flip	n	$n-1$	$\sim n/4$

Fractal Landscapes

Another characteristic of fitness landscapes is the connection between correlation and self-similarity. A landscape is said to be fractal if the variance of the difference in fitness between two points in the landscape scales as a power law with their distance from each other. More formally, a landscape is fractal if $\langle |f(x) - f(y)|^2 \rangle \propto d(x, y)^{2h}$ for all pairs of points (x, y) in the search space. Examples of fractal landscapes with $h=1/2$ include *NK*-Landscapes, TSP with edge-exchange, and the GBP. Fractal landscapes can be separated into four classes according to Weinberger & Stadler [1993]. However, it is still unknown how this classification is related to the performance of heuristic search methods.

Landscape Ruggedness and Epistasis

For many combinatorial optimization problems, under a suitable representation, the fitness or the cost function can be easily decomposed into fitness contribution functions for each gene of the genome representing a solution of the problem. Such a decomposition allows us to identify the gene interactions of a given representation, or in other words, on which and how many other genes the fitness contribution of each gene depends. For example, if

$$f(x) = c \cdot \sum_{i=1}^{n} f_i(x_i, x_{i_1}, ..., x_{i_{k(i)}})$$

then the fitness contribution f_i depends on the allele (value) x_i of gene i and $k(i)$ other alleles at the loci $i_1, ..., i_{k(i)}$. Thus, the value of $k(i)$ determines the amount of interactions between the genes, called *epistasis*. In contrast to the model proposed by Davidor [1990], who defines epistasis variance for functions where such a decomposition is not known or obvious (for example, real valued function optimization using binary encodings), the amount of gene interaction is derived from the problem and the chosen representation itself, and there is no need for the use of statistical models.

Epistasis can be seen as a measure of problem difficulty since it determines the amount of nonlinearity of the problem. One would expect that for low epistasis search is easy: if there is no gene interaction, then there exists only one local optimum, but on the other hand, if the fitness contribution of a site depends on all other gene values, the fitness landscape becomes totally unstructured. It has been shown for *NK*-landscapes, where $K=k(i)$ determines the number of interacting genes, that there is one local optimum for $K=0$, and the expected number of local optima for $K=N-1$ is $2^N/(N+1)$. However, high epistasis (in terms of a high average number of interacting genes per locus) is not the only property making a problem hard to solve. For random geometric instances of the GBP, we have shown that search becomes easier with increasing epistasis (Merz & Freisleben [1998]), indicating that the number of the interactions is not the only important property. The gene interactions can be viewed as a directed graph (*graph of epistatic interactions*) with vertices representing the genes and edges defining the dependencies between the genes. An edge (i, j) indicates that the fitness contribution at gene j depends on the allele at gene i (f_i is of the form $f_i(..., x_i, ...)$). Thus, the average vertex degree reflects the average number of interacting genes per locus. We have shown for the GBP that the structure of the graph of epistatic interactions has a high influence on the structure of the fitness landscape.

Fitness Distance Correlation

The *fitness distance correlation* (FDC) coefficient has been proposed in Jones & Forrest [1995] as a measure of problem difficulty for genetic algorithms. It is defined as:

$$\chi(f, d_{opt}) = \frac{\langle f d_{opt} \rangle - \langle f \rangle \langle d_{opt} \rangle}{\sqrt{\left(\langle f^2 \rangle - \langle f \rangle^2\right)\left(\langle d_{opt}^2 \rangle - \langle d_{opt} \rangle^2\right)}} \tag{16.8}$$

The FDC coefficient determines how closely fitness and distance to the nearest optimum in the search space are related. If fitness increases when the distance to the optimum becomes smaller, then the search is expected to be easy for selection-based algorithms: the optimum can successively be approached via fitter individuals. An FDC coefficient value of $\chi = -1.0$ ($\chi = 1.0$) for a maximization (minimization) problem indicates that fitness and distance to the optimum are perfectly correlated, and therefore that search on such a landscape promises to be easy. On the other hand, correlation coefficients for a maximization (minimization) problem of $\chi = 1.0$ ($\chi = -1.0$) means that with increasing fitness the distance to the optimum increases too. This can be thought of as a fully deceptive problem, in which every step we make towards locally better fitness takes us further from the global optimum.

A *fitness distance plot* can be made to gain insight in the structure of the search space instead of simply calculating the correlation coefficient. The scatter plot contains much more information and can be interpreted easier than the coefficient and thus has been recommended for this type of analysis (Jones & Forrest [1995]). The scatter plot is generated by plotting the fitness of points in the search space against their distance to an optimum or best-known solution. Fitness distance analysis (FDA) has been applied by several researchers, including Kauffman [1993] for *NK*-landscapes, Boese [1995] for the TSP, Reeves [1998] for a flow-shop scheduling problem, Moscato [1993] for the binary perceptron problem, and Merz & Freisleben [1998] for the GBP.

The disadvantage of the FDA is that the optimum solution has to be known in advance. In many cases, the best known solution can be used instead, since it is an optimum solution or it lies close to the optimum in the search space. For totally uncorrelated landscapes, replacing the optimum by the best solution found may lead to a totally different fitness distance plot, and thus the FDA is of little help for performance prediction.

16.2.4 Local Search Neighbourhoods

Fitness landscapes and local search algorithms are directly related. Local search algorithms are characterized by the neighbourhoods they depend on. For a given landscape $\mathcal{L} = (S, f, d)$, the simplest neighbourhood is defined by $\mathcal{N}(s) = \{s' \in S : d(s, s') = d_{min}\}$, where $\mathcal{N}(s)$ is the set of all neighbouring points of the solution S in the landscape $\mathcal{L}$. In other words, the neighbourhood of S is defined as the set of solutions that can be obtained by applying the elementary operator ω of the landscape once. More generally, the k-opt neighbourhood is defined as:

$$\mathcal{N}_{k\text{-}opt}(s) = \{s' \in S : d(s, s') \leq k\} \qquad (16.9)$$

The 3-opt neighbourhood, for example, includes the 2-opt neighbourhood and for $k = d_{min}$ the neighbourhood is identical to the whole search space. The size of the k-opt neighbourhoods $|\mathcal{N}_{k\text{-}opt}|$ grows exponentially in k for many combinatorial optimization problems, so usually only neighbourhoods with small values for k are used in local search algorithms.

16.3 MEMETIC ALGORITHM DESIGN

Evolutionary algorithms such as genetic algorithms (Holland [1975], Goldberg [1989]), evolutionary programming (Fogel et al [1966]), evolution strategies (Rechenberg [1973]) and memetic algorithms (Moscato [1989]) share the advantage that existing algorithms can be easily adapted to new problem domains. Only the problem specific details have to be rewritten, such as the evaluation of the fitness function, the definition of recombination and mutation operators as well as the population initialization function. All other parts of the algorithm do not have to be modified, for example the general framework, the parent selection mechanism, the replacement schemes and the data structures for storing the individuals of the population. The following steps are thus necessary to design a memetic algorithm for a new problem domain.

Step 1: Find a suitable representation for the candidate solutions of a given problem and an evaluation function for calculating the fitness of a given solution based on the representation.

Step 2: Find an efficient local search algorithm.

Step 3: Find a suitable initialization method for the initial population.

Step 4: Define the genetic mutation and recombination operators.

These steps are discussed in the following subsections.

16.3.1 Representation and Local Search

Finding a suitable encoding for the solutions of the problem is tightly coupled with finding a good elementary operator for local search, since the elementary operator depends on the representation chosen. The elementary operator defines the landscape by inducing a distance metric over all pairs of points in the search space and thus is responsible for the performance of neighbourhood based search. Generally, the elementary operator should only change the elements or genes of a solution slightly, since this often results in a slight change of fitness. In some cases, however, it is necessary to change many of the genes to achieve a slight change in the fitness values. An example is the inversion operator on bit strings: here, the order of the bits between two positions is inverted.

To compare different combinations of operators and encodings, and thus to compare different landscapes for a given problem, an autocorrelation analysis can be carried out either mathematically or experimentally. The fitness landscape with the higher correlation length (higher correlation of neighbouring points in the search space) should be preferred over the other (Moscato [1989]). For example, consider two different fitness landscapes for the TSP as listed in Table 16.1. The landscape with the distance metric based on the elementary operator of exchanging two cities in the tour has a lower correlation length than the landscape based on the elementary operator of exchanging edges. It has been shown empirically that local search in the latter landscape is much better at finding near optimum solutions than a local search in the former landscape, see for example Reinelt [1994].

Another interesting example is the graph bi-partitioning problem. Enlarging the search space by allowing infeasible solutions leads to a smoother landscape if a suitable penalty function for reducing the fitness of infeasible solutions is incorporated. Angel & Zissimopoulos [1998] have derived a penalty function for which the landscape (α-FLIP) has a higher correlation length and hence becomes smoother compared to the commonly chosen SWAP landscape (see Table 16.1). Another advantage of the FLIP landscape is that the neighbourhood size $|\mathcal{N}|$ is lower and hence the time for searching the neighbourhood for fitter individuals is reduced. Again, it has been shown experimentally that a local search based on the FLIP operator is more effective than a local search based on the SWAP operator (Angel & Zissimopoulos [1998]). Thus, autocorrelation analysis appears to be a suitable approach for comparing fitness landscapes considered in steps 1 and 2 of the memetic algorithm design process.

Large Neighbourhoods

Although the smallest possible neighbourhood for a combinatorial problem is preferable, there are cases where larger neighbourhoods can be searched very efficiently. Consider the k-opt neighbourhoods $\mathcal{N}_{k\text{-}opt}$. All solutions in these sets cannot be examined during the search, but there are algorithms that are searching a small subset and are highly effective. For example, the Lin-Kernighan heuristic (Lin & Kernigham [1973]) for the TSP and the Kernighan-Lin heuristic (Kernighan & Lin [1972]) for the GBP exchange a variable number of edges and a variable size of subsets, respectively. Since in case of the TSP an exchange of k edges is realized by performing a sequence of exchanges of two edges, the same distance measure can be used as for 2-opt. Analogously, for the GBP the same distance measure is recommended as for the SWAP operator. To speed up the running times for k-opt search algorithms, special data structures are necessary for large problem sizes. For the TSP, several data structures have been investigated (Fredman et al [1995]), and for the GBP, a data structure developed by Fiduccia & Mattheyses [1982] increases the efficiency of the Kernighan-Lin heuristic tremendously.

16.3.2 Generating Starting Solutions

In evolutionary algorithms, the starting solutions are usually generated in a purely random fashion. Hence, it is straightforward to do this in memetic algorithms too. To operate on locally optimal solutions, after generation of the starting solutions a local search is applied to each solution. However, to exploit the structure of the problem, randomized heuristics can be used that (a) produce a large variety of solutions, and (b) are good for a combination with local search. The advantage is two-fold: first, the combination of a construction heuristic and local search may produce better solutions, and second, the combination may be faster than applying local search to randomly selected points in the landscape, since the number of iterations of the local search is reduced due to the much better starting point generated by the heuristic.

Greedy heuristics are often good candidates for the construction of feasible solutions. Viewing a solution of a combinatorial optimization problem as a genome of length $|x|=n$ (n denoting the problem size), a greedy heuristic determines in each step an allele value for a selected location in a genome without violating the feasibility constraints of the problem. After n steps, all genes have their values assigned and a feasible solution is constructed. Which allele and which location is chosen depends on a greedy selection criterion aimed to optimize the objective function.

Epistasis and Greedy Heuristics

The effectiveness of a greedy heuristic depends highly on the non-linearity of the problem. If epistasis is high, then the choice of a gene value at a step in the construction heuristic strongly influences the future choices of the remaining locations in the genome that have not been assigned. A wrong greedy choice at an early stage of the algorithm has fatal consequences and may lead to a low fitness. On the other hand, if epistasis is low, an unfavourable decision has a much smaller influence on the overall fitness of the solution being built, since most decisions in the future of the algorithm are not affected. In the extreme case where no interactions are present and hence the choice of a gene value in each step is independent of the choices in the other steps, the greedy algorithm is able to find the global optimum. Thus, for problems with low epistatic interactions, a greedy algorithm is preferable to a purely random generation of solutions.

The TSP is a good example where a greedy heuristic works extremely well in combination with local search. Due to the feasibility constraints of the problem, in the last steps of the algorithm arbitrarily long edges are included in the tour constructed, but a local search is able to compensate this effect. The greedy heuristic (Lawler et al [1985]) has been shown to be superior to all other heuristics when combined with local search (Johnson & McGeoch [1997], Reinelt [1994]). Furthermore, the number of iterations of the local search is reduced compared to random starting tours, since many short edges are already contained in the tour and have not to be discovered by local search.

Fitness Distance Analysis

The initial population is important for the performance of a population based algorithm, so special attention has to be paid when creating it. To investigate how the points represented by the initial population are distributed in the search space relative to the optimum solution, an analysis of the fitness distance correlation can be performed. The fitness distance plots can help in comparing heuristic construction algorithms and local search, and can provide hints of how the memetic algorithm will perform. For example, the fitness distance plots of some GBP instances show the effectiveness of a greedy heuristic called *Differential Greedy* (Battiti & Bertossi [1998]) compared to the Kernighan-Lin local search on structured graphs (instances with low epistasis), as shown in Figure 16.2.

Instead of the fitness, the cut size difference $\Delta c(x) = c(x) - c_{opt}$ is plotted in the figure (note that the GBP is a minimization problem). The plots on the left representing 2500 local optima produced by the Kernighan-Lin heuristic show a much lower correlation than the plots on the right produced by the differential greedy heuristic. In case of graph Cat.5252 there is *no* correlation of the local optima. In both cases, the objective values of the solutions produced by differential greedy are much closer to the optimum than in case of the Kernighan-Lin solutions.

But there are also graphs for which the greedy heuristic does not perform better than the local search, as shown in Figure 16.3. The first graph (G1000.0025) is an unstructured random graph. Here, Kernighan-Lin solutions and differential greedy solutions are distributed similarly in the search space. The second graph is a random geometric graph (U1000.40) with high epistasis. Here, only few Kernighan-Lin local minima exist and the chance to hit the global optimum is high, thus the Kernighan-Lin heuristic appears to be superior to the greedy approach.

Since the greedy strategy is good for problems with low epistasis and the Kernighan-Lin approach is better for structured problems with high epistasis, the combination of both is a good way to produce the initial population for the GBP.

As shown above, fitness distance analysis can help in finding the best initialization methods for a given problem. However, to compare algorithms, the analysis must be performed for each problem instance, and the optimum solution or a near optimum solution must be known.

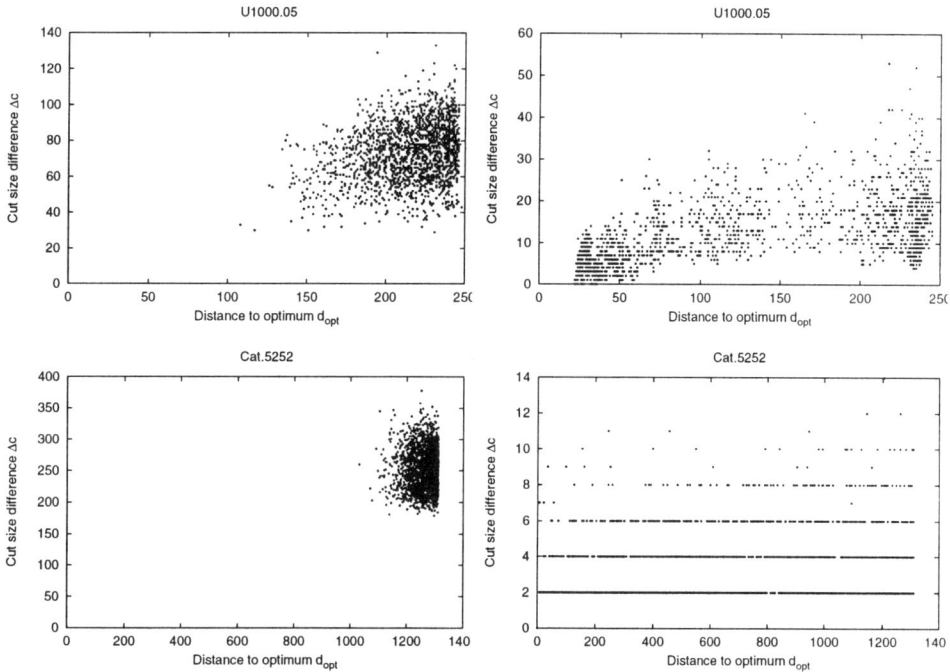

Fig. 16.2: Cut size difference vs. distance to optimum for Kernighan-Lin local optima (left) and Diff-Greedy solutions (right), on structured graphs with low epistasis.

16.3.3 Genetic Operators

In a memetic algorithm framework, mutation and recombination operators act as diversification strategies. By utilizing the information contained in the population – the individuals in the population may be located in a region of the search space containing local optima with high fitness – new starting points for a local search have to be discovered leading to even better local optima. Recombination and mutation operators hence perform jumps in the search space, leading from a local optimum away to a new point from which the next hill is climbed or (for minimization) the next valley is explored, as illustrated in Figure 16.4 for the TSP.

This implies that the distribution of the local optima has to be somehow structured. The design of mutation and recombination operators is discussed in the following.

Mutation

Mutation is an unary operator and has to be performed so that the subsequently applied local search does not revisit the parent solution by falling back into the same local optimum. The optimal jump distance depends at least on one property of the search space: the size of the attractor region of the current local optimum. For some landscapes it has been shown that the correlation length ℓ of a landscape is related to the average distance between local optima: in these landscapes there is one local optimum in a ball of radius

$R(\ell)$, where $R(s)$ denotes the expected distance of the start and end point of a simple random walk of s steps. Since the direction of the jump is random, no other properties can be exploited with the unary operator.

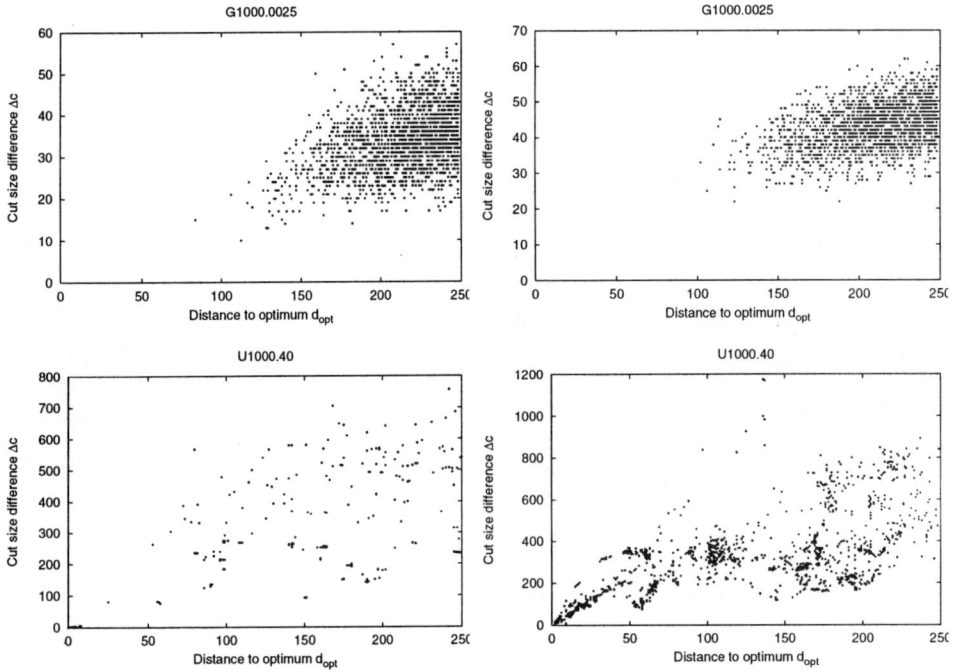

Fig. 16.3: Cut size difference vs. distance to optimum for Kernighan-Lin local optima (left) and Diff-Greedy solutions (right), on an unstructured random graph with high epistasis (G1000.0025) and a random geometric graph with high epistasis (U1000.40).

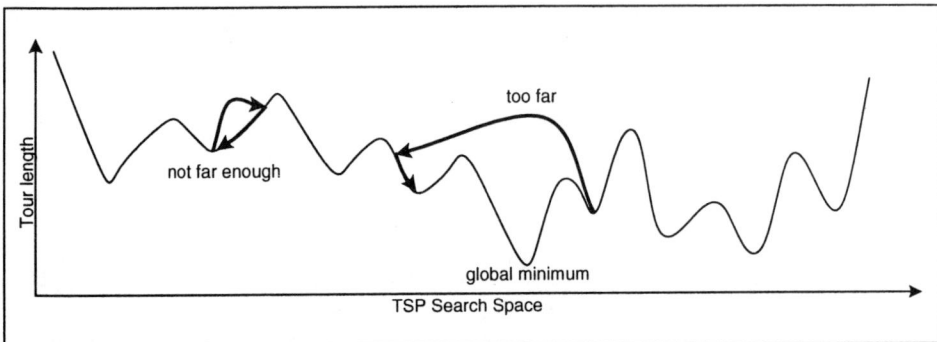

Fig. 16.4: Diversification by jumping in the search space.

Recombination

Recombination is a binary operator, and hence a jump can be performed with a predefined direction. In genetic algorithms, recombination is performed in analogy to biology by crossing over two parent bit vectors at a randomly selected position. Another widely used recombination mechanism is known under the name uniform crossover. Uniform crossover is a more general form of recombination, and single-point or k-point crossover are special cases (Syswerda [1989]). These crossover techniques applied to binary vectors have the following properties:

(i)   The bit values for the locations that are identical in both parents are preserved in the offspring.

(ii)   The hamming distance d_H between the parents x and y and the offspring z are lower or equal to the distance between the parents. Furthermore, we must also have $d_H(x, z) + d_H(z, y) = d_H(x, y)$.

For permutation search spaces, the first property can easily be fulfilled while the second can not. However, if (i) is obeyed, the following holds for all parents x and y and offspring z: $d(z, x) \leq d(x, y)$ and $d(z, y) \leq d(x, y)$, and furthermore $d(x, z) + d(z, y) \leq 2 \cdot d(x, y)$. Following the terminology of Radcliffe & Surry [1994, 1994a], a recombination operator obeying (i) is called *respectful*, while an operator obeying (ii) is called *assorting*. Recombination operators which fulfill (i) or even (ii) produce offspring that are contained in a region of the search space spanned by the two parents. The size of the region decreases during evolution since the individuals of the population move closer together from generation to generation. Hence, the direction of the jumps produced by respectful recombination operators is oriented towards a region between the parents, and the jump distance changes dynamically during the search.

Fitness Distance Analysis

To address the question of how a distance fitness analysis can help in designing genetic operators, it is instructive to look at some very different fitness landscapes. In Figure 16.5 plots are provided for landscapes of several combinatorial problems.

The first two plots (Cat.5252 and Breg5000.16) are taken from the analysis of instances of the GBP, and the second two are results of a fitness distance analysis for a TSP (att532) and a quadratic assignment problem (QAP) instance (tai80a), respectively. In all plots, 2500 local optima are displayed relative to the optimum or best-known solutions for the problem. While the first plot (Cat.5252) does not show correlation between fitness and distance, the second one (Breg5000.16) shows perfect correlation ($\chi=0.02$ and $\chi=0.99$, respectively). In the first case, the local optima have an average distance of nearly the maximum distance of the search space between each other. Hence, the local optima are uniformly distributed in the search space. Regarding the distribution of local optima, the search space does not exhibit a structure that could be exploited. The second landscape of the GBP is ideal for memetic algorithms. There is a 'path' to the global optimum from all local optima via fitter local optima. With increasing fitness (decreasing cut size), the local optima are closer to the global optimum. The fitness distance plot for the TSP landscape (att532) shows a correlation between fitness and distance to the optimum. Furthermore, the local optima are found in a small fraction of the search space, and they appear to be relatively close together. In this case, the maximum distance between two local optima is smaller than 1/3 of the maximum distance of the landscape. This landscape and the second landscape of the GBP (Breg5000.16) exhibit a structure that is called the *big valley* structure (Boese [1995]): the global optimum lies more or less central in the subspace containing the local optima. The last plot shows the relation between fitness and distance to the optimum of a typical QAP instance (tai80a). Here, points with optimum or near optimum fitness are arbitrarily far away from each other and most of the solutions have maximum distance to the optimum.

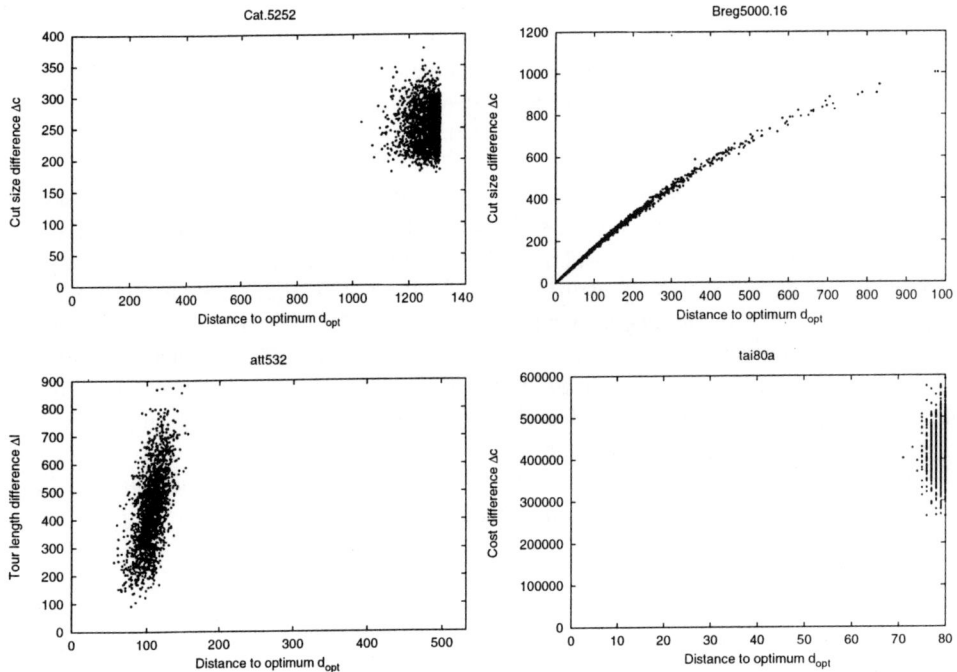

Fig. 16.5: Correlation of local optima for various combinatorial optimization problems.

Choice of Operators

If the landscape is structured, recombination operators are preferable to mutation operators since they are able to exploit the structure. Big valley characteristics are best exploited by directed jumps performed by respectful recombination operators, while these operators are not effective if the structure is missing. We have shown that for *NK*-landscapes with high epistasis mutation becomes favourable over crossover (Merz & Freisleben [1998a]). As shown in Merz & Freisleben [1999], for unstructured GBP instances (high epistasis) this also holds. We have made additional experiments for the TSP and for the QAP to show the relation between landscape structure and operator effectiveness. Table 16.2 shows the results for the TSP and Table 16.3 for the QAP. For the TSP, the average number of generations (gen) and the average time in seconds (t/s) to reach the optimum in 30 of 30 runs is provided. For the QAP, the average number of generations (gen), the best cost found averaged over 30 runs, and the time in seconds after the algorithm was terminated is given.

Table 16.2: Crossover vs. mutation based MA on 4 TSP instances.

Instance	tour length	DPX		Mutation	
		gen	t/s	gen	t/s
lin318	42029 (opt)	68	25	31	38
pcb442	50778 (opt)	99	35	92	63
att532	27686 (opt)	452	131	280	230
rat783	8806 (opt)	156	61	217	88

As expected, for the TSP, recombination is preferable to mutation, while for the QAP mutation outperforms recombination-based search.

Table 16.3: Crossover vs. mutation based MA on 5 QAP instances.

Instance	DPX		Mutation		
	gen	avg. cost (quality)	Gen	avg. cost (quality)	t/s
sko100a	16667	152804.6 (0.53%)	993	152210.4 (0.14%)	1800
tai100a	765	21667111.8 (2.56%)	1551	21366635.6 (1.14%)	1800
tai150b	244	504998950.4 (1.22%)	629	500976809.6 (0.42%)	3600
tho150	8936	8161583.4 (0.34%)	718	8150674.6 (0.21%)	3600
tai256c	875	44858227.6 (0.22%)	3431	44785102.8 (0.06%)	3600

In both cases, the recombination operator is distance preserving crossover DPX (Freisleben & Merz [1996], Merz & Freisleben [1997]). The operator is respectful but also highly disruptive: the distance of the jumps performed in the search space equals the distance between the two parents. The local search algorithm used for the TSP is the Lin-Kernighan heuristic (Lin & Kernighan [1973]) and a simple 2-opt local search was used for the QAP. Mutation in the TSP case is done with a non-sequential four-change operator (Lin & Kernighan [1973]), and random mutation of jump distance $d=30$ in the case of the QAP.

16.4 MEMETIC ALGORITHM PERFORMANCE

Memetic algorithms, in particular evolutionary algorithms incorporating local search, have been shown to outperform many other heuristic search algorithms for various problems: for the TSP, our memetic algorithm, also called genetic local search, has been shown to be one of the most effective algorithms (Bersini et al [1996], Freisleben & Merz [1996a], Merz & Freisleben [1997a]) – a predecessor of our improved approach has won the first international contest on evolutionary optimization (1st ICEO; Bersini et al [1996]). The results presented in Table 16.2 are even better than previously published (Merz & Freisleben [1997a]). In case of the QAP, our approach works extremely well and appears to be superior to tabu search, ant colonies, simulated annealing and also scatter search (Merz & Freisleben [1997, 1999a], Cung et al [1997]). For *NK*-landscapes we have shown that genetic local search is superior to genetic algorithms and multi-start local search (Merz & Freisleben [1998a]). Recently, we have shown for the GBP that our memetic algorithm is superior to other hybrid evolutionary approaches, simulated annealing, and in almost all cases superior to tabu search (Merz & Freisleben [1999]).

16.5 CONCLUSIONS

In this chapter, we have presented techniques to analyze combinatorial optimization problems to design highly effective search algorithms with special emphasis on memetic algorithms. The presented autocorrelation functions of fitness landscapes are well suited to determine the local structure of a landscape and thus help in finding preferable representations and local search neighbourhoods for a memetic algorithm. In particular, the correlation length of a landscape has been shown to be a good indicator for the effectiveness of representations in combination with local search. The correlation length of a landscape is based on the correlation of neighbouring points in the search space and can be determined either mathematically or experimentally. The higher the correlation length, the better the performance of a local search.

On the other hand, fitness distance analysis (FDA) is suited for analyzing global landscape structure. The distribution of local optima is important in memetic algorithm design because if a certain structure is present, it should be exploited by the genetic operators used. The conducted experiments have shown that if fitness and distance to the optimum are correlated, recombination operators are preferable to mutation operators. If no structure in the distribution can be observed, a mutation-based approach appears to be superior to recombination. Furthermore, FDA can be utilized to find suitable heuristics for initialization of the population. FDA allows a comparison of heuristics in terms of ability to adequately sample the search space and to predetermine promising features of solutions to a problem. However, our studies of landscapes of the graph bi-partitioning problem have shown that it is dangerous to perform FDA for only one type of instance of a given optimization problem. The results may not be generalized to other types of instances: some instances of the graph bi-partitioning problem show a high correlation between fitness and distance to the optimum, while for others no correlation could be observed.

Epistasis has been considered as an indicator of the hardness of an optimization problem. Our studies on the graph bi-partitioning problem have shown that the concept of modelling gene interactions by a *graph of epistatic interactions* can help in understanding the influence of epistasis on heuristic search.

Future work should address the question of how to design recombination operators that can best exploit certain properties of landscapes. Furthermore, it is desirable to be able to predict the optimum jump distances for mutation operators in unstructured landscapes. Here, we believe the correlation length of a landscape can be utilized beneficially.

Other statistical properties may be useful to predict the performance of memetic algorithms. For example, it should be investigated how the classification of fractal landscapes proposed by Weinberger & Stadler [1993] can help in classifying problems in terms of hardness for optimization algorithms.

Chapter Seventeen

The Number Partitioning Problem: An Open Challenge for Evolutionary Computation?

Regina Berretta and Pablo Moscato

17.1 INTRODUCTION

There have been many frustrated attempts to classify what makes a problem *hard* for Genetic Algorithms and this also extends to the whole field of Evolutionary Computation. Regarding the whole field of metaheuristics, from a scientific point of view it is frustrating to see that most results report 'successful' applications of a certain technique while many *negative* results and failures very seldom reach a published state. A notable exception to the rule was the study by Johnson, Aragon, McGeoch, and Schevon on the application of simulated annealing to the Number Partitioning problem (Johnson et al [1991]).

The Number Partitioning decision problem is *NP*-Complete and it certainly presents an open challenge for widely used metaheuristics such as genetic algorithms (GAs) (Jones & Beltramo [1991], Ruml [1993]) and simulated annealing (Johnson et al [1991], Sorkin [1992], Ruml et al [1996]), *problem space local search* (Storer et al [1996]), GRASP (Arguello et al [1996]) and tabu search (Glover & Laguna [1997]).

The purpose of this chapter is to help understand the reasons for this apparent failure, identify its causes and its extent, and provide new insights on the main mechanisms responsible for successful implementations, and failures, of memetic algorithms and general evolutionary computation based approaches for optimization. In particular, we will address the problem of the limitations of such an approach when a bad representation for the problem's solutions has been inadequately chosen.

17.1.1 The Problem

The Number Partitioning (D) problem is widely cited as being a conspicuous member of the *NP*-complete class. Following Garey and Johnson's style for its presentation, we can enunciate it as the following Input–Question pair:

Input: A set A of n positive integer numbers $\{a_1,...,a_n\}$.
Question: Can A be partitioned into two disjoint sets A_1, A_2 with $A = A_1 \cup A_2$ such that:

$$\sum_{a_i \in A_1} a_i = \sum_{a_j \in A_2} a_j \ ? \tag{17.1}$$

As stated, Number Partitioning (D) is a *decision* problem, this means that for every *instance* (each possible input set A of n numbers constitutes an instance $x \in I_P$ in our notation) the (unique) answer is either 'Yes' or 'No'. Associated to this problem there is a combinatorial *optimization* search problem or *optimization version* (denoted Min Number

Partitioning (O)). This related problem can be seen as the task of finding a set $y = \{v_1,...,v_n\}$, where v_i can be either 1 or -1, such that y minimizes the following function:

$$m_P(y,x) = \left| \sum_{i=1}^{n} a_i v_i \right| \tag{17.2}$$

Min Number Partitioning (O), is easy to state but hard to solve. It has been shown to be particularly difficult for metaheuristics like simulated annealing (Johnson et al [1991], Sorkin [1992]) and genetic algorithms (Jones & Beltramo [1991], Ruml [1993]).

17.1.2 Pseudopolynomial Algorithms and Weak *NP*-completeness

It is important to remark upon a difference between Min Number Partitioning (O) and other *NP* optimization problems. It can be solved with a *pseudopolynomial algorithm*. This means that if A is a set of n integers whose sum is B then there exists an algorithm which can find the minimum cost partition in time polynomial in nB. We say 'pseudopolynomial time' because nB is not bounded by any polynomial in $n \log B$ which is a measure of the space required to store the instance set A. The pseudopolynomial algorithm is based on dynamic programming and requires time and space at least linear in B, unfortunately it is of limited (or no) practical value when B is large.

Some other *NP*-complete decision problems (such as SAT, Hamiltonian Path, Bin Packing, and so on, as well as other studied in this book) remain *NP*-complete even if any instance of length n is restricted to contain integers of size at most $p(n)$. These problems are called *strongly NP*-complete. Under the conjecture that $P \neq NP$, strongly *NP*-complete problems have no pseudopolynomial algorithms that solve them (Garey & Johnson [1979]).

17.2 MOTIVATION

Following the previous discussion, our case study will be a member of the *NP*-complete class for which there exists a pseudo-polynomial algorithm, yet it has been shown to be very hard for local-searh-based metaheuristics (like SA) and population-based schemes (like GAs). It has also been a hard challenge for a metaheuristic known as GRASP (Arguello et al [1996]). We think that a better understanding of the deficiencies of these methods would lead to better, and probably more robust, algorithms. It would also point to inherent difficulties proper to *weakly NP*-complete problems. The latter, in turn, might help us achieve a better formal characterization of 'hardness'.

In (Johnson et al [1991]), Johnson, Aragon, McGeoch and Schevon studied Min Number Partitioning (O) as well as two other *NP*-hard problems: Min Graph Colouring and Min Graph Partitioning. In sharp contrast, the authors conclude

> The results for number partitioning were, as expected, decidedly negative, with annealing substantially outperformed by the much faster Karmarkar-Karp algorithm, and even beaten (on a time-equalized basis) by multiple-start local optimisation (MSLO).

Johnson et al [1991]

The Karmarkar-Karp algorithm is a fast constructive algorithm which, for the family of instances they studied, seemed to outperform SA. They conclude that:

> Thus, for NUMBER PARTITIONING, at least **for the types of random instances** we have been considering, illustrates the limitations of simulated annealing as a general technique. **When the solution space is sufficiently mountainous,** annealing's advantage over straightforward multiple start local optimization can be lost entirely. Moreover, **other approaches, not tied to the concept of navigating around a solution space**, may be able to outperform it substantially.
>
> Johnson et al [1991]

Emphasis has been added to stress our interest in investigating these conclusions. From a practical viewpoint, it is also interesting to see if what we may learn when addressing this problem can also be extended to other NP optimization problems. It is known that Min Number Partitioning (O) can be related to other decision problems like Bin Packing, Production Planning, Knapsack, Open-Shop Scheduling, Scheduling to Minimize Weighted Completion Time, and other problems listed in Appendix A of Garey & Johnson [1979].

Jones & Beltramo [1991] have used a GA for a generalization of Number Partitioning (O) which they called the 'equal piles problem' in which the objective is to divide a set of numbers into k partitions of exactly the same sum. Obviously Min Number Partitioning (O) is a special case of this problem when $k=2$.

17.3 THE KARMARKAR-KARP HEURISTIC

The Karmarkar-Karp (KK) heuristic (Karmarkar & Karp [1982]) works by repeatedly replacing the two largest numbers by their difference, until only one number remains. Each such replacement is accompanied by some book-keeping, via which a partition gradually grows. We illustrate it here with an example in Table 17.1. We start by replacing 15 and 12 with 3, which we accompany by forming a partition with 15 in one set and 12 in another. Next, we replace the 10 and 9 with 1, and also yield another partition (see row 3). The two largest numbers are now 3 and 4. Note that 3 represents a partition {{15}, {12}}, while 4 is from the original set; what happens here is that we place the 4 in the set with the smallest sum, hence yielding the partition {{15}, {12, 4}}. Finally, we replace the 1 and 1 with 0, and update the partition as follows. The 1's represent the partitions in row 4; we simply unite the set with the highest sum from one partition with that with the lowest from the other, and vice versa, yielding the partition given in row 5 of the table.

Table 17.1: An example using the Karmarkar-Karp heuristic.

Numbers	Partitions	Differences
15,12,10,9,4	-	-
3,10,9,4	{15} {12}	3
3,1,4	{15} {12} and {10}{9}	3,1
1,1	{15}{12,4}and{10}{9}	1,1
0	{15,10} {12,4,9}	0

An important optimal algorithm for this problems is called Complete Karmarkar Karp (CKK) (Korf [1995, 1998]). It is an exact algorithm which takes advantage of the KK and returns the optimal solution value.

17.4 PREVIOUS RESULTS

17.4.1 Asymptotic Expected Cost Formulae

For some types of instances, asymptotic expected cost formulae can be derived. Regarding the results of Karmarkar et al [1986], the authors of Johnson et al [1991] decided to set up several experiments using instances that we will call UI_n. Each one is a set of n real numbers generated at random with uniform probability in the interval $[0,1]$. This experimental arena was chosen since it was known a previous theoretical result that shows that if we call as $OPT(UI_n)$ the cost of the global minimum of an instance UI_n, then its average value over instances of this class is $\langle OPT(UI_n) \rangle = \mathcal{O}(2^{-n}\sqrt{n})$ (Karmarkar et al [1986]). The problem of evaluating the exact formula recently captured the attention of physicists who work on the statistical mechanics of disordered systems.

Ferreira & Fontanari [1998] used the *annealed approximation* to derive a rigorous lower bound:

$$\langle OPT(UI_n) \rangle \geq 2^{-n}\sqrt{\frac{\pi n}{6e^2}} \approx 0.266 \; 2^{-n}\sqrt{n} \tag{17.3}$$

Very recently, Mertens [1998] gave an exact expression for this quantity:

$$\langle OPT(UI_n) \rangle = \sqrt{\frac{2\pi}{3}} \; 2^{-n}\sqrt{n} \tag{17.4}$$

See also Lueker [1998] for results on this and the related subset-sum problem.

17.4.2 The Gap Between Local and Global Optimality

For the same type of instances, the expected value of the KK algorithm is $\mathcal{O}(1/n^{\alpha \log n})$ for some α. Fischetti & Martello [1987] did a worst-case analysis. It must be mentioned that Johnson et al [1991] remark that this result was actually proved for a variant of the KK algorithm described above. This variant simplified the analytical treatment and they noted that there are no reasons to believe that is somewhat better than the original algorithm. This subject has been recently addressed by Yakir [1996] (for previous research in these issues see Lueker [1987] and Coffman et al [1993]). It is easy to observe that there exists a great gap between optimal solutions and those provided by KK. The simulated annealing implementation by Johnson et al [1991] was not able to overcome this gap.

Johnson et al [1991] define a series of neighbourhood graphs to define the transition between configurations (in this case they are partitions). For instance, when we move an integer a_j from A_1 to A_2 that corresponds to a change of sign of the associated variable v_j (when we use the direct representation). The neighbourhood graph associated is named

SW_1. In general, they define the neighbourhood graph SW_k the one that is generated by connecting configurations that result from interchanging k or fewer elements.

17.4.3 The Failure of Simulated Annealing

We can then identify one of the factors that make the direct implementation of SA using the SW_1 neighbourhood graph a very unsuccessful one. Following the discussion of the previous chapter, we note that the failure is on a *fitness landscape* which combines the neighbourhood graph and the guiding function. In the general case, the expected value of the lowest cost difference between two neighbour configurations in SW_k is $1/n^k$. This is again in sharp contrast with the fact that the expected value of the optimal value for UI_n, $\langle OPT(UI_n) \rangle$, is approximately $1.447 \cdot 2^{-n} \sqrt{n}$. This said, it is clear that we expect that the best local minima are located in *'very deep valleys'* in configuration space, since they are surrounded by solutions of higher cost. This situation gets worse and worse as the size of the problem n increases.

For SA this is definitely not a good landscape; in order to move in SW_k we need 'temperatures' which are orders of magnitude higher (needed to 'jump' cost function steps of order $1/n^k$) than those necessary to 'efficiently sample' (using the underlying Metropolis algorithm) those configuration space regions which have good quality local minima (which are of the order $\mathcal{O}(\sqrt{n}/2^n)$). If the expected value of the residue of KK's algorithm is $\mathcal{O}(1/n^{\alpha \log n})$, asymptotically smaller than the value of the least cost in SW_k, then KK (although a constructive algorithm) is a remarkably competitive strategy when confronted with SA implementations based on the SW_k neighbourhood graphs.

The computational results in Johnson et al [1991] confirm these hypotheses. For an instance with 100 elements (see Figure 9 in Johnson et al [1991]) although the best solution found by SA was better than KK, the value to which the SA process converged (using SW_2) was radically worse than the KK (they had final residues of order 10^{-4} and 10^{-6} respectively). It must be emphasised that the final value of SA was only slightly worse than the average in the last 25% of the CPU time utilized by SA. One way of interpreting this fact is that SA was trapped in a not-so-promising region of configuration space after the temperature went lower than the expected value of the lowest cost interchange.

In experiments with 200 and 500 elements, they found that in contrast with Min Graph Partitioning and Min Graph Colouring, the final solution given by SA does not improve when we let the algorithm run for a long time. On the contrary, it remains in the neighbourhood of the expected value of the lowest interchange cost, that is well above the cost given by KK. The best solution tend to the cost of KK when it used 10,000 more CPU time that that used by KK (1.1 seconds!!). That computer time would be enough for attempting 100,000 local search steps (MSLO)! For 200 elements instances SW_1-based SA and MSLO gave approximately the same results while SW_2 MSLO is clearly superior to SA and is competitive with KK. For 500 elements instances KK is a clear winner since MSLO using SW_2 is not competitive due to the fact that its complexity is quadratic in time. In addition, an SW_1-based MSLO is clearly superior to SA.

The Average Number of Local Minima

Ferreira & Fontanari [1998] calculated the number of local minima for the SW_1 neighbourhood. Their result was that from a total of 2^n configurations a huge number:

$$\sqrt{\frac{24}{\pi}} \cdot \frac{2^n}{n^{3/2}} \approx 2.764 \frac{2^n}{n^{3/2}} \qquad (17.5)$$

were local minima. Note that the ratio of local minima to total number of configurations (informally, the 'density of local minima') decreases as $\mathcal{O}(n^{-1.5})$. This fact is in great contrast with similar measures for many other combinatorial optimization problems, for which decay is exponential.

Motivated by the unfavourable results of Johnson et al [1991] for SA and those of Jones & Beltramo [1991], using GAs, Ruml [1993] conducted a series of experiments with the objective of finding a better representation for this problem which would make SA competitive with KK. The representation used in Johnson et al [1991] was called '*direct*' and we will use that denomination too. The results with many different GA implementations were disappointing and showed the problems that both SA and GA had even using different representations.

Ruml's thesis, however, leaves open the possibility that a more appropriate representation would be better suited for SA and GAs. Ruml et al [1996] present an interesting way of blending KK with a representation which creates a *prepartitioning* of the items. They design it as a '*complete representation*'. They see this way of coding configurations as a more general design principle, and they denominate it as '*parameterised constraints*'.

The authors remark that the selection of the annealing schedule may even improve these values, however they conjecture that a behaviour they call 'gravitation' is the main reason behind a possible failure (Ruml et al [1996]).

17.5 THE EVOLUTIONARY ALGORITHMS PROPOSED

In this section, we will explain the algorithms we have implemented. The entire notation will be consistent with the one we have used in chapter fourteen. We remark that our implementation of a GA is different from the ones used by Ruml [1993]. One reason for this change is that he had already well established the poor performance of those 'traditional', nature-inspired GA implementations using the direct representation. In our case, our GA will be just the same basic MA strategy without any use of local search as there is no improvement period after recombination or mutations. These GAs have been introduced for methodological completeness and for comparison purposes.

17.5.1 Representation and Search Space

One of the aims of this investigation was to evaluate if the *direct representation* (Ruml et al [1996]) is definitely not appropriate for stochastic search algorithms as is implied by the results of Ruml et al [1996]. The direct representation ρ_D is *complete* since it can generate all possible partitions (the associated search space has 2^n configurations). We note, however, that any given partition (any solution $y \in sol_P(x)$) is represented by two configurations $s, s' \in S$. For instance, $s = \{1, -1, -1, -1, -1\}$ and $s' = \{-1, 1, 1, 1, 1\}$ both represent the same partition (the same feasible solution $y \in sol_P(x)$) of five integers.

Another representation we have used can be called *ternary direct* ρ_{TD} since it allows alleles to take one out of three different values, '0', '1', or '−1'. Obviously, the associated search space is also complete since it contains the search space of the ρ_D.

For both representations, we have used the same guiding function, which is actually the objective function $m_P(y, x)$. However, when we are using ρ_{TD} any allele values having '0' value must be 'decided', i.e. given either a '−1' or a '1' in order to compute $m_P(y, x)$. We have chosen to do that using a *greedy* procedure. At each step it takes the largest integer with a '0' and gives it a value (either a '1' or '−1') which minimizes the actual imbalance of all integers already decided.

The intuition here is that ρ_{TD} corresponds to another 'partition state' that can be assigned to an integer. Researchers in the GA field might like to think of the search space associated with ρ_{TD} as a space of *genotypes*. Then, the greedy decoding procedure is viewed as the development of a *phenotype*.

Greedy procedures like this one have been called *growth functions* in the GA literature (Radcliffe [1994]). We note in passing that a growth function that uses the KK algorithm can be a natural choice. However, we decided not to include computational results using it since it might be an unfair comparison.

17.5.2 Population Size and Structure

The population (used in both the GA and MA implementations) has a fixed size of 13 individuals. The neighbourhood relationship among individuals is based on a complete ternary tree of three levels (see Figure 17.1) and is also fixed.

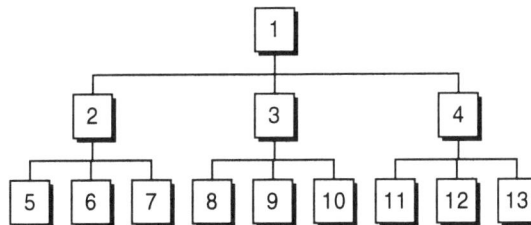

Fig. 17.1: Population Structure (ternary tree) used in all GAs and MAs in this study.

The population structure can be interpreted as a variant of *island models* of GAs in which each subpopulation has four individuals while individuals at an intermediate level (those which are neither the root nor the leaves of the tree) are *shared* by two subpopulations. Each subpopulation is composed of one '*leader*' node and three '*supporters*' which are one level below in the hierarchy. Individual 1, the root of the tree, is the leader of the top subpopulation and has as supporters Individuals 2, 3, and 4. Individual 2 has as supporters Individuals 5, 6, and 7, etc. Note that Individuals 2, 3, and 4 play both leader and supporter roles.

Each individual of the population is handling two chromosomes (two configurations in the associated search space). One is named '*Pocket*' and the other one '*Current*'. Whenever within an individual the Current has less cost than Pocket, they are switched, so the latter plays a role of a 'memory' of good solutions. Analogously, another procedure named

PocketPropagation changes two Pocket solutions if the leader has a Pocket solution which is worse than one of its followers. These two mechanisms are all that is needed to guarantee the flow of the best solutions towards the individual at the top of the hierarchy.

In our MA implementation, individuals optimize their Current chromosomes with periods of local search which alternate with recombination. As we mentioned before, we will call a 'GA' an implementation that differs from the MA just in the absence of the use of local search while all other rules of the algorithm remain the same. We call as one *generation* the process in which individuals have evolved their Current chromosomes to be local minima and afterwards they engage in recombination (in total agreement with the pseudo-code of chapter fourteen).

17.5.3 The initializePopulation Command

For ρ_D, the **initializePopulation** command creates 13 individuals, each with a Pocket and Current chromosome. Each chromosome represents a feasible partition $y \in sol_P(x)$. The search space $S(\rho_D)$ is the set of 2^n chromosomes, and allele values are chosen to be either '1' or '−1', with equal probability. For ρ_{TD} the initialization procedure is the same, but the search space (denoted $S(\rho_{TD})$) has 3^n configurations and the allele value '0' is selected at random with a probability of 0.5 while the two other values ('1' and '−1') have equal probability of 0.25.

17.5.4 The Recombine( ) Procedures

At each generation step, the Current chromosome of each individual is replaced with a new one generated by the Recombine( ) procedure acting on the Pocket chromosome of the individual and its leader. For example, the Current of the Individual 2, in Figure 17.1, will be replaced by the output of the Recombine( ) procedure having as input the Pocket of the Individual 1 and the Pocket of the Individual 2; the Current of the individual 9, will be replaced by the Recombine( ) using the Pocket of the Individual 3 and the Pocket of the Individual 9; etc. Then in a single iteration of the generation loop, all individuals except Individual 1, will replace its Current chromosome. Regarding the pseudo-code of the first chapter, the number *#recombinations* performed at each generation step is 12. Moreover, the **selectToMerge** command can be regarded as *totally constrained*, since each agent always engages in recombination with the same agents.

The ternary-tree neighbourhood topology for individuals always obliges supporters to recombine with their leaders. The population structure and this rule suggest that the island models of GAs (taken as a metaphor for evolution with colonization and diffusion) are not the most representative. Instead, the approach better resembles a hierarchical organisation in which "ideas" are discussed only with the immediate leader member of the group.

Behaviours

Before a leader recombines its solution with any of its three supporters, a different type of *behaviour* is assigned to each one. A behaviour can be understood as one extra control parameter in the control set of a given recombination operator (Radcliffe & Surry [1994a]). Each supporter will have different behaviour, which will be decided randomly with equal probability. The three types of behaviours used are described below, and are summarized in Table 17.2. To simplify the presentation, let us suppose that the direct representation is being used and parent P_1 is the leader and the parent P_2 is one of the supporters.

Table 17.2: Different behaviours in leader/supporter recombination.

Behaviour	First copied in the offspring
rebel	alleles of P_2 which are different from P_1
conciliator	alleles in common to P_1 and P_2
obsequent	alleles of P_1 which are different from P_2

For example, consider $P_1=\{-1,-1,1,-1,1\}$ and $P_2=\{1,-1,1,1,-1\}$, the recombinations using the same parents as input and each type of behaviour are as follows. Here the 'x' stands for a value that will be decided by algorithms which we will explain at a later stage.

rebel	$\{ 1 \quad x \quad x \quad 1 \quad -1 \}$
conciliator	$\{ x \quad -1 \quad 1 \quad x \quad x \}$
obsequent	$\{-1 \quad x \quad x \quad -1 \quad 1 \}$

The three names have been chosen with reference to the semantics of their preservation of information (allele values). The *conciliator* behaviour is an example of a recombination procedure that *respects* the representation (Radcliffe & Surry [1994], Radcliffe [1994]) since '*every child it produces contains all the alleles common to its two parents*' (i.e. those in $A \cap B$). It shares the property of being a *respectful* recombination as it is also the case of *uniform crossover*. In this case, since all alleles not in $A \cap B$ have either the value '-1' or '1', the recombination with conciliator behaviour is said also to *transmit alleles* (Radcliffe, 1994) since '*each allele in the offspring is present in at least one of its parents*'.

Both the *rebel* and the *obsequent* behaviours do not respect (in the sense postulated by Radcliffe) binary representations since they may not include allele values in $A \cap B$. Also since it is allowed to create allele values not present in both parents the *rebel* and *obsequent* behaviours gave types of recombinations which do not transmit alleles.

In order to decide the positions in the *offspring* where no allele was chosen (the 'x' marks) we have investigated several different variants. For the ρ_D representation, three types of algorithms have been used: *generalised transmission (GT)*, *GT with greedy repairing (GTgr)*, and *GT random seeded - greedy repairing (GTrsgr)*.

GT decides at random between either '-1' or '1' with equal probability. *GTgr* uses a greedy algorithm, i.e. a deterministic rule which sequentially decides between '-1' or '1' in order to minimize the actual imbalance. The order is based in a non-decreasing order of the sequence of not yet decided integers. *GTrsgr* starts by randomly selecting an integer such that its allele value has to be decided first and again this is done in such a way that it minimizes the imbalance. Then it continues in a deterministic way as *GTgr* does. According to the definitions, all of them are crossover operators, while *GT* is the only one which is blind since it does not use information from the instance of the problem.

For example, consider again the instance $A = \{15,12,10,9,4\}$ and the two parents P_1 and P_2 with conciliator behaviour. The *offspring* first receives the common allele values, i.e. $O=\{x, -1, 1, x, x\}$. With *GT*, each 'x' will be decided at random with the same probability (in this case we have the traditional *uniform crossover*). With *GTgr*, we chose $O[1] = 1$, $O[4] = -1$ and $O[5] = -1$, in this order. Note that in this case we decided for '1' or '−1' accordingly to the actual absolute difference of the partial partition.

For ρ_{TD} we have investigated two blind crossover operators. One is analogous to the *GT* but, since we are dealing with ρ_{TD} we can name it *GT*(0.5). It transmits allele values regarding behaviours in exactly the same way that *GT* does, however the remaining values are decided with random uniform probability where an *a priori* probability of 0.5 is assigned to value '0' and '0.25' is assigned to both '−1' and '1' values. The other crossover operator assigns a value of '0' to any non-transmitted allele, so we have chosen to call it *GT*(1.0) since it is as if we were selecting a '0' with a probability of one.

For example, consider $P_1 = \{1,-1,0,0,1\}$ and $P_2 = \{1,0,0,0,-1\}$. The offspring with obsequent behaviour will be $O = \{x,-1,x,x,1\}$. With *GT*(0.5) the $O[1]$, $O[3]$ and $O[4]$ will be randomly decided, but with probability 0.5 for '0' and 0.25 both for '1' and '−1'. Using *GT*(1.0) the offspring will be $O = \{0,-1,0,0,1\}$, i.e. '0' for all '*x*'.

17.5.5 The Mutate( ) Procedures

For both representations, we have implemented two types of mutations, *Simple* and *Minimal*. When using ρ_D the *Simple* mutation receives as input an individual and for all allele values it decides whether to 'flip' it (change from '−1' to '1' or from '1' to '−1') with a fixed probability of 0.1. For ρ_{TD}, whenever one allele value is decided to be changed (again with a fixed probability of 0.1), if it is either '−1' or '1' it is changed to '0', but if its value is '0' it is changed either to '−1' or '1' with equal probability.

The *Minimal* mutation was inspired by *Binomial Minimal Mutation* as discussed in Radcliffe & Surry [1994a]. However, a remarkable difference is that in our case we have taken into account the characteristics of the objective function (to which the label 'minimal' actually refers in this case). For ρ_D, we decide if an allele will have its sign changed not with the same *a priori* probability used by the *Simple* mutation (i.e. 0.1). Let us suppose allele i has sign $v_i = 1$ and has been selected to be mutated. Let us suppose we have represented the chromosomes with the traditional linear array of allele values, such that the indexing corresponds with a non-increasing order of the integers of the instance A. This means that the allele value of v_1 corresponds to the partition assigned to the largest integer in A (integer a_1). We then proceed to identify the index of the first allele in the '*left direction*' (referring to the linear array) j_l and the first allele in the '*right direction*' j_r which have different signs (i.e. $v_{j_r} = v_{j_l} = -1$). Then v_{j_l} is the allele of the smallest integer which is higher or equal than integer a_i and assigned to a different partition. Analogously, v_{j_r} is the allele of the largest integer which is smaller or equal to integer a_i but in a different partition. Then we select which one of j_r and j_l minimises $|a_i - a_j|$. We then swap its allele with the value of v_i. For ρ_{TD}, the procedure is the same, but if allele i has sign $v_i = 1$ we identify allele j such that either $v_j = -1$ or $v_j = 0$ and that it minimizes $|a_i - a_j|$; we then swap their allele values.

17.5.6 The Local-Search-Engine( ) procedures

We have implemented two different types of local search algorithms. One was called *GreedyImprovement* and the other one was called *TabuImprovement*. For both of them, the input is one chromosome, and the output is a chromosome with the same or better objective function value $m_P(y, x)$.

Using *GreedyImprovement* with the ρ_D representation we start by selecting one allele i at random. Then, as we did with the minimal mutation, we identify the position of the first allele in the *right direction* (j_r) and the position of the first allele in the *left direction* (j_l) such that $v_{j_r} = v_{j_l} \neq v_i$ (it may be possible to find only one satisfying the condition). We decide to swap the values of v_i with either v_{j_l} or v_{j_r} if the objective function value is reduced. If both can do that, we choose between v_{j_l} and v_{j_r} that one that causes the largest reduction in the objective function value. We repeat this process until ($FailuresTries - SuccessTries) > MaxNumberOfTries$, where *SuccessTries* is the number of tries that causes better $m_P(y, x)$ value and *FailuresTries* counts the opposite. We have used several values of the parameter *MaxNumberOfTries* and we will comment on that later.

With ρ_{TD} the procedure is the same, but we only select alleles to swap values '1' and '−1'. However, at each trial we need to calculate $m_P(y, x)$ with another greedy procedure, i.e. any allele value '0' is 'decided' to have either '−1' or '1' in order to compute $m_P(y, x)$.

The *TabuImprovement* uses the same idea of *GreedyImprovement*. The difference is that in this case we use a basic tabu search metaheuristic (Glover & Laguna [1997]) inside the *GreedyImprovement*. Each swap done between i and j, a tabu matrix (*TABU*) of integers stores, in the position $TABU[i][j]$, the number of trials that the swap between i and j will be tabu. In *TabuImprovement* we can allow swaps which do not reduce the value of $m_P(y, x)$, but the output of this procedure is the configuration with the best $m_P(y, x)$ found. We repeat this process until ($FailuresTries - SuccessTries) > MaxNumberOfTries$. The variable *SuccessTries*, in this case, is the number of tries that could be done, i.e. the number of times a try was not tabu. In addition, we use simple aspiration criteria (Glover & Laguna [1997]). If a swap causes an improvement in the objective function that has never been reached before, we do this swap, even if it was declared 'tabu'.

17.5.7 RestartPop( )

During the evolution of the population, individuals recombine only within their own subpopulation. More specifically, an individual only recombines with its leader individual. However, they can involve individuals of different subpopulations when a '*diversity crisis*' occurs. This happens when three supporters of the same subpopulation all have very similar configurations.

The criterion we used to define a diversity crisis is the following. We select at random 20% of the alleles of the Current chromosome of the three supporters. If the three individuals have the same values in these alleles, then a *DiversityCrisis* happened.

If *DiversityCrisis* is detected, the leader will not recombine with its three supporters, but the three supporters will recombine with supporters which belong to different subpopulations. For example, in general, individual 2 recombines with its three supporters, i.e. individuals 5, 6 and 7, but if *DiversityCrisis* is detected (i.e. 5, 6, and 7, all have similar configurations), then the recombination will be done between {5, 6, and 7} and {8, 9, and 10} or between {5, 6, and 7} and {11, 12, and 13}. Three recombinations will modify the Current chromosomes of individuals 5, 6, and 7; i.e. if the recombinations are to be done between {5, 6, and 7} and {8, 9, and 10} (the other subpopulation was chosen randomly), the recombination pairs can be: 5 with 9, 6 with 10, and 7 with 8. Pair assignments are chosen at random too.

With this *external mating* we get some extra diversity. Its potential benefits are incorporated from the bottom of the tree since further recombinations, involving the leader nodes will take place in the next generations.

17.6 COMPUTATIONAL EXPERIMENTS

We performed experiments using what can be considered *hard instances* of this problem, in order to identify reasons for the failure of direct implementations of GAs. The aim was to get some insights on the problems identified in Jones & Beltramo [1991] and Ruml [1993].

We wanted to convince ourselves that there is indeed no hope for good results while using the direct representation, even when more sophisticated selection and recombination methods are used. From this initial perspective, the final results have been a surprise.

17.6.1 Instances

Our first decision was which instances of the problem we should use. One possibility was to use the UI_n floating-point instances used by Johnson et al [1991]. Another possibility was to work with a multi-precision numerical package as was done by the authors of Ruml et al [1996], and to rely on the asymptotic expected cost formulae for comparing results.

Instead, due to the availability of Korf's code, we were able to solve instances with 10 decimal digits in a reasonable time. We are referring here to the hardest instances in the set.

We have created a set of 100 instances which was used in all the experiments that will be reported. This set is composed of 10 subsets containing 10 instances each. Each subset has the same value of n, i.e. 10 instances with $n=15$, 10 instances with $n=25$, etc., up to $n=105$. Each instance is composed of n positive integers of up to $d=10$ significant digits. This allows us to use Korf's code to find optimal solutions for all the instances, including instances near the '*phase-transition*'.

To avoid any possible correlation between the integers (due to the structure of the random number generators we are using) we decided to create each individual digit at random with uniform distribution probability between 0 and 9.

17.6.2 First Results

We first ran Korf's optimal code (CKK) using our set of instances (see Figure 17.2). In the figure, each point represents the average value over the set of ten instances that have that particular value of n and we use logarithmic scale for the vertical axis. The points have been linked with a line to help illustrate the trends for increasing values of n.

We verified the existence of the so-called *phase-transition* (Korf [1995]) around $n=35$ as was expected from theoretical analysis (Gent & Walsh [1998]). For some combinatorial optimization problems, when we use an optimal algorithm (like CKK), if we increase the size of the instance it becomes more difficult until a certain critical size is reached. After this, the problem is easier. These phenomena are called *phase-transitions*, and in this case we have an *easy-hard-easy* transition.

For this case, the *phase-transition* occurs when the probability to find a perfect partition is 1/2. Karmarkar et al [1986] showed that in a set of independent trials to find a partition in n numbers between '0' and '1', the average minimal difference is $\sqrt{n}/2^n$. Since in our case the instances have 10 decimal digits, the median value of the cost is $c10^n\sqrt{n}/2^n$, for some constant c. Korf [1998] was not aware of the result by Mertens, and he solves for c in the equation $c10^{10}\sqrt{35}/2^{35}=1$ obtaining $c=1.72$ and $c=0.873$ for $n=36$. This means that the instances with $n=35$ will be the hardest instances for CKK in our proposed test set.

With $n>35$ most of the time the instances have a perfect partition (one of optimal cost 0 or 1). For instances with $n<35$ is highly improbable to have a perfect partition. As a result, the optimal partition tends to have larger costs with decreasing n. An interesting side of these effects is reflected by counting the number of nodes used in the exact procedure (see Figure 17.2). For $n\geq45$, the problem starts to be easier for the exact method, apparently at a linear rate on a logarithmic scale.

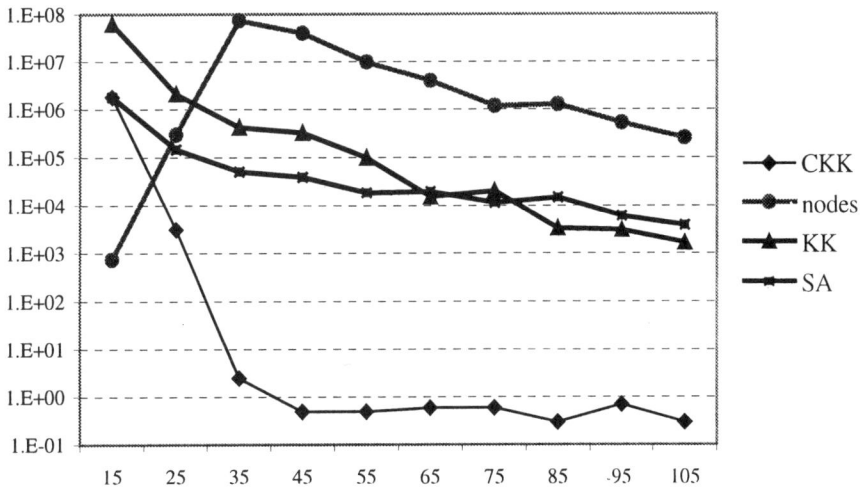

Fig. 17.2: Simulated annealing (SA), Karmarkar-Karp heuristic (KK), and Korf's exact method (CKK, nodes).

The KK algorithm seems to be improving with increasing n. This is possibly due to the fact that the number of perfect partitions increases with increasing n (Mertens [1998]), and possibly the KK gets some benefit from this fact too. The values obtained by KK appear to follow the theoretical prediction of being $O(1/n^{\alpha\log n})$ (Yakir [1996]) with $\alpha\approx0.702$ fitted from our experimental data. Our SA algorithm was coded for comparison purposes and exactly follows the implementation proposed in Johnson et al [1991]. It seems that for this set of instances SA is a better alternative than KK for $n\leq50$.

17.6.3 Results with the Evolutionary Algorithms Proposed

The next experiments show the performance of the GAs (in each case being our MAs without the Local-Search-Engine()) with the ρ_D and ρ_{TD} representations, with 4000 generations. We report the results of the algorithms which used *GTrsgr*, for $S(\rho_D)$ and

$GT(1.0)$ for $S(\rho_{TD})$, since they obtained the best results. These experiments are shown in Figure 17.3 where we have used the notation summarised in Table 17.3.

Table 17.3: Notation for experimental results shown in Figure 17.3.

Notation	Representation	Mutation
GA-Ds	ρ_D	Simple
GA-Dm	ρ_D	Minimal
GA-TDs	ρ_{TD}	Simple
GA-TDm	ρ_{TD}	Minimal

The results using the direct representation ρ_D using the minimal mutation (the curve labelled GA-Ds) were significantly bad, as expected from the previous results by Ruml [1993]. It is not even able to compete against the KK heuristic. It can be considered as a benchmark to compare the other GAs. Note that the use of the *Minimal* mutation (even when we are using the same representation) significantly improved the results, being only worse than KK for $n>75$. On the contrary, the use of the *Simple* mutation significantly improved the results when the $S(\rho_{TD})$ representation was used, being better than KK for $n<75$. The results appear to be better than the same algorithm using the *Minimal* mutation.

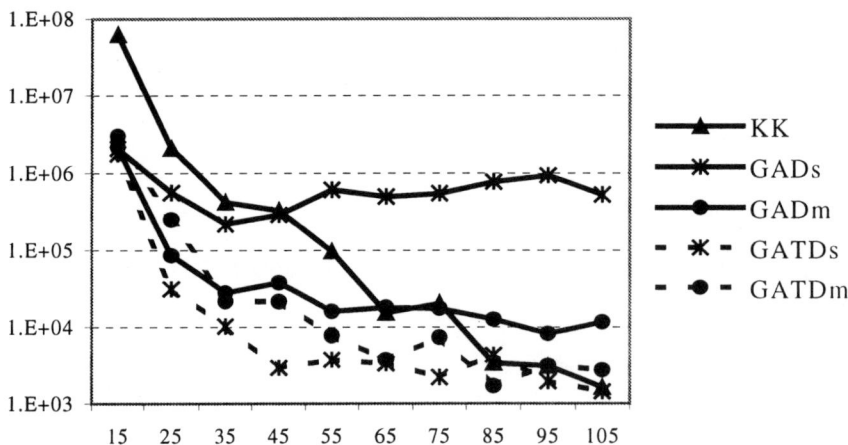

Fig. 17.3: GAs performance vs. Karmarkar-Karp heuristic.

We then incorporated the Local-Search-Engine(), and tested *GreedyImprovement* and *TabuImprovement* with *MaxNumberOfTries* = 10. In addition, in this case, we set a limit of 4000 generations. The results of the introduction of the *GreedyImprovement* are presented in Figure 17.4, where we show with dashed lines the values obtained by GA-Dm and GA-TDs (which were also shown in Figure 17.3 and are included in Figure 17.4 as a reference). The resulting two algorithms, ME-Dm and ME-TDs do not show any particularly impressive improvement over the GA-Dm and GA-TDs which do not use local search.

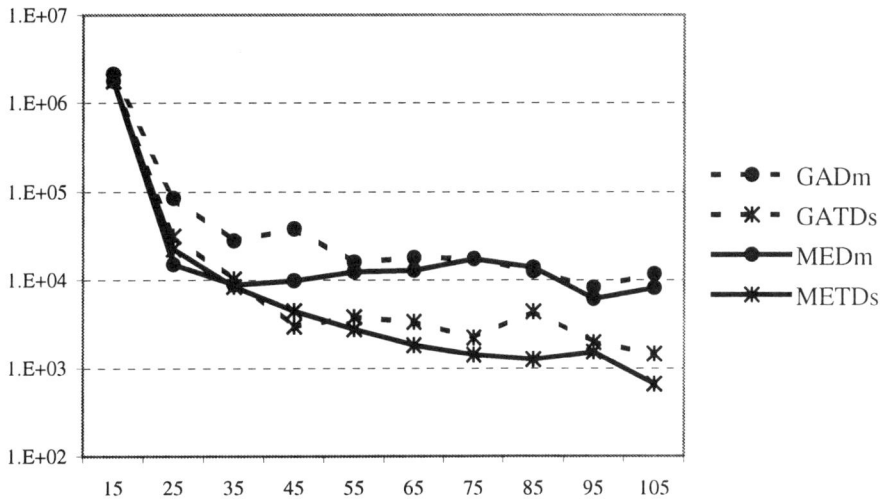

Fig. 17.4: GAs and MAs performance for two different representations.

Both in Figures 17.3 and 17.4, we note that use of the ρ_{TD} representation seems to outperform ρ_D in these experiments. At this point, we were a little frustrated with the results since the two memetic algorithms ME-Dm and ME-TDs where not showing strong improvements. Results using *TabuImprovement* with *MaxNumberOfTries*= 10 were similar to those using *GreedyImprovement* and are not included in the figure.

In the next experiment, we decided to use the Local-Search-Engine() with a greater value of *MaxNumberOfTries*. However, we decided not to apply Local-Search-Engine() for each generation, but after a fixed number of iterations (*GenerationForLocal*). This approach has some analogies with the one presented in Moscato [1993] for the binary perceptron learning problem. The essential idea is to less frequently use the tabu-based local search and, as a tradeoff, make it more exhaustive when applied.

Our experiments included three types of values for *GenerationForLocal* (10, 50, and 100). This means that after 10, 50, or 100 generations the Local-Search-Engine() is applied to the Pocket configuration of all individuals. The values of *MaxNumberOfTries* tested were 1000, 10000, 50000, and 100000. Seeking a fair comparison between these different methods, we decided that the best thing was to have a time limit which was set to 120 seconds. When we used *GreedyImprovement* the results were not sensitive to which representation was being used. However, when we used *TabuImprovement* with ρ_D the results improved significantly over the use of ρ_{TD}. The reason for this is that the ρ_{TD} representation requires the greedy decoding procedure to decide the values of the 'zeroes' and this consumes a precious amount of time when a time limit of 120 seconds is used.

In Figure 17.5, we show the results of the same two algorithms GA-Dm, and GA-TDs. We also present the two variants that add local search ME-Dm and ME-TDs. These curves have been shown in Figure 17.4 too. As a comparison, now we add the curve ME-Dm/100, a memetic algorithm which starts a Tabu Search (with *MaxNumberOfTries*=50000) as a diversification step every 100 generations. These results are now for the 120-seconds limit. The curves for GA-Dm and ME-Dm are very similar. However, for the ρ_m the GA-TDs appears to be outperforming the ME-TDs.

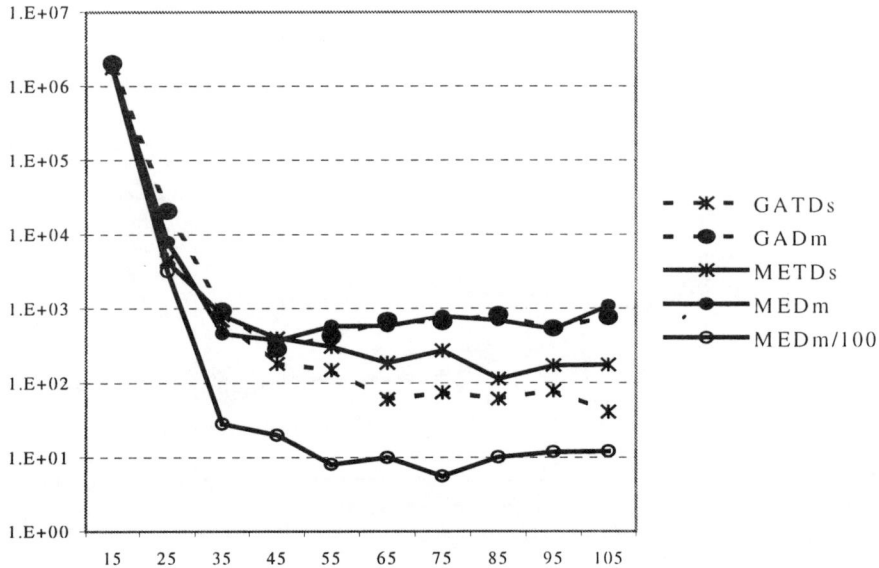

Fig. 17.5: MAs and GAs results (ME-Dm/100 uses Tabu Search for diversification).

Regarding these results, we might conclude that local search, at least in the way it has been implemented in the direct representations is of little use. However, the best curve in Figure 17.5 is a memetic algorithm using ρ_D, with *Minimal* mutation and a *TabuImprovement* period having *MaxNumberOfTrials*=50000 and executed every 100 generations. The results are significantly better. Most of the other variants of MAs for different combinations of values of *MaxNumberOfTrials* and *GenerationForLocal* gave similar results.

The results of the best memetic algorithm presented in Figure 17.5 led us to conduct an experiment to test the performance of a 'single-agent' *TabuImprovement* procedure. In this case, no population-based method was used. The results were very good (see the curve TB in Figure 17.6) but not very robust and in no case dominate the results of the memetic algorithm which uses Tabu.

In Figure 17.6, we can see a summary of some of the results to have a broad picture. The figure displays the results of the Karmarkar-Karp heuristic (KK). The other curves correspond to 120-seconds runs (all using ρ_D) of the simulated annealing implementation (SA), tabu search (TB), and the memetic algorithm that uses the same tabu search strategy of Figure 17.5 (ME-Dm/100 with (100, 50000)). In addition, we present the results of the random-generate-and-test strategy for ρ_{TD} using the greedy decoding procedure (curve RGT-TD in the figure).

We have been surprised by the performance of ME-Dm/100 which uses sporadic periods of tabu search. The performance of the simple tabu search procedure, although less robust, is also remarkable due to its simplicity. However, we note it has not been able to find optimal solutions for the instances with $n \leq 25$ as is the case with ME-Dm/100. We present in Table 17.4 the values (each one being the average over 10 instances, truncated to the nearest integer) obtained with the different methods. CKK gives optimal values and is the only method which has been not constrained to the 120-seconds limit.

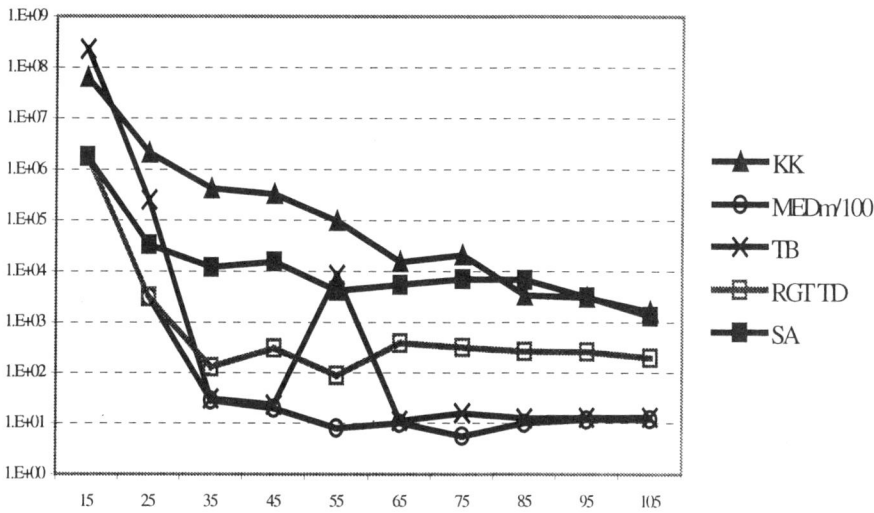

Fig. 17.6: Results for Karmarkar-Karp (KK), an MA with Tabu Search (MEDm/100), Simulated Annealing (SA), Single-agent Tabu Search (TB), and Random-Generate-and-Test (RGT-TD).

Table 17.4: Summarizing the performance of each method on each instance.

N	CKK	KK	SA	RGT-TD	GA-TDs	TB	MED m/100
15	1785469	62529719	1785469	1785469	1785469	27423824	1785469
25	3161	2087226	32958	3161	4610	255580	3161
35	3	422345	11996	129	688	31	28
45	1	329255	15492	309	181	23	20
55	1	97390	4177	87	150	8498	8
65	1	15250	5478	388	60	11	10
75	1	20488	6995	321	74	16	6
85	0	3389	6755	269	61	13	10
95	1	3122	3180	260	79	13	12
105	0	1656	1332	198	41	13	12

17.7 CONCLUSIONS

From our experiments we can conclude that this problem is still a source of interesting open questions. The random instances with 10 decimal digits still are challenging for GAs and other metaheuristics using the direct encoding. However, an MA which uses several

278 THE NUMBER PARTITIONING PROBLEM: AN OPEN CHALLENGE

novel ideas has dominated all other metaheuristics in this study. Contrary to expectations, the best MAs rely on the direct (binary) encoding, use a *Minimal* mutation and simple tabu search for diversification (Moscato [1993]). Nevertheless, we do not exclude the possibility of even better results using other representations.

We also note that no 'seeding' of the population or the SA has been used. It is part of the MA philosophy to introduce all possible knowledge and it would have been a valid option. The KK method would have been a good heuristic to make a randomized algorithm for the initial population. It is also a good constructive method to use instead of the greedy procedure in the recombination. We have tested these ideas experimentally but we have chosen not to include them in this study to make a clear comparison.

The gap from local optimality to global optimality is very high for this problem and presented a hard challenge for metaheuristics. The nature of this challenge seems to be lying on the strong dependence of several metaheuristics on the value of the objective function $m_P(y,x)$ when it is used as a guiding function. This fact, together with the exponential number of local minima found in the direct encoding representation is a hard to tame combination. Our MA, combined with tabu search steps, seems a good alternative (even in this unfavourable fitness landscape), particularly where the hard instances for CKK appear to be, i.e. for $n \approx 35$. For larger n, since we expect an exponential number of perfect partitions (Mertens [1998]), the performance of CKK can hardly be challenged.

The results of the simple tabu search technique have been surprising for us and we wonder why this simple method was not previously applied in other comparison studies. We note that the problem of finding the minimum cost configuration for this problem (when the objective function is $m_P(y,x)$ in the introduction) is equivalent to the problem of finding the ground state of the Hamiltonian:

$$H = (m_P(y,x))^2 = \sum_{i,j=1}^{N} v_i a_i a_j v_j \qquad (17.6)$$

which is an infinite range Ising spin glass with Mattis-like antiferromagnetic couplings $J_{ij} = -a_i a_j$ (Mertens [1998]). The good results of tabu search reported in Laguna & Laguna [1995] for the 2-dimensional Ising spin glass also correlate with our findings. Due to the more robust performance of our memetic algorithm which uses TS as a diversification strategy, we think that the method presented here can also have interesting applications in the physics of disordered systems.

Acknowledgements

P. Moscato wants to acknowledge G. Sorkin for first calling his attention to this problem in November of 1991 and for giving him a draft copy of his thesis at that time. He also wants to acknowledge D.S. Johnson for sending him several reprints in 1992. We also thank R. Korf for letting us use his source code and for sending us his paper. We would also like to thank F.F. Ferreira, J.F. Fontanari, I. Gent, W. Ruml, T. Walsh; for preprints and/or discussions while preparing this chapter. This work is supported by FAPESP, Brazil.

Chapter Eighteen

On Worst-Case and Comparative Analysis as Design Principles for Efficient Recombination Operators: A Graph Colouring Case Study

Pablo E. Coll, Guillermo A. Durán, and Pablo Moscato

18.1 INTRODUCTION, MOTIVATION AND PREVIOUS WORK

In 1995, Costa, Hertz and Dubuis, introduced a new metaheuristic for graph colouring problems (Costa et al [1995]) and they named it EDM (for Evolutionary Descent Method). Graph colouring is a problem with many applications and it naturally arises in a variety of different areas like scheduling, assignments and timetabling and it is associated to other problems in the NP-Hard class. The graph colouring problem arises in classical areas of Graph Theory like finding the minimum number of colours to colour a given map, scheduling of exams in a university (see also Paechter et al [1996]), as well as others coming from the advances of technology like frequency assignment of TV broadcasting stations to channels and to model problems arising in the development of efficient compilers for computer programs.

The metaheuristic can be classified as a *memetic algorithm* since it is based on a population search in which periods of local optimization are interspersed with phases in which new configurations are created from earlier, well-developed configurations or local minima of the previous iterative improvement process. The new population is created using *crossover* or *recombination* operators as in genetic algorithms. In this chapter we will discuss how a methodology inspired in *Competitive Analysis* and the recently introduced *Comparative Analysis* can lead to tight theoretical bounds and also be relevant to the problem of the design of recombination operators with better worst-case performance.

The term *'memetic'* was introduced in Moscato [1989] to encompass a class of metaheuristics for combinatorial optimization problems which are based on the use of a population of 'agents' engaged in periods of local-search-based optimization interspersed with phases in which new points in configuration space are created using crossover or recombination operators (see chapter fourteen and references therein). They are also known as *hybrid genetic algorithms*, although the former denomination is preferred to emphasize the difference with standard genetic algorithms. The latter do not include local search or other forms of *a priori* knowledge of the problem at hand.

Costa and coworkers remarked that their method: 'differs from most of the hybrid algorithms which have been recently developed in the sense that it uses a simple descent method instead of a refined sequential method which accepts non-improvement moves'.

Although Moscato [1993] is referenced as an example of such a method (those which accept non-improvement moves at the local optimization phases), in Moscato [1993] the binary perceptron learning problem is first addressed with a simple descent method (see also Eshelman [1991]). Regardless of these minor comments, the techniques have many analogies with new 'hybrid' genetic algorithms as well as former methods like variants of scatter search (see chapter nineteen). New results on memetic algorithms for timetabling problems can be found in Burke et al [1996] and Paechter et al [1996]. Also, the home page for memetic algorithms has been mentioned in chapter fourteen. It is worth mentioning here that it contains links to many on-line references and papers cited in this chapter.

The impact that a suitable, custom design of the recombination operator has on the overall performance of memetic and genetic approaches had been previously identified and it was well recognized in Hofmann [1993], Moscato [1989, 1993], Radcliffe & Surry [1994, 1994a]. However, we face an intrinsic practical difficulty in evaluating the effect that the recombination has by itself and to disassociate its benefits from the other components of a complex metaheuristic. Sometimes the recombination is just a small part of a highly complex algorithmic framework and sometimes, frustrating the hope for a more quantitative treatment of the issue, it seems that some researchers even enjoy having dozens of free parameters they fix on the basis of some preliminary computational experiments. All these facts finally conspire, they foil and disable us from achieving a proper comparison of results. Moreover, they do not allow a clear understanding of the key beneficial mechanisms of each implementation. This said, a good recombination may be part of a complex algorithmic framework and it seems to be very hard to find a reasonable way to evaluate its performance against a different recombination if we can only rely on the results of computer experiments.

The main problem we face is that we are making a comparison which may be biased by many other algorithmic decisions in a memetic framework like the type of local search used, the neighbourhood definition for moves among different configurations, the different parameters used, etc. A similar line of argument can be established for implementations of genetic algorithms, since they are not free of other *ad-hoc* parameterized decisions like the rate of mutation, probabilities for selection for recombination, mating strategies, avoidance of inbreeding solutions, etc. Indeed, these problems are part of the still not developed methodological procedures related to the proper performance analysis of metaheuristics techniques. However, we should mention at least one good step forward in this direction regarding memetic algorithms. It was the work on the Euclidean Travelling Salesman Problem (ETSP) by Hofmann [1993] followed by Radcliffe & Surry [1994a]. Their work, although it also relied on experimental issues, was based on the use of *Forma Analysis* and *correlation within formae experiments* using solved instances of the ETSP. This technique, which still relies on computational experimentation, attempted to isolate the benefits of recombination *per se*. The practicality of these approaches had been anticipated in Moscato [1989, 1993].

In this chapter, we present a novel methodology for the analysis and the design strategy of recombination operators. As a case study, which will illustrate the technique, we will discuss the principal recombination of the algorithm for the graph colouring problem introduced in Costa et al [1995]. Part of our motivation is based on the good results obtained by Costa and coworkers on large random graphs of the class $G_{n,p}$ (graphs with n vertices and density p) as well as some of the limitations of their method. Our approach to the evaluation of the performance of a recombination is inspired on *Competitive Analysis* and *Comparative Analysis* (Koutsoupias & Papadimitriou [1994]), two techniques developed in connection with *on-line* algorithms. In the next section we will discuss some of the main aspects of the heuristic proposed in Costa et al [1995] and with more detail the recombination procedure we will analyze. In a later section we will discuss in some detail the reasons which lead us to propose this approach.

18.2 THE RECOMBINATION PROCEDURE AND ASSOCIATED DEFINITIONS

In order to understand the problem and the recombination procedure we need to introduce some definitions. Our notation convention will follow that of Costa et al [1995] for clarity. Let $G=(V,E)$ be an undirected graph of vertex set V and edge set E. An *independent set* is a set $I \subseteq V$ such that every pair in I is not adjacent in G, i.e. $\{x,y\} \subset I \Rightarrow (x,y) \notin E$. A *partial q-colouring* of G is a partition $(V_1, V_2, ..., V_q)$ of a subset $V' \subseteq V$ into q disjoint independent sets. If we assign a colour $c(x)=i$ to each vertex $x \in V_i$ then a *partial colouring with q colours* can be interpreted as the problem of colouring with q colours a set $V' \subseteq V$ such that no two adjacent vertices have the same colour. The *dimension of a partial colouring with q colours* is the cardinality of the set $V' = V_1 \cup V_2 ... \cup V_q$. A *partial colouring with q colours of dimension* $n = |V|$ is known as a *q-colouring of G*. The associated optimization problem is the task of finding a colouring with the minimum q. The *chromatic number* of a graph is the minimum q for which a q-colouring exists.

The algorithm introduced by Costa, Hertz and Dubuis has two phases that can be included in a memetic framework. The first phase tries to find a partial q'-colouring. To achieve that goal, a recombination procedure is used and combined with local search descent steps. The second phase, which is the essential part of the algorithm, tries to find a feasible q-colouring of the yet uncoloured graph. It is this recombination procedure the one we are analyzing in this chapter. Clearly, the algorithm would use $q+q'$ colours to finally produce a colouring in this way. In Costa et al [1995], the authors claim that they need to use the two-phase approach since they believe (based on their own experiments and other work which exists in the literature) that they would not be able to find a feasible q-colouring using only the second phase. At least, they find it really improbable when addressing problems with more than 300 nodes.

The recombination procedure we are going to analyze has as input two parent colourings S_1 and S_2 of a graph $G(V,E)$ which are not necessarily feasible. That is, it is accepted the existence of *conflicting edges,* that is edges which have both extremes coloured using the same colour. Let $c_i(v)$ be the colour assigned to vertex v in the colouring S_i and let $NCE_i(v,d)$ be the *number of conflicting edges* which are at a distance d from v in S_i. To each vertex v a penalty $p_i(v)$ is associated with v which measures how 'close' vertex v is to conflicting edges in S_i. More explicitly:

$$p_i(v) = \sum_{d=0}^{2} \omega_d NCE_i(v,d) \qquad (18.1)$$

where ω_d are weights which balance the importance of conflicting edges located at different distances from vertex v. Costa and coworkers have decided that $\omega_0 > \omega_1 > \omega_2$ and not to take into account the cases where $d>2$ regarding some preliminary, qualitative 'cost/benefit' computational experiments they performed. From two 'parent' colourings S_1 and S_2 one 'child' colouring S_3 will be created such that each vertex $v \in S_3$ will be coloured either with $c_1(v)$ or $c_2(v)$ and preference is given to the colour with the smallest penalty $p_i(v)$ in S_1 or S_2. When $p_1(v) = p_2(v)$, we will consider the vertices of v which have been already coloured in the current partial colouring of S_3, choosing the colour $c \in \{c_1(v), c_2(v)\}$ which minimizes $nadj(v, c)$, the number of adjacent vertices to v coloured c in S_3. If we can not decide between $c_1(v)$ and $c_2(v)$ then we break ties choosing between them at random with the same probability. The following pseudocode from Costa et al [1995] will certainly help to clarify the procedure.

Input: $S_1, S_2 \in X$; **Output**: $S_3 = (V_1, ..., V_q) \in X$

$nadj(v, c) = 0;\ \forall v \in V, \forall c = 1, ..., q$;

$V_c \leftarrow \{\};\ \forall c = 1, ..., q$;

for (each vertex $v \in V$) **do**

    if $p_1(v) < p_2(v)$ **then** $c_3(v) = c_1(v)$

    else if $p_2(v) < p_1(v)$ **then** $c_3(v) = c_2(v)$

        else { $p_1(v) = p_2(v)$ *and we need to break ties* }

        if $nadj(v, c_1(v)) < nadj(v, c_2(v))$ **then** $c_3(v) = c_1(v)$

        else if $nadj(v, c_2(v)) < nadj(v, c_1(v))$ **then** $c_3(v) = c_2(v)$

           else { *then* $nadj(v, c_1(v)) = nadj(v, c_2(v))$ }

           { *now we break ties at random* }

           $c_3(v) = random(c_1(v), c_2(v), 0.5)$;

    $nadj(v', c_3(v)) = nadj(v', c_3(v)) + 1,\ \forall v'$ adjacent to v ;

    $V_{c_3(v)} = V_{c_3(v)} \cup \{v\}$

To be fair, this randomized procedure is actually defining not one but a family of recombinations since it has ω_0, ω_1 and ω_2 as free parameters. After a series of preliminary computational experiments with 20 graphs belonging to the class $G_{100,0.5}$, Costa and co-workers have observed that the best results have been obtained using $\omega_0 = 100$, $\omega_1 = 3$ and $\omega_2 = 1$. Undoubtedly, this selection leaves many open questions since it may be the case that this values are *instance-dependent*, that is they may be optimal just for the input distributions of the instances used in their computational study. Finite size effect associated to the use of $|V| = 100$ might have also influenced this selection.

18.3 A 'COMPETITIVE-INSPIRED' ANALYSIS

We will discuss two cases, where the principal recombination introduced in Costa et al [1995] is studied. The analysis is inspired by the concept of *Competitive Analysis* which was first introduced to analyze the performance of *on-line* algorithms.

A problem is said to be *on-line* if it requires that irrevocable decisions which influence the output must be made before having a complete knowledge of the entire input. Some examples of this class of problems can be found in robot motion planning, maintaining dynamic data structures, video on demand, network routing, etc. These problems are a real challenge to standard worst-case analysis since, after examination of the characteristics of an algorithmic procedure an '*adversary*' can choose an input sequence which can foil the performance of the on-line algorithm.

One way to overcome the problem of dealing with the distribution of inputs and still make a relevant worst-case analysis is to use the method known as *Competitive Analysis*, developed by Sleator & Tarjan [1985] although the concept can be found in the earlier literature of bin packing (Johnson [1974], Yao [1980]). The key idea is to compare an on-line algorithm with the optimal *off-line* algorithm, i.e. one that can see the entire input in advance thus it will have a complete knowledge of the future events. This comparison is done on an input-by-input basis. If we denote as A an on-line algorithm and ξ an input sequence we denote with $A(\xi)$ the cost of algorithm A on ξ. If $A_{opt}(\xi)$ is the cost of the optimal off-line algorithm on input ξ then we say that A is a *k-competitive algorithm* if for all ξ, $A(\xi) - k \cdot A_{opt}(\xi)$ remains bounded by a constant. The term k-competitive was coined in Karlin et al [1988]. For a randomized algorithm A is replaced by $\langle A(\xi) \rangle_a$, which stands for the expectation value over A's random choices. The *competitiveness of A*, denoted β_A, is the infimum of k such that A is k-competitive.

Under this perspective, the quality of a specific algorithm is given by the maximum ratio between the cost of an on-line problem and the cost incurred by the optimal algorithm for the off-line problem. Competitive analysis, although it is still a kind of worst-case analysis, implied a conceptual break-through, since by the definition of competitiveness it liberates from any kind of probabilistic assumptions about the input data. It allowed to view an on-line problem as a game between an *on-line player* and an *adversary* who will choose the input of the problem so as to maximize the ratio between the algorithm's cost and that of the optimal off-line algorithm (Manasse et al [1988]).

With these concepts in mind, we will give an example of the kind of analysis we propose for recombination design; we will act as an adversary of the recombination we want to study. We will first consider the problem of colouring $K_{6,6}$, a bipartite complete graph with six vertices in each partition. The vertices are numbered such that $\{v_1,...,v_6\}$ and $\{v_7,...,v_{12}\}$ belong to the first and the second partition, respectively. Note that the recombination of Costa et al [1995] specifies a number of operations which are executed in an order given by the vertex numbering. This said, thinking as a game in which we are the adversaries, we have chosen the input graph and the sequence of events. The input to the recombination procedure will be two parent configurations S_1 and S_2 with no conflicting edges, two feasible colourings. Vertices in each partition have the same colours, and we will also require that $c_1(v_1) = c_2(v_7) = B$ (B for blue) and $c_1(v_7) = c_2(v_1) = R$ (R for red). A natural cost measure of the performance of the recombination would be the number of conflicting edges present in the child colouring.

It is obvious to remark that the chromatic number for $K_{6,6}$ is two, so the discussion may look irrelevant since it may seem that there is no sense in crossing two optimal solutions. However, the example must be regarded as a subgraph of a larger graph. The decision to work out an example case for only two colours is motivated by the fact that the subgraph can be part of a well-developed configuration since those are the ones engaged in recombination in a memetic algorithm. We will see for this example how the recombination generates a child S_3 from two parent colourings S_1 and S_2. For each verex v in V, $p_1(v) = p_2(v) = 0$, so we need to take into account $nadj(v, c_i(v))$ to break ties. Starting from v_1, clearly $nadj(v_1, c_1(v_1)) = nadj(v_1, c_2(v_1)) = 0$, thus we need to arbitrarily select the colour of v_1 in S_3. The same situation will occur for all vertices in the same partition if we follow the index order in the **for** loop of the pseudocode which defines the recombination. Due to the randomized procedure, we may end up with a worst-case scenario in which we have $c_3(v_1) = c_3(v_2) = c_3(v_3) = B$ and $c_3(v_4) = c_3(v_5) = c_3(v_6) = R$. When we attempt to colour vertices v_7 to v_{12} we note that $nadj(v_j, c_1(v_j)) = nadj(v_j, c_2(v_j)) = 3$ for $7 \leq j \leq 12$, so we must break ties again to colour it. Again, it may be possible that $c_3(v_7) = c_3(v_8) = c_3(v_9) = B$ and $c_3(v_{10}) = c_3(v_{11}) = c_3(v_9) = R$. In conclusion, starting from two colourings of a graph with 36 edges without conflicts we end up having a new colouring S_3 which has 18 conflicting edges ($|E|/2$ in this case), (see Figure 18.1).

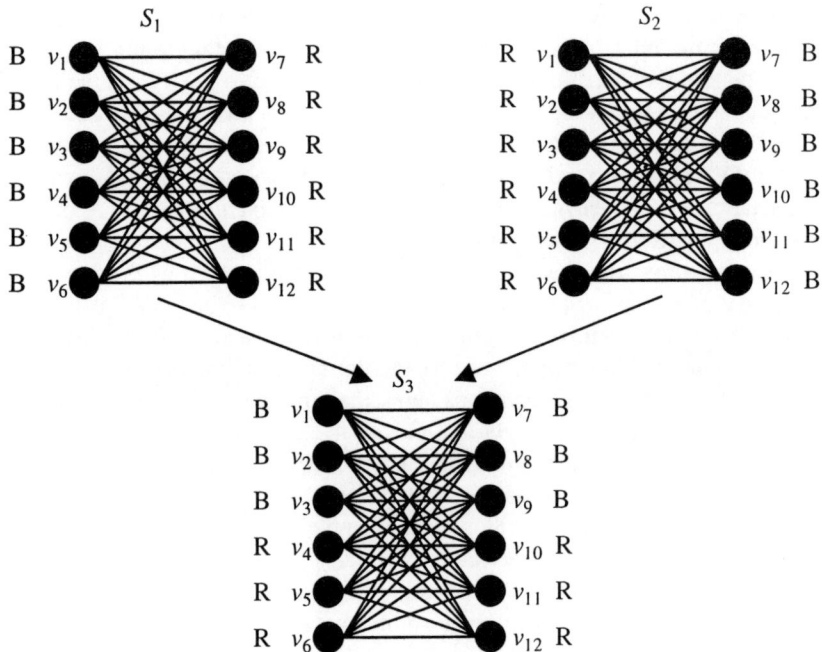

Fig. 18.1: The figure shows two parent colourings S_1 and S_2 and one child colouring S_3 which can be the result by the application of the graph colouring recombination introduced in Costa et al [1995]. For this particular instance of the problem, two feasible colourings (without conflicting edges) can create an output that has half of the edges in conflict.

It is clear that the situation described above has already identified the problem of creating new configurations which have at least $|E|/2$ new conflicting edges even when coming from two well-developed solutions. This may constitute a simple instance of a more general case. Let $K_{i1,...,ik}$ be a k-partite complete graph such that $j1 = j2 = ... = jk = j$. To simplify the discussion we will suppose that j and k are even. We will start again with a situation in which S_1 and S_2 have no conflicting edges. Let V_i be the ith partition, ($|V_i| = ji = j$). Let $c_1(v_l) = 1 + int((l-1)/i)$ and $c_2(v_l) = k + 1 - c_1(v_l)$ where $int(x)$ is the integer part of x. In this case the chromatic number for this graph is k but again we must recall that it can be regarded as a subgraph of a larger graph which is the one we would like to colour. Again to generate S_3, for all v in V, $p_1(v) = p_2(v) = 0$, since the two parents have no conflicting edges. Starting from v_1, clearly $nadj(v_1, c_1(v_1)) = nadj(v_1, c_2(v_1)) = 0$ with $c_1(v_1) = 1$ and $c_2(v_1) = k$, thus we need to arbitrarily select among them. The same situation will occur for all vertices $v_2,...,v_j \in V_1$ if we follow the index order. Due to randomization, we may end up with a worst-case scenario in which we have $c_3(v_1) = c_3(v_2) = ...$ $= c_2(v_{(j/2)}) = c_1(v_1) = 1$ and $c_3(v_{(j/2)+1}) = ... = c_3(v_j) = c_2(v_{(j/2)+1}) = k$. Again, due to the randomization procedure we may end up with a situation in which the first half of the vertices of partition V_i are coloured with colour i in S_3 and the second half are coloured with colour $k-i+1$ (note that for v_l with $l > kj/2$, the argument still holds but with $nadj(v_1, c_i(v_1)) = j/2$). In conclusion, starting with two colourings of $K_{j,...,j}$, a k-partite complete graph with $|V| = kj$ vertices and $|E| = |V| \times (|V|-j)/2$ edges which have no conflicting edges, we end up having a new colouring S_3 which has $|E|/(2(k-1))$ conflicting edges. This number is $\mathcal{O}(|E|)$ for 'small' k and $\mathcal{O}(|V|)$ for larger values of k. For $k=2$ we recover the result we presented in the first example.

18.4 UPPER BOUND

In this section we will prove that the first example of the preceding section is a worst-case example for the principal recombination method used by Costa et al [1995].

Lemma

Given a graph $G(V,E)$ and two feasible q-colourings of G, S_1 and S_2, let S_3 be the q-colouring of G (not necessarily feasible) created by the recombination of Costa et al [1995]. For a node $v \in V$ we denote as $NCE_3(v)$ the number of conflicting edges created in S_3 at the moment of colouring node v with either $c_1(v)$ or $c_2(v)$ the colour assigned to vertex v in the colourings S_1 and S_2, respectively. We will denote as $|AC(v)|$ the number of nodes adjacent to node v in G which have already been chosen for colouring in S_3 when we are colouring node v. Then the following is true:

$$NCE_3(v) \leq |AC(v)|/2$$

Proof

Let $c_1(v)$, $c_2(v)$ be the colours assigned to node v in S_1 and S_2, respectively. Let's suppose without losing generality, that node v will be coloured as in parent colouring S_1, that is $c_3(v) = c_1(v) = R$. We face two possibilities here. Let's first consider what happens when $c_2(v) = c_1(v) = R$. In this case, we are sure that no other vertex adjacent to vertex v has been coloured with colour R since by hypothesis we have assumed that both S_1 and S_2 are feasible colourings, then they have no conflicting edges. Then, $NCE_3(v) = 0$, and, since $|AC(v)| \geq 0$, then $NCE_3(v) \leq |AC(v)|/2$, which proves the result in this case. Now let's consider what happens in the case when $c_2(v) \neq c_1(v)$. We will suppose that $NCE_3(v) \geq \text{int}(|AC(v)|/2) + 1$, and we will prove the sought result via *reductio-ad-absurdum*. First note that $p_1(v) = p_2(v) = 0$, since S_1 and S_2 are two *feasible* colourings of G. Then the colouring of v in S_3 was decided as a consequence of two possibilities according to the recombination of Costa et al [1995]:

1. $nadj(v, c_1(v)) < nadj(v, c_2(v))$, or

2. $nadj(v, c_1(v)) = nadj(v, c_2(v))$,

and the selection of $c_3(v)$ was made at random with probability 0.5.

Since we have supposed that $NCE_3(v) \geq int(|AC(v)|/2)+1$ then we can also write $nadj(v, c_1(v)) > \Sigma_x \, nadj(v, x)$ where x runs through all the colours. Now, since it is also true that $\Sigma_x \, nadj(v, x) \geq nadj(v, c_2(v))$, we get $nadj(v, c_1(v)) \geq nadj(v, c_2(v))$, which contradicts the two cases above. This finally proves the lemma.

Now we are able to prove the following worst-case upper bound.

Theorem

Given a graph $G(V,E)$ and two parent colourings as defined in the lemma above, the number of conflicting edges NCE_3 in the final colouring S_3 generated by the recombination of Costa et al [1995], is bounded by $|E|/2$.

Proof:

Directly following from the Lemma:

$$NCE_3 = \sum_{i=1}^{|V|} NCE_3(v_i) \leq \sum_{i=1}^{|V|} |AC(v_i)|/2 = |E|/2$$

hence proving the theorem.

18.5 A WEAKER ADVERSARY

In our previous analysis we have used randomization for the benefits of our thesis. We have shown that we can get an extremely bad result due to the application of the standard procedure given in Costa et al [1995]. An open question that motivates this section is: How relevant were these random choices? How well would the recombination procedure do if it would not face such an extremely 'unfair' sequence of events?

In a certain way, we are making an analysis with a weaker adversary, one that can not control at will those random choices. However, the order in which the vertices are going to be coloured is at the control of the adversary and it will be the same as we have used in the previous worst-case analysis. In a certain way, we see some analogies with the relevance that knowing the future has for certain on-line problems (Karp [1992]).

In our previous analysis, the selection of colours for vertices in S_3 was random, but we were always choosing among the two possibilities the one which would be more 'unfair' for the recombination of Costa et al [1995]. We will now analyze what happens when the selection of which colour to use (B or R) is equiprobable (that is, it has probability of selection 0.5), whenever ties must be broken. It is a way of relaxing the worst case scenario by reducing the 'strength' of the adversary (using jargon from Competitive Analysis).

We will maintain the same numbering order for the vertices. We want to calculate the expected value of conflicting edges in S_3 for a $K_{2t,2t}$ graph coloured with two colours, where each node (whenever ties must be broken) can take colour c_1 with probability 0.5. Colours start to be assigned to vertices starting with v_1 and following the same indexing order we used before. This leads to the fact that the $V_1 = \{v_1, v_2, ..., v_{2t}\}$ partition can get 2^{2t} different configurations of two colours.

Let's denote with NCE_3 the number of conflicting edges in S_3. When the first partition is finally coloured, we have to consider two different cases:

(a) The number of nodes with colour c_1 is different to the number of nodes with colour c_2. Without losing generality, we can suppose that there are more nodes coloured with c_1 than with c_2, the other case is analogous. When colouring the other partition, and according to the algorithm proposed in Costa et al [1995], all other nodes will be assigned colour c_2, so the number of conflicting edges would be $2t \mid c_2 \mid_{(1)}$, where $\mid c_2 \mid_{(1)}$ is the number of nodes with colour c_2 in V_1. The distribution of the number of nodes coloured with colour c_2 in V_1 is a binomial distribution with parameters $2t$ and $\mid c_2 \mid_{(1)}$ ($B(2t, \mid c_2 \mid_{(1)})$). Since the total number of different ways in which we can colour V_1 with 2 colours is equal to 2^{2t}, then the probability of having $2kt$ conflicting edges is given by:

$$p(NCE_3 = 2kt) = 2 \binom{2t}{k} 2^{-2t}, \quad \text{for } k = 0,1,...,t-1$$

where the factor of 2 is due to the fact that k can be either $\mid c_1 \mid$ or $\mid c_2 \mid$ according to which one is the minimum of the two.

(b) The number of nodes coloured with c_1 and c_2 is the same. Then the nodes of V_2 will have colours which will be randomly chosen, but any of the 2^{2t} final configurations of V_2 will have the same number of conflicting edges, exactly $2t^2$. Then the probability of having exactly $2t^2$ conflicting edges is given by:

$$p(NCE_3 = 2t^2) = \binom{2t}{t} 2^{-2t}$$

For $k > t$ this is zero. Then the expected value of conflicting edges is given by:

$$E(NCE_3) = \sum_{i=1}^{2t^2} iP(\mid CE \mid = i)$$

and then:

$$E(NCE_3) = \frac{2t}{2^{2t}} \left(2\sum_{j=1}^{t-1} j \binom{2t}{j} + t \binom{2t}{t} \right).$$

Using the equality

$$\binom{j}{1}\binom{2t}{j} = \binom{2t}{1}\binom{2t-1}{j-1}$$

we have:

$$\sum_{j=1}^{t-1} j \binom{2t}{j} = 2t \sum_{j=1}^{t-1} \binom{2t-1}{j-1} = 2t \frac{2^{2t-1} - 2\binom{2t-1}{t-1}}{2},$$

and finally we reach the sought result

$$E(NCE_3) = 2t^2 \left(1 - \frac{1}{2^{2t}} \binom{2t}{t} \right).$$

The relation between $|E|$ and t is given by $|E| = 4t^2$ which allows us to say that $E(NCE_3) \geq |E|/3$ for $t \geq 3$, which can be easily proved by induction on t. Figure 18.2 shows the difference between both functions up to $|E| = 600$.

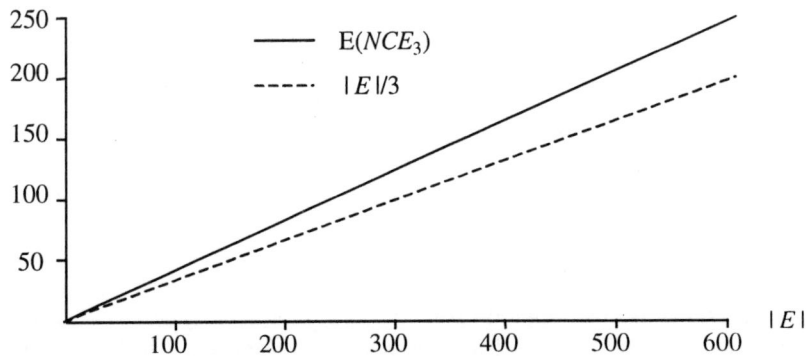

Fig. 18.2: The difference between E(NCE_3) and $|E|/3$.

For the specific example given above (a $K_{6,6}$ graph coloured with two colours) the expected value of conflicting edges in S_3 is 99/8. This result lets us claim that if the same indexing order is used, then the expected value of conflicting edges is at least of the same order than the number of edges. We have proved that in this average case scenario, breaking ties uniformly at random does not help significantly over the worst-case bound.

18.6 OPTIMAL MARRIAGES

The previous analysis has led us to consider the introduction of another procedure before recombining two parent colourings S_1 and S_2 to create a new child colouring S_3. Since the colour names are arbitrarily chosen, any given colouring with q colours is basically equivalent to $q!$ different assignments (coming from the $q!$ possible permutations of the colours' indices). It is quite evident from the two examples introduced above that an optimal 'off-line' algorithm would recognize that, in both cases, the two colourings are actually the same and would act accordingly. We remark here that the previous quotation marks have been used since the problem is definitely not an on-line problem. The characteristics of the problem faced by Costa and coworkers leave us free to design any type of recombination and for that purpose we can benefit from the fact that the complete colourings S_1 and S_2 are completely known in advance. It is the 'myopia' introduced by the sequential operations in the recombination we are currently studying which is the core source of the inefficiency.

We will see in the rest of this section how the previous analysis suggests the use of another procedure. It must be a fast heuristic to address the problem of reindexing the colours in one of the parents, say S_2, in order to maximize the number of vertices which have the same colour in both parents before using them to create a new colouring S_3.

Again, we will have as input two colourings (which are not necessarily feasible) $S_1 = (V_{1,(1)},...,V_{q,(1)})$ and $S_2 = (V_{1,(2)},...,V_{q,(2)})$ where $V_{j,(i)}$ denotes the set of vertices coloured with colour j in parent S_i. We will create an auxiliary graph $K_{q,q}$, a bipartite complete graph with q vertices in each partition and with weighted edges. The first partition is the set $\{V_{1,(1)},...,V_{q,(1)}\}$ and the second one is $\{V_{1,(2)},...,V_{q,(2)}\}$. The weight w_{ij} of the edge identified by $(v_{i,(1)}, v_{j,(2)})$ stands for the number of vertices in common between $V_{i,(1)}$ and $V_{j,(2)}$ (Figure 18.3). This said, if we find a *maximum weighted perfect matching* (in this case, it is clear that the maximum weighted matching will be perfect because the bipartite complete graph has non negative weights in the edges) of $K_{q,q}$, as defined above, and then we relabel the set of indexes of $\{V_{j,(2)}\}$ according to the best matching found, we have a way to overcome some of the problems discussed in the previous section.

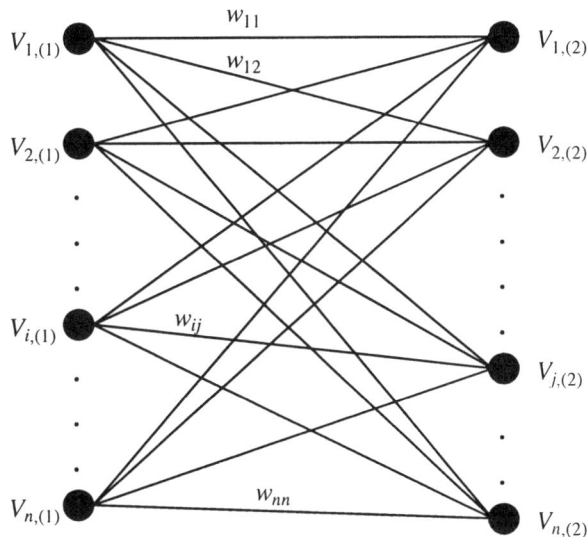

Fig. 18.3: An auxiliary graph used for reindexing the colours before crossing two parent colourings. It is a $K_{q,q}$, a bipartite complete graph. Each vertex of a given partition represents a given colour in one of the parents. The weight w_{ij} of an edge which connects vertices representing colours i and j in partitions 1 and 2 stands for the number of vertices coloured with colour i in parent 1 which are coloured with colour j in parent 2.

For example, we will discuss again the first example which involved $K_{6,6}$. Both parents have two colours so we will need to construct an auxiliary graph $K_{2,2}$. The first partition of $K_{2,2}$ is $\{V_{1,(1)}, V_{2,(1)}\}$ and the second one is $\{V_{1,(2)}, V_{2,(2)}\}$. The weights of the edges are $(v_{i,(1)}, v_{i,(2)}) = 0$ where $i = \{1, 2\}$ and the other weights have a value of 6. Clearly, there are only two possible perfect matchings. Obviously, the one that has the maximum weight is the one composed by the two edges with weight equal to 6 (Figure 18.4). This gives a proper relabeling of the colours in S_2. We leave as an exercise for the reader to work out what is the situation for the second example which involves $K_{j,...,j}$.

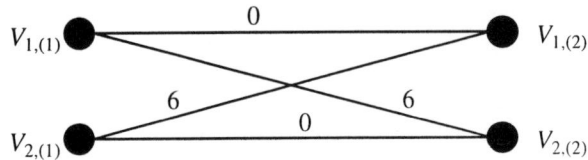

Fig. 18.4: The auxiliary graph $K_{2,2}$ which can be created for the case posed in Figure 18.1.

Despite the polynomial time complexity of the maximum weighted perfect matching problem, we think that we should constrain ourselves to lower order greedy heuristics for it. The reason is that in a memetic algorithm we expect to have a low order complexity procedure for recombination, having as a natural upper bound the time-complexity of the local search steps used. Also, we are not seeking for the ultimate best algorithm to solve the maximum weighted perfect matching since this is just one possible way to deal with the problem of indexing the colours in one of the parents as we discussed in the previous sections. In a certain way, its formulation is just a model, another heuristic to solve a problem. On the other hand, there is a clear advantage to using a greedy randomized heuristic for this problem since it would deliver different solutions from the same input parents. This, in turn, guarantees that we will efficiently explore neighbouring configurations between local minima when intensification steps are needed in the memetic paradigm (Moscato [1993], Radcliffe & Surry [1994]).

18.7 COMPARATIVE ANALYSIS

The competitive analysis of on-line algorithms has been criticized as being too crude and unrealistic. In 1994, Koutsoupias and Papadimitriou proposed two refinements of competitive analysis in two directions: The first restricts the power of the adversary by allowing only certain input distributions. The second one allows for comparisons between different information regimes for on-line decision-making. This latter refinement was used to explore the power of lookahead in server and task systems (Koutsoupias & Papadimitriou [1994]).

To understand their proposal, which they named *comparative analysis*, it will be good to follow their discussion. Suppose that A and B are classes of algorithms where typically but not necessarily $A \subseteq B$, that is B is usually a broader class of algorithms, a more powerful information regime. Then, the *comparative ratio* $R(A, B)$ is defined as:

$$R(A, B) = \max_{b \in B} \min_{a \in A} \max_{\xi} \frac{a(\xi)}{b(\xi)}$$

where $a(\xi)$ and $b(\xi)$ are the costs of algorithms a and b on input ξ. Koutsoupias and Papadimitriou have proposed a game-theoretic interpretation of this formula: B wants to demonstrate to A that it is a more powerful class of algorithms. With this purpose, B chooses an algorithm $b \in B$ among its own. Then, responding to this choice, A comes up with an algorithm $a \in A$. Then B chooses an input problem ξ. After this sequence, A must pay B the ratio $a(\xi)/b(\xi)$. It is assumed that the larger this ratio, the more powerful B is in comparison to $\mathcal{A}$. It should be remarked that if we let $\mathcal{A}$ be the class of on-line algorithms and $\mathcal{B}$ be the class of all algorithms – on-line or off-line – then the equation for the comparative ratio reduces to the standard definition of competitive ratio of a problem.

We will now discuss our results on the graph colouring recombination problem we have studied having in mind the definition of competitive ratio. We have analyzed the problem of creating a new (child) colouring for a graph $G(V, E)$, using two (parent) colourings S_1 and S_2. Since the recombination procedure to be analyzed was the one introduced by Costa et al [1995], in fact we have studied a class of algorithms $\mathcal{A}$ which is composed of only one algorithm, named a, which is this same recombination. Acting as an adversary of the algorithm a (or class $\mathcal{A}$) we have selected a class $\mathcal{B}$ composed of all possible reindexings of colours in one of the parent colourings. Note that in this case $\mathcal{A} \subseteq \mathcal{B}$ since when no reindexing is done, we apply the same basic recombination procedure a, and so $a \in \mathcal{B}$. Using the graph-theoretic interpretation, we have selected an algorithm $b \in \mathcal{B}$ which is composed of a reindexing (based on a best-matching procedure for reindexing the colours in one of the parent colourings) followed by the application of the standard recombination procedure (algorithm a). The input problem chosen has as input two feasible colourings of a bipartite complete graph. We have used as a measure of performance of the recombination procedures (i.e. cost) the number of conflicting edges, which is a natural choice in the memetic framework. Our worst-case theorem, and the fact that the class $\mathcal{A}$ has only one element, then indicates that the comparative ratio $R(\mathcal{A}, \mathcal{B}) = |E|/2$ (though a slightly different definition of cost should be used to avoid the denominator being zero).

18.8 CONCLUSIONS

There is a growing interest in a more scientific approach to the usual methodology behind computational experimentation. J.N Hooker has clearly depicted the situation in two of his most recent papers (see Hooker [1994, 1996]). C.C. McGeogh [1996, 1996a] has also discussed issues regarding analysis of algorithms in the context of computer experimentation. Barr et al [1995] have also discussed some issues for the proper design and analysis of computational experiments to analyze heuristics.

The aim of establishing a proper methodology for the analysis of heuristics is far from being a new interest, see for example Johnson & Papadimitriou [1985] and Golden & Stewart [1985]. In comparison, the theoretical analysis of metaheuristics for combinatorial optimization problems is still in its infancy. One of the intrinsic difficulties to be faced in order to develop a more scientific approach resides on the fact that the more widespread methodology, being currently used, only relies on the results of computer experiments. It is evident that this methodology has many flaws. Perhaps the most recurring one takes place when two metaheuristics, say $M1$ and $M2$, are compared based on the results of computer experiments on some set of instances of a problem P. Not only one of the metaheuristics may be more suitable for P than the other, the main concern is that $M1$ and $M2$ are *instantiated*, i.e. we are actually comparing them after some parameterized decisions which govern the metaheuristic behaviour are chosen; we can then denote that we are comparing $M1(p_1, ..., p_n)$ against $M2(q_1, ..., q_m)$. For instance, if $M1$ represents standard genetic algorithms (those that do not use local search, but are not restricted to binary representations), then, in our proposed notation, the parameters can be numbers (population size, mutation rate, etc.) but can also denote other algorithmic procedures like the recombination operators for example. If $M2$ represents a memetic algorithm, some of the parameters can be the same (population size, for instance), but others may not belong to $M1$ (the type of neighbourhood used for the local search technique is one good example).

This said, when the two metaheuristics are instantiated, we are comparing two heuristic algorithms $M1(p_1,...,p_n)$ and $M2(q_1,...,q_m)$ on a particular problem P, which takes us back to the issues of comparison. Unfortunately this whole picture is often not perceived and many researchers; if $M1(p_1,...,p_n)$ performs better than $M2(q_1,...,q_m)$ in their particular setting, they just report $M1$ as a successful metaheuristic and $M2$ as a failure, which is clearly a mistake due to the improper, or at least unjustified, generalization. On the other hand, comparison between the performance of heuristics $M1(p_1,...,p_n)$ and $M2(q_1,...,q_m)$ on problem P does not escape the usual problems we face when comparing heuristics.

In this chapter we have shown, using a particular example of a graph colouring recombination, that a novel design methodology and theoretical analysis inspired in some concepts of *Competitive Analysis* and *Comparative Analysis* may be very useful to provide some worst-case bounds to understand the performance of at least one characteristic of metaheuristics, the recombination or recombination operators. We should also remark that it might be possible to extend this type of analysis to other type of recombinations between feasible solutions, most notably the *Path Relinking* and *Structured Weighted Combinations* procedures in tabu search (Glover [1996]). The approach described here would be very useful when the input distribution of instances is unknown or can vary widely. It will also help in the cases where there are not many studied instances available in the literature. Also, tight upper and lower bounds on the 'competitiveness' of the recombinations (when properly defined) would lead to avoid cumbersome computational experiments and doubtful comparisons. However, we must warn the reader that we are still far from developing a complete formal theory since such an analysis currently seems only linked with the 'myopia' generated by the introduction of some sequential processes in the design of the recombination. But we must remark again that to act as an '*adversary*', as is generally the case in competitive and comparative analysis, would be beneficial to design more robust recombination operators by analyzing their comparative ratios.

We should also mention that we envision some other alternatives to formulate what constitutes a 'best' matching to induce a reindexing before recombination. In this chapter we have selected a criterion based on finding the maximum weight perfect matching. However, we would like to remark that it might be possible to use the concept of a *stable marriage* and use the *Proposal Algorithm* due to Gale & Shapley [1962] for reindexing (for a comprehensive treatment of this problem and its applications see Gusfield & Irwing [1989] and Knuth [1976], and also the analysis in Motwani & Raghavan [1995]). Instead of working with the actual value of the weights of the auxiliary graph $K_{q,q}$ we would be working with a set of preference lists indicating a partial order, a ranking among preferences. An important result to be mentioned is that it can be shown that for every choice of preference lists there is at least one stable marriage and that the Proposal Algorithm always terminates with one of them. However, it is evident that our results will not change if reindexing based on the stable marriage formulation is used.

On the usefulness of our result for the graph colouring problem itself, in Costa et al [1995] we can read: '... it is difficult, if not impossible, to find a q-colouring of a large graph G (more than 300 nodes) with q close to the chromatic number of G by applying directly a given algorithm A on the graph G.' In connection with this, other algorithms are referenced that consists in consecutively constructing colour (stable) sets of G 'which are as large as possible until we are left with at most a certain number n_{left} of vertices. The algorithm A is then invoked to colour the remaining vertices. [...] we generalize this approach by removing consecutively partial q'-colourings ($1 \leq q' \leq q$) instead of independent sets ($q'=1$) of G.' After their satisfactory results and the theoretical analysis presented in this chapter, we think the challenge of finding such an algorithm is still wide open for future research.

Addendum

After this chapter was finally completed we received a letter from Prof. Jin-Kao Hao calling our attention to two papers he had finished on graph colouring using a memetic algorithm approach (Dorne & Hao [1998], Galinier & Hao [1999]). Most remarkable was the fact that Hao and co-workers have identified the same limitations of *assignment approach* for recombination procedures on which our worst-case and comparative analysis is based. Computational experiments using DIMACS challenge benchmark instances showed the benefits of *reindexing* the colours before recombination, as we proposed in our theoretical analysis. These *partition-based* recombination procedures are reported to deliver highly effective MAs outperforming previous results with several metaheuristics.

It has been very exciting to find out that the theoretical worst-case analysis and the experimental results are not contradictory but also coherent. Indeed, it seems that theory can help at its best, being a prediction tool to avoid unnecessary research efforts. It is evident that there is hope for a better, more rational theory for the design of recombination operators for evolutionary computation. We consider it a *novel* approach, being explored here for the first time. But how *new* can a *good* idea be? We have recently found the following excerpt from R. Karp's contribution in a panel discussion which appeared in the same book that contains his seminal work on *NP*-completeness:

> The so-called adversary approach in which we think of an algorithm as a dialogue between somebody who is executing the algorithm step by step by asking questions like: 'Is this key bigger than that key or not?' and an adversary who tries to throw him off (a kind of a game theoretic approach to this worst case analysis of algorithms) is very important to keep in mind and very fruitful.

Karp [1972; p. 176]

We can do little more than humbly subscribe his point of view.

Acknowledgements

We would like to thank D. Costa, J.K. Hao, R. Dorne, P. Galinier, and E. Koutsoupias for sharing with us their preprints and results before publication. P.M. wants to thank CICPBA for supporting this work at its initial stages. He wants to acknowledge current support by FAPESP, Brazil. This work is also supported by UBA, Argentina.

Part Five

Scatter Search and Path Relinking

Co-ordinating Editor:

Fred Glover

Contributors:

Bahram Alidaee

Mohammad M. Amini

Vicente Campos

Fred Glover

Gary A. Kochenberger

Manuel Laguna

Rafael Martí

Colin R. Reeves

Takeshi Yamada

Chapter Nineteen

Scatter Search and Path Relinking

Fred Glover

19.1 INTRODUCTION

The evolutionary approach called scatter search, and its generalized form called path relinking, originated from strategies for creating composite decision rules and surrogate constraints. Recent studies demonstrate the practical advantages of these approaches for solving a diverse array of problems from both classical and real world settings.

Scatter search and path relinking contrast with other evolutionary procedures, such as genetic algorithms, by providing unifying principles for joining solutions based on generalized path constructions (in both Euclidean and neighbourhood spaces) and by using strategic designs where other approaches resort to randomization. Additional advantages are given by intensification and diversification mechanisms that exploit adaptive memory, drawing on foundations that link scatter search and path relinking to tabu search. The goal here is to clarify the connection between these developments in evolutionary methods, and to highlight key ideas and research issues that offer promise of yielding future advances.

Scatter search and path relinking have recently been investigated in a number of studies, disclosing the promise of these methods for solving difficult problems in discrete and nonlinear optimization. Recent applications of these methods (and of selected component strategies within these methods) are shown in Table 19.1.

Table 19.1: Illustrative applications of scatter search and path relinking strategies

Vehicle Routing	Rochat & Taillard [1995], Taillard [1996], Rego [1999]
Quadratic Assignment	Cung et al [1997]
Financial Product Design	Consiglio & Zenios [1997]
Neural Network Training	Kelly et al [1996]
Job Shop Scheduling	Yamada & Nakano [1996], Jain & Meeran [1998]
Flow Shop Scheduling	Yamada & Reeves [1997, and chapter twenty-two], Jain & Meeran [1998a]
Crew Scheduling	Lourenço et al [1998]
Graph Drawing	Laguna & Martí [1997]
Linear Ordering	Laguna et al [1997], Campos et al [chapter twenty-one]
Unconstrained Optimization	Fleurent et al [1996]
Bit Representation	Rana & Whitley [1997]
Multi-objective Assignment	Laguna et al [1999]
Optimizing Simulation	Glover et al [1996]
Complex Control Systems	Laguna [1997]
Mixed Integer Programming	Glover et al [1999]

Improved benchmarks for solving a variety of classical problems have resulted from these applications, along with new advances for solving a significant range of commercial problems, particularly those attended by uncertainty and complex nonlinearities.

Scatter search and path relinking derive their foundations from earlier strategies for combining decision rules and constraints, with the goal of enabling a solution procedure based on the combined elements to yield better solutions than one based only on the original elements. An examination of these origins sheds light on the character of these methods.

19.1.1 Combining Decision Rules

Historically, the antecedent strategies for combining decision rules were introduced in the context of scheduling methods to obtain improved local decision rules for job shop scheduling problems (Glover [1963]). New rules were generated by creating numerically weighted combinations of existing rules, suitably restructured so that their evaluations embodied a common metric.

The approach was motivated by the supposition that information about the relative desirability of alternative choices is captured in different forms by different rules, and that this information can be exploited more effectively when integrated by means of a combination mechanism than when treated by the standard strategy of selecting different rules one at a time, in isolation from each other. In addition, the method departed from the customary approach of stopping upon reaching a local optimum, and instead continued to vary the parameters that determined the combined rules, as a basis for producing additional trial solutions (this latter strategy also became a fundamental component of tabu search; see, e.g. Glover & Laguna [1997]).

The decision rules created from such combination strategies produced better empirical outcomes than standard applications of local decision rules, and also proved superior to a 'probabilistic learning approach' that selected different rules probabilistically at different junctures, but without the integration effect provided by generating combined rules (Crowston et al [1963]).

19.1.2 Combining Constraints

The associated procedures for combining constraints likewise employed a mechanism of generating weighted combinations, in this case applied in the setting of integer and nonlinear programming, by introducing nonnegative weights to create new constraint inequalities, called surrogate constraints (Glover [1965]). The approach isolated subsets of constraints that were gauged to be most critical, relative to trial solutions based on the surrogate constraints, and produced new weights that reflected the degree to which the component constraints were satisfied or violated.

A principal function of surrogate constraints, in common with the approaches for combining decision rules, was to provide ways to evaluate choices that could be used to generate and modify trial solutions. From this foundation, a variety of heuristic processes evolved that made use of surrogate constraints and their evaluations. Accordingly, these processes led to the complementary strategy of combining solutions, as a primal counterpart to the dual strategy of combining constraints, which became manifest in scatter search and its path relinking generalization. (The primal/dual distinction stems from the fact that surrogate constraint methods give rise to a mathematical duality theory associated with their role as relaxation methods for optimization. For example, see Greenberg & Pierskalla [1970, 1973], Glover [1965, 1975], Karwan & Rardin [1976, 1979], Freville & Plateau [1986, 1993].)

19.2 ELEMENTS OF SCATTER SEARCH AND PATH RELINKING

19.2.1 Scatter Search

The scatter search process, building on the principles that underlie the surrogate constraint design, is organized to capture information not contained separately in the original vectors, and to take advantage of auxiliary heuristic methods both for selecting the elements to be combined and for generating new vectors.[1]

The original form of scatter search (Glover [1977]) may be sketched as follows.

1. Generate a starting set of solution vectors by heuristic processes designed for the problem considered, and designate a subset of the best vectors to be reference solutions. (Subsequent iterations of this step, transferring from Step 3 below, incorporate advanced starting solutions and best solutions from previous history as candidates for the reference solutions.)

2. Create new points consisting of linear combinations of subsets of the current reference solutions. The linear combinations are chosen to produce points both inside and outside the convex regions spanned by the reference solutions, modified by generalized rounding processes to yield integer values for integer-constrained vector components.

3. Extract a collection of the best solutions generated in Step 2 to be used as starting points for a new application of the heuristic processes of Step 1. Repeat these steps until reaching a specified iteration limit.

Three particular features of scatter search deserve mention. First, the linear combinations are structured according to the goal of generating weighted centres of selected subregions, allowing for nonconvex combinations that project these centres into regions external to the original reference solutions. (The dispersion patterns created by such centres and their external projections is particularly useful for mixed integer optimization.) Second, the strategies for selecting particular subsets of solutions to combine in Step 2 are designed to make use of clustering, which allows different types of strategic variation by generating new solutions 'within clusters' and 'across clusters'. Third, the method is organized to use supporting heuristics that are able to start from infeasible solutions, and which removes the restriction that solutions selected as starting points for re-applying the heuristic processes must be feasible.

A simple two-dimensional illustration of a type of distribution of points that might be generated by scatter search is shown in Figure 19.1, by a criterion of selecting weighted centres of subregions. Here, for example, the parent solutions might consist of the three heavily shaded points or the three unshaded points, depending on whether an emphasis is given to generating points inside or outside the region spanned by the reference solutions. Generally speaking, the perspectives of these two types of emphasis are combined, although only a subset of the points produced by patterns such as depicted in Figure 19.1 are generated, and the offspring are skewed or displaced by the influence of the heuristics applied.[2] Larger number of reference points can be selected, and can be used to influence the character of the displacement.

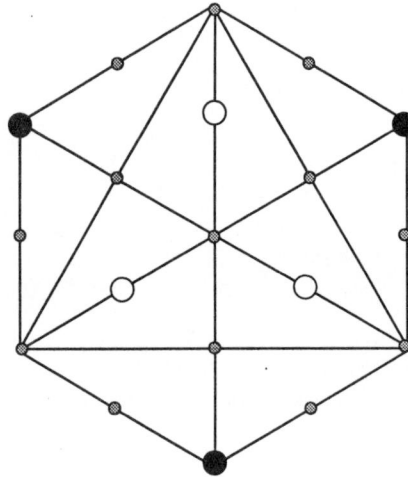

Fig. 19.1: Illustration of a scatter search problem.

In sum, scatter search is founded on the following premises.

(P1): Useful information about the form (or location) of optimal solutions is typically contained in a suitably diverse collection of elite solutions.

(P2): When solutions are combined as a strategy for exploiting such information, increased diversity and quality become possible by including combinations that extrapolate beyond the regions spanned by the reference solutions, and further by incorporating heuristic processes to map combined solutions into new points.

(P3): The opportunity to exploit information contained in the union of elite solutions is enhanced by taking account of multiple reference solutions simultaneously.

The fact that the heuristic processes of scatter search are not confined to a single uniform design, but represent a varied collection of procedures, affords extra strategic possibilities.

19.2.1 Scatter Search and Parametric Search

The approach described in section 19.1.1 for creating combined decision rules, which restructures component rules for compatibility and then joins them by weighted combinations, can be viewed not only as a precursor to scatter search, but also as a model for wider applications of the method. In particular, scatter search strategies can be applied to a variety of problems by the use of approaches that parameterize rules or problem data, and which then generate solutions based on strategic manipulation of the parameters.

A strategy of this type has proved effective in a workforce planning application by Glover & McMillan [1986], where useful gains in solution quality are obtained by replacing the original objective function by one containing a smoothing criterion, whose role is gradually diminished until the original objective dominates. The notion of parametrically modifying an objective function to create a smoothing effect has more recently been examined in the travelling salesman setting by Gu & Huang [1994], Schneider et al [1997], and Coy et al [1998]. These types of approaches can be extended by the use of strategic oscillation, as described later, which periodically phases in and phases out the modified objective.

The application of scatter search with smoothed objectives, and likewise with smoothed constraints, can be formalized by means of the class of approaches called ghost image (GI) processes (Glover [1994a]). In the form applicable to our present discussion, the GI approach modifies constraint coefficients, objective function coefficients and/or bounds, to generate a model that initially has an idealized structure which is easy to solve. For example, in covering or matching problems, constraint coefficients can be modified so that they all initially equal 1. In graph partitioning problems, weighted clique problems and travelling salesman problems, the weights (or costs) of edges can be modified so that all initially take the same value, accompanied by adding edges where necessary (penalized in the 'true' formulation) so that the graph has an easily identified optimal or near optimal solution. As illustrated in Glover [1994a], these types of starting points can be progressively transformed in a variety of ways to gradually recover the true problem structure, while generating trial solutions for the original problem based on associated solutions to the transformed problems.

Figure 19.2 depicts how selected types of problem data can be progressively transformed from an initial idealized state where subsets of coefficients are made uniform ('smoothed' on chosen dimensions) and gradually made to recover their original unmodified form.

The moving threshold in Figure 19.2 consists of a single value such that all associated data values (costs, resource availabilities, etc.) that lie on a specified side of the threshold are treated 'as if' they are the same as the threshold. For example, the moving threshold can begin at the maximum of the data values, with the stipulation that all values smaller than the threshold are treated as equal to the threshold, while all values larger than the threshold are not affected. Therefore, to begin, all values equal the maximum data value. Subsequently, on successive steps the threshold is dropped and an increasing number of data values receive their true values, until finally all do so. The same approach can be applied in reverse, by starting the threshold at the minimum data value and treating all values larger than the threshold as equal to the threshold.

Such a procedure may be applied in conjunction with rules that initially either 'spread out' or 'contract' the data values, again adopting the ghost image approach to gradually recover the true representation. For example, a special set covering problem described in Glover [1977] proves to be more readily solvable by spreading out the original cost data, in this case by squaring its values. Raising data (and weighted sums of data) to powers and fractional powers has also proved effective in creating data normalizations for surrogate constraint methods in optimization (Løkketangen & Glover [1997]). Similarly, Coy et al [1998a] have shown that the ideas of spreading out and contracting data are useful in smoothing methods for the well-known travelling salesman problem.

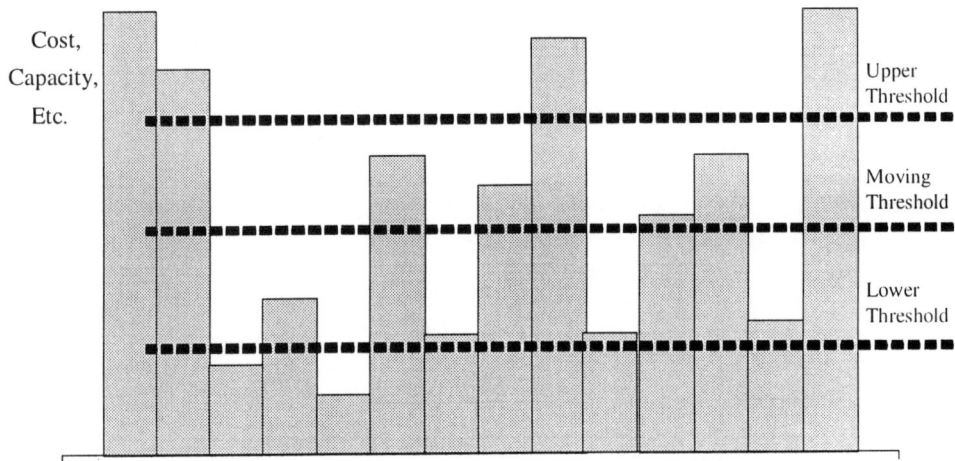

Fig. 19.2: All costs (or capacities, resource levels, etc.) above – or alternatively below – the Moving Threshold are treated as if equal to the threshold value.

The thresholding approach can be applied more generally by reference to paired upper and lower thresholds, as also depicted in Figure 19.2. In this case, data values above the upper threshold are treated as equal to the upper threshold and those below the lower threshold are treated as equal to the lower threshold, while all other values are unaffected. The paired threshold approach allows the two thresholds to begin equal (in the 'mid-range', or in the lower or upper quartile of values, for example) and then to be gradually separated. This approach includes the single moving threshold approach as a special case. To refine the process, modifications of the data which are based on recency and frequency memory provide us with a set of strategies that are able to generate changes with additional selectivity.

Within this framework, scatter search can then be applied to the different sets of changed data exactly as it would be applied to the solutions created on the basis of this data. Thus, by such a design, the data sets that have led to the best solutions become the reference points for generation of new solutions: selected collections of these points are joined by linear combinations to generate new data sets, which in turn are processed by the associated heuristics to generate new trial solutions.

19.3 PATH RELINKING

Features that have been added to scatter search, by extension of its basic philosophy, are captured in the path relinking framework. From a spatial orientation, the process of generating linear combinations of a set of reference solutions may be characterized as generating paths between and beyond these solutions, where solutions on such paths also serve as sources for generating additional paths. This leads to a broader conception of the notion of creating combinations of solutions. By natural extension, these may be conceived to arise by generating paths between and beyond selected solutions in neighbourhood space, rather than in Euclidean space (Glover [1994], Glover & Laguna [1995]).

This conception is reinforced by the fact that a path between solutions in a neighbourhood space will generally yield new solutions that share a significant subset of attributes contained in the parent solutions, in varying 'mixes' according to the path selected and the location on the path that determines the solution currently considered. The character of such paths is easily specified by reference to solution attributes that are added, dropped or otherwise modified by the moves executed in neighbourhood space. Examples of such attributes include edges and nodes of a graph, sequence positions in a schedule, vectors contained in linear programming basic solutions, and values of variables and functions of variables.

To generate the desired paths, it is only necessary to select moves that perform the following role: upon starting from an initiating solution, the moves must progressively introduce attributes contributed by a guiding solution (or reduce the distance between attributes of the initiating and guiding solutions). The roles of the initiating and guiding solutions are interchangeable; each solution can also be induced to move simultaneously toward the other as a way of generating combinations.

The incorporation of attributes from elite parents in partially or fully constructed solutions was foreshadowed by another aspect of scatter search, embodied in an accompanying proposal to assign preferred values to subsets of consistent and strongly determined variables. The theme is to isolate assignments that frequently or influentially occur in high quality solutions, and then to introduce compatible subsets of these assignments into other solutions that are generated or amended by heuristic procedures. (Such a process implicitly relies on a form of frequency based memory to identify and exploit variables that qualify as consistent.)

Multiparent path generation possibilities emerge in path relinking by considering the combined attributes provided by a set of guiding solutions, where these attributes are weighted to determine which moves are given higher priority. The generation of such paths in neighbourrhood space characteristically 'relinks' previous points in ways not achieved in the previous search history, hence giving the approach its name.

19.3.1 Initial Steps

First consider the creation of paths that join two selected solutions x' and x'', restricting attention to the part of the path that lies 'between' the solutions, producing a solution sequence $x = x(1), x(2), \ldots, x(r)$. To reduce the number of options to be considered, the solution $x(i + 1)$ may be created from $x(i)$ at each step by choosing a move that leaves a reduced number of moves remaining to reach x (or more aggressively, a 'fewest' number of moves). This policy, even if applied without exception, can permit a significant number of alternative choices for generating the next solution at each step. Consequently, additional criteria are relevant to creating the path, as indicated shortly.

It is possible, as in applying scatter search, that x' and x'' were previously joined by a search trajectory produced by a heuristic method (or by a metaheuristic such as tabu search). In this event, the new trajectory created by path relinking is likely to be somewhat different than the one initially established, representing a 'more direct route' between the solutions. An illustration of this is given in Figure 19.3. It may also be the case that x' and x'' were not previously joined by a search path at all, but were instead generated on different search paths. These different paths may have been produced either by a heuristic or by a previous relinking process. Such a situation is depicted in Figure 19.4.

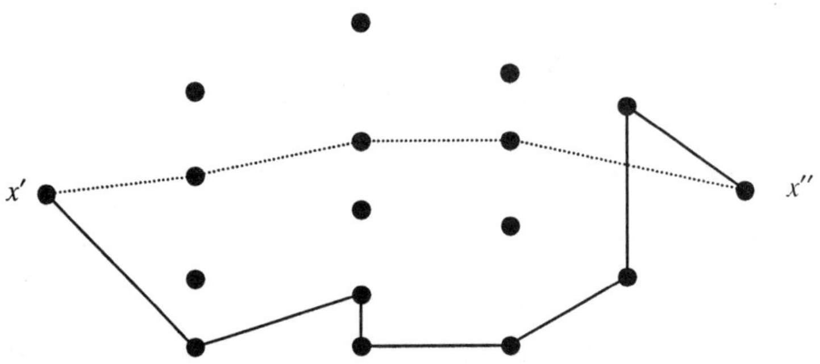

Fig. 19.3: Path relinking. Original path shown by heavy line; relinked path (one possibility) shown by dotted line.

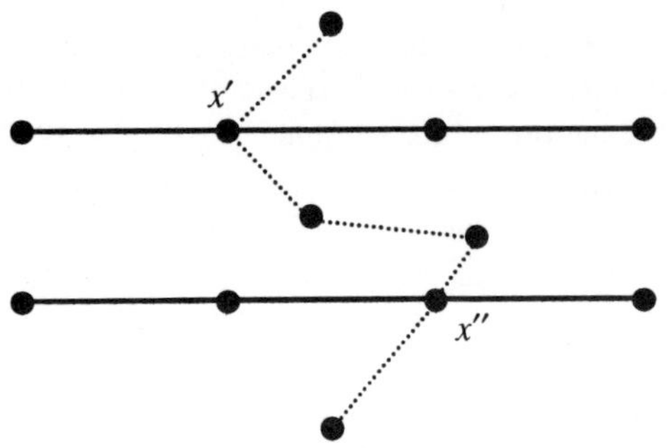

Fig. 19.4: Path relinking: Previously generated paths shown by heavy lines; relinked path shown by dotted line. (Multiple additional points in the space are not shown.)

In this case, the path between x' and x'' performs a relinking function by changing the connections that generated x' and x'' originally. The relinking path of this diagram is shown as extending beyond the points x' and x''. We discuss this type of construction subsequently under the heading of *extrapolated relinking*.

To choose among the different paths that may be possible in going from x' and x'', let $c(x)$ denote an objective function which is to be minimized. Selecting unattractive moves relative to $c(x)$, from the moves that are candidates to generate the path at each step, will tend to produce a final series of strongly improving moves to complete the path. Correspondingly, selecting attractive moves at each step will tend to produce lower quality moves at the end. (The last move, however, will be improving, or leave $c(x)$ unchanged, if x'' is selected to be a local optimum.) Thus, choosing best, worst or average moves, provides options that produce contrasting effects in generating the indicated sequence. An aspiration criterion may be used as in tabu search to override choices in the last two cases if a sufficiently attractive solution is available. (In general, it appears reasonable to select best moves at each step, and then to allow the option of reinitiating the process in the opposite direction by interchanging x' and x''.)

The choice of one or more solutions $x(i)$ to become reference points for launching a new search phase will preferably be made to depend not only on $c(x(i))$ but also on the values $c(x)$ of those solutions x that can be reached by a move from $x(i)$.

The process can additionally be varied to allow solutions to be evaluated other than those that yield $x(i + 1)$ closer to x''. Aspiration criteria again are relevant for deciding whether such solutions qualify as candidates for selection.

To elaborate the process, let $x^*(i)$ denote a neighbour of $x(i)$ that yields a minimum $c(x)$ value during an evaluation step, excluding $x^*(i) = x(i+1)$. If the choice rules do not automatically eliminate the possibility $x^*(i)=x(h)$ for $h<i$, then a simple tabu restriction can be used to do this (for example, see Glover & Laguna [1997]). Then the method selects a solution $x^*(i)$ that yields a minimum value for $c(x^*(i))$ as a new point to launch the search. If only a limited set of neighbours of $x(i)$ are examined to identify $x^*(i)$, then a superior least cost solution $x(i)$, excluding x' and x'', may be selected instead. Early termination becomes possible (though is not compulsory) upon encountering an $x^*(i)$ that yields $c(x^*(i))<\min\{c(x'),c(x''),c(x(p))\}$, where $x(p)$ is the minimum cost $x(h)$ for all $h<i$. The procedure will continue if $x(i)$, in contrast to $x^*(i)$, yields a smaller $c(x)$ value than x' and x'', since $x(i)$ effectively adopts the role of x''.

19.3.2 Variation and Tunnelling

A variant of the path relinking approach starts with both endpoints x' and x'' simultaneously producing two sequences $x' = x'(1),\ldots, x'(r)$ and $x''= x''(1), \ldots, x''(s)$. The choices in this case are designed to yield $x'(r)=x''(s)$, for final values of r and s. To progress toward this outcome, either $x'(r)$ is selected to create $x'(r+1)$ by the criterion of minimizing (reducing) the number of moves remaining to reach $x''(s)$, or $x''(s)$ is chosen to create $x''(s+1)$ by the criterion of minimizing (reducing) the number of moves remaining to reach $x'(r)$. From these options, the move is selected that produces the smallest $c(x)$ value, thus also determining which of r or s is incremented on the next step. Useful variation is also produced by basing the relinking process on more than one neighbourhood.

The path relinking approach benefits by a tunnelling strategy that often encourages a different neighbourhood structure to be used than in the standard search phase. For example, moves for path relinking may be periodically allowed that normally would be excluded due to creating infeasibility. Such a practice is protected against the possibility of becoming 'lost' in an infeasible region, since feasibility evidently must be recovered by the time x'' is reached. The tunnelling effect therefore offers a chance to reach solutions that might otherwise be bypassed. In the variant that starts from both x' and x'', at least one of $x'(r)$ and $x''(s)$ may be kept feasible. An example of tunnelling is shown in Figure 19.5.

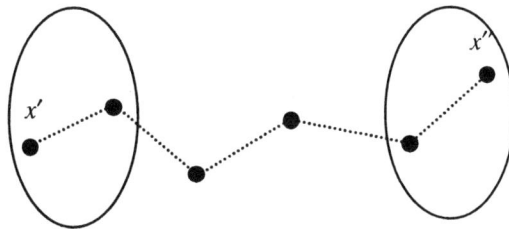

Fig. 19.5: Feasible region consists of disconnected components. The path 'tunnels through' the infeasible region to regain feasibility.

As in the case of the strategies used in tabu search for achieving intensification and diversification, it is appropriate here to select the points x' and x'' by reference to clusters of solutions that are created according to criteria of similarity or affinity. Choosing x' and x'' from the same cluster then stimulates intensification, while choosing them from two 'widely separated' clusters stimulates diversification. Alternately, parents can be chosen by 'anti-clustering'. In 'anti-clustering', each parent is selected so as to be as distant as possible from those solutions previously chosen within the same 'family' of parents. A separation criterion such as maximizing the minimum distance to previous points can be used, for example.

19.3.3 Extrapolated Relinking

The path relinking approach goes beyond consideration of points 'between' x' and x'' in the same way that linear combinations extend beyond points that are expressed as convex combinations of two endpoints. In seeking a path that continues beyond x'' (starting from the point x') we invoke a tabu search concept, referring to sets of attributes associated with the solutions generated, as a basis for choosing a move that 'approximately' leaves the fewest moves remaining to reach x''. Let $A(x)$ denote the set of solution attributes associated with ('contained in') x, and let A_{drop} denote the set of solution attributes that are dropped by moves performed to reach the current solution $x'(i)$, starting from x'. (Such attributes may be components of the x vectors themselves, or may be related to these components by appropriately defined mappings.)

Define a *to-attribute* of a move to be an attribute of the solution which was produced by the move, but not an attribute of the solution that initiated the move. Similarly, define a *from-attribute* to be an attribute of the initiating solution, but not an attribute of the new solution produced. Then we seek a move at each step to maximize the number of *to-attributes* belonging to $A(x'')-A(x(i))$, and subject to this to minimize the number that belong to $A_{drop}-A(x'')$. Such a rule generally can be implemented very efficiently by appropriate data structures.

Once the 'endpoint' $x(r)=x''$ has been reached, the process continues by using a modification of the choice rule as follows. The criterion now selects a move to maximize the number of its *to-attributes* not in A_{drop} minus the number of its *to-attributes* that are in A_{drop}, and subject to this to minimize the number of its *from-attributes* that belong to $A(x'')$. The combination of these criteria establishes an effect analogous to that achieved by the standard algebraic formula for extending a line segment beyond an endpoint. (The secondary minimization criterion is probably less important in this determination.) The path then stops whenever no choice remains that permits the maximization criterion to be positive. The maximization goals of these two criteria are of course approximate, and can be relaxed.

In cases in which we have neighbourhoods that allow relatively unrestricted choices of moves, this extrapolated relinking approach yields a path extending beyond x'' that introduces new attributes, without reincorporating any old attributes, until there is no move remaining that satisfies this condition. The ability to go beyond the previously limiting points x' and x'' creates a form of diversification analogous to that provided by the original scatter search approach. At the same time the exterior points are influenced by the trajectory that links x' and x''.

19.3.4 Multiple Parents

New points can be generated from multiple parents as follows. Instead of moving from a point x' to (or through) a second point x'', we replace x' by a collection of solutions X'. Upon generating a point $x(i)$, the options for determining a next point $x(i+1)$ are given by the union of the solutions in X', or more precisely, by the union A' of the attribute sets $A(x)$, for $x \in X'$. A' takes the role of $A(x)$ in the attribute-based approach previously described, with the added stipulation that each attribute is counted (weighted) in accordance with the number of times it appears in elements $A(x)$ of the collection. Still more generally, we may assign a weight to $A(x)$, which thus translates into a sum of weights over A'' applicable to each attribute, creating an effect analogous to that of creating a weighted linear combination in Euclidean space. Parallel processing can be applied to operate on an entire collection of points $x' \in X'$ relative to a second collection $x'' \in X''$ by this approach. Further considerations that build on these ideas, and that go beyond the scope of our present development, are detailed in Glover [1994b].

This multiparent path relinking approach generates new elements by a process that emulates the strategies of the original scatter search approach at a higher level of generalization. The reference to neighbourhood spaces makes it possible to preserve desirable solution properties (such as complex feasibility conditions in scheduling and routing), without requiring artificial mechanisms to recover these properties in situations where they may otherwise become lost.

Promising regions may be searched more thoroughly in path relinking by modifying the weights attached to attributes of guiding solutions, and by altering the bias associated with solution quality and selected solution features. Figure 19.6 depicts the type of variation that can result, where X represents an initiating solution and the points A, B, and C represent guiding solutions. For appropriate choices of reference points (and neighbourhoods for generating paths from them), principles such as those discussed in Glover & Laguna [1997] suggest that additional elite points are likely to be found in the regions traversed by the paths, upon launching new searches from high quality points on these paths.

19.3.5 Constructive Neighbourhoods and Vocabulary Building

A natural variation of path relinking occurs by using constructive neighbourhoods for creating offspring from a collection of parent solutions. In this case the guiding solutions consist of subsets of elite solutions, as before, but the initiating solution begins as a partial (incomplete) solution or even as a null solution, where some of the components of the solutions, such as values for variables, are not yet assigned. The use of a constructive neighbourhood permits such an initiating solution to 'move toward' the guiding solutions, by a neighbourhood path that progressively introduces elements of the guiding solutions, or that are evaluated as attractive based on the composition of the guiding solutions.

The evaluations can be conceived as produced by a process where the guiding solutions vote for attributes to be included in the initiating solution. It is possible, for example, that a certain partial configuration may be reached where none of the attributes of the guiding solutions can be incorporated within the existing solution, relative to a given constructive neighbourhood. Then it is important to still be able to select a next constructive step, by relying upon the voting process for evaluating moves. This same consideration can arise in transition neighbourhoods, though it is encountered less frequently there.

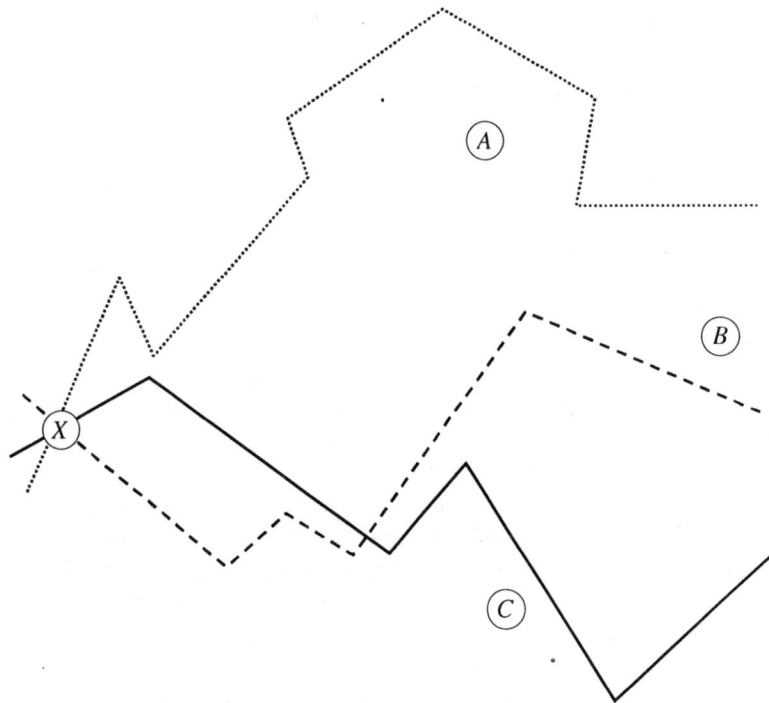

Fig. 19.6: Neighbourhood space paths with different attribute trade-offs. The solution X has been selected to generate a relinked path (A, B and C may also interchange roles with X alternately or simultaneously).

Combinations created in this way are called structured combinations, and their generation rests upon three properties.

Property 1 (representation property). Each guiding solution represents a vector of votes for particular decisions (e.g. the decision of assigning a specific value to a particular variable).

Property 2 (trial solution property). The votes prescribed by a guiding solution translate into a trial solution to the problem of interest by a well-defined process (determined by the neighbourhood structure).

Property 3 (update property). If a decision is made according to the votes of a given vector, a clearly defined rule exists to update all voting vectors for the residual problem so that Properties 1 and 2 continue to hold.

Features of these properties in particular contexts may be clarified as follows.

Elaboration of Property 1: Standard solution vectors for many problems can directly operate as voting vectors, or can be expanded in a natural way to create such vectors.

For instance, a solution vector for a job shop scheduling problem can be interpreted as a set of 0–1 votes for predecessor decisions in scheduling specific jobs on particular machines.

Elaboration of Property 2: A set of 'yes-no' votes for items to include in a knapsack, for instance, can be translated into a trial solution according to a designated sequence for processing the votes (such as determined by benefit-to-weight ratios), until either the knapsack is full or all votes are considered. More general numerical votes for the same problem may additionally prescribe the sequence to be employed, as where knapsack items are rearranged so the votes occur in descending order. (The voting vectors are not required to represent feasible solutions to the problems considered, or even represent solutions in a customary sense at all. Thus, for example, the scheme can also operate to combine decision rules as in the approach for doing this described in section 19.1.1.)

Elaboration of Property 3: Upon assigning a specific value to a particular variable, all votes for assigning different values to this variable effectively become cancelled. Property 3 then implies that the remaining updated votes of each vector retain the ability to be translated into a trial solution for the residual problem in which the assignment has been made.

Concrete illustrations of processes for generating structured combinations by reference to these properties are provided in Glover [1994b]. These same kinds of processes can be implemented by reference to destructive neighbourhoods – that is, neighbourhoods that allow the removal of less attractive elements. Typically, destructive processes are applied to solutions that begin with an 'excessive assignment' (such as too many elements to satisfy cardinality or capacity restrictions).

19.3.6 Vocabulary Building

The vocabulary building process creates structured combinations not only by using the primitive elements of customary neighbourhoods, but also building and joining more complex assemblies of such elements. The process receives its name by analogy with the process of building words progressively into useful phrases, sentences and paragraphs, where valuable constructions at each level can be visualized as represented by 'higher order words', just as natural languages generate new words to take the place of collections of words that embody useful concepts.

The motive underlying vocabulary building is to take advantage of those contexts where certain partial configurations of solutions often occur as components of good complete solutions. A strategy of seeking 'good partial configurations' – good vocabulary elements – can help to circumvent the combinatorial explosion that potentially results by manipulating only the most primitive elements by themselves. The process also avoids the need to reinvent (or rediscover) the structure of a partial configuration as a basis for building a good complete solution. (The same principle operates in mathematical analysis generally, where basic premises are organized to produce useful lemmas, which in turn facilitate the generation of more complex theorems.)

Vocabulary building has an additional useful feature in some problem settings by providing compound elements linked by special neighbourhoods that are more exploitable than the neighbourhoods which operate on the primitive elements. For example, a vocabulary building proposal of Glover [1992] discloses that certain subassemblies (partial 'tours') for travelling salesman problems can be linked by exact algorithms to produce optimal unions of these components. Variants of this strategy have more recently been introduced by Aggarwal et al [1997] as a proposal for modifying traditional genetic algorithms, and have also been applied to weighted clique problems by Balas & Niehaus [1998]. A particularly interesting application occurs in the work of Lourenço et al [1998], who use such concepts to create 'perfect children' for crew scheduling problems.

In general, vocabulary building relies on destructive as well as constructive processes to generate desirable partial solutions, as in the early proposals for exploiting strongly determined and consistent variables – which essentially 'break apart' good solutions to extract good component assignments, and then subject these assignments to heuristics to rebuild them into complete solutions. The construction and destruction processes therefore operate hand in hand in these approaches. An illustration of this vocabulary building process is depicted in Figure 19.7.

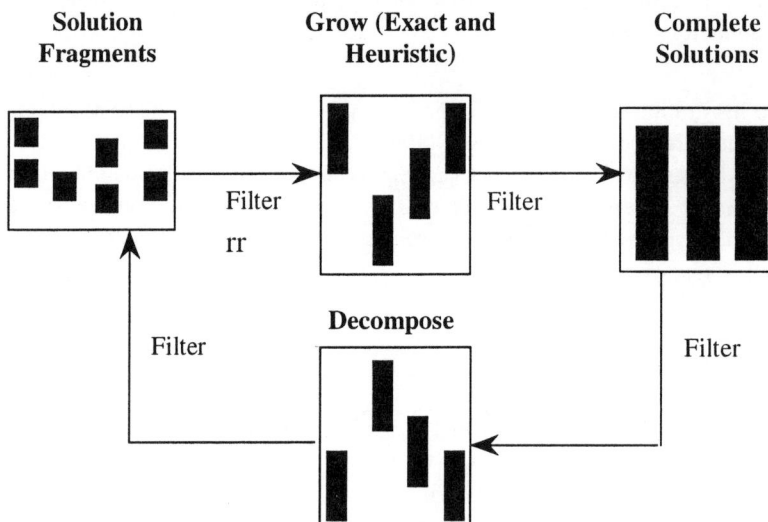

Fig. 19.7: The vocabulary building process.

19.4 IMPLICATIONS FOR FUTURE DEVELOPMENTS

The focus and emphasis of the scatter search and path relinking approaches several specific implications for the goal of designing improved optimization procedures. To understand these implications, it is useful to consider certain contrasts between the highly exploitable meaning of 'solution combination' provided by path relinking and the rather amorphous concept of 'crossover' used in genetic algorithms. Originally, GAs were founded on precise notions of crossover, using definitions based on binary stings and motivated by analogies with genetics. Although many GA researchers favour the types of crossover models originally proposed – since these give rise to the theorems that have helped to popularize GAs – many others have largely abandoned these ideas and have sought, on a case-by-case basis, to replace them with something different. The well-defined earlier notions of crossover have not been abandoned without a price. The literature is rife with examples where a new problem (or a new variant of an old one) has compelled the search for an appropriate 'crossover' to begin anew.[3]

Due to this lack of an organizing principle, many less-than-suitable modes of combination have been produced, some eventually replacing others, without a clear basis for taking advantage of context – in contrast to the strong context-exploiting emphasis embodied in the concept of search neighbourhoods. The difficulty of devising a unifying basis for understanding or exploiting context in GAs was inherited from its original theme, which had the goal of making GAs context free.

A few of the more conspicuous features of 'genetic crossover' and path relinking that embody such contrasts appear in Table 19.2.

Table 19.2: Constrast between genetic crossover and path relinking.

'Genetic Crossover' Features	Contrasting Path Relinking Features
Contains no integrated framework	Embodies a unifying 'path combination' principle
Each new 'crossover' is separate, with no guidance for the next	Each implementation of path relinking derives from a common foundation
No basis exists to systematically exploit context	Context inheres in neighbourhood structures and is directly exploitable by them
Advances are piecemeal, without clear sources of potential for transfer	Advances in neighbourhood search foster advances in path relinking (and reciprocally)
There is no design plan that is subject to analysis or improvement	A cohesive framework exists for developing progressively improved methods

The differences identified in Table 19.2 have important consequences for research to yield improved methods. Specific research areas for developing improved solution strategies that emerge directly from the path relinking orientation are listed in Table 19.3.

These research opportunities carry with them an emphasis on producing systematic and strategically designed rules, rather than following the policy of relegating decisions to random choices, as often is fashionable in evolutionary methods. The strategic orientation underlying path relinking is motivated by connections with the tabu search setting where these ideas first were proposed, and invites the use of adaptive memory structures in determining the strategies produced. The learning approach called target analysis (Glover & Laguna [1997]) gives a particularly useful basis for pursuing such research.

Table 19.3: Research areas providing opportunities for improved methods

Connections and complementarities between neighbourhoods for search methods and neighbourhoods for path relinking
Rules for generating paths to different depths and thresholds of quality
Strategies for generating multiple paths between and beyond reference solutions (with parallel processing applications)
Path interpolations and extrapolations that are effective for intensification and diversification goals
Strategies for clustering and anti-clustering, to generate candidate sets of solutions to be combined
Rules for multi-parent compositions
Isolating and assembling solution components by means of constructive linking and vocabulary building

19.5 INTENSIFICATION AND DIVERSIFICATION

A significant feature that distinguishes scatter search and path relinking from other evolutionary approaches is that intensification and diversification are not conceived to be embedded solely within the mechanisms for combining solutions, or within supplementary 'mutation' strategies based on randomly varying offspring to produce new solutions.[4]

Evidently, except where hybrids are being created with tabu search, alternative evolutionary computation approaches do not undertake to control search paths by adaptive memory strategies such as those based on measures of recency, frequency and influence.

The initial connections between scatter search and strategies involving these types of measures have already been noted in reference to exploiting consistent and strongly determined variables. Such strategies naturally fall in the category of intensification strategies, in the sense that they undertake to take advantage of features associated with good solutions. They are predicated on highly explicit analysis of the frequencies that attributes belong to high quality solutions, supplemented by considerations such as clustering the solutions to give increased meaning to the frequencies. This stands in notable contrast to the philosophy of other mainstream evolutionary procedures, where the relevance of attribute membership in solutions is left to be 'discovered' chiefly by the device of shuffling and combining solutions.

An approach called strategic oscillation introduced with the original scatter search proposal is important for linking intensification and diversification. The basic idea of this approach is to identify critical regions of search, and to induce the search pattern to visit these regions to various depths within their boundaries, by a variable pattern that approaches and retreats from the boundaries in oscillating waves. Examples of such regions and their associated boundaries are indicated in Table 19.4.

A number of variations of the regions and associated boundaries are evident, such as replacing the feasible/infeasible dichotomy by a focus on selected critical constraints to define varying domains of 'partial infeasibility'. In each case, the strategic oscillation approach operates by moving through one region to approach the boundary, and then either crosses the boundary or reverses direction to move back into the region just traversed (in the case of a 'one-sided' oscillation).

Table 19.4: Applications of strategic oscillation.

Regions	Boundary
Feasible and infeasible	Determined by constraints
Partial (sometimes 'Excessive') constructions	Complete construction (tree, clique, tour, etc.)
Underfilled or overfilled schedules	Satisfactorily filled schedules
Local optima and suboptima	Solutions with no immediate improvement
Elite solution clusters (or partitioned spaces)	Zones between clusters (or between partitions)
Alternative neighbourhoods	Transitions among move types

Often there are advantages to crossing boundaries to descend for varying depths within different regions and then doubling back to return again to the boundary. For example, in a number of discrete optimization problems the solutions that are most readily accessible from the feasible and infeasible regions differ – and, quite significantly the types of moves and choice criteria for traversing feasible and infeasible regions also differ. The ability to exploit these differences by rules that are specific to the regions traversed and the direction of movement within these regions (e.g. toward or away from their boundaries) provides an enriched set of options for carrying out the search. Similar characteristics are found in processes that build solutions by constructive processes and then dismantle them by destructive processes. In many settings, classical heuristics have been restricted to using only constructive processes for generating solutions, and in these cases strategic oscillation entails the creation of additional destructive moves in order to complement the constructive moves.

From the perspective of intensification and diversification, greater diversification is normally achieved by penetrating to greater depths beyond regional boundaries, while greater intensification is normally achieved by spending more time in the vicinity of such boundaries. However, the spatial image of remaining close to a boundary is misleading, because oscillations of small depths can create significant changes. For example, even when only few destructive moves are made to reverse a constructive process, the portions of the construction dismantled can significantly influence the solution structure and composition, which can become magnified after a few oscillation cycles. The guidance of memory as used in tabu search allows the oscillations to avoid becoming mired in local optima or in a process that unproductively wastes time in examining similar points in a common locale.

An extreme application of strategic oscillation in the context of a constructive approach is to employ destructive steps to completely dismantle the solution built by the constructive phase, which thus simply reduces the approach to a 'restart' procedure. However, the use of memory to guide the successively restarted constructions produces significantly different outcomes than those produced by customary restarting procedures based on randomization. These outcomes also contrast sharply with those produced by 'randomized greedy' construction schemes. The comparative advantages of memory-based strategies for rebuilding solutions are documented in a number of research papers including, for example, Fleurent & Glover [1999].

Intensification is often associated with shallow oscillations because in many settings the best solutions are found on or near the boundary. This is clearly true for multidimensional knapsack and covering problems, for instance, and it is also true by definition where the boundary is established to segregate local optima from suboptimal solutions. In such cases the oscillation process is augmented by spending additional time in the proximity of the boundary, as by shifting from a simple neighbourhood to a more complex neighbourhood. For instance, simple 'add/drop' or 'increment/decrement' moves may be augmented by a series of 'exchange' or 'paired increment/decrement' moves upon reaching (or drawing close to) the boundary. Candidate list strategies are important when complex neighbourhoods are used, in order to achieve proper tradeoffs between time spent looking for moves and the quality of the moves found (principal approaches of this type are described in Glover & Laguna [1997]).

19.5.1 Randomization and the Intensification/Diversification Dichotomy

The emphasis on systematic strategies in achieving intensification and diversification does not preclude the use of randomized selection schemes, which are often motivated by the fact that they require little thought or sophistication to apply. By the same token, deterministic rules that are constructed with no more reflection than devoted to creating a simple randomized rule can be quite risky, because they can easily embody oversights that will cause them to perform poorly. A randomized rule can then offer a safety net, by preventing a bad decision from being applied persistently and without exception.

Yet a somewhat different perspective suggests that deterministic rules can offer important advantages in the longer run. A 'foolish mistake' incorporated into a deterministic rule becomes highly visible by its consequences, whereas such a mistake in a randomized rule may be buried from view – obscured by the patternless fluctuations that surround it. Deterministic rules afford the opportunity to profit by mistakes and learn to do better. The character of randomized rules, that provides the chance to escape from repetitive folly, also inhibits the chance to identify more effective decisions.

The concepts of intensification and diversification are predicated on the view that intelligent variation and randomized variation are rarely the same.[5] This clearly contrasts with the prevailing perspective in the literature of evolutionary methods although, perhaps surprisingly, the intensification and diversification terminology has been appearing with steadily increasing frequency in this literature. Nevertheless, a number of the fundamental strategies for achieving the goals of intensification and diversification in scatter search and path relinking applications have still escaped the purview of other evolutionary methods.

Perhaps one of the factors that is slowing a more complete assimilation of these ideas is a confusion between the terminology of intensification and diversification and the terminology of 'exploitation versus exploration' popularized in association with genetic algorithms. The exploitation/exploration distinction comes from control theory, where exploitation refers to following a particular recipe (traditionally memoryless) until it fails to be effective, and exploration then refers to instituting a series of random changes – typically via multi-armed bandit schemes – before reverting to the tactical recipe. The issue of exploitation versus exploration concerns how often and under what circumstances the randomized departures are launched.

By contrast, intensification and diversification are mutually reinforcing (rather than being mutually opposed), and can be implemented in conjunction as well as in alternation. In longer term strategies, intensification and diversification are both activated when simpler tactics lose their effectiveness. Characteristically, they are designed to profit from memory, rather than to rely solely on indirect 'inheritance effects'.

19.6. CONCLUSION

It is not possible within the limited scope of this chapter to detail completely the aspects of scatter search and its path relinking generalization that warrant further investigation. Additional implementation considerations, including associated intensification and diversification processes, and the design of accompanying methods to improve solutions produced by combination strategies, may be found in the template for scatter search and path relinking in Glover [1998].

However, a key observation deserves to be stressed. The literature often contrasts evolutionary methods – especially those based on combining solutions – with local search methods, as though these two types of approaches are fundamentally different. In addition, evolutionary procedures are conceived to be independent of any reliance on memory, except in the very limited sense where solutions forged from combinations of others carry the imprint of their parents. Yet as previously noted, the foundations of scatter search strongly overlap with those of tabu search and, in addition, path relinking was initiated as a strategy to be applied with the guidance of adaptive memory processes. By means of these connections, a wide range of strategic possibilities exist for implementing scatter search and path relinking.

Very little computational investigation of these methods has been done by comparison to other evolutionary methods, and a great deal remains to be learned about the most effective implementations for various classes of problems. The highly promising outcomes of studies such as those cited in section 19.1 suggest that these approaches may offer a useful potential for applications in areas beyond those investigated up to now.

Acknowledgements

This research was supported in part by the Air Force Office of Scientific Research Grant #F49620-97-1-0271.

NOTES

1. One group of researchers has argued that the coupling of heuristic improvement with solution combination strategies should be given an entirely new name, and accordingly has inaugurated the term *memetic algorithms* to designate such a coupling (see, e.g., Moscato [1989], Radcliffe & Surry [1994]).
2. In some contexts, high quality solutions are found more often near the boundaries of a feasible region than deep in the interior of the region. For problems that technically have no interior due to the presence of equality constraints, the indicated phenomenon

nevertheless can occur relative to a subset of constraints that are inequalities, or relative to a space created by identifying and removing variables that may take the role of slack variables for certain equalities, thus transforming them into inequalities. Then linear combinations may reasonably be biased to generate points that lie within a chosen proximity to the feasible boundary.

3. The disadvantage of lacking a clear and unified model for combining solutions has had its compensations for academic researchers, since each new application creates an opportunity to publish another form of crossover! The resulting abundance of papers has done nothing to tarnish the image of a dynamic and prospering field.

4. Within the last few years, some researchers in the evolutionary computation field have begun to adopt aspects of scatter search and path relinking by incorporating systematic strategies for achieving intensification and diversification, instead of relying on randomization to achieve less purposeful forms of variation. However, some of the latest literature still disallows this type of approach as a legitimate feature of evolutionary computation. For example, Fogel [1998a] says that the main disciplines of evolutionary computation all involve a process whereby "New solutions are created by randomly varying the existing solutions".

5. Intelligence can sometimes mean quickly doing something mildly clever, rather than slowly doing something profound. This can occur where the quality of a single move obtained by extended analysis is not enough to match the quality of multiple moves obtained by more superficial analysis. Randomized moves, which are quick, sometimes gain a reputation for effectiveness because of this phenomenon. In such setting, a different perspective may result by investigating comparably fast mechanisms that replace randomization with intelligent variation.

Chapter Twenty

A Scatter Search Approach to Unconstrained Quadratic Binary Programs

Mohammad M. Amini, Bahram Alidaee, and Gary A. Kochenberger

20.1 INTRODUCTION

Scatter Search is an evolutionary method whose origins go back to the 1970s when it was first proposed to combine solutions, via linear combinations and generalized rounding, from an evolving population of candidate solutions in the pursuit of further attractive solutions. In recent years, various applications of scatter search have proven to be successful in a wide variety of combinatorial (and other) optimization problems. In this chapter, we introduce an implementation of scatter search designed to solve unconstrained quadratic binary programs, and provide an extensive computational study that discloses the effectiveness of the method. The study consisted of the largest and most comprehensive testbed of problems examined to date. Our approach obtained solutions whose quality matched or exceeded that previously obtained for every problem tested. The method proved especially effective for larger problems, where we obtained new best solutions for 12 problems out of a total of 114 in the set. We also examined problems larger than those examined in previous studies.

Scatter search, formally introduced by Glover [1977], is a population based approach to solving combinatorial (and other) optimization problems that evolves to new solutions by taking weighted combinations of trial solutions from a reference set of current solutions, together with applying strategic rounding processes to discrete variables. The search for improved solutions is aided by the use of heuristic improvement routines applied to the new solutions before the reference set is updated and further weighted combinations are explored. The evolution of the reference set of solutions is influenced by the search history via the use of adaptive memory functions associated with those used in tabu search.

Several researchers have recently reported on the use of scatter search to solve a variety of optimization problems. Successful applications have been reported in vehicle routing, the design of financial products, shop scheduling, optimizing discrete event simulations, and a variety of other diverse areas. For a comprehensive set of references to these applications, the reader is referred to chapter nineteen and to Glover [1998].

We apply scatter search to the unconstrained quadratic binary program:

$$QP: \max xQx, \text{ with } x \in \{0,1\} \tag{20.1}$$

This model has an ability to represent a diverse set of important combinatorial optimization problems, and has been the object of several research efforts in recent years. Notable recent papers addressing QP are Pardalos & Rodgers [1990], Chardaire & Sutter [1995], Glover et al [1998, 1998a], Alidaee et al [1998], Lodi et al [1997], and Alkhamis et al [1998]. These various papers approach the problem by branch and bound (Pardalos & Rodgers [1990]), tabu search (Glover et al [1998, 1998a]), decomposition heuristic (Chardaire & Sutter

[1995]), evolutionary algorithms (Lodi et al [1997]), and simulated annealing (Alkhamis et al [1998]). Each of these approaches exhibits some degree of success. The tabu search methods and the evolutionary algorithm show the most promise to date for solving difficult and large problems.

The work reported here is the first to approach QP via scatter search. In this chapter, we introduce an implementation of scatter search designed to solve unconstrained quadratic binary programs, and provide an extensive computational study that discloses the effectiveness of the method. The study consisted of the largest and most comprehensive testbed of problems examined to date. Our approach obtained solutions whose quality matched or exceeded that previously obtained for every problem tested. The method proved especially effective for larger problems, where we obtained new best solutions for 12 problems out of a total of 114 in the set. We also examined problems larger than those examined in previous studies.

20.2 BASIC SCATTER SEARCH NOTIONS

Scatter search methods evolve one collection of solutions into another by maintaining and enhancing a diverse set of trial solutions. Our approach is built around the following five key components:

(i) Diversification Generator: A routine designed to generate a collection of diverse trial solutions.

(ii) An Improvement Method: A routine designed to transform a trial solution into one or more enhanced trial solutions.

(iii) A Reference Set Update Method: A routine designed to maintain and manage a reference set of the best solutions found.

(iv) A Subset Generation Method: A routine designed to produce a subset of the reference set solutions for the purpose of creating combined solutions.

(v) A Solution Combination Method: A routine designed to transform a given subset of solutions into one or more combined solutions.

Our particular implementation of scatter search incorporates these five components into the following two-phase method. The purpose of Phase I is to produce a high quality reference set as an input to Phase II. Phase II performs the evolution via recombination and improvement, using scatter search.

PHASE I (produce initial reference set of solutions):

Step 1. Seed Solution Step: Create one or more seed solutions.

Step 2. Diversification Step: Use the Diversification Generator to produce diverse trial solutions from the seed solutions.

Step 3. Improvement/Reference Set Update Step: For each trial solution, use an improvement method to create one or more enhanced trial solutions. Maintain and update a reference set of the best solutions found.

Step 4. Reference Set Completion step: Repeat Steps (2) and (3) until the desired total number of enhanced trial solutions is obtained.

PHASE II (implement scatter search evolution):

Step 5. Subset Generation Step: Use the subset generation method to selectively produce subsets of the reference set solutions.

Step 6. Solution Combination Step: Use the combination method to produce one or more combined solutions by operating on each subset formed in step (5).

Step 7. Improvement/Reference Update Step: Apply the improvement method to each trial solution produced in step (6) to create one or more enhanced trial solutions. Apply the reference set update method to maintain and update the reference set of solutions.

Step 8. Solution Evolution Step: Repeat steps (5) through (7) until a specified iteration limit is reached.

Following the structure of this overview, we present a specific framework of our implementation in Figure 20.1, accompanied by explanatory remarks.

20.2.1 Phase I Implementation

The main purpose of Phase I is to systematically search the solution neighbourhood for a collection of diverse quality solutions and create a reference solution set to be applied in the Phase II for generation of further solutions through solution combination approach.

Step A: Generate Initial seed Solution(s)

Phase I can be initiated with a 0, 1, fractional 0/1, or previously known quality n-vector solution. Also, the method allows applying single or multiple initial solutions in Phase I. If an initial solution is a fractional 0/1 n-vector, we round the solution prior to the application of diversification generator. In our experiments, we observed the effectiveness of two types of seeds for diversification and sampling of the solution neighbourhood: the 0 n-vector, and solutions to problems in the same class, e.g. problem with the same size, density, cost ranges, etc. In solving 'large' and/or 'difficult' problem instances, the previously known quality solutions proved to be more effective seeds than the 0 n-vectors. This suggests the potential value of a more thorough investigation of seeds that incorporate an embedded quality structure, but since the seed solutions are transformed by the diversification generator we did not organize our study to address this issue.

Step B: Diversification Generator

The goal of diversification is to produce solutions that differ from each other in significant ways, and that yield productive (or 'interesting') alternatives in the context of the problem considered. Also, this can be viewed as sampling the solution space in a systematic fashion to identify high quality solutions with controllable degrees of differences.

PHASE I	PHASE II
	A. Set $i=0$.
	B. Identify the subsets of '*new*' and '*old*' solutions in the *Reference Set*.
A. Generate initial seed solution(s).	C. Is the subset of '*new*' solutions null?
	YES: Terminate the search!
B. Apply *Diversification Generator* to create a new seed solution and its complement.	NO: Go to Step D.
	D. Add 1 to i. If $i>4$ then set i to 1. Apply *Subset Generator i* as follows:
C. Apply *Improvement Method* to the new seed solution and its complement.	1. Select and combine k solutions from '*new*' and '*old*' to generate a new solution. If list of candidate solutions is exhausted, then go to Step B.
D. Does the improved solution duplicate any of the current solutions in the *Reference Set*?	2. Apply a *Rounding Method* to round the combined solution.
YES: Go to Step E.	3. Does the rounded solution duplicate a member of the *Recency Set*?
NO: Is the improved solution better than any solutions in the *Reference Set*?	YES: Go to Step 6.
YES: Add the improved Solution to the *Reference Set*.	NO: Add it to the *Recency Set*.
NO: Go to Step E.	4. Apply *Improvement Method* to the rounded solution.
E. Does the total number of seed solutions generated by the *Diversification Generator* exceed a predetermined limit?	5. Does the improved solution duplicate anything in the *Reference Set*?
	YES: Go to Step 6.
YES: Go to **PHASE II**.	NO: Is the improved solution better than any in *Reference Set*?
NO: Go to Step B.	YES: Add it to *Reference Set*.
	NO: Go to Step 6.
	6. Does the total number of combined solutions generated exceed a predetermined limit?
	YES: Terminate the search!
	NO: Go to Step 1.

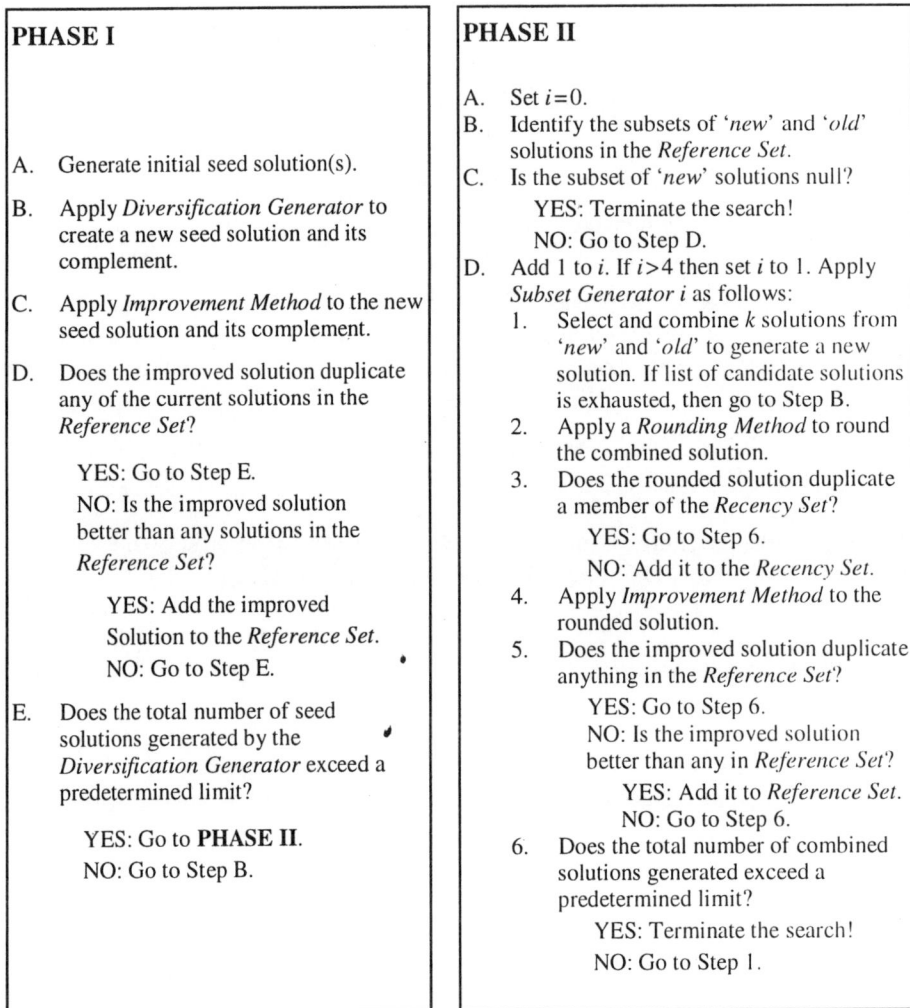

Fig. 20.1: A General Framework for the Scatter Search Method.

Glover [1998] introduced two diversification generators for creating 0–1 solutions. We sketch the ideas behind the methods briefly as follows and refer the reader to the source paper for further details. Given a seed solution, let say a 0 n-vector, the first generator uses an incremental parameter to determine the distance between 0/1 elements, where the distance is measured by the number of 0 elements to skip. For each value of the incremental parameter a new 0–1 solution is generated. In addition, the same parameter is applied to the complement of the initial seed solution to generate further solutions. If further variety is sought, a simple modification of the first generator creates additional seed solutions. For each value of the incremental parameter that is defined by $n/5$, four seed solutions can be generated. For example, for a problem with $n=100$, the method generates 420 different seed solutions.

The second method for generating 0–1 solutions is called Sequential (Max/Min) Diversification Generator. This method is based on the ideas of Sequential Diversification (Glover & Laguna [1997]), where a 'diverse sequence' can be composed by a rule that selects each successive seed to maximize the minimum Hamming distance from all solutions previously considered, according to a chosen metric (the rule has a nested component to break 'ties'.

In our implementation, we applied the first diversification generator in Phase I to create seed solutions and the second method is utilized to introduce further diversification in the Phase II. A discussion on the strategic use of the second method is included in the discussion of the Phase II.

Step C: Applying Improvement Method

As a metaheuristic, scatter search can house a variety of optimization-based or heuristic-based improvement approaches. Here for the sake of space we describe a particular approach we found to be effective, but note that other types of improvement methods are possible.

Our approach, which we called an Ascent Method with Subdivision, is an ascent method that utilizes a special subdivision strategy to allow consideration of non-improving moves. The method employs a candidate list strategy to consider different subsets of variables to generate and evaluate compound moves, moves that change the value of more than one variable at a time. The candidate list applied in the current study is dynamic in size and adaptive to the problem at hand. Although it allows effective evaluation of multi-component moves, our implementation limits consideration to one-, two-, and three-component moves. Given an initial solution, the improvement method cycles through these moves in a sequential order and it terminates when no further attractive moves can be identified. Our approach can be considered a special instance of the Fan and Filter method described by Glover [1998].

Step D: Generating and maintaining a Reference Solution Set

There are two primary purposes of creating and maintaining a reference solution set for the Phase II of our search: (1) to have a current collection of the top quality solutions at hand for generating further solutions through a combination strategy; and (2) to utilize the set as the Critical Event Memory construct for rounding fractional variables in the combined solutions. We discuss the first purpose here and the second purpose in the description of Phase II. A solution generated by the improvement method is considered as a potential candidate for inclusion in the reference set, where the inclusion decision depends on the predetermined size of the set and the quality of candidate solution relative to the quality of the current members of the set.

Step E: Terminating Phase I

The termination criteria applied for the Phase I is based on a predetermined limit on the number of seed solutions to be generated by the diversification generator. In our experiments with the class of binary quadratic problems, we applied n or $2n$ as the limit on the number of seed solutions to generate. Interestingly, the generation of more seed solutions does not translate into higher quality final solutions; in some problem instances the inverse is true.

20.2.2 Phase II Implementation

The primary objectives of Phase II are to: (1) apply the subset generator to systematically create different subsets of the current reference solution set; (2) combine the solutions within each subset to create new solutions; (3) round the combined solutions; (4) generate and maintain a Recency Solution Set; (4) subject the rounded solutions to the improvement method; (5) decide to include the improved solutions in the reference set; and (6) terminate the search process.

Step A: Initialize Subset Generator Index

At this stage of the search, we have the reference solution set that includes the top quality solutions identified in the Phase I. As a convention, we set the Subset Generator index to 0.

Step B: Classify the Solutions in the Reference Set

Three out of four subset generators implemented in this study operate on two main subsets of the reference solution set: 'new' and 'old' solution subsets. When a subset generator is about to be applied, a solution in the reference set is considered to be 'new' if it was added to the reference set after the same generator was utilized in the previous sequential cycle of the four subset generators. If a solution is not 'new' then it is considered 'old'.

Step C: Terminating Phase II

If the subset of 'new' solutions is null, then all combinations of the four types of subsets have been examined for their current compositions without generating any new solutions, and so the scatter search method can be terminated as a result of exhaustively considering all relevant subsets of the reference set in its final composition.

In our implementation, we observed that at this stage of the search that introducing the Sequential (Max/Min) Diversification Generator (for further solution diversification), and simultaneously increasing the reference solution set size, improved the final solution quality of 'large' or/and 'difficult' problem instances. This outcome was achieved by using some of the current solutions in the reference set as the seeds for the diversification generator. The final termination of the search occurs when such diversification has no further impact on generating the 'new' solutions.

Step D.1: Applying Subset Generator: Creating a New Solution

There are four subset generators that are considered in this implementation. From the two solution subsets 'new' and 'old', the first subset generator creates subsets of two solutions, which consist of pairs in which both members are 'new' solutions, or one member is a 'new' solution and one member is an 'old' solution. The second subset generator generates triples that join the top quality solution in the reference set with pairs of other solutions from the reference set, subject to the requirement that at least one member of the triple is a 'new' solution. The third subset generator selects the two top quality solutions from the reference set and joins them with pairs of remaining solutions, again requiring that one member of the collection is 'new'. The fourth subset generator chooses the five top quality solutions from the reference set and cumulatively adds the remaining solutions in the reference set one at a time. A subset is skipped if all members are 'old'. Given a subset of solutions, a linear combination is applied to create a combined solution. If the list of candidate solutions in the reference set for generating new combinations is exhausted, then we return to Step B to identify new sets of 'new' and 'old' solutions and apply the next subset generator.

While the subset generators can be applied in any order, in our implementation a sequential order from one to four (i.e. the order in which the methods are described) is utilized. Preliminary experimentation suggested that a reverse sequential order does not lead to higher quality final solutions.

Step D.2: Applying Subset Generator: Applying a Rounding Approach

A combined solution generated by a subset generator includes 0–1 as well as fractional variables. The fractional variables in these solutions must be rounded to integers prior to applying the improvement method. Three rounding approaches are considered and tested in this study. The first method, which we call the Best Local Choice Rule, rounds the fractional variables one at a time, at each step choosing the variable and direction of rounding that produces the best change in the objective function. The Critical Event Memory (CEM) technique in tabu search (see Glover et al [1998a] and Glover & Laguna [1997]) provides the structure of the second rounding approach. The third approach is new, constituting a modification of CEM that we call Conditional Critical Event Memory (CCEM). We briefly discuss the two CEM approaches here.

In general, a reference set-based CEM is a construct initiated by creating and maintaining a vector sum of solutions in the reference set, referred to as Critical Solutions. The value of a variable in the vector sum indicates the frequency that the variable received a value of 1, and the difference between the reference set size and the sum determines the frequency that the variable received a value of 0. The CEM approach then creates 'up' and 'down' penalties for rounding to 1 and 0 which are multiplied by the associated frequency to determine the total penalty for each rounding decision. The Best Local Choice Rule is then applied, upon adding the indicated total penalties to the customary evaluations. The stated CEM approach decreases the chance of creating rounded solutions that are duplicates of current solutions in the reference set. The CCEM approach is a more adaptive approach for achieving this outcome, which uses a modified vector sum to determine penalties. Every solution in the reference set that receives an assignment which matches the results of a previous rounding decision is excluded from the modified vector sum (i.e. these solutions are subtracted from the original sum). For additional flexibility, only a small subset of the fractional variables is rounded by the CCEM and the remaining ones are assigned binary values by the Best Local Choice Rule.

In our experimentation, we observed that a CCEM approach that included vectors from both Recency Solution Set, discussed in the next step, and Reference Solution Set offers a more effective approach than one which includes vectors from any of the two individual sets. Also, comparison of the CEM and CCEM indicates that while the two methods perform similarly on the 'smaller' and less 'difficult' test problems the CCEM approach is more effective on the 'large' and /or more 'difficult' problem instances.

Step D.3: Applying Subset Generator: Checking Duplication of the Rounded Solution

The Recency Solution Set constitutes the most recent m rounded solutions generated by the subset generators. The purpose of the Recency solution set is twofold. First, it helps to avoid duplicating most of the rounded solutions that are subjected to the improvement method. Second, it plays a role in the CEM approach, as noted above, by augmenting the vector sum to include its members, which therefore increases the collection of solution that are avoided during the CEM process. This dual role significantly improves the effectiveness of the search method.

The Recency Solution Set is updated by dropping each new current rounded solution, and (after the set reaches a described size) dropping the oldest solution is from the set. However, this update is bypassed if the current solution duplicates one already in the set.

Step D.4: Applying Subset Generator: Applying the Improvement Method

A rounded solution arriving at this stage is twice subjected to the improving method. In the first effort, we fix the values of the small subset of variables that are rounded by the CCEM method while allowing the other variables to change values. The solution obtained from the first application of the improvement method is utilized as an initial solution for the second stage where all variables all permitted to change values.

Steps D.5 and D.6: Applying Subset Generator: Checking Duplication and Termination

The solution obtained from the completed (second stage) application of the improvement method is checked against the current reference solution set. If the solution does not duplicate any member of the set and further it is better than the worst member, then it enters the set and the worst member is removed.

We apply two termination criteria. The first stops the method when the reference set contains no more 'new' solutions. The second stops the method, even if 'new' solutions remain, by placing an externally predetermined limit on the number of combined solutions generated. In our experiments, unexpectedly the first termination criterion terminated the search process for all test problem instances.

In testing the implementation described above, we experimented with several variants and strategies. We discuss the most notable ones. Within phase I, we conducted experiments with both types of diversification generators previously described. Our experiments with reversing the sequence of generating subsets of the reference set in phase II disclosed that this change in order has a negative impact on the quality of final solutions. Also, our comparisons of the three rounding methods disclose that the most consistent approach for providing high quality solutions is the third method, based on using conditional critical event memory. We also found that further diversification of the pre-rounding and post-rounding solutions did not improve the final solution quality, employing either of the two diversification approaches used in phase I, or simply by considering the complements of solutions produced.

In applying the rounding process based on conditional critical event memory, our experiments revealed that having both the reference solution set and the Recency solution set in the memory structure provides results superior to those obtained by incorporating only one of these two sets. Finally, an examination of several alternative improvement methods indicates that for the classes of problems considered here the ascent method with subdivision process is highly effective. These observations (along with many additional minor ones) arise from extensive experimentation, as discussed in the following sections.

20.3 COMPUTATIONAL EXPERIENCE

Our scatter search method was tested on a set of 114 testbed problems, which vary in both size and density, which constitute the largest and more comprehensive test to appear in the literature to date. For each problem, we report problem characteristics, the phase I and phase II solutions, and the best known solution. The results tables are supplemented by remarks to highlight and clarify the results shown in tabular form.

Table 20.1 presents the results for random problems that were created by using the generator provided by Pardalos & Rodgers [1990]. These problems, generated with characteristics designed to make them challenging, were previously solved by tabu search as reported in Glover et al [1998a]. The 'g' and 'h' problems are of particular interest as they represent the largest general test problems to appear in the literature to date.

One of the most interesting observations is that the solutions to problem sets 'a' through 'd' are obtained in phase I, while the best known solutions to problems in sets 'e', 'f', and 'g' are obtained in phase II. The problems of sets 'a' through 'f' are solved simply by the basic scatter search implementation, which does not make use of the critical event memory rounding method or further diversification effort as applied in phase II. Some of the 'f' and all 'g' problems required the inclusion of the more advanced strategies to obtain the best results. In addition, when the solutions to some of the 'g' problems were applied as initial seeds for solving other 'g' problems, the quality of the final solutions was improved.

Tables 20.2 and 20.3 report results on test problems obtained by recasting quadratic knapsack problems as equivalent QP problems, using the reformulation technique of Alidaee et al [1998]. These problems range in size from 10 to 500 variables and are all 100% dense; previous experience with them is reported in Alidaee et al [1998], which obtained the previous best known solutions to these problems via tabu search (as indicated earlier, aspects of this tabu search approach are also used in our present procedure).

In this case, our current approach matched the best known solutions to problem sets 'a' through 'c' and problems 'd4', 'd6', 'd7', and 'd8'. Also, we improved the previously best known solutions for the remaining problems, which indicates that our scatter search approach is robust as problem size increases.

Test results for the final two groups of problems we examined are given in Table 20.4. The five 'NUG' problems are quadratic assignment problems (QA) (from the Nugent test bed) reformulated as unconstrained quadratic binary programs. The best known solutions reported for these problems are in fact known to be optimal. The remaining 10 problems of Table 20.4, problem sets 'h' and 'i' are general QP problems obtained by using the Pardalos and Rodgers generator to create problems of size $n = 2000$ and 3000, respectively, with density varying from 10% to 50%. These problems are substantially larger than any yet reported in the literature.

Table 20.1: Quadratic binary test problems.

Problem id	Size	Density	Best Known Solution	Phase I Solution	Phase II Solution
1a	50	0.10	3414	3414	3414
2a	60	0.1	6063	6063	6063
3a	70	0.1	6037	6037	6037
4a	80	0.1	8589	8598	8598
5a	50	0.2	5737	5737	5737
6a	30	0.4	3980	3980	3980
7a	30	0.5	4541	4541	4541
8a	100	0.0625	11109	11109	11109
1b	20	1.0	133	133	133
2b	30	1.0	121	121	121
3b	40	1.0	118	118	118
4b	50	1.0	129	129	129
5b	60	1.0	150	150	150
6b	70	1.0	146	146	146
7b	80	1.0	160	160	160
8b	90	1.0	145	145	145
9b	100	1.0	137	137	137
10b	125	1.0	154	154	154
1c	40	0.8	5058	5058	5058
2c	50	0.6	6213	6213	6213
3c	60	0.4	6665	6665	6665
4c	70	0.3	7398	7398	7398
5c	80	0.2	7362	7362	7362
6c	90	0.1	5824	5824	5824
7c	100	0.1	7225	7225	7225
1d	100	0.1	6333	6333	6333
2d	100	0.2	6579	6579	6579
3d	100	0.3	9261	9261	9261
4d	100	0.4	10727	10727	10727
5d	100	0.5	11626	11613	11626
6d	100	0.6	14207	14207	14207
7d	100	0.7	14476	14476	14476
8d	100	0.8	16353	16353	16353
9d	100	0.9	15656	15656	15656
10d	100	1.0	19102	19102	19102
1e	200	0.1	16464	16458	16458
2e	200	0.2	23395	23351	23395
3e	200	0.3	25243	25228	25243
4e	200	0.4	35594	35594	35594
5e	200	0.5	35154	35126	35154
1f	500	0.1	61194	61039	61194
2f	500	0.25	100161	100015	100161
3f	500	0.5	138035	137755	138035
4f	500	0.75	172771	172362	172771
5f	500	1.0	190507	190037	190507
1g	1000	0.1	131456	130767	131456
2g	1000	0.2	172788	171620	172788
3g	1000	0.3	192565	189980	192565
4g	1000	0.4	215679	213776	215679
5g	1000	0.5	242367	240962	242367
6g	1000	0.6	243293	240324	243293
7g	1000	0.7	253590	251575	253590
8g	1000	0.8	264268	262992	264268
9g	1000	0.9	262658	259432	262658
10g	1000	1.0	274375	271867	274375

Table 20.2: Quadratic binary test problems (cont.)

Problem id	Size	Best Known Solution	Phase I Solution	Phase II Solution
qk_a1	16	6220*	6179	6220
qk_a2	16	24373*	24348	24373
qk_a3	16	1357*	1357	1357
qk_a4	16	45342*	45342	45342
qk_a5	16	3408*	3408	3408
qk_a6	16	34220*	34220	34220
qk_a7	16	58612*	58612	58612
qk_a8	16	42462*	42642	42462
qk_b1	26	180947*	180850	180947
qk_b2	26	76794*	76736	76794
qk_b3	26	73279*	73262	73279
qk_b4	26	226432*	226368	226432
qk_b5	26	347331*	347201	347331
qk_b6	26	55570*	55570	55570
qk_b7	26	194715*	194715	194715
qk_b8	26	4570*	4570	4570
qk_c1	36	5284*	5284	5284
qk_c2	36	2635*	2635	2635
qk_c3	36	254824	254702	254824
qk_c4	36	164548*	164498	164548
qk_c5	36	4631*	4631	4631
qk_c6	36	55748*	55748	55748
qk_c7	36	86359*	86359	86359
qk_c8	36	6472*	6472	6472

* Solutions known to be optimal.
** These are transformed Quadratic Knapsack problems.

Again, our scatter search method matched the previous best known solutions to the QA. It also found solutions for the new general QP testbed 'h' and 'I' problems with 2000 and 3000 variables respectively. Use of the critical event memory structure and the second diversification approach were essential for higher quality to these problems.

20.4 SUMMARY AND CONCLUSIONS

We have discussed the design and testing of a scatter search heuristic for the unconstrained quadratic binary program (QP). The various components of our method are designed to be flexible, allowing alternatives to be tested and additional strategic components to be easily incorporated over time. The computational tests reported are preliminary but nonetheless extensive, clearly illustrating the promise of scatter search for this class of problems. Across the 109 test problems addressed, which represent three problem classes, the scatter search method was very robust. It succeeded in matching the best known solutions on 88 problems, and obtained new best solutions for 16 problems. Also, the current method solved five problems that are substantially larger than any yet reported in the literature. It worked particularly well on large problems, where we found 12 new best solutions.

Table 20.3: Quadratic binary test problems (cont.)

Problem id	Size	Best Known Solution	Phase I Solution	Phase II Solution
qk_d1	46	888033	888057	**888200***
qk_d2	46	1607975	1608035	**1608054**
qk_d3	46	177190	177298	**177311**
qk_d4	46	1272126	1272126	1272126
qk_d5	46	1076775	1076774	**1076808**
qk_d6	46	1389799	1389799	1389799
qk_d7	46	1549279	1549279	1549279
qk_d8	46	40931	40931	40931
qk_e1	106	2659975	2659945	**2660125**
qk_e2	106	1953310	1953359	**1953780**
qk_e3	106	4241440	4242078	**4242166**
qk_e4	106	10993576	10996619	**10996856**
qk_e5	106	2119812	2120568	**2120568**
qk_e6	106	11040166	11043060	**11043060**
qk_e7	106	13696762	13699166	**13699512**
qk_e8	106	5943174	5944995	**5945128**
qk_f1	506	35491046	35494920	**35495308**
qk_f2	506	35544448	35548572	**35548572**
qk_f3	506	76078805	76085456	**76085616**
qk_f4	506	76145674	76159360	**76159416**

* **New best solution.**
** These are transformed Quadratic Knapsack problems.

Table 20.4: Quadratic Binary Test Problems (cont.)

Problem id	Size	Density	Best Known Solution	Phase I Solution	Phase II Solution
Nug07	49		7692	7692	7692
Nug08	64		10026	10022	10026
Nug12	144		28222	28186	28222
Nug15	225		52850	52812	52850
Nug20_2	400		17430	17390	17430
1h	2000	0.1	**	153079	153342
2h	2000	0.2	**	215491	216333
3h	2000	0.3	**	265999	266912
4h	2000	0.4	**	301121	302020
5h	2000	0.5	**	342460	343492
1i	3000	0.1	**	275277	276384
2i	3000	0.2	**	386742	388421
3i	3000	0.3	**	477578	479580
4i	3000	0.4	**	550677	552075
5i	3000	0.5	**	620363	621670

* 'NUG' problems are transformed Nugent problems.
**The 'h' and 'i' problem sets are the new substantially large QB problems.

The performance of our scatter search QP method remains very high independent of problem density. This is important because the ability to solve dense QP problems efficiently also makes it possible to solve constrained 0–1 quadratic programming problems efficiently. Perhaps surprisingly, as shown in Glover et al [1998a], this ability provides a more effective method for QP problem with a knapsack constraint than the methods previously developed which were explicitly designed to exploit the presence of the additional constraint.

While we have reported results for problems substantially larger than previously addressed in the literature, we remark that the application of special candidate list strategies is highly important for larger problems, and this provides an area of future research. Our continuing work is directed toward understanding how to tune and otherwise enhance the various components of our method, giving way to even greater efficiencies and success on even larger problems. The core of this process is to design and implement a target analysis learning approach (see Glover & Laguna [1997]) to understand the relationships among the run parameters.

From a practical standpoint, the relevance of the advances obtained by this preliminary scatter search study is amplified by the mathematical conversions presented in Alidaee et al [1998]. By these conversions, we are able to solve combinatorial problems different from QP (but reformulated as QPs) more effectively than previous approaches that have been tailored to solve the original (unconverted) forms of these problems. This opens the door to using our method to solve additional classes of problems without changing the underlying computer code to adapt it to different formulations.

Chapter Twenty-One

Scatter Search for the Linear Ordering Problem

Vicente Campos, Manuel Laguna, and Rafael Martí

21.1 INTRODUCTION

The goal of the research work presented in this paper is to expand the scatter search methodology by implementing innovative strategies within a scatter search procedure for the linear ordering problem. Before we address the contributions of our research in terms of advancing the scatter search methodology, we briefly discuss our problem setting.

The linear ordering problem (or LOP) has enjoyed a fair amount of research interest over the years, as documented in Grotschel et al [1984] and Chanas & Kobylanski [1996]. We use this problem as a test case for our strategies and search mechanisms. The problem can be described as follows.

Given a matrix of weights $E = \{e_{ij}\}_{m \times m}$, the LOP consists of finding a permutation p of the columns (and rows) in order to maximize the sum of the weights in the upper triangle. In mathematical terms, we seek to maximize:

$$C_E(p) = \sum_{i=1}^{m-1} \sum_{j=i+1}^{m} e_{p(i)p(j)}$$

where $p(i)$ is the index of the column (and row) in position i in the permutation. Note that in the Linear Ordering Problem, the permutation p provides the ordering of both the columns and the rows. The equivalent problem in graph theory consists of finding, in a complete weighted graph, an acyclic tournament with a maximal sum of arc weights (Reinelt [1985]).

In economics, the LOP is equivalent to the so-called *triangulation problem for input-output tables*, which can be described as follows. The economy of a region (generally a country) is divided into m sectors and an $m \times m$ input-output table E is constructed where the entry e_{ij} denotes the amount of deliveries (in monetary value) from sector i to sector j in a given year. The triangulation problem then consists of simultaneously permuting the rows and columns of E, such that the sum of the entries above the main diagonal is as large as possible. An optimal solution then orders the sectors in such a way that the suppliers (i.e., sectors that tend to produce materials for other industries) come first followed by the consumers (i.e. sectors that tend to be final-product industries that deliver their output mostly to end users).

Instances of the LOP, consisting of input-output tables from sectors in the European Economy can be found in the public-domain library LOLIB [1997]. In the computational experiments section, we employ these problem instances to test the merit of our scatter search implementation.

21.2 MAIN SCATTER SEARCH ELEMENTS

Scatter search, from the standpoint of metaheuristic classification, may be viewed as an evolutionary (or also called population-based) algorithm that constructs solutions by combining others. It derives its foundations from strategies originally proposed for combining decision rules and constraints (in the context of integer programming). The goal of this methodology is to enable the implementation of solution procedures that can derive new solutions from combined elements in order to yield better solutions than those procedures that base their combinations only on a set of original elements.

Our solution method for the linear ordering problem is based on the scatter search template in Glover [1998]. The procedure combines the following elements:

a. Diversification Generator

b. Improvement Method

c. Reference Set Update Method

d. Subset Generation Method

e. Solution Combination Method

We now describe the implementation of each of these elements, as adapted in the context of the linear ordering problem.

21.2.1 Diversification Generator

The generator that we implemented is based on the notion of constructing solutions employing modified frequencies. The generator exploits the permutation nature of a linear ordering. A frequency counter is maintained to record the number of times an element i appears in position j. The frequency counters are used to penalize the 'attractiveness' of an element with respect to a given position. To illustrate, suppose the generator has created 30 solutions to be included in a population of solutions P. If 20 of these have element 3 in position 5, then the frequency counter $Freq(3,5)=20$. This frequency value is used to bias the potential assignment of element 3 in position 5 during subsequent constructions, and therefore, to induce diversification with respect to the solutions already in P.

The attractiveness of assigning element i to position j is given by the greedy function $G(i,j)$, as proposed in Becker [1967]. We modify the value of $G(i,j)$ to reflect previous assignments of element i to position j, as follows:

$$G'(i, j) = G(i, j) - \beta(MaxG / MaxF)Freq(i, j)$$

where $MaxF$ is the maximum $Freq(i,j)$ value for all i and j, and $MaxG$ is the maximum $G(i,j)$ value for all i and j.

It is important to point out that in each iteration of the construction procedure, $G(i,j)$ is an adaptive function since its value depends on attributes of the unassigned elements. A pseudo-code version of the diversification generator to produce a population P with $PSize$ solutions, appears in Figure 21.1.

1. $P = \{\}$.
2. $Freq(i,j) = 0$ for all i and j.
While $(|P| < Psize)$ **do**
       3. $P(i)=1$ for all i.
       4. $N = \{1,...,m\}$ (the set of unassigned elements).
       5. $j = Maxf = MaxG = 1$.
       While $(N = \{\})$ **do**
              6. $G(i,j) = G(i,j) - \beta(MaxG/MaxF)Freq(i,j)$ for all $i \in N$.

              7. $i^* = \arg \max_{i}(G(i,j), i \in N)$.

              8. $MaxG = G(i^*,j)$.
              9. $N = N - \{i^*\}$.
              10. $P(i^*) = j$.
              11. $j = j + 1$.
       End While
       12. $Freq(i,p(i)) = Freq(i,p(i)) + 1$, for all i.

       13. $MaxF = \max_{i,j}(Freq(i,j), i \in N, j \in \{1,...,m\})$.

       If $(p \notin P)$ **then** $P = P \cup \{p\}$.

End While

Fig. 21.1: Pseudo-code of diversification generator.

The pseudo-code in Figure 21.1 uses general mathematical notation. However, our implementation takes advantage of quick updating mechanisms that are hard to represent mathematically. For example, the value of *MaxF* in step 13 can be maintained by keeping track of the updates of the frequency matrix *Freq*.

The performance of the diversification generator depends on the value of β. To determine effective values for this parameter, we created a measure of diversity for a set of solutions. The diversity measure is calculated as follows:

1. Calculate the median position of each sector i in the solutions in P.
2. Calculate the dissimilarity of each solution in the population with respect to the median position. The dissimilarity is calculated as the sum of the absolute difference between the position in the solution under consideration and the median solution.
3. Calculate d as the sum of all the individual dissimilarities.

To illustrate, suppose P consists of the orderings: (A,B,C,D), (B,D,C,A), (C,B,A,D). Then the median position of sector A is 3, since it occupies positions 1, 3 and 4 in the given orderings. In the same way, the median positions of B, C and D are 2, 3 and 4. Note that the median positions might not induce an ordering, as in this example. The dissimilarity of the first solution is then calculated as: $d_1 = |1-3| + |2-2| + |3-3| + |4-4| = 2$. In the same way, the dissimilarities of the other two solutions are $d_2 = 4$ and $d_3 = 2$. The diversity measure for P is then given by $d = 2 + 4 + 2 = 8$.

Since we are interested in finding a β-value that generates balanced populations, we use two relative measures: one based on the diversity value d, and one based on the objective function value C. Given a set of populations $\Pi = \{P_1, P_2,..., P_n\}$, we calculate $\Delta d(i)$ and $\Delta C(i)$ for each population P_iP_i as follows:

$$\Delta d(i) = \frac{d(i) - d_{min}}{d_{max} - d_{min}}, \text{ where } d(i) = \sum_{j \in P_i} d_j, \ d_{min} = \min_i\{d(i)\} \text{ and } d_{max} = \max_i\{d(i)\}$$

$$\Delta C(i) = \frac{C(i) - C_{min}}{C_{max} - C_{min}}, \text{ where } C(i) = \sum_{j \in P_i} C_j, \ C_{min} = \min_i\{C(i)\} \text{ and } C_{max} = \max_i\{C(i)\}$$

Figure 21.2 shows the values of our relative measures of quality and diversity when the diversification generator is executed with different β-values.

The legends in Figure 21.2 are such that costdev=ΔC, disdev=Δd and sum=costdev+disdev. This figure discloses that a value of 0.3 for β provides a good balance between diversity and quality in the population. As β increases, the diversity increases but the quality decreases. Therefore the value of sum is highest at β=0.3, with a similar contribution from both relative deviation measures.

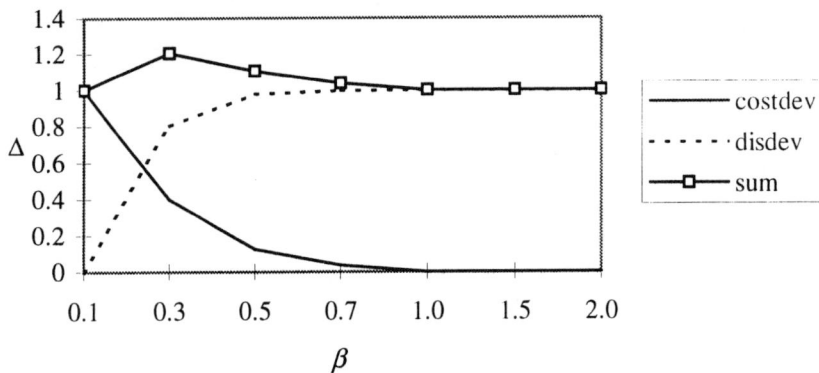

Fig. 21.2: Diversity vs. quality for different β-values.

21.2.2 Improvement Method

The improvement method is based on the neighbourhood search developed for the LOP in Laguna et al [1998]. Two neighbourhoods were considered in that study:

$$\mathcal{N}_1 = \{p': \text{INSERT\_MOVE}(p(j), i), \text{ for } j = 1,..., m-1, i = j+1\}$$

$$\mathcal{N}_2 = \{p': \text{INSERT\_MOVE}(p(j), i), \text{ for } j = 1,..., m, i = 1, 2,..., j-1, j+1,..., m\}$$

$\mathcal{N}_1$ consists of permutations that are reached by switching the positions of contiguous sectors $p(j)$ and $p(j+1)$. $\mathcal{N}_2$ consists of all permutations resulting from executing general insertion moves, as defined above. In conjunction with these neighbourhoods, two strategies are defined. The *best* strategy selects the move with the largest move value among all the moves in the neighbourhood. The *first* strategy, on the other hand, scans the list of sectors (in the order given by the current permutation) in search for the first sector $p(f)$ whose movement results in an strictly positive move value (i.e. a move such that $(C_E(p') > C_E(p))$. The move selected by the *first* strategy is then INSERT_MOVE($p(f)$, i^*), where i^* is the position that maximizes $C_E(p')$. Note that for $\mathcal{N}_1$, $i^* = f+1$, while for $\mathcal{N}_2$, i^* is chosen from $i = 1, 2, ..., f-1, f+1, ..., m$. Therefore, the *first* strategy used in combination with $\mathcal{N}_1$ is equivalent to searching for the first improving move in the neighbourhood.

Combining the selection strategies with the neighbourhood definitions results in four greedy local search procedures *first*($\mathcal{N}_1$), *best*($\mathcal{N}_1$), *first*($\mathcal{N}_2$), and *best*($\mathcal{N}_2$), the experimentation in Laguna et al [1998] showed that the greedy procedure *first*($\mathcal{N}_2$) was the most effective. Based on this finding, we partition $\mathcal{N}_2$ into m $\mathcal{N}_2^j$ neighbourhoods:

$$\mathcal{N}_2^j = \{p' : \text{INSERT\_MOVE}(p(j), i), \text{for } i = 1, 2, ..., j-1, j+1, ..., m\}$$

associated with each sector $p(j)$, for $j = 1, ..., m$. We therefore base our improvement method on choosing the best insertion associated with a given sector as proposed in Laguna et al [1998].

21.2.3 Reference Set Update Method

The Reference Set Update Method accompanies each application of the Improvement Method. The Reference Update Method is generally examined right after the Improvement Method, because of its linking role with the Subset Generation Method. The update operation consists of maintaining a record of the b best solutions found, where the value of b is treated as a constant search parameter. The issues associated with this updating function are conceptually straightforward and are addressed with extensive detail in Glover [1998], where a concrete design for such a procedure is given.

Accompanying this design is a detailed pseudo-code description of the procedure for maintaining *RefSet* (i.e. the Reference Set), which is called the *RefSet* Update Routine. This routine is organized to handle vectors of 0–1 variables. We have adapted this *RefSet* Update Routine to handle permutation vectors, as needed in our current application.

21.2.4 Subset Generation Method

This Subset Generation procedure consists of creating different subsets X of *RefSet*, as a basis for implementing the subsequent combination method. The scatter search methodology prescribes that the set of combined solutions (i.e. the set of all combined solutions that the implementation intends to generate) is produced in its entirety at the point where X is created. Therefore, once a given subset X is created, there is no merit in creating it again. This creates a situation that differs noticeably from those considered in the context of genetic algorithms, where the combinations are typically determined by the spin of a roulette wheel.

The procedure seeks to generate subsets X of *RefSet* that have useful properties, while avoiding the duplication of subsets previously generated. The approach for doing this is organized to generate four different collections of subsets of *RefSet*, which Glover [1998] refers to as *SubSetType* = 1, 2, 3 and 4, with the following characteristics:

SubsetType = 1:	all 2-element subsets.
SubsetType = 2:	3-element subsets derived from the 2-element subsets by augmenting each 2-element subset to include the best solution not in this subset.
SubsetType = 3:	4-element subsets derived from the 3-element subsets by augmenting each 3-element subset to include the best solutions not in this subset.
SubsetType = 4:	the subsets consisting of the best i elements, for $i = 5$ to b.

A central consideration of this design is that *RefSet* itself might not be static, because it might ·be changing as new solutions are added to replace old ones (when these new solutions qualify to be among the current b best solutions found). In our implementation, however, we maintain a static updating of *RefSet*, but use a broad definition of 'best' for the membership in this set. In other words, we do not allow RefSet to dynamically change its size, but we use two criteria to allow solutions to become members of this set. One criterion is the quality of the solution (as given by the objective function value) and the other is the diversity of the solution (as given by the dissimilarity measure). In this sense, our definition of 'best' is broader than one that considers only the objective function value.

21.2.5 Solution Combination Method

The Solution Combination Method as well as the Improvement Method are elements of scatter search that are context-dependent. Although it is possible to design 'generic' combination procedures, it is more effective to base the design on specific characteristics of the problem setting. Our Solution Combination Method, which is applied to each subset generated in the previous step, uses a min-max construction based on votes.

The method scans (left to right) each reference permutation in the subset, and uses the rule that each reference permutation votes for its first element that is still not included in the combined permutation (referred to as the 'incipient element'). The voting determines the next element to enter the first still unassigned position of the combined permutation. This is a min-max rule in the sense that if any element of the reference permutation is chosen other than the incipient element, then it would increase the deviation between the reference and the combined permutations. Similarly, if the incipient element were placed later in the combined permutation than its next available position, this deviation would also increase. So the rule attempts to minimize the maximum deviation of the combined solution from the reference solution, subject to the fact that other reference solutions in the subset are also competing to contribute.

This voting scheme can be implemented with a couple of variations depending on how votes are modified:

(V1) The vote of a given reference solution is weighted according to the incipient element's position (the 'incipient position'). A smaller incipient position gets a higher vote. For example, if the element in the first position of some reference permutation is not assigned to the combined permutation during the first four assignments, then the vote is weighted more heavily to increase the chances of having that element assigned to position 5 of the combined permutation. The rule emphasizes the preference to this assignment versus having a later occurring element of some other reference permutation (which is the incipient element for that other permutation) become assigned.

(V2) A bias factor that gives more weight to the vote of a reference permutation with higher quality. In our current implementation, such a factor should be very slight since it is expected that high quality solutions will be strongly represented anyway.

21.3 OVERALL PROCEDURE

The proposed procedure can be summarized as follows:

1. Use the diversification generator to create a set P of $|P| = PSize$ distinct solutions.
2. Apply the improvement method to P, keeping all resulting distinct solutions. The diversification generator stops when it finds $PSize$ distinct 'improved' solutions.
3. Order the solutions in P according to their objective function value (best to worst).

For (*Iter* = 1 **to** *MaxIter*)

4. Build *RefSet* from P, with $|RefSet| = b_1 + b_2$ (i.e. $b = b_1 + b_2$). Take the first b_1 solutions in P and assign them to *RefSet*. For each solution x in P−*RefSet*, calculate the minimum dissimilarity $d(RefSet,x)$ to all solutions in *RefSet*. Select the solution x' with the maximum dissimilarity $d(RefSet,x')$ of all x in P−*RefSet*. Add x' to *RefSet*, until $|RefSet| = b_1 + b_2$. Make *SubsetCounter* = 0.

   While (*SubsetCounter* < *MaxSubset*) **do**

5. Generate the next subset r from *RefSet* with the Subset Generation Method. This method generates one of four types of subsets with number of elements ranging from 2 to $|RefSet|$. Let subset $r = \{r_1,..., r_k\}$, for $2 \le k \le |RefSet|$.
6. Apply the Solution Combination Method to r to obtain a new solution s_r.
7. Apply the Improvement Method to s_r to obtain the improved solution s_r^*.

   If (s_r^* is not in *RefSet* and the objective function value of s_r^* is better than the objective function value of the worst element in *RefSet*) **then**

8. Add s_r^* to *RefSet*, overwriting worst element, Let *SubsetCounter* = 0.

   Else

9. Make SubsetCounter = SubsetCounter + 1.

   End if
   End while

   If (*Iter* < *MaxIter*) **then**

10. Build a new set P using the diversification generator, but with the best b_1 solutions currently in *RefSet* becoming the first b_1 solutions in the new P.

   End if
End for

We now turn our attention to the computational experiments used to assess the merit of our scatter search implementations. Details are provided in the next section.

21.4 COMPUTATIONAL EXPERIMENTS

The procedure described in the previous section was implemented in C, and all experiments were performed on a Pentium 166 Mhz personal computer. In the following set of experiments we compare the performance of our scatter search implementation with three methods: Chanas & Kobylanski [1996], tabu search (Laguna et al [1998]) and a greedy procedure described below.

The greedy local search procedure is based on deleting a sector from its current position and inserting it in another position. An iteration of the algorithm consists of scanning the list of sectors in search for the first one whose movement results in an improvement of the objective function value. The algorithm ends when there is no improving move.

Preliminary tests were done to set the key parameters of the scatter search algorithm. After experimentation, the following values provide a balance between solution quality and run time: $PSize=100$, $\beta=0.3$, $b_1=10$ and $b_2=10$. Two different implementations are reported: the first with $MaxIter=1$ (SS), while the second with $MaxIter=10$ (SS10).

We have tested the procedures in two sets of instances: (1) the 49 instances in the public-domain library LOLIB [1997] which contains instances of input-output tables from sectors in the European Economy, and (2) 25 randomly generated instances. A uniform distribution with parameters (0, 25000) was used to generate the random instances of size 75.

To reduce the computational effort related to avoiding duplications in the population, we have implemented the following hash function to compare solutions and avoid duplications:

$$hash(p) = \sum_{i=1}^{m} i p(i)^2$$

We have empirically determined that two different solutions almost always have different hash values (except for some rare exceptions). Therefore, in our implementation, when two solutions have the same hash value we consider that both are the same and eliminate one of them from further consideration. This implementation results in average computational-time savings of about 7% in LOLIB instances and 1.5% in random instances when compared to a full duplication checking mechanism. The scatter search procedure yields significantly lower duplications in random instances than in real-world examples. Intuitively, this can be explained by the relationships between sectors in real-world examples, which tend to favour the generation of similar solutions.

Table 21.1 shows, for each procedure, the average objective function value, the average percent deviation from optimality, the number of optimal solutions, and the average CPU time in seconds. Since optimal solutions are not known for the random instances, the deviations for these are reported considering the best solution found during each experiment. Also for this table, the number of best solutions found is reported instead of the number of optimal solutions. We refer to Chanas and Kobylanskis' method as CK, and as CK10 to the application of the method from 10 randomly generated initial solutions. The tabu search method will be denoted as TS.

Table 21.1: Results with LOLIB instances and random instances.

LOLIB instances						
	Greedy	CK	CK10	TS	SS	SS10
Value	22033729.5	22018008.3	22040892.1	22040159.4	22041229.8	22041232.3
Optima dev.	0.15%	0.15%	0.02%	0.04%	0.01%	0.01%
Num Optima	11	11	27	30	42	43
Run time (s.)	0.01	0.10	1.06	0.33	3.82	14.28
Random instances						
Value	32713295.6	32678348.7	32800044.7	32890757.4	32903496.5	32908203.7
Best dev.	0.60%	0.71%	0.34%	0.04%	0.02%	0.01%
Num. Best	0	0	0	12	10	16
Run time (s.)	0.01	0.65	6.56	1.38	7.45	38.68

The greedy procedure is clearly inferior in terms of solution quality, although given its simplicity, its performance is quite acceptable. The performance of the greedy and CK methods is very similar within each of the two problem sets, but their deviation from the optimal (or best) solutions is significantly higher in the case of random instances. TS and the SS variants, on the other hand, are quite robust, as evident by the negligible change in the deviation values from the LOLIB instances to the random instances.

Table 21.1 shows that the best solution quality is obtained by the SS variants with a mean deviation from optima of 0.01% in the LOLIB instances and 0.02% in the random instances. However, the SS variants use more computation time than the other methods.

TS is very competitive, considering that it is able to match 30 optima in the LOLIB and 12 best solutions in the random set, employing an average of 0.33 and 1.38 seconds, respectively. Also note the remarkable performance of SS10, which outperforms all other methods in terms of percent deviation as well as in terms of the number of optima matched.

21.5 CONCLUSIONS

The objective of our study has been to expand and advance the knowledge associated with the implementation of scatter search procedures. Unlike its close cousin, tabu search, scatter search has not yet become widely implemented and tested as a metaheuristic for solving complex optimization problems. Our study shows, however, that a careful scatter search implementation can be quite effective and rival the best procedures in the literature.

Acknowledgments

The authors wish to thank Fred Glover for his valuable comments on both content and presentation.

Chapter Twenty-Two

Goal-Oriented Path Tracing Methods

Colin R. Reeves and Takeshi Yamada

22.1 INTRODUCTION

As is now universally appreciated, it is not really likely that optimal solutions to large combinatorial problems (COPs) will be found reliably by any exact method, although it is possible to find classes of instances where problem-specific methods can achieve good results. However, for problems that are *NP*-hard (Garey & Johnson [1979]), it is now customary to rely on the application of heuristic techniques (Reeves [1993, 1996a]. These techniques include what some call the 'metaheuristics' - simulated annealing (SA) and tabu search (TS) - as well as the popular approach of genetic algorithms (GAs).

Central to most heuristic search techniques is the concept of neighbourhood search (GAs are apparently an exception to this, but in fact the resemblances are greater than the differences, as we shall discuss later). If we assume that a solution is specified by a vector, that the set of all (feasible) solutions is denoted by X (which we shall also call the *search space*), and the cost of solution x is denoted by $c(x)$, then every solution $x \in X$ has an associated set of *neighbours*, $\mathcal{N}(x) \subset X$, called the neighbourhood of x. Each solution $x' \in \mathcal{N}(x)$ can be reached directly from x by an operation called a *move*. Many different types of move are possible in any particular case, and we can view a move as being generated by the application of an operator ω. For example, if X is the binary hypercube Z_2^l, a simple operator is the bit flip $\phi(k)$

$$\phi(k) : Z_2^l \rightarrow Z_2^l \qquad \begin{cases} z_k \rightarrow 1 - z_k \\ z_i \rightarrow z_i & \text{if } k \neq i \end{cases}$$

where z is a binary vector of length l.

As another example, which we shall refer to later, we can take the forward shift operator for the case where X is Π_n – the space of permutations π of length n. The forward shift operator $\mathcal{FSH}(i, j)$ (where we assume $i < j$) is

$$\mathcal{FSH}(i, j): \Pi_n \rightarrow \Pi_n \qquad \begin{cases} \pi_k \mapsto \pi_{k-1} & \text{if } i < k \leq j \\ \pi_i \mapsto \pi_j \\ \pi_k \mapsto \pi_k & \text{otherwise} \end{cases}$$

An analogous backward shift operator $\mathcal{BSH}(i, j)$ can similarly be described; the composite of $\mathcal{BSH}$ and $\mathcal{FSH}$ is denoted by $\mathcal{SH}$. Another alternative for such problems is an exchange operator $\mathcal{EX}(i, j)$ which simply exchanges the elements in the ith and jth positions.

A typical neighbourhood search (NS) heuristic operates by generating neighbours in an iterative process where a move to a new solution is made whenever certain criteria are fulfilled. There is a great variety of ways in which candidate moves can be chosen for consideration, and in defining criteria for accepting candidate moves. Perhaps the most common case is that of *descent*, in which the only moves accepted are to neighbours that improve the current solution. *Steepest* descent corresponds to the case where all neighbours are evaluated before a move is made - that move being the best available. *Next* descent is similar, but the next candidate (in some pre-defined sequence) that improves the current solution is accepted, without necessarily examining the complete neighbourhood. Normally, the search terminates when no moves can be accepted.

The trouble with NS is that the solution it generates is usually only a *local* optimum - a vector none of whose neighbours offer an improved solution. It is thus clear that the idea of a local optimum only has meaning with respect to a particular neighbourhood. Other associated concepts are those of 'landscapes', 'valleys', and 'basins of attraction' of a particular local optimum. However, these may alter in subtle ways, depending on the neighbourhood used, and the strategy employed for searching it.

The landscape is not an invariant of the search space, but recent empirical analyses (Boese et al [1994], Reeves [1998], Merz & Freisleben [1998]) have shown that, for many problem instances, the landscapes induced by some commonly-used operators have a 'big valley' structure, where the local optima occur relatively close to each other, and to a global optimum. This obviously suggests that in developing algorithms, rather than merely being content with landscape as a metaphor, we should try to understand and exploit its structure.

There is as yet no well-defined mathematical description of what it means for a landscape to possess a 'big valley'. The idea is a fairly informal one, based on the observation that in many combinatorial optimization problems local optima are indeed not distributed uniformly throughout the landscape. In the context of landscapes defined on binary strings, Kauffman [1993] has been the pioneer of such experiments, from which he suggested several descriptors of a 'big valley' landscape (because he was dealing with fitness maximization, he used the term 'central massif', but it is clear that it is the same phenomenon).

22.2 AVOIDING LOCAL OPTIMA

In recent years many techniques have been suggested for the avoidance of local optima. A comprehensive introduction to these methods can be found in Reeves [1993, 1996a]. For completeness, we refer here briefly to some of the most popular principles.

At the most basic level, we could use iterative restarts of NS from many different initial points, thus generating a collection of local optima from which the best can be selected.

Simulated annealing uses a controlled randomization strategy – inferior moves are accepted probabilistically, the chance of such acceptance decreasing slowly over the course of a search. By relaxing the acceptance criterion in this way, it becomes possible to move out of the basin of attraction of a local optimum.

Tabu search adopts a deterministic approach, whereby a 'memory' is implemented by the recording of previously-seen solutions. This record could be explicit, but is often an implicit one, making use of simple but effective data structures. These can be thought of as a 'tabu list' of moves which have been made in the recent past of the search, and which are 'tabu' or forbidden for a certain number of iterations. This prevents cycling, and also helps to promote a diversified coverage of the search space.

Perturbation methods improve the restart strategy: instead of retreating to an unrelated and randomly chosen initial solution, the current local optimum is perturbed in some way and the heuristic restarted from the new solution. Perhaps the most widely-known of such techniques is the 'iterated Lin-Kernighan' (ILK) method introduced by Johnson [1990] for the travelling salesman problem. On reaching a local optimum, a set of links is randomly chosen for removal and re-connection, in such a way that a new search can start relatively close to a new local optimum. Such techniques can perhaps best be described as perturbation methods.

Genetic algorithms differ in using a population of solutions rather than moving from one point to the next. Furthermore, new solutions are generated from two (or, rarely) more solutions by applying a 'crossover' operator. However, they can also be encompassed within an NS framework, as is shown in Reeves & Höhn [1996], and as we shall discuss at length later in this chapter.

However, there are other possibilities besides a random perturbation of the population. Glover and coworkers use and investigate the notion of 'path relinking' (see chapter nineteen), which suggests an alternative means for exploring the landscape.

22.3 PATHS IN A LANDSCAPE

Suppose we have two locally-optimal solutions to a COP. If the operators we are using induce a big valley structure, then it is a reasonable hypothesis that a local search that traces out a path from one such solution to another one will at some point enter the basin of attraction of a third local optimum. Even if no better solution is found on such a path, at least we have gained some knowledge about the relative size of the basins of attraction of the original local optima along one trajectory in the landscape.

Of course, there are many paths that could be taken, and many strategies that could be adopted to trace them out. One possibility is that used by Rana & Whitley [1997] in investigating the idea of 'optima linking' in the context of a binary search space. Here a path was traced by finding at each step the *best* move among all those that would take the current point one step nearer (in the sense of Hamming distance) to the target solution.

If the representation space X is not the binary hypercube, distance between solutions may not be so easily measured, and several different approaches can be adopted. Later in this chapter we shall describe some experimental work carried out in permutation spaces. First, however, we review the terminology, and then consider some links between the idea of path tracing and other techniques.

22.3.1 Terminology

Glover originally used the term path *relinking* to describe a method for linking solutions previously discovered during the course of a local search such as TS. The reasoning behind this nomenclature was the concept that the points that are produced are inherited from 'heuristic paths' as well as from 'linking paths' generated earlier in a point-based search procedure, so in a sense the whole process he described becomes one of 'path relinking'.

However, in the approach we have taken, the emphasis is somewhat wider: we are not confined to linking points previously visited on a search and stored for further reference (although this is not excluded). In the case of a GA, for example, the points currently being linked may have a totally unrelated history. Nor would it be appropriate to use the term 'optima linking', since the points being linked are not necessarily optima. In Glover [1994], Glover uses the simple phrase 'the notion of tracing paths', and this seems the most straightforward term to adopt, as one that encompasses all the variations suggested. However, in one sense it may be too vague, as any NS method – even a random walk – traces out a path in a landscape. To provide a little more precision, we propose as a fuller description the term 'goal-oriented path tracing', since this captures the idea of having a point to aim at (without specifying its nature), although for simplicity the shortened version 'path tracing' will generally be used in this chapter.

22.3.2 Links to Tabu Search

The idea of path tracing had its genesis in the work of Glover [1989], and so was introduced in a TS context, but the reason why it is appropriate to TS may not be immediately obvious. One of the main aims of TS is to discourage revisiting of previously evaluated points on the landscape - something that is wasteful of computing resources in itself, and which also means the search is not adequately diversified (readers of Glover's works will realize the importance of the concept of diversification in his development of TS). This can be accomplished by means of an explicit 'tabu list' of points previously visited, but normally it is easier, and more efficient, to record specific attributes of such points, or of moves that would lead towards them.

In path tracing strategies, starting from one local optimum (the initial point), the other (the goal) is used to define an orientation for the search. By using points from the path that links them to initiate new descent phases, new local optima may be discovered. It is clear that the algorithm can only return to one or other of the original optima if a new search is commenced from a point on the path that is still within its basin of attraction. If we restrict new searches to points 'sufficiently far' from the end points, and if the big valley exists, this is not likely to occur. If it does occur, it suggests that the landscape may have few local optima in any case, with a corresponding likelihood that the endpoints are themselves very good solutions already. We can thus argue that path tracing qualifies as an *implicit* tabu method, since revisiting is clearly discouraged, without need of the apparatus of tabu lists.

22.3.3 Links to Perturbation Methods

The ILK algorithm is fairly well-known, but several similar methods have recently been proposed: a discussion of some of the work that fits under this general rubric can be found in Reeves [1996]. Of course, the success of this procedure is likely to depend on the existence of a big valley structure in the landscape, but if such a structure exists, and the right perturbation is used, the new initial solution tends to be both in the basin of attraction of a different local optimum, and also relatively close to it. Thus a new search can commence rapidly without having to begin from an unrelated and randomly chosen initial solution. However, such methods generally need user-specified parameters in order to control the perturbation, and getting it right might require much experimentation in practice

– if the perturbation is too great, the search reverts almost to an iterated random restart; if it is too little, the search is not shifted from the current basin of attraction and nothing is gained.

Path tracing can obviously be viewed as a means of directing (and to some extent controlling) the perturbation necessary in order to allow a successful new search to commence.

22.3.4 Links to Genetic Algorithms

If we consider the case of crossover of strings in Z_2^l, it is easily seen that any child produced from two parents will lie on a path that leads from one parent to another. As an (extreme) example, every point clearly lies between (0 0 ... 0 0) and (1 1 ... 1 1). In an earlier paper (Reeves [1994]), we described such points as 'intermediate vectors': intermediate not merely in some analogical 'genetic' sense, but also precisely in the sense of being an intermediate point on an underlying landscape – in this case, the Hamming landscape.

In the case of non-binary strings, the distance measure may be more complicated, but the principle is still relevant. However, while crossover (of whatever variety) will generate a string that is intermediate between its parents, it pays no attention to the cost function. It is also true that some crossover operators sample the set of all intermediate points in what might be seen as a rather eccentric way. This is discussed in Reeves [1994], where it is suggested that some sort of local optimization should be attempted to find a 'good' intermediate point instead of making what is (in terms of the cost landscape) a rather arbitrary move. This led to the proposal for a 'neighbourhood search crossover' (NSX) that was found to produce good results in certain scheduling and graph problems (Reeves & Höhn [1996]). Subsequently, Yamada & Nakano [1996] extended this idea to 'multi-step crossover with fusion' (MSXF) which gave excellent results for some job-shop scheduling problems.

Clearly, path tracing from one parent to another is also a reasonable candidate for a more 'intelligent' approach to recombination.

22.4 APPLICATIONS

Three applications of goal-oriented path tracing methods are now reported in flowshop scheduling. First, a fairly simple application to the $n/m/P/C_{sum}$ problem will be discussed; then an approach that builds on the earlier work reported in Reeves [1994] and Yamada & Nakano [1996] in which path tracing methods are embedded in a genetic algorithm for the $n/m/P/C_{max}$ problem. Some of this work has appeared previously (Reeves & Yamada [1998, 1998a] and Yamada & Reeves [1998]) and further details can be found in those papers. However, sufficient introductory and explanatory detail will be included to make this chapter self-contained.

Finally, returning to $n/m/P/C_{sum}$, a sophisticated implementation is described that allows elements of simulated annealing and tabu search to be incorporated. As Glover has remarked (private communication to the authors) the relevance of path tracing as a strategy for combining solutions gives a useful foundation for integrating concepts of TS and GAs.

Perhaps surprisingly, as he also remarked, no TS method had yet applied such a strategy to scheduling, and so our work represents a new contribution from the TS as well as the GA perspective.

Before these applications are described, we first remind readers of the nature of the permutation flowshop scheduling problem (PFSP). This is the following: given n jobs to be processed on m machines, where we have processing times $p(i, j)$ for job i on machine j, and a job permutation $\pi = \{\pi_1, \pi_2, ..., \pi_n\}$ representing the (same) order of processing on each machine, then we calculate the completion times $C(\pi_i, j)$ as follows:

$$C(\pi_1, 1) = p(\pi_i, 1)$$
$$C(\pi_i, 1) = C(\pi_{i-1}, 1) + p(\pi_i, 1), \qquad\qquad \text{for } i = 2, ..., n$$
$$C(\pi_1, j) = C(\pi_1, j-1) + p(\pi_1, j), \qquad\qquad \text{for } j = 2, ..., m$$
$$C(\pi_i, j) = \max\{C(\pi_{i-1}, j), C(\pi_i, j-1)\} + p(\pi_i, j), \quad \text{for } i = 2, ..., n; \ j = 2, ..., m$$

Finally, we define the *makespan* as $C_{\max}(\pi) = C(\pi_n, m)$.

The *makespan* version of the PFSP is then to find a permutation π^* such that:

$$C_{\max}(\pi^*) \le C_{\max}(\pi), \ \forall \pi \in \Pi_n$$

While it is the problem with the makespan objective that has received most attention, other objectives can also be defined. For example, we could seek to minimize the mean *flow-time* (the time a job spends in process), or the mean *tardiness* (assuming some deadline for each job). If the release dates of all jobs are zero (i.e. all jobs are available at the outset), the mean flow-time objective reduces to minimizing:

$$C_{\text{sum}}(\pi) = \sum_{i=1}^{n} C(\pi_i, m)$$

We call this the *flowsum version* of the PFSP.

22.5 SIMPLE APPLICATION TO $N/M/P/C_{\text{SUM}}$

There are clearly many ways in which a path tracing approach can be implemented. For example, it may not be necessary to start from a local optimum; perhaps a 'good' solution will do. The question of how to measure the distance between sequences is also one that has to be considered. Here we used ideas tested elsewhere (Reeves [1998]) and found to be helpful, basing our distance measure on differences in precedence relations between the two sequences. The next step is the implementation of a strategy for creating a path that gets steadily close to its goal.

Many possibilities exist for this aspect. The earlier path relinking proposal (Glover & Laguna [1995]) suggests more generally (in arbitrary landscapes) the idea of choosing each move to minimize the number of moves remaining to reach the target solution, and discusses the relevance of choosing the best such move at each step – although of course, what 'best' means is also context-dependent. In this more general setting, alternative ways of choosing moves are also discussed that involve reducing the numbers of attributes that differ between the current solution and the goal. Related, more advanced options, are suggested in Glover [1994, 1994b].

In the context of the flowsum problem, the path is very easily traced out by using a steepest descent approach successively to modify the initial point, where the objective is not C_{sum} itself, but the distance measured between the current point and the goal. This is what we have carried out.

At some point, the path should be abandoned for a new NS phase. Again, there are many possibilities. Our current implementation initiates a new search for a local optimum from the mid-point of the path. This has two advantages: it is not necessary at each stage to trace the complete path, and it is likely that the search starts in a new basin of attraction, as desired. However, alternatives exist, such as using the best point found.

In each case reported here, we initially generated three local optima using the $\mathcal{FSH}$ operator, adding each new local optimum as it was generated to the 'selection pool'. A maximum of 50 local optima were allowed in the pool; when the pool was full, each new local optimum replaced the one to which it was closest. At each stage, points were randomly selected from this pool as initial and target solutions. It was thought sensible to prevent the choice of linking points that were too close. Here we defined 'too close' to mean less than 5% of the maximum distance possible between two permutations. In fact, no solutions were ever detected that were this close – typical distances were around 20 – 30% of this maximum.

The method described above was implemented and tested on the well-known benchmark problems introduced by Taillard [1993a]. Global optima are not known for these problems, and in any case, we are more interested initially in generating high-quality solutions quickly. With this in mind, the results were compared with those generated by the three constructive methods proposed by Wang et al [1997]. The best solution obtained from each of these methods was used for comparison, with the results shown in Table 22.1.

Table 22.1: Results of applying goal-oriented path tracing to Taillard's 20-job and 50-job benchmarks, averaged over each group of ten instances. The C_{sum} values are reported relative to the values obtained as the best generated by Wang's constructive methods in each case.

	Ratios		
Problem Group	Min	Mean	Sd
20×5	0.941	0.962	0.015
20×10	0.945	0.967	0.011
20×20	0.955	0.969	0.009
50×5	0.961	0.982	0.010
50×10	0.928	0.961	0.013
50×20	0.957	0.969	0.007

These three solutions are generated fairly quickly, and the time allowed for the path-tracing solutions was fixed at the same level. However, if a local search was in progress, it was allowed to continue, so that the path-tracing approach generally had a little more computation time than the constructive methods. Nevertheless, the time allowed was of the same order of magnitude, and it can be seen that the solutions are of higher quality, with an average C_{sum} value (based on ten different initial random sets of sequences) that is 2 – 3%

better than the best of Wang's methods, and a best performance that improves these solutions by 5 – 7%. The standard deviation is small, so there is a low risk of finding a really poor solution (relative to Wang's results).

22.6 ADVANCED IMPLEMENTATION FOR $N/M/P/C_{MAX}$

Our second application of path tracing methods takes up the links discussed earlier with genetic algorithms. In earlier work on flowshop problems (Reeves [1995a]), a fairly simple GA provided encouragingly good results, but integrating path tracing into such a GA offered the prospect of significant improvement.

The GA used was a steady-state GA in which parents were selected probabilistically, the probability of selection being based on a linear ranking of their makespan values. In the earlier work crossover was the PMX operator of Goldberg & Lingle [1985] or a variant of Davis's order operator (Davis [1985]). Mutation was implemented by an application of $\mathcal{BSH}(i, j)$ or $\mathcal{FSH}(i, j)$ with i, j chosen randomly. An adaptive mutation rate was used to prevent premature convergence. A newly generated solution was inserted into the population only if its makespan is better than the worst in the current population (which is deleted).

However, the nature of the changes to be made were such that not all the prescriptions used previously were suitable. Both crossover and mutation have to be re-defined (as will be explained below), and the populations used were smaller. Also, in order to avoid premature convergence, no two individuals were allowed to have the same makespan.

22.6.1 'Crossover'

As proposed in section 22.3.4, crossover in the conventional sense was replaced by path tracing. The approach taken was a development of the MSXF operator mentioned above. MSXF carries out a short-term local search starting from one of the parent solutions (the initial point) and moving in the direction of the other parent (the goal). It clearly, therefore, needs a neighbourhood, and a strategy for deciding whether or not to move to a candidate neighbour. The method adopted in Yamada & Nakano [1996], and also used here was as shown in Figure 22.1, which describes the approach in a generic way. The neighbours of solution x are sorted in *ascending* order of their $d(y_i, \pi_2)$ values, and those which are closer to π_2 are probabilistically preferred. The objective C_{max} can of course be replaced by whatever is appropriate to the problem given. The termination condition can be given by, for example, a fixed number of iterations L in the outer loop. The best solution q is used for the next generation.

The neighbourhood used in our experiments was a restricted version of that generated by the $\mathcal{SH}$ operator, which made use of the concept of *critical blocks*. This critical block-based neighbourhood is commonly used for the problem (Nowicki & Smutnicki [1996]). The reasons for this and further details of this idea can be found in Reeves & Yamada [1998a], where experiments are reported that demonstrate that this neighbourhood also appears to induce a big valley.

- Let π_1, π_2 be the relevant solutions. Set $x = q = \pi_1$.

do

    - For each neighbour $y_i \in \mathcal{N}(x)$, calculate $d(y_i, \pi_2)$.
    - Sort $\{y_i\}$ in ascending order of $d(y_i, \pi_2)$.

    do

        1. Select y_i from $\mathcal{N}(x)$ with a probability inversely proportional to the index i.
        2. Calculate $C_{max}(y_i)$ if it is unknown.
        3. Accept y_i with probability 1 if $C_{max}(y_i) \leq C_{max}(x)$, and with probability $P_c(y_i)$ otherwise.
        4. Change the index of y_i from i to n, and the indices of y_k ($k \in \{i+1, \dots, n\}$) from k to $k-1$.

    until y_i is accepted.
    - Set $x = y_i$.
    - If $C_{max}(x) < C_{max}(q)$ then set $q = x$.

until some termination condition is satisfied.

- q is used for the next generation.

Fig. 22.1: Path tracing crossover. The initial point on the path is π_1 and π_2 is the goal. The neighbourhood of solution x is denoted by $\mathcal{N}(x)$; neighbours that are closer to π_2 are probabilistically preferred; better neighbours (smaller C_{max} values) are always accepted, otherwise y_i may be accepted with probability $P_c(y_i) = \exp(-\Delta C_{max}/c)$, where $\Delta C_{max} = C_{max}(y_i) - C_{max}(x)$. This last prescription is similar to the approach of simulated annealing, corresponding to annealing at a constant temperature $T = c$.

22.6.2 'Mutation'

It is also relevant to ask whether there is a path-tracing analogue for the mutation operator. To answer this, we need to consider the purpose of mutation. Most would probably agree that if crossover promotes the 'intensification' of the search, mutation promotes 'diversification' (where we use Glover's terminology: see chapter nineteen, and also Glover & Laguna [1995]). That is, mutation tends to move the population away from the region to which crossover has brought it. In the analogy to path tracing, this corresponds to extrapolation of a path between parents, where crossover corresponds to interpolation – an interpretation also suggested by Glover [1994].

This idea can be implemented by a simple modification to the algorithm illustrated in Figure 22.1, where the neighbours of x are sorted in *descending* order of $d(y_i, \pi_2)$ and the most *distant* solution is stored and used in the next generation instead of q, if q does not improve the parent solutions. However, 'mutation' was only invoked if the distance between parents was less than a value d_{min}. This is reasonable, because if the parents are too close together, 'crossover' accomplishes little, since the potential neighbours and paths are very few – in the limit, where the distance is one unit, there is of course no path at all.

22.6.3 Local search

Early in the search, even the best members of the population are unlikely to be local optima. They may even be in quite the 'wrong' part of the landscape – some distance from the 'big valley'. This is in fact a criticism often made of GAs, and many authors have experimented with various ways of incorporating local neighbourhood search into a GA. There is good reason therefore for including NS explicitly in the algorithm. In other words, the path is used as a jumping-off point for an attempted improvement phase within the main GA loop, in a very similar way to the simple implementation of path tracing described in section 22.5. This has two benefits: it means that the big valley region can be found quickly, so it is important early on; it is also important later, in searching the big valley more thoroughly than might be done by path tracing alone.

As it was not clear exactly how much local search should be done, we decided to make the choice a probabilistic one – with probability P_X the algorithm would use path tracing (either interpolatory or extrapolatory, depending on the distance between the parents), otherwise NS was used on the first parent selected. However, a complete search to full local optimality could require considerable computation, so a balance was struck by making the NS stochastic (as in simulated annealing, but with a constant `temperature' P_c), and fixing the number of iterations at a limit L. The resulting NS is like the path tracing crossover described in Figure 22.1, but the order of searching neighbours is now just random. Figure 22.2 gives an idealized picture of the concept.

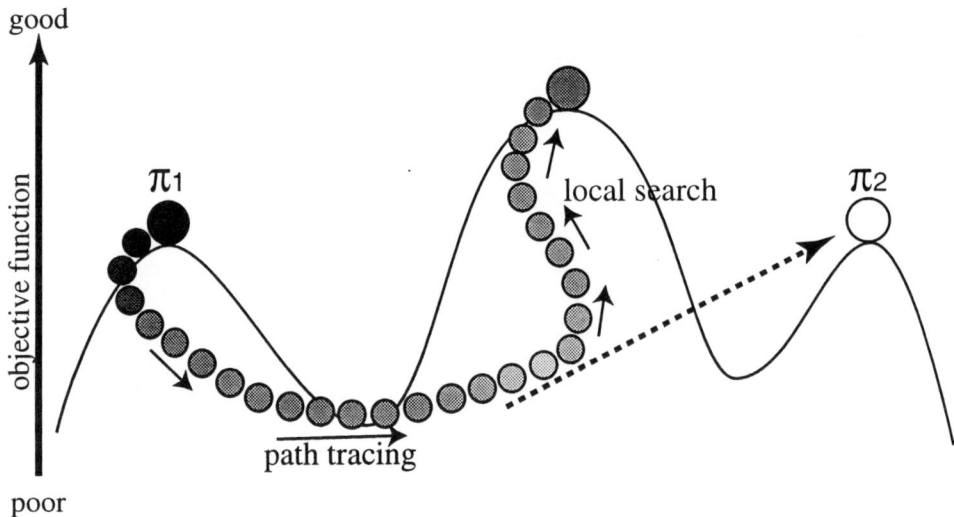

Fig. 22.2: Path tracing and local search: The search traces a path from the initial parent towards the goal. In the 'middle' of the search, good solutions may be found somewhere between the parents. A local search can then exploit this new starting point by climbing towards the top of a hill (or the bottom of a valley, if it is a minimization problem) – a new local optimum.

- Initialize population: randomly generate a set of permutation schedules. Sort the population members in descending order of their makespan values.

do

1. Select two sequences π_1, π_2 from the population inversely proportional to their ranks.
2. Do step (a) with probability P_X, otherwise do Step (b).

    (a) If the precedence-based distance between π_1 and π_2 is less than d_{min}, extrapolate from π_1 and generate q. **Otherwise**, apply path-tracing between π_1 and π_2 using the reduced neighbourhood and the precedence-based distance and generate a new schedule q.

    (b) Apply neighbourhood search to π_1 with acceptance probability P_c and the reduced neighbourhood. q is the best solution found during L iterations.

3. If q's makespan is less than the worst in the population, and no member of the current population has the same makespan as q, replace the worst individual with q.

until some termination condition is satisfied.

- Output the best schedule in the population.

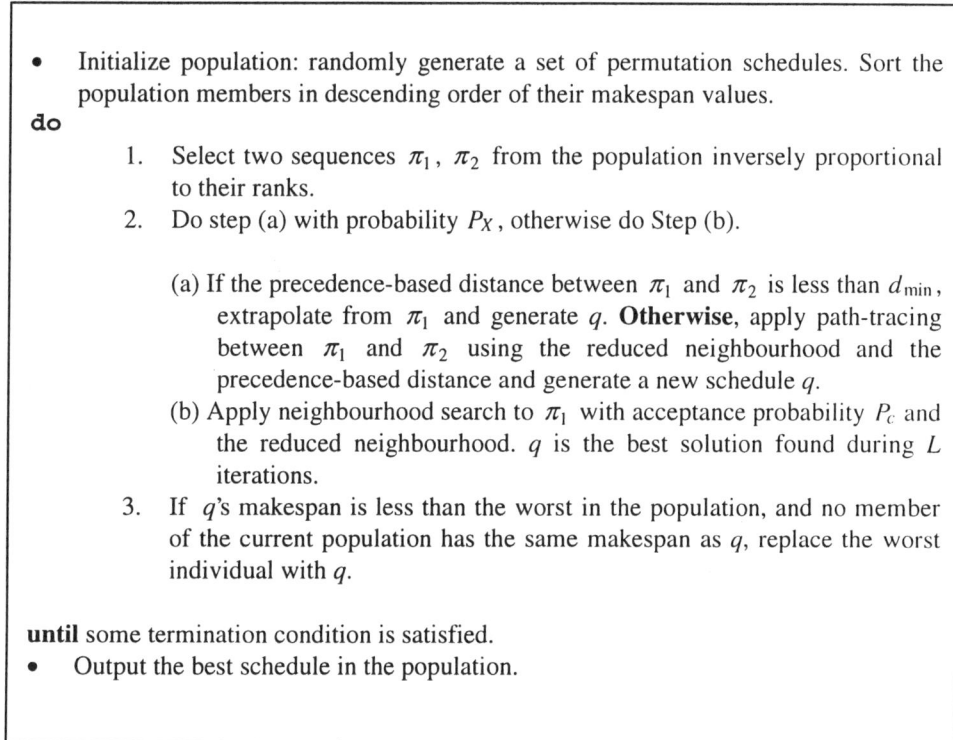

Fig. 22.3: The GA with embedded path tracing and neighbourhood search for the PFSP.

22.7 RESULTS

The above ideas were incorporated into a C program and implemented on a DEC Alpha 600 5/226 computer. A template summarizing the final version of the algorithm is given in Figure 22.3.

The parameter values used were as follows (no attempt was made to investigate whether these were in any sense 'optimal'). The population size is 15, constant temperature $c=3$, number of iterations for each path tracing or local search phase $L=1000$, and $d_{min}=n/2$. The probability $P_X=0.5$.

Global optima are now known for all Taillard's smaller PFSP benchmarks (instances ranging from 20×5 to 50×10 in size). The algorithm was run on these, and in every case it quite quickly found a solution within about 1% of the global optimum.

Of more interest are the larger problem instances, where global optima are still unknown. Table 22.2 summarizes the performance statistics for a subset of Taillard's larger benchmarks, together with the results found by Nowicki & Smutnicki [1996] using their TS implementation, and the lower and upper bounds taken from the OR-library (Beasley [1990]; these upper bounds are the currently best-known makespans, most of them found by a branch and bound technique with computational time unknown).

Table 22.2: Results of the Taillard benchmark problems: *best*, *mean*, *std* denote the best, average and standard deviation of our 30 makespan values ; *nowi* denotes the results of Nowicki & Smutnicki [1996]; {*lb*, *ub*} are the theoretical lower bounds and currently best known makespan values taken from the OR-library; **bold** figures are those which are better than the current *ub*.

50×20	Best	mean	std	nowi	lb–ub
1	**3861**	3880	9.3	3875	3771–3875
2	**3709**	3716	2.9	3715	3661–3715
3	**3651**	3668	6.2	3668	3591–3668
4	**3726**	3744	6.1	3752	3631–3752
5	**3614**	3636	8.9	3635	3551–3635
6	3690	3701	6.7	3698	3667–3687
7	3711	3723	5.6	3716	3672–3706
8	**3699**	3721	7.7	3709	3627–3700
9	3760	3769	5.2	3765	3645–3755
10	3767	3772	4.2	3777	3696–3767
100×20	Best	mean	std	nowi	lb–ub
1	6242	6259	9.6	6286	6106–6228
2	6217	6234	8.9	6241	6183–6210
3	6299	6312	7.8	6329	6252–6271
4	6288	6303	2.7	6306	6254–6269
5	6329	6354	11.3	6377	6262–6319
6	**6380**	6417	12.7	6437	6302–6403
7	6302	6319	11.0	6346	6184–6292
8	6433	6466	17.3	6481	6315–6423
9	6297	6323	11.4	6358	6204–6275
10	6448	6471	10.6	6465	6404–6434
200×20	Best	mean	std	nowi	lb–ub
1	11272	11316	20.8	11294	11152–11195
2	11299	11346	21.4	11420	11143–11223
3	11410	11458	25.2	11446	11281–11337
4	11347	11400	29.9	11347	11275–11299
5	11290	11320	16.6	11311	11259–11260
6	11250	11288	23.4	11282	11176–11189
7	11438	11455	9.3	11456	11337–11386
8	11395	11426	16.4	11415	11301–11334
9	11263	11306	21.5	11343	11145–11192
10	11335	11409	31.3	11422	11284–11313

It is clear that the GA with embedded path tracing has achieved results of outstandingly high quality, especially for the 50×20 instances The results for larger problems are not as good, but still good enough to support our view that implementing crossover as path tracing offers an effective way to improve GA performance significantly.

Some further experiments were carried out on the 50×20 set of instances, where CPU time was increased by a factor of about 4. The results of these experiments (based on 10 replications, rather than 30) are shown in Table 22.3.

Table 22.3: Results of longer runs (approx. 45 mins.) for the 50×20 instances.

No.	best	avg.	nowi	lb–ub
1	3855	3863	3875	3771–3875
2	3708	3713	3715	3661–3715
3	3647	3657	3668	3591–3668
4	3731	3735	3752	3631–3752
5	3614	3621	3635	3551–3635
6	3686	3692	3698	3667–3687
7	3707	3713	3716	3672–3706
8	3701	3712	3709	3627–3700
9	3743	3761	3765	3645–3755
10	3767	3768	3777	3696–3767

It appears from Table 22.3 that longer runs are able to improve the quality of solution even more – in six cases, further new best solutions have been obtained. (Altogether, seven new best solutions have been found, and in the other cases the difference is either 0 or 1 unit.) Perhaps of almost equal significance is the very good average performance, which in many cases is within a few units of the best. This suggests that the result of just a single long run is likely to be very close to the global optimum.

22.8 ADVANCED IMPLEMENTATION FOR $N/M/P/C_{\text{SUM}}$

The flowsum version of the PFSP has not been subject to the same intensity of investigation as the makespan version. Optimal solutions for the Taillard benchmarks are not known for this case. The problems are more difficult to optimize, mainly because the calculation of the objective function is more time consuming, good lower bounds are hard to generate, and problem specific knowledge such as critical blocks cannot be used. Some constructive algorithms based on heuristic rules have been suggested (Wang et al [1997]), but better solutions can be generated by the simple path tracing approach described earlier.

However, the success on the makespan version of the GA hybrid suggests that further improvement should be possible. Some differences in implementation are inevitable – for example, it is not possible to use critical blocks. The use of a restricted neighbourhood is however an important part of the algorithm, since it prevents computation in the path tracing and local search stages from becoming too large. In this case, we used a reduced neighbourhood as follows k members of the neighbourhood were chosen (at random) and tested. The best move in this candidate subset is then chosen. A mechanism for doing this efficiently is given in Reeves [1993]. Of course, the selected move may not be an improving one, and in order to prevent the acceptance of a really bad move, the local search is made stochastic as before, but with a modification: the neighbourhood is partitioned into p subsets, one of which is selected at random and all its members are evaluated; the best move in the subset is accepted probabilistically; if it is rejected, then another subset is selected at random. For more detail, please refer to Yamada & Reeves [1998]. The other potential problem is that the search could cycle, revisiting points using a standard pattern of moves. This is classic tabu search territory, and this implementation enables us to use TS ideas of adaptive memory (Glover & Laguna [1995]); in particular the concept of *recency*.

If a solution is generated from the current solution π by moving a job $j = \pi_i$ to a new position, the pair (j, i), i.e. the job and its original position, is recorded as tabu for the next l iterations. Thus subsequent moves cannot generate a solution in which job j is in position i until at least l iterations have passed: such moves are excluded from the calculation of the best move above. The number of iterations of the local search or path tracing component was limited to a value L as before, while the GA (the 'outer loop') was allowed L' 'events' (i.e. step 2 of Figure 22.3).

The method was applied to some of Taillard's benchmark problems. For the relatively easy problems (20×5, 20×10 and 20×20) six runs were carried out for each problem with different random seeds. The parameters in these experiments were: population size=5, $L=1000$, $L'=700$, $P_X=0.5$ and the tabu tenure $l=7$.

Quite consistent results were obtained, i.e. almost all of the six runs converged to the same job sequence in a short time (from a few seconds to a few minutes) before the limit of $L'=700$ was reached on an HP workstation. The best results (and they are also the average results in most cases) are reported in Table 22.4 together with the results obtained by the simple approach described in section 22.5.

Table 22.4: Taillard's benchmark results (20 jobs) for the flowsum version; *simple* denotes the results obtained by the simple path tracing implementation described earlier

	20×5			20×10			20×20	
prob	best	simple	prob	Best	simple	prob	best	simple
1	14033	14043	11	20911	21032	21	33623	33882
2	15151	15372	12	22440	22799	22	31587	31891
3	13301	13513	13	19833	19915	23	33920	34082
4	15447	15518	14	18710	18977	24	31661	31722
5	13529	13529	15	18641	18771	25	34557	34622
6	13123	13256	16	19245	19377	26	32564	32758
7	13548	13712	17	18363	18465	27	32922	33272
8	13948	14011	18	20241	20275	28	32412	32575
9	14295	14593	19	20330	20354	29	33600	33744
10	12943	13056	20	21320	21389	30	32262	32380

The next group of problems (50×5 and 50×10) are much more difficult. In each run the best results were different. Ten runs were carried out for each problem with different random seeds. The parameters used in these experiments were: population size=30, $L=10000$, $L'=700$, $P_X=0.5$. It takes 45 minutes per run for 50×5 instances and 90 minutes for 50×10 instances.

It is not certain how good these solutions are. Certainly, they improve on the simple method by a useful margin, but the lower bounds are some way off (on average around 30% – but they are probably not very good bounds). Even for the easier problems in Table 22.4 there is no guarantee that the best solutions obtained so far are optimal, although they are closer to their lower bounds. For the problems in Table 22.5, the best results could probably still be improved by increasing the amount of computation. For example, a solution to problem 31 was found with $C_{sum} = 64803$ by an overnight run.

Table 22.5: Taillard's benchmark results (50 jobs) for the flowsum version; *simple* denotes the results obtained by the simple path tracing implementation described earlier.

50×5				50×10			
prob	best	mean	simple	prob	best	mean	simple
31	64860	64934.8	66514	41	87430	87561.4	90423
32	68134	68247.2	70200	42	83157	83305.8	85869
33	63304	63523.2	64963	43	79996	80303.4	83361
34	68259	68502.7	70480	44	86725	86822.4	89670
35	69491	69619.6	71200	45	86448	86703.7	89854
36	67006	67127.6	68631	46	86651	86888.0	89656
37	66311	66450.0	67933	47	89042	89220.7	90869
38	64412	64550.1	66625	48	86924	87180.5	89856
39	63156	63223.8	65605	49	85674	85924.3	88628
40	68994	69137.4	71244	50	88215	88438.6	91391

Summarizing, we can say that although the absolute quality of these results is unknown, they certainly improve on existing procedures by a significant margin, and on the evidence of the makespan version, we expect them to be of generally high quality.

22.9 CONCLUSIONS

We have shown that the idea of a landscape need not simply be a useful metaphor for heuristic search, but that we can use neighbourhoods that induce a structure that is helpful to the search and can be exploited profitably. The concept of goal-oriented path tracing is such an approach. A simple procedure has been implemented for the flowsum version of the PFSP, and shown to produce excellent results. The approach has then been applied in the context of a genetic algorithm, where it has proved capable of generating extremely high-quality solutions to the makespan version of the PFSP. Finally it has been observed that the path tracing perspective offers an opportunity for an almost seamless integration of the capabilities of several 'metaheuristics'. This is demonstrated in the context of the flowsum PFSP, where path tracing has allowed the integration of elements of GAs, TS and SA in order to generate solutions that are currently the best known for some benchmark instances of this problem.

The quality of the results obtained is certainly high, but in our view this is not the most interesting aspect of goal-oriented path tracing. Rather it is the methodological aspect: that it is based in a fundamental way on the concept of the problem landscape, so that it becomes natural to develop algorithms that generalize concepts of existing popular metaheuristics. Our understanding of the nature of search landscapes and how to exploit them is something that promises to become an important area of future research.

Part Six

Emerging Ideas and Extensions

Co-ordinating Editors:

David Corne

Riccardo Poli

Contributors:

Russell Eberhart

Gusz Eiben

Jano van Hemert

James Kennedy

Jan Paredis

Riccardo Poli

Robert Reynolds

Rafal Salustowicz

Jürgen Schmidhuber

Chapter Twenty-Three

Constraint Satisfaction with Coevolution

Jan Paredis

23.1 INTRODUCTION

The Oxford Dictionary of Natural History provides the following definition of coevolution:

> **coevolution** Complementary evolution of closely associated species. The interlocking adaptations of many flowering plants and their pollinating insects provide some striking examples of coevolution. In a broader sense, predator-prey relationships also involve coevolution, with an evolutionary advance in the predator, for instance, triggering an evolutionary response in the prey.

Allaby [1985, p. 150]

According to the description above, coevolution involves closely interacting species. In predator-prey systems, for example, this form of species interaction is known as an *inverse fitness interaction:* success on one side is felt by the other side as failure to which must be responded in order to maintain one's chances of survival. There is a strong evolutionary pressure for prey to defend themselves better (e.g. by running faster, improved eye-sight, etc.) in response to which predators will develop better attacking strategies (such as stronger claws, faster diving, etc.). This typically results in an *arms race* in which the complexity of both predator and prey increases stepwise. Or, in other words, predator-prey interactions are an important driving force behind evolution, leading to highly complex adaptations. This chapter describes the use of coevolution within genetic algorithms (GAs) in order to obtain improved performance when solving constraint satisfaction problems (CSPs). The resulting algorithm is called a Coevolutionary Genetic Algorithm (CGA).

Genetic algorithms are computational optimization processes inspired by the process of natural selection. They use an artificial form of evolution to address optimization problems coming from various disciplines such as: engineering, computer science, artificial intelligence and operations research. GAs typically start with a population of randomly generated objects – often represented as binary strings. Each individual object has a fitness value which represents its quality. This usually is the value of the objective function one wants to optimize. The initial population is replaced by new individuals which – through the application of genetic operators such as crossover and mutation – inherit genes (e.g. bits) from the objects of the previous generations. Crossover typically constructs the genetic material of a child from the genetic material of the parents. This result is then passed on to a low probability mutation operator which mutates individual 'genes'. The better a solution is, the higher the chance that it will be chosen as parent. This way good solutions pass their genes on to new individuals which, hopefully, combine good partial solutions of their parents into a better solution.

In spite of their analogy with natural selection, there are some clear differences between the 'fitness calculation' in GAs and in nature. Standard GAs apply an à priori defined fitness function (e.g. the function one wants to optimize) to an individual. They typically use an 'all at once' calculation: individuals are evaluated immediately after their creation (i.e. birth). Fitness calculation in nature is substantially different. It consists of a continuous series of tests during an individual's life. These tests originate from a complex environment influenced by the animal's own actions, by the other individuals as well as other processes occurring in the world (e.g. climatological or geophysical changes). In this chapter we will see that the fitness calculation of CGAs is much closer to that of nature than that of standard GAs.

CGAs are well suited to solve *test-solution problems*. This large class of problems involves the search for a solution which satisfies given tests. A CGA uses two populations to solve test-solution problems. One contains the tests which a solution should satisfy. The other consists of potential solutions to the problem. CGAs have been applied to various test-solution problems, such as: classification (Paredis [1994]), process control (Paredis [1998]), path planning (Paredis & Westra [1997]), and the evolution of cellular automata (CA) for density classification (Paredis [1997]). Here, the approach is illustrated on constraint satisfaction problems. The main purpose of the applications described above is to help us understand, explore, and illustrate the operation of CGAs. Recently, researchers have been using CGAs in real-world applications such as object motion estimation from video images (Dixon et al [1997]) and timetabling of medical doctors associated with an emergency service (Kragelund [1997]). Paredis [1998a] provides an overview of the use of coevolution for computational purposes starting from the early days of computing. Here, only aspects directly relevant to constraint satisfaction will be discussed.

The structure of this chapter is as follows. The next section introduces constraint satisfaction problems (CSPs) as well as the bench-mark problem on which the algorithm will be tested. Section 23.3 describes the CGA. Section 23.4 concentrates on the empirical results. Next, the timetabling application is briefly described. Finally, this chapter closes with conclusions and discusses relations with other approaches and proposes some extensions to the CGA framework.

23.2 CONSTRAINT SATISFACTION PROBLEMS

Constraint Satisfaction Problems (CSPs) typically consist of a set of n variables x_i $(i \leq n)$ which have an associated domain D_i of possible values. There is also a set of constraints, called C, which describe relations between the values of the x_i (e.g. the value of x_1 should be different from the value of x_3). A *solution* consists of an assignment of values to the x_i such that all constraints in C are satisfied, i.e. the solution is valid.

In this chapter we use the n-queens problem to illustrate the operation of a CGA. This problem involves placing n queens on an $n \times n$ chess board in such a way that no two queens attack each other (i.e. they are not in the same row, column, or diagonal). A frequently used representation of this problem – which we use as well – consists of n variables x_i. Each such variable represents one column on the chess board. The assignment $x_2 = 3$, for example, indicates that a queen is positioned in the third row of the second column. Hence, each of the x_i takes a value from the set $\{1,2, ...,n\}$. The constraints for this problem are simple, and we can set them out as follows.

$$x_i \neq x_j \qquad\qquad i \neq j \qquad\qquad \text{'row-constraints'}$$
$$| x_i - x_j | \neq | i - j | \qquad\qquad i \neq j \qquad\qquad \text{'diagonal-constraints'}$$

The first line above prohibits two queens to be placed in the same row. The second line ensures that no two queens are on a same diagonal. Note that the column constraint (only one queen is allowed per column) is implicit in the representation. Here, we test our approach on a 50-queens CSP. Hence, a solution consists of 50 variables. Each of which has to be assigned a value from the set $\{1, 2, ..., 50\}$.

23.3 THE COEVOLUTIONARY GENETIC ALGORITHM

The algorithm involves two populations. The first one contains potential – possibly invalid – solutions to the CSP to be solved. The second population contains the constraints. Just as in predator-prey models the selection pressure on members of one population depends on the members of the other population. Or, more precisely, there is an inverse fitness interaction between both populations.

Figure 23.1 depicts the data structures used. The 'genetic representation' of both types of individuals is quite simple. The solutions are represented as 50-dimensional vectors containing integers from the set $\{1,2,3 ..., 50\}$. A constraint, on the other hand, is an a priori defined piece of code which checks whether it is violated by a given solution. The constraints can be taken directly from the problem specification. For each x_i two constraints are used. A first one checks whether any of the other columns have a queen positioned at the same row as x_i. The second one checks the diagonal constraint. Or, in a more formal way: for each $i \in \{1,2,3 ..., 50\}$ the following two constraints are present in the constraint population:

$$\forall j \in \{1,2,...,50\} : i = j \ \text{ or } \ x_i \neq x_j$$
$$\forall j \in \{1,2,...,50\} : i = j \ \text{ or } \ | x_i - x_j | \neq | i - j |$$

As we discuss in more detail below, the constraint population contains all the time the same hundred constraints. This in contrast to the population of solutions in which new solutions – created through reproduction – gradually replace older ones. Hence, the constraints do not form a real population in a strict sense. In other CGA applications (Dixon et al [1997], Paredis [1997, 1998], Paredis & Westra [1997]) both populations evolve. This is because in these applications the number of tests is too large to be listed exhaustively. Hence, problem characteristics determine whether both populations really evolve or only one of them.

An important novelty, in comparison with standard GAs, is the notion of an *encounter* between a solution and a test (i.e. constraint). During such an encounter the solution is checked with respect to the constraint it encounters. The solution receives a reward when it satisfies the constraint, it receives a penalty in case the constraint is violated. For the constraint involved in an encounter the result of an encounter is opposite: it gets a penalty when the solution encountered satisfies it and a reward in case of violation. In our implementation rewards have a value of 1 and penalties have a value of -1. Both can be interpreted as the *pay-off* resulting from an encounter. Each individual – whether constraint or solution – has an associated history containing the rewards and penalties it received during its most recent encounters. Here we use a history of length 20. Hence, the fitness of an individual is defined as the sum of the pay-off it received during the 20 most recent encounters it was involved in. Consequently, the fitness of an individual is approximated through a continuous series of tests during its lifetime. This in contrast with the traditional 'once and for all' fitness calculation. Hence, the fitness calculation of a CGA is called lifetime fitness evaluation (LTFE). The limited length of the histories ensures that only the most recent encounters are taken into account. That is why LTFE is said to provide a partial fitness measure.

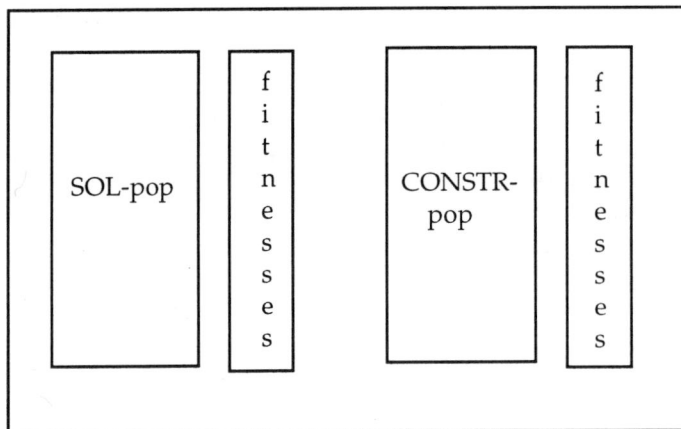

```
┌─────────────────────────────────────────────────────────────┐
│  ┌──────────┐  ┌───┐      ┌──────────┐  ┌───┐                │
│  │          │  │ f │      │          │  │ f │                │
│  │          │  │ i │      │          │  │ i │                │
│  │          │  │ t │      │          │  │ t │                │
│  │          │  │ n │      │          │  │ n │                │
│  │ SOL-pop  │  │ e │      │ CONSTR-  │  │ e │                │
│  │          │  │ s │      │   pop    │  │ s │                │
│  │          │  │ s │      │          │  │ s │                │
│  │          │  │ e │      │          │  │ e │                │
│  │          │  │ s │      │          │  │ s │                │
│  └──────────┘  └───┘      └──────────┘  └───┘                │
└─────────────────────────────────────────────────────────────┘
```

Fig. 23.1: Coevolving solutions and constraints.

The algorithm starts by creating the initial populations. The solutions are 50-dimensional vectors containing integers randomly drawn from the set {1,2,3 ..., 50}. The 100 constraints described above constitute the test population. In order to determine the fitness of the tests and solutions their histories are filled with the pay-offs received during 20 encounters with individuals randomly chosen from the other population. The fitness is then the sum of these 20 pay-offs. Once the fitness of the initial populations is calculated, the individuals are sorted on fitness, i.e. the fitter solutions and tests are located at the top of their respective populations. Next, the basic cycle described below is iterated. First 20[1] constraint-solution encounters are executed. The function which SELECTs the individuals to be involved in an encounter is biased towards highly ranking individuals: the most fit individual is 1.5 times more likely to be selected than the individual with median fitness. This way, fit solutions and constraints are often involved in an encounter. Or in other words, good solutions have to prove themselves more often. At the same time, the algorithm concentrates on satisfying difficult, i.e. not yet solved, constraints. This is because constraints have a high fitness when they are violated by many members of the solution population. The function ENCOUNTER returns 1 if the solution satisfies the constraint. In the other case, −1 is returned. Next, the histories of the solution and constraint involved in the encounter are UPDATEd[2]. This is done by pushing the pay-off associated with the current encounter on the history of the individuals. At the same time the pay-off associated with the least recent encounter is removed from these histories. Finally, the fitness of an individual – which is defined as the sum of pay-offs in its history – is updated. As the populations are continually kept sorted on fitness, this change of fitness might move the individual up or down in its population.

DO 20 TIMES
    sol ← SELECT (*sol-pop*)
    constr ← SELECT (*constr-pop*)
    res ← ENCOUNTER (*sol, constr*)
    UPDATE-HISTORY-AND-FITNESS (*sol, res*)
    UPDATE-HISTORY-AND-FITNESS (*constr, −res*)
    sol1 ← SELECT (*sol-pop*)   ; parent1
    sol2 ← SELECT (*sol-pop*)   ; parent2
    child ← MUTATE-CROSSOVER (*sol1, sol2*)
    f ← FITNESS (*child*)
    INSERT (*child, f, sol-pop*)

After the execution of the 20 encounters one new solution is created. This involves the following steps: (1) two parent solutions are SELECTed. This selection is – again – biased towards fitter individuals. (2) a new solution is generated from these parents through the application of MUTATION (which replaces a value by a randomly drawn member from the set {1,2, ..., 50}) and CROSSOVER (two-point crossover is used here), (3) the initial FITNESS of this child is calculated by having it to encounter 20 SELECTed constraints. The pay-offs associated with these encounters are pushed on the history. Again, the fitness of the newly created solution is the sum of these pay-offs[3], (4) if this fitness is higher than the minimum fitness in the population then the child is INSERTed at the appropriate rank in the solution population. At the same time, the individual with the minimum fitness is removed. As mentioned above the members of the constraint population do not change. Hence, no selection and reproduction operates on the constraint population.

The fitness interaction between solutions and constraints keeps both populations in constant flux. As soon as the solutions are becoming successful on a certain set of constraints then these constraints get a lower fitness. As a consequence, other, not yet satisfied constraints, move up in the population and will be selected more often. This forces the solutions to concentrate on these 'more difficult' constraints (because of the fitness proportional selection of the individuals involved in an encounter). In our test problem, for example, the diagonal-constraints rapidly move up in the population. This is because they check both diagonals. Hence, for every occupied board location, they constrain 2×49 other locations. The row-constraints, on the other hand, only constrain the 49 board locations in one row.

Let us now look at the benefits gained from the use of LTFE. Its continuous partial nature allows for an early detection of good and bad solutions: the solutions need not evaluate all 100 constraints at once. A few, well chosen, i.e. highly informative, constraint-checks provide sufficient information. This is true during different stages of the genetic search. Initially, all solutions are rather bad. In this case, one does not need extensive testing. A rough indication of their quality is sufficient. Even if – due to an unlucky choice of constraints in its initial encounters – the fitness is rated a bit too low then future encounters will certainly raise this fitness. At later stages – during which more mutation occurs[4] – LTFE is advantageous as well: it immediately weeds out clearly inferior offspring at minimal computational expense. When almost all solutions have a high fitness, e.g. they satisfy more than 80% of the constraints, then clearly inferior solutions can be spotted quite easily. Here too, one does not need to check all constraints. In addition, the biased selection of constraints allows to focus on the most relevant ones. In this way, LTFE and the negative fitness interaction of coevolution nicely complement each other.

Obviously the fitness of an individual – based on 20 encounters – is only approximate. The continuous lifetime fitness feedback together with the limited history length limits the effect of unrepresentative pay-off. Moreover, the same mechanisms allow the individuals to keep up with the changing individuals or rankings in the other population. This is the role of the 20 encounters executed in the **DO**-loop in the pseudo-code given above. As the empirical results of the next section show, the combined use of coevolution and LTFE considerably focuses the genetic search.

23.4 EMPIRICAL RESULTS

This section compares the CGA with two other genetic approaches called: TRAD and CGA-. TRAD is a traditional single population GA. It uses only a population of solutions. The fitness of a solution is defined as the number of constraints (out of 100) it satisfies. Hence, TRAD uses the traditional once-and-for-all fitness evaluation (instead of LTFE) and no coevolution. The code of the basic cycle of TRAD is given below (compare this with the code in the previous section).

$$sol1 \leftarrow \text{SELECT}(sol\text{-}pop) \qquad ; \text{parent1}$$
$$sol2 \leftarrow \text{SELECT}(sol\text{-}pop) \qquad ; \text{parent2}$$
$$child \leftarrow \text{MUTATE-CROSSOVER}(sol1, sol2)$$
$$f \leftarrow \text{FITNESS}(child)$$
$$\text{INSERT}(child, f, sol\text{-}pop)$$

The second algorithm, called CGA-, is identical to CGA except for the population structure of the constraints. In CGA- the constraints do not have any fitness. Hence, the selection of constraints involved in an encounter is not biased towards 'difficult' constraints. Or, in other words, the constraints form a set instead of a sorted 'population'. The main difference between CGA- and TRAD is that the former uses LTFE. CGA-, however, does not use coevolution. In this way an empirical comparison of these three systems can point out the relative merits of LTFE, coevolution, and their combination.

All three approaches were run ten times. Each run used a population size of 250. A run is stopped after the creation of 200000 offspring. In terms of solution quality both, CGA- and TRAD, are poor performers. On the ten runs, TRAD never found a global solution satisfying all constraints. CGA- found such a solution only once. CGA, on the other hand, was seven out of ten times successful. And this after having created, on average, 125000 offspring which is significantly less than the maximally allowed 200000. In the three other runs CGA found solutions which satisfy 98 out of the 100 constraints. This is also consistently higher than the quality obtained by TRAD and CGA-. Even after the generation of 200000 offspring TRAD and CGA-, on average, only found solutions satisfying 95.7 and 97.2 constraints, respectively. For CGA this average is 99.4. This comparison between TRAD, CGA-, and CGA gives a good indication of the increase in performance as a result of the combined use of LTFE and coevolution.

23.5 TIMETABLING

Kragelund [1997] applied CGAs to a timetabling problem which consists of scheduling medical doctors associated with an emergency service. He distinguishes two types of constraints: hard and soft constraints. The former *must* be satisfied, the latter are *preferably* to be satisfied. The personal preferences of the doctors are implemented as soft constraints. Both types of constraints result in pay-offs of a different magnitude. The absolute value of the pay-off resulting from an encounter involving a hard constraint is larger than that involving a soft constraint.

Kragelund compared six different GAs and four non-GA approaches. The best algorithm was a distributed CGA. It divides the solution population in a number of subpopulations which evolve in parallel. Occasionally, fit individuals are exchanged between the subpopulations. Kragelund concluded that:

> the CGA technique is better at locating the valid solutions. This should not surprise us since one is more likely to solve a problem if concentrating on the difficult aspects first and the easy aspects last.

> Kragelund [1997]

23.6 CONCLUSIONS AND DISCUSSION

Earlier work (Paredis [1994]) showed that the integrated use of LTFE and coevolution clearly boosts the performance of genetic neural net search. Here, we have illustrated the power of the combination of these same techniques in the completely different field of constraint satisfaction. The empirical results presented in both papers confirm the potential of the approach. The observed performance increase can be attributed to two factors. Primo, the partial nature of lifetime fitness evaluation allows for early detection of particularly good or bad solutions. Secundo, co-evolution concentrates its effort on the constraints which are most relevant at a given moment of the search. Furthermore, the combination of LTFE and coevolution has a clearly beneficial effect. The partial and continuous nature of LTFE – which only takes into account the most recent encounters – is well suited when dealing with coupled fitness landscapes. Here the fitnesses of solutions and constraints are coupled because changes in one population (through a different ranking or through the introduction of new individuals) clearly affect the fitness of the members of the other population. For this reason only the pay-off resulting from the most recent encounters provides an up-to-date approximation of the fitness of an individual.

In recent years a number of methods for constraint handling have been proposed within the GA community. One – genetic repair (Mühlenbein [1992]) – removes constraint violations in invalid solutions generated by the genetic operators (such as mutation and crossover). Another uses decoders such that all possible representations give rise to a valid solution (Davis [1988]). A third method uses penalty functions, see for example Richardson et al [1989]. This approach defines the fitness function as the objective function one tries to optimize minus the penalty function which represents the 'degree of invalidity' of a solution. Hence, the search process is allowed to wander around in portions of the search space containing only invalid solutions. The rationale being that it might be easier to find a solution if one is allowed to reach it from both sides of the valid/invalid border.

All these have a major disadvantage: they are all problem specific. For every CSP one has to determine a good decoder, a good genetic repair method or a penalty function which balances between convergence towards suboptimal valid solutions (when the penalty function is too harsh) or towards invalid solutions (too tolerant a penalty function is used).

In a CGA, however, coevolution gives rise to an 'auto-adjusting' penalty function. This is because fitness evaluation, which counts constraint violations, is a kind of a penalty function. The changing ranking and biased selection of constraints on which solutions are tested leads CGA to focus on the more difficult constraints. In other words, the penalty function becomes more and more harsh as better solutions are found. Informally, one could say that the penalty function coevolves in step with the quality of the solution population. Various researchers, for example Schoenauer & Xanthakis [1993], already observed that gradually adding constraints during the evolutionary search improves the results obtained. A CGA automatically performs such gradual tightening of the problem. Further, recent research by Pagie & Hogeweg [1997] has shown that 'all at once' fitness evaluation, based on all tests, selects too severely against errors. Partial fitness evaluation (such as LTFE), however, increases the freedom of the evolutionary process to traverse the space of possible solutions. Hence, partial evaluation helps (rather than hinders) the search process.

As well as via application to other tasks the current framework can be extended in yet another way. All examples discussed above have used predator-prey based ideas. Obviously, many other mechanisms – not necessarily based on inverse fitness interaction – exist in nature. Symbiosis is an important and widely occurring example. It consists of a positive fitness feedback in which success on one side improves the chances of survival of the other. Paredis [1995, 1996] describes a first investigation into the symbiotic evolution of solutions and their genetic representation (i.e. the gene ordering). A representation adapted to the solutions currently in the population speeds up the search for even better solutions which in turn might progress optimally when yet another representation is used.

NOTES

1. In all CGA applications the same number of encounters per cycle was used. This is also the case for the history length.
2. Note the inversion of the sign which implements the inverse fitness interaction between tests and solutions.
3. It should also be noted that the encounters used to calculate the fitness of a newly generated solution do not result in a fitness feedback for the tests involved. This is in order to avoid unreliable fitness feedback resulting from possibly mediocre offspring.
4. The probability of mutation is linearly proportional to the 'genetic similarity' of the parents. This is known as adaptive mutation.

Chapter Twenty-Four

Cultural Algorithms: Theory and Applications

Robert G. Reynolds

24.1 EXPLORING THE ORIGINS OF CULTURE WITH CULTURAL ALGORITHMS

Evolutionary computation (EC) methods have been successful in solving many diverse problems in search and optimization due to the unbiased nature of their operations which can still perform well in situations with little or no domain knowledge (Fogel [1995]). However, there can be considerable improvement in their performance when problem specific knowledge is used to bias the problem solving process in order to identify patterns in their performance environment. These patterns are used to promote more instances of desirable candidates or to reduce the number of less desirable candidates in the population (Sebag et al [1996]). In either case, this can afford the system an opportunity to reach the desired solution more quickly.

Adaptive Evolutionary Computation takes place when an EC system is able to incorporate such information into its representation and operators in order to facilitate the pruning and promoting activities mentioned above. For example, Bäck suggest that self-adaptation can be a powerful force in population-based evolutionary computational models such as Evolution Strategies (Bäck [1996]). Angeline [1995] has shown that self-adaptation can take place on several levels within a system such as the population level, the individual level, and the component level. At the population level, aspects of the system parameters that control all elements of the population can be modified. At the individual level, aspects of the system that control the action of specific individuals can be modified. If the individual is specified as a collection of components then component level adaptation is possible. This involves the adaptation of parameters that control the operation of one or more components that make up an individual.

In human societies, culture can be a vehicle for the storage of information in a form that is independent of the individual or individuals that generated and is potentially accessible to all members of the society. As such culture is useful in guiding the problem solving activities and social interaction of individuals in the population. This allows self-adaptive information as well as other knowledge to be stored and manipulated separately from the individuals in the social population. This provides a systematic way of utilizing self-adaptive knowledge to direct the evolution of a social population. Thus, cultural systems are viewed as a dual inheritance system where, at each time step, knowledge at both the population level and the level of acquired beliefs is transmitted to the next generation (Durham [1991]). This acquired knowledge is viewed to act as beacons by which to guide individuals towards perceived good solutions to problems and away from less desirable ones at a given time step. Cultural algorithms have been developed by Reynolds [1997] in order to model the evolution of cultural systems based upon principles of human social evolution taken from the social science literature. In the next section the theoretical basis for cultural algorithms is presented.

24.2 THE BASIS FOR CULTURAL ALGORITHMS

Edward B. Tylor was the first to introduce the term 'culture' in his two volume book on Primitive Culture published in 1871 (Tylor [1871]). There, he described culture as 'that complex whole which includes knowledge, beliefs, art, morals, customs, and any other capabilities and habits acquired by man as a member of society'. Since then there has been considerable debate as to the nature of the 'complex whole'. An approach often taken in these early efforts was to identify what Tylor called 'adhesions' between cultural elements. The goal was to see whether there were predictable sets of adhesions with and between different cultures. The presence of these adhesions would then provide the basis for a general classification mechanism for the world's cultures.

This early work was more concerned with the classification and description of cultures than the processes by which cultures developed and evolved. For comprehensive reviews of this work the reader is referred to Kroeber & Kluckhohn [1952], Harris [1968], and Moore [1974]. These approaches often resulted in a 'catalog' of those cultural components. For example, the world ethnographic survey of George Murdoch compared 565 cultures based upon 30 sample characteristics taken from available ethnographies (Murdoch [1957]). The characteristics included the following: the use of cultivated plants, the use of domesticated animals, economic dominance of agriculture, division of labour in economic activities, settlement patterns, community organization, family organization, household organization, marriage rules and marriage residence rules, kinship terminology, social stratification, political integration, and succession rules.

Research in cybernetics and systems theory in the late 1950s and early 1960s done by Maruyama [1963] and others provided a framework in which the functional aspects of cultural systems could be assessed relative to their environments. This spawned a view of culture as a system that can interact with the environmental subsystems in which it is embedded. From this perspective culture was seen as providing basic regulatory mechanisms in the form of positive and negative feedback that can respectively amplify and counteract behavioural deviations of individuals within the culture. The result of these feedback cycles was seen to produce long- and short-term equilibrium relations between the cultural system and its environment such as those demonstrated by Flannery [1971] for the Valley of Oaxaca, Mexico.

As a result, models of cultural systems and cultural change began to take a decidedly process-based form in the early 1970's. These new models began to emphasize how cultural elements produced and directed the flow of information within and between a cultural system and its environment, a generalization of the control activities suggested by the cultural ecologists. Thus, culture began to be viewed as a 'guidance system'. As suggested by Morris Freilich:

> Culture belongs to the family 'guidance system'. A guide is a bit of information that makes one type of behaviour more probable than [another...]. People who share a common space – members of the same geographic community – share a number of guides. Among such shared guides I will distinguish natural guides ([physiological...] drives, climate, etc) from standards (guides which are man-

made and developed as byproducts of social interaction). Culture as a member of the family guidance system belongs to the subfamily standards.

Freilich [1977]

While Freilich and others emphasized the use of culture primarily in a normative role and suggested that culture represents 'proper behaviour' for individuals in the society (Goodenough [1981; page 56] a broader interpretation was suggested by Clifford Geertz [1973; pp. 144–145]. He described culture as an 'ordered system of meaning and symbols in which social interaction takes place. Culture is the fabric of meaning in terms of which human beings interpret their experience and guide their action'. His definition supports the normative role but also views it from more of an information systems perspective, as a system in which individual experiences can be expressed, compared, and interpreted.

Subsequent work in the 1970s and 1980s provided additional support for Geertz's view. In surveying that work Durham [1991; page 3] concludes that there is strong evidence to believe that culture consists of 'shared ideational phenomena (values, ideas, beliefs, and the like) that can be used to interpret individual experience and guide individual behaviour'. This definition of culture provides a strong information systems perspective and fits well with the computational model that will be constructed around it here. We can view the cultural evolution process as a vehicle for amplifying individual or group behaviour and building consensus. In other words, during cultural evolution, 'conceptual beacons' that symbolize acceptable and unacceptable behaviour for individuals in a population are accumulated

24.3 CULTURAL ALGORITHMS

Cultural Algorithms are a class of algorithms that support the basic mechanisms for cultural change as described above (Reynolds [1994]) – a pseudocode description of cultural algorithms is given in Figure 24.1. Individuals are first *evaluated* using a performance function. The performance information represents the problem-solving experience of an individual. An *acceptance function* determines which individuals in the current population are able to impact, or to be *voted* to contribute, to the current beliefs. The experience of these selected individuals is used to *adjust* the current group beliefs. These group beliefs are then used to guide and *influence* the evolution of the population at the next step, where parameters for self-adaptation can be determined from the belief space. Information that is stored in the belief space can pertain to any of the lower levels, e.g. population, individual, or component. As a result, the belief space can be used to control self-adaptation at any or all of these levels.

The cultural algorithm is a dual inheritance system with evolution taking place at the population level and at the belief level. The two components interact through a communications protocol. The protocol determines the set of 'acceptable' individuals that are able to update the belief space. Likewise the protocol determines how the updated beliefs are able to impact and 'influence' the adaptation of the population component.

The belief space in cultural algorithms is then a natural repository for information concerning the self-adaptation process. Information stored in the belief space can relate to various global parameters that can be used to direct the population through the specified communications protocol. A cultural algorithm framework is denoted as an 8-tuple:

$$CA = \langle P, S, V_c, f, B, Accept, Adjust, Influence \rangle$$

where: P is a population; S is a selection operator; V_c is a variation operator; f is the performance function; B is the belief space; *Accept* is the acceptance function; *Adjust* is a belief space operator that adjusts or updates the belief space knowledge, B; and *Influence* is a set of influence functions to be used to influence the variation operator V_c. *Accept* and *Influence* together represent the communication protocol for a cultural algorithm. Each basic CA component and its relationships are depicted in Figure 24.2.

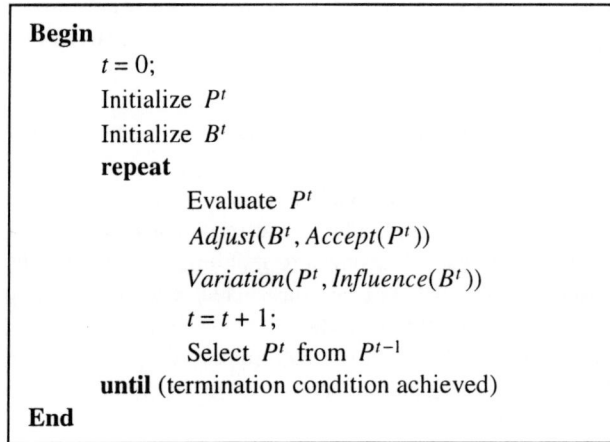

Begin
        $t = 0$;
        Initialize P^t
        Initialize B^t
        repeat
                Evaluate P^t
                $Adjust(B^t, Accept(P^t))$
                $Variation(P^t, Influence(B^t))$
                $t = t + 1$;
                Select P^t from P^{t-1}
        until (termination condition achieved)
End

Fig. 24.1: Cultural algorithms pseudocode.

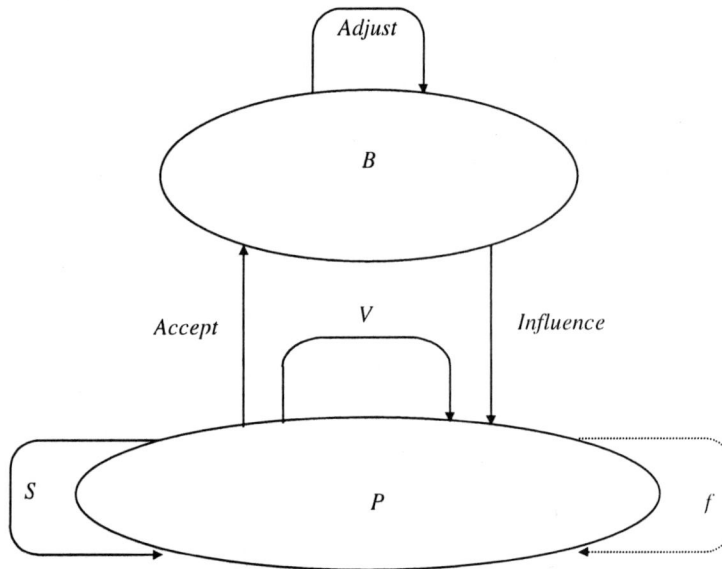

Fig. 24.2: Cultural algorithm framework.

In the following sections we briefly describe the basic application areas to which cultural algorithms have been applied in their order of development.

24.4 RESOURCE SCHEDULING AND THE EVOLUTION OF AGRICULTURE

Cultural algorithms as described above consist of three components. First, there is a population component that contains the social population to be evolved and the mechanisms for its evaluation, reproduction, and modification. Second there is a belief space that represents the bias that has been acquired by the population during its problem-solving process. The third component is the communications protocol that is used to determine the interaction between the population and their beliefs

For the population component, any existing Evolutionary Computational model for a population can be viewed as an analogue model for the social component. For example, early mathematical models of cultural evolution viewed each type of trait as analogous to a gene, and different values for a trait corresponded to alleles for a given gene. Thus, an individual consisted of a vector of traits. These traits could be affected by the interaction with other individuals. The basic operators were viewed to be analogous to the standard genetic operations, but other more socially motivated operators such as copying were also introduced by Boyd & Richerson [1985] and Cavilli-Sforza & Feldman [1969]. Thus, the spread of traits could be modelled mathematically in terms of population genetics.

The earliest model for the population component that was used by Reynolds [1979], was motivated by this early work. The population model used was the Genetic Algorithm of Holland [1975] and it was used as the basis for modelling the evolution of agriculture in the Valley of Oaxaca, Mexico. The model was used to show that agriculture could have evolved as the accumulation of small-scale resource scheduling decisions over a long period of time in the Valley. Thus, the need to resort to external causes was not necessary in this case.

The belief space in these early models corresponded to knowledge about the utility of a given social-learning operator (Reynolds [1986]). The probability of applying an operator was increased for an individual when use of the operator produced a new trait sequence with improved performance. Likewise, it was decreased for an individual if its use produced an individual with decreased performance. In these models, the acceptance function was 100%, since all individuals were used. The influence function affected the probability of applying an operator based upon the current belief about the operators utility. This allowed the social system to adjust its social learning practices to reflect the current evolutionary stage.

24.5 CONCEPT LEARNING APPLICATIONS

A second generation of models was used to acquire knowledge about the structure of the population elements in addition to information about population parameters (Sverdlik et al [1992]). The goal was to learn general concepts about aspects of individuals in a population. Again using a symbolic Genetic Algorithm population, the most natural way of representing generalizations about individuals in the social model was in terms of schema. For example, assume that two individuals, 10100 and 00100, were viewed to have above average performance. Then, we can infer that the schema #0100 has above average performance. The belief space itself was then organized as a lattice, where each schema was viewed as specifying a subset if individuals. The root of the lattice was the most general schema, ##### for our example. The leaf nodes were explicit population members such as 10100 here.

Learning in the belief space was done using Mitchell's Version Space Algorithms (Mitchell [1978]). The result of learning was to identify regions of the lattice where above average individuals were present, and areas where below average individuals were present. The performance scores for individuals in the population were promoted or demoted depending on the type of beliefs (above or below average) that they were associated with in the belief space. This served to prune the space of search to those regions that were more likely to yield above average results. As the average score increased over time, these regions also decreased in size. The generalization/specialization process was accelerated by the use of local search procedures that took a population element and systematically changed the bits in order to determine which bits were not important for the production of the observed above or below average behaviour for that individual. The resultant description of the individual contained don't cares, #, to represent those bits whose value when flipped made no change in the performance category for the individual. These descriptions were called stable classes since their performance was unchanged for the specified bits. These generalized individuals were then integrated into the existing set of beliefs to produce more generalized classes. A schema theorem for Version Space Guided Genetic Algorithms has been developed to illustrate how Culture can speed up the learning rate for a Genetic Algorithm population (Reynolds [1997]).

One major operation in the belief space is the combination of existing beliefs to produce more general ones. Without such an operation the power of the belief space to guide the population can be diminished. Sverdlik [1993] has demonstrated the probabilistic correctness of one such operator, combine, which takes two sub-lattices in a version space defined over a set of binary schema and produces a new sub lattice that is a generalization of them both. His analysis demonstrated that the correctness of combine was a probabilistic function of the size of the sub-lattices to be combined. Sub-lattice size was measured in terms of the number of leaf nodes that it contained.

Often for these models the acceptance function used either took all individuals, or often just the above average individuals (top 50%). The influence function involved the modification of the performance of individuals rather than directly modifying the structure of the individuals. This can be viewed as a type of Baldwin effect as suggested by Bala et al [1996] and Whitley et al [1994]. VGAs have been applied to the solution of a diverse set of concept learning problems such as the Boole problem (Reynolds & Maletic [1993]), and program understanding (Reynolds & Sverdlik [1995]) to name a few.

24.6 REAL-VALUED FUNCTION OPTIMIZATION

A third generation of models was developed to deal with real-valued Genetic Algorithms such as those proposed by Michalewicz [1994]. Here, the traits associated with individuals in the social population were real-valued in nature. Other population models that support the representation of real-valued traits, such as Evolutionary Programming and Evolution Strategies were also used here as well. Specifically we will focus on CAEP, cultural algorithms with Evolutionary Programming, systems here. A description of the basic CAEP framework is given below.

The belief space for these models was derived from work by Eschelman & Schaffer [1993] on real-valued schemata, a counterpart of the symbolic schema used with VGAs (Reynolds et al [1995]). Each of the traits in the population corresponded to a real-valued interval in the belief space. Initially the interval was set to equal the range constraint for the variable. They were subsequently adjusted based upon the parameter values for the subset of accepted individuals. The values of the traits for each of the accepted individuals are used to adjust the range for each parameter for that time step. Reducing the range corresponded to specialization, and range expansion corresponded to specialization. In addition to this normative knowledge, generalized descriptions of the current best individual found so far was used to guide the direction in which the range was adjusted.

As an example of how the CAEP process works, consider a function $f(x) = x_1^2 + x_2^2$ with the domain constraints $-1 < x_1 < 1$ and $-1 < x_2 < 1$. When we assume $p=5$, the initial population consists of five candidate solutions and would look like the Figure 24.3.

	1	2	$f(x)$
1	−0.1	0.2	0.05
2	0.0	0.1	0.01
3	−0.8	0.9	1.45
4	−0.3	0.7	0.58
5	−0.2	0.6	0.4

Fig. 24.3: An example of the initial population.

The situational knowledge component, S, of the Belief Space will consist of the best individual from the initial population as shown in Figure 24.4.

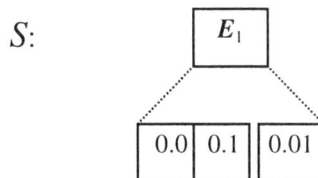

S: E_1 — 0.0 0.1 0.01

Fig. 24.4: An example of Situational Knowledge in the Belief Space.

The normative knowledge component, N, will be initialized with the range constraints for each of the problem parameters as shown in Figure 24.5.

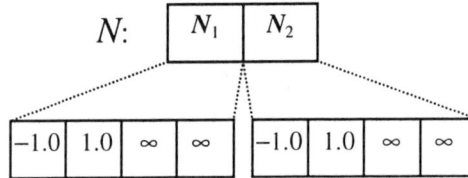

Fig. 24.5: An example of initial Normative Knowledge in the Belief Space.

Figure 24.6 shows the population structure after generating the p offspring solutions by applying the mutation operators with an influence function. Now, there are $2p$ solutions. Figure 24.7 shows the result of tournament selection.

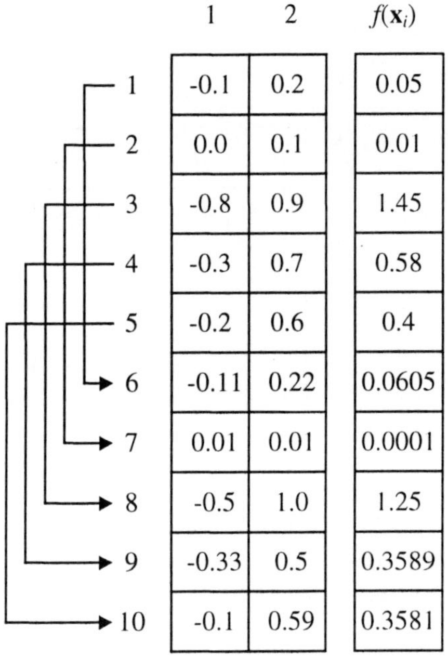

	1	2	$f(\mathbf{x}_i)$
1	-0.1	0.2	0.05
2	0.0	0.1	0.01
3	-0.8	0.9	1.45
4	-0.3	0.7	0.58
5	-0.2	0.6	0.4
6	-0.11	0.22	0.0605
7	0.01	0.01	0.0001
8	-0.5	1.0	1.25
9	-0.33	0.5	0.3589
10	-0.1	0.59	0.3581

Fig. 24.6: An example of generating offspring solutions

Assuming a top 40% acceptance function, the two best performers are accepted into the belief space as shown in the *accept* column in Figure 24.8. The best of the two is a candidate for replacing the current best (the *update*E column). Both of them can contribute to updating the normative range of values for x_1 and x_2 as shown in the *update*N column in Figure 24.8.

Figure 24.9 shows a result of adjusting situational knowledge from the population illustrated in Figure 24.8. Since the best individual has better as performance value (0.0001) than that of the current exemplar, the current exemplar is replaced with the current best, <0.01, 0.01>, in the population space.

	1	2	$f(x)$
1	0.01	0.01	0.0001
2	0.0	0.1	0.01
3	−0.1	0.2	0.05
4	−0.11	0.22	0.0605
5	−0.1	0.59	0.3581

Fig. 24.7: An example of tournament selection.

	1	2	$f(x)$	accept	updateE	updateN
1	0.01	0.01	0.0001	1	1	1
2	0.0	0.1	0.01	1	0	1
3	−0.1	0.2	0.05	0	0	0
4	−0.11	0.22	0.0605	0	0	0
5	−0.1	0.59	0.3581	0	0	0

Fig. 24.8: Individuals in a population for updating the Belief Space.

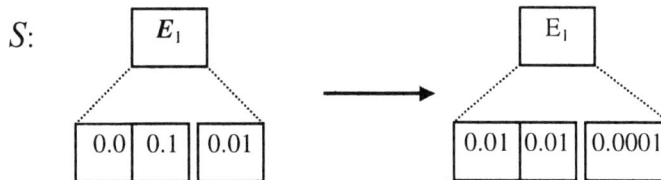

Fig. 24.9: An example result of adjusting Situational Knowledge.

Figure 24.10 shows a result of adjusting normative knowledge according to the adjustment rules from the population in Figure 24.8. The top 2 individuals, <0.01, 0.01> with performance score 0.0001 and < 0.0, 0.1> with performance score 0.01 are used to adjust the current normative knowledge from the population.

N:

N_1	N_2			

-1.0	1.0	∞	∞

-1.0	1.0	∞	∞

N_1	N_2

0.0	0.01	0.01	0.0001

0.01	0.1	0.0001	0.01

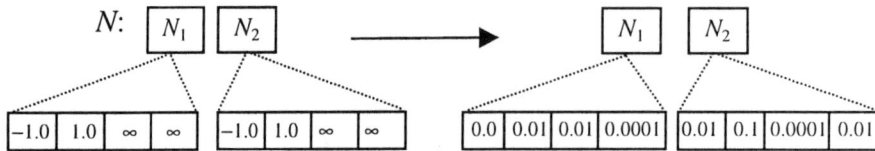

Fig. 24.10: An example result of adjusting Normative Knowledge

The individuals in Figure 24.8 are then become the parents for the next generation and the cycle begins again.

In general, for many problems the top 20% worked well for the acceptance function. This value is analogous to Rechenberg's 1/5 rule (see Bäck [1996]). Values higher than this were appropriate for more complex functions, especially those with a stochastic component. Recent work by Chung [1997] employed a fuzzy acceptance function, where the values can vary from 10 to 30% depending upon the stage of the evolution process. For example, at the beginning of the process the value is close to 30% while at the end it nears 10%. Reynolds & Zhu [1998] recently developed an alternative fuzzy acceptance function that accepted few individuals at the beginning and more at the end. His experiments suggested that this function was especially suitable for problems whose performance landscape was characterized by large basins and/or valleys. In these situations, it was found that it was better to sample small until a good direction was found, and then sample larger. In addition, other experiments by Chung suggest that for certain problems one type of knowledge is more useful than another in guiding the search process. For example, highly multi-modal problems were more likely to benefit from normative knowledge whereas problems with large basins and/or plateaus were likely to benefit from the use of situational knowledge (Reynolds & Chung [1997]).

Various CAEP configurations were applied not only to a variety of unconstrained linear and nonlinear optimization problems but to other problems as well. These problems include learning among cooperating agents on a robot soccer team (Reynolds & Chung [1997a]), parameter learning for gradient-based approaches to image segmentation (Reynolds & Rolnick [1995]), data mining of large-scale spatial-temporal databases (Al-Shehri [1998]), and re-engineering rule-based systems (Reynolds & Sternberg [1997]).

24.7 CULTURING GENETIC PROGRAMS

A fourth category of models uses sub-graphs as the population elements. These graphs can be viewed as decision structures within which social agents interact to solve problems. The belief space consists of a collection of sub-graphs that are frequently found in the subset of acceptable individuals. The acceptance function for this was set at in the 20% range. The influence function worked to reduce the probability that crossover would break apart one of the sub-trees currently found in the belief space. The more frequently the sub-tree was found in acceptable solutions the more the probability was reduced. The probability values ranged between 0 and 100, where the initial values were often set to 0.5 (Zannoni [1996]). This category of models was applied to the learning of programming concepts in a genetic programming environment. The concepts can then be reused to guide program evolution in related situations. This aproach was found to significantly reduce the amount of bloat generated by the crossing over of random programs.

24.8 FUTURE WORK

The principal economic activity for over 99% of man's existence has been as a hunter-gatherer. That is, collecting wild plants and hunting game. It is within this economic context that man's cultural capabilities evolved. The long-term focus of the cultural algorithms project is to investigate how and why cultural man's cultural capacity emerged during this period. It is hoped that by better understanding the reasons behind the emergence of Cultural Systems, we will be able to develop better human and artificial cultural systems in the future. Within this context future work will focus on how the structure and representation of knowledge in the belief space can evolve over time in response to challenges faced by individuals in the social population.

Chapter Twenty-Five

The Particle Swarm: Social Adaptation in Information-Processing Systems

James Kennedy and Russell C. Eberhart

25.1 INTRODUCTION

Even though an algorithm is in fact a purely algebraic event, it seems that even computer scientists find it easier to grasp an abstract phenomenon when it is grounded in a familiar metaphor, whether it is evolution, insect swarming, immune systems, pheromone following, or neural dynamics. The method described in the present chapter draws from the metaphor of human sociality. One of the authors is a social psychologist, while the other is an electrical engineer. As we asked questions about how human intelligence might arise in a social context, some experimentation with generic simulations found that social interaction, which has been theorized to play a crucial role in human cognition (for example: Hutchins [1995], Levine et al [1993]) is able, in a computer program, to find optimal solutions to hard mathematical problems.

The particle swarm algorithm models the exploration of a problem space by a population of individuals; individuals' successes influence the searches of their peers. Though it originated as a simulation of social behaviour, particle swarm optimization can be used with many kinds of continuous and binary problems. The algorithm is a general function optimizer, able to work on a wide range of problem domains. This chapter focuses on the relevance of such an algorithm to cognition, in particular the representation of semantic knowledge in neural networks; particle swarm optimization successfully optimizes the weights in networks, simulating the sharing of representations among social collaborators. The metaphor though is of course only an aid to understanding the system, as an artificial neural network is a way to understand cognition; the particle swarm is frequently used to optimize functions that are only remotely cognitive, if at all.

25.2 TRAJECTORIES IN HYPERSPACE

We assume a multidimensional problem space. In the current example this space is a hyperspace of connections among nodes in a neural network; thus an individual particle's position at any moment is described using connection weights as coordinates. The weights for each individual i on dimension d will be called x_{id}, or $\bar{x}_i$.

Individuals conduct repeated experiments, modeled in an iterative simulation, passing data through a network of weights $\bar{x}_i$ which are initially random. The outcome of each experiment is a measure of error, or the distance between calculated outputs and desired outputs as specified in the data. At each iteration the individual's position in hyperspace is changed by adding a velocity $\vec{v}_i$ to the coordinates. Thus, iteratively,

$$\vec{x}_i(t) = \vec{x}_i(t-1) + \vec{v}_i(t)$$

Unaltered, the velocity vector would move individuals in a straight line through the hyperspace. The particle swarm algorithm optimizes by operating upon the velocity of change.

25.2.1 The Individual Best

Each individual in the population enters the coordinates of its current position into the formulas for the neural network and measures the error of the estimate, then moves to a new position and repeats. As individuals move through space, they compare their current error value to the best they have attained at any point up to that iteration. We call the best, that is lowest, error term that i has encountered thus far $pbest_i$, and the position where that evaluation was attained is represented as a vector $\vec{p}_i$. Thus:

$$\text{if } f(\vec{x}_i) < pbest_i \text{ then } \vec{p}_i = \vec{x}_i$$

The position of the individual particle in any iteration differs from the previous best by some amount $(\vec{p}_i - \vec{x}_i)$. This difference can be used to define the direction and distance that the particle should go to return to the previous best. Of course it would not work to have:

$$\vec{x}_i(t) = \vec{x}_i(t-1) + (\vec{p}_i - \vec{x}_i(t-1))$$

as the particle would only return immediately to the previous best and the search would be ended.

In the algorithm, each element in the vector of differences is weighted by a random number ρ, whose upper limit is a constant parameter of the system, usually set to a value of 2.0. This new vector is added to the velocity of change, so that:

$$\vec{v}_i(t) = \vec{v}_i(t-1) + \rho \cdot (\vec{p}_i - \vec{x}_i(t-1))$$

This change-of-change vector introduces a tendency to return toward the previous best position: in one early paper (Kennedy and Eberhart, 1995) we called this 'simple nostalgia'. Psychologically it represents the tendency of organisms to repeat past behaviours that have been reinforced, or to return to past successes; it is a tendency to search regions that have demonstrated promise.

25.2.2 The Neighbourhood Best

Thus far the algorithm has no social component, but rather comprises individual search focusing on regions of the problem space that have shown promise (and doesn't perform very well). The next term of the formula introduces social influence and makes the particle swarm work.

A neighbourhood is defined for each individual. Though there are an infinite number of sociometric possibilities, our research has focused on two methods for defining neighbourhoods (Eberhart et al [1996]). The first method, which we call the $gbest$ method, simply counts the entire population as a neighbourhood. The second method, called *lbest*, defines a subset of the population surrounding individual *i*, usually one neighbour on each side, as the neighbourhood. Thus for each individual an *lbest* neighbourhood, where neighbourhood size = 3, is composed of individuals *i*−1, *i*, and *i*+1.

All individuals search the space simultaneously; each has its own *pbest$_i$* and $\bar{p}_i$. For the social term of the algorithm, individual *i* looks at its neighbours to determine which one has achieved the best *pbest$_i$* so far: the index of the neighbour who has found the best position so far is assigned to *g*, so that the neighbourhood's best position can be referred to as $\bar{p}_g$.

Thus the vector ($\bar{p}_g - \bar{x}_i$) represents the difference between *i*'s current position and the best position that has been found by any member of the neighbourhood. The particle swarm algorithm weights every element of this vector, as before, with a random number defined by an upper limit, and adds this vector of social influence to the change vector $\bar{v}_i$, along with the individual-best term described above. This term represents the social-psychological tendency of individuals to emulate the successes of others, which is fundamental to human sociality.

In sum, the particle swarm iterates through the following formulae:

$$\bar{v}_i(t) = \bar{v}_i(t-1) + \rho_1 \cdot (\bar{p}_i - \bar{x}_i(t-1)) + \rho_2 \cdot (\bar{p}_g - \bar{x}_i(t-1))$$

$$\bar{x}_i(t) = \bar{x}_i(t-1) + \bar{v}_i(t)$$

The only additional rule is that elements in $\bar{v}_i$ must be limited by some value $V_{\max}$. Without this limit the system can explode due to the randomness.

Other methods have been developed for controlling the tendency of the system to explode. French mathematician Maurice Clerc has suggested a system of 'constriction coefficients' which may be applied to various terms of the formulas in order to ensure convergence and prevent explosion. Clerc's analyses are currently under review, but it does appear that his work might result in adjustments to the particle swarm algorithm which will make the $V_{\max}$ constraint unnecessary.

25.3 BINARY PARTICLE SWARM

With a simple modification the particle swam algorithm can be made to operate on binary problems, such as those traditionally optimized by genetic algorithms. In the binary particle swarm, $\bar{x}_i$ and $\bar{p}_i$ can take on values of 0 or 1 only, and elements in $\bar{v}_i$ function as probability thresholds. A sigmoid function:

$$S(v_{id}) = \frac{1}{1 + \exp(-v_{id})}$$

squashes $\bar{v}_i$ values to the [0,1] range. Then we can generate a random number in the same range; if that number is less than $S(v_{id})$ then x_{id} will be evaluated as a 1, else $x_{id} = 0$. In other words, as v_{id} increases, the probability that x_{id} will be evaluated as a 1 increases. Of course v_{id} will tend to increase when the ($p - x$) terms – the values that are added to $\bar{v}_i$ on each iteration – are positive, i.e. when p_{id} or $p_{gd} = 1$, and decreases when p_{id} or $p_{gd} = 0$. Thus $\bar{x}_i$ tends to approximate $\bar{p}_i$ and $\bar{p}_g$, the previous best positions.

Kennedy & Eberhart [1997] showed that the binary particle swarm was able to successfully optimize the De Jong [1975] suite of test functions. Further, Kennedy &

Spears [1998] compared the binary particle swarm algorithm to genetic algorithms comprising crossover only, mutation only, and both crossover and mutation, in Spears' multimodal random problem generator. It was seen that the particle swarm found global optima faster than any of the three kinds of GAs in all conditions except for problems featuring low dimensionality. On those problems the mutation-only GA found optima slightly faster; it fell far behind on harder problems, though. The binary particle swarm appears to be a very powerful approach to optimization of binary functions, such as are frequently found in real-world applications.

25.4 PERFORMANCE OF THE ALGORITHM

A standard XOR feedforward network maps two binary input variables to an output classification. The inputs in {0, 1} map to an output of one if one of the inputs equals one and the other is zero, and to a zero if both equal one or both equal zero. This is a common benchmark problem for neural networks. With three hidden nodes, optimization of the network requires the estimation of 13 free parameters. Thus in the current paradigm a population of individuals must optimize a thirteen-dimensional nonlinear function. Twenty trials run with populations of 20 individuals, using the *lbest* neighbourhood=3 method, met a criterion of average squared error < 0.02 after a median of 50.5 iterations. The *gbest* method met the criterion in a median of 37.5 iterations. Note that these iterations consist of $50.5 \times 20 = 1,010$, and $37.5 \times 20 = 750$ actual evaluations respectively; this may be a better number to keep in mind for making comparisons with other algorithms.

Shi & Eberhart [1998] have developed a method to use particle swarm to optimize the structure as well as the weights of a feedforward neural network. In their unpublished tests on the Fisher [1936] iris data set, they were able to correctly classify a mean of 147.85 of the 150 records, averaged over forty trials. This is well above the usual neural net performance on this difficult, classic data analysis problem.

The theoretical view of learning as backpropagation of error differs from the particle swarm view in two important ways. First, from the psychological perspective the individual is considered by connectionist theorists to be a kind of sealed container, with information processing going on inside it. The particle swarm shifts the locus of information processing out into interpersonal space, with individuals learning from one another how to process information. The individual particle evaluates its position in the neighbourhood but it does not 'do' anything toward solving the problem. This has some important implications for the way we define minds and intelligence. Secondly, backpropagation of error is a deterministic hill-climbing algorithm (after a random start). A gradient descent heuristic determines the direction and degree of change in the weight matrix which immediately reduces error. The system iterates until a minimum has been reached and improvement stops. The present method more closely resembles stochastic algorithms such as the genetic algorithms, evolutionary programming (Fogel [1995]), simulated annealing, etc., exploiting randomness in the search of the problem space. Individuals in the population are pulled toward optimal positions, but do not climb hills in optimal neighbourhoods. Backprop is a rational model of thought: people continually move to improve their cognitive state. The particle swarm on the other hand is truly an irrational model of cognition, where individuals continually imitate others. Problem-solving is epiphenomenal.

25.5 SYSTEM PARAMETERS

There are several parameters to the particle swarm system. These include

- Dimensionality of the problem;
- Number of individuals;
- Upper limit to ρ;
- V_{max};
- Neighbourhood size;
- Inertia weight.

These parameters are each described in turn in the following.

25.5.1 Dimensionality

Dimensionality is probably the single most influential problem parameter in determining the hardness of a problem. The algorithm has been shown to perform very well on a wide variety of hard, high-dimensional test functions such as the De Jong suite and other hard problems such as Schaffer's f6 and Griewank, Ackley, Rastrigin, and Rosenbrock functions (Angeline [1998], Kennedy & Eberhart [1997], Shi & Eberhart [1998a]). In one set of tests, Angeline [1998a] varied the dimensionality of problems, and found that the particle swarm actually performed relatively better on higher-dimensional versions of some test functions than on versions with fewer dimensions.

25.5.2 Number of Individuals

As expected, there is an inverse relationship between the size of the population and the number of iterations required to meet a criterion, which appears to approximate an inverse power function (for a social-psychological analogue, see Latané [1981]). This relationship is clearer for the *gbest* versions of the algorithm, with the entire population considered as the neighbourhood, than with the noisier *lbest* versions. Table 25.1 shows the number of iterations required for an XOR network to meet error<0.02 for different population sizes.

Table 25.1: Comparison of population sizes. Median number of iterations required to attain error<0.02 on an XOR neural network, after 20 trials.

	Pop=5	Pop=10	Pop=20	Pop=50	Pop=75	Pop=100
Lbest, nb=3	67	39	50.5	25	13.5	17
Gbest	95	48	37.5	10.5	9	7

Increasing population size generally speeds up convergence, as measured in number of iterations, with the contribution of each additional individual inversely correlated with population size. It is seen, however, that the number of actual evaluations required increases with population size. Most of our implementations use twenty to sixty individuals.

25.5.3 Upper Limit of ρ

Each element added to the change vector $\vec{v}_i$ is weighted by a positive random number $\rho_k : k \in \{1,2\}$ whose upper limit is specified to the system. Varying this parameter has the effect of varying the strength of the pull toward the two bests. For instance, when ρ_k is near zero, individuals' trajectories move in smooth, wide cycles through the hyperspace, passing the bests and looping back toward them. The small weight means that the velocity vector is adapted by a relatively small amount on each iteration; of course over many iterations these small increments add up, and the trajectory is eventually reversed toward the best positions. When ρ_k is high the trajectories tend to oscillate sharply, as the vector $\vec{v}_i$ is overwhelmed by the large values added to it.

Kennedy [1998] described the effect of ρ_k on a particle's trajectory. Any time the sum of the two ρ_k coefficients exceeds the value 4.0, both the velocities and positions explode toward infinity. Thus almost all implementations of the particle swarm limit each of the two ρ_ks to 2.0.

25.5.4 V_{MAX}

On any given iteration, it is likely that the velocity on some individual particle on some dimensions will be limited to V_{max}. This upper limit on the rate of change prevents individuals from moving too rapidly from one region of the problem space to another, racing past potentially good combinations of coordinates. A deleterious effect of the limit, however, is that, when the rule is:

$$\text{if} \quad v_{id} > V_{max} \quad \text{then} \quad v_{id} = V_{max}$$
$$\text{else if} \quad v_{id} < -V_{max} \quad \text{then} \quad v_{id} = -V_{max}$$

a particle may revisit points on any dimension as it moves in steps that are the same size. This effect is not too terrible, though, as it is tempered by the fact that particle swarms are usually implemented in high-dimensional spaces where the chance of visiting a *multivariate* point more than once is remote.

The value assigned to V_{max} may be arbitrary. At best it is a function of the scale of the problem, and hopefully the researcher finds a value that is large enough to allow the particle to jump out of local optima, but small enough to influence the granularity of the search in a beneficial way. It is recommended to set V_{max} to a value that is determined by the dynamic range of the problem, that is, if x_{id} can range between -100 and $+100$, as in Schaffer's f6, then V_{max} should be proportional to ±100. A lower V_{max} such as 10 per cent of the dynamic range, is sometimes used by one of the authors (RCE).

The recent analyses by Clerc have explained why the V_{max} limit is necessary, and suggest the application of 'constriction coefficients' to control the explosion of the system. It is expected that these coefficients will eventually result in the discarding of the V_{max} parameter in particle swarm implementations.

For instance, Clerc shows that a coefficient χ can be defined such that:

$$\chi = \frac{\kappa}{abs\left(\dfrac{1-\dfrac{\rho}{2}-\sqrt{abs(\rho^2-4\rho)}}{2}\right)}$$

where $\kappa \in (0,1]$ (a value of 1.0 works well), ρ in this formula is the sum of the $\rho_1 + \rho_2$ in the formula as it was given above, and the limit of ρ should be greater than 4 (e.g. limit each ρ_k to 2.05 for this particular kind of constriction coefficient). When the entire right side of the update formula for $\vec{v}_i$ is weighted by χ:

$$\vec{v}_i(t) = \chi(\vec{v}_i(t-1) + \rho_1 \cdot (\vec{p}_i - \vec{x}_i(t-1)) + \rho_2 \cdot (\vec{p}_g - \vec{x}_i(t-1)))$$

the system converges without any need for V_{max} at all. This is only the simplest, and not the most elegant or most effective, application of constriction to the algorithm, but it gives some idea of a future direction we expect the paradigm to take.

25.5.5 Neighbourhood Size

In this chapter we describe two kinds of neighbourhoods, those with fewer than N sequential members and those comprising the entire population (20 in these examples), called *lbest* and *gbest* respectively. Intermediate neighbourhood sizes have also been tested.

The *gbest* model considers the entire population as a single neighbourhood; $\vec{v}_i$ is adapted toward the individual's previous best and the best position found by any member of the population. The method, as seen in the tables above, leads to faster convergence on a problem such as XOR, but it may be susceptible to local optima when these are numerous or good. When one individual finds a powerful local optimum, the entire population is attracted to it, with the consequence that other regions of the problem space may remain unexamined. On the other hand, for many real problems the *gbest* version probably performs better than the *lbest* version, and as it is computationally more efficient – $\vec{p}_g$ can be saved as a single vector for all particles, whereas in the *lbest* version the entire neighbourhood must be searched for every individual in the population on every iteration – the *gbest* particle swarm should probably be the first choice for an optimization problem.

The *lbest* version is slower to find good solutions, but is more hardy in the face of local optima. When one individual has found a local optimum, it might draw its immediate neighbours into it, and they may draw others into it, but other subpopulations continue to explore different promising regions of the problem space. Thus the population tends to flow around inferior local optima and toward better ones.

One phenomenon that is observed in *lbest* version is the emergence of like-minded 'cultures' within the population. This is consistent with social science models that include population members' mutual imitation (Nowak et al [1990], Axelrod [1997]). Those simulations result in a stabilized configuration comprising homogeneous subpopulations; individuals within a sociometric region tend to become identical to one another but different from individuals in other regions. Typically in an *lbest* particle swarm trial when there are multiple optima a string of consecutive individuals in the array will arrive at very similar vectors of weights – exactly the same phenomenon that Nowak et al [1990] call 'polarization'. In other words, because of the 'upward comparison' feature of the particle swarm (not found in the simulations cited above), individuals in a particle swarm do more than just converge: they converge in optimal regions of the problem space. The implication for psychology is that interactions among individuals can result in optimal cognitive structures; people come to understand the world by discussing it with one another. The implication for computer science is that hard mathematical problems can be solved reliably through use of a robust and simple algorithm.

25.5.6 The Inertia Weight

Shi and Eberhart [1998a] proposed a modification of the algorithm that resulted in improved performance. They applied an inertia weight w to the previous velocity $\vec{v}_i(t-1)$, so that :

$$\vec{v}_i(t) = w(\vec{v}_i(t-1)) + \rho_1 \cdot (\vec{p}_i - \vec{x}_i(t-1)) + \rho_2 \cdot (\vec{p}_g - \vec{x}_i(t-1))$$

The inertia weight w is employed to control the impact of the previous history of velocities on the current velocity, thus to influence the trade-off between global (wide-ranging) and local (nearby) exploration abilities of the particles. A larger inertia weight w facilitates global exploration (searching new areas) while a smaller inertia weight tends to facilitate local exploration to fine-tune the current search area. The inertia weight is typically decreased over time, to enable the particle to focus on a wider area early and a smaller area late in the search. Research is continuing on this adjustment to the particle swarm algorithm.

25.6 PARTICLE SWARMS AND EVOLUTIONARY COMPUTATION

The particle swarm algorithm is often presented in the context of evolutionary paradigms such as genetic algorithms, evolutionary programming, and evolutionary strategies. These methods share the quality of adaptation, that is the modification of structures which results in improvement of performance; all implement probabilistic methods for searching the problem space; all comprise populations of individuals – there are in fact many similarities.

The particle swarm differs from evolutionary algorithms in an important way, however. Evolution has no memory, but particle swarm individuals do. Evolution leads to improvement through the operation of selection, wherein only the fittest population members survive from one generation to the next, in the particle swarm all population members survive. Instead of selection, particle swarms adapt through learning, which is a process that modifies enduring structures. The metaphor driving the particle swarm is social interaction, that is, individuals learning from one another, changing to become more similar to their neighbours.

Angeline [1998] added selection to the particle swarm and found that it improved the performance of the algorithm. In his method, the swarm iterates as usual, except that at every iteration the poorer-performing half of the population is replaced with the better half. In a social-psychological context, selection might be seen as the kind of attrition that occurs in groups, as members who are less well adjusted to the group's norms tend to drift away or be rejected.

25.7 IMPLICATIONS AND APPLICATIONS

The future for this new paradigm appears to lead in two directions, which may or may not remain parallel. As a metatheory of human social behaviour, it ties together findings from various fields of social science research, and as a function optimizer it can be used for engineering and other mathematical applications.

The particle swarm model suggests a social theory. If social interaction is so good for solving problems, we reason, perhaps this model can help us understand why human social behaviour has evolved as it has. We note that humans are a species which has proven its ability to survive under many diverse environmental conditions. This ability to survive is a direct result of our excellent ability to understand the natural, artificial, and abstract dynamics of the world. Further, it is noted that humans are fundamentally and thoroughly social animals. Solitary confinement is after all our severest punishment short of death.

If we theorize that cognitive optimization at least partly explains our sociality, then certain social-psychological hypotheses are suggested. One hypothesis, mentioned above, concerns the social construction of semantic knowledge. As in the connectionist examples used here, individuals endeavouring to make sense of things do well to learn from one another. Interestingly, social science research has tended to emphasize the errors and bizarre behaviours that result from social influence and conformity. While clever laboratory research can exaggerate the fallibility of human social behaviour, the present paradigm suggests that social influence can result in good solutions to hard problems, as individuals communicate their information-processing strategies to one another. The topic clearly deserves serious research attention.

The other direction for the future regards the exploitation of this powerful mathematical method. Several researchers are working on analyses of the algorithm's dynamical performance, and a number of researchers are using the particle swarm to optimize complex systems. For instance, Shi and Eberhart, in an extension of work reported in Shi & Eberhart [1998], have used particle swarm optimization to evolve a neural network that distinguishes between sleep and wake stages using only actigraph (motion) data. Work is underway to apply this methodology to a diagnostic tool that quantifies tremors in Parkinson's Disease.

25.8 SUMMARY

The social metaphor provides new insights that allow collaborative search with excellent results. In the particle swarm algorithm, the movements of individuals through a search space are influenced by their own past successes and by the successes of their neighbours. A simple formula adjusts trajectories toward regions that have proven relatively successful, resulting in efficient discovery of optima. Exploration between as well as beyond known optima results in a collaborative effort which is able to solve hard numerical optimization problems. Particle swarm optimization of neural networks simulates the social construction of semantic knowledge, and suggests directions for research into the applications and implications of this metatheoretical paradigm. Mathematical analyses and empirical studies are shedding light on the operation of the algorithm, and its use in software applications is increasing, as its potential comes to be understood.

Chapter Twenty-Six

SAW-ing EAs: Adapting the Fitness Function for Solving Constrained Problems

Gusz Eiben and Jano van Hemert

26.1 INTRODUCTION

The common opinion about evolutionary algorithms (EAs) is that they are good optimizers, but cannot handle constraints well. This opinion is based on the observation that the variation operators, mutation and recombination, are 'blind' to constraints. In other words, if the parents satisfy certain constraints the offspring obtained by mutation and/or recombination might violate them. In the last couple of years several options have been proposed to overcome this problem.

Before discussing these options, let us have a closer look on the notion of a constrained problem. A natural classification of problems can be found in Eiben & Ruttkay [1997]. This classification distinguishes free optimization problems, where no constraints are present, and constraint satisfaction and constrained optimization problems that do have constraints to be satisfied. A *free optimization problem* (FOP) is a pair $\langle S, f \rangle$, where S is a free search space (i.e. $S = D_1,..., D_n$ is a Cartesian product of sets) and f is a (real valued) objective function on S, which has to be minimized. A solution of a free optimization problem is an $s \in S$ with an optimal (minimal) f-value. A *constrained optimization problem* (COP) is a triple $\langle S, f, \phi \rangle$, where S is a free search space, f is a (real valued) objective function on S and ϕ is a formula (Boolean function on S). A solution of a constrained optimization problem is an $s \in S$ with $\phi(s) = true$ and an optimal f-value. A *constraint satisfaction problem* (CSP) is a pair $\langle S, \phi \rangle$, where S is a free search space and ϕ is a formula (Boolean function on S). A solution of a constraint satisfaction problem is an $s \in S$ with $\phi(s) = true$. Usually ϕ is called the *feasibility condition*, and it is defined by a number of constraints (relations) $c_1,..., c_m$ on the domain, that is the formula ϕ is the conjunction of the given constraints. Satisfying the constraints means finding an instantiation of variables $v_1,..., v_n$ within the domains $D_1,..., D_n$ such that the relations $c_1,..., c_m$ hold. Solving a CSP means finding one feasible element of the search space, solving a COP means finding a feasible and optimal element. Solving COPs by EAs is extensively treated in Michalewicz [1995, 1995a], Michalewicz & Attia [1994], Michalewicz & Michalewicz [1995], and Michalewicz & Schoenauer [1996], where different options for constraint handling are given and an experimental comparison of various options can be found. Such surveys or comparative investigations on EAs and CSPs in general are more seldom, at this moment we are only aware of Eiben & Ruttkay [1997] and Eiben et al [1998].

Let us note that the problem of handling constraints is present in both COPs and CSPs. For both cases the commonly listed options for treating this problem are the following (after Eiben [1997], Eiben & Ruttkay [1997], Michalewicz & Michalewicz [1995])

1. **Eliminating** infeasible individuals/chromosomes.
2. **Penalizing** infeasible individuals/chromosomes.
3. **Repairing** infeasible individuals/chromosomes.
4. **Special variation operators** preserving the feasibility of the parents.
5. **Special representation/decoding** such that chromosomes always stand for feasible individuals.

It is obvious that options 3, 4 and 5 are problem dependent. In a given problem context they might provide a powerful algorithm, but only little can be said in general about handling constraints this way. Options number 1 and 2 are problem independent, but it is clear that the first one leads to a very inefficient algorithm. Penalizing infeasible individuals/chromosomes has many advantages. First of all, if it is applied to all constraints then minimizing the total penalty is the 'only' thing to be done. In other words, it transforms a COP/CSP into an FOP. Considering that EAs have a 'basic instinct' to optimize, this is a very natural choice. It is also very transparent. Penalties can be defined independently for each constraint and the total penalty of a chromosome can be the weighted sum of these local penalties. Using weights also allows the user to distinguish between difficult (important) and easy (less important) constraints by giving them a relatively high, respectively low weight. There are, of course, also disadvantages of using penalties. First of all, packing all knowledge on violated constraints into a single number causes a loss of information. Besides, if one is willing to distinguish between constraints, it can be difficult to determine appropriate weights without substantial insight in the problem. Finally, this approach is said not to work in case of sparse problems with only a few solutions (Richardson et al [1989]).

26.2 DETERMINING PENALTIES

Let us summarize the properties of penalty based constraint handling in EAs:

1. Conceptually simple, transparent,
2. Problem independent,
3. Reduces problem to 'simple' optimization,
4. Allows user to tune on his/her preferences by weights,
5. Loss of information by packing everything in a single number,
6. Might require knowledge about the problem (if weights are used),
7. Said not to work well for sparse problems.

Looking carefully at the advantages (items 1 to 4) and disadvantages (5 to 7) of penalty based constraint handling discloses that using appropriate penalties is crucial for the success of this approach. Namely, if the constraints that are more difficult to satisfy have a relatively high weight, then satisfying them gives a relatively high reward to the algorithm. Thus, the EA will be 'more motivated' to satisfy these constraints. For a good performance it is thus essential that the weights reflect the hardness of constraints properly. This causes two difficulties. First, determining the relative hardness of constraints, and thereby the appropriate weights, requires domain knowledge. Second, the definition of appropriate weights can be problem solver dependent – a constraint that is hard for method A can be easy for method B and vice versa. A natural way to handle these problems is to let the problem solver determine the penalties. In case of evolutionary algorithms, this amounts to having the EA determining its own fitness function.

Our first efforts in this direction are reported in Eiben et al [1994, 1995], and Eiben & Ruttkay [1996]. This approach, called 'learning penalty functions' is based on adjusting the weights of constraints in an off-line fashion, i.e. *after* finishing a run with an EA on a given problem. The basic algorithm for this *offline weight update mechanism* is below:

> set initial weights (thus initially define fitness function f)
> **for** x test runs **do**
>   run the GA with this f
>   redefine f after termination
> **end for**

Redefining the fitness function happens by raising the weights of those constraints that are violated by the best individual at termination (thus only in case of unsuccessful runs). Experiments on the so-called Zebra puzzle compare the number of successful runs (out of 100) with and without the learning feature mentioned above. The results turn out to depend on the applied crossover operator, but typically the performance is doubled by using this learning mechanism (in case of one negative outlier the performance does not change, in case of one positive outlier the performance increases by a factor of 6). Inspection of the weights after the whole series of 100 runs with learning shows that they are to a great extent independent of the applied crossover operator and also of their initial values. In Figure 26.1 we reproduce the curves from Eiben & Ruttkay [1996] indicating these outcomes.

These curves show that the learning mechanism is robust, that is insensitive to the specific algorithm setup. This supports the conclusion that the weights learned reflect properties of the problem itself, and are not artifacts of the algorithm or the experimentation.

Subsequent work has been based on the insight that (evolutionary) search is a dynamic process passing different phases. Even though these phases cannot be crisply distinguished, it is widely acknowledged that population dynamics and the corresponding (near) optimal algorithm parameter values are changing during a run. Using the terminology of the beginning of this section one could say that the definition of what appropriate weights are may change during problem solving. Adapting the basic idea of letting the problem solver determine the penalties to this view implies that the weights are redefined in an on-line fashion, i.e. *during* a run of the EA on a given problem. The resulting mechanism, called *Stepwise Adaptation of Weights* (SAW), is presented below.

> set initial weights (thus initially defining fitness function f)
> **while not** termination **do**
>   **for** the next T_p fitness evaluations **do**
>   let the GA go with this f
>   **end for**
>   redefine f and recalculate fitness of individuals
> **end while**

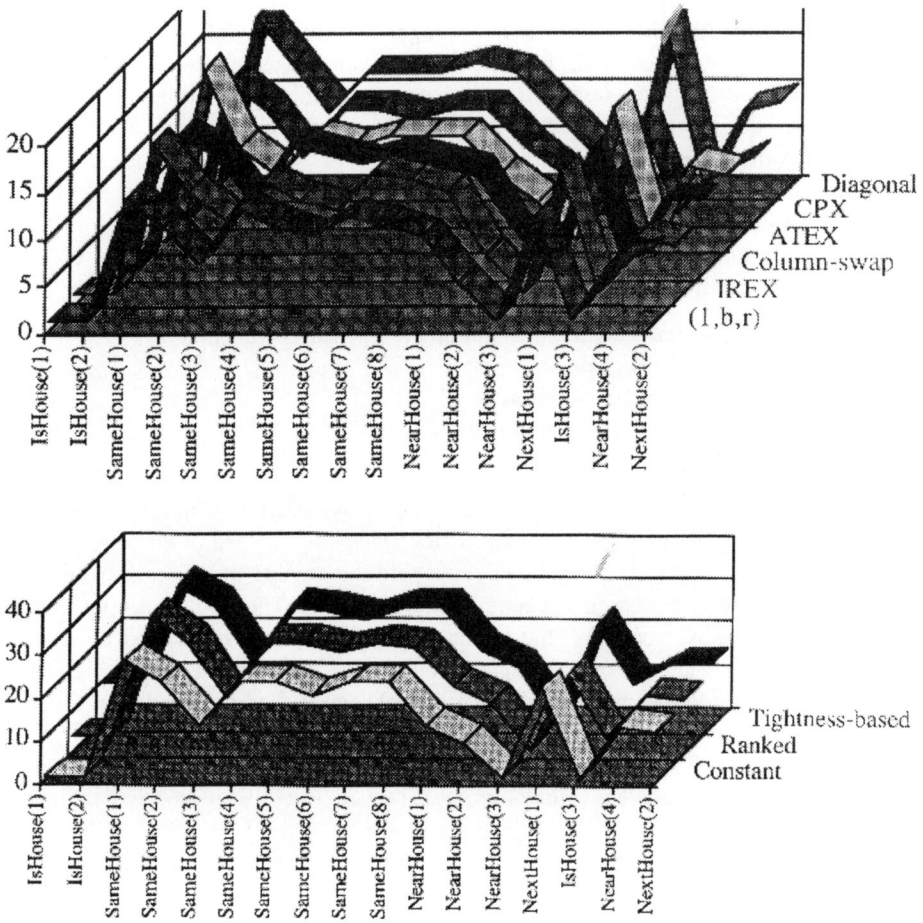

Fig. 26.1: Constraint weights learned on the Zebra puzzle. X-axis: constraints, Z-axis: weights obtained after 100 runs, Y-axis left figure: different crossover operators, Y-axis right figure: different weight initialization methods.

Redefining the fitness function happens by adding a value Δw to the weights of those constraints that are violated by the best individual at the end of each period of T_p fitness evaluations. The SAW-ing mechanism clearly adds two new parameters to an EA, the length of the update period T_p and the level of weight increase Δw. Extensive tests on graph colouring and 3-SAT (Eiben & van der Hauw [1996], van der Hauw [1996]) suggested that algorithm performance is relatively insensitive to these values.

26.3 SAW-ING EVOLUTIONARY ALGORITHMS

The SAW-ing mechanism has been applied to various constraint satisfaction problems: graph colouring, satisfiability, and binary CSPs. In this section we briefly summarize the most important results of these studies.

26.3.1 Graph Colouring

The first application of SAW-ing concerns graph 3-colouring (Eiben & van der Hauw [1996, 1997], Eiben et al [1998]). The problem of graph 3-colouring is to colour each vertex $v \in V$ of a given undirected graph $G=(V, E)$ with one of three colours so that no two vertices connected by an edge $e \in E$ are coloured with the same colour.

For this problem an order-based EA has been developed where the individuals are permutations of nodes and a decoder constructs a colouring from a permutation. As a decoder a simple greedy algorithm is used which colours a node with the lowest colour (colours are represented by integers) that does not violate constraints and leaves nodes uncoloured when this is not possible. Somewhat deviating from the general idea of using the weighted sum of unsatisfied constraints as fitness. Evaluation of a permutation is based on the number of uncoloured nodes in the colouring belonging to it. Formally, the function f is defined as:

$$f(x) = \sum_{i=1}^{n} w_i \cdot \chi(x,i) \qquad (26.1)$$

where w_i is the penalty (or weight) assigned with node i and:

$$\chi(x,i) = \begin{cases} 1 & \text{if node } x_i \text{ is left uncoloured because of a constraint violation} \\ 0 & \text{otherwise} \end{cases}$$

Initial weights are set at 1, and are increased with a step size of one during updates.

The effect of the SAW-ing mechanism on the EA performance has been tested using swap mutation as the only search operator, a (1+1) selection scheme and the SAW mechanism with $T_p=250$ and $\Delta w=1$ on graphs generated with the graph generator written by Joe Culberson[1] using four different seeds. The results on equipartite graphs with $n=1000$ nodes and $p=0.010$ edge connectivity are summarized in Table 26.1. The table shows the results for Falkenauer's Grouping GA (Falkenauer [1994, 1996]), Brélaz' DSatur algorithm with backtracking (Brélaz [1979]), an EA without SAW-ing, a hybrid EA+DSatur algorithm and the EA with SAW-ing.

Table 26.1: Success rates (SR) and the average number of evaluations to a solution (AES) for the Grouping GA, (1+1) EA using SWAP, DSatur with backtracking, the hybrid EA+DSatur and the (1+1) SAW-ing EA using SWAP.

Method	SR	AES
Grouping GA	0.00	300000
EA	0.09	261221
DSatur	0.22	220033
EA+DSatur	0.33	201354
EA+SAW	0.92	113099

These experiments (not all results repeated here) show not only that a SAW-ing EA highly outperforms the other techniques, but also that the performance is rather independent from the random seeds. Thus, the SAW mechanism is not only highly effective, obtaining much better success rates at lower costs, but also very robust.

A thorough comparison between DSatur with backtracking and a SAW-ing EA is performed on graph instances with three different topologies (arbitrary 3-colourable, equi-partite 3-colourable and flat 3 colourable graphs), three different sizes ($n=200$, 500, 1000) and for different values of edge connectivities around the phase transition where the hardest instances are located. Globally, the conclusions are that DSatur is better on the 'easy' instances (small graphs, the easier topologies and large graphs far from the phase transition), while the SAW-ing EA is better on the hardest instances. The SAW-ing EA is often able to find solutions where DSatur does not find any. As for speed, in general the EA needs fewer steps.

It is very interesting to see the fitness curve of a run of the EA with the SAW mechanism. Figure 26.2 shows a run when a solution is found. The left curve has a higher resolution, displaying the fitness of the best individual between 0–10000 evaluations, the right curve shows the range 0–80000. The higher resolution curve shows that within each period the fitness (actually, the penalty) drops as the EA is making progress and then sharply rises when the weights are updated, giving the image of a *saw*.

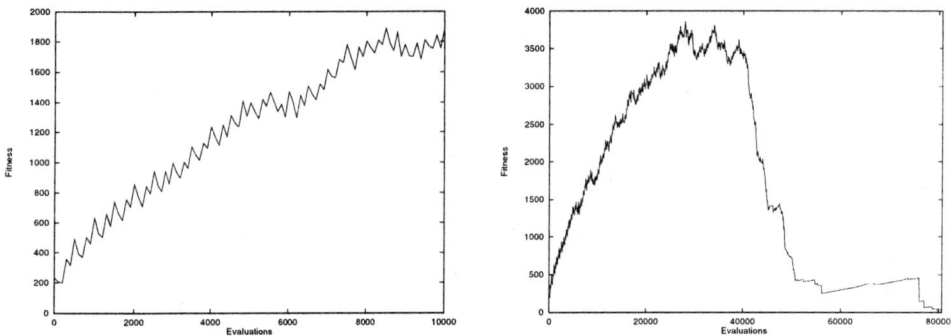

Fig. 26.2: Fitness curve for the SAW-ing EA on graph colouring.

26.3.2 Satisfiability

In a propositional satisfiability problem (SAT) a propositional formula is given and a truth assignment for its variables is sought for that makes the formula true. This problem was the first computational task shown to be *NP*-hard (Cook [1971]). Without loss of generality it can be assumed that the given formula is in conjunctive normal form (CNF), i.e. it is a conjunction of clauses where a clause is a disjunction of literals. In the 3-SAT version, it is also assumed that the clauses consist of exactly three literals. In the common notation, a formula has l clauses and n variables. Mitchell et al [1992] report that the phase transition, where the hardest problem instances are located, is found when $l=4.3n$.

In Eiben & van der Hauw [1997a] and van der Hauw [1996] several conclusions on SAW-ing EAs for graph colouring are validated on 3-SAT problems. A straightforward bit-string representation (one literal – one bit) and fitness function (the weighted sum of unsatisfied clauses) in a steady-state style form the basis of the algorithm. Similarly to graph colouring, an EA with population size 1 and mutation only works best for 3-SAT. The relative insensitivity of the SAW-ing mechanism to the parameters T_p and Δw is confirmed, and the particular behaviour of the fitness function can also be observed. Figure 26.3, after van der Hauw [1996], shows the development of fitness values (the weighted sum of unsatisfied clauses, to be minimized) during a typical run. Although the oscillations in this case are heavier than occurs in the graph colouring case, the general tendency is similar: the fitness curve is increasing first, then it is suddenly decreasing and hits the optimum level of zero.

The paper Eiben & van der Hauw [1997a] is concerned with developing a suitable version of the general SAW-ing EA and comparing this algorithm with traditional AI heuristics for solving 3-SAT. The best heuristic algorithms belong to the GenSAT family, such as GSAT proposed by Selman et al [1992], HSAT by Gent & Walsh [1993, 1993a] that outperformed GSAT, and Frank's WGSAT that was shown to be better than HSAT (Frank [1996], Gent & Walsh [1995]). The comparison of these techniques on Frank's set of 1000 satisfiable instances (SeedSet1) as well as on 1000 random instances (SeedSet2) show that the SAW-ing EA is superior. The results are given in Table 26.2 after Eiben & van der Hauw [1997a].

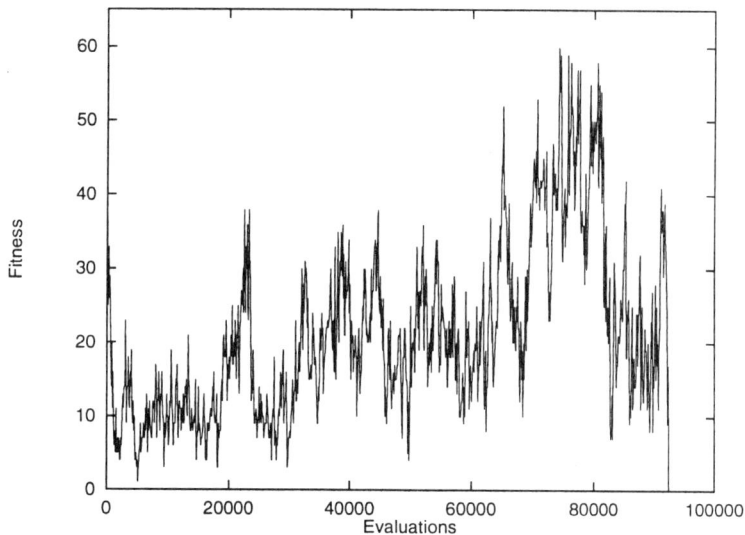

Fig. 26.3: Fitness curve for the SAW-ing EA on 3-SAT.

Table 26.2: Comparison between WGSAT and different SAW-ing EAs on 3-SAT

Method	SeedSet1		SeedSet2	
	SR	AES	SR	AES
WGSAT	0.30	110507	0.53	119262
SAW-ing EA without fine tuning	0.37	88359	0.68	97751
SAW-ing EA with fine tuning	0.48	70182	0.88	73166

An interesting aspect of these comparisons is that the family of GenSAT based methods is actually very similar to an asexual EA with extinctive $(1, \lambda)$ selection strategy (that has been used as SAW-ing EA with fine tuning on λ in the above experiments). Moreover, the WGSAT algorithm looks very much like a SAW-ing EA, since both methods are using an adaptive weighting mechanism on the clauses to be satisfied. But while WGSAT does an exhaustive search on each neighbour (in EA terms: on each child that can be obtained by one bit-flip mutation), the $(1, \lambda)$ EA only generates λ offspring before selecting the next generation (consisting of one single candidate solution). Despite the similarities in the search mechanisms there are significant differences in performance between WGSAT and this SAW-ing EA. These are most probably caused by the fact that the EAs makes locally suboptimal decisions by not performing exhaustive neighbourhood search, while WGSAT enumerates all neighbours (mutants) around a given trial solution and becomes sensitive for local optima. Apparently, the locally suboptimal choices of the EAs prevent getting stuck in local optima and on the long run this leads to a better overall performance.

A standard way of circumventing the local optimum problem of hill-climbers is using them with restarts. In Eiben & van der Hauw [1997a], WGSAT is used without restarts in order to keep the differences between the SAW-ing EA and the WGSAT algorithm minimal. Fair as this may seem, this can cause suboptimal performance for WGSAT and thus unfair comparisons. In Bäck et al [1998], WGSAT with restarts is considered and the frequency of restarts is fine tuned by numerous tests. Additionally, a second competitor of the SAW-ing EA is added to the contest: an evolution strategy, based on a hint of Z. Michalewicz (personal communication). The basic idea is to make the originally discrete SAT problem continuous and apply an evolution strategy that has the reputation of a good EA variant in case of continuous variables.

For an experimental comparison solvable problem instances are used which were created by the generator mkcnf.c by Allen van Gelder[3]. To ensure that the problem instances are 'interesting' the relationship $l=4.3n$ is maintained in this investigation. Tests are performed on three instances for each of the four different problem sizes ($n=30, 40, 50$ and 100). The results obtained by the fine tuned versions of all three algorithms are summarized below in Table 26.3.

Table 26.3: Summary of the results for ES, SAW-ing EA and WGSAT.

Method	30		40		50		100	
	SR	AES	SR	AES	SR	AES	SR	AES
ES	0.31	18725	0.45	10946	0.38	18068	0.15	85670
SAW	1.00	34015	0.93	45272	0.85	40836	0.72	50896
WGSAT	0.99	38316	0.98	31747	0.77	58386	0.36	124744

Here we can again see that the SAW-ing EA seems to be the best algorithm overall among those examined. On the smaller test cases the difference between SAW and WGSAT is small. In fact, for $n=40$ WGSAT is slightly better, but the SAW-ing EA clearly scales up better, that is on the largest test cases it has a significantly higher SR and lower AES than WGSAT.

26.3.3 Random Binary CSPs

A binary constraint satisfaction problem is a CSP where each constraint is binary, that is concerns exactly two variables. Restricting a study to binary CSPs does not lead to loss of generality, because every CSP can be equivalently transformed into a binary CSP (Tsang [1993]). Binary CSPs have been the subject of research by many others, among which Smith [1994] played an important role by trying to estimate the difficulty of CSP instances using four parameters:

1. the number of variables,

2. the domain sizes of these variables,

3. the constraint density of the given problem and

4. the tightness of the constraints.

Constraint density is defined as the probability that a constraint exists given two variables; this is a feature of the problem as a whole. Constraint tightness is a measure defined for each individual constraint, being the probability that two values for the variables are in a conflict. Fixing the number of variables and the domain size, the constraint density and the average constraint tightness largely determine the hardness of the problem instances. In Figure 26.4 we show the landscape of solvability exhibiting the theoretically predicted probability (Z-axis) that an instance has a solution as a function of the constraint density (X-axis) and constraint tightness (Y-axis). In this landscape three different areas can be distinguished. First, the high plateau belonging to low density and tightness values, where the probability of finding a solution is one. Second, the low plateau belonging to high density and tightness values, where the probability of finding a solution is zero. Between these two parts there is a third area of phase transition called the *mushy region* (Smith [1994]), where it is very hard to predict if a particular instance does or does not have a solution.

For the experiments on binary CSPs and SAW-ing, a problem instance generator called RandomCsp^2 has been built loosely based on G. Dozier's work. The generator is parameterized using the four parameters discussed above. Two series of experiments have been done, an extensive comparison between three adaptive EAs on 25 different density and tightness combinations, and an experiment where only the number of variables is varied to find out the scale-up behaviour of the two best algorithms from the previous experiment. The three methods participating in the first experiment are the coevolutionary GA applied to constraint satisfaction (CCS) (see chapter twenty-three, as well as Paredis [1994, 1997]), the microgenetic method (MID) (Bowen & Dozier [1995], Dozier et al [1994, 1995]) and the SAW-ing method. The SAW-ing EA used here (Eiben et al [1998], van Hemert [1998]) is the same as the best found in the investigation on graph colouring, using order-based representation with a simple greedy decoder to assign values to variables, a population size of one and one genetic mutation operator that swaps two variables.

For the first series of experiments the number of variables and the domain size of each variable are fixed at 15. Both the density and the tightness values are ranged over {0.1, 0.3, 0.5, 0.7, 0.9}, resulting in 25 combinations and for each of these combinations 25 instances are generated randomly for the tests. Each algorithm is ran on each instance 10 times and the average success rate and the corresponding AES are recorded for each combination. The success rate results for both MID and SAW show a landscape very similar to the theoretically estimated landscape of solvability. The success rates for CCS drop far sooner than for the other two methods. By the time MID and SAW first have a SR lower than one, CCS is already at SR=0, i.e. not finding any solutions. In Table 26.4 we reproduce the most interesting results from this experiment, leaving out CCS and showing only the density-tightness combinations from the mushy region. For other combinations MID and SAW almost had equal performance. The results indicate that MID finds more solutions in this region, but SAW is always faster, sometimes even two and a half times as fast as MID.

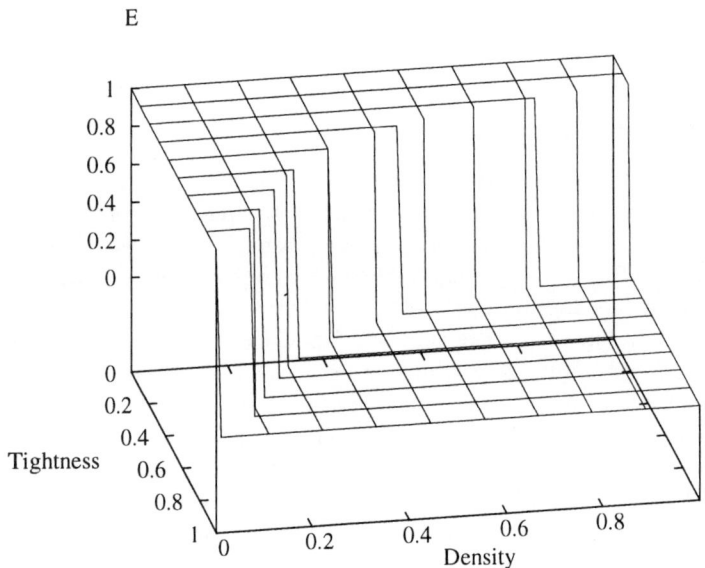

Fig. 26.4: Landscape of solvability as predicted theoretically.

Table 26.4: Comparison of MID and SAW. Showing the results for parameter settings that resulted in the biggest difference in performance.

Method	(density, tightness)							
	(0.9, 0.3)		(0.5, 0.5)		(0.3, 0.7)		(0.1, 0.9)	
	SR	AES	SR	AES	SR	AES	SR	AES
MID	1.00	8136	0.90	26792	0.52	32412	0.96	2923
SAW	1.00	3848	0.74	10722	0.23	21281	0.64	1159

The second experiment consists of a scale-up test comparing MID and SAW. By fixing the domain size (15), density (0.3) and tightness (0.3) values and varying the number of variables (n) from 10 to 40 with a step size of 5, the variance of performance as a function of the problem size can be observed. Figure 26.5 exhibits the AES results numerically (left) as well as graphically (right). Let us note that the corresponding success rates are constantly 1.0 for for both algorithms. These results show that SAW scales up much better than MID up to $n=35$, but for $n=40$ MID is faster, beating SAW by almost 1500 fitness evaluations.

Recall the particular behaviour of the fitness curves of the SAW-ing EA on graph colouring (Figure 26.2) and 3-SAT (Figure 26.3). We have recorded the fitness values during a run on a randomly generated CSP ($n=m=15$, $d=t=0.4$) and show the result in Figure 26.6. Here again, the left curve has a higher resolution, displaying the fitness of the best individual between 0–10000 evaluations, the right curve shows the range 0–100000. The fitness curves show that SAW repeatedly finds local optima resulting in a sudden drop of the fitness. Between these fitness drops SAW shows the same image as it does on the other problems, a periodical rise of the fitness because of an update of the weights that makes the plot look like a saw.

n	MID	SAW
10	10	1
15	52	2
20	163	5
25	410	30
30	1039	190
35	3462	1465
40	17252	18668

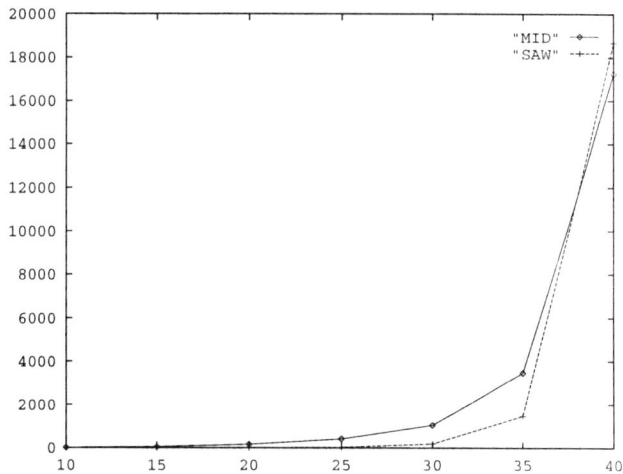

Fig. 26.5: AES results for the scale-up tests of MID and SAW. The density and tightness are set to 0.3 and the domain size of each variable to 15.

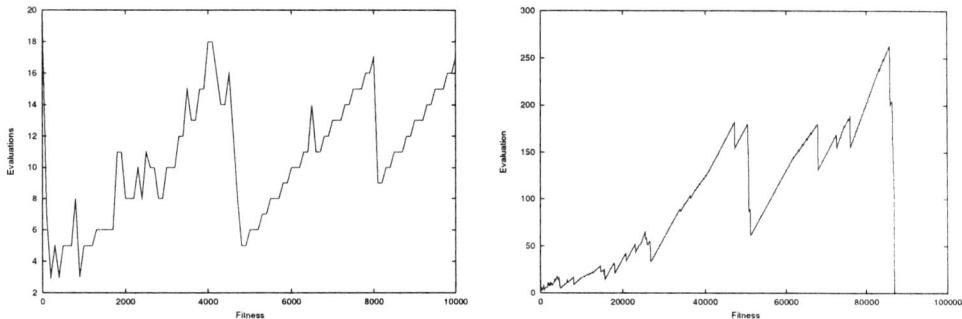

Fig. 26.6: Fitness curves for the SAW-ing EA on binary CSP.

26.4 RELATED WORK

The basic idea behind SAW-ing is the re-definition of the function to be optimized, triggered by observed failure in optimizing the current function. The freedom to do so comes from the nature of the objective function representing a CSP. Namely, the objective function must have the property that an optimal function value implies that no constraints are violated. Obviously, there are many functions satisfying this property and as long as this property holds the user is free to choose different variants. It is interesting to note that besides EAs based on penalties other heuristic techniques use a similar idea to solve CSPs by an estimation of the error in a solution that has to be minimized. Also the idea of redefining the heuristic estimation function on-the-fly has been propagated seemingly independently by a number of researchers. In this section we give a brief overview of related work along these lines.

Morris' breakout mechanism is a well-known Artificial Intelligence method in this spirit (Morris [1993]). The algorithm Morris used in experiments applies an iterative improvement method which proceeds as usual until a local optimum is reached. The function to be optimized is the weighted sum of nogoods, where a nogood is a set of prohibited values. When trapped in a local optimum, the breakout mechanism increases all weights of the current nogoods. When the algorithm breaks out of the local optimum, it resumes with iterative improvement. Good results are obtained on 3-SAT and fair results on graph colouring for three and four colours. Interesting in this paper is the proof that an idealized version of the method will eventually always find a solution for finite CSPs, although this method is not efficient.

Selman & Kautz [1993] describe a GenSAT type method in which GSAT associates a weight with each clause. The weights of all clauses that remain unsatisfied at the end of a *try* are incremented. This very much resembles the off-line weight update mechanism used in the EA for the Zebra problem, see section 26.2. Recently, Frank adapted this mechanism by updating the weights after each *flip* instead of after each run (Frank [1996, 1996a]) and achieved very good results with this version called WGSAT. This method is based on the same rationale as our SAW mechanism. Frank envisions his weight adaptation as repeatedly changing the search heuristics. We see SAW-ing as a problem independent way to handle constraints, in evolutionary terms a way to adapt the fitness landscape during the search.

Recent developments in (probabilistic) tabu search (Glover [1996a]), show similarity with this adaptive spirit too. The memory and learning structures described by Løkketangen & Glover [1997] embody an adaptive mechanism similar to SAW in the context of surrogate constraint analysis.

There are also a number of techniques within the field of evolutionary computation that modify the definition of fitness during the run. The first one we know of is that of Bean & Hadj-Alouane [1992], which utilizes feedback from the search process. Technically, the method decreases the penalties for the generation $t+1$ if all best individuals in the last k generations were feasible, and increases penalties, if all best individuals in the last k generations were infeasible. If there are some feasible and infeasible individuals as best individuals in the last k generations, then the weights remain without change.

We have mentioned the microgenetic algorithm with iterative descent from Bowen & Dozier [1995] and Dozier et al [1994, 1995]. In this EA a small population is used together with a system of breakouts à la Morris. A breakout consists of a nogood (i.e. a pair of values causing a constraint violation) and an associated weight. The standard fitness being the number of violated constraints is extended by the weighted sum of nogoods as an extra penalty for candidate solutions consisting nogoods. The list of nogoods is created and updated during the run, thus the definition of fitness is also changing during a run. The weight of a breakout is increased every time the pair of values is involved in a constraint violation when the algorithm is in a local optimum. This system is used to make sure the algorithm does not get stuck in local optima.

A different approach to adaptive fitness is represented by coevolutionary methods. This method, also used in the comparison discussed in section 26.3, is based on two populations in an arms race with each other, as proposed by Paredis (see chapter twenty-three, as well as Paredis [1994, 1997]). The first population consists of candidate solutions for the given CSP, while the second one contains the constraints. The fitness of an individual is determined by a number of encounters with members of the other population. Individuals are selected for encounters randomly, but biased by their fitness. An encounter is successful (resulting in better fitness) for a solution if it satisfies the encountered constraint. In turn, an encounter is successful for a constraint if the encountered solution cannot satisfy it. This causes the arms race, where the fitness in both populations is continuously varying depending on the (randomized) encounters.

26.5 CONCLUDING REMARKS

Looking at all research done so far on the SAW-ing method we can highlight the following findings as most important. First of all that a small population size, counterintuitive as it may seem, happens to work very well on the problems that have been tested. Second is the insensitivity that SAW-ing has to its parameters T_p and Δw. This insensitivity has been found in experiments on graph-colouring and satisfiability. Third, the fitness curves from the three problem classes shown in Figures 26.2, 26.3, and 26.4, all share the same features and exhibit the shape of a saw. This shape comes from alternating periods of decreasing and increasing fitness values, which are caused by converging to (local) optima and the periodic increase of weights, respectively.

Let us also make a note on the constraint weights the SAW-ing EA finds. The plots of the fitness curves suggest that problem solving with the SAW mechanism happens in two phases. In the first phase the penalty increases a lot because of the increased weights. This is followed by a phase where the penalty drops sharply and hits the optimum. A possible explanation for this behaviour is that in the first phase the EA is learning a good setting for the weights (that is, an appropriate fitness function) thereby making the problem 'easy'. In the second phase the EA is solving the problem, exploiting the knowledge (appropriate weights) learned in the first phase. This interpretation of the fitness curves is a plausible hypothesis. However, suggesting that the EA could learn universally good weights for the given problem instance would go too far. In the first place, another problem solver might need other weights to solve the problem. Besides, we have performed tests on graph colouring and binary CSPs to check this working hypothesis. In particular, we have applied a SAW-ing EA to a problem instance, thus learning a setting of the weights, and then applied an EA to the same problem instance using the learned weights non-adaptively, i.e. keeping them constant along the evolution. The results showed *worse* performance than in the first run when adaptive weights were used. This occurred for both graph colouring and binary CSPs. This refutes the above hypothesis and suggests that the SAW mechanism does not work because it enables the problem solver to discover some hidden, universally good weights. Rather, SAW-ing allows the EA to shift the focus of search (quasi) continuously, and thus amounting to implicit problem decomposition that guides the population through the search space.

Further research on SAW-ing includes other weight update mechanisms and other application areas for this technique. As for the first issue, also decreasing weights instead of only increasing them is a straightforward modification that needs to be assessed. Concerning other application areas, currently we are using genetic programming for data mining where the fitness (to be minimized) is the weighted sum of misclassified cases from the data base.

NOTES

1. Source code is for Joe Culberson's graph generator is available at ftp://ftp.cs.ualberta.ca/pub/joe/GraphGenerator/generate.tar.gz .
2. The problem instance generator called RandomCsp is available at the book's WWW site, and also at http://www.wi.leidenuniv.nl/~jvhemert/csp-ea/ .
3. Allen van Gelder's problem instance generator is available from the following address: ftp://dimacs.rutgers.edu/pub/challenge/satisfiability/contributed/UCSC/instances.

Chapter Twenty-Seven

Parallel Distributed Genetic Programming

Riccardo Poli

27.1 INTRODUCTION

Genetic Programming (GP) is an extension of Genetic Algorithms (GAs) in which the structures that make up the population to be optimized are not fixed-length character strings that encode possible solutions to a problem, but *programs* that, when executed, *are* the candidate solutions to the problem (Koza [1992]). Programs are expressed in GP as parse trees, rather than as lines of code. For example, the simple expression $\max(x*y,3+x*y)$ would be represented as shown in Figure 27.1(left). The set of possible internal (non-leaf) nodes used in GP parse trees is called the *function set*, $\mathcal{F}=\{f_1,...,f_{N_F}\}$. $\mathcal{F}$ can include almost any kind of programming construct: arithmetic operators, mathematical and Boolean functions, conditionals, looping constructs, procedures with side effects, etc. The set of terminal (leaf) nodes in the parse trees is called the *terminal set*, $\mathcal{T}=\{t_1,...,t_{N_T}\}$. $\mathcal{T}$ can include: variables, constants, 0-arity functions with or without side effects, random constants, etc. The basic search algorithm used in GP is a classical GA with mutation and crossover specifically designed to handle parse trees. For example, in their simplest form, crossover works by replacing a random subtree in one parent program with another randomly selected subtree taken from another parent program, while mutation replaces a random subtree with a new randomly generated subtree. To increase the modularity of the programs discovered by GP and the efficiency of the algorithm, it is possible to use a technique known as Automatically Defined Functions (ADFs) (Koza [1992, 1994]). When ADFs are used one branch of the root node is interpreted as the main program, while the other branches are interpreted as subroutines which the main program can call (ADFs are part of the function set of the main program). ADFs can be seen as individual-specific parametrized building blocks. Sometimes ADFs are part of the function set of other ADFs, which allows the evolution of complex hierarchies of functions. When ADFs are used, crossover and mutation are modified to ensure that nodes in the main program are never mixed with subroutine nodes (this is necessary since ADFs normally use a terminal set including only dummy arguments). For a more detailed introduction to standard Genetic Programming see Koza [1992, 1994], Banzhaf et al [1998], and Langdon [1998].

This form of GP has been applied successfully to a large number of difficult problems like automated design, pattern recognition, robot control, symbolic regression, music generation, image compression, image analysis, etc. (Koza [1992, 1994], Kinnear [1994], Koza et al [1996, 1997, 1998], Banzhaf et al [1998a]). However, tree-based GP is not very well suited to the evolution of parallel computational structures such as parallel programs, neural networks, logic circuits, and so on.

This chapter describes Parallel Distributed Genetic Programming (PDGP), a new form of GP which is suitable for the development of programs with a high degree of parallelism and distributedness[1].

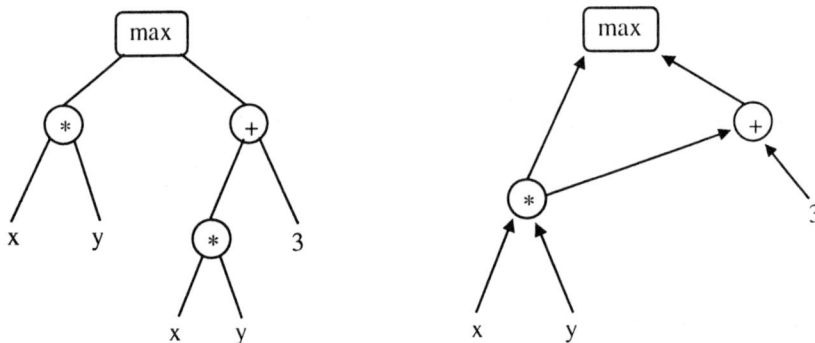

Fig. 27.1: Parse-tree representation of the expression $\max(x*y, 3+x*y)$ (left) and graph-like representation of the same expression (right).

Programs are represented in PDGP as graphs with nodes representing functions and terminals, and links representing the flow of control and results. In the simplest form of PDGP, links are directed and unlabelled, in which case PDGP can be considered a generalization of standard GP since PDGP uses the same kind of nodes as GP, and trees are a special kind of graphs. However, PDGP can use more complex (direct) representations, which allow the development of symbolic, neuro-symbolic and neural networks, recurrent transition networks, finite state automata, etc. Like GP, PDGP allows the development of programs of any size and shape (within predefined limits). However, it also allows the user to control the degree of parallelism of the programs to be developed. In PDGP, programs are manipulated by special crossover and mutation operators which, like the ones used in GP, guarantee the syntactic correctness of the offspring. This leads to a very efficient search of the space of possible parallel distributed programs. PDGP programs can be executed in different ways, depending on whether nodes with side effects are used or not.

The chapter is organized as follows. First, in section 27.2, we describe the basic representation used in PDGP. Then we report on genetic operators and initialization strategies (section 27.3) and describe the basic interpreters used in PDGP (section 27.4). Then, we describe some extensions to the basic representation and operators used in PDGP (section 27.5) and we illustrate the behaviour of PDGP on a number of problems (sections 27.6 and 27.7). In section 27.8 we describe work related to PDGP. Finally, we draw some conclusions and describe promising directions for future work in section 27.9.

27.2 REPRESENTATION

As mentioned above, usually programs in GP are represented as parse trees. Taking inspiration from the parallel distributed processing performed in neural nets (Rumelhart & McClelland [1986]), we decided to explore the possibility of representing programs as graphs with labelled nodes and oriented links. The idea was that nodes could be the functions and terminals used in a program while the links would determine which arguments to use in each function-node when it is next evaluated. We hoped in this way to obtain a form of parallel distributed programming with some of the useful features shown by artificial neural nets.

Figure 27.1 (right) shows an example of a parallel distributed program represented as a graph. The program implements the same function as the one shown in Figure 27.1 (left). i.e. max($x*y$, $3+x*y$). For now, its execution should be imagined as a 'wave of computations' starting from the terminals and propagating upwards along the graph, more or less like the updating of the activations of the neurons in a multi-layer feed-forward neural net. This tiny-scale example shows that graph-like representations of programs can be more compact (in term of number of nodes) and more efficient (the sub-expression $x*y$ is computed only once instead of twice) than tree-like representations. Also, this representation can be used to express a much bigger class of programs (trees are special kinds of graphs) which are parallel in nature: we call them *parallel distributed programs*. Unfortunately, the direct handling of graphs within a genetic algorithm presents some problems.

Several direct representations for graphs exist in graph theory. For each of them one could imagine operators that select a random sub-graph in one parent and then swap it with a *properly* selected sub-graph in the other parent or a *properly* generated random sub-graph (by 'proper sub-graph' we mean a sub-graph with the correct number of input and output links). However, as shown by the considerable work done in the field of neural networks, it is not easy to produce good genetic operators for direct graph encodings. In particular it is hard to produce a crossover operator such that: (a) when parents share a common characteristic their offspring inherit such a characteristic, (b) when parents have different characteristics their offspring can inherit both such characteristics, (c) every offspring is a valid solution, (d) crossover is efficient.

PDGP uses a direct representation of graphs which allows the definition of crossover operators which respect all the criteria listed above (in particular efficiency and offspring validity). The representation is based on the idea of assigning each node in the graph to a physical location in a multi-dimensional (evenly spaced) grid with a pre-fixed (regular or irregular) shape and limiting the connections between nodes to be upwards. Also, we allow connections to exist only between nodes belonging to adjacent rows, like the connections in a standard feed-forward multi-layer neural network. This representation for parallel distributed programs is illustrated in Figure 27.2 (left), where we assumed that the program has a single output at coordinates (0,0) (the y axis is pointing downwards) and that the grid is two-dimensional and includes $6\times6+1$ cells[2].

By adding the identity function I (that is, a wire or pass-through node) to the function set, any parallel distributed program (equivalently, any directed acyclic graph) can be rearranged in such a way that it can be described with this grid-based graph representation. For example, the program illustrated in Figure 27.1 (right) can be transformed into the layered network illustrated in Figure 27.3 (left).

In this representation it is possible to describe any program by listing the following parameters for each node: (1) the label of the node, (2) the coordinates of the node, and (3) the horizontal displacement of the nodes in the previous layer (if any) whose values are used as arguments for the node. For example, the program illustrated in Figure 27.3 (left) could be described by the list given in Figure 27.3 (right).

The basic representation described above will allow us to define very efficient forms of crossover and mutation. However, in order to study all the possibilities offered by our network-based representation of programs, we decided to expand the representation to explicitly include introns ('unexpressed' parts of code). In particular we assumed that, once the size and shape of the grid is fixed, a function or a terminal be associated to *every* node in the grid, i.e. also to the nodes that are not directly or indirectly connected to the output. We call them *inactive nodes* or *introns*. The others are called *active nodes*. For example, the program shown in Figure 27.2 (left) could have an expanded representation like the one in Figure 27.2 (right).

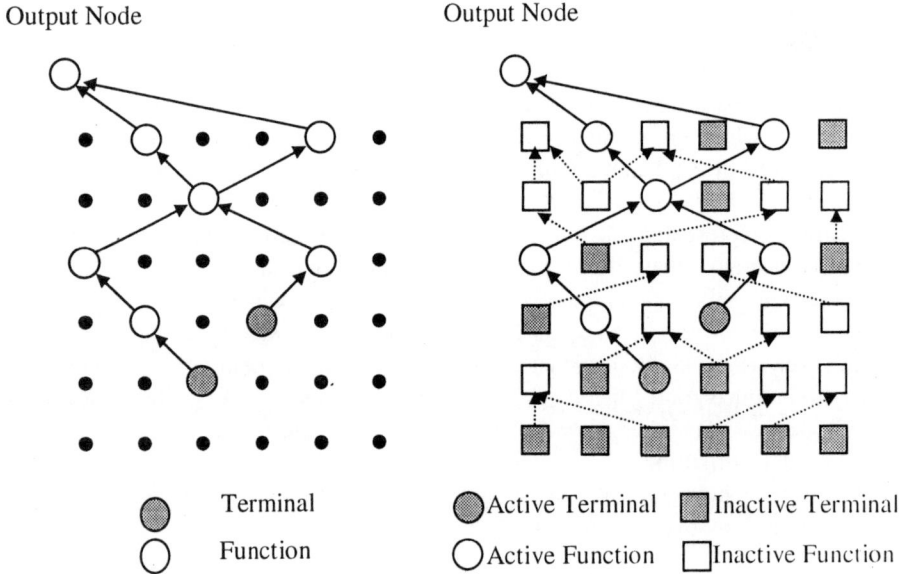

Fig. 27.2: Grid-based representation of graphs representing programs in PDGP (left) and intron-augmented representation of programs in PDGP (right).

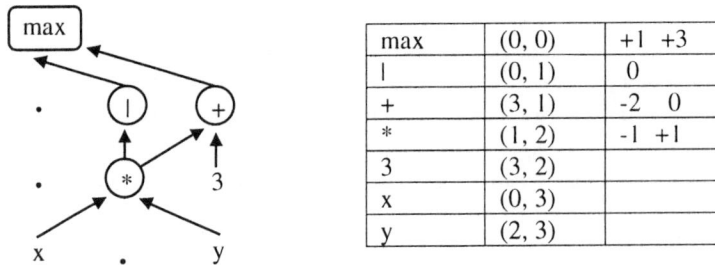

max	(0, 0)	+1 +3
		(0, 1)	0
+	(3, 1)	-2 0
*	(1, 2)	-1 +1
3	(3, 2)	
x	(0, 3)	
y	(2, 3)	

Fig. 27.3: Grid-based representation of the expression max($x*y$,3+$x*y$) (left) and an equivalent description using labels, coordinates and displacements (right).

It should be noted that inactive nodes can receive as input the results computed by both active and inactive nodes. It should also be noted that by using an array with the same topology as the grid, it is possible to store in each cell of the array only the label and the input connections of each node and omit the coordinates from the representation. This can lead to more efficient implementations.

This basic representation can be and has been extended in various ways. We will briefly describe these extensions after introducing the standard genetic operators and interpreters of PDGP. We will also present some examples of programs using these representations.

27.3 GENETIC OPERATORS

Several kinds of crossover, mutation and initialization strategies can be defined for the basic representation used in PDGP. We describe some of them in the following sections.

27.3.1 Random Program Generation

In standard GP, it is possible to obtain balanced or unbalanced random initial trees with the 'full' method and the 'grow' method, respectively (Koza [1992]). In the 'grow' method trees are build recursively (starting from the root node) by randomly selecting each node either from the function set or the terminal set. When a node is drawn from the function set the procedure is recursively applied to its arguments. When the desired maximum depth for the initial trees has been reached, only nodes from the terminal set are selected. The 'full' method works in the same way, except that until the maximum depth has been reached nodes are selected only from the function set.

Similarly, in PDGP it is possible to obtain 'balanced' or 'unbalanced' random graphs depending on whether we allow terminals to be at a pre-fixed maximum distance from the output node(s) only or whether they can occur anywhere in the initial programs.

In PDGP the generation of random programs can proceed in several ways, depending on whether introns are used or not. If introns are used, then the grid can be filled with random functions and terminals. When functions are inserted, a corresponding number of random input-links are also generated. Alternatively, it is possible to build random graphs recursively (like in standard GP) starting from the output nodes and selecting random functions (with their input links) or terminals depending on the kind of graphs we want to build (balanced or not) and on the depth reached with recursion.

In standard GP, during a run trees can grow bigger than the initial maximum depth. Normally the growth is limited by a second depth threshold. In most examples described here we have used relatively 'shallow' grids (that is, grids with a small number of rows). In experience with such grids, maintaining a distinction between the maximum depth of graphs (the number of rows) and the maximum depth for the initial graphs makes little difference. For this reason we have always given the same value to the two parameters.

27.3.2 Crossover

The basic crossover operator of PDGP, which we call *Sub-graph Active-Active Node* (SAAN) *crossover*, is basically a generalization to graphs of the crossover used in GP to recombine trees. SAAN crossover works as follows:

1. A random active node is selected in each parent (crossover point).

2.   A sub-graph including all the active nodes which are used to compute the output value of the crossover point in the first parent is extracted.

3.   The sub-graph is inserted in the second parent to generate the offspring. If the x coordinate of the insertion node in the second parent is not compatible with the width of the sub-graph, the sub-graph is wrapped around.

An example of the SAAN crossover operation is shown in Figure 27.4 (note that inactive nodes play no role in SAAN crossover, so they are not shown in the figure). The idea behind this form of crossover is that connected sub-graphs are functional units whose output is used by other functional units. Therefore, by replacing a sub-graph with another sub-graph, we tend to explore different ways of combining the functional units discovered during evolution.

Obviously, for the SAAN crossover to work properly some care has to be taken to ensure that the depth of the sub-graph being inserted in the second parent is compatible with the maximum allowed depth, that is, the number of rows in the grid. A simple way to do this is, for example, to select one of the two crossover points at random and choose the other with the coordinates of the first crossover point and the depth of the sub-graph in mind.

Several different forms of crossover can be defined by modifying SAAN crossover (a number of them have been described and tested in Poli [1996]). In some operators incomplete subgraphs or *sub-sub-graphs* are transfered to form the offspring. By sub-sub-graph we mean a graph fragment which includes only a connected sub-set of the active nodes used to compute the output value of the crossover point selected in the first parent. This behaviour allows the insertion of any parts of a parent programs into any other locations of the other parent. In other operators the selection of the crossover points is not limited to the active nodes. This can be useful in the presence of dynamic fitness functions or epistatic problems. The best operators in our experience are two in which the above-mentioned features are somehow combined:

Sub-Sub-graph Active-Active Node (SSAAN) Crossover

This is a form of crossover where both crossover points are selected at random among the active nodes. Conceptually, the operator works in two stages. Firstly, it extracts a complete sub-graph from the first parent (like the SAAN crossover) disregarding the problems possibly caused by its depth. If the depth of the sub-graph is too big for it to be copied into the second parent, in a second phase the lowest nodes of the sub-graph are pruned to make it fit. In doing so, care is taken to preserve terminals which are exactly at the maximum allowed sub-graph depth. Figure 27.5 illustrates this process. In order for this type of crossover to work properly introns are essential, in particular the inactive terminals in the lowest row of the second parent (unlike other introns, they have been explicitly shown in the figure to clarify the interaction between them and the functions and terminals in the sub-graph).

Sub-sub-graph Inactive-Active Node (SSIAN) Crossover

This is like the SSAAN crossover but selects the first crossover point among both the active and the inactive nodes.

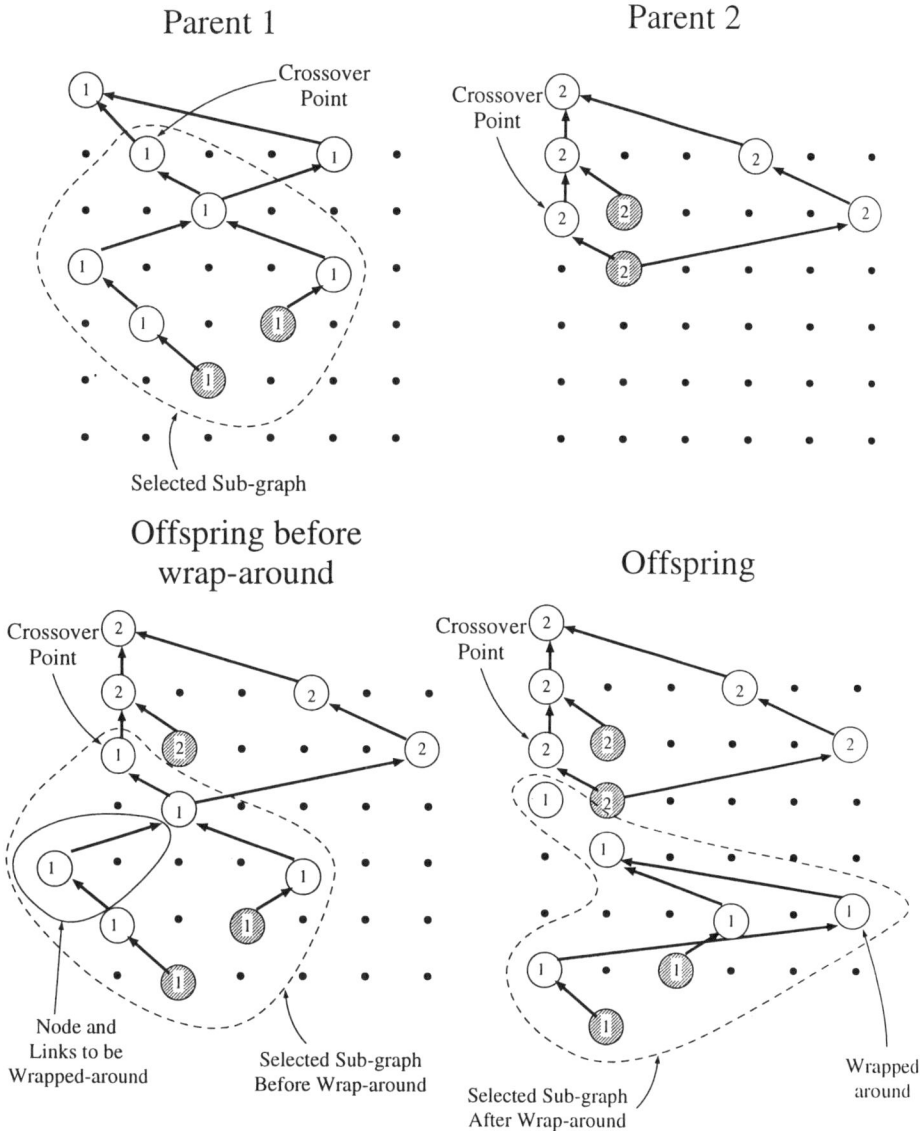

Fig. 27.4: Sub-graph active-active node (SAAN) crossover.

All the experiments reported in the following sections have been carried out with one of the two afore-mentioned operators.

27.3.3 Mutation

The standard GP mutation can be naturally extended to PDGP. It is sufficient to select a random active node in a program, generate a sub-graph which can be inserted into it, and perform the insertion. We call this form of mutation, *global mutation*[3]. We have also found quite useful another form of mutation, *link mutation*, which makes local modifications to the connection topology of the graph. Link mutation selects a random function-node, then a random input-link of such a node and alters the offset associated to the link, that is, it changes a connection in the graph. Other forms of mutation can easily be defined for the basic PDGP representation (e.g. node mutation).

27.4 INTERPRETERS

If no functions or terminals with side effects are used, it is possible to evaluate a PDGP program just as a feed-forward neural net, starting from the input-layer (the lowest row of nodes), which always contains only terminals, and proceeding layer by layer upwards until the output nodes are reached. However, this approach has some limitations (Poli [1996]).

The current PDGP interpreter overcomes these limitations by using a totally different approach based on recursion and a hash table which stores partial results and control information. Let us first consider the case of nodes with no side effects. Then, the interpreter, the procedure eval(*program*), can be thought of as having the structure outlined in Figure 27.6.

The interpreter starts the evaluation of a program from the output nodes and calls recursively the procedure microeval(*node*) to perform the evaluation of each node. microeval checks to see if the value of a node is already known, if not it executes the corresponding primitive (calling itself recursively to get the values for the arguments, if any), otherwise it returns the value stored in a hash table. This is illustrated in Figure 27.7.

It should be noted that the use of a hash table allows a total freedom in the connection topology of PDGP programs. In the absence of nodes with side effects accessing the hash table is, however, slightly slower than accessing a vector of values (not much slower as we hash on an integer key obtained by combining the coordinates of the node, and hashing on integers is very fast). This overhead could be removed by using an array with the same topology as the grid instead of the hash table.

It is also worth noting that, although the interpreter described in Figure 27.6 performs a sequential evaluation of programs, this process is inherently parallel. In fact, if we imagine each node to be a processor (with some memory to store its state and current value) and each link to be a communication channel, the evaluation of a program is equivalent to the parallel downward propagation of control messages requesting a value followed by an upward propagation of return values.

In order to imagine ways in which to add the handling of nodes with side effects it is now sufficient to consider what would happen if such nodes were used in conjunction with this simple interpreter. Obviously, the nodes in the program would work on a 'read-many-execute-once' (RMEO) basis: they would perform their action (if any) only the first time they are called (that is, once per fitness case) as their value would then be cached and used thereafter. In some cases this might be a desirable property, but in general we want more freedom. Also, if the RMEO policy may work with functions, it can produce some really strange behaviours with macros. For example, the standard IFLTE(*arg1,arg2,arg3*) macro (which executes *arg2* if eval(*arg1*) is less than or equal to zero, *arg3* otherwise) would never check again the value of *arg1* to see which branch to execute and/or which value to return (the one returned by *arg2* or the one returned by *arg3* ?).

Parent 1

Crossover Point

Selected Sub-graph

Parent 2

Crossover Point

Other Introns

Inactive Terminals (introns)

Offspring before sub-graph pruning

Crossover Point

Inactivated Node

Original Sub-graph

Nodes to be pruned before recombination

Offspring

Crossover Point

Reactivated Terminal

Inserted Sub-graph

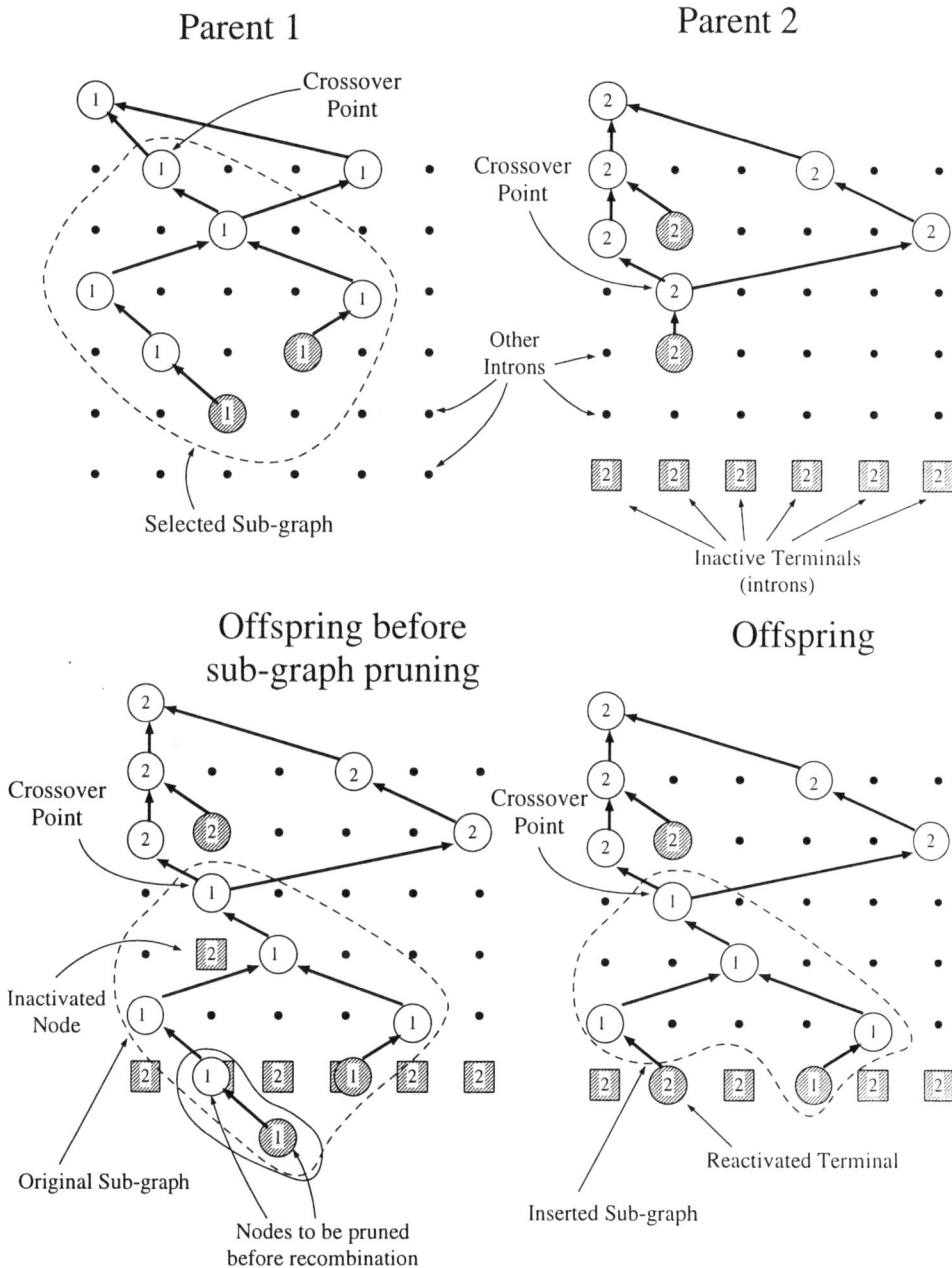

Fig. 27.5: Sub-sub-graph active-active node (SSAAN) crossover with random crossover points.

Total freedom can be obtained by using terminals, functions and macros with different re-execution policies and letting evolution choose which combinations are best for a particular application. For example, in addition to nodes with the standard RMEO policy we could define: nodes with an 'execute-always' (EA) policy, nodes with a combination of

EA and RMEO (for example *arg1* in IFLTE could be of type EA), nodes which are executed for a finite number of times or when certain conditions are satisfied (this would allow for example the handling of conflicts if PDGP programs with side effects were executed on a parallel machine), and so on.

```
eval(program):
Begin
        Reset the hash table NodeValue.
        For each node N in the first layer (the output nodes) do
                Call the procedure microeval(N)
                Store the results in a temporary output vector Out
        Return(Out)
End
Microeval(N):
Begin
        If NodeValue(N) is 'unknown' then
                If N is a function then
                        For each node M connected (as an argument) to node N do
                                Call the procedure microeval(M)
                                Store the results in a temporary output vector Out
                        Call the procedure N(Out)
                        Store the result R in NodeVal(N)
                        Return(R)
                Elseif N is a macro then
                        Call the procedure N(M1,...Mn) where M1...Mn are the
                                nodes connected (as arguments) to node N
                        Store the result R in NodeVal(N)
                        Return(R)
                else /* N is a variable or a constant */
                        Return(valof(N))
                Endif
        else /* N has been already evaluated */
                Return(NodeVal(N))
        Endif
End
```

Fig. 27.6: Pseudo-code for the PDGP interpreter (in the absence of nodes with side effects).

Introducing non-RMEO execution is trivial, requiring only more conditions microeval. For example, the only change needed by EA macros and functions is to copy the pseudo-code for standard RMEO nodes and remove lines which store the result R in $NodeVal(N)$.

27.5 EXTENDED REPRESENTATIONS

It is possible to imagine many ways in which some of the constraints imposed on the graphs produced by PDGP could be removed without reducing the search efficiency significantly. In the following we briefly describe the extended representations and operators we have implemented.

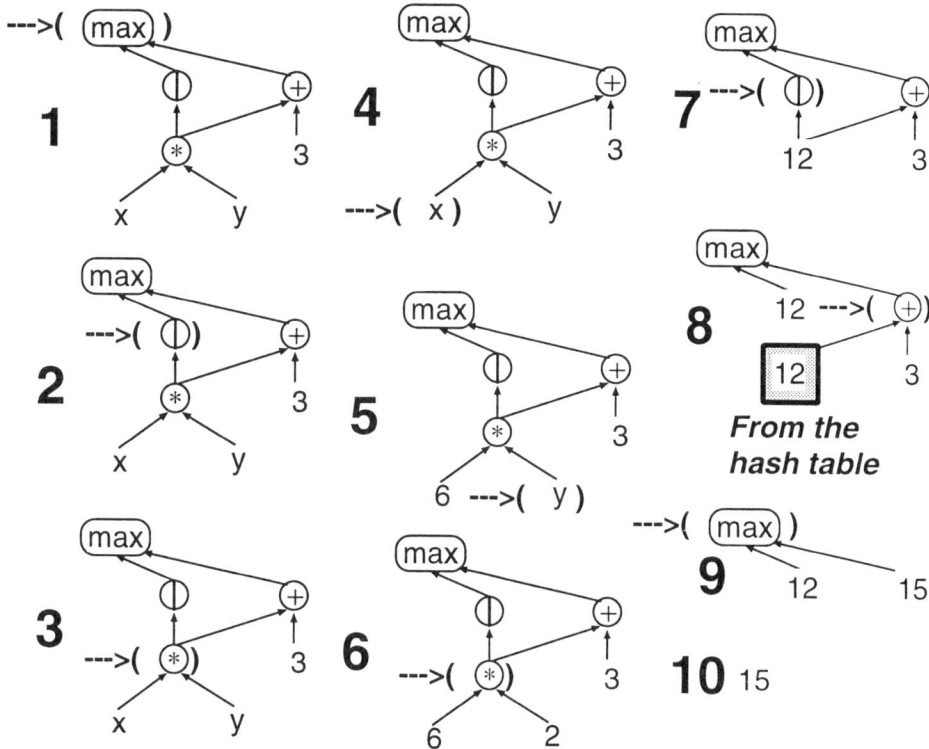

Fig. 27.7: Sample evaluation of the program in Figure 27.3 (left). The horizontal arrow indicates which node is evaluated by the microeval function at different time steps (indicated by the number, 1 through 10, in boldface).

A first obvious extension of the basic representation is allowing feed-forward connections between non-adjacent layers. With this representation any directed acyclic graph can be naturally represented within the grid of nodes, without requiring the presence of pass-through nodes. In order to implement this it is sufficient to store within each node also the vertical displacements of the nodes whose values are used as arguments by such a node. The link mutation operator has to consider these additional parameters when deciding where to reconnect a mutated link.

Once the previous extension is implemented, it becomes trivial to represent graphs with backward connections as well, for example with cycles. It is sufficient to accept negative or zero vertical displacements. Obviously, the presence of recurrent connections requires some changes to the interpreter and to the crossover operator. The interpreter must be able to detect infinite loops and to terminate them somehow gracefully, for example by returning a default value after a given number of evaluations of the same node. With the present interpreter this is trivial to implement as it is sufficient to store in the hash table how many times a node has been evaluated in addition to its value. Also the change to the crossover operator is surprisingly simple: it is sufficient to perform a wrap-around of nodes and connection in the vertical direction before doing the wrap around in the horizontal one.

Adding labels to links is another extension of the basic representation which we have explored. The labels for the links are contained in a *link set*, $\mathcal{L}$, which is used in the initialization phase and also during mutation. If $\mathcal{L}$ contains a random constant generator only, this technique allows the direct development of neural networks. The interpreter requires only minor changes: it has to multiply the value obtained via a link by the corresponding weight before using it as an argument for a node, and it has to pass the value of the label as an additional argument to macros.

However, the link set can really contain anything: if the labels are symbols of a language the representation can be used to develop finite state automata, transition nets, semantic nets, etc. In these cases the semantics of the evaluation is application specific. However, no change to the interpreter is necessary once the link labels are implemented, as virtually any semantics can be obtained by using macros.

The addition of labels to links allows the definition of additional operators, like *label mutation* which substitutes the label of a link with a randomly selected label from $\mathcal{L}$. If $\mathcal{L}$ contains the random constant generator, label mutation gives a mechanism to alter the weights of PDGP programs representing neural nets.

Examples in which some of the above-mentioned extensions are used and more details on the interpretation process will be given in the next section.

27.6 EXAMPLES

In this section we will describe some experiments which show the representational power and efficiency of PDGP. Other examples can be found in Poli [1996].

27.6.1 Exclusive-Or Problem

In order to show the representational capabilities of PDGP, in this section, we report on some experimental results obtained by applying PDGP to the exclusive-or problem (a sort of benchmark problem in the neural networks community), using different function and terminal sets. The problem is finding a parallel distributed program that implements the function:

$$XOR(x_1, x_2) = \begin{cases} 1 & \text{if } x_1 \neq x_2 \\ 0 & \text{otherwise} \end{cases}$$

Given the simplicity of the problem, in all the experiments reported in this section, the population size was very small (in normal Genetic Programming terms) at $P=200$ individuals. The maximum number of generations was $G=20$, the crossover probability was 0.7, the global mutation probability was 0.25 while the link mutation probability was 0.25 (we used a generational genetic algorithm in which mutation was applied to all individuals produced by crossover and reproduction). The GA used tournament selection with tournament size 7. The other parameters were the 'grow' initialization method and SSIAN crossover. The fitness of a solution was the number of correct predictions of the entries in the XOR truth-table. With each function and terminal set we performed 20 runs (with different random number seeds) with three different grid sizes: 2×2, 2×3 and 3×4.

In initial tests we tried to evolve *logic solutions* to the problem by using the function set $\mathcal{F}=\{AND, OR, NAND, NOR, I\}$ and the terminal set $\mathcal{T}=\{x1, x2\}$. Apart from the use of I

(identity function), these are the primitives normally used in GP to solve Boolean classification problems. Figure 27.8 shows three typical solutions to the XOR problem obtained by PDGP, showing the actual output produced by our Pop-11 implementation of PDGP[4]. Active nodes and links are drawn with thick lines, all the rest are introns (note also that the output node, having coordinates (0,0), should be in the top-left corner; but in the figure it is centred horizontally for clarity). These examples show how PDGP tends to reuse nodes (in this case only terminals) and therefore tends to be parsimonious.

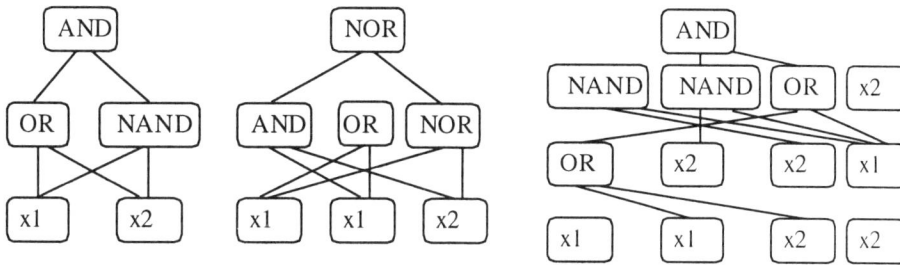

Fig. 27.8: Symbolic networks implementing the exclusive-or function with Boolean processing elements (introns are drawn with thin lines).

In other experiments we used the function set $\mathcal{F}=\{+,-,*, PDIV, I\}$ (*PDIV* is the protected division operator, which returns its first argument if the second is zero) and the terminal set $\mathcal{T}=\{x1, x2\}$ to evolve *algebraic solutions* to the XOR problem. In these and the other experiments involving analogue functions we used a 'wrapper' that transformed the output of the program into *true* if it was greater than 0.5, *false* otherwise. Figure 27.9 shows two typical solutions to the XOR problem obtained using algebraic operators. Note that, for the sake of clarity, in this and the following figures introns are not drawn – they are simply represented by small crosses. Both networks represent the same quite interesting solution $XOR(x1,x2)=(x1-x2)/(x1-x2)$ which returns zero if the divisor is zero by exploiting the protection in *PDIV*. However, in the first network this is achieved more efficiently by reusing the value $(x1-x2)$ without computing it twice. It should also be noted that in general the interpretation of the non-commutative nodes (like '−' and '*PDIV*') requires knowledge of the order of evaluation of their arguments (the incoming links). However, for clarity, we have preferred not to add this information to the figures in this section, as the order of evaluation could easily be inferred given the simplicity of the examples reported.

Inspired by these 'creative' analogue solutions we tried to develop *neuro-algebraic solutions* using the same function and terminal set but adding random weights in the range $[-1,1]$ to the links. As explained earlier, the weights acted as multipliers for the arguments of functions in $\mathcal{F}$. Figure 27.10 shows two typical XOR solutions obtained using neuro-algebraic operators. Judging from these, the addition of weights seems to enlarge the space of solutions available to PDGP. However, it is clear that neuro-algebraic solutions present the same kind of 'black-boxness' typical of neural nets: they are hard to understand.

In part, this negative feature may also be present in the *weight-less neural solutions* obtained by using the function set $\mathcal{F} =\{+,-, S2, S3, P2, P3, I\}$, where S2 and S3 are neurons with sigmoid activation function, P2 and P3 are Π neurons (which compute the product of their inputs) and '+' and '−' simulate linear neurons. The terminal set included also a random constant generator, to create biases in the range $[-1.0,+1.0]$. The links had no weights. Figure 27.11 shows three typical solutions to the XOR problem obtained with these operators. It is interesting to note that the solutions developed with smaller grids are again understandable quite easily as they do not use numeric coefficients. Actually the solution in the centre of the figure, $XOR(x1,x2)=(x1-x2)^2$, is quite clever and efficient. As soon as biases are used solutions become much harder to understand.

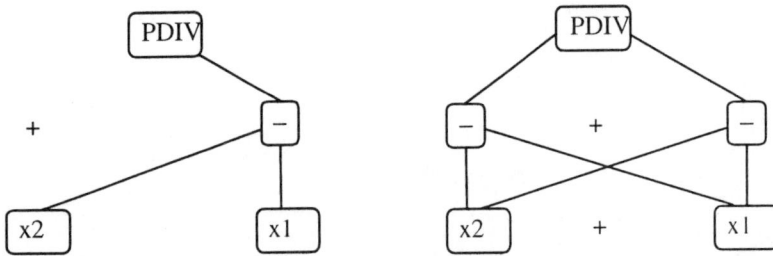

Fig. 27.9: Algebraic network-like realisations of the exclusive-or function.

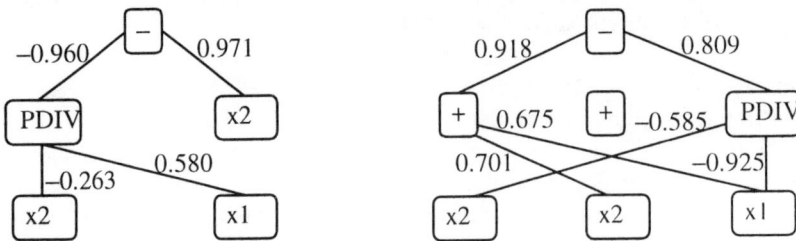

Fig. 27.10: Exclusive-or implementations based on neuro-algebraic parallel distributed programs.

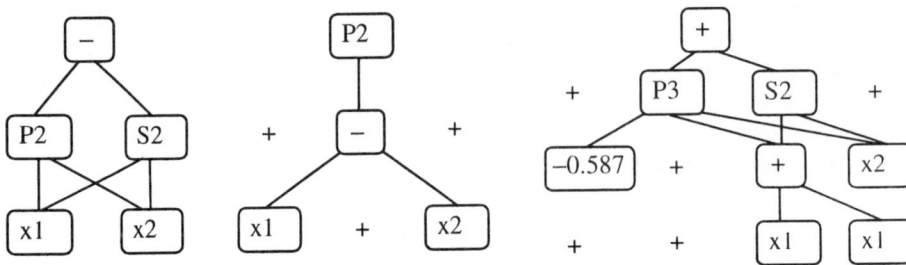

Fig. 27.11: Weight-less neural networks implementing the exclusive-or function.

More standard forms of *neural solutions* can also be obtained with PDGP by using the same function set and terminal set as above but adding weights (in the range $[-1,1]$) to the links. For example, Figure 27.12 shows two typical solutions to the XOR problem obtained with these choices. Unfortunately, although perfectly valid, these solutions can only be understood with pen, paper and a pocket calculator.

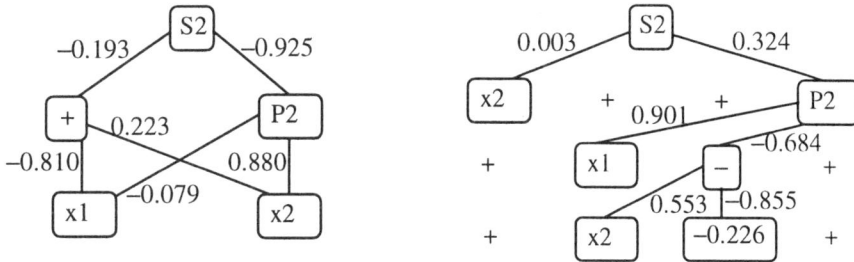

Fig. 27.12: Neural realizations of the exclusive-or function.

In terms of computational effort different representations show quite different behaviours as detailed in Table 27.1. One of the criteria we used to assess the performance of PDGP was the computational effort E used in the GP literature (E is the minimum number of fitness evaluations necessary to get a correct program, in multiple runs, with probability 99%). As the effort of evaluating each individual (at least on a sequential machine) depends on the number of nodes it includes, we also used as a criterion the total number of nodes N to be evaluated in order to get a solution with 99% probability. In the table, the columns reporting the computational effort E indicate that increasing the size of the grid tends to reduce the number of fitness evaluations necessary to get a solution.

Table 27.1: Computational effort for the XOR problem for different PDGP representations. The E figure gives thousands ('000s) of evaluations, and the N figure gives thousands ('000s) of nodes.

Grid Size	Logic		Algebraic		Neuro-Algebraic		Weight-less Neural		Neural	
	E	N	E	N	E	N	E	N	E	N
2×2	5.2	26	2.4	12	9.6	48	10.2	54	342	1,710
2×3	4.2	29.4	2.8	19.6	12	84	6.8	47.6	378	2,646
3×4	1.6	20.8	1.6	20.8	7	91	6	78	46.2	600.6

This improvement with increasing grid size seems reasonable considering that smaller grids impose harder constraints on the search. However, if we look at the results in terms of total number of nodes to be evaluated N, the advantage of larger grids is not clear at all. In fact, in most cases N is smaller for smaller grids and, in general, it seems anyway worth spending a few percent more evaluations of nodes and get a better solution in terms of size, execution speed and (possibly) generalization.

In the case of neuro-algebraic solutions, the table indicates that the use of random weights makes the search much harder and that again increasing the size of the grid reduces the number of fitness evaluations but not necessarily the number of nodes to be evaluated. This might seem surprising at first as in theory by adding weights to the connections we can explore a much larger space of programs. However, enlarging the search space does not necessarily mean to increase the frequency of solutions. As PDGP, like any other incomplete search method, can only explore part of the search space, it is quite likely that, at least for this problem, by adding weights we make a less efficient use of the available resources (the fitness evaluations).

A similarly increased computational effort is necessary to get weight-less neural solutions. This is probably due to the limited expressive power of neurons with respect to other classes of functions, at least for Boolean classification problems.

The combination of the negative effects of weights and neural processing elements leads to a considerable degradation of the performance of PDGP when searching the space of possible neural nets. In this case a large grid seems to be a relative advantage.

In general the increased computational effort required to develop programs with weighted links seems to indicate that the operators used by PDGP to optimize the topology and the processing elements of parallel distributed programs are probably ineffective in optimizing the connection weights. Specialized operators can solve this problem (Pujol & Poli [1998, 1998a, 1998b]).

In summary, the results with the XOR problem show how PDGP can explore (although with different degrees of efficiency) a large space of programs which ranges from non-recurrent neural nets to classical tree-like programs without discontinuities. They also suggest that, when looking for logic and algebraic solutions, PDGP can compete, in terms of computational effort, with other well-established machine learning techniques, like the standard back-propagation algorithm which requires from several hundreds to a few thousands training epochs to solve the XOR problem (Rumelhart & McClelland [1986]).

27.6.2 The Lawnmower Problem

In this section we describe some experiments in which nodes with side effects were used. For our experiments we selected a well-known, extensively studied problem: the lawnmower problem. The problem consists of finding a program which can control the movements of a lawnmower so that it cuts all the grass in a lawn (Koza [1994], pages 225–273). In the lawnmower problem the lawn is a rectangular array of grass tiles. Figure 27.13 (left) shows the initial configuration for the problem. The lawnmower has a direction of movement which can take only four different values (0, 90, 180 and 270 degrees). The mower can only be rotated towards left, moved forward one step (in its current direction) or lifted and repositioned on another tile. Figure 27.13 (middle) shows the effect of a sequences of forward moves. The lawn is considered to be toroidal, as indicated in Figure 27.13 (right) which depicts the situation after two additional forward moves, a turn left and a sequence of forward moves.

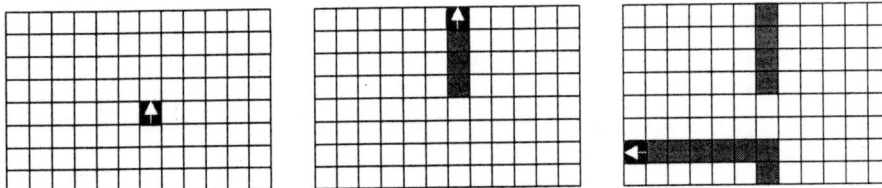

Fig. 27.13: Illustrating the lawnmower problem.

The interesting facts about this problem are: (a) its difficulty can be varied indefinitely just by changing the size of the lawn, (b) although it can become very hard to solve for GP, the evaluation of the fitness of each individual requires only one interpretation of the program (the program must contain all the operations needed to solve the problem), (c) it is a problem with a lot of regularities which GP without ADFs seems unable to exploit, (d) GP with ADFs does very well on this problem.

In order to make the comparison with the results described in Koza [1994] possible, we used the terminal set $T=\{MOW, LEFT, random\}$ and the function set $F=(V8A, FROG, PROG2, PROG3\}$. The operation *MOW* performs a step forward, mows the new grass patch and returns the pair of coordinates (0,0). *LEFT* performs a left rotation of the mower and returns (0,0). *random* returns a random pair of coordinates (x, y) with $x,y \in \{0,...,7\}$. V8A performs the addition modulo 8 of two pairs of coordinates. FROG lifts and moves the mower to a new cell whose displacement in horizontal and vertical direction is indicated by the single argument of FROG, mows the new grass patch and returns its argument. PROG2 (PROG3) is the usual LISP programming construct which executes its two (three) arguments in their order and then returns the value returned by the second (third) argument. The other parameters of PDGP were: SSIAN crossover with probability 0.7, link mutation with probability 0.009, global mutation with probability 0.001, population with size $P=1000$, a maximum number of generations $G=50$, a grid with 8 rows and 2 columns and the 'grow' initialization method. All functions with side effects used an 'execute-always' policy.

Figure 27.14 shows a typical program obtained in our experiments with an 8×8 lawn. The numeric labels near the links represent the order in which the arguments of each node are evaluated. For example, they show that the function PROG3 in the output node first twice invokes the subgraph on its left and then executes once the sub-graph on the right.

The program is extremely parsimonious (it includes only 11 nodes out of the possible 17) and shows one of the features of PDGP: the extensive reuse of sub-graphs. In fact, each sub-graph of this program is called over and over again by the nodes above it and the program is therefore organised as a complex hierarchy of nine non-parametrized subroutines (the non-terminal nodes) calling each other multiple times (note the prevalence of PROG3 nodes). This tends to be a common feature in PDGP programs: sub-graphs act as building blocks for other sub-graphs. Despite its small size, the depth of the nested function calls makes this program execute hundreds of actions during its interpretation.

In order to assess the performance of PDGP on the lawnmower problem, we varied the width of the lawn from 4 to 16, while keeping its height constant (8 cells), thus varying the lawn size from 32 to 128 grass tiles. For each lawn size we performed 20 runs with different random seeds. The results were amazing. Standard GP (without ADFs) requires $E=19,000$ for a lawn size of 32, $E=56,000$ for a size of 48, $E=100,000$ for a size of 64, $E=561,000$ for a size of 80, and 4,692,000 for a size of 96 cells, with an exponential growth in the effort as the difficulty of the problem increases. On the contrary, PDGP is solving the same problems with an effort ranging from 4,000 to 6,000, which seems to grow linearly even beyond the sizes on which standard GP was tried. The linear regression equation for PDGP is $E=3286 + 26.8 \times L$, where L is the size of the lawn (regression coefficient $r=0.949$). A comparison between the linear regression for PDGP and the linear regression for standard GP (Koza [1994], page 266) shows that PDGP scales up about 2,300 times better. The average structural complexity of PDGP solutions is approximately 15 nodes, and it does not vary significantly (it really could not) as the complexity of the problem changes. If we compare this with the average structural complexity of standard GP programs (which ranges from 145.0 for the 32-cell lawn to 408.8 for the 96-cell one) we observe an improvement of 10.5 to 29.2 times.

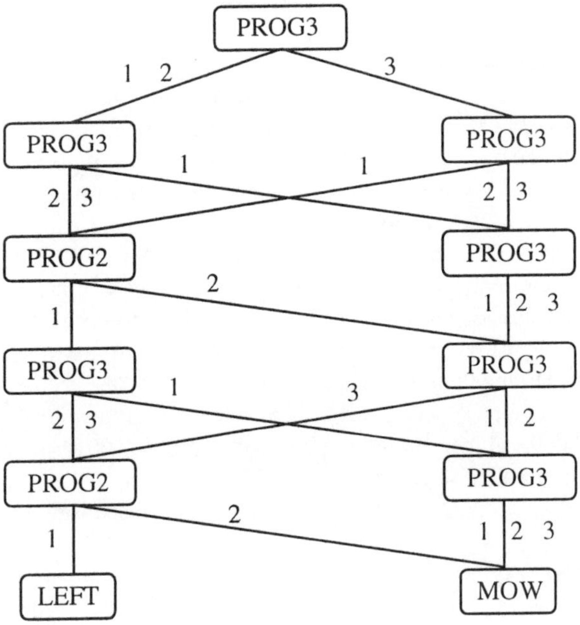

Fig. 27.14: Parallel distributed program solving the lawnmower problem with a lawn of 8×8=64 cells.

PDGP clearly outperforms GP without ADFs. The situation for GP improves somehow when ADFs are added. For example, the computational effort drops to values from 5,000 (for the 32-cell lawn) to 20,000 (for the 96-cell lawn) while the average structural complexities range from 66.3 to 84.9. However, the analysis of the linear regression equations reveals that PDGP still scales up about 9 times better than GP with ADFs and that the structural complexity of PDGP programs is 4.7 to 6.1 times smaller. We believe that the power of PDGP on this problem derives from its ability to discover and reuse building blocks. The fact that it outperforms GP with ADFs suggests that parameterized reuse is not necessarily an advantage with respect to the non-parameterized reuse of standard PDGP (that is, PDGP without ADFs).

In order to understand whether these levels of performance were due to the ability of the SSIAN crossover or to the particularly narrow grid used, which enforces strongly graph-like (as opposed to tree-like) solutions, in Poli [1997] we studied the behaviour of PDGP as the width of the grid was varied from 2 to 64. The analysis showed that by increasing the width of the grid, the 'treeness' of the programs increases (when the grid is very large PDGP really tends to behave like a kind of standard GP with a special form of crossover). As somehow expected by the results mentioned above, PDGP performance decreased quite dramatically as the size of the grid grew. This suggests that favouring reuse through small grids may make the search in the space of programs much easier. More details on the experiments described in this section can be found in Poli [1996, 1997].

27.6.3 Symbolic Regression

To investigate further the matter of parameterized vs. non-parameterized reuse, we applied PDGP to a symbolic regression problem on which GP performance was approximately the same with (E=1,440,000) or without (E=1,176,000) ADFs with a population of P=4,000 individuals (see Koza [1994, pages 110–122]).

The problem is to find a function (that is, a program) which fits 50 data samples obtained from the sextic polynomial $p(x) = x^6 - 2x^4 + x^2$. The samples are obtained by selecting 50 random values x_i in the range $[-1,1]$ and associating them with the corresponding value of $p_i = p(x_i)$. The fitness function is:

$$\sum_i |\, p_i - \text{eval}(prog, x_i)\,|$$

The stopping criterion for a run is the discovery of a program that fits all the datapoints with an absolute error smaller than 0.01.

The parameters we used for PDGP were: population size P=1000, maximum number of generations G=100, SSIAN crossover, the 'grow' initialization method, no mutation, and a grid with 3 columns and 6 rows. The terminal set was T={x, random} (where random is a constant random generator with values in the range $[-1,1]$) while the function set was the standard $\mathcal{F}$={+,–,*, PDIV, I}.

Figure 27.15 shows a typical program discovered by PDGP which fully solves the problem. With a very clever use of 'pieces of wire' (the identity function I), the program is actually computing the expression $(x - x^3)(1 - x^2)x$ which is equivalent to $p(x)$.

The computational effort shown in 20 runs with different random seeds was surprisingly small: E=91,000. While improvement over standard GP was expected (we obtained a nearly 16-fold reduction of E), we did not expect such a large improvement (about 13 times) over GP with ADFs. A possible explanation is that in some problems the use of parameterized ADFs allows GP to explore a much larger space in which, however, the frequency of solutions is not significantly higher. This is understandable if we consider, for example, that ADFs have different behaviours in different parts of a program (since they receive different arguments). So, in order to discover if an ADF is good or not, GP has also to 'understand' with which kind of arguments the ADF can be used properly. On the contrary the non-parameterized reuse available in standard PDGP seems to increase the size of the space of possible programs (it allows the development of graph-like in addition to tree-like programs) in a direction in which the frequency of solutions increases as well.

27.6.4 The Encoder-Decoder Problem

In all the work described in this chapter we have used two-dimensional grids with a rectangular shape. This is not a limitation of PDGP: it just seemed to be the most natural choice for the particular experiments we performed. For other applications it might make sense to use other shapes. For example, it would make sense to use triangular grids with layers of increasing width if one wanted to develop classification programs or to develop tree-like structures. In this section we present an interesting application of irregular grids to the 4-bit binary encoder-decoder problem.

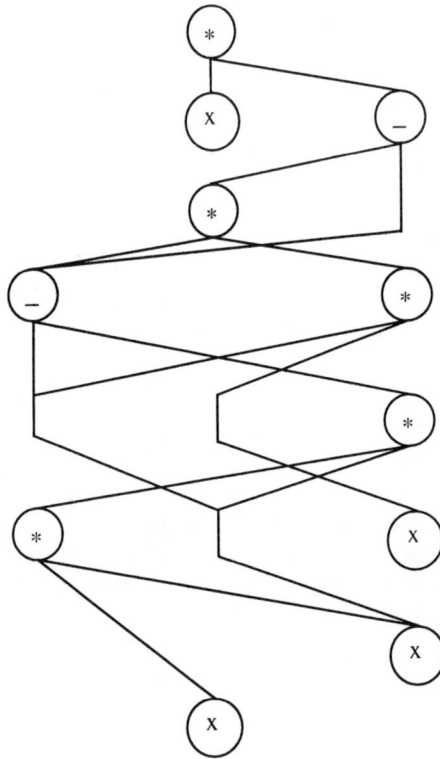

Fig. 27.15: Parallel distributed program implementing the sextic polynomial $p(x) = x^6 - 2x^4 + x^2$.

The problem is to find a program capable of first encoding (with a 2 bit binary code) and then decoding binary input vectors of the form $\{1,0,0,0\}$, $\{0,1,0,0\}$, etc. The programs to be evolved have four output nodes and four input variables. In order to force PDGP to develop programs that could encode and decode the input patterns we used a sand-glass-like grid obtained by creating a narrowing in the middle of a rectangular grid. In particular, the grid had nine rows with the following widths: 4, 4, 4, 4, 2, 4, 4, 4 and 4. The objective of the experiment was to discover a program whose outputs reproduced the inputs and in which no terminals were above the narrowing in the grid. Such a program would guarantee that the sub-graph in the lower part of the grid would perform some form of encoding of the input patterns while the upper sub-graph would decode them.

The function set was $\mathcal{F}=\{AND, OR, NOR, NAND, I\}$ while the terminal set was $\mathcal{T} = \{x1, x2, x3, x4\}$. We used 'full' initialization, a relatively large population with $P=4,000$ individuals, a maximum number of generations $G=200$, a link mutation probability of 0.045 and a global mutation probability of 0.005. As usual, the crossover probability was 0.7. In preliminary tests we immediately realized that, with the normal crossover and mutation operators, PDGP tended to discover the invalid solution in which the terminals were positioned in the first row of the grid (the output layer). For this reason we used a specialized form of crossover and mutation which simply kept trying generating new offspring until one was produced in which all the terminals were not above the narrowing. Note that much more efficient forms of crossover and mutation could have been used if this one did not work. For example, a SSAAN crossover which does not move terminals would have guaranteed validity of all offspring.

Figure 27.16 shows a 100% correct program produced in the second run of PDGP with these operators. The binary code used in the nodes in the narrowing is the somewhat unusual code:

Input	Code
1000	01
0100	11
0010	10
0001	00

It is interesting to note that exactly the same idea used here to discover binary encoder-decoders could be used to discover compression and decompression algorithms, dimensionality-reduction algorithms, visualization algorithms, tools for statistical analysis, non-linear principal component algorithms, clustering algorithms, and so forth.

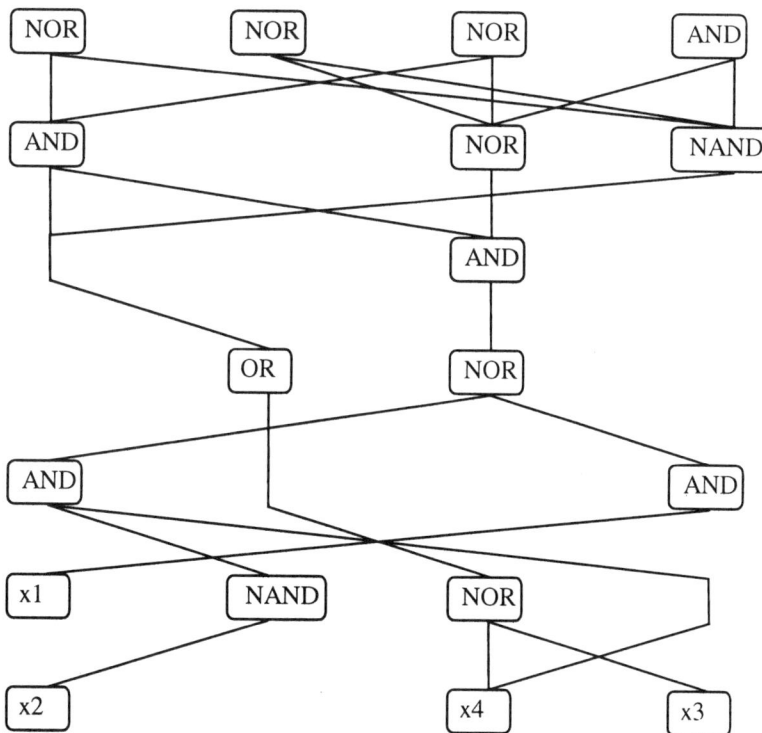

Fig. 27.16: Solution to the 4-bit binary encoder-decoder problem produced by PDGP.

27.6.5 The Finite State Automata Induction Problem

Until now we have presented results involving the basic PDGP representation for directed acyclic graphs without and with labelled links. In this section we want to show how, by using all the extensions presented in section 27.5, PDGP can actually search very efficiently the space of directed (cyclic and acyclic) graphs.

The problem on which we applied the full PDGP representation was inducing, from positive and negative examples, a deterministic finite state automaton capable of recognizing a prefixed language (for more details on the problem and on past and recent results see Brave [1996]). The language we chose for our tests was the regular language $L=a*b*a*b*$ consisting of all sentences with zero or more a symbols, followed by zero or more b symbols, followed by zero or more a symbols followed finally by zero or more b symbols. For example, the sentence *abbbbab* is in L while the sentence *babab* is not.

For these experiments we use a population with $P=2,000$ individuals, a maximum number of generations $G=200$, a regular 4×4 grid in which the node in the top left corner was considered to be the start node, and the 'grow' initialisation method. The crossover operator was a form of SAAN crossover with wrap around of nodes and links in both horizontal and vertical direction. The probability of crossover was 0.7, the probability of link mutation was 0.09, and the probability of global mutation was 0.01. The link set included the labels A and B, which represented the two different kinds of input symbols. The function set included the macros $N1$, $N2$, $E1$, and $E2$. The macros $N1$ and $N2$ represent non-stop states in the finite state machine with one and two outgoing links, respectively. When called they just check to see if the current symbol in the input sentence is present on one of their links. If this is the case they remove the symbol from the input stream and pass control to (that is, evaluate) the node connected to the link labelled with the matching symbol. If no link has the correct label, *false* is returned to the calling node. The same happens if no more symbols are available in the input stream. The nodes $E1$ and $E2$ represent terminal states. They have exactly the same behaviour as the N nodes except that if the end of the sentence is reached they return *true*. We also used a nonempty terminal set $T=\{DONE\}$ where the node $DONE$ behaves like a terminal state without output links.

With these macros (whose execution policy is of type 'execute always') no change is required to the standard PDGP interpreter. It is only necessary to reset the symbol stream before the eval procedure is called by the fitness function.

In the experiments we used 165 positive and 485 negative example sentences including up to 20 symbols. In 10 runs, all successful in developing a general automaton (not just a 100% fit automaton), we measured a computational effort $E=22,000$ and an average structural complexity of 4.2 nodes (in 2 runs out of 10 there was a trailing $DONE$ in the automaton) which compare very favourably with the results reported by others. Figure 27.17 shows one of the solutions found by PDGP (this has been hand drawn for display purposes). The execution of the automaton starts from the node in the upper left corner and proceeds following the outgoing links (which depart from the bottom of the nodes).

27.6.6 A Natural Language Recognition Problem

In this section we will show how the representations, operators and interpreters used in PDGP can be tailored to solve a much harder problem: the induction of a recognizer for natural language from positive and negative examples. A recognizer for natural language is a program that given a sentence (say in English) returns *true* if the sentence is grammatical, *false* otherwise. The problem of inducing recognizers (and parsers) from actual sentences of a language, also known as language acquisition, is a very hard machine learning problem (see Shapiro [1992, pages 443–451] for a survey on the topic).

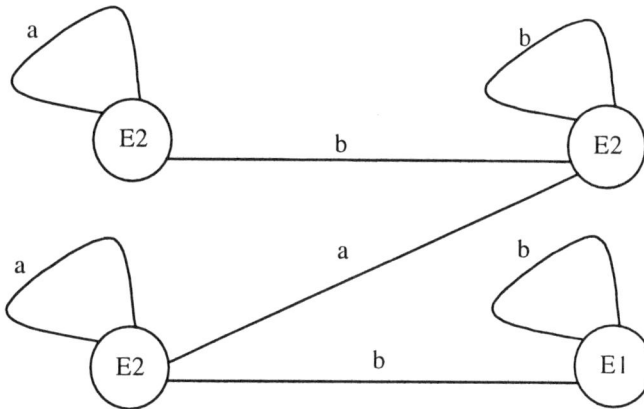

Fig. 27.17: Finite state automaton capable of recognising the language $L=a*b*a*b*$.

Deterministic finite state automata are well suited to build recognizers for simple regular languages. However, they are not particularly suited to represent the recursive nature of natural-language grammars. Indeed, the language used in the previous section has nothing to do with the complexity of natural language. For this reason we have decided to use PDGP to evolve recognizers based on Recursive Transition Networks (RTNs). RTNs are extensions of finite state automata, in which the label associated to a link can represent either symbols of the language, like in standard finite state automata or other RTNs possibly including the RTN containing the link.

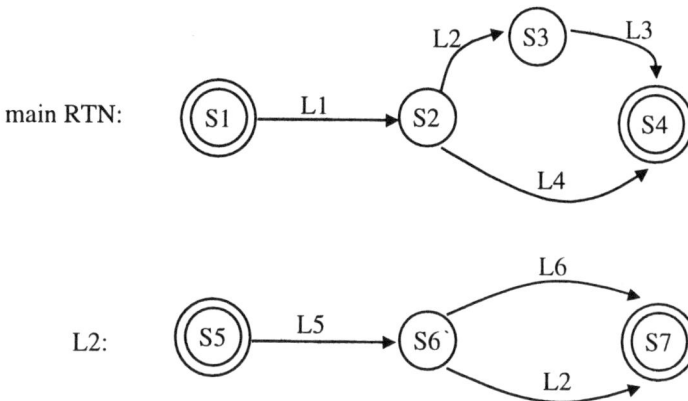

Fig. 27.18: Sample recursive transition network

To understand how RTNs work let us consider the example in Figure 27.18. In the figure, the double circles represent initial and end states. The labels *L1*, *L3*, *L4*, *L5*, and *L6* are symbols of the language, while *L2* represents another RTN. In the presence of the input sequence [*L1 L5 L6 L3*] the following happens. Starting from *S1*, *L1* is read and *S2* is reached. Since *S2* has no outgoing link labelled *L5*, the sub RTN *L2* is invoked to check whether the subsequence starting from *L5* can be parsed. So, control passes to state *S5*. Since *S5* has an outgoing link labelled *L5*, *S6* is reached, then *L6* is read and *S7* is reached. Since *S7* is an end state, control is returned to *S3*, causing *L3* to be read and the end state *S4* to be reached. If instead of just one *L5*, the sequence had several contiguous *L5*s, the sub-RTN *L2* would invoke itself several times before returning control to the main RTN.

While standard PDGP can evolve networks of any topology, in order to evolve RTNs for natural language processing we decided to use a technique unique to PDGP, called Automatically Defined Links (ADLs). ADLs can be seen as the dual of ADFs. ADLs work in a very similar way to ADFs. Basically, they are ADFs which, instead of being part of the function set of the main program, are part of the link set, and instead of being tree-like are graph-like subprograms. For example, if the label of a link is the symbol *ADL0*, the interpreter will 'invoke' the parallel distributed program (which in this case is an RTN) corresponding to the first ADL. Note that PDGP allows the use of both ADFs and ADLs.

For our experiments we generated 67 grammatical sentences and 181 ungrammatical ones, all with different syntactic structures, using the following grammar, in which *S* stands for sentence, *NP* stands for noun phrase, *VP* stands for verb phrase, *SNP* indicates a simple noun phrase, *PP* indicates a prepostional phrase, *DET* stands for a determiner, *ADJ* for an adjective, *TVERB* means a transitive verb, and *IVERB* means an intransitive verb:

$$
\begin{array}{lll}
S & \rightarrow & NP \ VP \\
NP & \rightarrow & SNP \ | \ SNP \ PP \\
SNP & \rightarrow & DET \ NOUN \ | \ DET \ ADJ \ NOUN \ | \ DET \ ADJ \ ADJ \ NOUN \\
PP & \rightarrow & PREP \ SNP \\
VP & \rightarrow & TVERB \ NP \ | \ IVERB
\end{array}
$$

The words in the examples were assigned a lexical category (like 'noun', 'verb', 'adjective', and so on) so that the actual examples were sequences of lexical categories like '*DET ADJ NOUN TVERB DET ADJ NOUN PREP DET ADJ NOUN*' rather than, for example, 'the little kitten frightened the big mouse with a sudden jump'.

Experiments used a population of 4,000, a maximum number of generations of 200, two ADLs, a 4×7 grid for the main RTN and two 4×5 grids for the ADLs. Recombination was a form of SSAAN crossover, applied with probability 0.7, and the probability of mutation was 0.1. The start node was that in the top left corner of the main grid.

The following link set was used for both the main RTN and the two ADLs: {*NOUN, TVERB, IVERB, PREP, DET, ADJ, ADL0, ADL1*}. It includes the different kinds of lexical categories and the names of the two ADLs. The function set included the macros {*N1, N2*} which represent non-stop states in the RTN, with one and two outgoing links, respectively. When called they just check to see if the current symbol in the input sentence is present on one of their links. If this is the case they remove the symbol from the input stream and pass control to the node connected to the link labelled with the matching symbol. If the label is an ADL, then control is passed to the corresponding RTN. If no link has the correct label, *false* is returned to the calling node. The same happens if no more symbols are available in the input stream.

The main RTN terminal set used only nodes of type *DONE*, which behave as *N1* nodes without output links except that if the end of the sentence is reached they return *true*. The terminal set for the ADLs included only nodes of type *RETURN*, which simply return *true*.

The fitness of an RTN was $f = 67 - n_s - 10^{-5} \times n_w$, where n_s is the number of sentences incorrectly classified and n_w is the number of words not read by the RTN in the sentences incorrectly classified. The value 67 corresponds to the number of grammatical sentences in the training set. The term $10^{-5} \times n_w$ has the function of smoothing the fitness landscape created by the term n_s. The coefficient 10^{-5} is chosen so that $10^{-5} \times n_w < 1$. This ensures that evolution will always favour solutions with smaller n_s whatever the value of n_w.

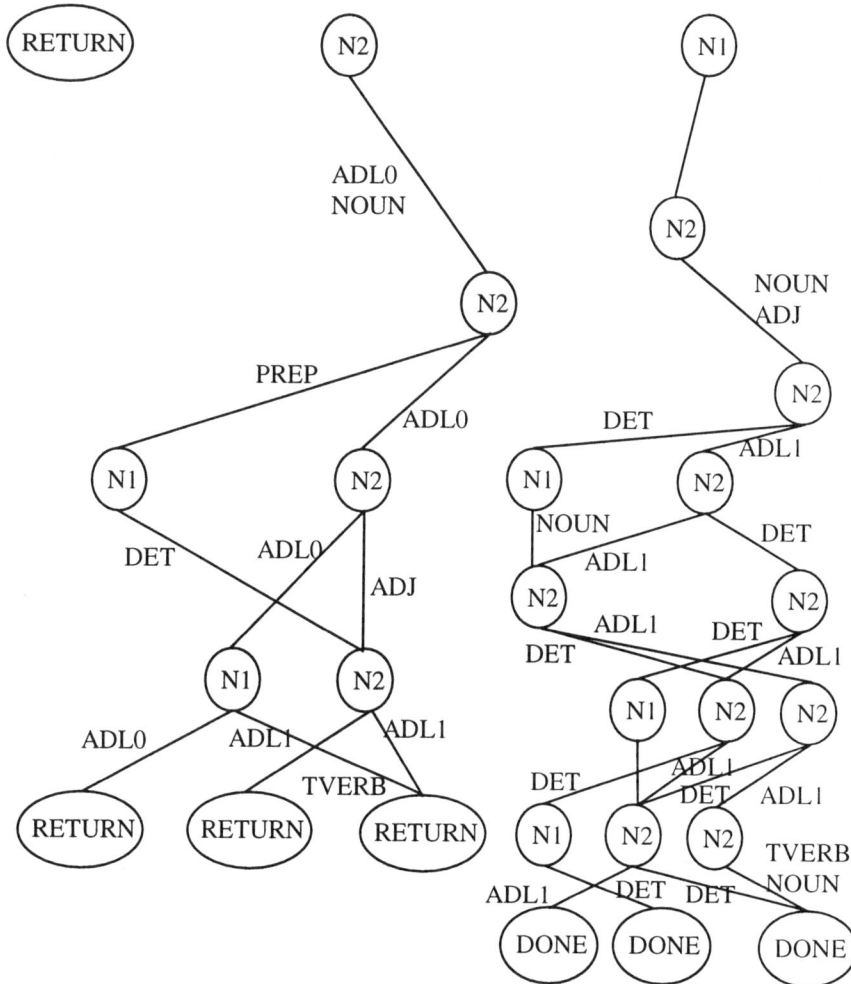

Fig. 27.19: Recursive transition network for recognizing grammatical English sentences evolved by PDGP. The main RTN is on the right, *ADL0* on the left and *ADL1* in the centre.

Figure 27.19 shows the 100%-correct solution found by PDGP following two unsuccessful runs. The performance of this RTN has been tested with 156 different grammatical sentences (all with different structure), which the system classified correctly, and 12066 different random ungrammatical sentence types, of which the system correctly classified 12008 (note that the disparity between the number of grammatical and ungrammatical sentences is due to the impossibility of generating more grammatical sentence types with the grammar above). This would suggest the system has sensitivity of 100% and specificity of 99.5%. However, tests with 156 different slightly ungrammatical sentence types (obtained by modifying one lexical category in a valid sentence) revealed a lower specificity, 68.6%, which seems still good for a system 100% sensitive.

The recognizer works in a very complicated and rather unusual way, by using ADL0 to move from node to node without changing the symbol to be parsed, and by using ADL1 mainly to parse propositional phrases or fragments of them. For example, the output produced by the Pop-11 tracer when recognizing the sentence 'the kitten on the small mat frightened a mouse' is shown in Figure 27.20. The parse tree for this sentence is in Figure 27.21 together with the parts of the RTN responsible for the recognition of each word.

It should be noted that for very difficult problems which have never been solved before, at least with evolutionary techniques, such as the one considered in this chapter or the evolution of electronic circuits (see for example Koza et al [1997a]), it is usually impossible to perform more than a few runs (in this case three). This is normally considered more than acceptable because, in these cases, the research focus is not assessing the performance of GP through the usual statistics used in the GP literature (like the computational effort, the percentage of successful runs, etc.), but rather showing how GP can reach new horizons and studying the characteristics of the solutions evolved.

> DET DET	!!> ADJ ADJ	!< PREP <false>	!< ADL0 <true>
< DET <true>	!!< ADJ <true>	!> ADL0 END	!> TVERB END
> ADJ NOUN	!!> ADL1 NOUN	!< ADL0 <true>	!< TVERB <false>
< ADJ <false>	!!!> NOUN NOUN	!> ADJ END	!> ADL0 END
> NOUN NOUN	!!!< NOUN <true>	!< ADJ <false>	!< ADL0 <true>
< NOUN <true>	!!!> PREP TVERB	!> ADL0 END	< ADL1 <true>
> DET PREP	!!!< PREP <false>	!< ADL0 <true>	> DET END
< DET <false>	!!!> ADL0 TVERB	!> TVERB END	< DET <false>
> ADL1 PREP	!!!< ADL0 <true>	!< TVERB <false>	> ADL1 END
!> NOUN PREP	!!!> ADJ TVERB	!> ADL0 END	!> NOUN END
!< NOUN <false>	!!!< ADJ <false>	!< ADL0 <true>	!< NOUN <false>
!> ADL0 PREP	!!!> ADL0 TVERB	< ADL1 <true>	!> ADL0 END
!< ADL0 <true>	!!!< ADL0 <true>	> DET END	!< ADL0 <true>
!> PREP PREP	!!!> TVERB TVERB	< DET <false>	!> PREP END
!< PREP <true>	!!!< TVERB <true>	> ADL1 END	!< PREP <false>
!> DET DET	!!< ADL1 <true>	!> NOUN END	!> ADL0 END
!< DET <true>	!< ADL1 <true>	!< NOUN <false>	!< ADL0 <true>
!> ADL1 ADJ	< ADL1 <true>	!> ADL0 END	!> ADJ END
!!> NOUN ADJ	> DET DET	!< ADL0 <true>	!< ADJ <false>
!!< NOUN <false>	< DET <true>	!> PREP END	!> ADL0 END
!!> ADL0 ADJ	> DET NOUN	!< PREP <false>	!< ADL0 <true>
!!< ADL0 <true>	< DET <false>	!> ADL0 END	!> TVERB END
!!> PREP ADJ	> ADL1 NOUN	!< ADL0 <true>	!< TVERB <false>
!!< PREP <false>	!> NOUN NOUN	!> ADJ END	!> ADL0 END
!!> ADL0 ADJ	!< NOUN <true>	!< ADJ <false>	!< ADL0 <true>
!!< ADL0 <true>	!> PREP END	!> ADL0 END	< ADL1 <true>

Fig. 27.20: Functions invoked by the parsing of the sentence: 'the kitten on the small mat frightened a mouse'.

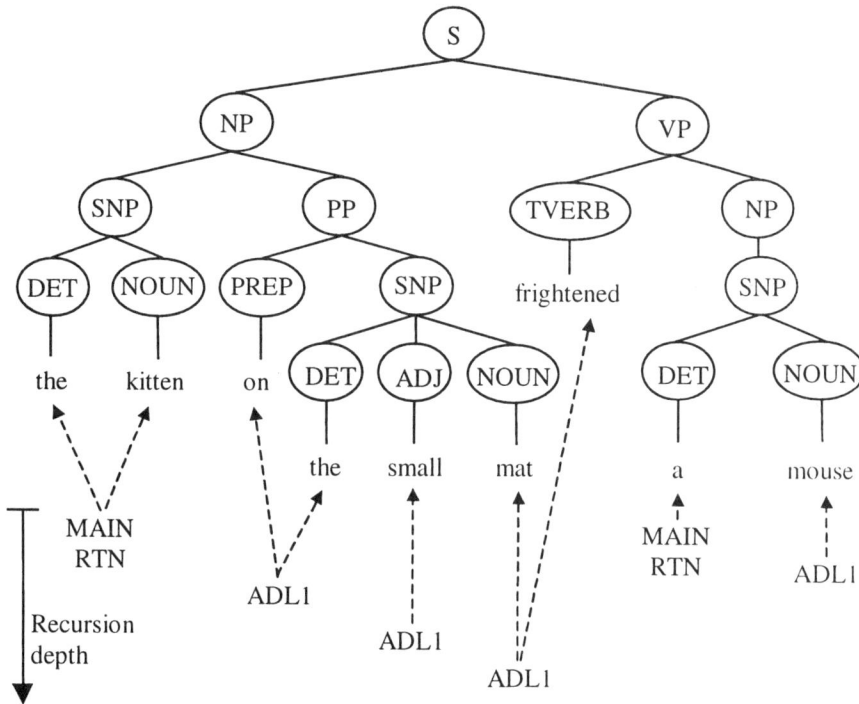

Fig. 27.21: Parse tree for the sentence 'the kitten on the small mat frightened a mouse' and parts of the RTN responsible for its recognition (calls to *ADL0* are not shown).

27.7 RELATED WORK

When appropriate terminals, functions and/or interpreters are defined, standard GP can go beyond the production of sequential tree-like programs. For example using cellular encoding (CE) GP can be used to develop (grow) structures, like neural nets (Gruau & Whitley [1993], Gruau [1994]) or electronic circuits (Koza et al [1996a, 1996b, 1998a]), which can be thought of as performing some form of parallel analogue computation. In CE a program, rather than being executed directly, is interpreted as a sequence of instructions which modify (grow) a simple initial structure (embryo). Once the program terminates the resulting structure is executed to evaluate the program's fitness. Although this has never been done, nothing would prevent the use of CE to evolve parallel distributed programs.

One of the advantages of indirect graph representations, like CE or its variants (e.g. edge encoding – Luke & Spector [1996]), is that the standard GP operators can be used on CE programs. However, such representations require an additional genotype-to-phenotype decoding step before the interpretation of the graphs being optimized can start, as the search is not performed in the space of possible graphs, but in the space of sequential programs that produce graphs. When the fitness function involves complex calculations with many fitness cases the decoding step can have a limited relative effect on the evaluation of each individual in terms of computational cost. However, the meta-encoding of the graphs seems to make the search more costly by increasing the total number of individuals that must be evaluated (see for example the comparison between cellular and direct encodings of neural nets in Gruau et al [1996]).

In conjunction with an interpreter implementing a parallel virtual machine, GP can be used to translate sequential programs into parallel ones (Walsh & Ryan [1996]) or to develop some kinds of parallel programs. Note however that the development of parallel programs should not be confused with parallel implementations of GP, which are essentially methods of speeding-up the genetic search of standard tree-like programs (Andre & Koza [1996], Dracopoulos & Kent [1996], Oussaidene et al [1996], Juille & Pollack [1996], Stoffel & Spector [1996]). These methods are usually based on the use of multiple processors, each one handling a separate population, a subset of fitness evaluations or a subset of fitness cases.

Returning to the issue of parallel programs, rather than parallelized GP, Bennett [1996] used a parallel virtual machine in which several standard tree-like programs (called 'agents') had their nodes executed in parallel with a two stage mechanism simulating parallelism of sensing actions and simple conflict resolution (prioritization) for actions with side effects. Andre et al [1996] used GP to discover rules for cellular automata which could solve large majority-classification problems. In a system called PADO (Parallel Algorithm Discovery and Orchestration), Teller & Veloso [1995, 1995a, 1996], and Teller [1996] used a combination of GP and linear discrimination to obtain classification programs for signals and images.

Other work which has some relation with ours is based on the idea, first proposed by Handley [1994] and later improved by Ehrenburg [1996], of storing the population of parse trees as a single directed acyclic graph, rather than as a forest of trees. This leads to considerable savings of memory (structurally identical subtrees are not duplicated) and computation (the value computed by each subtree for each fitness case is cached). However, it is important to emphasize that this technique can only be applied when using *primitives with no side effects* and that it is conceptually equivalent to the evolution of tree-like programs as standard GP; that is, it is not about the evolution of parallel programs.

27.8 CONCLUSIONS

In this chapter we have presented PDGP, a new form of genetic programming which is suitable for the automatic discovery of parallel network-like programs in which symbolic and sub-symbolic (neural, numeric, etc.) primitives can be combined in a free and natural way as can primitives with and without side effects.

The grid-based representation of programs used in PDGP allowed us to develop efficient forms of crossover and mutation. By changing the size, shape and dimensionality of the grid, this representation allows a fine control on the size and shape of the programs being developed. For example it is possible to control the degree of parallelism and the reuse of building blocks by changing the number of columns in the grid. In future, it would be interesting to study the idea of evolving the shape and size of the grid during PDGP runs.

When programs do not include functions or terminals with side-effects, our grid-based representation of programs can be directly mapped onto the nodes of some kinds of fine-grained parallel machines. This can lead to a very efficient evaluation of fitness cases as

PDGP programs could produce a new result at every clock tick. PDGP programs (possibly developed with some additional constraints) could also be used to define the functions of field programmable gate arrays. This, for example, could lead to new ways of doing research in the field of evolvable hardware.

In this chapter we have gone beyond our initial simple form of program interpretation inspired to the propagation of activation in the neurons of feed-forward neural nets. By using a more sophisticated interpreter we have been able to solve the problems of executing general graph-like programs, possibly including recurrent connections and nodes with side effects, on a sequential computer. We also think that, through the use of macros, functions and terminals that use special execution policies, like 'execute-if-no-clash' or 'lock-execute-unlock', PDGP could naturally be used to develop parallel distributed programs for any kind of parallel machine.

The programs developed by PDGP are fine-grained, but the representation used is also suitable for the development of medium-grained parallel programs via use of automatically defined functions and automatically defined links: a new technique unique to PDGP.

The experimental results with the evolution of recursive transition nets for natural language recognition obtained using this technique are very promising and show how evolutionary computation with the use of little prior knowledge can now tackle higher and higher level problems usually considered to require special AI techniques.

It should be noted that ADLs are just one of the new representational possibilities opened by PDGP. PDGP is an efficient paradigm to optimize general graphs (with or without cycles, possibly recursively nested via ADFs and ADLs, with or without labelled links, with or without directions, etc.). These graphs need not be interpreted as programs. They can be interpreted as engineering designs, semantic nets, neural networks, etc. Also, cellular encoding can naturally be extended to PDGP, thus creating a very large set of new possibilities (the weirdest of all possibly being using the direct graph representation of PDGP to develop GP trees).

Acknowledgements

The author wishes to thank Bill Langdon and the other members of the Evolutionary and Emergent Behaviour Intelligence and Computation (EEBIC) group at Birmingham for useful discussions and comments.

NOTES

1. The work described in this chapter has been previously reported in more extensive form in Poli [1996, 1996a, 1996b, 1996c, 1997, 1997a] and has been extended in Pujol & Poli [1998, 1998a, 1998b].
2. In this chapter (if not otherwise stated) we have adopted the convention that the first row of the grid includes as many cells as the number of outputs of the program.
3. In the current implementation of PDGP we use a less efficient mutation operator which is however equivalent to global mutation: we perform the crossover of an individual with a randomly generated new individual, which is then discarded.
4. Pop-11 is an AI language with features similar to Lisp, which is quite widespread in the UK where it was originally developed.

Chapter Twenty-Eight

From Probabilities to Programs with Probabilistic Incremental Program Evolution

Rafal Salustowicz and Jürgen Schmidhuber

28.1 INTRODUCTION

Probabilistic Incremental Program Evolution (PIPE – Salustowicz & Schmidhuber [1997][1])
is a recent method for synthesizing programs. PIPE searches spaces of tree-structured,
functional programs that can be constructed from predefined instruction sets. PIPE applies
a generational model: Starting with a population of randomly generated programs, it
iteratively generates successive program populations (generations). To create better and
better programs PIPE uses an adaptive probability distribution over all possible programs
with respect to a predefined instruction set. Initially the probability distribution is random.
It is then successively adapted as follows: (1) Each generation, the probability of generating
the best program in the current population is increased; (2) occasionally the probability of
generating the best program found so far (elitist) is increased; (3) sometimes, single
probabilities are mutated to better explore the search space.

28.1.1 Sources of Inspiration

PIPE emerged from three major sources of inspiration: (1) Probabilistic Programming
Languages; (2) Genetic Programming; (3) Population-Based Incremental Learning.

Probabilistic Programming Languages

Probabilistic Programming Languages (PPLs) have been recently introduced in the field of
reinforcement learning (Schmidhuber [1994], Wiering & Schmidhuber [1996], Zhao &
Schmidhuber [1996], Schmidhuber et al [1997, 1997a]). With PPLs, instruction sequences
are generated and executed according to sets of variables, initially uniform probability
distributions. The distributions are modified either by a fixed learning algorithm such as
Adaptive Levin Search (ALS – Wiering & Schmidhuber [1996], Schmidhuber et al
[1997a]) or an evolving, self-modifying, probabilistic learning algorithm (SMPLA)
embedded within the distributions themselves (Schmidhuber et al [1997]). ALS extends
Levin Search (LS – Levin [1973, 1984]), a theoretically optimal algorithm for
nonincremental search in program space, to the incremental case. SMPLAs go one step
further – they try to improve the way they learn by modifying their learning algorithm.

PIPE encodes programs in variable probability distributions, but it is not an on-line
reinforcement learning method and does not use SMPLAs, or ALS. It is an evolutionary

method based on successive program generations comparable to Genetic Programming (e.g.. Cramer [1985], Dickmanns et al [1987], Koza [1992]).

Genetic Programming (GP)

GP is a Genetic Algorithm for evolving programs. It starts with a population of random programs. Each program's quality is evaluated on a given task. Selected programs may (1) immediately join the next generation, or (2) exchange code with other programs ('crossover'). Programs with high quality have higher probability of being selected than others. The procedure is repeated for a fixed number of generations or until a satisfactory solution has been found. Koza's GP variant (Koza [1992]) encodes programs in parse trees. So does PIPE. Thus, both can be applied to the same problems. GP, however, stores domain knowledge in program populations, whereas PIPE captures this knowledge in a probability distribution. GP relies on crossover to generate better and better programs, whereas PIPE uses a learning method similar to Population-Based Incremental Learning (Baluja & Caruana [1995]).

Population-Based Incremental Learning (PBIL)

PBIL generates a population of fixed-length bitstrings (solution candidates for a given task) according to a vector of probabilities (initially 0.5). The probabilities are then adjusted to increase the probability of the current population's best individual and to decrease the probability of the current population's worst individual. This procedure is repeated until all probabilities are either 1.0 or 0.0. Thus, PBIL does not store domain knowledge in a population, but in a probability distribution.

PIPE follows PBIL's update algorithm but uses a different representation. PIBL stores the probability distribution in a fixed-length probability vector that encodes probabilities for bits in the solution representation being set. PIPE, however, needs to handle tree-coded programs of varying size and uses an incrementally growing and shrinking *Probabilistic Prototype Tree* (PPT) which contains the probability distribution over all possible programs with respect to a predefined instruction set. Furthermore, PIPE significantly extends PBIL's initialization and update rules to accommodate tree-coded programs.

28.1.2 Outline

The remainder of this chapter is organized as follows: section 28.2 defines instructions – the basic program elements – and describes the tree-structure of programs. Section 28.3 is then dedicated to the *Probabilistic Prototype Tree* (PPT) that stores the probability distribution used by PIPE. Section 28.4 then introduces the learning algorithm used by PIPE, and explains all of the update rules. Section 28.5 contains a step by step description of how to set up PIPE for an application, based on much empirical experience. Section 28.6 then presents three applications in detail, describing the setup for each, and results using PIPE. These applications are, in turn, function regression, 6-bit parity, and 3+8-bit multiplexer. Section 28.7 then concludes.

28.2 PROGRAMS

Programs are made of instructions from an instruction set $S = \{I_1,...,I_z\}$ with z instructions. Instructions are user-defined. Each instruction is either a *function* or a *terminal*. Instruction set S therefore consists of a function set $F = \{f_1,...,f_k\}$ with k functions and a terminal set $T = \{t_1,...,t_l\}$ with l terminals, where $z=k+l$ holds. Functions and terminals differ in that the former have one or more arguments and the latter have zero. For instance, to solve a one-dimensional function regression task one might use $F=\{+, -, *, \%, \sin, \cos, \exp, rlog\}$ and $T=\{x, R\}$, where $\%$ denotes protected division (when $z\neq0$: $y\%z = y/z$, and $y\%0=1$); $rlog$ denotes protected logarithm (when $y\neq0$, $rlog(y)=\log(abs(y))$, and $rlog(0)=0$); x is an input variable; and R is a *generic random constant* (GRC). GRCs are to allow random constants in programs. A GRC (like an 'ephemeral random constant' – Koza [1992]) is a no-argument function (a terminal). When accessed during program creation, it is either instantiated to a random value from a predefined, problem-dependent set of constants or a value previously stored in the *PPT* (see section 28.3).

The instruction set must comply with the *closure* principle (Koza [1992]). The closure principle ensures that all created programs are syntactically correct. To ensure closure for PIPE every terminal and every output of a function must be acceptable as another function's argument with respect to type and value.

Programs are encoded in *n*-ary trees, with *n* being the maximal number of function arguments. Each nonleaf node encodes a function from *F* and each leaf node a terminal from *T*. The number of subtrees each node has corresponds to the number of arguments of its function. Each argument is calculated by a subtree. Trees are parsed depth first from left to right. Sample trees for function regression (section 28.2.1) are shown in Figure 28.1.

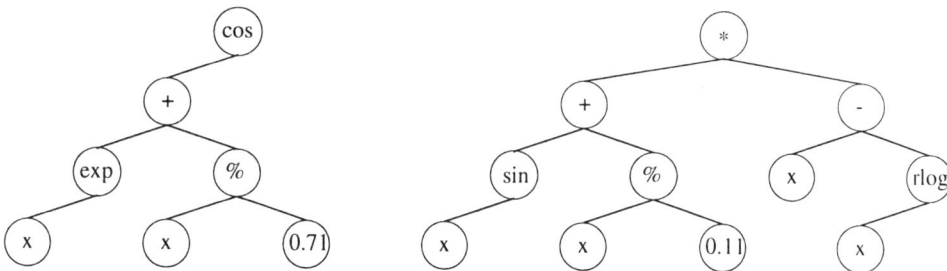

Fig. 28.1: Sample program trees for function regression. (left: $f(x)=\cos(\exp(x)+(x\%0.71))$; right: $f(x)=((\sin(x)+(x\%0.11))*(x-rlog(x))$.

28.3 PROBABILISTIC PROTOTYPE TREE (*PPT*)

The *PPT* stores the knowledge gained from experiences with programs and guides the evolutionary search. It holds random constants and the probability distribution over all possible programs that can be constructed from a predefined instruction set. The *PPT* is generally a complete *n*-ary tree with infinitely many nodes, where *n* is again the maximal number of function arguments.

28.3.1 Nodes

All *PPT* nodes are created equal. Each node N_j with $j \le 0$ contains a random constant R_j and a variable probability vector $\vec{P}_j$. Each $\vec{P}_j$ has z components, where z is the number of instructions in instruction set S. Each component $P_j(I)$ of $\vec{P}_j$ denotes the probability of choosing instruction $I \in S$ at node N_j. All components of vector $\vec{P}_j$ sum to one.

28.3.2 Initialization

Each *PPT* node N_j requires an initial random constant R_j and an initial probability $P_j(I)$ for each instruction $I \in S$. A value for R_j is randomly taken from the same predefined, problem-dependent set of constants, from which also the GRC function draws its instantiations (see section 28.2). To initialize instruction probabilities a predefined, constant probability P_T for selecting an instruction from T (the terminal set) and $(1 - P_T)$ for selecting an instruction from F (the function set) are used. Each vector $\vec{P}_j$ is then initialized as follows:

$$P_j(I) \leftarrow \frac{P_T}{l}, \forall I \in T \quad \text{and} \quad P_j(I) \leftarrow \frac{1 - P_T}{k}, \forall I \in F$$

where l is the total number of terminals in T and k is the total number of functions in F. Figure 28.2 shows an initialized *PPT* node for the function regression task defined in section 28.2.1 with $P_T=0.6$ and R_j picked uniformly random from $[0;1)$.

```
P(x)    = 0.3
P(R)    = 0.3
P(+)    = 0.05
P(-)    = 0.05
P(*)    = 0.05
P(%)    = 0.05
P(sin)  = 0.05
P(cos)  = 0.05
P(exp)  = 0.05
P(rlog) = 0.05

R_j     = 0.45      N_j
```

Fig. 28.2: Initialized *PPT* node N_j with $P_T=0.6$ and R_j random in $[0;1)$. N_j holds $P_j(I)$ for each instruction $I \in S$ (see section 28.2.1) and a random constant R_j to allow for GRCs.

28.3.3 Program Generation

Programs are generated according to the probability distribution stored in the *PPT*. To generate a program PROG from *PPT*, an instruction $I \in S$ is selected with probability $P_j(I)$ for each accessed node N_j of *PPT*. This instruction is denoted as I_j. Nodes are accessed in a depth-first way, starting at the root node and traversing *PPT* from left to right. Once $I_j \in F$ (a function) is selected, a subtree is created for each argument of I_j. If $I_j = R$ (the GRC), then an instance of R, called $V_j(R)$, replaces R in PROG. If $P_j(R)$ exceeds a threshold T_R, then $V_j(R) = R_j$ (the value stored in the *PPT*). Otherwise $V_j(R)$ is generated uniformly random from a problem-dependent set of constants. Starting with N_0 (root node) the program generation process can be recursively written as follows:

```
create_program_node_from_PPT_node(*ppt_node, *program_node) {
    probabilistically select instruction I_j according to P⃗_j ;
    /* special treatment, if instruction is a GRC */
    if I_j = R then {
        if P_j(R) > T_R then I_j ← V_j(R) = R_j ;
        else I_j ← V_j(R) = 'random value from problem-dependent set';}
    for ( i ← 0 ; i < 'number of I_j's arguments'; i ← i+1)
        create_program_node_from_PPT_node(ppt_node→next[i], program_node→next[i]); }
```

Figure 28.3 illustrates the relation between a *PPT* and a possible program tree for the function regression example of section 28.2.1.

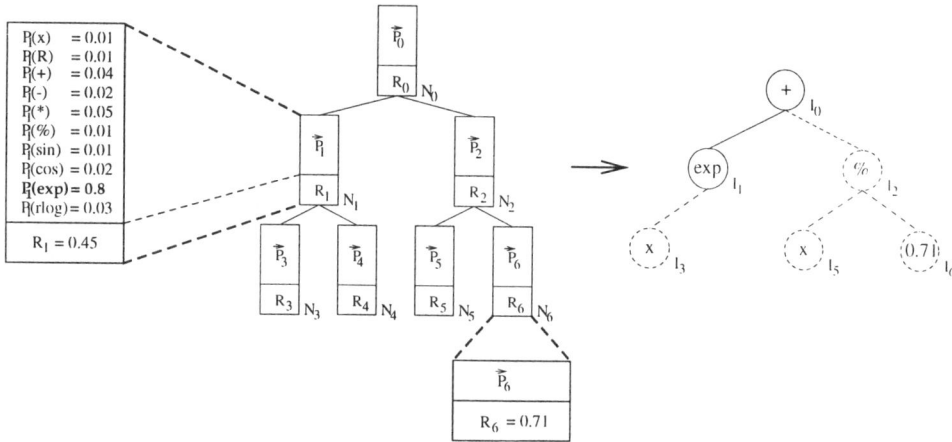

Fig. 28.3: Left: Example of node N_1's instruction probability vector $\vec{P}_1$ and random constant R_1. Middle: Probabilistic prototype tree *PPT* with details of node N_6. Right: Possible extracted program PROG. At the time of creation of instruction I_1, the dashed part of PROG did not yet exist. $I_6 = R$ is instantiated to $I_6 \leftarrow V_6(R) \leftarrow R_6 = 0.71$ because probability $P_6(R)$ (not shown) exceeds the random constant threshold T_R.

28.3.4 Memory Management

A *complete PPT* is infinite. A 'large' *PPT* is memory intensive. Recall that each *PPT* node holds a probability for each instruction, a random constant, and n pointers to following nodes, where n is *PPT*s arity. Empirical evidence, however, indicates that it suffices to maintain a *PPT* with on average roughly two to three times as many nodes as in the current best solution (best program of generation). To reduce memory requirements, it is thus possible to incrementally grow and prune the *PPT*.

Growing

Initially, the *PPT* contains only the root node. Further nodes are created 'on demand' whenever $I_j \in F$ is selected and the subtree for an argument of I_j is missing. Figure 28.4 shows how the *PPT* grows incrementally.

Pruning

PPT subtrees attached to nodes that contain at least one probability vector component above a threshold T_P can be pruned. If T_P is set to a sufficiently high value (e.g. $T_P=0.99999$) only parts of the *PPT* will be pruned that have a very low probability of being accessed. In case of functions, only those subtrees should be pruned that are *not* required as function arguments (see Figure 28.5). Apart from reducing memory requirements, pruning also helps to discard elements of the probability distribution that have become irrelevant over time.

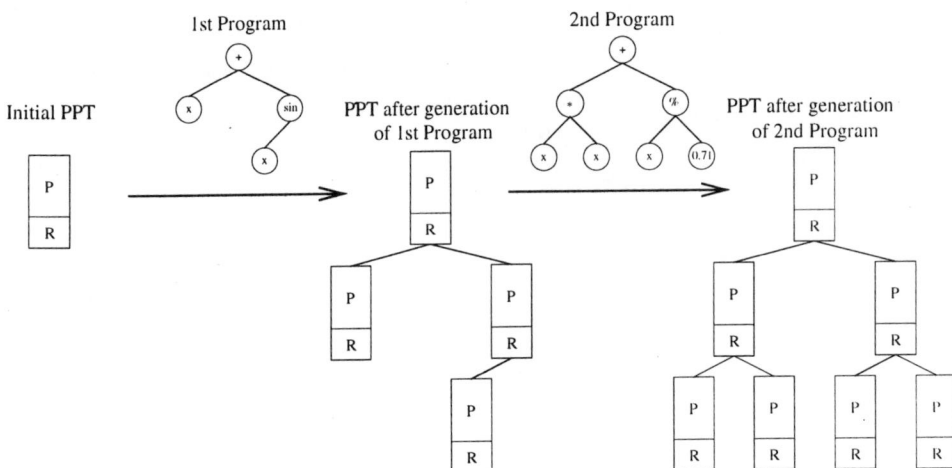

Fig. 28.4: Growing the *PPT* 'on demand'. Initially the *PPT* contains only the root node (left). Additional nodes are created with each program that accesses non-existing nodes during its generation.

28.4 LEARNING

PIPE attempts to find better and better programs by biasing its search towards programs that are statistically similar to previous best solutions.

28.4.1 Fitness Functions

What makes a program better than another? In order to answer this question it is necessary to setup a quality measure for programs. PIPE uses *fitness functions*. A fitness function is problem-dependent and user-defined. It defines the task to be solved. A fitness function maps programs to scalar, real-valued fitness values that reflect the programs' performances on a given task. For PIPE to work properly fitness functions need to comply with the following: (a) Fitness values must not be negative. (b) Programs embodying better solutions need to be mapped to smaller fitness values. Thus, PIPE seeks to minimize fitness and PIPE's fitness functions can therefore be seen as 'error measures'.

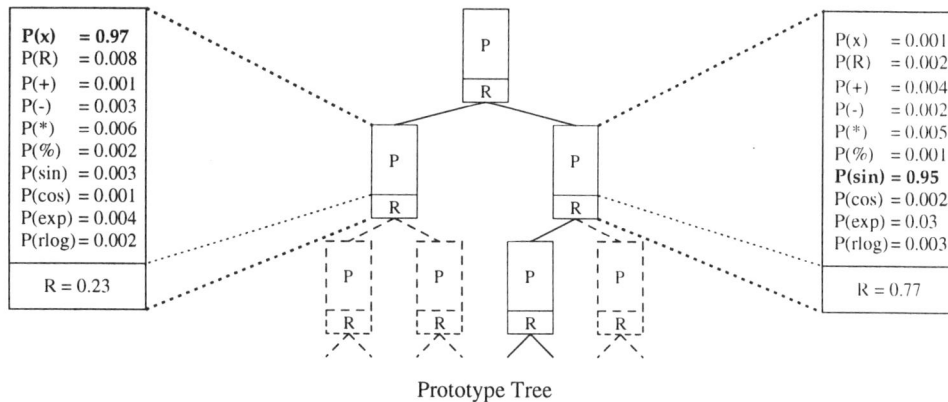

Prototype Tree

Fig. 28.5: The dashed parts of the prototype tree can be pruned because the probabilities of the adjacent nodes exceed threshold value $T_P = 0.9$ and contain high probabilities for a terminal (left) and a single function with one argument (right).

A secondary non-user-defined objective for which PIPE always optimizes programs is program size as measured by number of nodes. Among programs with equal fitness smaller ones are *always* preferred. This objective constitutes PIPE's built-in Occam's razor.

28.4.2 Learning Framework

PIPE combines two forms of learning: Generation-Based Learning (GBL) and Elitist Learning (EL). GBL is PIPE's main learning algorithm. EL's purpose is to make the best program found so far an attractor. PIPE executes:

> GBL
> **REPEAT**
>> with probability P_{el} **DO** EL
>> otherwise **DO** GBL
> **UNTIL** termination criterion is reached

Here, P_{el} is a user-defined constant in [0;1].

28.4.3 Generation-Based Learning

PIPE learns in successive generations, each comprising five distinct phases: (1) creation of program population, (2) population evaluation, (3) learning from population, (4) mutation of prototype tree, and (5) prototype tree pruning.

(1) Creation of Program Population

A population of programs PROG$_j$ (0<j≤PS); *PS* is population size) is generated using the prototype tree *PPT*, as described in section 28.3.3. The *PPT* is grown 'on demand' (see section 28.3.4).

(2) Population Evaluation

Each program PROG$_j$ of the current population is evaluated on the given task and assigned a fitness value *FIT*(*PROG$_j$*) according to the predefined fitness function (see section 28.4.1). The best program of the current population (the one with the smallest fitness value) is denoted *PROG$_b$*. The best program found so far (elitist) is preserved in *PROG^{el}*.

(3) Learning from Population

Prototype tree probabilities are modified such that the probability *P*(*PROG$_b$*) of creating *PROG$_b$* increases. This procedure is called adapt_PPT_towards(*PROG$_b$*). It increases *P*(*PROG$_b$*) independently of *PROG$_b$*'s length. This is important as otherwise a strong bias towards creating short programs is induced and hampers evolution. Procedure adapt_PPT_towards(*PROG$_b$*) works as follows:

First *P*(*PROG$_b$*) is computed by looking at all *PPT* nodes N_j used to generate *PROG$_b$*:

$$P(PROG_b) = \prod_{j \in N_j \text{ used to generate } PROG_b} P_j(I_j(PROG_b))$$

where $I_j(PROG_b)$ denotes the instruction of program *PROG$_b$* at node position *j*. Then a target probability P_{TARGET} for *PROG$_b$* is calculated:

$$P_{TARGET} = P(PROG_b) + (1 - P(PROG_b)) \cdot lr \cdot \frac{\varepsilon + FIT(PROG^{el})}{\varepsilon + FIT(PROG_b)}$$

Here *lr* is a constant learning rate and ε a positive user-defined constant. The fraction on the right implements *fitness-dependent learning (fdl)*. Larger steps are taken towards programs with higher quality (lower fitness) than towards programs with lower quality (higher fitness). Constant ε determines the degree of *fdl*'s influence. If ε is always significantly smaller than *FIT*(*PROG^{el}*), then PIPE can use small population sizes because generations containing only low-quality individuals do not affect the *PPT* much.

Given P_{TARGET}, *all* single node probabilities $P_j(I_j(PROG_b))$ are increased iteratively (in parallel):

REPEAT UNTIL $P(PROG_b) \geq P_{TARGET}$:

$$P_j(I_j(PROG_b)) \leftarrow P_j(I_j(PROG_b)) + c^{lr} \cdot lr \cdot (1 - P_j(I_j(PROG_b)))$$

Here c^{lr} is a constant influencing the number of iterations. The smaller c^{lr}, the higher the approximation precision of P_{TARGET} and the number of required iterations. Setting $c^{lr}=0.1$ turned out to be a good compromise between precision and speed. Finally, all adapted vectors $\vec{P}_j$ are renormalized and each random constant in PROG$_b$ is copied to the appropriate node in the *PPT*: if $I_j(PROG_b) = R$ then $R_j = V_j(R)$.

(4) Mutation of Prototype Tree

Mutation is one of PIPE's major exploration mechanisms. Mutation of *PPT* probabilities is guided by the current best solution *PROG$_b$*. PIPE explores the area 'around' *PROG$_b$*. All probabilities $P_j(I)$ stored in nodes N_j that were accessed to generate program *PROG$_b$* are mutated with probability P_{M_P}:

$$P_{M_P} = \frac{P_M}{z \cdot \sqrt{|PROG_b|}}$$

where the user-defined parameter P_M defines the overall mutation probability, z is the number of instructions in instruction set S (see section 28.2.1) and $|PROG_b|$ denotes the number of nodes in program *PROG$_b$*. To prevent rapid growth of mutation probability P_{M_P}, it is made dependent on *PROG$_b$*'s size. The justification of the square root is empirical: Larger programs improve faster with higher mutation probability. Selected probability vector components are then mutated as follows:

$$P_j(I) \leftarrow P_j(I) + mr \cdot (1 - P_j(I))$$

where *mr* is the mutation rate, another user-defined parameter. All mutated vectors $\vec{P}_j$ are finally renormalized. One can see that small probabilities (close to 0) are subject to stronger mutations than high probabilities. Otherwise, mutations would tend to have little effect on the next generation.

(5) Prototype Tree Pruning

At the end of each generation the prototype tree is pruned, as described in section 28.3.4.

28.4.4 Elitist Learning

During elitist learning (EL), the *PPT* is adapted towards the elitist program *PROG^{el}* by calling adapt_PPT_towards(*PROG^{el}*); then the *PPT* is pruned. However, neither is a population created and evaluated nor are the probabilities of the *PPT* mutated, making EL computationally cheap. EL focuses search on previously discovered promising parts of the search space. It is particularly useful with small population sizes and works efficiently in the case of noise-free problems.

28.4.5 Termination Criteria

PIPE is run either for a fixed number of program evaluations (*PE* – time constraint) or until a solution with fitness better than *FIT$_s$* is found (quality constraint).

28.4.6 Summary of User-Defined Parameters

The following above-mentioned parameters have to be set by the user:

P_T : *Initial Terminal Probability*. The initial probability of selecting an instruction from terminal set T at each node N_j. High P_T forces PIPE to start with small programs (containing few nodes) and prevents programs from growing rapidly.

P_{el}: *Elitist Update Probability*. Probability of learning from the elitist program $PROG^{el}$ instead of a new generation of programs.

PS : *Population Size*. The number of programs created and evaluated during one generation.

lr : *Learning Rate*. This influences the step size for adapting the probabilities of PPT during each learning phase.

ε : *Fitness Constant*. This determines the impact of fitness dependent learning by introducing an absolute fitness scale.

P_M : *Mutation Probability*. Probability of mutating probabilities in PPT. High P_M stimulates exploration but may destabilize learning.

mr : *Mutation Rate*. Strength of mutation of a single selected probability vector component of the PPT. A large mr ensures high impact of mutations on future generations. Many small mutations tend to make all PPT probability distributions uniform (see mutation probability above).

T_R : *Random Constant Threshold*. Probability threshold that defines when to try new values for R_js. A too high T_R tends to make PIPE forget previously discovered good random constants.

T_P : *Prune Threshold*. Probability threshold used in the pruning procedure to reduce memory requirements.

PE : *Program Evaluations*. Maximum number of programs tested during system life (time constraint).

FIT_s : *Satisfactory Fitness*. Fitness of a satisfactory solution. Once a satisfactory solution is found, the search can be stopped (quality constraint).

28.5 APPLYING PIPE

Applying PIPE needs various steps, which are now described in turn.

Training and Test Environment Setup

A training and test environment that allows for establishing program quality needs to be derived from the problem definition. An environment in this context can be, e.g. a training and a test data set.

Fitness Function Definition

The fitness function must define the goal of PIPE's optimization process. It needs to be setup following the guidelines from section 28.4.1.

Instruction Set Selection

The choice of the instruction set has great influence on PIPE's performance. In general there is no recipe which instructions to pick, since the choice of an appropriate instruction set is problem-dependent. Only a 'weak' guideline can be given as to how to choose a terminal and function set.

Terminal Set Selection

The terminal set must at least include all relevant input variables. It may also include a GRC and further terminal instructions. The minimal constraint on the GRC is to insure closure with respect to type and value range.

Function Set Selection

To select an appropriate function set a priori knowledge about the problem is required. Choosing an inappropriate function set will prevent PIPE from finding a useful solution. Many problems, however, can be solved using a single *basic function set* (*bfs*) as a basis and enriching it with further instructions when necessary. Establishing a *bfs* that serves well for a particular group of problems is non-trivial and beyond the scope of this chapter. A *bfs* that has been empirically shown to work well for a wide variety of problems is the function set presented in section 28.2.1. It has been successfully applied to: function approximation, parity problems, learning in partially observable environments (Salustowicz & Schmidhuber [1997]), learning soccer strategies (Salustowicz et al [1998]) and time series prediction (Salustowicz & Schmidhuber [1998]).

Output Interface Definition

The result of applying *PROG* to data x is denoted as *PROG*(x). For some problems *PROG*(x) needs to be transformed to a different output value and/or type to constitute a solution. This is what a predefined output interface does (compare also with 'wrappers' – Koza [1992]). If, for example, the instruction set from section 28.2.1 is used to evolve solutions for a Boolean problem requiring a 'true' or 'false' as an output, *PROG*(x) can be transformed to accommodate for the Boolean nature of the problem by using the following output interface:

$$\text{if } PROG(x) < 0 \text{ then } \textit{false} \text{ else } \textit{true}$$

Parameter Setup

In general the optimal parameter setting is problem-dependent. There are, however, a few 'rules of thumb' that have empirically been proven to work well:

- Initial terminal probability P_T is the most important parameter. It should be initially set to a high value (e.g. 0.8) to focus the search on small programs first, as smaller programs require less evaluation time. In case PIPE cannot improve its solutions and no larger programs are tired after some generations, PIPE needs to be restarted with a smaller value for P_T that favours larger programs.

- Elitist update probability P_{el} needs to be set to 0 for problems with a noisy program evaluation.
- Population size PS should be kept small (exceptions exist for obtaining speed-ups through parallelization) in favour of an increased number of generations.
- Apart from program evaluations PE and satisfactory fitness FIT_s which are the termination criteria, all remaining parameters tend to work well with 'standard' values (see section 28.6).

28.6 APPLICATIONS

Three distinct problems have been selected to demonstrate how PIPE can be applied: function regression, 6-bit parity, and the 3+8-bit multiplexer. All selected problems verify empirically that the 'rules of thumb' from section 28.5.5 work. Each experiment on its own adds more insight into how PIPE works.

Function Regression

The task is to evolve a program constituting an approximation to a continuous, one-dimensional function. A non-trivial function is selected to prevent PIPE from simply guessing it. Since the function is continuous, infinite many fitness values exist and allow for a slow incremental adaptation.

6-Bit Parity

The 6-bit parity problem is a discrete task involving just 65 distinct fitness values. The limited number of fitness values allows for testing PIPE's built-in Occam's razor. Furthermore, 6-bit parity has been selected to show that the same basic function set as for the function regression problem can be applied. Finally, an output interface is presented.

3+8-Bit Multiplexer

The 3+8-bit multiplexer problem has been chosen to verify that PIPE works well with different function sets and program trees of various arities.

28.6.1 Function Regression

The test function we use is: $f(x) = x^3 \cdot e^{-x} \cdot \cos(x) \cdot \sin(x) \cdot (\sin^2(x) \cdot \cos(x) - 1)$ which is plotted in Figure 28.6.

Training and Test Environment Setup

The training data set D_{tr} samples F at 101 equidistant points in the interval $[0;10]$. The test data set D_{te} samples F at 101 equidistant points in the interval $[0.05;10.05]$. D_{tr} is used to calculate fitness values during program evolution, and D_{te} is used to test how well the best evolved programs generalize.

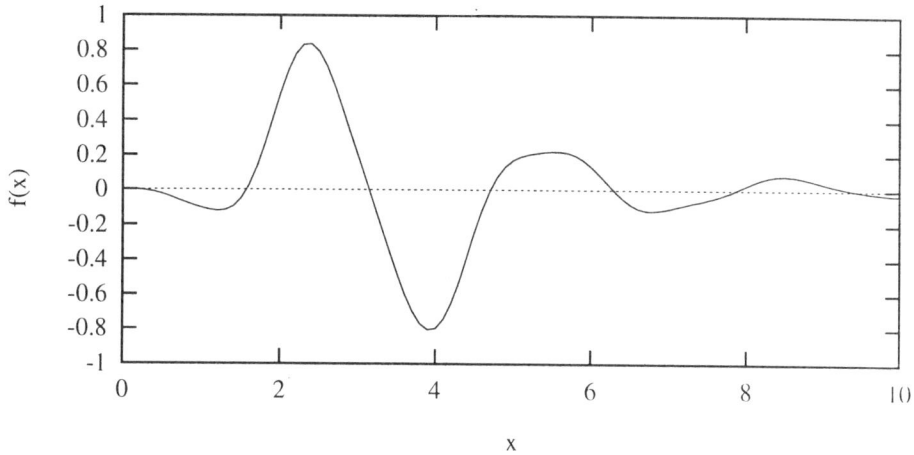

Fig. 28.6: Test function for application of PIPE to function regression.

Fitness Function Definition

The fitness value of each program PROG is as follows:

$$FIT(PROG) = \sum_{x \in D_{tr}} | f(x) - PROG(x) |$$

To verify how an evolved program generalizes its generalization performance is calculated as follows:

$$GEN(PROG) = \sum_{x \in D_{te}} | f(x) - PROG(x) |$$

To obtain an idea how generalization performances relate to function approximation quality, consider Figure 28.7. The graphs show that with increasing *GEN*(PROG) approximation quality becomes worse.

Instruction Set Selection

The following function and terminal sets have been used: F = {+, −, *, %, sin, cos, exp, rlog} and T = {x, R} (see section 28.2.1). R denotes the generic random constant in [0;1).

Output Interface Definition

No specific output interface is required in this case.

Parameter Setup

The termination criteria are set to: *PE*=100,000 and *FIT_s*=0.001. The initial terminal probability is P_T=0.8. The remaining parameters are set to what we call 'standard' values, with ε=0.000001, P_{el}=0.01, *PS*=10, *lr*=0.01, P_M=0.4, *mr*=0.4, T_R=0.3, T_P=0.999999.

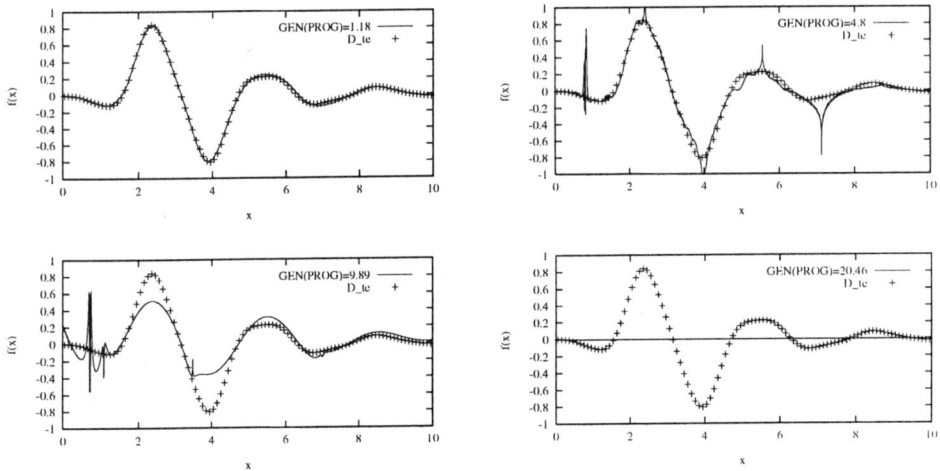

Fig. 28.7: Test data set D_{te} and approximations with GEN(PROG)=1.18 (upper left), GEN(PROG) = 4.8 (upper right), GEN(PROG) = 9.89 (lower left), and GEN(PROG) = 20.46 (lower right).

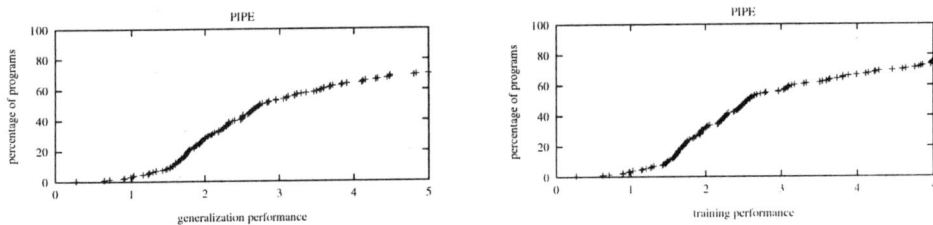

Fig. 28.8: Cumulative histograms of PIPE's performance on the training (left) and test (right) data sets for the function regression problem. The plots show the range with the best performing programs. Programs with *FIT(PROG)*>5 and *GEN(PROG)*>5 are of little interest due to the bad solution quality they embody (see Figure 28.7 for reference).

Results

Since PIPE is a stochastic learning algorithm it does not always deliver a solution of the same quality. 200 independent runs have been conducted to obtain statistics which enable an overview over the best solutions evolved by PIPE. The performance of PIPE on both the training and test data sets is summarized in Figure 28.8. Performance, *v,* is plotted against the percentage of programs with *FIT(PROG)*≤*v* and *GEN(PROG)*≤*v*. As can be seen, PIPE's performance is very similar on both data sets. The evolved programs generalize almost as well as they learn. Though not all evolved programs constitute a good solution, 50% of all runs achieved solutions with *FIT(PROG)*<2.6 and *GEN(PROG)*<2.8 (see Figure 28.7 for reference).

The following is an example of program evolved by PIPE for this problem. This program had a generalization performance *GEN(PROG)*=1.18, and it was found by PIPE after 99,390 program evaluations. It contains 248 nodes and computes: the following function:

(sin(((x−(cos(((sin((sin(cos((rlog(sin(0.350466))*((((cos(sin((cos((x−((rlog(cos(((0.359722+cos(x))+(x−
0.082538))))*(x−(0.039232−((x%0.440611)%0.499641))))*0.025812)))−(0.914140*(x*(0.506207%0.3
79995))))))*(x−((x%sin(rlog(0.334052)))+rlog(((x+x)*x)))))%exp(exp((0.743179−0.128703))))+x))))%((
(0.507077*((exp((x−x))−((cos(sin((x−(cos((0.915233%x))−exp(0.709387)))))−0.492354)%0.840741))
%cos((x*0.981004))))*((x%cos(x))*(0.091520*(0.112682+sin(sin(x))))))+x)))%x)%(sin((((cos(sin(rlog((
exp(x)%cos(0.712427)))))+0.933998)%0.609029)−cos(0.936381)))%(((cos(0.790039)−(x−0.069650)
)*sin(x))−x))))+sin(exp(rlog(x))))−((sin(0.375208)*(exp(rlog(exp(0.697598)))%cos((cos(0.585192)−0.0
95603))))+(((0.395458−(0.282354*sin(0.822447)))%(0.533448%(0.785156*0.918876)))*cos((x−(0.63
9372%0.524799)))))))))−sin((sin(sin((sin(sin(sin(x)))%sin(cos(0.287498)))))+x))))*(cos(((0.482642+((0.1
83318*(0.338145+0.069478))*cos((x+0.496698))))+(cos((x*0.649953))%cos(0.151858))))%(sin(sin((0
.470205+(x%((exp(rlog(x))%(x+0.684205))+0.058088)))))+((exp(rlog((x%0.994150))%cos(0.178977)
)*(cos(0.785409)*0.700799)))))

Conclusion

PIPE exhibits a stochastic learning behaviour. Solution quality varies for every evolutionary run. In 50% of all runs, however, PIPE finds programs embodying high quality solutions. Generalization performances are similar to training performances. Programs that perform well on the trainings set also generalize well. Much like programs evolved by Koza's GP variant (Koza [1992]), PIPE's programs differ much from programs created by human programmers.

28.6.2 6-Bit Parity

The 6-bit parity function has six Boolean arguments represented by integers: 1 for true and 0 for false. It returns 1 if the number of non-zero arguments is odd and 0 otherwise.

Training and Test Environment Setup

All 64 patterns are used for training.

Fitness Function Definition

The fitness of a program is the number of patterns it classifies *incorrectly*. Best fitness for classifying all patterns correctly is 0 and worst fitness for classifying no patterns correctly is 64.

Instructions Set Selection

The terminal set is set to $T = \{ x_0, x_1, x_2\ x_3, x_4, x_5, R \}$, where $x_0, x_1, x_2\ x_3, x_4, x_5$ are input variables and R the GRC in [0;1]. Function set F (and GRC interval) is identical to the function set used for the function regression task in section 28.6.1.

Output Interface Definition

To fit the Boolean nature of the problem the real-valued output of a program is mapped to 0 if negative and to 1 otherwise.

Parameter Setup

The termination criteria are set to: $PE = 500,000$ and $FIT_s = 0.001$. The initial terminal probability is $P_T = 0.6$. The remaining parameters are set to 'standard' values: $\varepsilon = 0.000001$, $P_{el} = 0.01$, $PS = 10$, $lr = 0.01$, $P_M = 0.4$, $mr = 0.4$, $T_R = 0.3$, $T_P = 0.999999$.

Results

100 independent test runs were conducted. Table 28.1 summarizes the results.

Table 28.1: Summary of 6-bit parity results.

Solved	Program Evaluations			Nodes		
	Min	Med	Max	Min	Med	Max
71%	8,100	**75,210**	483,790	25	**63**	231

In 71% of all runs PIPE found a perfect solution within the given time. The median successful run took 75,210 program evaluations. Solutions differs wildly. Perfect solutions are made of 25 to 231 nodes, while 63 nodes are needed in the median.

Conclusion

Due to its built-in Occam's razor PIPE solves 6-bit parity in 71% of runs. Tests without the Occam's razor (not presented) do not deliver such favourable results. Further, given an appropriate output interface, a basic function set (as for function regression) can be used.

28.6.3 3+8-Bit Multiplexer

The input of the Boolean $x+y$ multiplexer function consists of x address bits a_i and $y = 2^x$ data bits d_j. The target is to output the data bit d_j addressed by the address bits $j_{10} = (a_0, ..., a_{x-1})_2$. The 3+8-bit multiplexer function has therefore 11 Boolean arguments. Figure 28.9 shows a possible input/output configuration for the 3+8-bit multiplexer.

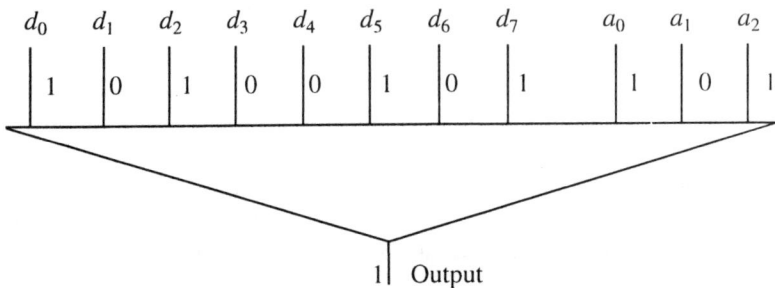

Fig. 28.9: The 3+8-bit Boolean multiplexer function with address lines a_0, a_1, a_2 and data lines $d_0, d_1, d_2, d_3, d_4, d_5, d_6, d_7$. The output is the value of data bit d_5, which is singled out by address bits $a_1 a_2 a_3$ that are set to $101_2 = 5_{10}$ respectively.

Training and Test Environment Setup

All 2048 possible patterns are used for training.

Fitness Function Definition

The fitness of a program is the number of incorrect outputs when applying all input patterns. Best fitness, if a program evaluates to the correct output for each input pattern, is 0 and worst fitness for not achieving a single correct output is 2048.

Instruction Set Selection

The terminal set is set to $T=\{a_0, a_1, a_2, d_0, d_1, d_2, d_3, d_4, d_5, d_6, d_7\}$, where each is an input variable. No distinction is made between address and data inputs. The function set $F=\{and, or, not, if\}$ was used, where *if* is a three argument function that returns the second argument, if the first argument evaluates to 1, and the third argument otherwise.

Output Interface Definition

An output mapping is not required. Only terminals and functions outputting 1 or 0 are used.

Parameter Setup

The termination criteria are set to: $PE=500,000$ and $FIT_s=0.001$. The initial terminal probability is $P_T=0.8$. The remaining parameters are set to 'standard' values: $\varepsilon = 0.000001$, $P_{el}=0.01$, $PS=10$, $lr=0.01$, $P_M=0.4$, $mr=0.4$, $T_R=0.3$, $T_P=0.999999$.

Results

100 independent test runs were conducted. Table 28.2 summarizes the results.

Table 28.2: Summary of 3+8-bit multiplexer results.

Solved	Program Evaluations			Nodes		
	Min	Med	Max	Min	Med	Max
93%	17,290	**130,210**	484,400	29	**53**	132

In 93% of all runs PIPE found a perfect solution within the given time frame. The median successful run took 130,210 program evaluations. The appearance of solutions differs. Perfect solutions are made of 29 to 132 nodes, while 53 nodes are needed in the median.

Conclusion

PIPE is not bound to the function set used for the function regression and the 6-bit parity task. PIPE works well with a completely different, for Boolean problems more intuitive function set. The increased arity of program trees and *PPT* (recall that instruction *if* has three arguments) does not prevent PIPE from solving the 3+8-bit multiplexer problem.

28.7 CONCLUSION

This chapter has given a basic introduction to PIPE – a novel method for automatic program synthesis which searches program space by generating successive populations of programs according to a probability distribution over all possible programs with respect to a predefined instruction set. The distribution guides the search and is adapted according to the results. Further, a step by step description on how to setup and apply PIPE was given.

The latter parts of this chapter were dedicated to some basic applications to illustrate PIPE and its performance characteristics. These were: function approximation, 6-bit parity, and 3+8-bit multiplexer. PIPE found programs embodying good solutions for all of them. Solution programs had a similar form to those evolved by Koza's GP (Koza [1992]) and differed much from human-designed programs. Comparing across applications suggests that PIPE can use 'standard' settings for most of its parameters, which facilitates setup for other problems. It also reveals that a basic function set can be applied to various problems such as function approximation and 6-bit parity, however this is not always the case; to solve the 3+8-bit multiplexer problem a different, more suitable function set was used. This verified that PIPE can successfully use different instruction sets and deal with program trees of various arities. Further applications such as path problems in partially observable environments, soccer strategy learning and prediction tasks that include memory, output cells, recurrent links and different output interfaces can be found in Salustowicz & Schmidhuber [1998] and Salustowicz et al [1998].

Two principal extensions to PIPE have been developed: Hierarchical PIPE (H-PIPE) Salustowicz & Schmidhuber [1998a] and *filtering* (Salustowicz & Schmidhuber [1998]). H-PIPE is based on restricting the program search space by context free grammars (Whigham [1995], Gruau [1996]). Programs are a priori structured by defining the order of instructions. Certain instructions cannot contain certain other instructions in their argument subtrees. Additionally 'skip nodes' are used to rapidly turn program parts on or off. *Filtering* is a learning algorithm independent, automatic task decomposition method. In connection with PIPE it first evolves programs, which constitute partial solutions by splitting the training data set into learnable chunks. Then programs are evolved, which assemble the learned partial solutions to a final solution.

There are also many yet untried PIPE variants. For instance, PIPE may be applied to programs with automatically defined functions (Koza [1992]) or to programs with even more general jump instructions (Dickmanns et al [1987]). Instead of coding programs by parse trees one may also use grids or directed acyclic graphs (DAGs). In principle, jump instructions and DAGs allow for automatic evolution of modular structures that cannot be represented by trees. It might also be possible to improve PIPE by updating the probability distribution based on information conveyed by programs other than the best, and by incorporating second-order statistics similar to those used in string-based evolution (De Bonet et al [1997], Baluja & Davies [1997]).

A free software package containing the basic PIPE engine can be downloaded from this book's WWW-site, or can be obtained from: ftp://ftp.idsia.ch/pub/rafal/PIPE_v1.0.tar.gz.

NOTES

1. Extended excerpts of this chapter are © MIT press. Reprinted, with permission, from Salustowicz & Schmidhuber [1997].

References

Aarts & Korst [1989]: E.H.L. Aarts, J. Korst, *Simulated Annealing and Boltzmann Machines: A Stochastic Approach to Combinatorial Optimization and Neural Computing*, John Wiley & Sons Ltd.

Aggarwal et al [1997]: C.C. Aggarwal, J.B. Orlin, R.P. Tai, Optimized Crossover for the Independent Set Problem, *Operations Research* **45**(2), pp. 226–234.

Al–Shehri [1998]: H. Al–Shehri, *Evolution–Based Decision Tree Optimization Using Cultural Algorithms*, PhD thesis, Wayne State University, Detroit, Michigan.

Aldous & Vazirani [1994]: D. Aldous, U. Vazirani, 'Go with the winners' algorithms, in *Proceedings of the 35th Annual Symposium on Foundations of Computer Science*, Santa Fe, New Mexico, IEEE Press, pp, 492–501.

Alidaee et al [1998]: B. Alidaee, M.M. Amini, G. Kochenberger, *Applications of the Unconstrained Binary Quadratic Program*, Working Paper, University of Colorado (at Denver).

Alkhamis et al [1998]: T.M. Alkhamis, M. Hasan, M.A. Ahmed, Simulated Annealing for the Unconstrained Quadratic Pseudo–Boolean Function, *European Journal of Operations Research* **108**, pp. 641–652.

Allaby [1985]: M. Allaby, *The Oxford Dictionary of Natural History*, Oxford University Press.

Andre & Koza [1996]: D. Andre, J.R. Koza, Parallel genetic programming: A scalable implementation using the transputer network architecture, in P.J. Angeline, K.E. Kinnear Jr (eds.), *Advances in Genetic Programming 2*, MIT Press, Chapter 16, pp. 317–338.

Andre et al [1996]: D. Andre, F.H. Bennett III, J.R. Koza, Discovery by genetic programming of a cellular automata rule that is better than any known rule for the majority classification problem, in J.R. Koza, D.E. Goldberg, D.B. Fogel, R.L. Riolo (eds.) *Genetic Programming 1996: Proceedings of the First Annual Conference*, MIT Press, pp. 3–11.

Angel & Zissimopoulos [1998]: E. Angel, V. Zissimopoulos, Autocorrelation Coefficient for the Graph Bipartitioning Problem, *Theoretical Computer Science* **191**, pp. 229–243.

Angeline [1995]: P. Angeline, Adaptive and self–adaptive computation, in M. Palaniswami, Y. Attikiouzel, R. Marks II, D.B. Fogel, T. Fukuda (eds.), *Computational Intelligence: A Dynamic System Perspective*, IEEE Press, Piscataway, NJ, pp. 152–163.

Angeline [1998]: P.J. Angeline, Using selection to improve particle swarm optimization, in *Proceedings of the 1998 IEEE International Conference on Evolutionary Computation*, IEEE Press, pp. 84–89.

Angeline [1998a]: P.J. Angeline, Evolutionary optimization versus particle swarm optimization: Philosophy and performance differences, in V.W. Porto, N. Saravanan, D. Waagen (eds.), *Evolutionary Programming VII: 7th International Conference (EP98)*, San Diego, California, USA, Springer Verlag LNCS 1447, pp. 601–610.

Angeline & Pollack [1993]: P.J. Angeline, J.B. Pollack, Competitive Environments Evolve Better Solutions for Complex Tasks, in *Proceedings of the 5th International Conference on Genetic Algorithms*, University of Illinois, Morgan Kaufman.

Arguello et al [1996]: M.F. Arguello, T.A. Feo, O. Goldschmidt, Randomized Methods for the Number Partitioning Problem, *Computers and Operations Research* **23**(2), pp. 103–111.

Axelrod [1997]: R. Axelrod, The dissemination of culture: A model with local convergence and global polarization, *Journal of Conflict Resolution* **41**, pp. 203–226, reprinted in R. Axelrod [1997], The Complexity of Cooperation, Princeton University Press.

Axelrod & Hamilton [1981]: R. Axelrod, W.D. Hamilton, The Evolution of Cooperation, *Science* **211**, pp. 1390–1396.

Bäck [1996]: T. Bäck, *Evolutionary Algorithms in Theory and Practice*, Oxford University Press.

Bäck et al [1998]: T. Bäck, A.E. Eiben, M.E. Vink, A superior evolutionary algorithm for 3–SAT, in V.W. Porto, N. Saravanan, D. Waagen (eds.), *Evolutionary Programming VII: 7th International Conference (EP98)*, San Diego, California, USA, Springer Verlag LNCS 1447, pp. 125–136.

Badeau et al [1997]: P. Badeau, M. Gendreau, F. Guertin, J.-Y. Potvin, É.D. Taillard, A Parallel Tabu Search Heuristic for the Vehicle Routing Problem with Time Windows, *Transportation Research– C* **5**, pp. 109–122.

Bala et al [1996]: J. Bala, K. De Jong, J. Huang, H. Vafaie, H. Wechsler, Using learning to facilitate the evolution of features for recognizing visual concepts, *Evolutionary Computation* **4**(3), pp. 297–312.

Balas & Niehaus [1998]: E. Balas, E.W. Niehaus, Optimized Crossover–Based Genetic Algorithms for the Maximum Cardinality and Maximum Weight Clique Problems, *Journal of Heuristics* **4**(2), pp. 107–124.

Baluja & Caruana [1995]: S. Baluja, R. Caruana, Removing the Genetics from the Standard Genetic Algorithm, in A. Prieditis, S. Russell (eds.), *Machine Learning: Proceedings of the Twelfth International Conference*, Morgan Kaufmann Publishers, San Francisco, CA, pp. 38–46.

Baluja & Davies [1997]: S. Baluja, S. Davies, *Using Optimal Dependency–Trees for Combinatorial Optimization: Learning the Structure of the Search Space*, Technical Report CMU–CS–97–107, Carnegie Mellon University.

Banzhaf et al [1998]: W. Banzhaf, P. Nordin, R.E. Keller, F.D. Francone, *Genetic Programming: An Introduction: On the Automatic Evolution of Computer Programs and its Applications*, Morgan Kaufmann.

Banzhaf et al [1998a]: W. Banzhaf, R. Poli, M. Schoenauer, T.C. Fogarty (eds.), *Genetic Programming*, Springer LNCS volume 1391.

Barr et al [1995]: R.S. Barr, B.L. Golden, J.P. Kelly, M.G.C. Resende, W. Stewart, Designing and reporting on computational experiments with heuristic methods, *Journal of Heuristics* **1**(1), pp. 9–32.

Battiti & Bertossi [1998]: R. Battiti, A. Bertossi, Differential Greedy for the 0–1 Equicut Problem, in D.Z. Du, P.M. Pardalos (eds.), *Proceedings of the DIMACS Workshop on Network Design: Connectivity and Facilities Location*, American Mathematical Society.

Battiti & Tecchiolli [1994]: R. Battiti, G. Tecchiolli, The Reactive Tabu Search, *ORSA Journal on Computing* **6**(2), pp. 126–140.

Bauer et al [1999]: A. Bauer, B. Bullnheimer, R.F. Hartl, C. Strauss, An Ant Colony Optimization Approach for the Single Machine Total Tardiness Problem, in *Proceedings of the 1999 Congress on Evolutionary Computation (CEC'99)*, Washington, USA.

Bean & Hadj–Alouane [1992]: J.C. Bean, A.B. Hadj–Alouane, *A dual genetic algorithm for bounded integer programs*, Technical Report TR–92–53, Department of Industrial and Operations Engineering, The University of Michigan.

Beasley [1990]: J.E. Beasley, OR–Library: Distributing test problems by electronic mail, *European Journal of Operational Research* **41**, pp. 1069–1072.

Beasley & Chu [1996]: J. Beasley, P.C. Chu, A genetic algorithm for the set covering problem, *European Journal of Operational Research* **94**(2), pp. 393–404.

Beasley & Chu [1998]: J. Beasley, P.C. Chu, A genetic algorithm for the multidimensional knapsack problem, *Journal of Heuristics* **4**, pp. 63–86.

Becker [1967]: O. Becker, Das Helmstädtersche Reihenfolgeproblem – die Effizienz verschiedener Näherungsverfahren, in *Computer uses in the Social Sciences*, Bericht einer Working Conference, Wien.

Belasco [1973]: A. Belasco, *Chess and Draughts: How to Play Scientifically*, Foulsham.

Bennett [1996]: F.H. Bennett III, Automatic creation of an efficient multi–agent architecture using genetic programming with architecture–altering operations, in J.R. Koza, D.E. Goldberg, D.B. Fogel, R.L. Riolo (eds.) *Genetic Programming 1996: Proceedings of the First Annual Conference*, MIT Press, pp. 30–38.

Bentley [1992]: J.L. Bentley, Fast Algorithms for Geometric Traveling Salesman Problems, *ORSA Journal on Computing* **4**(4), pp. 387–411.

Berliner [1973]: H.J. Berliner, Some Necessary Conditions for a Master Chess Program, in *Proceedings of the 3rd International Joint Conference on Artificial Intelligence, CA.*

Bersini & Varela [1991]: H. Bersini, F.J. Varela, The immune recruitment mechanism: A selective evolutionary strategy, in R. K. Belew, L. B. Booker, (eds.), *Proceedings of the Fourth International Conference on Genetic Algorithms*, Morgan Kaufmann, pp. 520–526.

Bersini et al [1996]: H. Bersini, M. Dorigo, L. Gambardella, S. Langerman, G. Seront, Results of the First International Contest on Evolutionary Optimisation (1st ICEO), in *Proceedings of the 1996 IEEE International Conference on Evolutionary Computation*, Nayoga, Japan.

Bertsekas [1995]: D. Bertsekas, *Dynamic Programming and Optimal Control*, Athena Scientific.

Boese [1995]: K.D. Boese, *Cost versus Distance in the Traveling Salesman Problem*, Technical Report TR–950018, UCLA Computer Science Department, 1995.

Boese et al [1994]: K.D. Boese, A.B. Kahng, S. Muddu, A New Adaptive Multi–Start Technique for Combinatorial Global Optimization, *Operations Research Letters* **16**, pp. 101–113.

Bolondi & Bondanza [1993]: M. Bolondi, M. Bondanza, *Parallelizzazione di un algoritmo per la risoluzione del problema del commesso viaggiatore*, Technical Report, Dipartimento di Elettronica, Politecnico di Milano, Italy.

Bonabeau et al [1998]: E. Bonabeau, F. Henaux, S. Guérin, D. Snyers, P. Kuntz, G. Théraulaz, Routing in Telecommunication Networks with 'Smart' Ant–Like Agents, in *Proceedings of IATA '98: Second Int. Workshop on Intelligent Agents for Telecommunication Applications*, Lecture Notes in AI vol. 1437, Springer Verlag.

Bonabeau et al [1999]: E. Bonabeau, M. Dorigo, G. Théraulaz, *From Natural to Artificial Swarm Intelligence*, Oxford University Press.

Bonnizoni et al [1994]: P. Bonnizoni, M. Duella, G. Mauri, *Approximation complexity of longest common subsequence and shortest common supersequence over fixed alphabet*, Technical Report 117/94, Dipartimento di Scienze dell' Informazione, Universitá degli Studi di Milano.

Bovet & Crescenzi [1994]: D. P. Bovet, P. Crescenzi, *Introduction to the Theory of Complexity*, Prentice Hall International (UK) Ltd.

Bowen & Dozier [1995]: J. Bowen, G. Dozier, Solving constraint satisfaction problems using a genetic/systematic search hybride that realizes when to quit, in L.J. Eshelman (ed.) *Proceedings of the 6th International Conference on Genetic Algorithms*, Morgan Kaufmann, pp. 122–129.

Boyd & Richerson [1985]: R. Boyd, P. Richerson. *Culture and the Evolutionary Process*, The University of Chicago Press, London.

Brady [1985]: R.M. Brady, Optimization strategies gleaned from biological evolution, *Nature* **317**, pp. 804–806.

Branke et al [1998]: J. Branke, M. Middendorf, F. Schneider, Improved heuristics and a genetic algorithm for finding short supersequences, *OR–Spektrum* **20**, pp. 39–46.

Braun [1991]: H. Braun, On Solving Traveling Salesman Problems by Genetic Algorithms, in H.–P. Schwefel, R. Männer (eds.), *Parallel Problem Solving from Nature PPSN I*, Springer Verlag LNCS 496, pp. 129–133.

Brave [1996]: S. Brave, Evolving deterministic finite automata using cellular encoding, in J.R. Koza, D.E. Goldberg, D.B. Fogel, R.L. Riolo (eds.), *Genetic Programming 1996: Proceedings of the First Annual Conference*, MIT Press, pp. 39–44.

Brélaz [1979]: D. Brélaz, New methods to color vertices of a graph, *Communications of the ACM* **22**, pp. 251–256.

Bui & Moon [1996]: T.N. Bui, B.R. Moon, Genetic algorithm and graph partitioning, *IEEE Transactions on Computers* **45**(7), pp. 841–855.

Bui & Moon [1998]: T.N. Bui, B.R. Moon, GRCA: A hybrid genetic algorithm for circuit ratio–cut partitioning, *IEEE Transactions on Computer–Aided Design of Integrated Circuits and Systems* **17**(3), pp. 193–204.

Bullnheimer & Strauss [1996]: B. Bullnheimer, C. Strauss, *Tourenplanung mit dem Ant System*, Technical Report 6, Institut für Betriebwirtschaftslehre, University of Vienna, Austria.

Bullnheimer et al [1997]: B. Bullnheimer, R.F. Hartl, C. Strauss, *A New Rank–Based Version of the Ant System: A Computational Study*, Technical Report POM–03/97 Institute of Management Science, University of Vienna, Austria.

Bullnheimer et al [1997a]: B. Bullnheimer, G. Kotsis, C. Strauss, *Parallelization Strategies for the Ant System*, Technical Report POM 9–97, Institute of Management Science, University of Vienna, Austria.

Bullnheimer et al [1997b]: B. Bullnheimer, R.F. Hartl, C. Strauss, An Improved Ant System Algorithm for the Vehicle Routing Problem, Technical Report POM–10/97, Institute of Management Science, University of Vienna, Austria (accepted for publication in *Annals of Operations Research*).

Bullnheimer et al [1999]: B. Bullnheimer, R.F. Hartl, C. Strauss, Applying the Ant System to the Vehicle Routing Problem, in S.Voss, S. Martello, I.H. Osman, C. Roucairol (eds.), *Meta–heuristics: Advances and Trends in Local Search for Optimization*, Kluwer Academic Publishers, Boston, pp. 285–296.

Burkard & Offermann [1977]: R.E. Burkard, J. Offermann, Entwurf von Schreibmaschinentastaturen mittels quadratischer Zuordnungsprobleme, *Zeitschrift für Operations Research* 21, pp. B121–B132.

Burkard & Rendl [1984]: R.E. Burkard, F. Rendl, A Thermodynamically Motivated Simulation Procedure for Combinatorial Optimization Problems, *European Journal of Operational Research* 17, pp. 169–174.

Burke & Smith [1997]: E.K. Burke, A.J. Smith, A Memetic Algorithm for the Maintenance Scheduling Problem, in *Proceedings of the ICONIP/ANZIIS/ANNES'97 Conference*, Dunedin, New Zealand, Springer, pp. 469–472.

Burke et al [1995]: E.K. Burke, D.G. Elliman, R.F. Weare, A Hybrid Genetic Algorithm for Highly Constrained Timetabling Problems, in L.J. Eshelman (ed.) *Proceedings of the Sixth International Conference on Genetic Algorithms*, Morgan Kaufmann, pp. 605–610.

Burke et al [1996]: E.K. Burke, J.P. Newall, R.F. Weare, A Memetic Algorithm for Univerisity Exam Timetabling, in E.K. Burke & P. Ross (eds.), *The Practice and Theory of Automated Timetabling*, Springer Verlag LNCS 1153, pp. 241–250.

Cao & Wu [1997]: Y.J. Cao, Q.H. Wu, Mechanical design optimization by mixed–variable evolutionary programming, in *Proceedings of the 1997 IEEE Conference on Evolutionary Computation*, IEEE Press, pp. 443–446.

Cardinale & O'Donnell [1999]: K.J. Cardinale, H. O'Donnell, *A Constructive Induction Approach to Computer Immunology*, Masters Thesis, Technical Report AFIT/GCE/ENG/99M–02, Graduate School of Engineering, Air Force Institute of Technology, Wright–Patterson AFB.

Carrizo et al [1992]: J. Carrizo, F.G. Tinetti, P. Moscato, A Computational Ecology for the Quadratic Assignment Problem, in *Proceedings of the 21st Meeting on Informatics and Operations Research*, SADIO, Buenos Aires.

Cavalli–Sforza & Feldman [1969]: L.L. Cavalli–Sforza, M.W. Feldman, Models for Cultural Inheritance, *Theoretical Population Biology* 4.

Chanas & Kobylanski [1996]: S. Chanas, P. Kobylanski, A New Heuristic Algorithm Solving the Linear Ordering Problem, *Computational Optimization and Applications* 6, pp. 191–205.

Chardaire & Sutter [1995]: P. Chardaire, A. Sutter, A Decomposition Method for Quadratic Zero–One Programming, *Management Science* 41, pp. 704–712.

Chen & Tsao [1993]: J.L. Chen, Y.C. Tsao, Optimal design of machine elements using genetic algorithms. *Journal of the Chinese Society of Mechanical Engineers* 14(2), pp. 193–199.

Cheng & Gen [1997]: R.W. Cheng, M. Gen, Parallel machine scheduling problems using memetic algorithms, *Computers & Industrial Engineering* 33(34), pp. 761–764.

Chiang & Russel [1993]: W.C. Chiang, R. Russel, *Hybrid Heuristics for the Vehicle Routing Problem with Time Windows*, Working Paper, Department of Quantitative Methods, University of Tulsa, OK, USA.

Chisholm [1976]: K.J. Chisholm, *DRAFT5: A Learning Draughts Program*, B.Sc. Thesis, University of Edinburgh.

Chisholm & Bradbeer [1997]: K.J. Chisholm, P.V.G. Bradbeer, Machine Learning Using a Genetic Algorithm to Optimise a Draughts Program Board Evaluation Function, in *Proceedings of the IEEE International Conference on Evolutionary Computation (ICEC '97)*, Indianapolis, USA, IEEE Press.

Chu & Beasley [1997]: P.C. Chu & J. Beasley, A genetic algorithm for the generalised assignment problem, *Computers & Operations Research* **24**, pp. 17–23.

Chung [1997]: C.J. Chung, *Knowledge–Based Approaches to Self–Adaptation in Cultural Algorithms*, PhD thesis, Wayne State University, Detroit, Michigan.

Coffman et al [1993]: E.G. Coffman, D.S. Johnson, G.S. Lueker, P.W. Shor, Probabilistic Analysis of Packing and Related Partitioning Problems, *Statistical Science* **8**(1), pp. 40–47.

Connolly [1990]: D.T. Connolly, An Improved Annealing Scheme for the QAP, *European Journal of Operational Research* **49**, pp. 93–100.

Consiglio & Zenios [1997]: A. Consiglio, S.A. Zenios, A Model for Designing Callable Bonds and its Solution Using Tabu Search. *Journal of Economic Dynamics and Control* **21**, pp. 1445–1470.

Cook [1971]: S.A. Cook, The complexity of theorem–proving procedures, in *Proceedings of the 3rd Annual ACM Symposium on the Theory of Computing*, pp. 151–158.

Cordone & Wolfler–Calvo [1997]: R.Cordone, R.Wolfler–Calvo, *A Heuristic Algorithm for the Vehicle Routing Problem with Time Windows*, Technical Report 97–012, Dipartimento di Elettronica, Politecnico di Milano, Italy.

Costa [1995]: D. Costa, An evolutionary tabu search algorithm and the NHL scheduling problem, *INFOR* **33**(3), pp. 161–178.

Costa & Hertz [1997]: D. Costa, A. Hertz, Ants Can Colour Graphs, *Journal of the Operational Research Society* **48**, pp. 295–305.

Costa et al [1995]: D. Costa, N. Dubuis, A. Hertz, Embedding of a sequential procedure within an evolutionary algorithm for coloring problems in graphs, *Journal of Heuristics* **1**(1), pp. 105–128.

Cottarelli & Gobbi [1997]: M. Cottarelli, A. Gobbi, *Estensioni dell'algoritmo formiche per il problema del commesso viaggiatore*, Master's thesis, Dipartimento di Elettronica e Informazione, Politecnico di Milano, Italy.

Coy et al [1998]: S.P. Coy, B.L. Golden, G. Runger, E. Wasil, See the Forest Before the Trees: Finetuned Learning and its Application to the Traveling Salesman Problem, *IEEE Transactions on Systems, Man, and Cybernetics* **28**(4), pp. 454–464.

Coy et al [1998a]: S.P Coy, B.L Golden, E. Wasil, A Computational Study of Smoothing Heuristics for the Traveling Salesman Problem, Research report, University of Maryland, to appear in *European Journal of Operational Research*.

Cramer [1985]: N.L. Cramer, A Representation for the Adaptive Generation of Simple Sequential Programs, in J.J. Grefenstette (ed.), *Proceedings of an International Conference on Genetic Algorithms and Their Applications*, Lawrence Erlbaum Associates, Hillsdale NJ, pp. 183–187.

Crowston et al [1963]: W.B. Crowston, F. Glover, G.L. Thompson, J.D. Trawick, Probabilistic and Parametric Learning Combinations of Local Job Shop Scheduling Rules, in *ONR Research Memorandum No. 117*, GSIA, Carnegie Mellon University, Pittsburgh, PA.

Cung et al [1997]: V.D. Cung, T. Mautor, P. Michelon, A. Tavares, A Scatter Search Based Approach for the Quadratic Assignment Problem, in T. Bäck, Z. Michalewicz, X. Yao (eds.), *Proceedings of ICEC'97*, IEEE Press, pp. 165–170.

Dasgupta [1998]: D. Dasgupta, An Artificial Immune System as a Multi–Agent Decision Support System, in *Proceedings of the 1998 IEEE International Conference on Systems, Man, and Cybernetics*, IEEE Press, pp. 3816–3820.

Dasgupta [1999]: D. Dasgupta (ed.), *Artificial Immune Systems and Their Applications*, Springer–Verlag.

Dasgupta & Attoh–Okine [1997]: D. Dasgupta, N. Attoh–Okine, Immunity–Based Systems: A Survey, in *Proceedings of the IEEE International Conference on Systems, Man and Cybernetics (SMC'97)*, Volume 1, pp. 369–374.

Davidor [1990]: Y. Davidor, Epistasis Variance: Suitability of a Representation to Genetic Algorithms, *Complex Systems* **4**(4), pp. 369–383.

Davis [1985]: L Davis, Job shop scheduling with genetic algorithms, in J.J Grefenstette (ed.), *Proceedings of the 1st International Conference on Genetic Algorithms and Their Applications*, Lawrence Erlbaum Associates, Hillsdale New Jersey, pp. 136–140.

Davis [1988]: L.D. Davis, Applying Adaptive Algorithms to Epistatic Domains, in *Proceedings of the International Joint Conference on Artificial Intelligence – IJCAI–88*.

Dawkins [1990]: R. Dawkins, *The Selfish Gene*, Oxford University Press.

De Bonet et al [1997]: J.S. De Bonet, C.L. Isbell Jr., P. Viola, MIMIC: Finding Optima by Estimating Probability Densities, in M. Jordan, M. Mozer, M. Perrone (eds.), *Advances in Neural Information Processing Systems*, volume 9, MIT Press, pp. 424–430.

De Jong [1975]: K.A. De Jong, *An analysis of the behavior of a class of genetic adaptive systems*, PhD thesis, University of Michigan.

De Jong [1993]: K. De Jong, Genetic Algorithms are NOT function optimizers, in D. Whitley (ed.), *Foundations of Genetic Algorithms 2*, Morgan Kaufmann, pp. 5–17.

Di Caro & Dorigo [1997]: G. Di Caro, M. Dorigo, *AntNet: A mobile agents approach to adaptive routing*, Technical Report IRIDIA/97–12, IRIDIA, Université Libre de Bruxelles, Belgium.

Di Caro & Dorigo [1998]: G. Di Caro, M. Dorigo, AntNet: Distributed Stigmergetic Control for Communications Networks, *Journal of Artificial Intelligence Research (JAIR)* **9**, pp. 317–365.

Di Caro & Dorigo [1998a]: G. Di Caro, M. Dorigo, Two Ant Colony Algorithms for Best–Effort Routing in Datagram Networks, in *Proceedings of the Tenth IASTED International Conference on Parallel and Distributed Computing and Systems (PDCS'98)*, IASTED/ACTA Press, pp. 541–546.

Di Caro & Dorigo [1998b]: G. Di Caro, M. Dorigo, Extending AntNet for best–effort Quality–of–Service routing, unpublished presentation at *ANTS'98: From Ant Colonies to Artificial Ants: First International Workshop on Ant Colony Optimization*, Bruxelles, Belgium, October 15–16.

Dickey & Hopkins [1972]: J.W. Dickey, J.W. Hopkins, Campus Building Arrangement Using TOPAZ, *Transportation Science* **6**, pp. 59–68.

Dickmanns et al [1987]: D. Dickmanns, J. Schmidhuber, A. Winklhofer, *Der genetische Algorithmus: Eine Implementierung in Prolog*. Fortgeschrittenenpraktikum, Institut für Informatik, Lehrstuhl Prof. Radig, Technische Universität München.

Dixon et al [1997]: E.L. Dixon, C. Pantsios Markhauser, K.R. Rao, Object motion estimation technique for video images based on a genetic algorithm, *IEEE Transactions on Consumer Electronics* **43**(3).

Dongarra [1997]: J.J. Dongarra, *Performance of Various Computers Using Standard Linear Equations Software*, Technical Report CS–89–85, Computer Science Department, University of Tennesse, USA.

Donnelly et al [1994]: P. Donnelly, P. Corr, D. Crookes, Evolving Go Playing Strategy in Neural Networks, in T.C. Fogarty (ed.), *Evolutionary Computing: Selected Papers from the 1994 AISB Workshop*, Springer Verlag LNCS 865.

Dorigo [1992]: M. Dorigo, *Optimization, Learning and Natural Algorithms*, PhD Thesis (in Italian), Dipartimento di Elettronica, Politecnico di Milano, Italy.

Dorigo [1993]: M. Dorigo, *Parallel Ant System: An Experimental Study*, unpublished manuscript.

Dorigo & Gambardella [1997]: M. Dorigo and L.M. Gambardella, Ant Colony System: A Cooperative Learning Approach to the Traveling Salesman Problem, *IEEE Transactions on Evolutionary Computation* **1**(1), pp. 53–66.

Dorigo & Gambardella [1997a]: M. Dorigo and L.M. Gambardella, Ant Colonies for the Traveling Salesman Problem, *BioSystems* **43**, pp. 73–81.

Dorigo et al [1991]: M. Dorigo, V. Maniezzo, A. Colorni, *Positive feedback as a search strategy*, Technical Report 91–016, Dipartimento di Elettronica, Politecnico di Milano, Italy.

Dorigo et al [1996]: M. Dorigo, V. Maniezzo, A. Colorni, The Ant System: Optimization by a colony of cooperating agents, *IEEE Transactions on Systems, Man, and Cybernetics: Part B*, **26**(1), pp. 29–41.

Dorigo et al [1998]: M. Dorigo, G. Di Caro, L.M. Gambardella, Ant Algorithms for Discrete Optimization, Technical Report IRIDIA/98–10, Université Libre de Bruxelles, Belgium (accepted for publication in *Artificial Life*).

Dorne & Hao [1998]: R. Dorne, J.K. Hao, A New Genetic Local Search Algorithm for Graph Coloring, in A.E. Eiben, T. Bäck, M. Schoenauer, H.–P. Schwefel (eds.), *Parallel Problem Solving from Nature – PPSN V*, Springer–Verlag LNCS 1498, pp. 745–754.

Dozier et al [1994]: G. Dozier, J. Bowen, D. Bahler, Solving small and large constraint satisfaction problems using a heuristic–based microgenetic algorithm, in *Proceedings of the 1st IEEE International Conference on Evolutionary Computation*, IEEE Press, pp. 306–311.

Dozier et al [1995]: G. Dozier, J. Bowen, D. Bahler, Solving randomly generated constraint satisfaction problems using a micro–evolutionary hybrid that evolves a population of hill–climbers, in *Proceedings of the 2nd IEEE International Conference on Evolutionary Computation*, IEEE Press, pp. 614–619.

Dracopoulos & Kent [1996]: D.C. Dracopoulos, S. Kent, Speeding up genetic programming: A parallel BSP implementation, in J.R. Koza, D.E. Goldberg, D.B. Fogel, R.L. Riolo (eds.) *Genetic Programming 1996: Proceedings of the First Annual Conference*, MIT Press, page 421.

Dunham et al [1961]: Dunham, Fridshal, Fridshal, North, *Design by Natural Selection*, RC 476, IBM Research Department, June 20th.

Durham [1991]: W. Durham, *Co–evolution: Genes, Culture, and Human Diversity*, Stanford University Press.

Dzubera & Whitley [1994]: J. Dzubera, D. Whitley, Advanced Correlation Analysis of Operators for the Traveling Salesman Problem, in H.–P. Schwefel, R. Männer (eds.), *Parallel Problem Solving from Nature – PPSN III*, Springer Verlag LNCS 866, pp. 68–77.

Eberhart et al [1996]: R.C. Eberhart, R. Dobbins, P. Simpson, *Computational Intelligence PC Tools*, Academic Press, Boston.

Ehrenburg [1996]: H. Ehrenburg, Improved direct acyclic graph handling and the combine operator in genetic programming, in J.R. Koza, D.E. Goldberg, D.B. Fogel, R.L. Riolo (eds.) *Genetic Programming 1996: Proceedings of the First Annual Conference*, MIT Press, pp. 285–291.

Eiben [1997]: A.E. Eiben, *Constraint satisfaction by evolutionary algorithms*, Leiden University Technical Report, July, available at www.wi.leidenuniv.nl/~gusz/icga97.ps.gz.

Eiben & van der Hauw [1996]: A.E. Eiben, J.K. van der Hauw, *Graph coloring with adaptive evolutionary algorithms*, Technical Report TR-96-11, Leiden University, also available as www.wi.leidenuniv.nl/~gusz/graphcol.ps.gz .

Eiben & van der Hauw [1997]: A.E. Eiben, J.K. van der Hauw, Adaptive penalties for evolutionary graph–coloring, in J.K. Hao, E.Lutton, E.Ronald, M.Schoenauer, D.Snyers (eds.), *Artificial Evolution '97*, Springer LNCS 1363, pp. 95–106.

Eiben & van der Hauw [1997a]: A.E. Eiben, J.K. van der Hauw, Solving 3–SAT with adaptive Genetic Algorithms, in *Proceedings of the 4th IEEE Conference on Evolutionary Computation*, IEEE Press, pp. 81–86.

Eiben & Ruttkay [1996]: A.E. Eiben, Zs. Ruttkay, Self–adaptivity for constraint satisfaction: Learning penalty functions, in *Proceedings of the 3rd IEEE Conference on Evolutionary Computation*, IEEE Press, pp. 258–261.

Eiben & Ruttkay [1997]: A.E. Eiben, Zs. Ruttkay, Constraint Satisfaction Problems, in T. Bäck, D. Fogel, M. Michalewicz (eds.), *Handbook of Evolutionary Computation*, IOP Publishing Ltd. and Oxford University Press, pp. C5.7:1–C5.7:8.

Eiben et al [1994]: A.E. Eiben, P.E. Raué, Zs. Ruttkay, Repairing, adding constraints and learning as a means of improving GA performance on CSPs, in J.C. Bioch, S.H. Nienhuiys–Cheng (eds.),

Proceedings of the 4th Belgian Dutch Conference on Machine Learning, Number 94–05 in EUR–CS, Erasmus University Press, pp. 112–123.

Eiben et al [1995]: A.E. Eiben, P.E. Raué, Zs. Ruttkay, Constrained Problems, in L. Chambers (ed.), *Practical Handbook of Genetic Algorithms*, CRC Press, pp. 307–365.

Eiben et al [1998]: A.E. Eiben, J.I. van Hemert, E. Marchiori, A.G. Steenbeek, Solving binary constraint satisfaction problems using evolutionary algorithms with an adaptive fitness function. in A.E. Eiben, T. Bäck, M. Schoenauer, H.–P. Schwefel (eds.), *Proceedings of the 5th Conference on Parallel Problem Solving from Nature*, Springer LNCS 1498, pp. 196–205.

Eiselt & Laporte [1991]: H.A. Eiselt, G. Laporte, A Combinatorial Optimization Problem Arising in Dartboard Design, *Journal of the Operational Research Society* 42, pp. 113–118.

Elshafei [1977]: A.N. Elshafei, Hospital Layout as a Quadratic Assignment Problem, *Operations Research Quarterly* 28, pp. 167–179.

Eshelman [1991]: L.J. Eshelman, The CHC Adaptive Search Algorithm: How to Have Safe Search When Engaging in Nontraditional Genetic Recombination, in G.J.E. Rawlins (ed.), *Foundations of Genetic Algorithms*, Morgan Kaufmann, pp. 265–283.

Eshelman & Schaffer [1991]: L.J. Eshelman, J.D. Schaffer, Preventing Premature Convergence in Genetic Algorithms by Preventing Incest, in R. K. Belew, L. B. Booker, (eds.), *Proceedings of the Fourth International Conference on Genetic Algorithms*, Morgan Kaufmann, pp. 115–122.

Eshelman & Schaffer [1993]: L.J. Eshelman, J.D. Schaffer, Real coded genetic algorithms and interval schemata, in L.D. Whitley (ed.), *Foundations of Genetic Algorithms* 2, Morgan Kaufmann, pp. 187–202.

Etzioni & Weld [1994]: O. Etzioni, D. Weld, A Softbot–Based Interface to the Internet, *Communications of the ACM* 37(7), pp. 72–80.

Falkenauer [1994]: E. Falkenauer, A new representation and operators for genetic algorithms applied to grouping problems, *Evolutionary Computation* 2(2), pp. 123–144.

Falkenauer [1996]: E. Falkenauer, A hybrid grouping genetic algorithm for bin packing, *Journal of Heuristics* 2, pp. 5–30.

Fang et al [1993]: H–L. Fang, P. Ross, D. Corne, A promising GA approach to job–shop scheduling, rescheduling and open–shop scheduling, in *Proceedings of 5th International Conference on Genetic Algorithms*, Morgan Kaufmann, San Mateo, pp. 375–382.

Farmer et al [1986]: J.D. Farmer, N.H. Packard, A.S. Perelson, The immune system, adaptation, and machine learning. *Physica D* 22, pp. 187–204.

Ferreira & Fontanari [1998]: F.F. Ferreira, J.F. Fontanari, Probabilistic analysis of the number partitioning problem, *Journal of Physics A: Math. Gen.*, pp. 3417–3428.

Ferreira & Zerovnik [1993]: A.G. Ferreira, J. Zerovnik, Bounding the probability of success of stochastic methods for global optimization, *Computers & Mathematics with Applications* 25 pp. 1–8.

Fiduccia & Mattheyses [1982]: C.M. Fiduccia, R.M. Mattheyses, A Linear–Time Heuristic for Improving Network Partitions, in *Proceedings of the 19th ACM/IEEE Design Automation Conference DAC 82*, pp. 175—181.

Fischer [1995]: S.T. Fischer, A note on the complexity of local search problems, *Information Processing Letters* 53(1), pp. 69–75.

Fischetti & Martello [1987]: M. Fischetti, S. Martello, Worst–Case Analysis Of The Differencing Method for the Partition Problem, *Mathematical Programming* 37(1), pp. 117–120.

Fisher [1936]: R.A. Fisher, The use of multiple measurements in taxonomic problems, *Annals of Eugenics* 7, pp. 179–188.

Fisher [1994]: M.L. Fisher, Optimal Solution of Vehicle Routing Problems Using Minimum K–trees, *Operations Research* 42, 1994, pp. 626–642.

Flannery [1971]: K. Flannery, Archaeological systems theory and early Meso–America, in S. Streuver (ed.), *Prehistoric Agriculture*, Natural History Press, Garden City, New York, pp. 80–100.

Fleurent & Ferland [1994]: C. Fleurent, J.A. Ferland, Genetic Hybrids for the Quadratic Assignment Problem, in P.M. Pardalos, H. Wolkowicz (eds.) *Quadratic assignment and related problems,*

DIMACS Series on Discrete Mathematics and Theoretical Computer Science, volume 16, American Mathematical Society, pp. 173–187.

Fleurent & Ferland [1996]: C. Fleurent, J.A. Ferland, Genetic and hybrid algorithms for graph coloring, *Annals of Operations Research* **63**, pp. 437–461.

Fleurent & Glover [1999]: C. Fleurent, F. Glover, Improved Constructive Multistart Strategies for the Quadratic Assignment Problem Using Adaptive Memory, *INFORMS Journal on Computing* **11**(2), pp. 198–204.

Fleurent et al [1996]: C. Fleurent, F. Glover, P. Michelon, Z. Valli, A Scatter Search Approach for Unconstrained Continuous Optimization, in *Proceedings of the 1996 IEEE International Conference on Evolutionary Computation*, IEEE Press, pp. 643–648.

Flood [1956]: M. M. Flood, The Traveling Salesman Problem, *Operations Research* **4**(1), pp. 61–75.

Fogel [1995]: D.B. Fogel, *Evolutionary Computation: Toward a New Philosophy of Machine Intelligence*, IEEE Press.

Fogel [1998]: D.B. Fogel (ed.), *Evolutionary Computation: The Fossil Record*, IEEE Press, 1998.

Fogel [1998a]: D.B. Fogel, An Introduction to Evolutionary Computation, in D.B. Fogel (ed.), *Evolutionary Computation: The Fossil Record*, IEEE Press, pp. 1–2.

Fogel et al [1966]: L.J. Fogel, A.J. Owens, M.J. Walsh, *Artificial Intelligence through Simulated Evolution*, John Wiley & Sons.

Forrest & Perelson [1991]: S. Forrest, A.S. Perelson, Genetic algorithms and the immune system, in *Proceedings of the 1st International Conference on Parallel Problem Solving from Nature* (*PPSN I*), Springer–Verlag, Berlin (Lecture Notes in Computer Science).

Forrest et al [1993]: S. Forrest, B. Javornik, R. Smith, A.S. Perelson, Using genetic algorithms to explore pattern recognition in the immune system, *Evolutionary Computation* **1**(3), pp. 191–211.

Forrest et al [1994]: S. Forrest, A.S. Perelson, L. Allen, R. Cherukuri, Self–Nonself Discrimination in a Computer, in *Proceedings of the IEEE Symposium on Research in Security and Privacy*, Oakland, CA, pp. 202–212.

Forrest et al [1997]: S. Forrest, S.A. Hofmeyr, A. Somayaji, Computer Immunology, *Communications of the ACM* **40**(10), pp. 88–96.

Fortman [1982]: R. Fortman, *Basic Checkers*, available from the American Checkers Federation.

Foulser et al [1992]: D.E. Foulser, M. Li, Q. Yang, Theory and algorithms for plan merging, *Artificial Intelligence* **57**, pp. 143–181.

Frank [1996]: J. Frank, Weighting for Godot: Learning heuristics for GSAT, in *Proceedings of the AAAI International Conference on Artificial Intelligence*, pp. 338–343.

Frank [1996a]: J. Frank, *Learning short–term weights for GSAT*, Technical report, University of California at Davis, available as http://rainier.cs.ucdavis.edu/~frank/decay.ml96.ps

Fraser [1995]: C.B. Fraser, *Subsequences and Supersequences of Strings*, PhD thesis, Dept. of Computer Science, University of Glasgow, UK.

Fredman et al [1995]: M.L. Fredman, D.S. Johnson, L.A. McGeoch, G. Ostheimer, Data Structures for Traveling Salesmen, *Journal of Algorithms* **18**, pp. 432–479.

Freilich [1977]: M. Freilich, The meaning of socio–cultural, in B. Bernardi (ed.), *The Concept and Dynamics of Culture*, Mouton Press, The Hague: pp 90–91.

Freisleben & Merz [1996]: B. Freisleben, P. Merz, New Genetic Local Search Operators for the Traveling Salesman Problem, in H.–M. Voigt, W. Ebeling, I. Rechenberg, H.–P. Schwefel (eds.), *Proceedings of the 4th International Conference on Parallel Problem Solving from Nature - PPSN IV*, Springer Verlag LNCS 1141, pp. 890–900.

Freisleben & Merz [1996a]: B. Freisleben, P. Merz, A Genetic Local Search Algorithm for Solving Symmetric and Asymmetric Traveling Salesman Problems, in *Proceedings of the 1996 IEEE International Conference on Evolutionary Computation*, IEEE Press, pp. 616–621.

Freville & Plateau [1986]: A. Freville, G. Plateau, Heuristics and Reduction Methods for Multiple Constraint 0–1 Linear Programming Problems, *European Journal of Operational Research* **24**, pp. 206–215.

Freville & Plateau [1993]: A. Freville, G. Plateau, An Exact Search for the Solution of the Surrogate Dual of the 0–1 Bidimensional Knapsack Problem, *European Journal of Operational Research* **68**, pp. 413–421.

Fu et al [1991]: J.–F. Fu, R.G. Fenton, W.L. Cleghorn, A mixed integer–discrete–continuous programming method and its application to engineering design optimization, *Engineering Optimization* **17**(4), pp. 263–280.

Gale & Shapley [1962]: D. Gale, L.S. Shapley, College admissions and the stability of marriage, *American Mathematical Monthly* **69**, pp. 6–15.

Galinier & Hao [1998]: P. Galinier, J.K. Hao, Hybrid Evolutionary Algorithms for Graph Coloring, submitted to the *Journal of Combinatorial Optimization*.

Gambardella & Dorigo [1995]: L.M. Gambardella, M. Dorigo, Ant–Q: A Reinforcement Learning Approach to the Traveling Salesman Problem, in *Proceedings of the Twelfth International Conference on Machine Learning, ML–95*, Morgan Kaufmann, Palo Alto, pp. 252–260.

Gambardella & Dorigo [1996]: L.M. Gambardella, M. Dorigo, Solving Symmetric and Asymmetric TSPs by Ant Colonies, in *Proceedings of the IEEE Conference on Evolutionary Computation, ICEC96*, IEEE Press, pp. 622–627.

Gambardella & Dorigo [1997]: L.M. Gambardella, M. Dorigo, HAS–SOP: *An Hybrid Ant System for the Sequential Ordering Problem*, IDSIA Technical Report IDSIA–11–97, IDSIA, Lugano, Switzerland.

Gambardella et al [1999]: M. Gambardella, É.D. Taillard, M. Dorigo, Ant Colonies for the Quadratic Assignment Problem, *Journal of the Operational Research Society* **50**, pp. 167–176.

Garey & Johnson [1979]: M.R. Garey, D.S. Johnson, *Computers and Intractability*, W.H. Freeman and Company.

Gargano et al [1993]: M.L. Gargano, P. Chamoun, D.L. von Kleeck, Using Genetic Algorithms to Solve Financial Portfolio Problems Related to Optimal Allocation, Portfolio Insurance and Performance Prediction, in *Proceedings of the Second Annual International Conference on AI Application on Wall Street: Tactical and Strategic Computing Technologies*, New York, NY, USA.

Geertz [1973]: C. Geertz, *The Interpretation of Culture: Selected Essays*, Basic Books, New York.

Gen & Cheng [1997]: M. Gen & R. Cheng, *Genetic Algorithms and Engineering Design*, John Wiley & Sons Ltd, Wiley Series in Engineering Design and Automation.

Gent & Walsh [1993]: I. Gent, T. Walsh, *The enigma of SAT hill–climbing procedures*, Technical Report 605, Department of Artificial Intelligence, University of Edinburgh.

Gent & Walsh [1993a]: I. Gent, T. Walsh, Towards an understanding of hill–climbing procedures for SAT, in *Proceedings of the AAAI Conference on Artificial Intelligence*, pp. 28–33.

Gent & Walsh [1995]: I. Gent, T. Walsh, Unsatisfied variables in local search, in J. Hallam (ed.), *Hybrid Problems, Hybrid Solutions*, IOS Press, pp. 73–85.

Gent & Walsh [1998]: I. Gent, T. Walsh, Analysis of heuristics for number partitioning, *Computational Intelligence* **14**(3), pp. 430–451.

Geoffrion & Graves [1976]: A.M. Geoffrion, G.W. Graves, Scheduling Parallel Production Lines with Changeover Costs: Practical Applications of a Quadratic Assignment/LP Approach, *Operations Research* **24**, pp. 595–610.

Gilmore [1962]: P.C. Gilmore, Optimal and Suboptimal Algorithms for the Quadratic Assignment Problem, *Journal of the SIAM* **10**, pp. 305–313.

Glover [1963]: F. Glover, Parametric Combinations of Local Job Shop Rules, in *ONR Research Memorandum no. 117*, GSIA, Carnegie Mellon University, Chapter IV.

Glover [1965]: F. Glover, A Multiphase Dual Algorithm for the Zero–One Integer Programming Problem, *Operations Research* **13**(6), p. 879.

Glover [1975]: F. Glover, Surrogate Constraint Duality in Mathematical Programming, *Operations Research* **23**, pp. 434–451.

Glover [1977]: F. Glover, Heuristics for Integer Programming Using Surrogate Constraints, *Decision Sciences* **8**(1), pp. 156–166.

Glover [1989]: F. Glover, Tabu Search Part I, *ORSA Journal on Computing* **1**, pp. 190–206.

Glover [1990]: F. Glover, Tabu Search Part II, *ORSA Journal on Computing* **2**, pp. 4–32.

Glover [1992]: F. Glover, Ejection Chains, Reference Structures and Alternating Path Methods for Traveling Salesman Problems, Research Report, University of Colorado. Shortened version published in *Discrete Applied Mathematics* **65**, pp. 223–253.

Glover [1994]: F. Glover, Genetic Algorithms And Scatter Search – Unsuspected Potentials. *Statistics and Computing* **4**(2), pp. 131–140.

Glover [1994a]: F. Glover, Optimization by Ghost Image Processes in Neural Networks, *Computers and Operations Research* **21**(8), pp. 801–822.

Glover [1994b]: F. Glover, Tabu Search for Nonlinear and Parametric Optimization (with links to genetic algorithms), *Discrete Applied Mathematics* **49**, pp. 231–255.

Glover [1995]: F. Glover, Scatter Search And Star–Paths: Beyond The Genetic Metaphor, *OR Spektrum* **17**(2–3), pp. 125–137.

Glover [1996]: F. Glover, Búsqueda Tabú, in *Optimización Heurística y Redes Neuronales*, (Belarmino Adenso Diaz, ed.), Editorial Paraninfo, Madrid, pp. 105–142.

Glover [1996a]: F. Glover, Tabu search and adaptive memory programming - advances, applications, and challenges, in R.S. Barr, R.V. Helgason, J.L. Kennington (eds.), *Interfaces in Computer Science and Operations Research*, Kluwer Academic Publishers, Norwell, MA, pp. 1–75.

Glover [1998]: F. Glover, A Template for Scatter Search and Path Relinking, in J.K. Hao, E. Lutton, E. Ronald, M. Schoenauer, D. Snyers (eds.), *Artificial Evolution*, Springer LNCS 1363, pp. 13–54.

Glover & Laguna [1995]: F. Glover, M. Laguna, *Tabu Search*, in C.R. Reeves (ed.), *Modern Heuristic Techniques for Combinatorial Problems*, Chapter 3, McGraw–Hill (originally published in 1993 by Blackwell Scientific).

Glover & Laguna [1997]: F. Glover, M. Laguna, *Tabu Search*, Kluwer Academic Publishers, Boston.

Glover & McMillan [1986]: F. Glover, C. McMillan, The General Employee Scheduling Problem: An Integration of MS and AI, *Computers and Operations Research* **13**(5), pp. 563–573.

Glover et al [1996]: F. Glover, J.P. Kelly, M. Laguna, New Advances and Applications of Combining Simulation and Optimization, in J.M. Charnes, D.J. Morrice, D.T. Brunner, J.J. Swain (eds.), *Proceedings of the 1996 Winter Simulation Conference*, pp. 144–152.

Glover et al [1998]: F. Glover, G. Kochenberger, B. Alidaee, Adaptive Memory Tabu Search for binary Quadratic Programs, *Management Science* **44**, pp. 336–345.

Glover et al [1998a]: F. Glover, B. Alidaee, M. Amini, G. Kochenberger, *Using Reformulation and Tabu Search to Solve Quadratic Knapsack Problems*, Working Paper, University of Colorado (at Denver).

Glover et al [1999]: F. Glover, A. Løkketangen, D. Woodruff, *Scatter Search to Generate Diverse MIP Solutions*, Research Report, University of Colorado, Boulder.

Goldberg [1989]: D.E. Goldberg, *Genetic Algorithms in Search, Optimization and Machine Learning*, Addison–Wesley.

Goldberg & Lingle [1985]: D.E. Goldberg, R. Lingle, Alleles, loci and the traveling salesman problem, in J.J Grefenstette (ed.), *Proceedings of the 1st International Conference on Genetic Algorithms and Their Applications*, Lawrence Erlbaum Associates, Hillsdale New Jersey, pp. 154–159.

Golden & Stewart [1985]: B.L. Golden, W.R. Stewart, Empirical analysis of heuristics, in E.L. Lawler, J.K. Lenstra, A.H.G. Rinnooy Kan, D.B. Shmoys (eds.), *The Traveling Salesman Problem: A Guided Tour of Combinatorial Optimization*, John Wiley & Sons, Chichester, pp. 207–249.

Goodenough [1981]: W. Goodenough. *Culture, language, and Society*, Benjamin/Cummings Press, Menlo Park, California.

Gorges–Schleuter [1989]: M. Gorges–Schleuter, ASPARAGOS: An Asynchronous Parallel Genetic Optimization Strategy, in J.D. Schaffer (ed.), *Proceedings of the 3rd International Conference on Genetic Algorithms*, Morgan Kaufmann, pp. 422–427.

Gorges–Schleuter [1991]: M. Gorges–Schleuter, Explicit Parallelism of Genetic Algorithms through Population Structures, in H. Schwefel, R. Männer (eds.), *Parallel Problem Solving from Nature*, Springer Verlag Lecture Notes in Computer Science, pp. 150–159.

Gorges–Schleuter [1991a]: M. Gorges–Schleuter, *Genetic Algorithms and Population Structures: A Massively Parallel Algorithm*, PhD thesis, University of Dortmund, Germany.

Goss et al [1989]: S. Goss, S. Aron, J.L. Deneubourg, J.M. Pasteels, Self–organized shortcuts in the Argentine ant, *Naturwissenschaften* **76**, pp. 579–581.

Grassé [1959]: P. P. Grassé, La reconstruction du nid et les coordinations interindividuelles chez Bellicositermes Natalensis et Cubitermes sp. La théorie de la stigmergie: essai d'interprétation du comportement des termites constructeurs, *Insectes Sociaux* **6**, pp. 41–81.

Greenberg & Pierskalla [1970]: H.J. Greenberg, W.P. Pierskalla, Surrogate Mathematical Programs, *Operations Research* **18**, pp. 924–939.

Greenberg & Pierskalla [1973]: H.J. Greenberg, W.P. Pierskalla, Quasi–conjugate Functions and Surrogate Duality, *Cahiers du Centre d'Etudes de Recherche Operationelle*, **15**, pp. 437–448.

Grefenstette [1984]: J.J Grefenstette, Genesis: A system for using genetic search procedures, in *Proceedings of a Conference on Intelligent Systems and Machines*, Rochester, MI, pp. 161–165.

Grefenstette [1987]: J.J. Grefenstette, Incorporating Problem Specific Knowledge into Genetic Algorithms, in L. Davis (ed.), *Genetic Algorithms and Simulated Annealing*, Morgan Kaufmann, pp. 42–60.

Grim [1997]: P. Grim, The undecidability of the spatialized prisoner's dilemma, *Theory and Decision* **42**(1), pp. 53–80.

Grötschel et al [1984]: M. Grötschel, M. Jünger, G. Reinelt, A Cutting Plane Algorithm for the Linear Ordering Problem, *Operations Research* **32**(6), pp. 1195–1220.

Gruau [1994]: F. Gruau, Genetic micro programming of neural networks, in K.E. Kinnear Jr. (ed.), *Advances in Genetic Programming*, MIT Press, Chapter 24, pp. 495–518.

Gruau [1996]: F. Gruau, On Using Syntactic Constraints with Genetic Programming, in P.J. Angeline, K.E. Kinnear Jr. (eds.), *Advances in Genetic Programming 2*, MIT Press, pp. 377–394.

Gruau & Whitley [1993]: F. Gruau, D. Whitley, Adding learning to the cellular development process: a comparative study, *Evolutionary Computation* **1**(3), pp. 213–233.

Gruau et al [1996]: F. Gruau, D. Whitley, L. Pyeatt, A comparison between cellular encoding and direct encoding for genetic neural networks, in J.R. Koza, D.E. Goldberg, D.B. Fogel, R.L. Riolo (eds.) *Genetic Programming 1996: Proceedings of the First Annual Conference*, MIT Press, pp. 81–89.

Gu & Huang [1994]: J. Gu, X. Huang, Efficient Local Search With Search Space Smoothing: A Case Study of the Traveling Salesman Problem, *IEEE Transactions on Systems, Man, and Cybernetics* **24**(5), pp. 728–735.

Gusfield & Irwing [1989]: D. Gusfield, R.W. Irwing, *The stable marriage problem: structure and algorithms*, MIT Press, Cambridge, MA.

Haase [1989]: J. Haase, *Entwurf digitaler Filter mit erhoehter Leistungsfaehigkeit oder verringertem Aufwand*, PhD thesis, Inst. of Networks and Systems Theory, University of Stuttgart.

Hajela [1990]: P. Hajela, Genetic Search – An Approach to the Nonconvex Optimization Problem, *AIAA Journal* **26**(7), pp. 1205–1210.

Hajela & Lee [1995]: P. Hajela, E. Lee, Genetic Algorithms in Truss Topological Optimization, *Journal of Solids and Structures* **32**(22), pp. 3341–3357.

Hajela & Lee [1996]: P. Hajela, J. Lee, Constrained Genetic Search Via Schema Adaptation: An Immune Network Solution, *Structural Optimization* **12**(1), pp. 11–15.

Hajela & Yoo [1996]: P. Hajela, J. Yoo, Constraint Handling in Genetic Search Using Expression Strategies, *AIAA Journal* **34**(11), pp. 2414–2420.

Hajela et al [1997]: P. Hajela, J. Yoo, J. Lee, GA Based Simulation of Immune Networks – Applications in Structural Optimization, *Journal of Engineering Optimization*.

Handley [1994]: S. Handley, On the use of a directed acyclic graph to represent a population of computer programs, in *Proceedings of the 1994 IEEE World Congress on Computational Intelligence*, IEEE Press, pp. 154–159.

Hansen & Mladenovic [1998]: P. Hansen, N. Mladenovic, An Introduction to Variable Neighborhood Search, in S. Voss et al. (eds.), *Proceedings of the 2nd International Conference on Metaheuristics – MIC97*, Kluwer, Dordrecht.

Harel [1987]: D. Harel, Algorithmics: *The Spirit of Computing*, Addison–Wesley.

Harris [1968]: M. Harris, *The Rise of Anthropological Theory*, Crowell Press, New York.

Hart & Belew [1991]: W.E. Hart, R.K. Belew, Optimizing an arbitrary function is hard for the genetic algorithm, in R.K. Belew, L.B. Booker, (eds.) *Proceedings of the Fourth International Conference on Genetic Algorithms*, San Mateo, CA: Morgan Kaufmann, pp. 190–195.

Hart & Ross [1999]: E. Hart, P. Ross, *Using an immune system model for pattern recognition*, Technical report, Department of Artificial Intelligence, University of Edinburgh, in preparation.

Hart et al [1998]: E. Hart, P. Ross, J. Nelson, Producing robust schedules via an Artificial Immune system, in *Proceedings of the 1998 IEEE International Conference on Evolutionary Computation*, Alaska, IEEE Press.

Hart et al [1998a]: E. Hart, P. Ross, J.A.D Nelson, Solving a real world problem using an evolving, heuristically driven schedule builder, *Evolutionary Computation* $6(1)$, pp. 61–81.

Hartmann & Grill [1996]: D. Hartmann, H. Grill, Mixed–Discrete Structural Optimization with Evolution Strategies: An Object Oriented Approach, presented at *Euromech Colloquium 345*, Liverpool, U.K.

van der Hauw [1996], J.K. van der Hauw, *Evaluating and improving steady state evolutionary algorithms on constraint satisfaction problems*, Master's thesis, Leiden University, this is also on the WWW via the following URL: http://www.wi.leidenuniv.nl/MScThesis/IR96–21.html.

van Hemert [1998]: J.I. van Hemert, *Applying adaptive evolutionary algorithms to hard problems*, Master's thesis, Leiden University, also available as http://www.wi.leidenuniv.nl/~jvhemert /publications/IR–98–19.ps.gz.

Heusse et al [1998]: M. Heusse, S. Guérin, D. Snyers, P. Kuntz, *Adaptive agent–driven routing and load balancing in communication networks*, Technical Report RR–98001–IASC, Départment Intelligence Artificielle et Sciences Cognitives, ENST Bretagne.

Hifi [1997]: M. Hifi, A genetic algorithm–based heuristic for solving the weighted maximum independent set and some equivalent problems, *Journal of the Operational Research Society* $48(6)$, pp. 612–622.

Hightower et al [1995]: R. Hightower, S. Forrest, A.S. Perelson, The evolution of emergent organization in immune system gene libraries, in L.J. Eshelman (ed.) *Proceedings of the 6th International Conference on Genetic Algorithms*, Morgan Kaufmann, pp. 344–350.

Hightower et al [1996]: R. Hightower, S. Forrest, A.S. Perelson, The Baldwin effect in the immune system: learning by somatic hypermutation, in R.K. Belew & M. Mitchell (eds.) *Adaptive Individuals in Evolving Populations*, Addison–Wesley, pp. 159–167.

Hillis [1982]: W. D. Hillis, *The Connection Machine*, MIT Press.

Hofmann [1992]: R. Hofmann, *Parallel Evolutionary Trajectories*, Research Report EPCC–SS92–11, Edinburgh Parallel Computing Centre, University of Edinburgh, UK.

Hofmann [1993]: R. Hofmann, *Examinations of the Algebra of Genetic Algorithms*, Diplomarbeit, Institut für Informatik, Technische Universität München, Germany.

Hofstadter [1983]: D.R. Hofstadter, Computer Tournaments of the Prisoners–Dilemma Suggest How Cooperation Evolves, *Scientific American* **248**(5), pp. 16–23.

Holland [1975]: J.H. Holland, *Adaptation in Natural and Artificial Systems*, University of Michigan Press, Ann Arbor.

Hooker [1994]: J.N. Hooker, Needed: An empirical science of algorithms, *Operations Research* **42**, pp. 201–212.

Hooker [1996]: J.N. Hooker, Testing heuristics: we have it all wrong, *Journal of Heuristics* **1**, pp. 33–42.

Hutchins [1995]: E. Hutchins, *Cognition in the Wild*, MIT Press.

ITU–CCIR [1985]: International Telecommunications Union Consultative Committee on International Radio (ITU–CCIR) Study Groups, Document 11/463–E.

Jain & Meeran [1998]: A.S. Jain, S. Meeran, An Improved Search Template for Job–Shop Scheduling, *INFORMS Spring Meeting*, Montreal, Quebec, Canada, April 26–29.

Jain & Meeran [1998a]: A.S. Jain, S. Meeran, *A Multi–Level Hybrid Framework for the General Flow–Shop Scheduling Problem*, Technical Report, Department of Applied Physics, Electronic and Mechanical Engineering, University of Dundee, Dundee, Scotland.

Janeway [1997]: C.A. Janeway, Jr., How the Immune System Recognizes Invaders, *Scientific American*, September, pp. 73–79.

Janzen [1980]: D.H. Janzen, When is it coevolution?, *Evolution* **34**, pp. 611–612.

Jerne [1973]: N.K. Jerne, The immune system, *Scientific American* **229**(1), pp. 52–60.

Johnson [1974]:D.S. Johnson, Fast algorithms for bin packing, *Journal of Computer and System Sciences* **8**, pp. 272–314.

Johnson [1990]: D.S. Johnson, Local Optimization and the travelling salesman problem, in M.S. Paterson (ed.) *Automata, Languages and Programming*, Lecture Notes in Computer Science 443, Springer, Berlin, pp. 446–461.

Johnson & McGeoch [1997]: D.S. Johnson, L.A. McGeoch, The Traveling Salesman Problem: A Case Study, in E.H. Aarts and J.K. Lenstra (eds.), *Local Search in Combinatorial Optimization*, John Wiley & Sons, Chichester, pp. 215–310.

Johnson & Papadimitriou [1985]: D.S. Johnson and C.H. Papadimitriou, Performance guarantees for heuristics, in E.L. Lawler, J.K. Lenstra, A.H.G. Rinnooy Kan, D.B. Shmoys (eds.), *The Traveling Salesman Problem: A Guided Tour of Combinatorial Optimization*, John Wiley & Sons, Chichester, pp. 145–180.

Johnson et al [1988]: D.S. Johnson, C.H. Papadimitriou, M. Yannakakis, How easy is local search?, *Journal of Computer and System Sciences* **37**(1), pp. 79–100.

Johnson et al [1991]: D.S. Johnson, C.R. Aragon, L.A. McGeoch, C. Schevon, Optimization by Simulated Annealing: An Experimental Evaluation; Part II, Graph Coloring and Number Partitioning, *Operations Research* **39**(3), pp. 378–406.

Jones & Beltramo [1991]: D.R. Jones, M.A. Beltramo, Solving partitioning problems with genetic algorithms, in R.K. Belew, L.B. Booker, (eds.), *Proceedings of the Fourth International Conference on Genetic Algorithms*, Morgan Kaufmann, pp. 442–449.

Jones & Forrest [1995]: T. Jones, S. Forrest, Fitness Distance Correlation as a Measure of Problem Difficulty for Genetic Algorithms, in L.J. Eshelman (ed.) *Proceedings of the Sixth International Conference on Genetic Algorithms*, Morgan Kaufmann, pp. 184–192.

Juille & Pollack [1996]: H. Juille, J.B. Pollack, Massively parallel genetic programming, in P.J. Angeline, K.E. Kinnear Jr. (eds.), *Advances in Genetic Programming 2*, MIT Press, Chapter 17, pp. 339–358.

Karlin et al [1988]: A. Karlin, M. Manasse, L. Rudolph, D.D. Sleator, Competitive snoopy caching, *Algorithmica* **3**, pp. 79–119.

Karmarkar & Karp [1982]: N. Karmarkar, R.M. Karp, *The Differencing Method of Set Partitioning*, Report UCB/CSD 82/113, University of California, Berkeley, CA, USA.

Karmarkar et al [1986]: N. Karmarkar, R.M. Karp, G.S. Lueker, A.M. Odlyzko, Probabilistic Analysis Of Optimum Partitions, *Journal of Applied Probability* **23**(3), pp. 226–245.

Karmouch [1998]: A. Karmouch (ed.), *IEEE Communications Magazine*, IEEE Press, July.

Karp [1972]: R.M. Karp, Reducibility among combinatorial problems, in R.E. Miller, J.W. Thatcher (eds.), *Complexity of Computer Computations*, Plenum Press, New York, pp. 85–103.

Karp [1992]: R.M. Karp, On–line algorithms versus off–line algorithms: how much is it worth to know the future?, Technical Report TR–92–044, ICSI, Berkeley.

Karwan & Rardin [1976]: M.H. Karwan, R.L. Rardin, *Surrogate Dual Multiplier Search Procedures in Integer Programming*, School of Industrial Systems Engineering, Report Series No. J–77–13, Georgia Institute of Technology.

Karwan & Rardin [1979]: M.H. Karwan, R.L. Rardin, Some Relationships Between Lagrangean and Surrogate Duality in Integer Programming, *Mathematical Programming* **17**, pp. 230–334.

Kase & Nishiyama [1964]: S. Kase, N. Nishiyama, An Industrial Engineering Game Model for Factory Layout, *The Journal of Industrial Engineering* **XV**(3), pp. 148–150.

Kauffman [1993]: S.A. Kauffman, *The Origins of Order: Self–Organization and Selection in Evolution*, Oxford University Press.

Kauffman & Levin [1987]: S.A. Kauffman, S. Levin, Towards a General Theory of Adaptive Walks on Rugged Landscapes, *Journal of Theoretical Biology* **128**, pp. 11–45.

Keinath [1992]: A. Keinath, *Entwurf digitaler Filter mit Forderungen an Betrag und Gruppenlaufzeit*, PhD thesis, Inst. of Networks and Systems Theory, University of Stuttgart.

Kelly et al [1996]: J. Kelly, B. Rangaswamy, J. Xu, A Scatter Search–Based Learning Algorithm for Neural Network Training, *Journal of Heuristics* **2**, pp. 129–146.

Kennedy [1998]: J. Kennedy, The behavior of particles, in V.W. Porto, N. Saravanan, D. Waagen (eds.), *Evolutionary Programming VII: Proceedings of the 7th International Conference (EP98)*, San Diego, California, USA, Springer Verlag LNCS 1447, pp. 581–589.

Kennedy & Eberhart [1997]: J. Kennedy, R.C. Eberhart, A discrete binary version of the particle swarm algorithm, in *Proceedings of the 1997 Conference on Systems, Man, and Cybernetics*, IEEE Press, pp. 4104–4109.

Kennedy & Spears [1998]: J. Kennedy, W.M. Spears, Matching algorithms to problems: an experimental test of the particle swarm and some genetic algorithms on the multimodal problem generator, in *Proceedings of the 1998 International Conference on Evolutionary Computation*, IEEE Press, pp. 78–83.

Kennedy et al [1997]: H.C. Kennedy, C. Chinniah, P. Bradbeer, L. Morse, The Construction and Evaluation of Decision Trees: a Comparison of Evolutionary and Concept Learning Methods, in D. Corne, J, Shapiro (eds.), *Evolutionary Computing: Selected Papers from the 1997 AISB Workshop*, Springer LNCS.

Kephart [1994]: J.O. Kephart, A Biologically Inspired Immune System for Computers, in *Proceedings on the 4th International Workshop on the Synthesis and Simulation of Living Systems and Artificial Life*, MIT Press, pp. 130–139.

Kephart et al [1997]: J.O. Kephart, G.B. Sorkin, D.M. Chess, S.R. White, Fighting Computer Viruses, *Scientific American*, November, pp. 88–93.

Kernighan & Lin [1972]: B. Kernighan, S. Lin, An Efficient Heuristic Procedure for Partitioning Graphs, *Bell Systems Technical Journal* **49**, pp. 291–307.

Kilby et al [1999]: P. Kilby, P. Prosser, P. Shaw, Guided Local Search for the Vehicle Routing Problems With Time Windows, in S.Voss, S. Martello, I.H. Osman, C. Roucairol (eds.), *Meta-heuristics: Advances and Trends in Local Search for Optimization*, Kluwer Academic Publishers, Boston, pp. 473–486.

Kinnear [1994]: Kenneth E. Kinnear, Jr. (ed.), *Advances in Genetic Programming*, MIT Press.

Klockgether & Schwefel [1977]: J. Klockgether, H.–P. Schwefel, Two phase nozzle and hollow core jet experiments, in D. Elliot (ed.), *Proceedings of the Eleventh Symposium on Engineering Aspects of Magnetohydrodynamics*, California Institute of Technology, Pasadena, CA, pp. 141–148.

Knuth [1976]: D.E. Knuth, *Marriages stables,* Les Presses de l'Université de Montréal, Montréal, Canada.

Knuth & Moore [1975]: D.E. Knuth & R.W. Moore, An Analysis of Alpha–Beta Pruning, *Artificial Intelligence* **6**(4).

Kohl et al [1997]: N. Kohl, J. Desrosiers, O.B.G. Madsen, M.M. Solomon, F. Soumis, *K–Path Cuts for the Vehicle Routing Problem with Time Windows*, Technical Report IMM–REP–1997–12, Technical University of Denmark.

Korf [1995]: R. Korf, From Approximate to Optimal Solutions: a case study of Number Partitioning, in C. S. Mellish (ed.), *Proceedings of 14th Joint Conference on Artificial Intelligence, (IJCAI–95)*, pp. 266–272, Morgan Kauffman.

Korf [1998]: R. Korf, A complete anytime algorithm for number partitioning, *Artificial Intelligence* **106**(2), pp. 181–203.

Koutsoupias & Papadimitriou [1994]: E. Koutsoupias, C.H. Papadimitriou, Beyond competitive analysis, in *Proceedings of the 35th Annual Symposium on Foundations of Computer Science*, Santa Fe, New Mexico, pp. 394–400.

Koza [1992]: J.R. Koza, *Genetic Programming*, MIT Press.

Koza [1994]: J.R. Koza, *Genetic Programming II: Automatic Discovery of Reusable Programs*. MIT Press, Cambridge, Massachusetts.

Koza et al [1996]: J.R. Koza, D.E. Goldberg, D.B. Fogel, R.L. Riolo (eds.), *Genetic Programming 1996: Proceedings of the First Annual Conference*, Stanford University, CA, USA, MIT Press.

Koza et al [1996a]: J.R. Koza, F.H. Bennett III, D. Andre, M.A. Keane, Automated WYWIWYG design of both the topology and component values of electrical circuits using genetic programming, in J.R. Koza, D.E. Goldberg, D.B. Fogel, R.L. Riolo (eds.) *Genetic Programming 1996: Proceedings of the First Annual Conference*, MIT Press, pp. 123–131.

Koza et al [1996b]: J.R. Koza, D. Andre, F.H. Bennett III, M.A. Keane, Use of automatically defined functions and architecture–altering operations in automated circuit synthesis using genetic programming, in J.R. Koza, D.E. Goldberg, D.B. Fogel, R.L. Riolo (eds.) *Genetic Programming 1996: Proceedings of the First Annual Conference*, MIT Press, pp. 132–149.

Koza et al [1997]: J.R. Koza, K. Deb, M. Dorigo, D.B. Fogel, M. Garzon, H. Iba, R.L. Riolo (eds.), *Genetic Programming 1997: Proceedings of the Second Annual Conference*, Stanford University, CA, USA. Morgan Kaufmann.

Koza et al [1997a]: J.R. Koza, F.H. Bennett III, J. Lohn, F. Dunlap, M.A. Keane, D. Andre, Use of architecture–altering operations to dynamically adapt a three–way analog source identification circuit to accommodate a new source, in J.R. Koza, K. Deb, M. Dorigo, D.B. Fogel, M. Garzon, H. Iba, R.L. Riolo (eds.), *Genetic Programming 1997: Proceedings of the Second Annual Conference*, Morgan Kaufmann, pp. 213–221.

Koza et al [1998]: J.R. Koza, W. Banzhaf, K. Chellapilla, K. Deb, M. Dorigo, D.B. Fogel, M.H. Garzon, D.E. Goldberg, H. Iba, R. Riolo (eds.), *Genetic Programming 1998: Proceedings of the Third Annual Conference*, University of Wisconsin, Madison, WI, USA. Morgan Kaufmann.

Koza et al [1998a], J.R. Koza, D. Andre, F.H. Bennett III, M.A. Keane, *Genetic Programming 3*, MIT Press.

Kragelund [1997]: Lars Vestergaard Kragelund, Solving a Timetabling Problem using Hybrid Genetic Algorithms, *Software – Practice & Experience* **27**(10), pp. 1121–1134.

Krarup & Pruzan [1978]: J. Krarup, M. Pruzan, Computer–aided Layout Design, *Mathematical Programming Study* **9**, pp. 75–94.

Kroeber & Kluckhohn [1952]: A. Kroeber, C. Kluckhohn, Culture, a critical review of the concepts and definitions, in *Papers of the Peabody Museum on American Archeological Ethnology* **47**(1), pp. 1–223.

Krüger et al [1998]: F. Krüger, D. Merkle, M. Middendorf, *Studies on a parallel ant system for the BSP model*, unpublished manuscript.

Kuby [1994]: J. Kuby, *Immunology* W. H. Freeman and Company, 2nd edition.

LOLIB [1997]: http://www.iwr.uni–heidelberg.de/iwr/comopt/soft/LOLIB/LOLIB.html.

Laguna [1997]: M. Laguna, *Optimizing Complex Systems with OptQuest*, Research Report, University of Colorado.

Laguna & Laguna [1995]: M. Laguna, P. Laguna, Applying Tabu Search to the 2–dimensional Ising Spin Glass, *International Journal of Modern Physics C – Physics and Computers* **6**(1), pp. 11–23.

Laguna & Martí [1997]: M. Laguna, R. Martí, *GRASP and Path Relinking for 2–Layer Straight Line Crossing Minimization*, Research Report, University of Colorado.

Laguna et al [1997]: M. Laguna, R. Martí, V. Campos, *Tabu Search with Path Relinking for the Linear Ordering Problem*, Research Report, University of Colorado.

Laguna et al [1998]: M. Laguna, R. Martí, V. Campos, Intensification and Diversification with Elite Tabu Search Solutions for the Linear Ordering Problem, to appear in *Computers and Operations Research*.

Laguna et al [1999]: M. Laguna, H. Lourenço, R. Martí, *Multi–objective scatter search for efficient assignments of proctors to examinations*, Working Paper, University of Colorado.

Lake et al [1994]: R. Lake, J. Schaeffer, P. Lu, Solving Large Retrograde–Analysis Problems Using a Network of Workstations, in H.J. van den Herik, I.S. Herschberg, J.W.H.M. Uiterwijk (eds.), *Advances in Computer Chess VII*, University of Limberg, Maastricht. Netherlands, pp. 135–162.

Langdon [1998]: W.B. Langdon, *Data Structures and Genetic Programming: Genetic Programming + Data Structures = Automatic Programming!*, Kluwer, Boston.

Laporte & Mercure [1988]: G. Laporte, H. Mercure, Balancing Hydraulic Turbine Runners: A Quadratic Assignment Problem, *European Journal of Operational Research* **35**, pp. 378–381.

Latané [1981]: B. Latané, The psychology of social impact, *American Psychologist* **36**, pp. 343–356.

Lawler [1963]: E.L. Lawler, The Quadratic Assignment Problem, *Management Science* **9**, pp. 586–599.

Lawler et al [1985]: E.J. Lawler, J.K. Lenstra, A.H.G. Rinnooy Kan, D.B. Shmoys (eds), *The Traveling Salesman Problem: A Guided Tour of Combinatorial Optimization*, Wiley, Chichester.

Le Riche & Haftka [1993]: R. Le Riche, R.T. Haftka, Optimization of Laminate Stacking Sequence for Buckling Load Maximization by Genetic Algorithms, *AIAA Journal* **31**(5), pp. 951–956.

Lee & Hajela [1996]: J. Lee, P. Hajela, GAs in Decomposition Based Design: Subsystem Interactions Through Immune Network Simulation, in *Proceedings of the 6th AIAA/NASA/USAF/ISSMO Conference on Multidisciplinary Analysis and Optimization*, September 4–6, 1996, Bellevue, Washington, pp. 1717–1726.

Lee & Hajela [1997]: J. Lee, P. Hajela, GAs in Decomposition Based Design: Subsystem Interactions Through Immune Network Simulation, *Structural Optimization*.

Leguizamón & Michalewicz [1999]: G. Leguizamón, Z. Michalewicz, A New Version of Ant Systrem for Subset Problems, in *Proceedings of the 1999 Congress on Evolutionary Computation (CEC'99)*, Washington, USA.

Levin [1973]: L.A. Levin, Universal sequential search problems, *Problems of Information Transmission* **9**(3), pp. 265–266.

Levin [1984]: L.A. Levin, Randomness Conservation Inequalities: Information and Independence in *Mathematical Theories, Information and Control* **61**, pp. 15–37.

Levine [1996]: D. Levine, A parallel genetic algorithm for the set partitioning problem, in I.H. Osman, J.P. Kelly (eds.), *Meta–Heuristics: Theory & Applications*, Kluwer Academic Publishers, pp. 23–35.

Levine et al [1993]: J.M. Levine, L.B. Resnick, E.T. Higgins, Social foundations of cognition, *Annual Review of Psychology* **44**, pp. 585–612.

Levy & Newborn [1991]: D. Levy, M. Newborn, *How Computers Play Chess*, Computer Science Press.

Lewis & Papadimitriou [1997]: H.R. Lewis, C.H. Papadimitriou, *Elements of the Theory of Computation*, Prentice Hall, 2nd edition.

Li & Chou [1994]: H.–L. Li, C.–T. Chou, A global approach for nonlinear mixed discrete programming in design optimization, *Engineering Optimization* **22**, pp. 109–122.

Li et al [1994]: Y. Li, P.M. Pardalos, M.G.C. Resende, A Greedy Randomized Adaptive Search Procedure for the Quadratic Assignment Problem, in P.M. Pardalos, H. Wolkowicz (eds.) *Quadratic assignment and related problems*, DIMACS Series on Discrete Mathematics and Theoretical Computer Science, volume 16, American Mathematical Society, pp. 237–261.

Liepins & Hilliard [1987]: G. E. Liepins, M. R. Hilliard, Greedy Genetics, in *Genetic Algorithms and their Applications: Proceedings of the Second International Conference on Genetic Algorithms*, Lawrence Erlbaum, pp. 90–99.

Lin [1965]: S. Lin, Computer Solutions of the Traveling Salesman Problem, *Bell Systems Technical Journal* **44**, pp. 2245–2269

Lin & Hajela [1993]: C.–Y. Lin, P. Hajela, Genetic Search Strategies in Large Scale Optimization, in *Proceedings of the 34th AIAA/ASME/ASCE/AHS/ASC SDM Conference*, La Jolla, California, pp. 2437–2447.

Lin & Kernighan [1973]: S. Lin, B.W. Kernighan, An effective heuristic algorithm for the traveling–salesman problem. *Operations Research* **21**, pp. 498–516.

Lin et al [1995]: S.–S. Lin, C. Zhang, H.–P. Wang, On mixed–discrete nonlinear optimization problems: A comparative study, *Engineering Optimization* **23**(4), pp. 287–300.

Lin et al [1997]: S.–C. Lin, E.D. Goodman, W.F. Punch, A genetic algorithm approach to dynamic job–shop scheduling problems, in T. Bäck (ed.), *Proceedings of the Seventh International Conference on Genetic Algorithms*, Morgan Kaufmann, pp. 481–489.

Lodi et al [1997]: A. Lodi, K. Allemand, T.M. Liebling, *An Evolutionary Heuristic for Quadratic 0–1 Programming*, Technical Report OR–97–12, D. E. I. S., University of Bollogna, Spain.

Lodish et al [1995]: H. Lodish, D. Baltimore, A. Berk, L. Zipurks (Contributor), J. Darnell (Contributor), *Molecular Cell Biology*, W.H. Freeman & Co., 3rd Edition.

Loh & Papalambros [1991]: H.T. Loh, P.Y. Papalambros, A sequential linearization approach for solving mixed–discrete nonlinear design optimization problems, *Transactions of the ASME, Journal of Mechanical Design*, **113**(3), pp. 325–334.

Loh & Papalambros [1991a]: H.T. Loh, P.Y. Papalambros, Computational implementation and tests of a sequential linearization algorithm for mixed–discrete nonlinear design optimization, *Transactions of the ASME, Journal of Mechanical Design* **113**(3), pp. 335–345.

Løkketangen & Glover [1997]: A. Løkketangen, F. Glover, Surrogate Constraint Analysis: New Heuristics and Learning Schemes for Satisfiability Problems, *DIMACS Series in Discrete Mathematics and Theoretical Computer Science* **35**, pp. 537–572.

Lourenço et al [1998]: H. Lourenço, J. Paixao, R. Portugal, *Metaheuristics for the bus–driver scheduling problem*, Economic Working Papers Series, no. 304, Universitat Pompeu Fabra, Spain.

Lueker [1987]: G.S. Lueker, A note on the average–case behaviour of a simple differencing method for partitioning, *Operations Research Letters* **6**(6), pp. 285–287.

Lueker [1998]: G.S. Lueker, Exponentially small bounds on the expected optimum of the partition and subset sum problems, *Random Structures and Algorithms* **12**(1), pp. 51–62.

Luke & Spector [1996]: S. Luke, L. Spector, Evolving graphs and networks with edge encoding: Preliminary report, in J.R. Koza (ed.), *Late Breaking Papers at the Genetic Programming 1996 Conference*, pp. 117–124.

Maes [1994]: P. Maes, Agents that Reduce Work and Information Overload, *Communications of the ACM* **37**(7), pp. 31–40.

Manasse et al [1988]: M.S. Manasse, L.A. McGeoch, D.D. Sleator, Competitive algorithms for on–line problems, in *Proc. of 20th ACM Symposium on Theory of Computing*, pp. 322–333.

Manderick et al [1991]: B. Manderick, M. de Weger, P. Spiessens, The Genetic Algorithm and the Structure of the Fitness Landscape, in R.K. Belew, L.B. Booker, (eds.), *Proceedings of the Fourth International Conference on Genetic Algorithms*, Morgan Kaufmann, pp. 143–150.

Maniezzo [1998]: V. Maniezzo, *Exact and Approximate Nondeterministic Tree–Search Procedures for the Quadratic Assignment Problem*, Technical Report CSR–98–1, Scienze dell'Informazione, Universitá di Bologna, sede di Cesena, Italy.

Maniezzo & Carbonaro [1998]: V. Maniezzo, A. Carbonaro, *An ANTS Heuristic for the Frequency Assignment Problem*, Technical Report CSR 98-4, Scienze dell'Informazione, Universitá di Bologna, sede di Cesena, Italy.

Maniezzo & Colorni [1999]: V. Maniezzo, A. Colorni, The Ant System Applied to the Quadratic Assignment Problem, *IEEE Trans. Knowledge and Data Engineering*.

Maniezzo et al [1994]: V. Maniezzo, A. Colorni, M. Dorigo, *The Ant System Applied to the Quadratic Assignment Problem*, IRIDIA Technical Report IRIDIA/94–28, Université Libre de Bruxelles, Belgium.

Mariano et al [1995]: A. Mariano, P. Moscato, M.G. Norman, Arbitrarily large planar ETSP instances with known optimal tours, *Pesquisa Operacional* **15**(1–2), pp. 89–96.

Marmelstein et al [1998]: R.E. Marmelstein, D.A. Van Veldhuizen, G.B. Lamont, A Distributed Architecture for an Adaptive Computer Virus Immune System, in *Proceedings of the 1998 IEEE International Conference on Systems, Man, and Cybernetics*, IEEE Press, pp. 3838–3843.

Marrack & Kappler [1993]: P. Marrack, J.W. Kappler, How the Immune System Recognizes the Body, *Scientific American* **269**(3), pp. 80–89.

Martin et al [1991]: O. Martin, S.W. Otto, E.W. Felten, Large–Step Markov Chains for the Traveling Salesman Problem, *Complex Systems* **5**(3), pp. 299–326.

Maruyama [1963]: M. Maruyama. The second cybernetics: deviation–amplifying mutual causal processes., *American Scientist* **5**(1), pp. 164–179.

Mathias & Whitley [1992]: K. Mathias, D. Whitley, Genetic operators, the Fitness Landscape and the Traveling Salesman Problem, in R. Männer, B. Manderick (eds.) *Parallel Problem Solving from Nature II*, Elsevier Science Press, pp. 219–228.

McGeogh [1996]: C.C. McGeogh, Towards an experimental method for algorithm simulation, *INFORMS Journal on Computing* **8**, pp. 1–15.

McGeogh [1996a]: C.C. McGeogh, Challenges in algorithm simulation, *INFORMS Journal on Computing* **8**, pp. 27–28.

Mertens [1998]: S. Mertens, Phase transition in the number partitioning problem, *Physical Review Letters* **81**(20), pp. 4281–4284.

Merz & Freisleben [1997]: P. Merz, B. Freisleben, A Genetic Local Search Approach to the Quadratic Assignment Problem, in T. Bäck (ed.), *Proceedings of the 7th International Conference on Genetic Algorithms (ICGA'97)*, Morgan Kaufmann, pp. 465–472.

Merz & Freisleben [1997a]: P. Merz, B. Freisleben, Genetic Local Search for the TSP: New Results, in *Proceedings of the 1997 IEEE International Conference on Evolutionary Computation*, IEEE Press, pp. 159–164.

Merz & Freisleben [1998]: P. Merz, B. Freisleben, Memetic algorithms and the fitness landscape of the graph bi–partitioning problem, in A.E. Eiben, T. Bäck, M. Schoenauer, H.–P. Schwefel (eds.), *Parallel Problem Solving from Nature: PPSN V*, Springer Verlag LNCS 1498, pp. 765–774.

Merz & Freisleben [1998a]: P. Merz, B. Freisleben, On the Effectiveness of Evolutionary Search in High—Dimensional *NK*–Landscapes, in *Proceedings of the 1998 IEEE International Conference on Evolutionary Computation*, IEEE Press, pp. 741–745.

Merz & Freisleben [1999]: P. Merz and B. Freisleben, Fitness Landscapes, Memetic Algorithms and Greedy Operators for Graph Bi–Partitioning, *Evolutionary Computation* (to appear).

Merz & Freisleben [1999a]: P. Merz, B. Freisleben, A Comparison of Memetic Algorithms, Tabu Search, and Ant Colonies for the Quadratic Assignment Problem, *in Proceedings of the 1999 International Congress of Evolutionary Computation (CEC99)*, Washington DC, USA (to appear).

Michalewicz [1994]: Z. Michalewicz, *Genetic Algorithms + Data Structures = Evolution Programs*, 2nd edn, Springer Verlag.

Michalewicz [1995]: Z. Michalewicz, A Survey of Constraint Handling Techniques in Evolutionary Computation Methods. in J.R. McDonnell, R.G. Reynolds, D.B. Fogel (eds.) *Proceedings of the 4th Annual Conference on Evolutionary Programming*, MIT Press, pp. 135–155.

Michalewicz [1995a] Z. Michalewicz, Genetic algorithms, numerical optimization, and constraints. in L.J. Eshelman (ed.), *Proceedings of the 6th International Conference on Genetic Algorithms*, Morgan Kaufmann, pp. 151–158.

Michalewicz & Attia [1994]: Z. Michalewicz, N. Attia, Evolutionary Optimization of Constrained Problems, in A.V. Sebald, L.J. Fogel (eds.), *Proceedings of the 3rd Annual Conference on Evolutionary Programming*, World Scientific, pp. 98–108.

Michalewicz & Janikow [1991]: Z. Michalewicz, C. Janikow, Handling Constraints in Genetic Algorithms, in R.K. Belew, L.B. Booker, (eds.), *Proceedings of the Fourth International Conference on Genetic Algorithms*, Morgan Kaufmann, pp. 151–157.

Michalewicz & Michalewicz [1995], Z. Michalewicz & M. Michalewicz, Pro–life versus pro–choice strategies in evolutionary computation techniques, in M. Palaniswami. Y. Attikiouzel, R.J. Marks, D. Fogel, T. Fukuda (eds.), *Computational Intelligence: A Dynamic System Perspective*, IEEE Press, pp. 137–151.

Michel & Middendorf [1998]: R. Michel, M. Middendorf, An Island Model based Ant System with Lookahead for the Shortest Supersequence Problem, in A.E. Eiben, T. Bäck. M. Schoenauer, H.–P.

Schwefel (eds.), *Parallel Problem Solving from Nature – PPSN V*, Springer–Verlag LNCS 1498, pp. 692–701.

Michalewicz & Schoenauer [1996]: Z. Michalewicz, M. Schoenauer, Evolutionary algorithms for constrained parameter optimization problems, *Evolutionary Computation* **4**(1), pp. 1–32.

Middendorf [1994]: M. Middendorf, More on the complexity on some common superstring and supersequence problems, *Theoret. Comput. Sci.* **125**, pp. 205–228.

Minsky [1994]: M. Minsky, Negative Expertise, *International Journal of Expert Systems* **7**(1), pp. 13–19.

Mitchell [1978]: T.M. Mitchell, *Version Spaces: An Approach to Concept Learning*, PhD thesis, Stanford University, Stanford, California.

Mitchell et al [1992]: D. Mitchell, B. Selman, H.J. Levesque, Hard and easy distributions of SAT problems, in *Proceedings of the AAAI Conference on Artificial Intelligence*, San Jose, CA, pp. 459–465.

Mitra & Kaiser [1993]: S.K. Mitra, J.F. Kaiser, *Handbook for digital signal processing*, John Wiley & Sons.

Moore [1974]: F.W. Moore, The culture concept as ideology, *American Ethnologist* **15**, pp. 37–49.

Mori et al [1996]: K. Mori, M. Tsukiyama, T. Fukuda, Multi–Optimization by Immune Algorithm with Diversity and Learning, in *Proceedings of ICMAS '96: Immunity Based Systems*, pp. 118–123.

Morris [1993]: P. Morris, The breakout method for escaping from local minima, in *Proceedings of the 11th National Conference on Artificial Intelligence AAAI–93*, AAAI press/MIT Press, pp. 40–45.

Morton & Pentico [1993]: T.E. Morton, D.W. Pentico, *Heuristic Scheduling Systems*, John Wiley & Sons.

Moscato [1989]: P. Moscato, *On Evolution, Search, Optimization, Genetic Algorithms and Martial Arts: Towards Memetic Algorithms*, Report 826, Caltech Concurrent Computation Program, California Institute of Technology, Pasadena, California, USA.

Moscato [1993]: P. Moscato, An Introduction to Population Approaches for Optimization and Hierarchical Objective Functions: The Role of Tabu Search, *Annals of Operations Research* **41**(14), pp. 85–121.

Moscato & Norman [1992]: P. Moscato & M.G. Norman, A Memetic Approach for the Traveling Salesman Problem Implementation of a Computational Ecology for Combinatorial Optimization on Message–Passing Systems, in M. Valero, E. Onate, M. Jane, J. L. Larriba, B. Suarez (eds.), *Parallel Computing and Transputer Applications*, IOS Press, Amsterdam, pp. 177–186.

Moscato & Norman [1998]: P. Moscato, M.G. Norman, On the Performance of Heuristics on Finite and Infinite Fractal Instances of the Euclidean Traveling Salesman Problem, *INFORMS Journal on Computing* **10**(2), pp. 121–132.

Motwani & Raghavan [1995]: R. Motwani, P. Raghavan, *Randomized Algorithms*, Cambridge University Press.

Mühlenbein [1989]: H. Mühlenbein, Parallel Genetic Algorithms, Population Genetics and Combinatorial Optimization, in J.D. Schaffer (ed.), *Proceedings of the 3rd International Conference on Genetic Algorithms*, Morgan Kaufmann, pp. 416–421.

Mühlenbein [1991]: H. Mühlenbein, Evolution in Time and Space – The Parallel Genetic Algorithm, in G.J.E. Rawlins (ed.), *Foundations of Genetic Algorithms*, Morgan Kaufmann, pp. 316–337.

Mühlenbein [1992]: H. Mühlenbein, Parallel Genetic Algorithms in Combinatorial Optimization, in *Proceedings of Computer Science and Operations Research: New Developments in Their Interfaces*, ORSA, Pergamon Press.

Mühlenbein & Schlierkamp–Voosen [1993]: H. Mühlenbein and D. Schlierkamp–Voosen, Predictive models for the breeder genetic algorithm I, *Evolutionary Computation*, **1**(1), pp. 25–50.

Mühlenbein et al [1988]: H. Mühlenbein, M. Gorges–Schleuter, O. Krämer, Evolution Algorithms in Combinatorial Optimization, *Parallel Computing* **7**, pp. 65–88.

Murdoch [1957]: G.P. Murdoch, World Ethnographic Sample, *American Anthropologist* **59**(4), pp. 664–687.

Nakamaru et al [1998]: M. Nakamaru, H. Nogami, Y. Iwasa, Score–dependent fertility model for the evolution of cooperation in a lattice, *Journal of Theoretical Biology* **194**(1), pp. 101–124.

Nakamaru et al [1998a]: M. Nakamaru, H. Matsuda, Y. Iwasa, The evolution of social interaction in lattice models, *Sociological Theory and Methods* **12**(2), pp. 149–162.

Navarro Varela & Sinclair [1999]: G. Navarro Varela, M.C. Sinclair, Ant Colony Optimisation for Virtual-Wavelength-Path Rouring and Wacelength Allocation, in *Proceedings of the 1999 Congress on Evolutionary Computation (CEC'99)*, Washington, USA.

Nissen [1994]: V. Nissen, Solving the Quadratic Assignment Problem with Clues from Nature, *IEEE Transactions on Neural Networks* **5**(1), pp, 66–72.

Norman & Moscato [1989]: M.G. Norman, P. Moscato, A Competitive and Cooperative Approach to Complex Combinatorial Search, Report 790, Caltech Concurrent Computation Program, California Institute of Technology, Pasadena, California, USA (expanded version published in the *Proceedings of the 20th Informatics and Operations Research Meeting, Buenos Aires (20th JAIIO)*, Aug. 1991, pp. 3.15–3.29.)

Norman & Moscato [1995]: M.G. Norman, P. Moscato, The Euclidean Traveling Salesman Problem and a Space–Filling Curve, *Chaos, Solitons and Fractals* **6**, pp. 389–397.

Nowak & Sigmund [1998]: M.A. Nowak, K. Sigmund, Evolution of indirect reciprocity by image scoring, *Nature* **393**(6685), pp. 573–577.

Nowak et al [1990]: A. Nowak, J. Szamrej, B. Latané, From private attitude to public opinion: A dynamic theory of social impact, *Psychological Review* **97**, pp. 362–376.

Nowicki & Smutnicki [1996]: E. Nowicki, C. Smutnicki, A fast tabu search algorithm for the permutation flow–shop problem, *European Journal of Operational Research* **91**, pp. 160–175.

Oussaidene et al [1996]: M. Oussaidene, B. Chopard, O.V. Pictet, M. Tomassini, Parallel genetic programming: An application to trading models evolution, in J.R. Koza, D.E. Goldberg, D.B. Fogel, R.L. Riolo (eds.) *Genetic Programming 1996: Proceedings of the First Annual Conference*, MIT Press, pp. 357–380.

Ozcan & Mohan [1998]: E. Ozcan & C.K. Mohan, Steady State Memetic Algorithm for Partial Shape Matching, in V.W. Porto, N. Saravanan, D. Waagen (eds.), *Evolutionary Programming VII: 7th International Conference (EP98)*, San Diego, California, USA, Springer Verlag LNCS 1447, pp. 527–536.

Paechter et al [1996]: B. Paechter, A. Cumming, M.G. Norman, H. Luchian, Extensions to a Memetic Timetabling System, in E.K. Burke & P. Ross (eds.), *The Practice and Theory of Automated Timetabling*, Springer Verlag LNCS 1153, pp. 251–265.

Pagie & Hogeweg [1997]: L. Pagie, P. Hogeweg, Evolutionary Consequences of Coevolving Targets, *Evolutionary Computation* **5**(4), pp. 401–418.

Papadimitriou & Steiglitz [1982]: C.H. Papadimitriou, K. Steiglitz, *Combinatorial Optimization: Algorithms and Complexity*, Prentice–Hall.

Papadimitriou et al [1990]: C. H. Papadimitriou, A. Schäffer, M. Yannakakis, On the Complexity of Local Search, in *Proceedings of the 22nd Annual ACM Symposium on Theory of Computing*, pp. 438–445.

Pardalos & Rodgers [1990]: P.M. Pardalos, G.P. Rodgers, Computational Aspects of a Branch and Bound Algorithm for Quadratic Zero–One programming, *Computing* **45**, pp. 131–144.

Paredis [1994]: J. Paredis, Steps towards Co–evolutionary Classification Neural Networks, in R. Brooks, P. Maes (eds.), *Artificial Life IV*, MIT Press/Bradford Books.

Paredis [1995]: J. Paredis, The Symbiotic Evolution of Solutions and their Representations, in L.J. Eshelman (ed.), *Proceedings of the 6th International Conference on Genetic Algorithms*, Morgan Kaufmann.

Paredis [1996]: J. Paredis, Symbiotic Coevolution for Epistatic Problems, in W. Wahlster (ed.), *Proceedings of the European Conference on Artificial Intelligence (ECAI–96)*, John Wiley & Sons.

Paredis [1997]: J. Paredis, Coevolving Cellular Automata: Be aware of the Red Queen!, in T. Bäck (ed.), *Proceedings of the 7th International Conference on Genetic Algorithms (ICGA97)*, Morgan Kaufmann.

Paredis [1998], J. Paredis, Coevolutionary Process Control, in *Proceedings of the International Conference on Artificial Neural Networks and Genetic Algorithms (ICANNGA97)*, Springer, Vienna.

Paredis [1998a]: J. Paredis, Coevolutionary Algorithms, in T. Bäck, D.B. Fogel, Z. Michalewicz (eds.), *The Handbook of Evolutionary Computation*, 2nd and later editions, Oxford University Press.

Paredis & Westra [1997]: J. Paredis, R. Westra, Coevolutionary Computation for Path Planning, in H.–J. Zimmermann (ed.), *Proceedings of the 5th European Congress on Intelligent Techniques and Soft Computing (EUFIT 97)*, Verlag Mainz, Aachen.

Peinado & Lengauer [1997]: M. Peinado, T. Lengauer, Parallel 'go with the winners' algorithms in the LogP Model, in *Proceedings of the 11th International Parallel Processing Symposium*, IEEE Computer Society Press, pp, 656–664.

Pham & Karmouch [1998]: V.A. Pham, A. Karmouch, Mobile Software Agents: An Overview, in A. Karmouch (ed.), *IEEE Communications Magazine*, pp. 26–37, July.

Poli [1996]: R. Poli, *Parallel distributed genetic programming*, Technical Report CSRP–96–15, School of Computer Science, University of Birmingham, B15 2TT, UK.

Poli [1996a]: R. Poli, Some steps towards a form of parallel distributed genetic programming, in *The 1st Online Workshop on Soft Computing (WSC1)*, http://www.bioele.nuee.nagoya–u.ac.jp/wsc1/. Nagoya University, Japan.

Poli [1996b]: R. Poli, *Discovery of symbolic, neuro–symbolic and neural networks with parallel distributed genetic programming*, Technical Report CSRP–96–14, University of Birmingham, School of Computer Science.

Poli [1996c]: R. Poli, *Evolution of recursive transistion networks for natural language recognition with parallel distributed genetic programming*, Technical Report CSRP–96–19, School of Computer Science, University of Birmingham, B15 2TT, UK.

Poli [1997]: R. Poli, Evolution of graph–like programs with parallel distributed genetic programming, in T. Bäck (ed.), *Genetic Algorithms: Proceedings of the Seventh International Conference*, Morgan Kaufmann, pp. 346–353.

Poli [1997a]: R. Poli, Evolution of recursive transistion networks for natural language recognition with parallel distributed genetic programming, in D. Corne, J.L. Shapiro (eds.), *Evolutionary Computing: Selected Papers of the 1997 AISB Workshop*, Springer Lecture Notes in Computer Science 1305, pp. 163–177.

Potter & De Jong [1998]: M.A. Potter, K.A. De Jong, The Coevolution of Antibodies for Concept Learning, in H.–M. Voigt, W. Ebeling, I. Rechenberg, H.–P. Schwefel (eds.), *Proceedings of the 4th International Conference on Parallel Problem Solving from Nature PPSN IV*, Springer Verlag LNCS 1141.

Potvin & Bengio [1996]: J.–Y. Potvin, S. Bengio, The Vehicle Routing Problem with Time Windows Part II: Genetic Search, *INFORMS Journal of Computing* 8, pp. 165–172.

Price [1994]: K.V. Price, Genetic Annealing, *Dr. Dobb's Journal*, October, pp. 127–132.

Price [1996]: K. Price, Differential evolution: a fast and simple numerical optimizer, in M. Smith, M. Lee, J. Keller, J. Yen (eds.), *1996 Biennial Conference of the North American Fuzzy Information Processing Society*, IEEE Press, New York, NY, pp. 524–527.

Price [1997]: K.V. Price, Differential Evolution vs. The Functions of the 2nd ICEO, in *Proceedings of the Fourth IEEE International Conference on Evolutionary Computation (ICEC97)*, Indianapolis, IEEE Press.

Pujol & Poli [1998]: J.C.F. Pujol, R. Poli, Efficient evolution of asymmetric recurrent neural networks using a PDGP–inspired two–dimensional representation, in W. Banzhaf, R. Poli, M. Schoenauer, T.C. Fogarty (eds.), *Proceedings of the First European Workshop on Genetic Programming*, Springer LNCS 1391, pp. 130–141.

Pujol & Poli [1998a]: J.C.F. Pujol, R. Poli, Evolution of the topology and the weights of neural networks using genetic programming with a dual representation, *Applied Intelligence* 8, pp. 73–84.

Pujol & Poli [1998b]: J.C.F. Pujol, R. Poli, Evolving neural networks using a dual representation with a combined crossover operator, in *Proceedings of the 1998 IEEE World Congress on Computational Intelligence*, Anchorage, Alaska, IEEE Press, pp. 416–421.

Rabiner & Gold [1975]: L.R. Rabiner, B. Gold, *Theory and Applications of Digital Signal Processing*, Prentice–Hall.

Radcliffe [1994]: N.J. Radcliffe, The Algebra of Genetic Algorithms, *Annals of Mathematics and Artificial Intelligence* **10**(IV).

Radcliffe & Surry [1994]: N.J. Radcliffe, P.D. Surry, Formal Memetic Algorithms, in T.C. Fogarty (ed.), *Evolutionary Computing: Selected Papers from the 1994 AISB Workshop*, Springer Verlag LNCS 865, pp. 1–16.

Radcliffe & Surry [1994a]: N.J. Radcliffe, P.D. Surry, Fitness Variance of Formae and Performance Prediction, in L.D. Whitley, M.D. Vose (eds.), *FOGA III – Proceedings of the 3rd Workshop on Foundations of Genetic Algorithms*, Morgan Kaufmann, San Francisco, pp. 51–72.

Räihä & Ukkonen [1981]: K.J. Räihä, E. Ukkonen, The shortest common supersequence problem over binary alphabet is NP–complete, *Theoret. Comput. Sci.* **16**, pp. 187–198.

Ramalhinho Lourenço & Serra [1998]: H. Ramalhinho Lourenço, D. Serra, *Adaptive Approach Heuristics for the Generalized Assignment Problem*, Technical Report 304, Economic Working Paper Series, Department of Economics and Management, Universitat Pompeu Fabra, Barcelona, Spain.

Rana & Whitley [1997]: S. Rana, D. Whitley, Bit Representations with a Twist, in T. Bäck (ed.), *Proceedings of the Seventh International Conference on Genetic Algorithms*, Morgan Kaufmann, pp. 188–196.

Rechenberg [1973]: I. Rechenberg, *Evolutionsstrategie: Optimierung technischer Systeme nach Prinzipien der biologischen Evolution*, Frommann–Holzboog, Stuttgart.

Reeves [1993]: C.R. Reeves, Improving the efficiency of tabu search in machine sequencing problems, *Journal of the Operations Research Society* **44**, pp. 375–382.

Reeves [1994]: C.R. Reeves, Genetic algorithms and neighbourhood Search, in T.C. Fogarty (ed.), *Evolutionary Computing: Selected Papers from the 1994 AISB Workshop*, Springer Verlag LNCS 865, pp. 115–130.

Reeves [1995]: C.R. Reeves (ed.), *Modern Heuristic Techniques for Combinatorial Problems*, McGraw–Hill (originally published in 1993 by Blackwell Scientific).

Reeves [1995a]: C.R. Reeves, A genetic algorithm for flowshop sequencing, *Computers & Operations Research* **22**, pp. 5–13.

Reeves [1996]: C.R. Reeves, Hybrid genetic algorithms for bin–packing and related problems, *Annals of Operations Research* **63**, pp. 371–396.

Reeves [1996a]: C.R. Reeves, Heuristic search methods: A review, in D.S. Johnson, F.O'Brien (eds.), *Operational Research: Keynote Papers 1996*, Operational Research Society, Birmingham, UK, 122–149.

Reeves [1998]: C.R. Reeves, Landscapes, Operators and Heuristic Search, *Annals of Operations Research* **86**, pp. 473–490.

Reeves & Höhn [1996]: C.R. Reeves & C. Höhn, Integrating local search into genetic Algorithms, in V.J. Rayward–Smith, I.H. Osman, C.R. Reeves, G.D. Smith (eds.), *Modern Heuristic Search Methods*, John Wiley & Sons, New York, pp. 99–115.

Reeves & Yamada [1998]: C.R. Reeves, T. Yamada, Implicit tabu search methods for flowshop sequencing, in P. Borne, M. Ksouri, A. El Kamel (eds.), *Proceedings of IMACS International Conference on Computational Engineering in Systems Applications*, IEEE Publishing, pp. 78–81.

Reeves & Yamada [1998a]: C.R. Reeves, T. Yamada, Genetic algorithms, path relinking and the flowshop sequencing problem, *Evolutionary Computation* **6**, pp. 45–60.

Rego [1999]: C. Rego, Integrating *Advanced Principles of Tabu Search for the Vehicle Routing Problem*, Working Paper, Faculty of Sciences, University of Lisbon.

Rego & Roucairol [1996]: C. Rego, C. Roucairol, A Parallel Tabu Search Algorithm Using Ejection Chains for the Vehicle Routing Problem, in L.H. Osman, J. Kelly (eds.), *Meta–heuristics: Theory and applications*, Kluwer Academic Publishers, Boston, 1996, pp. 661–675

Reinelt [1985]: G. Reinelt, The Linear Ordering Problem: Algorithms and Applications, in H.H. Hofmann, R. Wille (eds.) *Research and Exposition in Mathematics* 8, Heldermann Verlag, Berlin.

Reinelt [1994]: G. Reinelt, *The Traveling Salesman Problem: Computational Solutions for TSP Applications*, Springer–Verlag, Berlin.

Reynolds [1979]: R.G. Reynolds, *An Adaptive Computer Model of the Evolution of Agriculture*, PhD Thesis, University of Michigan, Ann Arbor, Michigan.

Reynolds [1986]: R.G. Reynolds, An adaptive computer–model for the evolution of plant collecting and early agriculture in the eastern valley of Oaxaca, in K.V. Flannery (ed.), *Guila Naquitz: Archaic Foraging and Early Agriculture in Oaxaca, Mexico*, Academic Press, Orlando, Florida, pp. 439–500.

Reynolds [1994]: R.G. Reynolds, An introduction to cultural algorithms, in A.V. Sebald, L.J. Fogel (eds.), *Proceedings of the 3rd Annual Conference on Evolutionary Programming*, World Scientific Press, Singapore, pp. 131–139.

Reynolds [1997]: R.G. Reynolds, Why does cultural evolution proceed at a faster rate than biological evolution?, in S. van der Leeuw, J. McQade (eds), *Time, Process and Structured Change in Archaeology*, Routledge Press, London, pp. 269–282.

Reynold & Chung [1997]: R.G. Reynolds, C.J. Chung, Knowledge–Based Self Adaptation in Evolutionary Search, in *Proceedings of the 1997 IEEE International Conference on Artificial Intelligence Tools*, Newport Beach.

Reynolds & Chung [1997a]: R.G. Reynolds, C.J. Chung, A Cultural Algorithm Framework for Evolving Multi–Agent Cooperation using Evolutionary Programming, in P. Angeline, R. Reynolds, I. McDonnell, R. Eberhart (eds.), *Evolutionary Programming VI: Proceedings of the 6th International Conference on Evolutionary Programming*, Springer–Verlag, Berlin, Germany, pp. 323–334.

Reynolds & Maletic [1993]: R.G. Reynolds, J. Maletic, The use of version space controlled genetic algorithms to solve the Boole problem, *International Journal on Artificial Intelligence Tools* 2(2), pp. 219–234.

Reynolds & Rolnick [1995]: R.G. Reynolds, S. Rolnick, Learning the Parameters for a Gradient–Based Approach to Image Segmentation using Cultural Algorithms, in *Proceedings of the 1995 International Conference on Evolutionary Computation*, IEEE Press, Los Alamitos, CA., pp. 819–824.

Reynolds & Sternberg [1997]: R.G. Reynolds, M. Sternberg, Using Cultural Algorithms to Support the Re–Engineering of Rule–Based Expert Systems in Dynamic Performance Environments: A Fraud Detection Example, *IEEE Transactions on Evolutionary Computation* 1(4), pp. 225–243.

Reynolds & Sverdlik [1995]: R.G. Reynolds, W. Sverdlik, An evolution–based approach to program understanding using cultural algorithms, *International Journal of Software Engineering and Knowledge Engineering* 5(2), pp. 211–226.

Reynolds & Zhu [1998]: R.G. Reynolds, S. Zhu, The Impact of Fuzzy Knowledge Representation on Problem Solving in Fuzzy Cultural Algorithms with Evolutionary Programming, in *Proceedings of the Genetic Programming Conference*, Madison, Wisconsin, Morgan Kaufmann.

Reynolds et al [1995]: R.G. Reynolds, Z. Michalewicz, M.J. Cavaretta, Using cultural algorithms for constraint handling in Genocop, in J. McDonnell, R.G. Reynolds, D.B. Fogel (eds.), *Evolutionary Programming IV – Proceedings of the 4th Annual Conference on Evolutionary Programming*, MIT Press, Cambridge Massachusetts, pp. 289–306.

Richardson et al [1989]: J.T. Richardson, M.R. Palmer, G. Liepins, M. Hilliard, Some Guidelines for Genetic Algorithms with Penalty Functions, in J.D. Schaffer (ed.), *Proceedings of the 3rd International Conference on Genetic Algorithms*, Morgan Kaufmann, pp. 191–197.

Rochat & Taillard [1995]: Y. Rochat, É.D. Taillard, Probabilistic Diversification and Intensification in Local Search for Vehicle Routing, *Journal of Heuristics* 1, 1995, 147–167.

Roitt et al [1998]: I. Roitt, B. Brostoff, D. Male, *Immunology*, Mosby International Ltd, 5th edition.

Rorabaugh [1993]: C.B. Rorabaugh, *Digital Filter Designers Handbook*, McGraw–Hill.

Rosin & Belew [1995]: C.D. Rosin, R.K. Belew, Methods for Competitive Coevolution: Finding Opponents Worth Beating, in L.J. Eshelman (ed.), *Proceedings of the 6th International Conference on Genetic Algorithms*, Morgan Kaufmann, pp. 373–380.

Rosin & Belew [1997]: C.D. Rosin, R.K. Belew, New Methods for Competitive Coevolution, *Evolutionary Computation* 5(1) pp. 1–29.

Rudolph [1992]: G. Rudolph, On correlated mutations in evolutionary strategies, in R. Männer, B. Manderick (eds.) *Parallel Problem Solving from Nature II*, Elsevier Science Press, pp. 105–114.

Rumelhart & McClelland [1986]: D. Rumelhart, J. McClelland (eds.), *Parallel Distributed Processing: Explorations in the Microstructure of Cognition*, Vols. 1–2, MIT Press, Cambridge, MA.

Ruml [1993]: W. Ruml, *Stochastic Approximation Algorithms for Number Partitioning*, Technical Report TR–17–93, Harvard University, Cambridge, MA, USA, available via ftp://dasftp.harvard.edu/techreports/tr–17–93.ps.gz.

Ruml et al [1996]: W. Ruml, J.T. Ngo, J. Marks, S.M. Shieber, Easily Searched Encodings for Number Partitioning, *Journal of Optimization Theory and Applications* 89(2), pp. 251–291.

SPEC [1995]: SPECint95 and SPECfp95 computer benchmarks, The Standard Performance Evaluation Corporation, *http://www.specbench.org/*

Sahni & Gonzalez [1976]: S. Sahni, T. Gonzalez, P–complete Approximation Problems, *Journal of the ACM* 23, pp. 555–565.

Sakamoto et al [1997]: A. Sakamoto, X.Z. Liu, T. Shimamoto, A genetic approach for maximum independent set problems, *IEICE Transactions on Fundamentals of Electronics Communications and Computer Sciences* E80A(3), pp. 551–556.

Salomon [1996]: R. Salomon, Reevaluating genetic algorithm performance under coordinate rotation of benchmark function; A survey of some theoretical and practical aspects of genetic algorithms, *Biosystems* 39(3), pp. 263–278.

Salomon [1997]: R. Salomon, Raising theoretical questions about the utility of genetic algorithms, in P. Angeline, R. Reynolds, J. McDonnell, R. Eberhart (eds.), *Evolutionary Programming VI: Proceedings of the 6th Annual Conference on Evolutionary Programming*, Springer Lecture notes in Computer Science 1213, pp. 275–284.

Salustowicz & Schmidhuber [1997]: R.P. Salustowicz, J. Schmidhuber, Probabilistic Incremental Program Evolution, *Evolutionary Computation* 5(2), pp. 123–141.

Salustowicz & Schmidhuber [1998]: R.P. Salustowicz, J. Schmidhuber, *Learning to Predict Through Probabilistic Incremental Program Evolution and Automatic Task Decomposition*, Technical Report IDSIA–11–98, IDSIA, Lugano, Switzerland.

Salustowicz & Schmidhuber [1998a]: R.P. Salustowicz, J. Schmidhuber, Evolving Structured Programs with Hierarchical Instructions and Skip Nodes, in J. Shavlik (ed.), *Machine Learning: Proceedings of the Fifteenth International Conference (ICML98)*, Morgan Kaufmann Publishers, San Francisco, pp. 488–496.

Salustowicz et al [1998], R.P. Salustowicz, M.A. Wiering, J. Schmidhuber, Learning Team Strategies: Soccer Case Studies, to appear in *Machine Learning*.

Samuel [1959]: A.L. Samuel, Some Studies in Machine Learning Using the Game of Checkers, *IBM Journal of Research and Development* 3(3).

Samuel [1967]: A.L. Samuel, Some Studies in Machine Learning Using the Game of Checkers II – Recent Progress, *IBM Journal of Research and Development* 11(6).

Sandgren [1990]: E. Sandgren, Nonlinear integer and discrete programming in mechanical design optimization, *Transactions of the ASME, Journal of Mechanical Design* 112(2), pp. 223–229.

Saravanan & Fogel [1996]: N. Saravanan, D. B. Fogel, An empirical comparison of methods for correlated mutations under self–adaptation, in L.J. Fogel, P.J. Angeline, T. Bäck (eds.), *Evolutionary Programming V: Proceedings of the 5th Annual Conference on Evolutionary Programming*, MIT Press, pp. 479–485.

Schaeffer et al [1992]: J. Schaeffer, B.K. Culberson, N. Treloar, P. Lu, D. Szafron, A World Championship Calibre Checkers Program, *Artificial Intelligence* **53**, pp. 273–289.

Schaeffer et al [1993]: J. Schaeffer, N. Treloar, P. Lu, R. Lake, Man Verses Machine for the World Checkers Championship, *AI Magazine* **4**(2), pp. 28–35.

Schäffer & Yannakakis [1991]: A. Schaffer, M. Yannakakis, Simple Local Search Problems That Are Hard to Solve, *SIAM Journal on Computing* **20**(1), pp. 56–87.

Schmidhuber [1994]: J. Schmidhuber, *On learning how to learn learning strategies*, Technical Report FKI–198–94, Fakultät für Informatik, Technische Universität München, Germany.

Schmidhuber et al [1997]: J. Schmidhuber, J. Zhao, N. Schraudolph, Reinforcement learning with self–modifying policies, in S. Thrun, L. Pratt (eds.), *Learning to learn*, Kluwer, Boston, pp. 293–309.

Schmidhuber et al [1997a]: J. Schmidhuber, J. Zhao, M. Wiering, Shifting inductive bias with success–story algorithm, adaptive Levin search, and incremental self–improvement, *Machine Learning* **28**, pp. 105–130.

Schneider et al [1997]: J. Schneider, M. Dankersreiter, W. Fettes, I. Morgenstern, M. Schmid, J. Singer, Search–space Smoothing for Combinatorial Optimization Problems, *Physica A Statistical and Theoretical Physics* **243**(12), pp. 77–112.

Schoenauer & Xanthakis [1993]: M. Schoenauer, S. Xanthakis, Constrained GA optimization, in *Proceedings of 5th International Conference on Genetic Algorithms*, Morgan Kaufmann, San Mateo.

Shonkwiler & van Vleck [1994]: R. Shonkwiler, E. van Vleck, Parallel speed–up of Monte Carlo Methods for Global Optimization, *Journal of Complexity* **10**, pp. 64–95.

Schoonderwoerd et al [1996]: R. Schoonderwoerd, O. Holland, J. Bruten, L. Rothkrantz, Ant–based Load Balancing in Telecommunications Networks, *Adaptive Behavior* **5**(2), pp. 169–207.

Schoonderwoerd et al [1997]: R. Schoonderwoerd, O. Holland, J. Bruten, Ant–like agents for load balancing in telecommunications networks, in *Proceedings of the First International Conference on Autonomous Agents*, Martina del Ray, California, ACM Press, pp. 209–216.

Schraudolph & Belew [1992]: N.N. Schraudolph, R.K. Belew, Dynamic Parameter Encoding for Genetic Algorithms, *Machine Learning* **9**, pp. 9–21.

Schwefel [1981] H.–P. Schwefel, *Numerical Optimization of Computer Models*, John Wiley & Sons Ltd, Chichester, U.K.

Schwefel [1995]: H.–P. Schwefel, *Evolution and Optimum Seeking*, John Wiley & Sons Inc., New York.

Sebag et al [1996]: M. Sebag, C. Ravise, M. Schoenauer, Controlling evolution by means of machine learning, in L.J. Fogel, P. Angeline, T. Bäck (eds.), *Evolutionary Programming V: Proceedings of the 5th Annual Conference on Evolutionary Programming*, MIT Press/Bradford Books, pp. 57–66.

Segel [1997]: L. Segel, The Immune System As a Prototype of Autonomous Decentralized Systems, in *Proceedings of the IEEE International Conference on Systems, Man, and Cybernetics* (SMC97), **1**, pp. 375–385.

Selman & Kautz [1993]: B. Selman, H. Kautz, Domain–independent extensions to GSAT: Solving large structured satisfiability problems, in *Proceedings of the International Joint Conference on Artificial Intelligence – IJCAI93*.

Selman et al [1992]: B. Selman, H. Levesque, D. Mitchell, A new method for solving hard satisfiability problems, in *Proceedings of the 10th AAAI National Conference on Artificial Intelligence*, pp. 440–446.

Shannon [1950]: C.E. Shannon, Programming a Digital Computer for Playing Chess, *Philosophy Magazine* **41**.

Shannon [1950a]: C.E. Shannon, Automatic Chess Player, *Scientific American* **182** (48).

Shapiro [1992]: S.C. Shapiro (ed.), *Encyclopedia of Artificial Intelligence*, Wiley, New York, second edition.

Shaw [1998]: P. Shaw, Using Constraint Programming and Local Search Methods to Solve Vehicle Routing Problems, in M. Maher and J.–F. Puget (eds.), *Proceedings of the Fourth International*

Conference on Principles and Practice of Constraint Programming (CP'98), Springer–Verlag, pp. 417–431.

Shi & Eberhart [1998]: Y. Shi, R.C. Eberhart, Using artificial neural network for sleep/wake discrimination from wrist activity: preliminary results, in *Proceedings of the 20th Annual International Conference of the IEEE Engineering in Medicine and Biology*.

Shi & Eberhart [1998a]: Y. Shi, R.C. Eberhart, Parameter Selection in Particle Swarm Optimization, in V.W. Porto, N. Saravanan, D. Waagen (eds.), *Evolutionary Programming VII: 7th International Conference (EP'98)*, San Diego, California, USA, Springer Verlag LNCS 1447, pp. 591–600.

Siddall [1992]: J.N. Siddall, *Optimal engineering design: principles and applications*, Mechanical engineering series 14. Marcel Dekker Inc.

Skorin–Kapov [1990]: J. Skorin–Kapov, Tabu Search Applied to the Quadratic Assignment Problem, *ORSA Journal on Computing* **2**, pp. 33–45.

Sleator & Tarjan [1985]: D.D. Sleator, R.E. Tarjan, Amortized efficiency of list update and paging rules, *Communications of the ACM* **28**, pp. 202–208.

Smith [1994]: B.M. Smith, Phase transitions and the mushy region in constraint satisfaction problems, in A.G. Cohn (ed.), *Proceedings of the 11th European Conference on Artificial Intelligence*, Wiley, pp. 100–104.

Smith et al [1993]: R.E Smith, S. Forrest, A.S. Perelson, Searching for diverse, cooperative populations with genetic algorithms, *Evolutionary Computation* **1**(2), pp. 127–149.

Smith et al [1997]: D.J Smith, S. Forrest, D.H Ackley, A.S Perelson, Modelling the effects of prior infection on vaccine efficacy. in *Proceedings of the IEEE International Conference on Systems, Man, and Cybernetics (SMC'97)* **1**, pp. 363–368.

Smith et al [1999]: D.J. Smith, S. Forrest, A.S. Perelson, Immunological Memory is Associative, in D. Dasgupta (ed.), *Artificial Immune Systems and their Applications*, Chapter 6, Springer–Verlag.

Solomon [1987]: M. Solomon, Algorithms for the Vehicle Routing and Scheduling Problem with Time Window Constraints, *Operations Research* **35**, pp. 254–365.

Sorkin [1992]: G. Sorkin, *Theory and Practice of Simulated Annealing on Special Energy Landscapes*, Ph.D. thesis, University of California at Berkeley, Berkeley, CA, USA.

Stadler [1992]: P.F. Stadler, Correlation in Landscapes of Combinatorial Optimization Problems, *Europhys. Letters* **20**, pp. 479–482.

Stadler [1995]: P.F. Stadler, Towards a Theory of Landscapes, in R. Lopéz–Peña, R. Capovilla, R. García–Pelayo, H. Waelbroeck, F. Zertuche (eds.), *Complex Systems and Binary Networks*, Springer Verlag Lecture Notes in Physics 461.

Stadler [1996]: P.F. Stadler, Landscapes and their Correlation Functions, *J. Math. Chem.* **20**, pp. 1–45.

Steiglitz & Weiner [1968]: K. Steiglitz, P. Weiner, Some Improved Algorithms for Computer Solution of the Travelling Salesman Problem, in *Proceedings of the 6th Annual Allerton Conference on Circuit and System Theory*, pp. 814–821.

Steinberg [1961]: L. Steinberg, The Backboard Wiring Problem: A Placement Algorithm, *SIAM Review* **3**, pp. 37–50.

Stoffel & Spector [1996]: K. Stoffel, L. Spector, High–performance, parallel, stack–based genetic programming, in J.R. Koza, D.E. Goldberg, D.B. Fogel, R.L. Riolo (eds.) *Genetic Programming 1996: Proceedings of the First Annual Conference*, MIT Press, pp. 224–229.

Storer et al [1996]: R.H. Storer, S.W. Flanders, S.D. Wu, Problem space local search for number partitioning, *Annals of Operations Research* **63**, pp. 465–487.

Storn [1996]: R. Storn, On the Usage of Differential Evolution for Function Optimization, *NAFIPS '96*, pp. 519–523.

Storn & Price [1996]: R. Storn, K.V. Price, Minimising the Real Functions of the ICEC96 Contest by Differential Evolution, *in Proceedings of the 1996 IEEE Conference on Evolutionary Computation*, Nagoya, Japan, IEEE Press.

Storn & Price [1997]: R. Storn, K. Price, Differential evolution – a fast and efficient heuristic for global optimization over continuous spaces, *Journal of Global Optimization* **11**, pp. 341–359.

Storn & Price [1997a]: R. Storn, K. Price, Differential Evolution – a simple evolution strategy for fast optimization, *Dr. Dobb's Journal*, April 97, pp. 18–24 and p. 78.

Stryer [1995]: L. Stryer, *Biochemistry*, W. H. Freeman and Company, New York, 4th edition.

Stützle [1997]: T. Stützle, MAX–MIN Ant System for Quadratic, Assignment Problems, Technical Report AIDA–97–04, Intellectics Group, Department of Computer Science, Darmstadt University of Technology, Germany.

Stützle [1998]: T. Stützle, Parallelization Strategies for Ant Colony Optimization, in A.E. Eiben, T. Bäck, M. Schoenauer, H.–P. Schwefel (eds.), *Parallel Problem Solving from Nature – PPSN V*, Springer–Verlag LNCS 1498, pp. 722–731.

Stützle [1998a]: T. Stützle, Local Search Algorithms for Combinatorial Problems: Analysis, Improvements, and New Applications, PhD thesis, Fachbereich Informatik, TU Darmstadt, Germany.

Stützle [1998b]: T. Stützle, An Ant Approach for the Flow Shop Problem, in *Proceedings of the 6th European Congress on Intelligent Techniques & Softcomputing (EUFIT'98)*, volume 3, Verlag Mainz, Wissenschaftsverlag, Aachen, pp. 1560–1564.

Stützle & Dorigo [1999]: T. Stützle, M. Dorigo, *ACO Algorithms for the Traveling Salesman Problem*, in P. Neittaanmäki, J. Periaux, K. Miettinen, M.M. Mäkelä (eds.), *Evolutionary Algorithms in Engineering and Computer Science: Recent Advances in Genetic Algorithms, Evolution Strategies, Evolutionary Programming, Genetic Programming and Industrial Applications*, John Wiley & Sons.

Stützle & Hoos [1997]: T. Stützle, H. Hoos, The MAX–MIN Ant system and local search for the traveling salesman problem, in T. Baeck and Z. Michalewicz and X. Yao (eds.), *Proceedings of IEEE–ICEC–EPS'97, IEEE International Conference on Evolutionary Computation and Evolutionary Programming Conference*, IEEE Press, pp. 309–314

Stützle & Hoos [1997a]: T. Stützle, H. Hoos, Improvements on the ant system: Introducing MAX–MIN ant system, in G.D. Smith, N.C. Steele, R.F. Albrecht (eds.) *Proceedings of the International Conference on Artificial Neural Networks and Genetic Algorithms*, Springer Verlag, Vienna, pp. 245–249.

Stützle & Hoos [1999]: T. Stützle, H. Hoos, MAX–MIN Ant System and Local Search for Combinatorial Optimization Problems, in S. Voss, S. Martello, I.H. Osman, C. Roucairol (eds.) *Meta–Heuristics: Advances and Trends in Local Search Paradigms for Optimization*, Kluwer Academics, Boston, pp. 313–329.

Subramanian et al [1997]: D. Subramanianm, P. Druschel, J. Chen, Ants and Reinforcement Learning: A Case Study in Routing in Dynamic Networks, in *Proceedings of IJCAI–97, International Joint Conference on Artificial Intelligence*, Morgan Kaufmann, pp. 832–838.

Suh & van Gucht [1987]: J.Y. Suh, D. van Gucht, Incorporating Heuristic Information into Genetic Search, in *Genetic Algorithms and their Applications: Proceedings of the Second International Conference on Genetic Algorithms*, Lawrence Erlbaum, pp. 100–107.

Surry & Radcliffe [1996]: P.D. Surry, N.J. Radcliffe, Inoculation to Initialise Evolutionary Search, in T.C. Fogarty (ed.), *Evolutionary Computing: Selected Papers of the 1996 AISB Workshop*, Springer Lecture Notes in Computer Science.

Sverdlik [1993]: W. Sverdlik, Dynamic Version Spaces in Machine Learning, Hybrid Boolean Learning Algorithms, Report DAI–B 53/12, Wayne State University.

Sverdlik et al [1992]: W. Sverdlik, R.G. Reynolds, E. Zannoni, HYBAL: A self–tutoring algorithm for concept learning in highly autonomous systems, in *Proceedings of the 3rd Annual Conference on Artificial Intelligence, Simulation, and Planning in High Autonomy Systems*, IEEE Computer Society Press, Los Alamitos, CA, pp. 15–22.

Syswerda [1989]: G. Syswerda, Uniform Crossover in Genetic Algorithms, in J.D. Schaffer (ed.), *Proceedings of the 3rd International Conference on Genetic Algorithms*, Morgan Kaufmann, pp. 2–9.

Taguchi et al [1998]: T. Taguchi, T. Yokota, M. Gen, Reliability optimal design problem with interval coefficients using Hybrid Genetic Algorithms, *Computers & Industrial Engineering* **35** (12), pp. 373–376.

Taillard [1991]: É.D. Taillard, Robust Taboo Search for the Quadratic Assignment Problem, *Parallel Computing* **17**, pp, 443–455.

Taillard [1993]: É.D. Taillard, Parallel Iterative Search Methods for Vehicle Routing Problems, *Networks* **23**, 1993, 661-673.

Taillard [1993a]: É.D. Taillard, Benchmarks for basic scheduling problems, *European Journal of Operational Research* **64**, pp. 278–285.

Taillard [1995]: É.D. Taillard, Comparison of Iterative Searches for the Quadratic Assignment Problem, *Location Science* **3**, pp. 87–105.

Taillard [1999]: É.D. Taillard, A Heuristic Column Generation for the Heterogeneous VRP, *Recherche Operationelle – RAIRO* **33**(1), pp. 1–14.

Taillard [1998]: É.D. Taillard, *FANT: Fast Ant System*, Technical Report IDSIA 46–98, IDSIA, Lugano, Switzerland.

Taillard & Gambardella [1997]: É.D. Taillard, L.M. Gambardella, *Adaptive Memories for the Quadratic Assignment Problem*, Technical Report IDSIA–87–97, IDSIA, Lugano, Switzerland.

Taillard et al [1997]: É.D. Taillard, P. Badeau, M. Gendreau, F. Guertin, J.-Y. Potvin, A Tabu Search Heuristic for the Vehicle Routing Problem with Soft Time Windows, *Transportation Science* **31**, pp. 170–186

Taillard et al [1998]: É.D. Taillard, L.M. Gambardella, M. Gendreau, J.-Y. Potvin, Adaptive Memory Programming: A Unified View of Meta–Heuristics, Technical Report IDSIA–19–98, IDSIA, Lugano, Switzerland. Also published in *EURO XVI Conference Tutorial and Research Reviews booklet* (semi–plenary session), Brussels, July 1998.

Tate & Smith [1995]: D.M. Tate, A.E. Smith, A Genetic Approach to the Quadratic Assignment Problem, *Computers & Operations Research* **22**(1), pp. 73–83.

Teller [1996]: A. Teller, Evolving programmers: The co–evolution of intelligent recombination operators, in P.J. Angeline, K.E. Kinnear Jr (eds.), *Advances in Genetic Programming 2*, MIT Press, Chapter 3, pp. 45–68.

Teller & Veloso [1995]: A. Teller, M. Veloso, *PADO: Learning tree structured algorithms for orchestration into an object recognition system*, Technical Report CMU–CS–95–101, Department of Computer Science, Carnegie Mellon University, Pittsburgh, PA, USA.

Teller & Veloso [1995a]: A. Teller, M. Veloso, A controlled experiment: Evolution for learning difficult image classification, in *Seventh Portuguese Conference On Artificial Intelligence*, Springer LNCS 990, pp. 165–176.

Teller & Veloso [1996]: A. Teller, M. Veloso, *Neural programming and an internal reinforcement policy*, in J.R. Koza (ed.), *Late Breaking Papers at the Genetic Programming 1996 Conference*, Stanford University July 28 to 31, 1996, Stanford Bookstore, pp. 186–192.

Thangiah et al [1994]: S.R. Thangiah, I.H. Osman, T. Sun, *Hybrid Genetic Algorithm Simulated Annealing and Tabu Search Methods for Vehicle Routing Problem with Time Windows*, Technical Report 27, Computer Science Department, Slippery Rock University, USA.

Thierauf & Cai [1997]: G. Thierauf, J. Cai, Evolution strategies – parallelization and application in engineering optimization, in B.H.V. Topping (ed.), *Parallel and distributed processing for computational mechanics*, Saxe–Coburg Publications, Edinburgh.

Timkovsky [1990]: V.G. Timkovsky, Complexity of common subsequence and supersequence problems and related problems, *Cybernetics* **25**, pp. 565–580 (translated from *Kibernetica*, **25**:1–13, 1989).

Toth & Vigo [1998]: P. Toth, D. Vigo, *The Granular Tabu Search (and its Application to the Vehicle Routing Problem)*, Technical Report, Dipartimento di Elettronica, Informatica e Sistemistica, Università di Bologna, Italy.

Tsang [1993]: E. Tsang, Foundations of Constraint Satisfaction, Academic Press.

480 REFERENCES

Turing [1953]: A.M. Turing, Digital Computers Applied to Games, in B.V. Bowden (ed.), *Faster Than Thought*, Pittman, pp. 186–310.

Tylor [1871]: E.B. Tylor, *Anthropology*, Henry Holt, London.

Ulder et al [1991]: N.L.J. Ulder, E.H.L. Aarts, H.–J. Bandelt, P.J.M. van Laarhoven, E. Pesch, Genetic Local Search Algorithms for the Traveling Salesman Problem, in H.–P. Schwefel. R. Männer (eds.), *Parallel Problem Solving from Nature – PPSN I*, Springer Verlag LNCS 496, pp. 109–116.

van der Put [1998]: R. van der Put, *Routing in the FaxFactory using mobile agents*, Technical Report R&D–SV–98–276, KPN Research, The Netherlands.

van der Put & Rothkrantz [1999]: R. van der Put, L. Rothkrantz, Routing in packet switched networks using agents, *Simulation Practice and Theory* (in press).

Verhoeven & Aarts [1995]: M.G.A. Verhoeven, E.H.L. Aarts, Parallel Local Search, *Journal of Heuristics* 1(1), pp. 43–65.

Voudouris [1997]: C. Voudouris, *Guided Local Search for Combinatorial Optimization Problems*, PhD thesis, Department of Computer Science, University of Essex, UK.

Voudouris & Tsang [1995]: C. Voudouris, E. Tsang, *Guided Local Search*, Technical Report CSM–247, Department of Computer Science, University of Essex, UK.

Voudouris & Tsang [1998]: C. Voudouris, E. Tsang, Guided local search and its application to the travelling salesman problem, *European Journal of Operational Research* 113(2), pp. 80–110.

Walsh & Ryan [1996]: P. Walsh, C. Ryan, Paragen: A novel technique for the autoparallelisation of sequential programs using genetic programming, in J.R. Koza, D.E. Goldberg, D.B. Fogel, R.L. Riolo (eds.) *Genetic Programming 1996: Proceedings of the First Annual Conference*, MIT Press, pp. 406–409.

Wang [1997]: F.–S. Wang, Differential evolution for dynamic optimization of differential–algebraic equations, in *Proceedings of the IEEE 1997 Conference on Evolutionary Computation*, IEEE Press, New York, NY, pp. 531–536.

Wang et al [1997]: C.Wang, C.Chu and J.–M.Proth, Heuristic approaches for $n / m / F / \Sigma C_i$ scheduling problems, *European Journal of Operational Research* 96, pp. 636–644.

Weinberger [1990]: E.D. Weinberger, Correlated and Uncorrelated Fitness Landscapes and How to Tell the Difference, *Biological Cybernetics* 63, pp. 325–336.

Weinberger & Stadler [1993]: E.D. Weinberger, P.F. Stadler, Why some Fitness Landscapes are Fractal, *J. Theor. Biol.* 163, pp. 255–275.

Whigham [1995]: P.A. Whigham, Grammatically–based genetic programming, in J.P. Rosca (ed.), *Proceedings of the Workshop on Genetic Programming: From Theory to Real–World Applications*, Tahoe City, California, pp. 33–41.

White et al [1998]: T. White, B. Pagurek, F. Oppacher, Connection management using adaptive mobile agents, in H.R. Arabnia (ed.), *Proceedings of the International Conference on Parallel and Distributed Processing Techniques and Applications (PDPTA98)*, CSREA Press, pp. 802–809.

Whitley et al [1994]: L.D. Whitley, V.S. Gordon, K. Mathias, Lamarkian evolution, the Baldwin effect, and function, optimization, in Y. Davidor, H.–P. Schwefel, R. Männer (eds.), *Parallel Problem Solving in Nature III*, Springer Verlag LNCS, pp. 453–469.

Wiering & Schmidhuber [1996]: M.A. Wiering, J. Schmidhuber, Solving POMDPs with Levin search and EIRA, in L. Saitta (ed.), *Machine Learning: Proceedings of the Thirteenth International Conference*, Morgan Kaufmann Publishers, San Francisco, CA, pp. 534–542.

Wright [1932]: S. Wright, The Roles of Mutation, Inbreeding, Crossbreeding, and Selection in Evolution, in *Proceedings of the 6th Congress on Genetics*, volume 1, p. 365.

Wu & Chow [1995]: S.–J. Wu, P.–T. Chow, Genetic algorithms for nonlinear mixed discrete–integer optimization problems via meta–genetic parameter optimization, *Engineering Optimization* 24(2), pp. 137–159.

Xu & Kelly [1996]: J. Xu, J. Kelly, A Network Flow–Based Tabu Search Heuristic for the Vehicle Routing Problem, *Transportation Science* 30, 1996, pp. 379–393

Yakir [1996]: B. Yakir, The differencing algorithm LDM for partitioning: A proof of a conjecture of Karmarkar and Karp, *Mathematics of Operations Research* **21**(1), pp. 85–99.

Yamada & Nakano [1996]: T. Yamada, R. Nakano, Scheduling by Genetic Local Search with Multi–Step Crossover, in H.–M. Voigt, W. Ebeling, I. Rechenberg, H.–P. Schwefel (eds.), *Proceedings of the 4th International Conference on Parallel Problem Solving from Nature: PPSN IV*, Springer Verlag LNCS 1141, pp. 960–969.

Yamada & Reeves [1997]: T. Yamada, C. Reeves, Permutation Flowshop Scheduling by Genetic Local Search, in *Proceedings of the 2nd IEE/IEEE International Conference on Genetic Algorithms in Engineering Systems (GALESIA '97)*, pp. 232–238.

Yamada & Reeves [1998]: T.Yamada and C.R.Reeves, Solving the C_{sum} permutation flowshop scheduling problem by genetic local search, in *Proceedings of the 1998 IEEE International Conference on Evolutionary Computation*, IEEE Press, pp. 230–234.

Yannakakis [1997]: M. Yannakakis, Computational Complexity of Local Search, in E.H.L. Aarts and J. K. Lenstra (eds.), *Local Search in Combinatorial Optimization*, John Wiley & Sons, Chichester.

Yao [1980]: A. Yao, New algorithms for bin packing, *Journal of the ACM* **27**, pp. 207–227.

Yoo & Hajela [1999]: J. Yoo, P. Hajela, Immune Network Simulations in Multicriterion Design, *Structural Optimization* (to appear).

Zannoni [1996]: E. Zannoni, *Cultural Algorithms with Genetic Programming, Learning to Control the Program Evolution Process*, PhD thesis, Wayne State University, Detroit, Michigan.

Zhang & Wang [1993]: C. Zhang, H.–P. Wang, Mixed–discrete nonlinear optimization with simulated annealing, *Engineering Optimization* **21**(4), pp. 277–291.

Zhao & Schmidhuber [1996]: J. Zhao, J. Schmidhuber, Incremental Self–Improvement for Life–Time Multi–Agent Reinforcement Learning, in P. Maes, M. Mataric, J. Arcady–Meyer, J. Pollack, S. Wilson (eds.), *From Animals to Animats 4: Proceedings of the Fourth International Conference on Simulation of Adaptive Behavior*, MIT Press, Bradford Books, pp. 516–525.

Index

E

F